Financial Accounting

D0082428

flatworld KNOWLEDGE

Financial Accounting

Published by:

Flat World Knowledge, Inc.
13 N. Mill Street
Nyack, NY 10960

Printed in the United States of America

Brief Contents

Contents

About the Authors

JOE BEN HOYLE, UNIVERSITY OF RICHMOND

Joe Hoyle is an associate professor of accounting at the Robins School of Business at the University of Richmond. In 2006, he was named by *BusinessWeek* as one of twenty-six favorite undergraduate business professors in the United States. In 2007, he was named Virginia Professor of the Year by the Carnegie Foundation for the Advancement of Teaching and the Council for the Advancement and Support of Education. In 2009, he was selected as one of the one hundred most influential members of the accounting profession by *Accounting Today*.

Joe has two market-leading textbooks published with McGraw-Hill—*Advanced Accounting* (10th edition, 2010) and *Essentials of Advanced Accounting* (4th edition, 2010), both coauthored with Tom Schaefer of the University of Notre Dame and Tim Doupnik of the University of South Carolina.

At the Robins School of Business, Joe teaches Fundamentals of Financial Accounting, Intermediate Financial Accounting I, Intermediate Financial Accounting II, and Advanced Financial Accounting. He earned his BA degree in accounting from Duke University and his MA degree in business and economics, with a minor in education, from Appalachian State University. He has written numerous articles and made many presentations around the country on teaching excellence.

Joe also has three decades of experience operating his own CPA review programs. In 2008, he created CPA Review for Free (http://www.CPAreviewforFREE.com), which provides thousands of free questions to help accountants around the world prepare for the CPA Exam.

Joe and his wife, Sarah, have four children and four grandchildren.

C. J. SKENDER, UNIVERSITY OF NORTH CAROLINA AT CHAPEL HILL

C. J. Skender has received multiple teaching awards at the University of North Carolina's Kenan-Flagler Business School (ten), at Duke University's Fuqua School of Business (five), and at North Carolina State University (five). He has been included among the outstanding Fuqua faculty in four editions of the *BusinessWeek Guide to the Best Business Schools*. C. J. also received the James M. Johnston Teaching Excellence Award at the University of North Carolina in 2005. His classes were featured on businessweek.com and sportsillustrated.cnn.com in 2006.

C. J. has served as a training consultant on three continents for Glaxo Wellcome, IBM, Nortel Networks, Paragon Trade Brands, Siemens, Starwood, and Wells Fargo. He has developed and delivered various executive education seminars as well as CPA, CMA, and CIA review courses. For six years, he lectured simultaneously in the State, Carolina, and Duke CPA preparatory classes. For seven years, C. J. taught Financial Accounting and Managerial Accounting on cable television in the Research Triangle area. His scholarly work has been published in TAXES and *Journal of Accounting Education*.

C. J. was born in Harrisburg, Pennsylvania, in 1954. He captained three sports at Susquehanna Township High School. C.J. holds academic degrees from Lehigh University and Duke University. He attended Lehigh on a basketball scholarship and graduated magna cum laude. C. J. worked as an auditor for Deloitte Haskins and Sells in Philadelphia. He has attained eleven professional designations in accounting, financial planning, insurance, and management: CPA (certified public accountant), CMA (certified management accountant), CCA (certified cost analyst), CIA (certified internal auditor), ChFC (chartered financial consultant), CLU (chartered life underwriter), CFP (certified financial planner), AIAF (associate in insurance accounting and finance), CFE (certified fraud examiner), CFM (certified in financial management), and CBM (certified business manager).

C. J. and his wife, Mary Anne, are the parents of two sons and one daughter: Charles (1979), Timothy (1983), and Corey (1987). They reside in Raleigh, North Carolina.

Acknowledgments

A textbook of this size owes a genuine debt of gratitude to a long list of wonderful people. We want to acknowledge the time, energy, ideas, and patience invested by each of the following individuals.

BOOK DEVELOPMENT AND SUPPORT

A warm thank you to Jeff Shelstad, Bradley Felix, Sharon Koch, Shannon Gattens, Jenn Yee, Stacy Claxton, Chrissy Chimi, John Britton, and Barbara Corbin.

TEXTBOOK REVIEWERS

- Pervaiz Alam, Kent State University
- Jane Austin, Oklahoma City University
- Richard Baldwin, Johnson & Wales University, Friedman Center, Graduate School
- Sheila Bedford, American University
- Bruce Branson, North Carolina State University
- Rada Brooks, University of California, Berkeley, Haas School of Business
- Charles Bunn, Wake Technical Community College
- Stan Clark, University of Southern Mississippi
- Sue Cunningham, Rowan Cabarrus Community College
- Betty David, Francis Marion University
- Carolyn Dreher, Southern Methodist University, Cox School of Business
- Wilbert Harri, Pima Community College
- Lori Holder-Webb, Simmons College School of Management
- Ethan Kinory, Baruch College, City University of New York
- Pamela Legner, College of DuPage
- Randall Lewis, Spring Arbor University
- Chao-Shin Liu, University of Notre Dame
- Mary Middleton, University of Richmond
- Jane Mooney, Simmons College
- David Sulzen, Ferrum College
- Diane Tanner, University of North Florida
- Steven Thoede, Texas State University
- Robin Thomas, North Carolina State University
- Wendy Wilson, Southern Methodist University
- Gregory Yost, University of West Florida

The authors also appreciate the efforts of Lydia Rosencrants, LaGrange College Accountancy and Business Programs, who has assisted the project by developing the end of chapter and supplementary material. We want to give a special word of thanks to Katie Fischer for reading the early chapters of this textbook and giving a wonderful perspective from a student's point of view.

Preface

HOW TO USE THIS BOOK: FROM THE AUTHORS TO THE STUDENTS

If we have done our job properly during the creation of this textbook, it will be like no other educational material that you have ever experienced. We literally set out to rethink the nature, structure, and purpose of college textbooks. Every feature that you find here was designed to enhance student learning. We want this material to be presented in a manner that is both innovative and effective.

The two of us have taught in college for over sixty years. Year in and year out, financial accounting has always seemed to us to be both interesting and relevant to everyday life. We believe it is knowledge well worth acquiring. From the day we started this project, we hoped to share our enthusiasm with you, to develop a book that you will find to be both readable and worth reading.

Historically, textbooks have been presented as dry monologues, a one-way conversation that often seems to talk to the teacher more than to the student. "Boring" and "confusing" should never be synonymous with any aspect of education. Instead, we seek to promote an active dialogue. Authors, teachers, and students should work together to create an environment where education flourishes. We want you, the student, to understand the nature of our endeavor. After all, the only reason that this book exists is to aid you in learning financial accounting. If you do not read the chapters because you find them boring or if you do not understand the material that is included, no one benefits. We will have wasted our time.

We view this textbook as a guide. In constructing these seventeen chapters, we have worked to guide you on a voyage through the world of business and financial reporting. We want to help you attain a usable knowledge of the principles of financial accounting as well as an appreciation for its importance and logic. By learning its theory, presentation, and procedures, individuals become capable of using financial accounting to make prudent business decisions. That is an important goal regardless of the direction of your career. We have relied on our experience as teachers to highlight the aspects of this material that make it interesting, logical, and relevant.

Talk, though, is cheap. Saying that this book is different and interesting does not make it so. Be a wise consumer. When someone tries to sell you something, force them to back up their claims.

SO HOW DOES THIS BOOK WORK? WHAT MAKES IT SPECIAL?

1. Every chapter is introduced with a short video in which one of the authors provides an overview of the material and a discussion of its importance. Thus, students are never forced to begin reading blindly, struggling to put new subjects into an understandable context. Even before the first written word, each chapter is explained through the opening video. Simply put, this introduction makes the subject matter more understandable and your reading more interesting and efficient. We attempt to remove the mystery from every aspect of financial accounting because we want you to be an effective learner.
2. This textbook is written entirely in a question and answer format. The Socratic method has been used successfully for thousands of years to help students develop critical thinking skills. We do that here on every page of every chapter. A question is posed and the answer is explained. Then, the next logical question is put forth to lead you through the material in a carefully constructed sequential pattern. Topics are presented and analyzed as through a conversation. This format breaks each chapter down into easy-to-understand components. A chapter is not thirty pages of seemingly unending material. Instead, it is twenty-forty questions and answers that put the information into manageable segments with each new question logically following the previous one.
3. All college textbooks present challenging material. However, that is no excuse for allowing readers to become lost. Educational materials should be designed to enhance learning and not befuddle students. At key points throughout each chapter, we have placed embedded multiple-choice questions along with our own carefully constructed answers. These questions allow you to pause at regular intervals to verify that you understand the material that has been covered. Immediate feedback is always a key ingredient in successful learning. These questions and answers are strategically placed throughout every chapter to permit ongoing review and reinforcement of knowledge.
4. For a course such as financial accounting, each subject should relate in some manner to the real world of business. Therefore, every chapter includes a discussion with a successful investment analyst about the material that has been presented. This expert provides an honest and open assessment of financial accounting straight from the daily world of high finance and serious business decisions. Every question, every answer, every topic need to connect directly to the world we all face. Students should always be curious about the relevance of every aspect of a textbook's coverage. We believe that it is helpful to consider this material from the perspective of a person already working in the business environment of the twenty-first century.
5. In many chapters, we also talk about the current evolution occurring in financial accounting as the United States moves from following U.S. rules (U.S. GAAP) to international standards (IFRS). The world is getting smaller as companies and their operations become more global. At the same time, technology makes the amount of available information from around

the world almost beyond comprehension. Consequently, throughout this textbook, we interview one of the partners of a large international accounting firm about the impact of possibly changing financial accounting in this country so that all reporting abides by international accounting rules rather than solely U.S. standards.

6. Each chapter ends with a final video. However, instead of merely reviewing the material one last time in a repetitive fashion, we challenge you to select the five most important elements of each chapter. Some coverage is simply more important than others. That is a reasonable expectation. Part of a successful education is gaining the insight to make such evaluations. Then, we provide you with our own top five. The lists do not need to match; in fact, it is unlikely that they will be the same. That is not the purpose. This exercise should encourage you to weigh the significance of the material. What really makes a difference based on your understanding of financial accounting? In what areas should you focus your attention?

IS THIS BOOK UNIQUE?

We truly believe so. We believe that it has an educationally creative structure that will promote your learning and make the educational process more effective and more interesting:

- Opening videos for the chapters
- Socratic method
- Embedded multiple-choice questions
- Discussions with both an investment analyst and an international accounting expert
- Closing videos establishing top-five lists for each chapter

Every page of this book, every word in fact, has been created to encourage and enhance your understanding. We want you to benefit from our coverage, but just as importantly, we want you to enjoy the process. When presented correctly, learning can be fun and, we believe, should be.

Please feel free to contact us if you have any suggestions for improvement. We would love to hear from you.

Finally, this book is dedicated to our wives and our families. It is also dedicated to the thousands of wonderful teachers across the world who walk into countless college classrooms each day and make learning happen for their students. You make the world better.

Joe Hoyle, University of Richmond (Jhoyle@richmond.edu)

C. J. Skender, University of North Carolina at Chapel Hill

CHAPTER 1
Why Is Financial Accounting Important?

Video Clip

Joe introduces the course objectives and Chapter 1.

View the video online at: http://blip.tv/play/sDyBv5YyAA

1. MAKING GOOD FINANCIAL DECISIONS ABOUT AN ORGANIZATION

LEARNING OBJECTIVES

At the end of this section, students should be able to meet the following objectives:

1. **Define financial accounting.**
2. **Understand the connection between financial accounting and the communication of information.**
3. **Explain the importance of learning to understand financial accounting.**
4. **List decisions that an individual might make about an organization.**
5. **Differentiate between financial accounting and managerial accounting.**
6. **Provide reasons for individuals to be interested in the financial accounting information supplied by their employers.**

*Question: This textbook professes to be an introduction to financial accounting? A logical place to begin such an exploration is to ask the obvious question: **What is financial accounting?***

Answer: In simplest terms, **financial accounting** is the communication of information about a business or other type of organization (such as a charity or government) so that individuals can assess its financial health and prospects. Probably no single word is more relevant to financial accounting than "information." Whether it is gathering financial information about a specific organization, putting that information into a structure designed to enhance communication, or working to understand the information being conveyed, financial accounting is intertwined with information.

In today's world, information is king. Financial accounting provides the rules and structure for the conveyance of financial information about businesses (and other organizations). At any point in time,

financial accounting

The communication of financial information about a business or other type of organization to external audiences in order to help them assess its financial health and prospects.

some businesses are poised to prosper while others teeter on the verge of failure. Many people are seriously interested in evaluating the degree of success achieved by a particular organization as well as its prospects for the future. They seek information. Financial accounting provides data that these individuals need and want.

organization → reports information based on the principles of financial accounting → individual assesses financial health

*Question: Every semester, most college students are enrolled in several courses as well as participate in numerous outside activities. All of these compete for the hours in each person's day. Why should a student invest valuable time to learn the principles of financial accounting? Why should anyone be concerned with the information communicated about an organization? More concisely, **what makes financial accounting important?***

Answer: Many possible benefits can be gained from acquiring a strong knowledge of financial accounting and the means by which information is communicated about an organization. In this book, justification for the serious study that is required to master the subject matter is simple and straightforward: Obtaining a working knowledge of financial accounting and its underlying principles enables a person to understand the information conveyed about an organization so that better decisions can be made.

Around the world, millions of individuals make critical judgments each day about the businesses and other organizations they encounter. Developing the ability to analyze financial information and then use that knowledge to arrive at sound decisions can be critically important. Whether an organization is as gigantic as Wal-Mart or as tiny as a local convenience store, a person could have many, varied reasons for making an assessment. As just a single example, a recent college graduate looking at full-time employment opportunities might want to determine the probability that Company A will have a brighter economic future than Company B. Although such decisions can never be correct 100 percent of the time, knowledge of financial accounting and the information being communicated greatly increases the likelihood of success. As Kofi Annan, former secretary-general of the United Nations has said, "Knowledge is power. Information is liberating."[1]

Thus, the ultimate purpose of this book is to provide students with a rich understanding of the rules and nuances of financial accounting so they can evaluate available information and then make good choices about those organizations. In the world of business, most successful individuals have developed this talent and are able to use it to achieve their investing and career objectives.

*Question: Knowledge of financial accounting assists individuals in making informed decisions about businesses and other organizations. What kinds of evaluations are typically made? For example, assume that a former student—one who recently graduated from college—has been assigned the task of analyzing financial data provided by Company C. **What real-life decisions could a person be facing where an understanding of financial accounting is beneficial?***

Answer: The number of possible judgments that an individual might need to make about a business or other organization is close to unlimited. However, many decisions deal with current financial health and the prospects for future success. In making assessments of available data, a working knowledge of financial accounting is invaluable. The more in-depth the understanding is of those principles, the more likely the person will be able to use the available information to arrive at the best possible choice. Common examples include the following:

interest

The charge for using money over time, often associated with long-term loans; even if not specifically mentioned in the debt agreement, U.S. GAAP requires it to be computed and reported based on a reasonable rate.

- The college graduate might be employed by a bank to work in its corporate lending department. Company C is a local business that has applied to the bank for a large loan. The graduate has been asked by bank management to prepare an assessment of Company C to determine if it is likely to be financially healthy in the future so that it will be able to repay the money when due. A correct decision to lend the money eventually earns the bank profit because Company C (the debtor) will be required to pay an extra amount (known as **interest**) on the money borrowed. Conversely, an incorrect analysis of the information could lead to a substantial loss if the loan is granted and Company C is unable to fulfill its obligation. Bank officials must weigh the potential for profit against the risk of loss. That is a daily challenge in virtually all businesses. The former student's career with the bank might depend on the ability to analyze financial accounting data and then make appropriate choices about the actions to be taken. Should a loan be made to this company?
- The college graduate might hold a job as a credit analyst for a manufacturing company that sells its products to retail stores. Company C is a relatively new retailer that wants to buy goods (inventory) for its stores on credit from this manufacturer. The former student must judge whether it is wise to permit Company C to buy goods now but wait until later to remit the

money. If payments are received on a timely basis, the manufacturer will have found a new outlet for its merchandise. Profits will likely increase. Unfortunately, another possibility also exists. Company C could make expensive purchases but then be unable to make payment, creating significant losses for the manufacturer. Should credit be extended to this company?

- The college graduate might be employed by an investment firm that provides financial advice to its clients. The firm is presently considering whether to recommend acquisition of the ownership shares of Company C as a good investment strategy. The former student has been assigned to gather and evaluate relevant financial information as a basis for this decision. If Company C is poised to become stronger and more profitable, its ownership shares will likely rise in value over time earning money for the firm's clients. Conversely, if the prospects for Company C appear to be less bright, the value of these shares might be expected to drop (possibly precipitously) so that the investment firm should avoid suggesting the purchase of an ownership interest in Company C. Should shares of this company be recommended for acquisition?

Success in life—especially in business—frequently results from making appropriate decisions. Many economic choices, such as those described above, depend on the ability to understand and make use of the financial information that is produced and presented about an organization in accordance with the rules and principles underlying financial accounting.

EXERCISE

Link to multiple-choice question for practice purposes: http://www.quia.com/quiz/2092614.html

Question: A great number of possible decisions could be addressed in connection with an organization. ***Is an understanding of financial accounting relevant to all business decisions?*** *What about the following?*

- *Should a business buy a building to serve as its new headquarters or rent a facility instead?*
- *What price should a data processing company charge customers for its services?*
- *Should advertisements to alert the public about a new product be carried on the Internet or on television?*

Answer: Organizational decisions such as these are extremely important for success. However, these examples are not made about the reporting organization. Rather, they are made within the organization in connection with some element of its operations.

The general term "accounting" refers to the communication of financial information for decision-making purposes. Accounting is then further subdivided into (a) financial accounting and (b) **managerial accounting**.[2] Financial accounting is the subject explored in this textbook. It focuses on conveying relevant data (primarily to external parties) so that decisions can be made about an organization (such as Motorola or Starbucks) as a whole. Thus, questions such as the following all fall within the discussion of financial accounting:

managerial accounting

The communication of financial information within an organization so internal decisions can be made in an appropriate manner.

- Do we loan money to Company C?
- Do we sell on credit to Company C?
- Do we recommend that our clients buy the ownership shares of Company C?

They relate to evaluating the financial health and prospects of Company C as a whole.

Managerial accounting is the subject of other books and other courses. This second branch of accounting refers to the communication of information within an organization so that internal decisions (such as whether to buy or rent a building) can be made in an appropriate manner. Individuals studying an organization as a whole have different goals than do internal parties making operational decisions. Thus, many unique characteristics have developed in connection with each of these two branches of accounting. Financial accounting and managerial accounting have evolved independently over the decades to address the specific needs of the users being served and the decisions being made. This textbook is designed to explain those attributes that are fundamental to attaining a useable understanding of financial accounting.

It is not that one of these areas of accounting is better, more useful, or more important than the other. Financial accounting and managerial accounting have simply been created to achieve different objectives. They both do their jobs well; they just do not have the same jobs.

EXERCISE

Link to multiple-choice question for practice purposes: http://www.quia.com/quiz/2092571.html

Question: Financial accounting refers to the conveyance of information about an organization as a whole and is most frequently directed to assisting outside decision makers. ***Is there any reason for a person who is employed by a company to care about the financial accounting data reported about that organization?*** *Why should an employee in the marketing or personnel department of Company C be interested in the financial information that it distributes?*

Answer: As indicated, financial accounting is designed to portray the overall financial condition and prospects of an organization. Every employee should be quite interested in assessing that information to judge future employment prospects. A company that is doing well will possibly award larger pay raises or perhaps significant end-of-year cash bonuses. A financially healthy organization can afford to hire new employees, buy additional equipment, or pursue major new initiatives. Conversely, when a company is struggling and prospects are dim, employees might anticipate layoffs, pay cuts, or reductions in resources.

Thus, although financial accounting information is often directed to outside decision makers, employees should be vitally interested in the financial health of their own organization. No one wants to be clueless as to whether their employer is headed for prosperity or bankruptcy. In reality, employees are often the most avid readers of the financial accounting information distributed by their employers because the results can have such an immediate and direct impact on their jobs and, hence, their lives.

KEY TAKEAWAY

Financial accounting encompasses the rules and procedures to convey financial information about an organization. Individuals who attain a proper level of knowledge of financial accounting can utilize this information to make decisions based on the organization's perceived financial health and outlook. Such decisions might include assessing employment potential, lending money, granting credit, and buying or selling ownership shares. However, financial accounting does not address issues that are purely of an internal nature such as whether an organization should buy or lease equipment or the level of pay raises. Information to guide such internal decisions is generated according to managerial accounting rules and procedures that are introduced in other books and courses. Despite not being directed toward the inner workings of an organization, employees are interested in financial accounting because it helps them to assess the future financial prospects of their employer.

2. INCORPORATION AND THE TRADING OF CAPITAL SHARES

LEARNING OBJECTIVES

At the end of this section, students should be able to meet the following objectives:

1. **Define incorporation.**
2. **Explain the popularity of investing in the capital stock of a corporation.**
3. **Discuss the necessity and purpose of a board of directors.**
4. **List the potential benefits gained from acquiring capital stock.**

Question: Above, in discussing the possible decisions that could be made about an organization, ownership shares were mentioned. Occasionally, on television, in newspapers, or on the Internet, mention is made that the shares of one company or another have gone up or down in price during that day because of trading on one of the stock markets. ***Why does a person or an organization acquire ownership shares of a business such as Capital One or Intel?***

Answer: In the United States, as well as in many other countries, owners of a business or other type of organization can apply to the state government to have it identified as an entity legally separate from its owners. This process is referred to as **incorporation**. Therefore, a **corporation** is an organization that has been formally recognized by the government as a legal entity. A business that has not been incorporated is legally either a **sole proprietorship** (one owner) or a **partnership** (more than one owner).

As will be discussed in detail in Chapter 16, several advantages can be gained from incorporation. For one, a corporation has the ability to issue (sell) shares to obtain monetary resources and allow investors to become owners (also known as **stockholders** or **shareholders**). The Walt Disney Company and General Electric, as just two examples, are corporations. They exist as legal entities completely distinct from the multitude of individuals and organizations that possess their ownership shares (also known as equity or **capital stock**).

Any investor who acquires one or more capital shares of a corporation is an owner and has rights that are specified by the state government or on the stock certificate. The number of shares and owners can be staggering. At the end of 2008, owners held over 2.3 billion shares of The Coca-Cola Company. Thus, possession of one share of The Coca-Cola Company at that time gave a person approximately a 1/2,300,000,000th part of the ownership.[3]

If traded on a stock exchange, shares of the capital stock of a corporation continually go up and down in value based on myriad factors including the perceived financial health and prospects of the organization. As an example, during trading on December 4, 2009, the price of an ownership share of Intel rose by $0.59 to $20.46, while a share of Capital One went up by $1.00 to $37.92.

incorporation

Legal process by which owners of an organization apply to a state government to have it identified as an entity legally separate from its owners (a corporation); corporations are the legal form of most businesses of any size in the United States.

corporation

An organization that has been formally recognized by the state government as a legal entity so that it can sell ownership shares to raise money for capital expenditures and operations; business is legally separated from its owners.

sole proprietorship

A business created, owned, and operated by a single individual; the business is not legally separate from its owner.

partnership

A business created, owned, and operated by more than one individual; business is not legally separate from its owners through incorporation.

stockholders

Individuals or organizations that hold the ownership shares of stock of a corporation; same as shareholders.

shareholders

Individuals or organizations that hold the ownership shares of stock of a corporation; same as stockholders.

capital stock

Ownership (equity) shares of stock in a corporation that are issued to raise financing for capital expenditures and operations.

common stock

A type of capital stock that is issued by every corporation; it provides rights to the owner that are specified by the laws of the state in which the organization is incorporated.

New York Stock Exchange

Organized stock market that efficiently matches buyers and sellers of capital stock at a mutually agreed-upon price allowing ownership in companies to change hands easily.

For countless individuals and groups around the world, the most popular method of investment is through the purchase and sell of these shares of corporate ownership. Although a number of other types of investment opportunities are available (such as the acquisition of gold or land), few evoke the level of interest of capital stock.[4] On the **New York Stock Exchange** alone, billions of shares are bought and sold every business day at a wide range of prices. As of December 4, 2009, an ownership share of Ford Motor Company was trading for $8.94, while a single share of Berkshire Hathaway sold for thousands of dollars.

EXERCISE

Link to multiple-choice question for practice purposes: http://www.quia.com/quiz/2092597.html

Question: In most cases, the owners of a small corporation should be able to operate the business effectively. For example, one person might hold one hundred shares of capital stock while another owns two hundred. Those two individuals must learn to work together to manage the business on a day-to-day basis. Large corporations offer a significantly different challenge. ***How could millions of investors possessing billions of capital shares of a single corporation ever serve in any reasonable capacity as the ownership of that organization?***

board of directors

A group that oversees the management of a corporation; the members are voted to this position by stockholders; it hires the management to run the company on a daily basis and then meets periodically to review operating and financing results and also approve policy and strategy.

Answer: Obviously, a great many companies like The Coca-Cola Company have an enormous quantity of capital shares outstanding. Virtually none of these owners can expect to have any impact on the daily operations of the corporation. In a vast number of such businesses, stockholders simply vote to elect a representative group to oversee the company for them. This body—called the **board of directors**[5] —is made up of approximately ten to twenty-five knowledgeable individuals. As shown in Figure 1.1, the board of directors hires the members of management to run the company on a daily basis and then meets periodically (often quarterly) to review operating and financing results as well as to approve strategic policy initiatives.

FIGURE 1.1 Company Operational Structure

Ownership	Each capital share is the equivalent of one unit of ownership.
Board of Directors	Elected by shareholders to hire and oversee the management of the company and make policy decisions.
Management	Officials such as the president, the chief financial officer, and the director of marketing who are in charge of daily operations.
Employees	All individuals who work for a company who are not deemed to be members of the management.

Occasionally, the original founders of a business (or their descendants) continue to hold enough shares to influence or actually control its operating and financial decisions. Or, wealthy outside investors may acquire enough shares to gain this same level of power. Such owners have genuine authority within the corporation. Because these cases are less common, the specific financial accounting issues involved with this degree of ownership will be deferred until a later chapter. In most cases, the hierarchy of owners, board of directors, management, and employees remains intact. Thus, stockholders are usually quite removed from the operations of any large corporation.

Question: The acquisition of capital shares is an extremely popular investment strategy across a wide range of the population. A buyer becomes one of the owners of the corporation. Why spend money in this way especially since very few stockholders can ever hope to hold enough shares to participate in managing or influencing the operations? Ownership shares sometimes cost small amounts but can also require hundreds if not thousands of dollars. ***What is the potential benefit of buying capital stock issued by a business organization?***

Answer: Capital shares of thousands of corporations trade each day on markets around the world such as the New York Stock Exchange or **NASDAQ (National Association of Securities Dealers Automated Quotation Service)**. One party is looking to sell shares whereas another is seeking shares to buy. Stock markets match up these buyers and sellers so that a mutually agreed-upon price can be negotiated. This bargaining process allows the ownership interest of all these companies to change hands with relative ease.

NASDAQ (National Association of Securities Dealers Automated Quotations)

An electronic market that allows for the trading of equity securities in approximately 4,000 companies, providing instantaneous price quotations to efficiently match buyers and sellers allowing ownership in companies to change hands.

When investors believe a company is financially healthy and its future is bright, they expect prosperity and growth. If that happens, the negotiated price for this company's capital stock should rise over time. Everyone attempts to anticipate such movements in order to buy the stock at a low price and sell it later at a higher one. Conversely, if predictions are not optimistic, then the share price is likely to drop and owners face the possibility of incurring losses in the value of their investments. Many factors affect the movement of stock prices such as the perceived quality of the management, historical trends in profitability, the viability of the industry in which it operates, and the health of the economy as a whole.

Financial accounting information plays an invaluable role in this market process as millions of investors attempt each day to assess the financial condition and prospects of corporate organizations. Being able to understand and make use of reported financial data helps improve the investor's knowledge of a company and, thus, the chance of making wise decisions that will generate profits from buying and selling capital shares. Ignorance can lead to poor decisions and much less lucrative outcomes.

In the United States, such investment gains—if successfully generated—are especially appealing to individuals if the shares are held for over twelve months before being sold. For income tax purposes, the difference between the buy and sale prices for such investments is referred to as a **long-term capital gain or loss**. Under certain circumstances, significant tax reductions are allowed in connection with long-term capital gains.[6] Congress created this tax incentive to encourage investment so that businesses could more easily obtain money for growth purposes.

long-term capital gain or loss

Occurs when certain investments are held for more than twelve months before being sold; a favorable tax treatment can result when gains are earned.

EXERCISE

Link to multiple-choice question for practice purposes: http://www.quia.com/quiz/2092598.html

Question: Investors acquire ownership shares of selected corporations hoping that the stock values will rise over time. This investment strategy is especially tempting because net long-term capital gains are taxed at a relatively low rate. ***Is the possibility for appreciation of stock prices the only reason that investors choose to acquire capital shares?***

Answer: Many corporations—although certainly not all—also pay cash **dividends** to their stockholders periodically. A dividend is a reward for being an owner of a business that is prospering. It is not a required payment; it is a sharing of profits with the stockholders. As an example, for 2008, Duke Energy reported earning profits (net income) of $1.36 billion. During that same period, the corporation distributed a total cash dividend of approximately $1.14 billion to the owners of its capital stock.[7]

dividends

Distributions made by a corporation to its shareholders as a reward when income has been earned; shareholders often receive favorable tax treatment when cash dividends are collected.

The board of directors determines whether to pay dividends. Some boards prefer to leave money within the business to stimulate future growth and additional profits. For example, Yahoo! Inc. reported profits (net income) for 2008 of over $424 million but paid no dividends to its owners.

Not surprisingly, a variety of investing strategies abound. Some investors acquire ownership shares almost exclusively in hopes of benefiting from the potential for significant appreciation of stock prices. Another large segment of the investing public is more interested in the possibility of dividend payments. Unless an owner has the chance to influence or control operations, only these two possible benefits can accrue: appreciation in the value of the stock price and cash dividends.

Question: An investor can put money into a savings account at a bank and earn a small but relatively risk free profit. For example, $100 could be invested on January 1 and then be worth $102 at the end of the year because interest is added. The extra $2 means that the investor is earning an annual return of 2 percent ($2 increase/$100 investment). ***How is the annual return computed when the capital stock of a corporation is acquired?***

Answer: Capital stock investments are certainly not risk free. Profits can be high, but losses are also always a possibility. Assume that on January 1, Year One, an investor spends $100 for one ownership share of Company A and another $100 for a share of Company B. During the year, Company A distributes a dividend of $1.00 per share to its owners while Company B pays $5.00 per share. On December

31, the stock of Company A is selling on the stock market for $108 per share whereas the stock of Company B is selling for $91 per share.

The investor now holds a total value of $109 as a result of the purchase of the share of Company A: the cash dividend of $1 and a share of stock worth $108. Total value has gone up $9 ($109 less $100) so that the annual return for the year was 9 percent ($9 increase/$100 investment).

The shares of Company B have not performed as well. Total value is now only $96: the cash dividend of $5 plus one share of stock worth $91. That is a drop of $4 during the year ($96 less $100). The annual return on this investment is a negative 4 percent ($4 decrease/$100 investment).

Clearly, investors want to have all the information they need in hopes of maximizing their potential profits each year. A careful analysis of the available data might have helped this investor to choose Company A rather than Company B.

KEY TAKEAWAY

Incorporation allows an organization to be viewed as a separate entity apart from its ownership. As a corporation, shares of capital stock can be issued that give the holder an ownership right. If the organization is financially healthy and prospering, these shares can increase in value—possibly by a significant amount. In addition, a profitable organization may well share its good fortune with the ownership through the distribution of cash dividends. In most large organizations, few owners want to be involved in the operational decision making. Instead, these stockholders elect a board of directors to oversee the company and direct the work of management.

3. USING FINANCIAL ACCOUNTING FOR WISE DECISION MAKING

LEARNING OBJECTIVES

At the end of this section, students should be able to meet the following objectives:

1. **List the predictions that investors and potential investors want to make.**
2. **List the predictions that creditors and potential creditors want to make.**
3. **Distinguish financial accounting information from other types of data about a business organization.**
4. **Explain how financial accounting information is enhanced and clarified by verbal explanations.**

Question: Investors are interested (sometimes almost obsessively interested) in the financial information that is produced by a company based on the rules and principles of financial accounting. They want to use this information to make wise investing decisions. ***What do investors actually hope to learn about a company from this financial information?***

Answer: The information reported by financial accounting is similar to a giant, complex portrait painted of the organization. There are probably hundreds, if not thousands, of aspects that can be examined, analyzed, and evaluated in assessing the financial health and future prospects of the model. Theories abound as to which pieces of information are best to use when studying a business. One investor might prefer to focus on a particular portion of the data almost exclusively (such as profitability) while another may believe that entirely different information is most significant (such as the sources and uses of cash during the period).

Ultimately, in connection with the buying and selling of capital stock, all investors are trying to arrive at the same two insights. They are attempting to use the provided data to estimate (1) the price of the corporation's stock in the future and (2) the amount of cash dividends that will be paid over time. Despite the complexity of the information, these two goals are rather simplistic. If an investor owns capital shares of a company and feels that the current accounting information signals either a rise in stock prices or strong dividend payments, holding the investment or even buying more shares is probably warranted. Conversely, if careful analysis indicates a possible drop in stock price or a reduction in dividend payments, sale of the stock is likely to be the appropriate action.

Interestingly, by the nature of the market, any exchange of ownership shares means that the buyer has studied available information and believes the future to be relatively optimistic for the business in question. In contrast, the seller has looked at similar data and arrived at a pessimistic outlook.

EXERCISE

Link to multiple-choice question for practice purposes: http://www.quia.com/quiz/2092616.html

Question: ***Are there reasons to analyze the financial accounting information produced by a particular business other than to help investors predict stock prices and cash dividend payments?***

Answer: The desire to analyze a company's financial situation is not limited to investors in the stock market. For example, as discussed previously, a loan might be requested from a bank or one company could be considering the sale of its merchandise to another on credit. Such obligations eventually require payment. Therefore, a sizeable portion of the parties that study the financial information reported by an organization is probably most interested in the likelihood that money will be available to pay its debts. Future stock prices and cash dividend distributions are much less significant speculations for a creditor.

The same financial data utilized by investors buying or selling stock will also be of benefit to current and potential creditors. However, this second group is likely to focus its attention on particular elements of the information such as the amount of the company's debt, when that debt is scheduled to come due, and the perceived ability to generate cash to meet those demands in a timely fashion. Ultimately, creditors attempt to anticipate the organization's cash flows to measure the risk that debt principal and interest payments might not be forthcoming when due.[8]

Therefore, millions of individuals use reported financial information to assess various business organizations in order to make three predictions:

- Future stock market prices for the capital shares issued by the company
- Future cash dividend distributions
- Future ability to generate sufficient cash to meet debts as they mature

The first two relate to investors in the capital stock of the company; the last is of more significance to a creditor.

Question: The term "financial information" comes up frequently in these discussions. ***What is meant by financial information?***

Answer: The financial information reported by and about an organization consists of data that can be measured in monetary terms. For example, if a building cost $4 million to acquire, that is financial information as is the assertion that a company owes a debt of $700,000 to a bank. In both cases, relevant information is communicated to decision makers as a monetary balance. However, if a company has eight thousand employees, that number might be interesting but it is not financial information. The figure is not a dollar amount; it is not stated in the form that is useful for decision-making purposes. Assuming that those workers were paid a total of $500 million during the current year, then that number is financial information because it is stated in terms of the money spent.

Likewise, a men's clothing store does not include in its financial information that it holds ten thousand shirts to be sold. Instead, the company reports that it currently owns shirts for sale (**inventory**) with a cost of, perhaps, $300,000. Or, after having sold these items to customers, the company could explain that it had made sales during the period for a total of $500,000.

inventory

A current asset bought or manufactured for the purpose of selling in order to generate revenue.

Question: The value of reported data seems somewhat restricted if it only includes dollar amounts. ***Is financial information limited solely to figures that can be stated in monetary terms?***

Answer: Although financial accounting starts by reporting balances as monetary amounts, the communication process does not stop there. Verbal explanations as well as additional numerical data are also provided to clarify or expand the information where necessary. To illustrate, assume that an organization is the subject of a lawsuit and estimates an eventual loss of $750,000. This is financial information to be reported based on the rules of financial accounting. However, the organization must also communicate other nonfinancial information such as the cause of the lawsuit and the likelihood that the loss will actually occur. Thus, accounting actually communicates to decision makers in two distinct steps:

1. Financial information is provided in monetary terms
2. Further explanation is given to clarify and expand on those monetary balances

KEY TAKEAWAY

Throughout the world, investors buy and sell the capital stock of thousands of businesses. Others choose to loan money to these same organizations. Such decisions are based on assessing potential risks and rewards. Financial accounting provides information to these interested parties to help them evaluate the possibility of stock value appreciation, cash dividend distributions, and the ability to generate cash to meet obligations as they come due. This information is financial in nature, meaning that it is stated in monetary terms. However, such numerical information alone is too limited. Thus, financial accounting provides financial information as well as clarifying verbal explanations to assist users in evaluating the financial health and potential of a particular organization.

Talking with a Real Investing Pro

Kevin G. Burns is a partner in his own registered investment advisory firm, the LLBH Private Wealth Management Group, an organization that specializes in asset management, concentrated stock strategies, and wealth transfer. LLBH consults on investing strategies for assets of nearly $1 billion. Before starting his own firm in October 2008, he was first vice president of Merrill Lynch Private Banking and Investment Group. Burns began his career on Wall Street in 1981 at Paine Webber. He has also worked at Oppenheimer & Co. and Smith Barney. Burns has appeared several times on the CBS Evening News. He has been kind enough to agree to be interviewed about his opinions and experiences in using accounting information. His firm's Web site is http://www.LLBHprivatewealthmanagement.com.

Question: You majored in accounting in college but you never worked in the accounting field. Instead, you became an investment advisor. If you never planned to become an accountant, why did you major in that subject?

Kevin Burns: In my view, accounting is the backbone of any business major in college. Being able to translate the information that a company provides, prepare a budget, understand the concept of revenues and expenses, and the like has been enormously helpful in my investment management business. Anyone majoring in any aspect of business needs that knowledge. I also liked being able to know I had the right answers on the tests that my accounting professors gave me when all the numbers added up properly.

Question: Why do you prefer to invest in the capital stock of a business rather than put your client's money in other forms of investment such as gold or real estate?

KB: I think it is very important to diversify investments. In my world, that includes stocks as well as other types of investments. Of course, there is a place for investments in real estate, commodities, and the like. My personal preference is to invest only in very liquid assets; those—such as stocks—that can be turned into cash quickly. I like to know, even if I am investing for the long term, that I can sell my investments five minutes after I buy them should I change my mind. I simply prefer liquid investments. Real estate is not very liquid. Gold, of course, is liquid. However, while it has appreciated lately, it was around $800 an ounce when I was in high school and is now about $900 an ounce. If my clients earned a total return of 10 or 12 percent on their money over forty years, they would fire me.

What Was Truly Important?

To students of financial accounting:

You have now read Chapter 1. What were the five that you encountered in this chapter that seemed most important to you? A lot of information is provided here. What stood out as truly significant? After you make your choices, go to the following link and watch a short video clip where one of the authors will make an analysis of the top five points presented here in Chapter 1. You can learn the rationale for these picks and see whether you agree or disagree with the selections.

Video Clip

Joe talks about the five most important points in Chapter 1.

View the video online at: http://blip.tv/play/sDyBv5RzAA

4. END-OF-CHAPTER EXERCISES

QUESTIONS

1. What is financial accounting?
2. How does financial accounting differ from managerial accounting?
3. List the potential users of the information provided by financial accounting.
4. What is a corporation?
5. How does a business become a corporation?
6. Why would a business want to become a corporation?
7. What is the board of directors of a corporation?
8. Why do individuals or entities choose to invest in the capital stock of corporations?
9. How does an investor differ from a creditor?
10. What is financial information?

TRUE OR FALSE

1. ____ Financial accounting helps with decisions made inside an organization.
2. ____ Typically, a sole proprietor will be able to raise money easier than a corporation.
3. ____ Employees are not users of the information provided by financial accounting.
4. ____ The board of directors of a corporation is elected by its shareholders.
5. ____ Investors who hold investments in a stock longer than a year may enjoy a tax benefit.
6. ____ Corporations are required by law to pay dividends to their shareholders.
7. ____ Purchasing stock is typically a riskier investment than opening a savings account.
8. ____ Financial information is communicated in monetary terms but may be explained verbally.
9. ____ Accountants are the only users of the information provided by financial accounting.
10. ____ An entity that loans a company money is referred to as a "shareholder."

MULTIPLE CHOICE

1. Ramon Sanchez is a loan officer at Washington Bank. He must decide whether or not to loan money to Medlock Corporation. Which of the following would Ramon most likely consider when making this decision?
    a. Medlock had positive cash flows last year.
    b. Medlock paid dividends last year.
    c. Medlock's stock price increased last year.
    d. The number of stockholders in Medlock increased last year.
2. Which of the following is not a reason an investor would purchase stock in a corporation?
    a. To receive dividend payments
    b. To sell the stock for a gain if the share price increases
    c. To earn a return on their investment
    d. To participate in the day-to-day operations of the business
3. Which of the following would not be considered an example of a decision made using financial accounting information?
    a. An investor decided to invest in the stock of Rayburn Corporation.
    b. A credit analyst at Mayfield Corporation rejected a request for credit from Rayburn Corporation.
    c. A Rayburn Corporation manager decided to increase production of widgets.
    d. A loan officer at Fairburn Bank chose to grant a loan request made by Rayburn Corporation.
4. Which of the following is most likely to have a say in the policy decision of a large corporation?
    a. A stockholder
    b. A member of the board of directors
    c. An employee
    d. A creditor
5. Leon Williams is an investor in Springfield Corporation. On September 1, Year One, he purchased 150 shares of stock at a price of $45 per share. On October 15, Year One, Springfield distributed dividends of $1.50 per share. On December 31, Year One, Springfield's stock is selling for $47 per share. Which of the following is the value of Leon's investment on December 31, Year One?
    a. $6,750
    b. $6,975
    c. $7,050
    d. $7,275

PROBLEMS

1. Explain how each of the following might use the information provided by the financial accounting of Nguyen Company.
   a. Bank loan officer considering loaning money to Nguyen Company.
   b. Current employee of Nguyen Company.
   c. Potential employee of Nguyen Company.
   d. Current investor in Nguyen Company.
   e. Potential investor in Nguyen Company.
   f. A credit analyst of company wanting to sell inventory to Nguyen Company.
2. Mark each of the following with an (F) to indicate if it is financial information or and (N) to indicate if it is nonfinancial information.

   Metro Corporation has:

   a. ____ Cash of $4,000,000
   b. ____ A building that cost $50,000,000
   c. ____ 2,000 employees
   d. ____ Inventory worth $16,000,000
   e. ____ 500 shares of capital stock
   f. ____ 1,000 trucks
   g. ____ Sales of $45,000,000

RESEARCH

1. The chapter introduced several forms of business, including a corporation, sole proprietorship, and partnership. Other forms of business exist as well. Do research to compare and contrast the following business forms:
   - Sole proprietorship
   - Partnership
   - Limited partnership
   - C corporation
   - S corporation
   - Limited liability corporation (LLC)

   Examine the following areas for each form of business: ease of organization and maintenance of form, number of people involved, government involvement, liability to owners, ease of exit, taxation, day-to-day management, and funding sources.
2. Corporations usually provide a good amount of financial information on their Web sites. Visit http://www.starbucks.com to access information about Starbucks. You will need to click "about us" at the top and then "investor relations" on the left.
   a. For what amount is Starbucks stock currently selling?
   b. Give the year for the most current annual report listed.
   c. Name three members of Starbucks board of directors.
   d. Click on "investor FAQ" on the left. Choose a question that interests you. Write it here and summarize the answer given.
3. Go the U.S. Department of Labor Web site at http://www.bls.gov/oco/ocos001.htm. Here you can learn about the profession of accounting.
   a. In general, what functions do accountants perform?
   b. Briefly list the different types of accountants and what they do.
   c. What education is required?
   d. What is a CPA?
   e. What are the typical requirements to become a CPA?
   f. What other certifications are available for accountants?
   g. What is the current job outlook for the accounting profession?

ENDNOTES

1. See http://www.deepsky.com/~madmagic/kofi.html.
2. Tax accounting serves as another distinct branch of accounting. It is less focused on decision making and more on providing the information needed to comply with all government rules and regulations. Even in tax accounting, though, decision making is important as companies seek to take all possible legal actions to minimize tax payments.
3. Sole proprietorships and partnerships rarely sell capital shares. Without the legal authority of incorporation, a clear distinction between owner and business often does not exist. For example, debts incurred by the business may ultimately have to be satisfied by the owner personally. Thus, individuals tend to avoid making investments in unincorporated businesses unless they can be involved directly in the management. For that reason, active trading of partnership and proprietorship ownership interests is usually limited or nonexistent. One of the great advantages of incorporation is the ease by which capital stock can usually be exchanged. Investors frequently buy or sell such shares on stock exchanges in a matter of moments. However, partnerships and sole proprietorships still remain popular because they are easy to create and offer possible income tax benefits as will be discussed in a future chapter.
4. The most prevalent form of capital stock is **common stock** so that these two terms have come to be used somewhat interchangeably. As will be discussed in a later chapter, the capital stock of some corporations is made up of both common stock and preferred stock.
5. A story produced by National Public Radio on the roles played by a board of directors can be found at http://www.npr.org/templates/story/story.php?storyId=105576374.
6. This same tax benefit is not available to corporate taxpayers, only individuals.
7. The receipt of cash dividends is additionally appealing to stockholders because, in most cases, they are taxed at the same reduced rates as are applied to net long-term capital gains.
8. Cash flows also influence stock prices and dividend payments and would, thus, be information useful for potential investors in the capital stock of a company as well as its creditors.

CHAPTER 2

What Should Decision-makers Know so That Good Decisions Can Be Made about an Organization?

Video Clip

Joe introduces Chapter 2 and speaks about the course in general.

View the video online at: http://blip.tv/play/sDyBvsxhAA

1. CREATING A PORTRAIT OF AN ORGANIZATION THAT CAN BE USED BY DECISION MAKERS

LEARNING OBJECTIVES

At the end of this section, students should be able to meet the following objectives:

1. **Explain the comparison of financial accounting to the painting of a portrait.**
2. **Understand the reasons why financial accounting information does not need to be exact.**
3. **Define the term "material" and describe its fundamental role in financial accounting.**
4. **Define the term "misstatement" and differentiate between the two types of misstatements.**

Question: In Chapter 1, mention was made that financial accounting is somewhat analogous to the painting of a giant, complex portrait. ***How could financial accounting possibly be compared to an artistic endeavor such as the creation of a painting?***

representative faithfulness

Agreement between a measure or description and the situation it purports to represent; in simpler terms, information that conveys an appropriate picture of underlying events or amounts.

presents fairly

Financial information that contains no material misstatements in accordance with U.S. generally accepted accounting principles (U.S. GAAP).

financial statements

Quantitative reports and related verbal disclosures describing and detailing the operations, financial position, and cash flows of an organization.

Answer: The purpose of a portrait—as might have been painted by Rembrandt, van Gogh, or even Picasso—is to capture a likeness of the artist's model. In a somewhat parallel fashion, financial accounting attempts to present a likeness of an organization that can be used by interested parties to assess its financial health and anticipate future stock prices, dividend payments, and cash flows. Accounting terms such as **representational faithfulness** and **presents fairly** are commonly used to indicate that reported financial information successfully provides a reasonable picture of the financial position, operations, cash flows, and overall economic vitality of a reporting organization.

In accounting, this portrait is created in the form of **financial statements**. These statements provide the form and structure for the conveyance of financial information to describe a particular organization. This textbook is about the preparation of those financial statements and the meaning of their contents.

A human portrait, even by a master such as Rembrandt, is not terribly precise. The shape of the person's chin or the turn of the neck may be off slightly; the color of the eyes and hair cannot possibly be a perfect replica of life. It is a painted portrait, not a photograph (which is much more mechanically accurate). However, absolute exactness is not a necessary element for capturing a proper likeness. Success is achieved when a viewer exclaims, "I know that person." Exact precision is not required to meet that objective.

Despite public perception, financial accounting information is rarely exact. For example, the reported cost of constructing a building may be off slightly because of the sheer volume of money being spent on the many different aspects of the project. No one expects the reported cost of a $50 million manufacturing plant to be accurate to the penny. As with the painted portrait, that does not necessarily reduce the usefulness of the data. If financial information is a fair representation, an interested party should be able to make use of it to arrive at the desired projections. A potential investor or creditor does not need numbers that are absolutely accurate in order to assert, "Based on the available financial information, I understand enough about this company to make informed decisions. Even if I could obtain figures that were precise, I believe that I would still take the same actions."

An artist applies oil paints, pastels, or watercolors to a canvas to capture the essence of a subject. An accountant does something quite similar by using numbers and words. The goal is much the same: to capture a likeness that truly reflects the essence of the model.

EXERCISE

Link to multiple-choice question for practice purposes: http://www.quia.com/quiz/2092599.html

Question: This is a surprising, possibly shocking, revelation. Financial accounting information has universally been branded as exhibiting rigid exactness. In fact, accountants are often referred to as "bean counters" because of their perceived need to count every bean in the bowl to arrive at obsessively accurate numbers. Here, though, the assertion is made that accounting information is not a precise picture but merely a fair representation of an organization's financial health and prospects. ***How correct or exact is the financial information that is reported by a business or other organization?***

materiality

The magnitude of an omission or misstatement of accounting information that makes it probable that the judgment of a reasonable person relying on the information would have been changed or influenced by that omission or misstatement.

Answer: In accounting, **materiality** has long been the underlying benchmark in the reporting of information. This concept requires that data presented by an organization to decision makers should never contain any material misstatementsmisstatements. For financial accounting information, this is the basic standard for the required level of accuracy. Decision makers want financial statements—such as those prepared by Starbucks or Intel—to contain no material misstatements. Because of their central role in this reporting process, understanding the terms "misstatement" and "material" is essential for any student seeking to understand financial accounting.

A misstatement is an **error** (made accidentally) or **fraud** (done intentionally) where reported figures or words actually differ from the underlying reality. For example, a company official could erroneously record a $100,000 expenditure that was made to acquire a new building as actually pertaining to the purchase of land. Consequently, the building's cost might be reported as $2.3 million when it was actually $2.4 million. This financial information is misstated. The balance presented for the building contains a $100,000 misstatement, as does the figure shown for land.

error

An unintentional misstatement of financial information.

fraud

An intentional misstatement of financial information; it can result from misappropriation of assets (theft) or fraudulent financial reporting.

A misstatement is judged to be material if it is so significant that its presence would impact a decision made by an interested party. Using the above illustration, assume the accidental $100,000 reduction in the reported cost of this building leads an outside decision maker to alter a choice being made (such as whether to buy or sell capital stock, the price to exchange for such shares, or whether to grant a loan). Because of that outcome, the misstatement is material by definition. Financial information can (and almost always does) contain misstatements. However, the reporting entity must take adequate precautions to ensure that the information holds no material misstatements for the simple reason that the data can no longer be considered fairly presented. The portrait of the company does not properly look like the model if it contains any material misstatements. The decision maker is being misled.

The concept of materiality can seem rather nebulous. For a small convenience store, a $10 misstatement is clearly not material whereas a $10 million one certainly is. For a company with real estate holdings of $30 billion, even a $10 million misstatement is probably not material. The problem for the accountant is determining where to draw the line for each organization. That is one of the most difficult decisions for any financial accountant. An exact dollar amount for materiality is virtually impossible to identify because it is a measure of the effect on an external party's judgment. Other than sheer magnitude, the cause of the problem must also be taken into consideration. An accidental mistake of $100,000 is probably less likely to be material than one of $100,000 that resulted from a fraudulent act. Both the size and cause should be weighed in judging whether the presence of a misstatement has the ability to impact a decision maker's actions.

Therefore, a financial accountant never claims that reported information is correct, accurate, or exact. Such precision is rarely possible and not needed when decision makers are analyzing the financial health and prospects of an organization. However, the accountant must take all precautions necessary to ensure that the data contains no material misstatements. Thus, financial figures are never released without reasonable assurance being obtained that no errors or other mistakes are present that could impact the decisions that will be made. All parties need to believe that reported information can be used with confidence in order to evaluate the financial condition and prospects of the organization as a whole.

When a company reports that a building was constructed at a cost of $2.3 million, the real message is that the cost was not materially different than $2.3 million. This figure is a fair representation of the amount spent, one that can be used in making decisions about the organization's current financial situation as well as its future prospects.

EXERCISE

Link to multiple-choice question for practice purposes: http://www.quia.com/quiz/2092618.html

KEY TAKEAWAY

Financial accounting does not attempt to provide exact numbers because such accuracy is often impossible to achieve and not really required by decision makers. Instead, reported accounting information is intended to provide a likeness of an organization and its operations, a type of portrait. To achieve this goal, the balances and other data cannot contain any material misstatements. A misstatement is inaccurate information reported by accident (an error) or intentionally (fraud). Materiality refers to the point at which the size or the nature of such misstatements would cause a change in the decisions made by an individual using that information. If all material misstatements can be eliminated, interested parties should be able to use the information to make considered decisions.

2. DEALING WITH UNCERTAINTY

LEARNING OBJECTIVES

At the end of this section, students should be able to meet the following objectives:

1. **Discuss the challenge created for financial accountants by the presence of uncertainty.**
2. **List examples of uncertainty that a financial accountant might face in reporting financial information.**
3. **Explain how financial accounting resembles a language.**

Question: Absolute accuracy is not necessary in order to estimate future stock prices, cash dividend payments, and cash flows. Thus, the concept of materiality as a standard guideline in reporting information is obviously quite important. However, financial accounting figures can still be exact. If a cash register is bought for $830.00, the cost is exactly $830.00. ***Even if not necessary, what prevents reported financial information from being precise?***

Answer: In truth, a reasonable percentage of the numbers reported in financial accounting are exact. Materiality is no issue in such cases. The cash register mentioned here will have a reported cost of $830.00—a precise measure of the amount paid. Likewise, a cash balance shown as $785.16 is exact to the penny. However, many of the other occurrences that must be reported by an organization do not lend themselves to such accuracy.

The primary reason that precision is not a goal—or often not even a possibility—in financial accounting can be summed up in a single word: uncertainty. Many of the events encountered every day by an organization contain some degree of uncertainty. Unfortunately, no technique exists to report uncertain events in precise terms.

When first introduced to financial accounting, many students assume that it is little more than the listing of cash receipts and disbursements in much the same way that elementary school children report how they spent their weekly allowances. That is a misconception. Financial accounting attempts to paint a fairly presented portrait of a company's overall operations, financial condition, and cash flows. This objective includes the reporting of events where a final resolution might not occur for years. Here are just a few examples of the kinds of uncertainty that virtually every business (and financial accountant) faces in reporting financial information.

- A company is the subject of a lawsuit. Perhaps a customer has filed this legal action claiming damage as a result of one of the company's products. Such legal proceedings are exceedingly common and can drag on in the courts for an extended period of time before a settlement is reached. The actual amount won or lost (if either occurs) might not be known for years. What should the company report *now*?
- A sale of merchandise is made today for $300 with the money to be collected from the customer in several months. Until the cash is received, the organization cannot be sure of the exact amount that will be collected. What should the company report *now*?
- An employee is promised a cash bonus next year that will be calculated based on any rise in the market price of the company's capital stock. Until the time passes and the actual increase (if any) is determined, the amount of this bonus remains a mystery. What should the company report *now*?
- A retail store sells a microwave oven today with a warranty. If the appliance breaks at any time during the next three years, the store has to pay for the repairs. No one knows whether the microwave will need to be fixed during this period. What should the company report *now*?

Any comprehensive list of the uncertainties faced regularly by most organizations would require pages to enumerate. Because of the quantity and variety of such unknowns, exact precision can simply not be an objective of financial reporting. For many accountants, dealing with so much uncertainty is the most interesting aspect of their job. Whenever the organization encounters a situation of this type, the accountant must first come to understand what has taken place and then determine a logical method to communicate a fair representation of that information within the appropriate framework provided by financial accounting. This is surely one of the major challenges of being a financial accountant.

Question: Accounting is sometimes referred to as the "language of business." However, the goal of financial accounting had already been identified as the painting of a fairly presented portrait of an organization. ***Given the references throughout this chapter to painting, is accounting really a type of language?*** *Is it possible for accounting to paint portraits and be a language?*

Answer: The simple answer to this question is that accounting is a language, one that enables an organization to communicate a portrait of its financial health and future prospects to interested parties by using words and numbers rather than oils or watercolors. That language becomes especially helpful when an organization faces the task of reporting complex uncertainties.

Any language, whether it is English, Spanish, Japanese or the like, has been developed through much use to allow for the effective transfer of information between two or more parties. If a sentence such as "I drive a red car" is spoken, communication occurs but only if both the speaker and the listener have an adequate understanding of the English language. Based solely on these five words, information can be passed from one person to the other. This process succeeds because English (as well as other languages) relies on relatively standardized terminology. Words like "red," "car," and "drive" have defined meanings that the speaker and the listener can each comprehend with a degree of certainty. In addition, grammar rules are utilized such as syntax and punctuation to provide a framework for the communication. Thus, effective communication is possible in a language when (1) set terminology exists and (2) structural rules and principles are applied.

As will be gradually introduced throughout this textbook, financial accounting has its own terminology. Many words and terms (such as "LIFO" and "accumulated depreciation") have very specific meanings. In addition, a comprehensive set of rules and principles has been established over the decades to provide structure and standardization. They guide the reporting process so that the resulting information will be fairly presented and can be readily understood by all interested parties, both inside and outside of the organization.

Some students who read this textbook will eventually become accountants. Those individuals must learn the terminology, rules, and principles in order to communicate financial information about an organization that is fairly presented. Other students will become external decision makers. They will make loans, buy stock, grant credit, make employment decisions, provide investment advice, and the like. They will not present financial information with all of its uncertainties but rather make use of it. The more such individuals know about financial accounting terminology, rules, and principles, the more likely it is that they will make appropriate decisions.

To communicate a portrait properly in any language, both the speaker and the listener must understand the terminology as well as the structural rules and principles. That holds even if the language is financial accounting.

KEY TAKEAWAY

At any point in time, organizations face numerous uncertain outcomes such as the settlement of litigation or the collection of a receivable. The conveyance of useful information about uncertain situations goes beyond the simple reporting of exact numbers. To convey a reasonable understanding of such uncertainty, financial accounting must serve as a language. Thus, it will have set terminology and structural rules much like that of any language.

3. THE NEED FOR GENERALLY ACCEPTED ACCOUNTING PRINCIPLES

LEARNING OBJECTIVES

At the end of this section, students should be able to meet the following objectives:

1. **Describe the purpose of U.S. generally accepted accounting principles (U.S. GAAP) and the benefits that these rules provide.**
2. **Explain the importance of U.S. GAAP to the development of a capitalistic economy.**
3. **Understand the role played by the Financial Accounting Standards Board (FASB) in the ongoing evolution of U.S. GAAP.**
4. **Discuss the advantages and the possibility of switching from U.S. GAAP to International Financial Reporting Standards (IFRS).**

Question: Rules and principles exist within financial accounting that must be followed. They provide the standard guidance necessary for achieving effective communication. For example, assume that a reporting organization encounters an uncertainty (such as a lawsuit) and is now preparing financial information to portray the reality of that event. ***When faced with complexity, how does the financial accountant***

know what reporting guidelines to follow? *How does a decision maker looking at reported information know what reporting guidelines have been followed?*

U.S. generally accepted accounting principles (U.S. GAAP)

A recognized set of accounting rules used and followed in the United States of America.

Answer: A significant body of **generally accepted accounting principles** (frequently referred to as **U.S. GAAP**) has been created in the United States over many decades to provide authoritative guidance and standardization for financial accounting. When faced with a reporting issue such as a lawsuit, the accountant consults U.S. GAAP to arrive at an appropriate resolution, one that results in fair presentation. If both the accountant and the decision maker understand U.S. GAAP, even the most complex financial information can be conveyed successfully. A proper likeness can be portrayed and communicated.

Thus, the financial information to be distributed by an organization in the form of financial statements is structured according to U.S. GAAP. This textbook is an exploration of those accounting principles that serve as the foundation for financial accounting in this country.[1]

Based on coverage here, students who seek to become accountants can learn to report financial information that is fairly presented. That means that it is reported according to U.S. GAAP so that it contains no material misstatements. Students who want to evaluate specific organizations in order to make decisions about them should learn U.S. GAAP in order to understand the data being reported.

Although some elements of U.S. GAAP have been in use almost throughout history, many of these rules and principles are relatively new—often developed within the last twenty to thirty years. Accounting principles evolve quite quickly as the nature of business changes and new issues, problems, and resolutions arise. Fairly important changes in U.S. GAAP occur virtually every year.

The existence of U.S. GAAP means that a business in Seattle, Washington, and a business in Atlanta, Georgia, will account for information in much the same manner.[2] Because of this standardization, any decision maker with an adequate knowledge of financial accounting—whether located in Phoenix, Arizona, or in Portland, Maine—should be able to understand the fairly presented financial information conveyed by a wide variety of companies. They all speak the same language. Put simply, U.S. GAAP enables organizations and other parties to communicate successfully.

EXERCISE

Link to multiple-choice question for practice purposes: http://www.quia.com/quiz/2092600.html

Question: An article in the Wall Street Journal *contained the following comment about U.S. GAAP: "When the intellectual achievements of the 20th century are tallied, GAAP should be on everyone's Top 10 list. The idea of GAAP—so simple yet so radical—is that there should be a standard way of accounting for profit and loss in public businesses, allowing investors to see how a public company manages its money. This transparency is what allows investors to compare businesses as different as McDonald's, IBM and Tupperware, and it makes U.S. markets the envy of the world."*[3]

Could U.S. GAAP be so very important? *Can the development of U.S. GAAP possibly be one of the ten most important intellectual achievements of the entire twentieth century? A list of other accomplishments during this period would include air travel, creation of computers, landing on the moon, and the development of penicillin. With that level of competition, U.S. GAAP does not seem an obvious choice to be in the top ten. How can it be so important?*

Answer: The United States has a capitalistic economy, which means that businesses are (for the most part) owned by private citizens and groups rather than by the government. To operate and grow, these companies must convince investors and creditors to contribute huge amounts of their own money voluntarily. Not surprisingly, such financing is only forthcoming if the possible risks and rewards can be assessed and then evaluated with sufficient reliability. Before handing over thousands or even millions of dollars, investors and creditors must believe that they have the reliable data required to make reasonable estimations of future stock prices, cash dividends, and cash flows. Otherwise, buying stocks and granting credit is no more than gambling. As this quote asserts, U.S. GAAP enables these outside parties to obtain the information they need to reduce their perceived risk to acceptable levels.

Without U.S. GAAP, investors and creditors would encounter significant difficulties in evaluating the financial health and future prospects of an organization.[4] They would face even greater uncertainty and be likely to hold on to their money or invest only in other, safer options. Consequently, if U.S. GAAP did not exist, the development and expansion of thousands of the businesses that have become a central part of today's society would be limited or impossible simply because of the lack of available resources.

By any standard, the explosive development of the U.S. economy during the twentieth century (especially following World War II) has been spectacular, close to unbelievable. This growth has been fueled by massive amounts of money flowing from inside and outside the United States into the country's businesses. Much of the vitality of the U.S. economy results from the willingness of people to risk their money by buying capital stock or making loans to such companies as McDonald's, IBM, and Tupperware. Without those resources, most businesses would be small or nonexistent and the United States would surely be a radically different country.

Question: ***If U.S. GAAP is so very important, who creates it?*** *If U.S. GAAP is constantly evolving, how does that occur?*

Answer: Since 1973, the primary authoritative body in charge of producing U.S. GAAP has been the Financial Accounting Standards Board (frequently referred to as FASB).[5] FASB is an independent group supported by the U.S. government, various accounting organizations, and private businesses. It is charged with establishing and improving the standards by which businesses and not-for-profit organizations (such as charities) produce the financial information that they distribute to decision makers.

Typically, accounting problems arise over time within various areas of financial reporting. New types of financial events can be created, for example, that are not covered by U.S. GAAP or, perhaps, weaknesses in earlier rules start to become evident. If such concerns grow to be serious, FASB will step in and study the issues and alternatives and possibly pass new rules or make amendments to previous ones. FASB is methodical in its deliberations and the entire process can take years. Changes, additions, and deletions to U.S. GAAP are not made without proper consideration.

Several other bodies also play important roles in the creation of U.S. GAAP. They are normally discussed in detail in upper-level accounting textbooks. However, the major authority for the ongoing evolution of U.S. GAAP lies with FASB and its seven-member board. It released approximately 170 official statements during its first thirty-six years of existence. The impact that those rulings—and other types of FASB pronouncements—has had on U.S. GAAP and the financial reporting process is almost impossible to overemphasize. In 2009, FASB combined all authoritative accounting literature into a single source for U.S. GAAP, which is known as the *Accounting Standards Codification*. By bringing together hundreds of official documents, FASB has made U.S. GAAP both more understandable and easier to access. Multiple sources have been woven together in a logical fashion so that all rules on each topic are in one location.

As just one example, FASB recently made a number of critical changes in the method by which businesses report the costs and obligations that arise from certain types of employee pension plans. Previous rules had been the subject of much criticism by the investing community for failing to properly portray the financial impact of such plans. After much discussion, the members of the board came to believe that new rules were needed to improve the method by which organizations reported these obligations to decision makers trying to predict stock prices, cash dividends, and cash flows.

KEY TAKEAWAY

No language can enable communication without some standardization and rules. In the United States, this structure is created by U.S. generally accepted accounting principles (U.S. GAAP). The availability of these authoritative guidelines has played a central role in the growth of the U.S. economy since the end of the Great Depression. U.S. GAAP is constantly evolving as accountants seek better methods of providing financial information in an ever changing business world. The main authority for the development of U.S. GAAP lies with the Financial Accounting Standards Board (FASB). Over the next decade, U.S. GAAP may be replaced by International Financial Reporting Standards (IFRS) to provide consistent accounting and financial reporting around the world.

Talking with an Independent Auditor about International Financial Reporting Standards

Robert A. Vallejo is a partner in the assurance (audit) practice of the public accounting firm PricewaterhouseCoopers (PWC).[6] From 2006 until 2008, he served as a consulting partner in PWC's national professional services group in Paris, France. He currently works out of the firm's Richmond, Virginia, office, but during his career with that organization, he also served clients in Amsterdam and Philadelphia. Rob is the founder of the Philadelphia Chapter of ALPFA (the Association of Latino Professionals in Finance and Accounting). Because of his years of work in Europe, he has extensive experience implementing International Financial Reporting Standards.

Question: Over the past fifty years or so, the accounting profession in the United States has developed a very comprehensive set of official guidelines referred to collectively as U.S. generally accepted accounting principles. Recently, a strong push has developed to move away from U.S. GAAP and adopt the pronouncements of the International Accounting Standards Board, which are known as International Financial Reporting Standards (IFRS). If U.S. GAAP has worked successfully for so many years, what is the need to abandon them in favor of a new system that is not necessarily well understood in the United States?

Rob Vallejo: Recent economic events have shown how interrelated the world's economies really are. Therefore, it makes common sense that all companies around the world should report their financial information in accordance with the same set of accounting standards. However, the United States is one of the few remaining jurisdictions that has not adopted IFRS. Switching to IFRS in the United States will allow for more comparable financial information across the globe. Another argument in favor of the adoption of IFRS is the complexity of U.S. GAAP. U.S. GAAP is a very rules-based set of standards that has evolved to address the ever-changing business world, creating a maze of standards that is difficult to navigate. IFRS is more principles-based, allowing the preparers of financial information more judgment in applying the standards to a wide variety of situations. Lastly, the U.S. standard setters are very likely to become more involved in the evolution of IFRS so that the U.S. perspective will be appropriately represented.

Question: Rob, at key spots throughout this textbook, you have agreed to help us understand the impact that a change to IFRS will have on financial reporting in the United States. Obviously, the future is always difficult to anticipate with precision. However, what is your best guess as to when IFRS will start to be used in the financial statements issued by U.S. companies? At a basic level, as is appropriate in an introductory financial accounting course, how much real difference will be created by a change from U.S. GAAP to IFRS?

RV: The move to IFRS is being driven by the Securities and Exchange Commission (SEC). In 2008, the SEC published a road map that calls for the largest U.S. publicly traded companies to publish their annual results for the year ending December 31, 2014, in accordance with IFRS. Some larger companies may begin much sooner. Smaller public companies will have a little more time, but all of these companies should be transitioned to IFRS by the year ending December 31, 2016. In practical terms, this timetable might be delayed due to other recent priorities at the SEC. Even if there is a delay, I believe the switch to IFRS will eventually happen in the United States. In general, the move to IFRS from U.S. GAAP will not have a substantial impact on the financial information being reported by most companies. However, because of the many subtle differences between IFRS and U.S. GAAP, the preparers of financial information will have a lot of work to do in order to transition their reporting properly. As is the case many times, the devil is in the details.

4. FOUR BASIC TERMS FOUND IN FINANCIAL ACCOUNTING

LEARNING OBJECTIVES

At the end of this section, students should be able to meet the following objectives:

1. **Define "asset" and provide examples in financial reporting.**
2. **Define "liability" and provide examples in financial reporting.**
3. **Define "revenue" and provide examples in financial reporting.**
4. **Define "expense" and provide examples in financial reporting.**

Question: Attaining a thorough understanding of financial accounting and U.S. GAAP is a worthwhile endeavor especially if a person hopes to become successful in analyzing businesses or other organizations. ***Where should the journey to gain knowledge of financial accounting and its principles begin?***

Answer: The study of a language usually starts with basic terminology. That is also an appropriate point of entry for an exploration into financial accounting. Consequently, four fundamental terms will be introduced here. Knowledge of these words is essential to understanding accounting because they serve as the foundation for a significant portion of the financial information provided by any business or other organization.

To illustrate, when examining the 2008 financial statements presented by Safeway Inc. (the large retail grocery store chain), four monetary balances stand out because of their enormous size. As of the end of that year, this corporation reported $17.5 billion in **assets** along with $10.7 billion in **liabilities**. During that year, Safeway generated **revenues** of $44.1 billion and incurred **expenses** of $43.1 billion.

- Assets
- Liabilities
- Revenues
- Expenses

There are thousands of words and concepts found in financial accounting. However, no terms are more crucial to a comprehensive understanding than these four. Almost all discussions concerning financial reporting, whether practical or theoretical, come back to one or more of these words.

assets

Future economic benefits owned or controlled by an organization.

liabilities

Future sacrifices of economic benefits arising from present obligations, the debts of an organization.

revenues

Measures of the increases in or inflows of net assets (assets minus liabilities) resulting from the sale of goods and services.

expenses

Measures of decreases in or outflows of net assets (assets minus liabilities) incurred in connection with the generation of revenues.

inventory

A current asset bought or manufactured for the purpose of selling in order to generate revenue.

*Question: The first term presented here is "asset." Is an asset a complicated accounting concept? **What general information is conveyed to a decision maker by the term "asset?"***

Answer: Simply put, an asset is a future economic benefit that an organization either owns or controls.[7] At the end of 2008, Safeway reported holding over $17.5 billion of these economic benefits. If a customer walks into one of that company's retail stores, many of the assets are easy to spot. The building itself may well be owned by the company and certainly provides a probable future economic benefit by allowing Safeway to display merchandise and make sales. Other visible assets are likely to include cash registers, the cash held in those machines, available merchandise from baby food to broccoli to paper towels (usually referred to as **inventory** in financial accounting), refrigerators, shopping carts, delivery trucks, and the shelves and display cases. Each of those assets will help the company to prosper in the future.

*Question: All decision makers evaluating the financial health of an organization should be quite interested in learning about its assets because those balances reflect the economic resources held at the present time. This is valuable information. To provide additional clarification, **what are the largest assets reported by Safeway?***

Answer: As a result of financial reporting, such information is readily available to anyone wanting to learn about virtually any business. At the end of 2008, the following four assets were reported by Safeway as having the highest dollar amounts:

Fixtures and Equipment	$7.8 billion
Buildings	$5.7 billion
Leasehold Improvements[8]	$3.8 billion
Merchandise Inventories	$2.6 billion

The underlying meaning of these four figures will be explained at later points in this textbook.

EXERCISE

Link to multiple-choice question for practice purposes: http://www.quia.com/quiz/2092633.html

*Question: Safeway also reported owing nearly $11 billion in liabilities at the end of 2008. Does this balance reflect the total amount that the company will eventually have to pay to outside parties? **Are liabilities the equivalent of monetary debts?***

Answer: A more formal definition of a liability is that it is a probable future sacrifice of economic benefits arising from present obligations but, for coverage here, liabilities can certainly be viewed as the debts of the organization.

The $11 billion liability total disclosed by Safeway probably includes (1) amounts owed to the vendors who supply merchandise to the company's stores, (2) notes due to banks as a result of loans, (3) income tax obligations, and (4) balances to be paid to employees, utility companies, advertising agencies, and the like. The amount of such liabilities reported by many businesses can be staggering. Wal-Mart, for example, disclosed approximately $98 billion in liabilities as of January 31, 2009. However, even that amount pales in comparison to the $684 billion liability total reported by General

Electric at the end of 2008.[9] To ensure that a fairly presented portrait is being produced, companies such as Safeway and General Electric must make certain that the reported data contains no material misstatements. Thus, all the information that is provided to decision makers about liabilities should be based on the rules and principles to be found in U.S. GAAP.

EXERCISE

Link to multiple-choice question for practice purposes: http://www.quia.com/quiz/2092634.html

Question: In financial accounting, a company reports its assets, which are future economic benefits such as buildings, equipment, and cash. Liabilities (debts) are also included in the financial information being disclosed. Both of these terms seem relatively straightforward. The third basic term to be discussed at this time—revenues—is one that initially appears to be a bit less clear. Safeway reported that its stores generated revenues of over $44 billion in 2008 alone. ***What information is conveyed by a company's revenue balance?***

Answer: The term "revenue" is a measure of the financial impact on a company resulting from a particular process. This process is a sale. A customer enters a Safeway grocery store and pays $20 to purchase items such as cookies, toothpaste, lettuce, and milk. The company receives an asset, possibly a $20 bill. This $20 asset inflow into the company results from a sale and is called revenue. Revenue is *not* an asset; it is a measure of the increase in the company's net assets[10] that results from sales of inventory and services. As will be discussed in more detail in Chapter 3, for reporting purposes, these sales must result from the primary or central operation of the business. Thus, for The Coca-Cola Company, revenues are derived from the sale of soft drinks. Sales resulting from noncentral parts of the company's operations (perhaps the disposal of a piece of land, for example) will be reported in a different manner.

Throughout each day of the year, Safeway makes sales to customers and accepts cash, checks, or credit card payments. The reported revenue figure is merely a total of all sales made during the period, clearly relevant information to any decision maker attempting to determine the financial prospects of this company. During 2008, the multitude of Safeway stores located both inside and outside of the United States sold inventory and received over $44 billion in assets in exchange. That is the information communicated by the reported revenue balance. To reiterate, this figure is not exact, precise, accurate, or correct. However, according to the company, it is a fairly presented total determined according to the rules of U.S. GAAP so that it contains no material misstatement. Any outside party analyzing Safeway should be able to rely on this number with confidence in making possible decisions about the company as a whole.

EXERCISE

Link to multiple-choice question for practice purposes: http://www.quia.com/quiz/2092619.html

EXERCISE

Link to multiple-choice question for practice purposes: http://www.quia.com/quiz/2092620.html

Question: That leaves "expense" as the last of the four basic accounting terms being introduced at this point. Safeway reported $43.1 billion in total expenses during 2008. This figure apparently is essential information that helps paint a proper portrait of the company. ***What is an expense?***

Answer: An expense is an outflow or reduction in net assets[11] that was incurred by an organization in hopes of generating revenues. To illustrate, assume that—at the end of a week—a local business pays its employees $12,000 for the work performed during the previous few days. A $12,000 salary expense must be reported. Cash (an asset) was reduced by that amount and this cost was incurred because the company employed those individuals to help generate revenues. The same general logic can be applied in recording insurance expense, rent expense, advertising expense, utility expense (such as for electricity and water), and many other similar costs.

In some ways, expenses are the opposite of revenues that measure the inflows or increases in net assets created by sales. Expense figures reflect outflows or decreases in net assets incurred in hopes of generating revenues.

EXERCISE

Link to multiple-choice question for practice purposes: http://www.quia.com/quiz/2092601.html

Question: To reiterate, four terms are basic to an understanding of financial accounting. Almost any coverage of accounting starts with these four. ***What is the meaning of asset, liability, revenue, and expense?***

Answer:

- *Asset.* A future economic benefit owned or controlled by the reporting company such as inventory, land, or equipment.
- *Liability.* A probable future economic sacrifice or, in simple terms, a debt.
- *Revenue.* A measure of the inflow or increase in net assets generated by the sales made by a company. It is a reflection of the amounts brought into the company by the sales process during a specified period of time.
- *Expense.* A measure of the outflow or reduction in net assets caused by the company's attempt to generate revenues and includes costs such as rent expense, salary expense, and insurance expense.

KEY TAKEAWAY

A strong knowledge of basic accounting terminology is essential for successful communication to take place in the reporting of financial information. Four terms provide a foundational core around which much of the accounting process is constructed. Assets are future economic benefits owned or controlled by an organization. Assets typically include cash, inventory, land, buildings, and equipment. Liabilities are the debts of the reporting entity such as salary payable, rent payable, and notes payable. Revenue figures indicate the increase in a company's net assets (its assets minus its liabilities) that is created by a sale of goods or services. Revenues are the lifeblood of any organization. Without the inflow of cash or receivables that comes from generating sales, a company cannot exist for long. Expenses are decreases in net assets that are incurred by a company in hopes of generating revenues. Expenses incurred by most companies run a full gamut from rent and salary to insurance and electricity.

Talking with a Real Investing Pro (Continued)

Following is a continuation of our interview with Kevin G. Burns.

Question: Financial accountants tend to place a heavy emphasis on the importance of generally accepted accounting principles (U.S. GAAP) to the world of business. After nearly three decades as an investment advisor, what is your opinion of the relevance of U.S. GAAP?

Kevin Burns: Before the accounting scandals of the late 1990s—such as Enron and WorldCom—financial information that adhered to U.S. GAAP was trusted worldwide. Investors around the globe took comfort in a standard that had such a great reputation for integrity. In the 1990s, though, I felt that U.S. GAAP become somewhat muddied because investors wanted to depend too heavily on one or two figures rather than judging the company as a whole. In the last several years, FASB has moved back to stressing clearer transparency for reported information. That objective enables investors to better see and understand the organization standing behind those statements. That is important in order to maintain investor confidence.

As for the current state of the U.S. GAAP, it is certainly superior to the majority of the world's standards. Unfortunately, it is getting more complicated every year, which is not always a good goal.

Question: Are you bothered by the fact that the financial information that is reported to you by a business is not terribly exact?

KB: No reporting system can ever be exact and many estimates are necessary in reporting any business. Am I bothered by the lack of precision? No, not particularly. I will say, though, that I tend to avoid companies that have an excessive quantity of notes to their financial statements. Many of those companies can be extremely difficult to evaluate because of the complexity of their operations. I prefer businesses where the analysis is a bit simpler and I am able to gain a genuine understanding of what is happening.

Question: When you begin to study the financial data reported by a company that you are analyzing as an investment possibility, which do you look at first: revenues, expenses, assets, or liabilities?

KB: For me, assets have always been the most important determination in the investments that I have chosen. However, that is because I have always been strictly a value investor. There are many different styles of investing. Value investors look at the value of a company's assets and then look for bargains based on current market prices. In comparison, growth investors look at earnings momentum and don't care too much about asset values. They like to see a consistent rise in profitability each year. Over the years, being a value investor has worked well for my clients and me.

Video Clip

Joe talks about the five most important points in Chapter 2.

View the video online at: http://blip.tv/play/sDyBv5URAA

5. END-OF-CHAPTER EXERCISES

QUESTIONS

1. Why is it acceptable for financial accounting to be imprecise?
2. What is materiality?
3. How is materiality determined?
4. What is a misstatement?
5. When is a misstatement considered fraud?
6. Give three examples of uncertainties faced by businesses.
7. Define U.S. GAAP.
8. Why is GAAP so important to the capital market system in the United States?
9. Who creates U.S. GAAP?
10. Define asset and give an example of one.
11. Define liability and give an example of one.
12. Define revenue.
13. Define expense.

TRUE OR FALSE

1. _____ Most countries require companies to follow U.S. GAAP in preparing their financial statements.
2. _____ Companies face many uncertainties when preparing their financial statements.
3. _____ A liability is defined as a future economic benefit that an organization owns or controls.
4. _____ Creation of U.S. GAAP is primarily done by the U.S. government.
5. _____ In order for investors to evaluate the financial information of a company, it is vital that the financial information be exact.
6. _____ Materiality depends on the size of the organization.
7. _____ Material misstatements made on financial statements are acceptable as long as there are only a few of them.
8. _____ An example of an uncertainty faced by companies in financial statements is a pending law suit.
9. _____ Only accountants need to understand the terminology of accounting.
10. _____ An employee is an example of an asset.
11. _____ A sale is usually considered revenue even if cash is not collected.
12. _____ The purchase of a building is recorded as an expense.
13. _____ A deliberate misstatement is known as fraud.

MULTIPLE CHOICE

1. Which of the following is not an example of an uncertainty companies face in their financial reporting?
   a. Sales that have not yet been collected in cash
   b. Warranties
   c. A loan due to a bank
   d. A law suit that has been filed against the company
2. Which is of the following is true about U.S. GAAP?
   a. S. GAAP has been developed over the past ten years.
   b. S. GAAP allows financial statement users to compare the financial information of companies around the world.
   c. S. GAAP helps accountants achieve an exact presentation of a company's financial results.
   d. S. GAAP helps investors and creditors evaluate the financial health of a company.

Questions 3, 4, and 5 are based on the following:

Mike Gomez owns a music store called "Mike's Music and More." The store has inventory that includes pianos, guitars, and other musical instruments. Mike rents the building in which his store is located, but owns the equipment and fixtures inside of it. Last week, Mike's Music made sales of $3,000. Some of the sales were made in cash. Some were made to customers who have an account with Mike's Music and are billed at the end of the month. Last month, Mike's Music borrowed $10,000 from a local bank to expand.

3. Which of the following is not an asset owned by Mike's Music?
   a. The inventory of musical instruments
   b. The building in which the store is located
   c. The amount owed to Mike's Music by its customers
   d. The equipment and fixtures in the store
4. Which of the following is a liability to Mike's Music?
   a. The loan amount that must be repaid to the bank
   b. The amount owed to Mike's Music by its customers
   c. The sales Mike's made last week
   d. The cash collected from customers on the sales made last week
5. Which of the following is a true statement?
   a. Mike's Music is too small for anyone to care about its financial information.
   b. The sales Mike's Music made last week are considered revenue.
   c. The intent of Mike's Music to expand is an asset.
   d. The sales Mike's Music made on credit last week cannot be considered revenue.

PROBLEM

Mark each of the following with an (A) to indicate it is an asset, an (L) to indicate it is a liability, an (R) to indicate it is revenue or an (E) to indicate it is an expense.

a. ____ Cash
b. ____ Building
c. ____ Loan due to the bank
d. ____ Inventory
e. ____ Salary expense
f. ____ Rent expense
g. ____ Amounts owed to employees for work done
h. ____ Equipment
i. ____ Amounts owed to suppliers
j. ____ Sales

RESEARCH

1. The chapter introduces the Financial Accounting Standards Board (FASB) as the body that has primary responsibility for determining U.S. GAAP. You can learn more about this organization at http://www.fasb.org. On the menu to the left, click on "Facts about FASB."
   a. How long has FASB been in existence?
   b. From which organization does FASB get its power?
   c. Why do you think it is important that FASB be independent?
   d. What role does the Financial Accounting Foundation play?
   e. Name two current members of FASB.
   f. What is the EITF?
2. Four fundamental accounting terms were introduced in Chapter 2: assets, liabilities, revenues, and expenses. We will explore these items further by examining the financial statements of Starbucks. You can access their financial statements by visiting http://www.starbucks.com. You will need to click "about us" at the top and then "investor relations" on the left. Click on "annual reports" in the menu on the left. Select the 2007 Annual Report—Financials. On the left side menu, select Item 8 (financial statements).
   a. The first page contains a statement showing the revenues and expenses for the year. What is this statement called?
   b. What was Starbucks total net revenue for the year?
   c. Based on your understanding of Chapter 2, can you say that this revenue number reported is the exact revenue earned by Starbucks in 2007? If not, what can you say about this revenue number?
   d. List two expenses reported by Starbucks.
   e. The statement on the next page reports Starbucks assets and liabilities. What is this statement called?
   f. Name two assets and two liabilities reported by Starbucks.

ENDNOTES

1. Many countries other than the United States have developed their own individual systems of generally accepted accounting principles. These alternatives are utilized in specific areas of the world. In addition, international accounting standards (created by the London-based International Accounting Standards Board) known formally as International Financial Reporting Standards, or IFRS, also exist and are now used in numerous countries. U.S. GAAP is by far the most sophisticated system in the world because a significant portion of the capital markets exist here. Unless noted otherwise, U.S. GAAP is being described in this textbook. However, in recent years, a strong push toward universal acceptance of IFRS has taken place. Therefore, their potential impact will be analyzed throughout this book in special discussions of relevant topics.

2. As will be discussed later in this textbook, key points exist within financial accounting where more than one approach can be used for reporting purposes. Rigid standardization is found in many areas of financial reporting but not in all.

3. Clay Shirky, "How Priceline Became a Real Business," *Wall Street Journal*, August 13, 2001, A-12.

4. The recent wide scale financial meltdown in the world economy has put a serious strain on the traditional capitalist model. The U.S. and other governments have had to spend billions of dollars to bailout (and, in some cases, takeover) major enterprises. Whether U.S. GAAP could have done a better job to help avoid this calamity will probably not be fully known for years.

5. Considerable information can be found about the Financial Accounting Standards Board by touring http://www.fasb.org. The tab "About FASB" is especially informative.

6. The role played in the U.S. economy by public accounting firms will be described in Chapter 6. Some of these organizations have grown to enormous size. According to its Web site as of July 9, 2009 (http://www.pwc.com), PricewaterhouseCoopers employs 155,000 individuals working in over 150 countries. During 2008, the firm received in excess of $28 billion from customers for the services it rendered to them.

7. This is an opening chapter in an introductory financial accounting textbook. Definitions are somewhat simplified here so as to be more understandable to students who are just beginning their exploration of accounting. Many terms and definitions will be expanded in later chapters of this textbook or in upper-level accounting courses.

8. Leasehold improvements represent the remaining cost of any structural changes that were made by the company to improve property that it was only renting and did not own. In many cases, for financing purposes and tax reasons, companies prefer to rent space—for example, in a shopping mall—rather than buy it. While renting, companies often spend significant amounts of money to adapt the facility to their own particular needs. This cost is reported as an asset because the changes will benefit the company in the future. In accounting, this asset is commonly known as a leasehold improvement.

9. To help fully comprehend the magnitude of the debt owed by General Electric, consider that 684 billion one-dollar bills laid end to end would circle Earth at the equator approximately 2,662 times, or about 66 million miles.

10. "Net assets" is a term that reflects a company's assets less its liabilities. Revenue can also be created by a decrease in a liability rather than an increase in an asset, but that rarely happens in the business world.

11. An expense can cause a reduction in assets, especially if cash is paid. Frequently, though, an expense creates an increase in liabilities if the cost is incurred but payment has not yet been conveyed. In either case—the reduction of an asset or the creation of a liability—the amount of net assets held by the organization decreases.

CHAPTER 3
In What Form Is Financial Information Actually Delivered to Decision Makers Such as Investors and Creditors?

Video Clip

Joe introduces Chapter 3 and speaks about the course in general.

View the video online at: http://blip.tv/play/sDyBv5ssAA

1. THE CONSTRUCTION OF AN INCOME STATEMENT

LEARNING OBJECTIVES

At the end of this section, students should be able to meet the following objectives:

1. **Understand that financial statements provide the structure for companies to report financial information to decision makers.**
2. **Identify each of the four financial statements typically reported by a company.**
3. **List the normal contents of an income statement.**
4. **Define gains and losses and explain how they differ from revenues and expenses.**
5. **Explain cost of goods sold.**
6. **Compute gross profit and the gross profit percentage.**
7. **Describe the location of income taxes within an income statement.**

Question: The revenues, expenses, assets, and liabilities reported by an organization provide data that is essential for decision making. The informational value of these figures enables a thorough analysis of an organization and its financial health and future prospects. How do outsiders learn of these amounts? ***How is financial data actually conveyed to interested parties?*** *For example, a company such as Marriott International Inc. (the hotel chain) has possibly millions of current and potential shareholders, creditors, and employees. How does such a company communicate vital financial information to all the groups and individuals that might want to make some type of considered evaluation?*

Answer: Businesses and other organizations periodically produce financial statements that provide a formal structure for conveying financial information to decision makers. Smaller organizations distribute such statements each year, frequently as part of an annual report prepared by management. Larger companies, like Marriott International, issue yearly statements but also prepare interim statements, usually on a quarterly basis.[1] Regardless of the frequency of preparation, financial statements serve as the vehicle to report all the monetary balances and explanatory information required according to the rules and principles of U.S. generally accepted accounting principles (U.S. GAAP). Based on these standards, such statements are intended as a fairly presented portrait of the organization—one that contains no material misstatements. In simple terms, a company's revenues, expenses, assets, and liabilities are reported to outsiders by means of its financial statements.

Typically, a complete set of financial statements produced by a business includes four separate statements along with comprehensive notes. When studied with knowledge and understanding, a vast array of information becomes available to aid decision makers who want to predict future stock prices, cash dividend payments, and cash flows.

1.1 Financial Statements and Accompanying Notes[2]

- **Income statement** (also called a statement of operations or a statement or earnings)[3]
- **Statement of retained earnings** (or the more inclusive statement of stockholders' equity)
- **Balance sheet** (also called a statement of financial position)
- **Statement of cash flows**

The four financial statements prepared by Marriott International as of January 2, 2009, and the year then ended were presented in just four pages of its annual report (pages forty-three through forty-six) whereas the notes accompanying those statements made up the next twenty-seven pages. Although decision makers often focus on a few individual figures found in financial statements, the vast wealth of information provided by the notes should never be ignored.

income statement

A listing of all revenues earned and expenses incurred during a specific period of time; also called statement of operations or statement of earnings.

statement of retained earnings

A reconciliation of a corporation's retained earnings account from the beginning of a period to the end; the account is increased by net income and decreased by net loss and/or dividends declared.

balance sheet

A listing of all asset, liability, and stockholders' equity accounts at a specific point in time; also called statement of financial position.

statement of cash flows

A listing of all cash inflows (sources) and cash outflows (uses) during a specific period of time categorized as operating activities, investing activities, and financing activities.

EXERCISE

Link to multiple-choice question for practice purposes: http://www.quia.com/quiz/2092635.html

Question: Assume that a financial investor is analyzing the latest income statement prepared by a company in hopes of deciding whether to buy its capital stock or, possibly, loan money to the company. Or, perhaps, a current employee must decide whether to stay with the company or take a job offer from another organization. Both of these individuals want to assess the company's financial health and future prospects. Certainly, all the available financial statements need to be studied but, initially, this person is looking at the income statement. ***What types of financial data will be available on a typical income statement such as might be produced by a business like IBM, Apple, Papa John's, or Pizza Hut?***

Answer: The main content of an income statement is rather straightforward: a listing of all revenues earned and expenses incurred by the reporting organization during the period specified. As indicated previously in Chapter 2, revenue figures disclose increases in net assets (assets minus liabilities) that were created by the sale of goods or services resulting from the primary operations of the organization. For IBM, revenues are derived from the sale and servicing of computers and the like (a total of nearly $104 billion in 2008) while, for Papa John's International, the reported revenue figure (a bit over $1.1 billion) measures the sale of pizzas and related items.

Conversely, expenses are decreases in net assets incurred by a reporting company in hopes of generating revenues. For example, salaries paid to sales people for the work they have done constitute an expense. The cost of facilities that have been rented is also an expense as is money paid for utilities such as electricity, heat, and water.

For example, IBM reported selling, general, and administrative expenses for 2008 of $23.4 billion. That was just one category of its expenses disclosed within the company's income statement.[4] During the same period, Papa John's reported salaries and benefits as an expense for its domestic company-owned restaurants of $158.3 million. Financial accounting focuses on providing information about an organization and both of these figures should help decision makers begin to glimpse a portrait of the underlying company. Accounting is often said to provide transparency—the ability to see straight through the words and numbers to gain a vision of the company and its operations.

Question: ***Is nothing else presented on an income statement other than revenues and expenses?***

Answer: An income statement also reports gains and losses for the same period of time. A gain is an increase in the net assets of an organization created by an occurrence outside of its primary or central operations. A loss is a decrease in net assets from a similar type of incidental event.

When Apple sells a computer to a customer, it reports revenue but if the company disposes of a piece of land adjacent to a warehouse, it reports a gain (if sold above cost) or a loss (if sold below cost). Selling computers falls within Apple's primary operations whereas selling land does not. If Pizza Hut sells a pepperoni pizza, the transaction brings in assets. Revenue has been earned and should be reported. If this same company disposes of one of its old stoves, the result is reflected as either a gain or loss. Pizza Hut is not in the business of selling appliances. This classification split between revenues/expenses and gains/losses helps provide decision makers with a clearer portrait of what actually happened to the company during the reporting period.

An example of an income statement for a small convenience store is shown in Figure 3.1. Note that the name of the company, the identity of the statement, and the period of time reflected are apparent. Although this is only an illustration, it is quite similar to the income statements created by virtually all business organizations in the United States and many other countries.

FIGURE 3.1 Income Statement

Davidson Groceries Income Statement for Year Ended December 31, 2XX4

Revenues:		
Sales of groceries		$1,400,000
Expenses:		
Cost of goods sold	$900,000	
Salary	120,000	
Rent	20,000	
Advertising	30,000	
Insurance	15,000	
Others	25,000	
Total Expenses		(1,110,000)
Operating income		290,000
Other gains and losses:		
Gain on sale of delivery truck	5,000	
Loss on sale of land behind building	(15,000)	(10,000)
Income before income taxes		280,000
Income tax expense		(50,000)
Net income		$230,000

EXERCISE

Link to multiple-choice question for practice purposes: http://www.quia.com/quiz/2092602.html

Question: A review of this sample income statement raises a number of questions. The meaning of balances such as salary expense, rent expense, advertising expense, and the like are relatively clear. These figures measure specific outflows or decreases in the company's net assets that were incurred in attempting to generate revenue. However, the largest expense reported on this income statement is called ***cost of goods sold. What does the $900,000 cost of goods sold figure represent?***

Answer: This convenience store generated sales of $1.4 million in Year 2XX4. Customers came in during that period of time and purchased merchandise at its sales price. That is the first step in the sale and is reflected within the revenue balance. The customers then took these goods with them and left the store; this merchandise no longer belongs to Davidson Groceries. In this second step, a decrease occurred in the company's net assets. Thus, an expense has occurred. As the title implies, "cost of goods sold" (sometimes referred to as "cost of sales") is an expense reflecting the cost of the merchandise that a company's customers purchased during the period. It is the amount that Davidson paid for inventory items such as apples, bread, soap, tuna fish, and cheese that were then sold.

Note that the timing of expense recognition is not tied to the payment of cash but rather to the loss of the asset. As a simple illustration, assume Davidson pays $2 in cash for a box of cookies on Monday and then sells it to a customer for $3 on Friday. The income statement will show revenue of $3 (the increase in the net assets created by the sale) and cost of goods sold of $2 (the decrease in net assets resulting from the sale). Both the revenue and the related expense are recorded on Friday when the sale took place and the inventory was removed.

gross profit

Difference between sales and cost of goods sold; also called gross margin or mark-up.

gross margin

Difference between sales and cost of goods sold; also called gross profit or mark-up.

mark-up

Difference between sales price and cost of goods sold on an item of inventory; also called gross profit or gross margin.

The difference in revenue and cost of goods sold is often referred to as the company's **gross profit**, **gross margin**, or **mark-up**. It is one of the reported figures studied carefully by decision makers. For this year, Davidson Groceries earned a gross profit of $500,000 ($1.4 million in revenues less $900,000 cost of goods sold). Its gross profit was 35.7 percent of sales ($500,000/$1.4 million).

For the year ending January 30, 2009, Lowe's Companies Inc., the home improvement company, reported net sales revenues of $48.2 billion along with cost of sales of $31.7 billion. Thus, Lowe's earned a gross margin (the company's term) during that period of $16.5 billion. Sales of merchandise ($48.2 billion) exceeded the cost of those same goods ($31.7 billion) by that amount. Its gross profit percentage was 34.2 percent ($16.5 million/$48.2 million). Any potential investor or creditor will find such numbers highly informative especially when compared with the company's prior years or with competing enterprises. For example, for the year ending February 1, 2009, the Home Depot Inc., a major competitor of Lowe's Companies, reported net sales of $71.3 billion, cost of sales of $47.3 billion, and gross profit (the company's term) of $24.0 billion. Its gross profit percentage was 33.7 percent ($24.0 million/$71.3 million). Such information allows decision makers to compare these two companies and their operations.

EXERCISE

Link to multiple-choice question for practice purposes: http://www.quia.com/quiz/2092636.html

Question: In Figure 3.1, revenues and expenses are listed first to arrive at an operating income figure. That is followed by gains and losses. This sequencing is appropriate since revenues and expenses relate to the primary or central operations of the business and gains and losses are created by more incidental events. ***Why then is income tax expense listed last, by itself, on the income statement and not with the other expenses?***

Answer: State and federal income taxes cost businesses in the United States considerable sums of money each year. Exxon Mobil Corporation reported income taxes of $36.5 billion at the bottom of its 2008 income statement. The income tax figure is segregated in this manner because it is not an expense in a traditional sense. As previously described, an expense—like cost of goods sold, advertising, or rent—is incurred in order to generate revenues. Income taxes do not create revenues at all. Instead, they are caused by the company's revenues and related profitability. Although referring to income taxes as an expense is common, probably a more apt title is "income taxes assessed by government." The financial impact is the same as an expense (an outflow or decrease in net assets); thus, "income tax expense" is often used for labeling purposes. However, because the nature of this "expense" is different, the reported income tax figure is frequently isolated at the bottom of the income statement, separate from true expenses.

KEY TAKEAWAY

Financial information can be gathered about an organization but the resulting figures must then be structured in some usable fashion to be conveyed to interested decision makers. Financial statements serve this purpose. A typical set of financial statements is made up of an income statement, statement of retained earnings, balance sheet, statement of cash flows, and explanatory notes. The income statement reports revenues from sales of goods and services as well as expenses such as rent expense and cost of goods sold. Gains and losses that arise from incidental activities of a company are also included on the income statement but separately so that the income generated from primary operations is apparent. Income tax expense is reported at the bottom of the income statement because it is actually a government assessment rather than a true expense.

2. REPORTED PROFITABILITY AND THE PRINCIPLE OF CONSERVATISM

LEARNING OBJECTIVES

At the end of this section, students should be able to meet the following objectives:

1. **Describe the method used to differentiate assets from expenses.**
2. **Discuss the rationale for the principle of conservatism and its effect on financial reporting.**
3. **Explain the reason dividend distributions are not reported within net income.**
4. **Discuss the need to study an entire set of financial statements rather than focus in obsessively on one or two numbers such as net income.**

Question: Previously, the term "asset" was defined as a future economic benefit owned or controlled by a reporting company. On an income statement, items such as rent and advertising are listed as expenses. Why are such costs not grouped with the assets on the balance sheet? For example, the rent paid for a building could provide a probable future economic benefit for the reporting organization but it is included in Figure 3.1 as an expense. The same is true for advertising. ***How does a company determine whether a cost represents an asset or an expense?***

Answer: Drawing a distinction that allows a cost to be classified as either an asset or an expense is not always easy for an accountant. If a company makes a $1,000 rent payment, an expense might have been incurred because an outflow of an asset has taken place. However, the cost of this rent could also be shown on the balance sheet as an asset if it provides future economic benefits.

A cost is identified as an asset if the benefit clearly has value in generating *future* revenues for the company whereas an expense is a cost that has already helped to earn revenues in the *past.*

With an asset, the utility will be consumed in the year. With an expense, the utility has already been consumed. To illustrate, assume that on December 31, Year One, a company pays $1,000 for rent on a building used during the previous month. The benefit gained from occupying that space has already occurred. Use of the building helped the company generate revenue during December. The outflow of this money is reflected on the income statement as a rent expense. The benefit is now in the past.

If on that same day, another $1,000 is paid to rent this building again during the upcoming month of January Year Two, the acquired benefit relates directly to the future. Until consumed, this second cost should be shown on the balance sheet as a $1,000 asset (referred to as prepaid rent).

- *Expense.* Cost that helped to generate revenues in the past.
- *Asset.* Cost expected to help generate revenues in the future.

When a cost is incurred, the accountant must investigate to determine when the related benefit is expected. This timing—which is guided by U.S. GAAP—indicates whether an asset should be recognized (shown on the balance sheet) or an expense (reported on the income statement).

EXERCISE

Link to multiple-choice question for practice purposes: http://www.quia.com/quiz/2092637.html

Question: A business or other organization can face many complicated situations. At times, the decision as to whether a specific cost will generate revenue in the future (and is reported as an asset) or has already helped to create revenue in the past (an expense) is difficult. When an accountant encounters a case that is "too close to call," what reporting is appropriate? For example, assume that a company has agreed to pay $24,000 but officials cannot ascertain the amount of the related benefit that has already occurred versus the amount that will take place in the future. ***When delineation between an asset and an expense appears to be impossible, what is reported?***

principle of conservatism

Preference of accountants to avoid making an organization look overly good; when faced with multiple reporting options that are equally likely, the worse possible outcome is reported to help protect the decision maker from being too optimistic.

Answer: Being an accountant is a relatively easy job when financial events are distinct and clearly understood. Unfortunately, in real life, situations often arise where two or more outcomes seem equally likely. The distinction raised in this question between an asset and an expense is simply one of numerous possibilities where multiple portraits could be envisioned. At such times, financial accounting has a long history of following the **principle of conservatism**.

The conservative nature of accounting influences many elements of U.S. GAAP and must be understood in order to appreciate the meaning of the financial information that is conveyed about an organization. Simply put, conservatism holds that whenever an accountant faces two or more *equally likely* possibilities, the one that makes the company look worse should be selected. In other words, financial accounting attempts to ensure that a reporting organization never looks significantly better than it actually is.

If a cost has been incurred that might have either a future value (an asset) or a past value (an expense), the accountant always reports the most likely possibility. That is the only appropriate way to paint a portrait of an organization that is the fairest representation. However, if neither scenario appears more likely to occur, the cost is classified as an expense rather than an asset because of the principle of conservatism. Reporting a past benefit rather than a future benefit has a detrimental impact on the company's appearance to an outside party. This handling reduces the reported net income as well as the amount shown as the total of the assets.

The principle of conservatism can be seen throughout financial accounting. When the chance of two possibilities is the same, accounting prefers that the more optimistic approach be avoided.

Question: ***Why does conservatism exist in financial accounting?*** *Companies must prefer to look as successful as possible. Why does a bias exist for reporting outcomes in a negative way?*

Answer: Accountants are well aware that the financial statements they produce are relied on by decision makers around the world to determine future actions that will place monetary resources at risk. For example, if a company appears to be prosperous, an investor might decide to allocate scarce cash resources to obtain shares of its capital stock. Similarly, a creditor is more willing to make a loan to a company that seems to be doing well economically.

Such decision makers face potential losses that can be significant. Accountants take their role in this process quite seriously. As a result, financial accounting has traditionally held that the users of financial statements are best protected if the reporting process is never overly optimistic in picturing an organization's financial health and future prospects. Money is less likely to be lost if the accountant paints a portrait that is no more rosy than necessary. The practice of conservatism is simply an attempt by financial accounting to help safeguard the public.

The problem that can occur when a company appears excessively profitable can be seen in the downfall of WorldCom where investors and creditors lost billions of dollars. A major cause of this accounting scandal, one of the biggest in history, was the fraudulent decision by members of the company's management to record a cost of nearly $4 billion as an asset rather than as an expense. Although any future benefit resulting from these expenditures was highly doubtful, the cost was reported to outsiders as an asset. Conservatism was clearly not followed.

Consequently, in its financial statements, WorldCom appeared to have more assets and be much more profitable than was actually the case. Investors and creditors risked their money based on the incorrect information they had received. Later, in 2002, when the truth **was** discovered, the stock price plummeted and the company went bankrupt. Even if the decision had been close as to whether these costs represented assets or expenses, the practice of conservatism would have dictated the need to record them as expenses to prevent an overly optimistic picture of the company and its financial health.

EXERCISE

Link to multiple-choice question for practice purposes: http://www.quia.com/quiz/2092638.html

Question: Previously, the term "dividends" was introduced and discussed. Dividend distributions reduce the net assets of a company. In Figure 3.1, a number of expenses are listed but no dividends are mentioned. ***Why are dividend payments not included as expenses on an income statement?***

Answer: Dividends are not expenses and, therefore, must be omitted in creating an income statement. Such payments obviously reduce the amount of net assets owned or controlled by a reporting company. However, they are not related in any way to generating revenues. A dividend is a reward distributed by a company (through the decision of its board of directors) to the owners of its capital stock. Thus, a dividend is a sharing of profits and not a cost incurred to create revenues.

In Figure 3.1, Davidson Groceries reports net income for the year of $230,000. The board of directors might look at that figure and opt to make a cash dividend distribution to company owners. That is one of the most important decisions for any board. Such payments usually please the owners but reduce the size of the company and—possibly—its future profitability.

An income statement reports revenues, expenses, gains, and losses. Dividend distributions do not qualify and must be reported elsewhere in the company's financial statements.

EXERCISE

Link to multiple-choice question for practice purposes: http://www.quia.com/quiz/2092622.html

Question: The final figure presented on the income statement is net income. This balance reflects the growth in a company's net assets during the period resulting from all revenues, expenses, gains, and losses. In evaluating the operations of any company, that figure seems to be incredibly significant. It reflects the profitability for the period. ***Is net income the most important number to be found in a set of financial statements?***

Answer: The net income figure reported for any business organization is an eagerly anticipated and carefully analyzed piece of financial information. It is the most discussed number disclosed by virtually any company. However, financial statements present a vast array of data and the importance of one balance should never be overemphasized. A portrait painted by an artist is not judged solely by the small section displaying the model's ear but rather by the representation made of the entire person. Likewise, only the analysis of all information conveyed by a complete set of financial statements enables an interested party to arrive at the most appropriate decisions about an organization.

Some creditors and investors seek shortcuts when making business decisions rather than doing the detailed analysis that is appropriate. Those individuals often spend an exorbitant amount of time focusing on reported net income. Such a narrow view shows a fundamental misunderstanding of financial reporting and the depth and breadth of the information being conveyed. In judging a company's financial health and future prospects, an evaluation should be carried out on the entity as a whole. Predicting stock prices, dividends, and cash flows requires a complete investigation. That is only possible by developing the capacity to work with all the data presented in a set of financial statements. If a single figure could be used reliably to evaluate a business organization, creditors and investors would never incur losses.

KEY TAKEAWAY

Conservatism is an often misunderstood term in financial reporting. Despite a reputation to the contrary, financial accounting is not radically conservative. However, when two reporting options are equally likely, the one that makes the company look best is avoided. In that way, the portrait created of a company is less likely to be overly optimistic so that decision makers are protected. Losses are less likely to occur. For example, expenses refer to costs that had value in the past while assets reflect future economic benefits. If this distinction cannot be drawn for a particular cost, it should be reported as an expense. That assignment reduces both reported income and assets. The resulting net income figure is useful in evaluating the financial health and prospects of a company but no single figure should be the sole source of information for a decision maker.

3. INCREASING THE NET ASSETS OF A COMPANY

LEARNING OBJECTIVES

At the end of this section, students should be able to meet the following objectives:

1. **Define retained earnings and explain its composition.**
2. **Define capital stock and explain the meaning of its reported account balance.**
3. **Understand the lack of financial impact that the exchange of ownership shares between investors has on a company.**

Question: The second financial statement is known as the statement of retained earnings[5]*. The term* ***retained earnings*** *has not yet been introduced.* ***What information does a retained earnings balance communicate to an outside decision maker?*** *For example, on January 31, 2009, Barnes & Noble Inc. reported retained earnings of nearly $721 million, one of the larger amounts found in the company's financial statements. What does that figure tell decision makers about this bookstore chain?*

Answer: Retained earnings is one of the most misunderstood accounts in all of financial reporting. In simplest terms, this balance is merely the total amount of net income reported by a company since it first began operations, less all dividends paid to stockholders during that same period. Thus, the figure provides a measure of the profits left in a business throughout its history to create growth.

FIGURE 3.2

Total net income since organization began operations
Less: total of all dividends paid to owners

Retained earnings balance

When a company earns income, it becomes larger because net assets have increased. Even if a portion of the profits is later distributed to shareholders as a dividend, the company has grown in size as a result of its own operations. The retained earnings figure informs decision makers of the amount of that internally generated expansion. The reported balance answers the question: How much of the company's net assets have been derived from operations during its life?

If a company reports net income of $10,000 each year and then pays a $2,000 dividend to its owners, it is growing in size at the rate of $8,000 per year. After four years, for example, $32,000 ($8,000 × four years) of its net assets were generated by its own operating activities. That information is communicated through the retained earnings balance.

As of January 31, 2009, Barnes & Noble reported total assets of $3.0 billion and liabilities of $2.1 billion. Thus, the company had net assets of $900 million. It held that many more assets than liabilities. Those additional assets did not appear by magic. They had to come from some source. One of the primary ways to increase the net assets of a company is through profitable operations. The balance for retained earnings shown by Barnes & Noble at this time lets decision makers know that approximately $721 million of its net assets were generated by the net income earned since the company's inception, after all dividend distributions to shareholders were subtracted.

EXERCISE

Link to multiple-choice question for practice purposes: http://www.quia.com/quiz/2092623.html

Question: In Figure 3.1, Davidson Groceries calculated its net income for 2XX4 as $230,000. Assume that this company began operations on January 1, 2XX1, and reported the following balances over the years:

FIGURE 3.3

Year	Reported Net Income	Dividends Distributed	Growth in Company (income minus dividends)
Past Years			
2XX1	$140,000	$50,000	$90,000
2XX2	180,000	70,000	110,000
2XX3	210,000	90,000	120,000
Totals	$530,000	$210,000	$320,000
Current Year			
2XX4	$230,000	$100,000	$130,000

How is this information reported? ***What is the structure of the statement of retained earnings as it appears within a company's financial statements?***

Answer: In its three prior years of existence, Davidson's net assets increased by a total of $320,000 as a result of its operating activities. As can be seen here, the company generated total profit during this period of $530,000 while distributing dividends to shareholders amounting to $210,000, an increase of $320,000. Net assets rose further during the current year (2XX4) as Davidson made an additional profit (see also Figure 3.1) of $230,000 but distributed $100,000 in dividends.

Figure 3.4 shows the format by which this information is conveyed to the decision makers who are evaluating Davidson Groceries.

FIGURE 3.4 Statement of Retained Earnings

Davidson Groceries Statement of Retained Earnings for Year Ended December 31, 2XX4		
Retained earnings balance, January 1, 2XX4		$320,000
Net income reported for 2XX4	$230,000	
Dividents distributed during 2XX4	100,000	
Net income less dividends for 2XX4		130,000
Retained earnings balance, December 31, 2XX4		$450,000

EXERCISE

Link to multiple-choice question for practice purposes: http://www.quia.com/quiz/2092624.html

Question: In the information given about Barnes & Noble, the company reported holding net assets of $900 million but only about $721 million of that amount was generated through operations as shown by its retained earnings balance. Clearly, additional sources must have helped the company to attain its growth in size. Increases in net assets of a company are not the result of magic or miracles. ***Other than through operations, how else does a company derive its net assets?***

capital stock

Ownership (equity) shares of stock in a corporation that are issued to raise financing for capital expenditures and operations.

common stock

A type of capital stock that is issued by every corporation; it provides rights to the owner that are specified by the laws of the state in which the organization is incorporated.

contributed capital

Amounts invested in a corporation by individuals or groups in order to attain ownership interests; balance is reported within stockholders' equity section of balance sheet to indicate the amount of the net assets that came from the owners.

retained earnings

Accumulated total of the net income earned by an organization during its existence in excess of dividends distributed to the owners; indicates the amount of the net assets currently held that came from operations over the life of the organization.

Answer: Beyond operations (as reflected by the retained earnings balance), a company accumulates net assets by receiving contributions from its owners in exchange for capital stock.[6] This is the other major method by which Barnes & Noble was able to gather its $900 million in net assets. On a balance sheet, the measure of this inflow is usually labeled something like **capital stock**, **common stock**, or **contributed capital**. The reported amount indicates the portion of the net assets that came into the business directly from stockholders.

The amount of a company's net assets is the excess of its assets over its liabilities. Two reported balances indicate the primary source of those net assets:

- *Capital stock (or contributed capital).* The amount invested in the business by individuals and groups in order to become owners. For example, as of December 31, 2008, Motorola Inc. reported having received a total of approximately $7.8 billion from its shareholders since its inception.
- **Retained earnings**. All the net income earned by the organization over its life less amounts distributed as dividends to owners. On December 31, 2008, Google Inc. reported a retained earnings balance of $13.6 billion (up over $4 billion in just one year).

Companies that seek to grow must be able to generate resources from owners, operations, or both.

Question: A corporation issues (sells) ownership shares to investors. The source of the resulting inflow of assets into the business is reflected on its balance sheet by the reporting of a capital stock (or contributed capital) balance. Thus, over its life, Motorola has received assets of $7.8 billion from stockholders in exchange for capital stock. ***Does the company receive money in this way when shares are sold each day on the New York Stock Exchange, NASDAQ (National Association of Securities Dealers Automated Quotation Service), or other stock exchanges?***

Answer: No, purchases and sales on stock markets normally occur between investors and not with the company. Only the initial issuance of the ownership shares to a stockholder creates the inflow of assets reported by the company's capital stock or contributed capital account.

To illustrate, assume that Investor A buys capital stock shares directly from Business B for $179,000 in cash. This transaction increases the net assets of Business B by that amount. The source of the increase is communicated to decision makers by adding $179,000 to the capital stock balance reported by the company. Subsequently, these shares may be exchanged between investors numerous times without any additional financial impact on Business B. For example, assume Investor A later sells the shares to Investor Z for $200,000 using a stock market such as the New York Stock Exchange. Investor A earns a $21,000 gain ($200,000 received less $179,000 cost) and Investor Z has replaced Investor A as an owner of Business B. However, the financial condition of the company has not been affected by this new exchange. Thus, the capital stock balance only measures the initial investment contributed directly to the business.

KEY TAKEAWAY

The source of a company's net assets (assets minus liabilities) is of interest to outside decision makers. The reported retained earnings figure indicates the amount of these net assets that came from the operations of the company. This growth in size was internally generated. Retained earnings is all the net income earned since operations began less all dividend distributions. Net assets can also be derived from contributions to the company made by parties seeking to become owners. The capital stock (or contributed capital) balance measures this source of net assets. To impact the company, the assets must come directly from the owners. Hence, exchanges between investors on a stock exchange do not affect the company's net assets or its financial reporting.

4. REPORTING A BALANCE SHEET AND A STATEMENT OF CASH FLOWS

LEARNING OBJECTIVES

At the end of this section, students should be able to meet the following objectives:

1. **List the types of accounts presented on a balance sheet.**
2. **Explain the difference between current assets and liabilities and noncurrent assets and liabilities.**
3. **Calculate working capital and the current ratio.**
4. **Provide the reason for a balance sheet to always balance.**
5. **Identify the three sections of a statement of cash flows and explain the types of events included in each.**

Question: The third financial statement is the balance sheet. ***If a decision maker studies a company's balance sheet (on its Web site, for example), what information can be discovered?***

Answer: The primary purpose of a balance sheet is to report an organization's assets and liabilities at a particular point in time. The format is quite simple. All assets are listed first—usually in order of liquidity[7] —followed by the liabilities. A picture is provided of each future economic benefit owned or controlled by the company (its assets) as well as its debts (liabilities).

A typical balance sheet is reported in Figure 3.5 for Davidson Groceries. Note that the assets are divided between current (those expected to be used or consumed within the next year) and noncurrent (those expected to remain within the company for longer than a year). Likewise, liabilities are split between current (to be paid during the next year) and noncurrent (not to be paid until after the next year). This labeling aids financial analysis because Davidson's current liabilities ($57,000) can be subtracted from its current assets ($161,000) to arrive at a figure often studied by interested parties known as working capital ($104,000 in this example). The current assets can also be divided by current liabilities ($161,000/$57,000) to determine the company's current ratio (2.82 to 1.00), another figure calculated by many decision makers as a useful measure of short-term operating strength.

The balance sheet shows the company's financial condition on one specific date. All the other financial statements report events occurring over a period of time (often a year or a quarter). The balance sheet discloses assets and liabilities as of the one specified date.

FIGURE 3.5 Balance Sheet[8]

Davidson Groceries Balance Sheet, December 31, 2XX4		
Assets		
Current Assets		
Cash	$22,000	
Accounts Receivable	24,000	
Inventory	103,000	
Prepaid Rent	12,000	
Total Current Assets		$161,000
Noncurrent Assets		
Land	210,000	
Equipment (net)	155,000	
Buildings (net)	680,000	
Total Noncurrent Assets		1,045,000
Total Assets		$1,206,000
Liabilities and Stockholders' Equity		
Liabilities		
Current Liabilities		
Accounts Payable	$33,000	
Salaries Payable	9,000	
Insurance Payable	15,000	
Total Current Liabilities		$57,000
Noncurrent Liabilities		
Note Payable—Third National Bank	300,000	
Note Payable—State Bank	220,000	
Total Current Liabilities		520,000
Total Liabilities		$577,000
Stockholders' Equity		
Capital Stock	$179,000	
Retained Earnings	450,000	
Total Stockholders' Equity		$629,000
Total Liabilities and Stockholders' Equity		$1,206,000

EXERCISE

Link to multiple-choice question for practice purposes: http://www.quia.com/quiz/2092603.html

Question: Considerable information is included on the balance sheet presented in Figure 3.5. Assets such as cash, inventory, and land provide future economic benefits for a company. Liabilities for salaries, insurance, and the like reflect debts that are owed at the end of year. The $179,000 capital stock figure indicates the amount of assets that the original owners contributed to the business. The retained earnings balance of $450,000 was computed earlier in Figure 3.4 and identifies the portion of the net assets generated by the company's own operations over the years. For convenience, a general term such as "stockholders' equity" or "shareholders' equity" encompasses the capital stock and the retained earnings balances.

Why does the balance sheet balance? *This agreement cannot be an accident. The asset total of $1,206,000 is exactly the same as the liabilities ($577,000) plus the two stockholders' equity accounts ($629,000—the total of capital stock and retained earnings). Thus, assets equal liabilities plus stockholders' equity. What creates that equilibrium?*

Answer: The balance sheet will always balance unless a mistake is made. This is known as the **accounting equation**:

assets = liabilities + stockholders' equity.

Or, if the stockholders' equity account is broken down into its component parts:

assets = liabilities + capital stock + retained earnings.

This equation stays in balance for one simple reason: assets must have a source. If a business or other organization has an increase in its total assets, that change can only be caused by (a) an increase in liabilities such as money being borrowed, (b) an increase in capital stock such as additional money being contributed by stockholders, or (c) an increase created by operations such as a sale that generates a rise in net income. There are no other ways to increase assets.

One way to understand the accounting equation is that the left side (the assets) presents a picture of the future economic benefits that the reporting company holds. The right side provides information to show how those assets were derived (from liabilities, from investors, or from operations). Because no assets are held by a company without a source, the equation (and, hence, the balance sheet) must balance.

assets = the total source of those assets

accounting equation

Assets = liabilities + stockholders' equity. The equation balances because all assets must have a source: a liability, a contribution from an owner (contributed capital), or from operations (retained earnings).

Question: The final financial statement is the statement of cash flows. Cash is so important to an organization and its financial health that a complete statement is devoted to presenting the changes that took place in that asset. As can be determined from the title, this statement provides a picture of the various ways in which the company generated cash during the year and the uses that were made of it. ***How is the statement of cash flows structured?***

Answer: Outside decision makers place considerable emphasis on a company's ability to create significant cash inflows and then wisely apply that money. Figure 3.6 presents an example of that information in a statement of cash flows for Davidson Groceries for the year ended December 31, 2XX4. Note that all the cash changes are divided into three specific sections: **operating activities**, **investing activities**, and **financing activities**.

operating activities

A statement of cash flow category used to disclose cash receipts and disbursements arising from the primary activities of the reporting organization.

investing activities

A statement of cash flow category used to disclose cash receipts and disbursements arising from an asset transaction other than one relating to the primary activities of the reporting organization.

financing activities

A statement of cash flow category used to disclose cash receipts and disbursements arising from a liability or stockholders' equity transaction other than one relating to the primary activities of the organization.

FIGURE 3.6 Statement of Cash Flows[9]

Davidson Groceries Statement of Cash Flows for Year Ended December 31, 2XX4

Cash Flows from Operating Activities		
Cash Collected from Customers	$1,075,000	
Cash Paid for Inventory	(420,000)	
Cash Paid for Salaries	(208,000)	
Cash Paid for Rent	(95,000)	
Cash Paid for Advertising	(81,000)	
Cash Paid for Insurance	(57,000)	
Cash Paid for Income Taxes	(52,000)	
Total Cash Inflow from Operating Activities		$162,000
Cash Flows from Investing Activities		
Cash Received from Sale of Delivery Truck	26,000	
Cash Received from Sale of Land	75,000	
Cash Paid in Purchase of Building	(300,000)	
Total Cash Outflow from Investing Activities		(199,000)
Cash Flows from Financing Activities		
Cash Paid to Owners as Dividends	(100,000)	
Cash Received from Bank on a Loan	120,000	
Total Cash Inflow from Financing Activities		20,000
Cash Reduction During Year		(17,000)
Cash Balance—January 1, 2XX4		39,000
Cash Balance—December 31, 2XX4		$22,000

Question: In studying the statement of cash flows, a company's individual cash flows relating to selling inventory, advertising, selling land, buying a building, paying dividends, and the like can be readily identified. For example, when the statement indicates that $120,000 was the "cash received from bank on a loan," a decision maker should have a clear picture of what happened. There is no mystery.

All the cash flows are divided into one of the three categories:

1. *Operating activities*
2. *Investing activities*
3. *Financing activities*

How are these distinctions drawn? ***On a statement of cash flows, what is the difference in an operating activity, an investing activity, and a financing activity?***

Answer: Cash flows listed as operating activities relate to receipts and disbursements that arose in connection with the central activity of the organization. For Davidson, these cash changes resulted from the daily operations carried out by the convenience store and include selling goods to customers, buying merchandise, paying salaries to employees, and the like. This section of the statement shows how much cash the primary function of the business was able to generate during this period of time, a figure that is watched closely by many financial analysts. Eventually, a company is only worth the cash that it can create from its operations.

Investing activities report cash flows from events that (1) are separate from the central or daily operations of the business and (2) involve an asset. Thus, the amount of cash collected when either equipment or land is sold is reported within this section. A convenience store does not participate in such transactions as a regular part of operations and both deal with an asset. Cash paid to buy a building or machinery will also be disclosed in this same category. Such purchases do not happen on a daily operating basis and an asset is involved.

Like investing activities, the third section of this statement—cash flows from financing activities—is unrelated to daily business operations but, here, the transactions relate to either a liability or a stockholders' equity balance. Borrowing money from a bank meets these criteria as does distributing a dividend to shareholders. Issuing stock to new owners for cash is another financing activity as is payment of a noncurrent liability.

Any decision maker can review the cash flows of a business within these three separate sections to receive a picture of how company officials managed to generate cash during the period and what use was made of it.

EXERCISE

Link to multiple-choice question for practice purposes: http://www.quia.com/quiz/2092604.html

KEY TAKEAWAY

The balance sheet is the only financial statement created for a specific point in time. It reports a company's assets as well as the source of those assets: liabilities, capital stock, and retained earnings. Assets and liabilities are divided between current and noncurrent amounts, which permits the company's working capital and current ratio to be computed for analysis purposes. The statement of cash flows explains how the company's cash balance changed during the year. All cash transactions are classified as falling within operating activities (daily activities), investing activities (nonoperating activities that affect an asset), or financing activities (nonoperating activities that affect either a liability or a stockholders' equity account).

Talking with a Real Investing Pro (Continued)

Following is a continuation of our interview with Kevin G. Burns.

Question: Warren Buffett is one of the most celebrated investors in history and ranks high on any list of the richest people in the world. When asked how he became so successful at investing, Buffett answered quite simply: "We read hundreds and hundreds of annual reports every year."[10]

Annual reports, as you well know, are the documents that companies produce each year containing their latest financial statements. You are an investor yourself, one who provides expert investment analysis for your clients. What is your opinion of Mr. Buffett's advice?

Kevin Burns: Warren Buffet—who is much richer and smarter than I am—is correct about the importance of annual reports. Once you get past the artwork and the slick photographs and into the "meat" of these reports, the financial statements are a treasure trove of information. Are sales going up or down? Are expenses as a percentage of sales increasing or decreasing? Is the company making money? How are the officers compensated? Do they own stock in the company? Are there many pages of notes explaining the financial statements?

I actually worry when there are too many pages of notes. I prefer companies that don't need so many pages to explain what is happening. I like companies that are able to keep their operations simple. Certainly, a great amount of important information can be gleaned from a careful study of the financial statements in any company's annual report.

Video Clip

Joe talks about what was most important in Chapter 3.

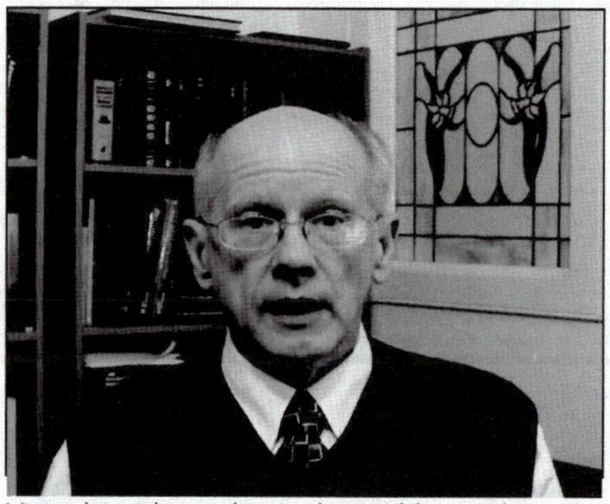

View the video online at: http://blip.tv/play/sDyBv5lkAA

5. END-OF-CHAPTER EXERCISES

QUESTIONS

1. Why do businesses produce financial statements?
2. What are the four financial statements typically produced by a company?
3. On which financial statement would one find revenues and expenses?
4. What is a gain?
5. How does a gain differ from a revenue?
6. What is a loss?
7. How does a loss differ from an expense?
8. Why are revenues and expenses reported separately from gains and losses?
9. What three items are typically listed at the top of a financial statement?
10. Define cost of goods sold.
11. Define gross profit.
12. How do companies determine if a cost is an expense or an asset?
13. Define conservatism.
14. Explain why dividends are not reported on the income statement.
15. What are retained earnings?
16. Define capital stock.
17. On which statement would assets and liabilities be reported?
18. What differentiates a current asset from a noncurrent asset?
19. Give the accounting equation and explain why it is true.
20. What are the three categories of cash flows on the cash flow statement?
21. How do operating, investing and financing cash flows differ from one another?

TRUE OR FALSE

1. _____ The income statement gives company's revenues and expenses for one particular day of the year.
2. _____ An increase in net assets of a business due to the sale of its inventory is a gain.
3. _____ Retained earnings represents amounts contributed to the business by its owners.
4. _____ Assets and liabilities can be broken down into the categories of current and noncurrent.
5. _____ Income tax expense is typically reported separately from other expenses.
6. _____ Conservatism helps companies look better to potential investors.
7. _____ Dividends paid are reported on the balance sheet.
8. _____ Companies receive money each time their stock is sold on a stock exchange.
9. _____ A balance sheet should always balance.
10. _____ The statement of cash flows is broken up into operating, investing, and financing activities.
11. _____ Notes are considered part of a complete set of financial statements.
12. _____ Sales revenue less cost of goods sold is referred to as net income.
13. _____ A gain is the amount of net income earned by a company over its life less any dividends it has paid.
14. _____ The purpose of the balance sheet is to report the assets and liabilities of a company on a specific date.

MULTIPLE CHOICE

1. You are the CEO of Fisher Corporation. You are very concerned with presenting the best financial picture possible to the owners of your company. Unfortunately, Fisher has a lawsuit pending at the end of the year, which could result in the company having to pay a large sum of money. On the bright side, Fisher also has business deal that might go through, which could result in the company making a large gain. The principle of conservatism would say that which of the following is true?
   a. Fisher should not report the potential loss related to the lawsuit.
   b. Fisher should report the possible gain from the business deal.
   c. Fisher should report the potential liability it has related to the lawsuit.
   d. Fisher should report the potential cash inflow it could receive from the business deal.
2. Henderson Inc. reports the following: assets of $500,000, liabilities of $350,000 and capital stock of $100,000. What is the balance in retained earnings?
   a. $450,000
   b. $50,000
   c. $250,000
   d. $750,000
3. Giles Corporation borrowed money from Midwest Bank during the year. Where would this event be reported on Giles's statement of cash flows?
   a. Operating activities
   b. Investing activities
   c. Financing activities
   d. It would not be reported on the statement of cash flows.
4. You are considering investing in the stock of Mogul Corporation. On which of the following statements would you find information about what a company has to help it generate revenue in the future and what the company owes to others?
   a. Income statement
   b. Statement of retained earnings
   c. Balance sheet
   d. Statement of cash flows
5. Which of the following is not a correct representation of the accounting equation?
   a. Assets = Liabilities + Capital Stock + Retained Earnings
   b. Assets – Liabilities = Owners' Equity
   c. Assets = Liabilities + Owners' Equity
   d. Assets + Liabilities = Owners' Equity

PROBLEMS

1. Use the following abbreviations to indicate on which statement you would find each item below. Some items may appear on more than one statement. Include all abbreviations that would apply.
   - IS: Income statement
   - SRE: Statement of retained earnings
   - BS: Balance sheet

   a. ____ Sales
   b. ____ Cash
   c. ____ Gain on sale of building
   d. ____ Retained earnings
   e. ____ Salary expense
   f. ____ Capital stock
   g. ____ Dividends paid
   h. ____ Loss on sale of investment
   i. ____ Income tax expense
   j. ____ Net income

2. The following relate to Farr Corporation for the month of April:

Sales Revenue	$140,000
Gain on the Sale of Land	$20,000
Cost of Goods Sold	$75,000
Tax Expense	$14,000
Advertising Expense	$10,000
Dividends Paid	$7,000
Loss on Lawsuit	$24,000

   a. Determine Farr's gross profit for the month of April.
   b. Determine Farr's net income for the month of April.
   c. If retained earnings at the beginning of April were $1,500,000, what would retained earnings be at the end of April?

3. Maverick Company has the following account balances at the end of December. Show that Maverick's balance sheet would balance using the accounting equation.

Cash	$8,000
Capital Stock	$120,000
Inventory	$16,000
Note Payable	$45,000
Retained Earnings	$29,000
Building	$150,000
Equipment	$20,000

4. Ramond Company has hired you to prepare financial statements for the year ending 12/31. On your first day of work, your assistant comes to you with several items that could be classified as expenses or could be classified as assets. Based on your knowledge of accounting so far, determine whether the following items should be recorded as an expense or an asset.
   a. On 12/31, Ramond paid $14,000 to rent office space for the next twelve months.
   b. On 10/1, Ramond paid $40,000 for insurance that covered the company's property for the last quarter of the year.
   c. On 6/1, Ramond purchased $27,000 in supplies, all of which were used by 12/31.
   d. On 12/31, Ramond purchased $5,000 worth of supplies for the coming month.

5. For each of the following, determine the missing balance.

a.

Net Income	$82,900
Cost of Goods Sold	$459,030
Advertising Expense	$56,000
Gain on Sale of Equipment	$5,000
Income Tax Expense	$50,000
Sales Revenue	?

b.

Net Income	$6,500
Retained Earnings, 12/31	$16,200
Dividends	$2,900
Retained Earnings, 1/1	?

c.

Cash	$460,000
Accounts Receivable	$540,200
Current Assets	$1,670,000
Inventory	?

d.

Total Assets	$54,000
Total Liabilities	$32,000
Capital Stock	$15,000
Retained Earnings	?

6. Rescue Records needs rescuing. The downloading of songs and other media are killing its business. The owners of Rescue want to know if they made a net income or a net loss for the year ended December 31. Given the following account balances, prepare an income statement for Rescue similar to Figure 3.1.

Advertising Expense	$4,600
Salary Expense	$25,470
Cost of Goods Sold	$109,000
Sales Revenue	$197,000
Income Tax Expense	$3,800
Loss on Sale of Stock	$12,090
Rent Expense	$35,000

7. Your lawn care business, A Cut Above, has grown beyond your wildest dreams—to the point where you would like to buy some new equipment and hire some people to help you. Unfortunately, you don't have that kind of money sitting around, so you are applying for a loan. The bank has requested financial statements, including, of course, a balance sheet. The following are the balances you have on 5/31. Prepare a classified balance sheet to submit to the bank.

Cash	$2,400
Prepaid Insurance	$1,400
Note Payable Due Two Years from Now (Loan from Mom)	$5,000
Capital Stock (Money You Invested to Start Business)	$2,000
Accounts Receivable	$500
Supplies Inventory	$300
Equipment, Net	$3,000
Accounts Payable	$300
Retained Earnings	$300

8. Maria Sanchez, an accountant by trade, moonlights as a personal trainer. Maria is curious about her cash inflows and outflows from her personal work for the month of February. Using the following information, prepare a statement of cash flows for Maria.

Cash for Supplies Inventory	$500
Cash for Advertising	$400
Cash Paid for Equipment	$900
Cash Received from Bank Loan	$1,000
Cash Paid for Insurance	$700
Cash Received from Customers	$2,200
Cash Paid for Taxes	$400
Cash Balance, 2/1	$500

RESEARCH

1. The U.S. Securities and Exchange Commission (SEC) is a governmental organization whose mission is to protect investors and oversee capital markets. The SEC requires companies whose stock is traded on U.S. public exchanges to submit financial statements like those introduced in this chapter on a quarterly and annual basis. Anyone can access these statements using the SEC's EDGAR (Electronic Data Gathering and Retrieval) database system. This exercise will allow you to learn more about the SEC and use its database to access a company's financial statements. You can access the SEC on the Internet at http://www.sec.gov.
   a. When and why was the SEC created?
   b. Name the main divisions of the SEC and briefly explain their function.
   c. From the home page, select "Forms and Filings (EDGAR)." Select "search for company filings." Select "companies and other filers." In the box beside "company name," enter the name or part of the name of a company about which you are interested in learning more. You should see a long list of strange letters and numbers like 8-K and 10-K. These designate the type of filing the company has made. Scroll down until you come to a 10-K filing. This is the annual report of the company. Select html and then select the document next to 10-K. Scroll down to the table of contents and select item 8. These are the company's financial statements. Which financial statements do you see?

ENDNOTES

1. Financial statements for many of the businesses that have their capital stock traded publicly on stock exchanges are readily available on corporate Web sites. For example, the statements released by Marriott International can be located through the following path. The financial statements issued by most large companies will be found by using similar steps.
   - Go to http://www.marriott.com.
   - Click on "company news & info" (probably at the bottom of the homepage).
   - Click on "investor relations."
   - Click on "financial information."
   - Click on "financial reports & proxy."
   - Click on "annual report" (for the year desired).
2. Because the final figures derived on the income statement and the statement of retained earnings are necessary to produce other statements, the preparation of financial statements is carried out in the sequential order shown here.
3. As will be discussed in a later chapter of this textbook, a statement of comprehensive income is also sometimes required to be attached to or presented with an income statement.
4. Financial information reported by large publicly traded companies tends to be highly aggregated. Thus, the expense figure shown by IBM is a summation of many somewhat related expenses. Those individual balances would be available within the company for internal decision making.
5. As indicated earlier, many companies actually report a broader statement of changes in stockholders' equity to present details on all the accounts appearing in the stockholders' equity section of the balance sheet. At this initial point in the coverage, focusing solely on retained earnings makes the learning process easier.
6. As with many aspects of the coverage at this introductory stage, other events can also impact the reported total of a company's net assets and will be discussed in later chapters. The two sources here—capital stock and retained earnings—are shown by all corporations and are normally significantly large amounts.
7. Liquidity refers to the ease with which assets can be converted into cash. Thus, cash is normally reported first followed by investments in stock that are expected to be sold soon, accounts receivable, inventory, and so on.
8. As will be discussed in detail later in this textbook, noncurrent assets such as buildings and equipment are initially recorded at cost. This figure is then systematically reduced as the amount is moved gradually each period into an expense account over the life of the asset. Thus, balance sheet figures for these accounts are reported as "net" to show that only a portion of the original cost still remains recorded as an asset. This shift of the cost from asset to expense is known as depreciation and mirrors the using up of the utility of the property. On this company's income statement—Figure 3.1—assume that depreciation for the period made up a portion of the "other" expense category.
9. The cash flows resulting from operating activities are being shown here using the direct method, an approach recommended by the Financial Accounting Standards Board (FASB). This format shows the actual amount of cash flows created by individual operating activities such as sales to customers and purchases of inventory. In the business world, an alternative known as the indirect method is more commonly encountered. This indirect method will be demonstrated in detail in Chapter 17.
10. See http://www.minterest.com/warren-buffet-quotes-quotations-on-investing/.

CHAPTER 4

How Does an Organization Accumulate and Organize the Information Necessary to Prepare Financial Statements?

Video Clip

Joe introduces Chapter 4 and speaks about the course in general.

View the video online at: http://blip.tv/play/sDyBv5srAA

1. THE ESSENTIAL ROLE OF TRANSACTION ANALYSIS

LEARNING OBJECTIVES

At the end of this section, students should be able to meet the following objectives:

1. **Define transaction and provide common examples.**
2. **Define transaction analysis and explain its importance to the accounting process.**
3. **Identify the account changes created by the purchase of inventory, the payment of a salary, and the borrowing of money.**
4. **Understand that accounting systems can be programmed to automatically record expenses such as salary as it accrues.**

Question: Information provided by a set of financial statements is essential to any individual analyzing a business or other organization. The availability of a fair representation of a company's financial position, operations, and cash flows is invaluable for a wide array of decision makers. However, the sheer volume of data that a company such as General Mills, McDonald's, or PepsiCo must gather in order to prepare these statements has to be astronomical. Even a small enterprise—a local convenience store, for example—generates a significant quantity of information virtually every day. ***How does an accountant begin the process of accumulating all the necessary data so that financial statements can eventually be produced?***

transactions

Events that have a financial impact on an organization that must be gathered, sorted, classified and turned into financial statements by means of an accounting system.

Answer: The accounting process starts by analyzing the effect of **transactions**—any event that has a financial impact on a company. Large organizations participate in literally millions of transactions each year that must be gathered, sorted, classified, and turned into a set of financial statements that cover a mere four or five pages. Over the decades, accountants have had to become very efficient to fulfill this seemingly impossible assignment. Despite the volume of transactions, the goal remains the same: to prepare financial statements that are presented fairly because they contain no material misstatements according to U.S. generally accepted accounting principles (U.S. GAAP).

For example, all the occurrences listed in Figure 4.1 are typical transactions that any company might encounter. Each causes some measurable effect on a company's assets, liabilities, revenues, expenses, gains, losses, capital stock, or dividends paid. The accounting process begins with an analysis of each transaction to determine the financial changes that took place. Was revenue earned? Did a liability increase? Has an asset been acquired?

FIGURE 4.1 Transactions Frequently Encountered

1—Buy inventory on credit for $2,000
2—Pay regular salary of $300 to an employee for work done during the past week; no amount had previously been recorded
3—Borrow $9,000 in cash from bank by signing a loan agreement
4—Make a sale of the inventory bought in (1) to a customer for $5,000 on credit
5—Pay $700 for insurance coverage for the past few months; this amount has previously been recognized in the company's accounting system as it was incurred
6—Buy a new automobile for the company for a price of $40,000 by paying $10,000 in cash and signing a note for the remainder
7—Issue ownership shares to a new stockholder for cash of $19,000
8—Collect cash from customer on earlier sale in (4)
9—Pay cash for the inventory acquired in (1)
10—Pay $4,000 to rent a building for the next four months

In any language, successful communication is only possible if the information to be conveyed is properly understood. Likewise, in accounting, transactions must be analyzed so their impact is understood. A vast majority of transactions are relatively straightforward so that, with experience, the accountant can ascertain the financial impact almost automatically. For transactions with greater complexity, the necessary analysis becomes more challenging. However, the importance of this initial step in the production of financial statements cannot be overstressed. The well-known computer aphorism captures the essence quite succinctly: "garbage in garbage out." There is little hope that financial statements can be fairly presented unless the entering data are based on an appropriate identification of the changes created by each transaction.

EXERCISE

Link to multiple-choice question for practice purposes: http://www.quia.com/quiz/2092626.html

1.1 Transaction Analysis

Question: Transaction 1—A company buys inventory on credit for $2,000. How does transaction analysis work here? ***What accounts are affected by this purchase?***

Answer: Inventory, which is an asset, increases by $2,000. The organization has more inventory than it did prior to the purchase. Because no money has yet been paid for these goods, a liability for the same amount has been created. The term **accounts payable** is often used in financial accounting to represent debts resulting from the acquisition of inventory and supplies.

accounts payable

Short-term liabilities to pay for goods and services that have been acquired.

inventory (asset) increases by $2,000

accounts payable (liability) increases by $2,000

Note that the accounting equation described in the previous chapter remains in balance. Assets have gone up by $2,000 while the liability side of the equation has also increased by the same amount to reflect the source of this increase in the company's assets.

EXERCISE

Link to multiple-choice question for practice purposes: http://www.quia.com/quiz/2092605.html

Question: Transaction 2—A company pays a salary of $300 to one of its employees for work performed during the past week. No amount had previously been recorded by the accounting system for this amount. ***What accounts are affected by this salary payment?***

Answer: Cash (an asset) is decreased here by $300. Whenever cash is involved in a transaction, determining that change is a good place to start the analysis. Increases and decreases in cash are often obvious.

The cash balance declined here because salary was paid to an employee. Assets were reduced as a result of the payment. That is a cost to the company. Thus, a salary expense of $300 is reported. Recognizing an expense is appropriate rather than an asset because the employee's work reflects a past benefit. The effort has already been carried out, generating revenues for the company in the previous week rather than in the future.

salary expense (expense) increases by $300

cash (asset) decreased by $300

The continued equilibrium of the accounting equation does exist here although it is less obvious. Assets are decreased. At the same time, an expense is recognized. This expense reduces reported net income. On the statement of retained earnings, current net income becomes a component of retained earnings. The reduction in income here serves to decrease retained earnings. Because both assets and retained earnings go down by the same amount, the accounting equation continues to balance.

Question: In Transaction 2, the company paid a salary of $300 that it owed to a worker. ***Why does a payment to an employee not reduce a salary payable balance?***

Answer: Costs such as salary, rent, or interest increase gradually over time and are often referred to as **accrued expenses** because the term "accrue" means "to grow." An accounting system can be mechanically structured to record such costs in either of two ways. The results are the same but the steps in the process differ.

- Some companies simply ignore accrued expenses until paid. At that time, the expense is recognized and cash is reduced. No liability is entered into the accounting system or removed. Because the information provided above indicates that nothing has been recorded to date, this approach is used here.
- Other companies choose to program their computer systems so that both the expense and the related liability are recognized automatically as the amount grows. For salary, as an example, this increase could literally be recorded each day or week based on the amount earned by employees. At the time payment is finally conveyed, the expense has already been recorded. Thus, the liability is removed because that debt is being settled. Below, in Transaction 5, this second possible approach to recording accrued expenses is illustrated.

A company can recognize an accrued expense (such as a salary) as incurred or wait until payment. This decision depends on the preference of company officials. The end result (an expense is reported and cash decreased) is the same, but the recording procedures differ. As will be discussed, if no entry has been made for such costs prior to the production of financial statements (the first alternative), both the expense and the payable do have to be recognized at that time so that all balances are properly stated for reporting purposes.

EXERCISE

Link to multiple-choice question for practice purposes: http://www.quia.com/quiz/2092606.html

Question: Transaction 3—A company borrows $9,000 from a bank. ***What is the impact of signing a loan agreement with a bank or other lending institution?***

Answer: Cash is increased by the amount of money received from the lender. The company is obligated to repay this balance and, thus, has incurred a new liability. As with many transactions, the financial impact is reasonably easy to ascertain.

cash (asset) increases by $9,000

note payable (liability) increases by $9,000

KEY TAKEAWAY

Most organizations must gather an enormous quantity of information as a prerequisite for preparing financial statements periodically. This process begins with an analysis of the impact of each transaction (financial event). After the effect on all account balances is ascertained, the recording of a transaction is relatively straightforward. The changes caused by most transactions—the purchase of inventory or the signing of a note, for example—can be determined quickly. For accrued expenses, such as salary or rent that grow over time, the accounting system can record the amounts gradually as incurred or only at the point of payment. However, the figures to be reported are not impacted by the specific mechanical steps that are taken.

2. THE EFFECTS CAUSED BY COMMON TRANSACTIONS

LEARNING OBJECTIVES

At the end of this section, students should be able to meet the following objectives:

1. **Explain the reason that a minimum of two accounts are impacted by every transaction.**
2. **Identify the account changes that are created by the payment of insurance and rent, the sale of merchandise, the acquisition of a long-lived asset, a capital contribution, the collection of a receivable, and the payment of a liability.**
3. **Separate the two events that occur when inventory is sold and determine the effect of each.**

Question: Transaction 4—The inventory items that were bought in Transaction 1 for $2,000 are now sold for $5,000 on account. ***What balances are impacted by the sale of merchandise in this manner?***

Answer: Two things actually happen in the sale of inventory. First, revenue of $5,000 is generated by the sale. Because the money will not be collected until a later date, accounts receivable (an asset) is initially increased. The reporting of receivable balance indicates that this amount is due from a customer and should be collected at some subsequent point in time.

accounts receivable (asset) increases by $5,000

sales (revenue) increases by $5,000

Second, the inventory is removed. Companies have an option in the method by which inventory balances are monitored. Here, a **perpetual inventory system** will be utilized. That approach has become extremely common due to the prevalence of computer systems in the business world. It maintains an ongoing record of the inventory held and the amount that has been sold to date. All changes in inventory are recorded immediately. However, in a later chapter, an alternative approach—still used by some companies—known as a **periodic inventory system** will also be demonstrated.

Since a perpetual system is being used here, the reduction in inventory is recorded simultaneously with the sale. An expense is incurred as inventory costing $2,000 is taken away by the customer. The company's assets are reduced by this amount. Cost of goods sold (an expense) is recognized to reflect this decrease in the amount of merchandise on hand.

perpetual inventory system

Accounting system that maintains an ongoing record of all inventory items; records increases and decreases in inventory accounts as they occur as well as the cost of goods sold to date.

periodic inventory system

Accounting system that does not maintain an ongoing record of all inventory items; instead, ending inventory is determined by a physical count so that a formula (beginning inventory plus purchases less ending inventory) can be used to determine cost of goods sold.

cost of goods sold (expense) increases by $2,000

inventory (asset) decreases by $2,000

The $3,000 difference between the sales revenue of $5,000 and the related cost of goods sold of $2,000 is known as the gross profit (or gross margin or mark up) on the sale.

EXERCISE

Link to multiple-choice question for practice purposes: http://www.quia.com/quiz/2092607.html

Question: In each event that has been studied so far, two accounts have been affected. ***Are two accounts impacted by every possible transaction?***

Answer: In every transaction, a cause and effect relationship is always present. For example, accounts receivable increases because of a sale. Cash decreases as a result of paying salary expense. No account can possibly change without some identifiable cause. Thus, every transaction must touch a minimum of two accounts. Many transactions actually affect more than two accounts but at least two are impacted by each of these financial events.

Question: Transaction 5—The reporting company pays $700 for insurance coverage relating to the past few months. The amount was previously recorded in the company's accounting system as the cost was incurred. Apparently, computers were programmed to accrue this expense periodically. ***What is the financial impact of paying for an expense if the balance has already been recognized over time as the liability grew larger?***

Answer: Several pieces of information should be noted here as part of the analysis.

- Cash declined by $700 as a result of the payment.
- This cost relates to a past benefit; thus, an expense has to be recorded. No future economic benefit is created by the insurance payment in this example. Cash was paid for coverage over the previous months.
- The company's accounting system has already recorded an accrual of this amount. Thus, insurance expense and the related liability were recognized as incurred. This is clearly a different mechanical procedure than that demonstrated in number 2 above for the salary payment.

The expense cannot be recorded again or it will be double-counted. Instead, cash is reduced along with the liability established through the accrual process. The expense was recorded already so no additional change in that balance is needed. Instead, the liability is removed and cash decreased.

insurance payable (liability) decreases by $700

cash (asset) decreases by $700

Note that accounting recognition is often dependent on the recording that has taken place. The final results should be the same (here an expense is recognized and cash decreased), but the steps in the process can vary.

EXERCISE

Link to multiple-choice question for practice purposes: http://www.quia.com/quiz/2092608.html

Question: Transaction 6—A truck is acquired for $40,000 but only $10,000 in cash is paid by the company. The other $30,000 is covered by signing a note payable. This transaction seems to be a bit more complicated because more than two figures are involved. ***What is the financial impact of buying an asset when only a portion of the cash is paid on that date?***

Answer: In this transaction, for the first time, three accounts are impacted. A truck is bought for $40,000 so the recorded balance for this asset is increased by that cost. Cash decreases $10,000 while the notes payable balance rises by $30,000. These events each happened. To achieve a fair presentation, the accounting process seeks to reflect the actual occurrences that took place. As long as the analysis is performed properly, recording a transaction is no more complicated when more than two accounts are affected.

truck (asset) increases by $40,000

cash (asset) decreases by $10,000

notes payable (liability) increases by $30,000

Question: Transaction 7—Assume that several individuals approach the company and offer to contribute $19,000 in cash to the business in exchange for capital stock so that they can join the ownership. The offer is accepted. ***What accounts are impacted by the issuance of capital stock to the owners of a business?***

Answer: When cash is contributed to a company for a portion of the ownership, cash obviously goes up by the amount received. This money was not generated by revenues or by liabilities but rather represents assets given freely so that new ownership shares could be issued. This inflow is reflected in the financial statements as increases in the cash and capital stock accounts. Outside decision makers can see that this amount of the company's net assets came from investments made by owners.

cash (asset) increases by $19,000

capital stock (stockholders' equity) increases by $19,000

EXERCISE

Link to multiple-choice question for practice purposes: http://www.quia.com/quiz/2092640.html

Question: Transaction 8—A sale of merchandise was made previously in Transaction 4 for $5,000. No cash was received at that time but is collected now. ***What accounts are affected by the receipt of money from an earlier sale?***

Answer: The revenue from this transaction was properly recorded previously in number 4 when the sale originally took place and the account receivable balance was established. Revenue should not be recorded again or it will be double-counted causing reported net income to be overstated. Instead, the accountant indicates that this increase in cash is caused by the decrease in the accounts receivable balance.

cash (asset) increases by $5,000

accounts receivable (asset) decreases by $5,000

Question: Transaction 9—Inventory was bought in Transaction 1 for $2,000 and later sold in Transaction 4. Now, however, the company is ready to make payment on the amount owed for this merchandise. ***When cash is delivered to settle a previous purchase of inventory, what is the financial effect of the transaction?***

Answer: As a result of the payment, cash is decreased by $2,000. The inventory was recorded previously when acquired. Therefore, this new transaction does not replicate that effect. Instead, the liability established in number 1 is removed from the books. The company is not buying the inventory again but simply paying the debt established for these goods.

accounts payable (liability) decreases by $2,000

cash (asset) decreases by $2,000

EXERCISE

Link to multiple-choice question for practice purposes: http://www.quia.com/quiz/2092627.html

Question: Transaction 10—The company wants to rent a building to use for the next four months and pays the property's owner $4,000 to cover this cost. ***When a rent or other payment provides the company with a future benefit, what recording is appropriate?***

Answer: In acquiring the use of this property, the company's cash decreases by $4,000. The money was paid in order to utilize the building for four months in the future. The anticipated economic benefit is an asset and should be reported to decision makers by establishing a prepaid rent balance. The reporting company has paid to use the property at a designated time in the future to help generate revenues.

prepaid rent (asset) increases $4,000

cash (asset) decreases by $4,000

KEY TAKEAWAY

Accountants cannot record transactions without understanding the impact that has occurred. Whether inventory is sold or an account receivable is collected, at least two accounts are always affected because all such events have both a cause and a financial effect. Individual balances rise or fall depending on the nature of each transaction. The payment of insurance, the collection of a receivable, a capital contribution, and the like all cause very specific changes in account balances. One of the most common is the sale of inventory where both an increase in revenue and the removal of the merchandise takes place. Increases and decreases in inventory are often monitored by a perpetual system that reflects all such changes immediately. In a perpetual system, cost of goods sold—the expense that measures the cost of inventory acquired by a company's customers—is recorded at the time of sale.

3. AN INTRODUCTION TO DOUBLE-ENTRY BOOKKEEPING

LEARNING OBJECTIVES

At the end of this section, students should be able to meet the following objectives:

1. **Explain the history of double-entry bookkeeping.**
2. **List the four steps followed in the accounting process.**
3. **Indicate the purpose of a T-account.**
4. **List the rules for using debits and credits.**
5. **Understand the reason that debits and credits are always equal.**

Question: Transaction analysis determines the changes in account balances as the events of each day take place. Financial statements provide a formal structure to communicate the resulting balances periodically to an array of interested parties. Revenues, expenses, gains, and losses are presented on an income statement where they are combined to arrive at reported net income for the period. Total income earned and dividends paid by the company over its entire life are netted to compute the current retained earnings balance. Assets, liabilities, capital stock, and retained earnings are all displayed on a balance sheet. Changes in cash are separated into operating activities, investing activities, and financing activities and disclosed on a statement of cash flows. Notes offer pages of additional explanatory information. The amount of financial data that is readily available is impressive.

The accountant for a business of any significant size faces a daunting challenge in creating financial statements: gathering, measuring, and reporting the impact of the many varied events that occur virtually every day. As an example, for 2008, Xerox Corporation disclosed revenues of over $17.6 billion and operating expenses and other costs of $17.4 billion. At the end of 2008, the Kellogg Company reported holding $897 million in inventory—which is a lot of cereal—and indicated that its operating activities that year generated a net cash inflow of nearly $1.3 billion. ***How can any organization possibly amass and maintain such an enormous volume of data so that financial statements can be produced with no material misstatements?***

double-entry bookkeeping

A mechanical process created over five hundred years ago and documented by Fra Luca Bartolomeo de Pacioli that facilitates the gathering and reporting of financial information.

Answer: Over five hundred years ago, Venetian merchants in Italy developed a system that continues to serve in the twenty-first century as the basis for accumulating financial data throughout much of the world. Today, when every aspect of modern society seems to be in a constant state of flux, a process that has remained in use for over five centuries is almost impossible to comprehend. However, the **double-entry bookkeeping** procedures that were first documented in 1494 by Fra Luca Bartolomeo de Pacioli (a friend of Leonardo da Vinci) remain virtually unchanged by time. Organizations, both small and large, use the fundamentals of double-entry bookkeeping to collect the information needed to produce financial statements that are fairly presented according to the rules of U.S. GAAP.

Question: This assertion sounds like science fiction. It hardly seems believable that Xerox keeps up with over $17.6 billion in revenue (approximately $48 million per day) using the same methods that Venetian merchants applied to their transactions during the Renaissance. ***How can a five-hundred-year-old bookkeeping system possibly be usable by today's modern businesses?***

Answer: State-of-the-art computers and other electronic devices are designed to refine and accelerate the financial accounting process but the same basic organizing procedures have been utilized now for hundreds of years. In simplest terms, accounting systems are all created to follow four sequential steps:

- Analyze
- Record
- Adjust
- Report

As explained previously, financial accounting starts by analyzing each transaction—every event that has a monetary impact on the organization—to ascertain the changes created in accounts such as rent expense, cash, inventory, and dividends paid. Fortunately, a vast majority of any company's transactions are repetitive so that many of the effects can be easily anticipated. A sale on credit always increases both accounts receivable and revenues. Regardless of the time or place, a cash purchase of equipment increases the balance reported for equipment while decreasing cash. Computer systems can be programmed to record the impact of these events automatically allowing the accountant to focus on analyzing more complex transactions.

Question: The second step in the accounting system is listed above as "recording." At the beginning of this chapter, a number of transactions were presented and their impact on individual accounts determined. Following this analysis, some method has to be devised to capture the information in an orderly fashion. Officials could just list the effect of each transaction on a sheet of paper: increase inventory $2,000 and increase accounts payable $2,000; increase salary expense $300 and decrease cash $300. However, this process is slow and poorly organized. A more efficient process is required. ***What is the key to recording transactions after all account changes are identified?***

accounts

Detailed records of the transactions and current balances of specific assets, liabilities, stockholders' equity, revenues and expenses.

Answer: An essential step in understanding the accounting process is to realize that financial information is accumulated by **accounts**. Every balance to be reported in a company's financial statements is maintained in a separate account. Thus, for assets, an individual account is established to monitor cash, accounts receivable, inventory, and so on. To keep track of expenses, a number of additional accounts are needed such as cost of goods sold, rent expense, salary expense, and repair expense. The same is true for revenues, liabilities, and other categories. A small organization might utilize only a few dozen accounts for its entire recordkeeping system. A large company could have thousands.

Based on the original Venetian model, the balance for each account is monitored in a form known as a **T-account** as displayed in Figure 4.2. This structure provides room for recording on both the left side (known as the **debit** side) and the right side (the **credit** side).

T-account

Used to maintain the monetary balance for each of the accounts reported by an organization with a left (debit) side and a right (credit) side.

debit

Left side of a T-account; it is used to show increases in assets, expenses, and dividends paid and decreases in liabilities, contributed capital, and revenues.

credit

Right side of a T-account used to show increases in liabilities, shareholders' equity, and revenues and decreases in assets, expenses, and dividends paid.

FIGURE 4.2 Common T-Accounts

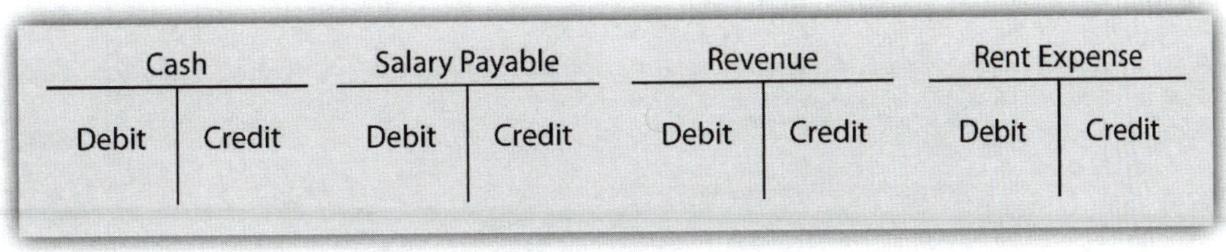

One side of each T-account records increases; the other side indicates decreases. For over five hundred years, the following rules have applied.

The following are accounts where debits reflect an increase and credits a decrease:

- Expenses and losses
- Assets
- Dividends paid[1]

The following are accounts where credits reflect an increase and debits a decrease:

- Liabilities
- Capital stock
- Revenues and gains
- Retained earnings[2]

The debit and credit rules for these seven general types of accounts provide a short-hand method for recording the financial impact that a transaction has on any account. They were constructed in this manner so that the following would be true:

debits must always equal credits for every transaction.

At first, the debit and credit rules might seem completely arbitrary. However, they are structured to mirror the cause and effect relationship found in every transaction. This is the basis of what the Venetian merchants came to understand so long ago: every effect must have a cause.

To illustrate:

- Assume an asset (such as cash) increases. As shown above, that is recorded on the debit side of the specific asset's T-account. What could cause an asset to become larger? A reason must exist. A liability—possibly a bank loan—could have been incurred (recorded as a credit); capital stock could have been issued to an owner (a credit); revenue could have been earned from a sale (a credit); another asset could have been sold (a credit). The list of possible reasons is relatively short. In each case, the debit (increase) to the asset is caused by an equal and offsetting credit.
- Assume an asset (such as cash) decreases. This change is recorded on the credit side of the asset's T-account. What might cause this reduction? An expense could have been paid (recorded as a debit); a dividend could have been distributed to shareholders (a debit); a liability could have been extinguished (a debit); another asset could have been acquired (a debit). Once again, the cause and effect relationship is reflected; the debits equal the credits. Each effect is set equal and opposite to every potential cause.

There are only seven types of accounts. Therefore, a mastery of debit and credit rules can be achieved with a moderate amount of practice. Because of the fundamental position of debits and credits within every accounting system, this knowledge is well worth the effort required.

EXERCISE

Link to multiple-choice question for practice purposes: http://www.quia.com/quiz/2092609.html

KEY TAKEAWAY

Most companies participate in numerous transactions each day that must be examined and organized so that financial statements can be prepared. This process requires four steps: analyze, record, adjust, and report. Over five hundred years ago, double-entry bookkeeping was created as a mechanical process to facilitate this gathering and reporting of financial information. A T-account is maintained for each of the accounts (such as cash, accounts payable, and rent expense) to be reported by a company. The left side of the T-account is the debit side, and the right side is the credit. Expenses and losses, assets, and dividends paid increase with debits. Liabilities, revenues and gains, capital stock, and retained earnings increase with credits. Debits always equal credits because every transaction must have both an effect and a cause for that effect.

4. PREPARING JOURNAL ENTRIES

LEARNING OBJECTIVES

At the end of this section, students should be able to meet the following objectives:

1. **Describe the purpose and structure of a journal entry.**
2. **Identify the purpose of a journal.**
3. **Define trial balance and indicate the source of its monetary balances.**
4. **Prepare journal entries to record the effect of acquiring inventory, paying salary, borrowing money, and selling merchandise.**
5. **Define accrual accounting and list its two components.**
6. **Explain the purpose of the revenue realization principle.**
7. **Explain the purpose of the matching principle.**

Question: In an accounting system, the impact of each transaction is analyzed and must then be recorded. Debits and credits are used for this purpose. ***How does the actual recording of a transaction take place?***

Answer: The effects produced on the various accounts by a transaction should be entered into the accounting system as quickly as possible so that information is not lost and mistakes have less time to occur. After analyzing each event, the financial changes caused by a transaction are initially recorded as a **journal entry**.[3] A list of all recorded journal entries is maintained in a **journal** (also referred to as a **general journal**), which is one of the most important components within any accounting system. The journal is the diary of the company: the history of the impact of the financial events as they took place.

A journal entry is no more than an indication of the accounts and balances that were changed by a transaction.

journal entry

The physical form used initially in double-entry bookkeeping to record the financial changes caused by a transaction; must have at least one debit and one credit and the total debit(s) always equal the total credit(s).

journal

The physical location of all journal entries; the diary of an organization capturing the impact of financial events as they took place; it is also referred to as the general journal

general journal

The physical location of all journal entries; the diary of a company capturing the impact of financial events as they took place; it is also referred to as the journal

Question: Debit and credit rules are best learned through practice. ***In order to grasp the use of debits and credits, how should the needed practice begin?***

Answer: When faced with debits and credits, everyone has to practice at first. That is normal and to be expected. These rules can be learned quickly but only by investing a bit of effort. Earlier in this chapter, a number of transactions were analyzed to determine their impact on account balances. Assume now that these same transactions are to be recorded as journal entries. To provide a bit more information for this illustration, the reporting company will be a small farm supply store known as the Lawndale Company that is located in a rural area. For convenience, assume that the company incurs these transactions during the final few days of Year One, just prior to preparing financial statements.

Assume further that this company already has the account balances presented in Figure 4.3 in its T-accounts before making this last group of journal entries. Note that the total of all the debit and credit balances do agree ($54,300) and that every account shows a positive balance. In other words, the figure being reported is either a debit or credit based on what makes that particular type of account increase. Few T-accounts contain negative balances.

This current listing of accounts is commonly referred to as a **trial balance**. Since T-accounts are kept together in a ledger (or general ledger), a trial balance reports the individual balances for each T-account maintained in the company's ledger.

trial balance

List of account balances as shown at a point in time for each of the T-accounts maintained in the company's ledger; eventually, financial statements are created using these balances.

FIGURE 4.3 Balances Taken From T-accounts in Ledger

Lawndale Company
Trial Balance (prior to recording new transactions)

Account	Debit Balance	Credit Balance
Cash	$20,000	
Accounts receivable	9,000	
Inventory	8,000	
Insurance payable		$700
Accounts payable		2,600
Notes payable (long term)		10,000
Capital stock		12,000
Retained earnings (beginning of year)		7,000
Sales of merchandise		22,000
Cost of goods sold	12,000	
Rent expense	3,600	
Salary expense	1,000	
Insurance expense	700	
Totals	$54,300	$54,300

Question: Assume that after the above balances were determined, several additional transactions took place. The first transaction analyzed at the start of this chapter was the purchase of inventory on credit for $2,000. This acquisition increases the record of the amount of inventory being held while also raising one of the company's liabilities, accounts payable. ***How is the acquisition of inventory on credit recorded in the form of a journal entry?***

Answer: Following the transactional analysis, a journal entry is prepared to record the impact that the event has on the Lawndale Company. Inventory is an asset that always uses a debit to note an increase. Accounts payable is a liability so that a credit indicates that an increase has occurred. Thus, the following journal entry is appropriate. [4]

FIGURE 4.4 Journal Entry 1: Inventory Acquired on Credit

Inventory	2,000		(increase an asset—debit)
Accounts Payable		2,000	(increase a liability—credit)

Notice that the word "inventory" is physically on the left of the journal entry and the words "accounts payable" are indented to the right. This positioning clearly shows which account is debited and which is credited. In the same way, the $2,000 numerical amount added to the inventory total appears on the left (debit) side whereas the $2,000 change in accounts payable is clearly on the right (credit) side.

Preparing journal entries is obviously a mechanical process but one that is fundamental to the gathering of information for financial reporting purposes. Any person familiar with accounting procedures could easily "read" the above entry: based on the debit and credit, both inventory and accounts payable have gone up so a purchase of merchandise for $2,000 on credit is indicated. Interestingly, with translation of the words, a Venetian merchant from the later part of the fifteenth century would be capable of understanding the information captured by this journal entry even if prepared by a modern company as large as Xerox or Kellogg.

Question: As a second example, the Lawndale Company pays its employees their regular salary of $300 for work performed during the past week. ***If no entry has been recorded previously, what journal entry is appropriate when a salary payment is made?***

Answer: Because no entry has yet been made, neither the $300 salary expense nor the related salary payable already exists in the accounting records. Apparently, the $1,000 salary expense appearing in the above trial balance reflects earlier payments made during the period by the company to its employees.

Payment is made here for past work so this cost represents an expense rather than an asset. Thus, the balance recorded as salary expense goes up by this amount while cash decreases. Increasing an expense is always shown by means of a debit; decreasing an asset is reflected through a credit.

FIGURE 4.5 Journal Entry 2: Salary Paid to Employees

Salary Expense	300		(increase an expense—debit)
Cash		300	(decrease an asset—credit)

In practice, the date of each transaction could also be included here. For illustration purposes, this extra information is not necessary.

Question: Assume $9,000 is borrowed from a local bank when officials sign a new note payable that will have to be repaid in several years. ***What journal entry is prepared by a company's accountant to reflect the inflow of cash received from a loan?***

Answer: As always, recording begins with an analysis of the transaction. Here, cash increases as the result of the incurred debt (notes payable). Cash—an asset—increases $9,000, which is shown as a debit. The company's notes payable balance also goes up by the same amount. As a liability, the increase is recorded through a credit. By using debits and credits in this way, the financial effects are entered into the accounting records.

FIGURE 4.6 Journal Entry 3: Money Borrowed from Bank

Cash	9,000		(increase an asset—debit)
Notes Payable		9,000	(increase a liability—credit)

EXERCISE

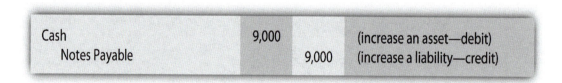

Link to multiple-choice question for practice purposes: http://www.quia.com/quiz/2092610.html

Question: In Transaction 1, inventory was bought for $2,000. That entry is recorded above. Assume now that these goods are sold for $5,000 to a customer on credit. ***How is the sale of merchandise on account recorded in journal entry form?***

Answer: As discussed previously, two events really happen when inventory is sold. First, the sale is made and, second, the customer takes possession of the merchandise from the company. Assuming again that a perpetual inventory system is in use, both the sale and the related expense are recorded immediately. In the initial part of the transaction, the accounts receivable balance goes up $5,000 because the money from the customer will not be collected until a later date. The increase in this asset is shown by means of a debit. The new receivable resulted from a sale. Revenue is also recorded (by a credit) to indicate the cause of that effect.

FIGURE 4.7 Journal Entry 4A: Sale Made on Account

Accounts Receivable	5,000		(increase an asset—debit)
Sales of Merchandise		5,000	(increase revenue—credit)

At the same time, inventory costing $2,000 is surrendered by the company. The reduction of any asset is recorded through a credit. The expense resulting from the asset outflow has been identified previously as "cost of goods sold." Like any expense, it is entered into the accounting system through a debit.

FIGURE 4.8 Journal Entry 4B: Merchandise Acquired by Customers

Cost of Goods Sold	2,000		(increase an expense—debit)
Inventory		2,000	(decrease an asset—credit)

Question: In the above transaction, the Lawndale Company made a sale but the cash will not be collected until some later date. ***Why is revenue reported at the time of sale rather than when the cash is eventually collected?*** *Accounting is conservative. Thus, delaying recognition of sales revenue (and the resulting increase in net income) until the $5,000 is physically received might have been expected.*

Answer: This question reflects a common misconception about the information conveyed through financial statements. As shown above in Journal Entry 4A, recognition of revenue is not tied directly to the receipt of cash. One of the most important elements comprising the structure of U.S. GAAP is **accrual accounting**, which serves as the basis for timing the reporting of revenues and expenses. Because of the direct impact on net income, such recognition issues are among the most complicated and controversial in accounting. The accountant must always determine the appropriate point in time for reporting each revenue and expense. Accrual accounting provides standard guidance (in the United States and throughout much of the world).

accrual accounting

System required by U.S. GAAP to standardize the timing of the recognition of revenues and expenses; it is made up of the revenue realization principle and the matching principle.

Accrual accounting is really made up of two distinct components. The **revenue realization principle** provides authoritative direction as to the proper timing for the recognition of revenue. The **matching principle** establishes guidelines for the reporting of expenses. These two principles have been utilized for decades in the application of U.S. GAAP. Their importance within financial accounting can hardly be overstated.

revenue realization principle

The portion of accrual accounting that guides the timing of revenue recognition; it states that revenue is properly recognized at the point that the earning process needed to generate the revenue is substantially complete and the amount to be received can be reasonably estimated.

Revenue realization principle. Revenue is properly recognized at the point that (1) the earning process needed to generate the revenue is substantially complete and (2) the amount eventually to be received can be reasonably estimated. As the study of financial accounting progresses into more complex situations, both of these criteria will require careful analysis and understanding.

Matching principle. Expenses are recognized in the same time period as the revenue they help to create. Thus, if specific revenue is to be recognized in the year 2019, any associated costs should be reported as expenses in that same time period. Expenses are matched with revenues. However, when a cost cannot be tied directly to identifiable revenue, matching is not possible. In those cases, the expense is recognized in the most logical time period, in some systematic fashion, or as incurred—depending on the situation.

matching principle

The portion of accrual accounting that guides the timing of expense recognition; states that expense is properly recognized in the same time period as the revenue that it helped to generate.

For the revenue reported in Journal Entry 4A, assuming that the Lawndale Company has substantially completed the work required of this sale and $5,000 is a reasonable estimate of the amount that will be collected, recognition at the time of sale is appropriate. Because the revenue is recognized at that moment, the related expense (cost of goods sold) should also be recorded as can be seen in Journal Entry 4B.

Accrual accounting provides an excellent example of how U.S. GAAP guides the reporting process in order to produce fairly presented financial statements that can be understood by all decision makers around the world.

EXERCISE

Link to multiple-choice question for practice purposes: http://www.quia.com/quiz/2092642.html

KEY TAKEAWAY

After the financial effects are analyzed, the impact of each transaction is recorded within a company's accounting system through a journal entry. The purchase of inventory, payment of a salary, and borrowing of money are all typical transactions that are recorded by means of debits and credits. All journal entries are maintained within the company's journal. The timing of this recognition is especially important in connection with revenues and expenses. Accrual accounting provides formal guidance within U.S. GAAP. Revenues are recognized when the earning process is substantially complete and the amount to be collected can be reasonably estimated. Expenses are recognized based on the matching principle, which holds that they should be reported in the same period as the revenue they help to generate.

5. THE CONNECTION OF THE JOURNAL AND THE LEDGER

LEARNING OBJECTIVES

At the end of this section, students should be able to meet the following objectives:

1. **Prepare journal entries for basic transactions such as the payment of insurance, the acquisition of a long-lived asset, the contribution of capital, the payment of a dividend, and the like.**
2. **Explain the recording of a gain or loss rather than revenue and cost of goods sold.**
3. **Describe the recording of an unearned revenue.**
4. **Understand the purpose of both the journal and the ledger.**
5. **Discuss the posting of journal entries to the ledger T-accounts and describe the purpose of that process.**

Question: The Lawndale Company pays $700 for insurance coverage received over the past few months. In this case, though, the amount has already been recognized by the company. Both the insurance expense and an insurance payable were recorded as incurred. Thus, the amounts can be seen on the trial balance in Figure 4.3. Apparently, Lawndale's accounting system was designed to recognize this particular expense as it grew over time. ***When an expense has already been recorded, what journal entry is appropriate at the time actual payment is made?***

Answer: Because of the previous recognition, the expense should not now be recorded a second time. Instead, this payment reduces the liability that was established by the accounting system. Cash—an asset—is decreased, which is shown by means of a credit. At the same time, the previously recorded payable is removed. Any reduction of a liability is communicated by a debit. To reiterate, no expense is included in this entry because that amount has already been recognized.

FIGURE 4.9 Journal Entry 5: Liability for Insurance Is Paid

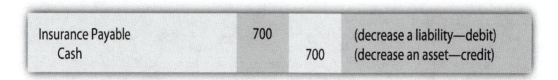

Insurance Payable	700		(decrease a liability—debit)
Cash		700	(decrease an asset—credit)

Note that Journal Entries 2 and 5 differ although the events are similar. As discussed previously, specific recording techniques can be influenced by the manner in which the accounting system has handled earlier events. In Journal Entry 2, neither the expense nor the payable had yet been recorded. Thus, the expense was recognized at the time of payment. For Journal Entry 5, both the expense and payable had already been entered into the records as the amount gradually grew over time. Hence, when paid, the liability is settled but no further expense is recognized. The proper amount is already present in the insurance expense T-account.

Question: Assume that a new truck is acquired by the Lawndale Company for $40,000. Cash of $10,000 is paid now but a note payable—due in several years—is signed for the remaining $30,000. This transaction impacts three accounts rather than just two. ***How is a journal entry constructed when more than two accounts have been affected?***

Answer: As has been discussed, every transaction changes at least two accounts because of the cause and effect relationship underlying all financial events. However, beyond that limit, any number of accounts can be impacted. Complex transactions often touch numerous accounts. Here, the truck account (an asset) is increased and must be debited. Part of the acquisition was funded by paying cash (an asset) with the decrease recorded as a credit. The remainder of the cost was covered by signing a note payable (a liability). A liability increase is recorded by means of a credit. Note that the debits do equal the credits even when more than two accounts are affected by a transaction.

FIGURE 4.10 Journal Entry 6: Truck Acquired for Cash and by Signing a Note

Truck	40,000		(increase an asset—debit)
Cash		10,000	(decrease an asset—credit)
Note Payable		30,000	(increase a liability—credit)

Question: Lawndale Company needs additional financing so officials go to current or potential shareholders and convince them to contribute cash of $19,000 in exchange for new shares of the company's capital stock. These individuals invest this money in order to join the ownership or increase the number of shares they already hold. ***What journal entry does a business record when capital stock is issued?***

Answer: The asset cash is increased in this transaction, a change that is always shown as a debit. Capital stock also goes up because new shares are issued to company owners. As indicated in the debit and credit rules, the capital stock account increases by means of a credit.

FIGURE 4.11 Journal Entry 7: Capital Stock Issued for Cash

Cash	19,000		(increase an asset—debit)
Capital Stock		19,000	(increase a capital stock—credit)

EXERCISE

Link to multiple-choice question for practice purposes: http://www.quia.com/quiz/2092643.html

Question: In Journal Entry 4A, a sale was made on credit. An account receivable was established at that time for $5,000. Assume that the customer now pays this amount to the Lawndale Company. ***How does the collection of an amount from an earlier sales transaction affect the account balances?***

Answer: When a customer makes payment on a previous sale, cash increases and accounts receivable decrease. Both are assets; one balance goes up (by a debit) while the other is reduced (by a credit).

FIGURE 4.12 Journal Entry 8: Money Collected on Account

Cash	5,000		(increase an asset—debit)
Accounts Receivable		5,000	(decrease an asset—credit)

Note that cash is collected here but no additional revenue is recorded. Based on the requirements of accrual accounting, revenue of $5,000 was recognized previously in Journal Entry 4A. Apparently, the revenue realization principle was met at that time, the earning process was substantially complete and a reasonable estimation could be made of the amount to be received. Recognizing the revenue again at the current date would incorrectly inflate reported net income. Instead, the previously created receivable balance is removed.

Question: In Journal Entry 1, inventory was purchased on credit for $2,000. Assume, now, that Lawndale makes payment of the entire amount that is due. ***How is a cash outflow to pay for inventory previously acquired shown in a company's journal?***

Answer: Inventory was bought at an earlier time and payment is now being made. The inventory was properly recorded when acquired and should not be entered again. The merchandise was only obtained that one time. Here, cash is reduced (a credit). The liability set up in Journal Entry 1 (accounts payable) is removed by means of a debit.

FIGURE 4.13 Journal Entry 9: Money Paid on Account

Accounts Payable	2,000		(decrease a liability—debit)
Cash		2,000	(decrease an asset—credit)

Question: Company officials like the building that is being used for operations and decide to rent it for four additional months at a rate of $1,000 per month. An immediate payment of $4,000 is made. This cost provides a future economic benefit for the company rather than a past value. Recognition of an expense is not yet appropriate. ***What is recorded when rent or other costs such as insurance or advertising are paid in advance?***

Answer: Cash is decreased by the payment made here to rent this building. As an asset, a reduction is reported in cash by means of a credit. However, this rent provides a future value for Lawndale Company. The cost is not for past usage of the building but rather for the upcoming four months. Therefore, the amount paid creates an asset. The probable economic benefit is the ability to make use of this facility during the future to generate new revenues. When the $4,000 is initially paid, an asset—normally called prepaid rent—is recorded through a debit.

FIGURE 4.14 Journal Entry 10: Money Paid for Future Rent

Prepaid Rent	4,000		(increase an asset—debit)
Cash		4,000	(decrease an asset—credit)

Note that this company does not record the building itself as the asset because it does not gain ownership or control (beyond these four months). The payment only provides the right to make use of the building for the specified period in the future so that a prepaid rent balance is appropriate.

Before this illustration of typical journal entries is completed, four additional transactions will be examined. In total, these fourteen provide an excellent cross-section of basic events encountered by most

businesses and the journal entries created to capture that information. Coming to understand the recording of these transactions is of paramount importance in mastering the debit and credit rules.

Question: Officials of the Lawndale Company decide to buy a small tract of land by paying $8,000 in cash. Perhaps they think the space might be used sometime in the future as a parking lot. ***What is recorded to reflect the cash purchase of a plot of land?***

Answer: The transaction here is straightforward. As an asset, land increases with a debit. Cash goes down because of the acquisition and is recorded using a credit. As stated previously, Venetian merchants would probably have made the same recording five hundred years ago (although not in U.S. dollars).

FIGURE 4.15 Journal Entry 11: Land Acquired for Cash

Land	8,000		(increase an asset—debit)
Cash		8,000	(decrease an asset—credit)

Question: Now, assume that—at a later time—this same piece of land is sold to an outside party for cash of $11,000. A sale occurs here but the land is not inventory. It was not bought specifically to be resold within the normal course of business. Selling land is not the primary operation of the Lawndale Company. ***Should revenue be recorded along with cost of goods sold when land is sold?*** *These accounts are used in journalizing the sale of inventory. Does the same reporting apply to the sale of other items such as land or equipment?*

Answer: Because the sale of land is not viewed as a central portion of this company's operations, neither revenue nor cost of goods sold is reported as in the sale of inventory. An $11,000 increase in cash is recorded along with the removal of the $8,000 cost of the land that was conveyed to the new buyer. However, to alert decision makers that a tangential or incidental event has taken place, a gain (if the sales price is more than the cost of the land) or a loss (if the sales price is less than cost) is recognized for the difference. The effect on net income is the same but the reporting has changed.

Often, the resulting gain or loss is then separated from revenues and expenses on the company's income statement to more clearly communicate information as to the nature of the transaction. Consequently, neither revenue nor cost of goods sold is found in the entry below as was shown above in Journal Entries 4A and 4B.

FIGURE 4.16 Journal Entry 12: Land Sold for Cash in Excess of Cost

Cash	11,000		(increase an asset—debit)
Land		8,000	(decrease an asset—credit)
Gain on Sale of Land		3,000	(increase revenue/gain—credit)

EXERCISE

Link to multiple-choice question for practice purposes: http://www.quia.com/quiz/2092628.html

Question: Accrual accounting, as specified in the revenue realization principle, mandates that revenues should not be recognized until the earning process is substantially complete. Assume a customer gives the Lawndale Company $3,000 in cash for some type of service to be performed at a future date. The work has not yet begun. Thus, Lawndale cannot report revenue of $3,000. ***How is a cash inflow recorded if it is received for work before the earning process is substantially complete?***

Answer: Although the company collected money, accrual accounting dictates that revenue cannot yet be recognized. The earning process here will not take place until sometime in the future. As an asset, the cash account is increased (debit) but no revenue can be recorded. Instead, an unearned revenue account is set up to recognize the $3,000 credit. This balance is reported by the Lawndale Company as a liability. Because the money has been accepted, the company is obliged to provide the service or return the $3,000 to the customer. Recording this liability mirrors the company's future responsibility.

FIGURE 4.17 Journal Entry 13: Money Received for Work to Be Done Later

Cash	3,000		(increase an asset—debit)
Unearned Revenue		3,000	(increase a liability—credit)

Here is one final transaction to provide a full range of basic examples at this preliminary stage of coverage. Many additional transactions and their journal entries will be introduced throughout this textbook, but these fourteen form a strong core of typical events encountered by most businesses.

Question: Assume that the Lawndale Company has been profitable. As a result, the board of directors votes to distribute a cash dividend to all owners, a reward that totals $600. Payment is made immediately. ***What recording is appropriate when a dividend is paid?***

Answer: Cash is reduced by this distribution to the company's owners. As an asset, a credit is appropriate. The cause of the decrease was payment of a dividend. Hence, a dividends paid account is established. According to the debit and credit rules, dividends paid is listed as one of the accounts that increases through a debit. Thus, the recording of this last illustration is as follows.

FIGURE 4.18 Journal Entry 14: Dividend Distributed to Owners

Dividends Paid	600		(increase dividends paid—debit)
Cash		600	(decrease an asset—credit)

Question: With practice, obtaining an understanding of the rules for debits and credits is a reasonable goal. However, these journal entries do not provide the current balance of any account. They record the effect of each transaction but not the updated account totals, figures that could change many times each day. ***How does an accountant determine the current balance of cash, inventory, rent expense, or the like?***

Answer: In an accounting system, the recording process is composed of two distinct steps.

1. After analyzing the financial impact of a transaction, a journal entry is created to reflect the impact on relevant accounts.
2. Then, each individual debit and credit is added to the specific T-account being altered, a process known as "posting." A debit to cash in a journal entry is listed as a debit in the cash T-account. A credit made to notes payable is recorded as a credit within the notes payable T-account. After all entries are posted, the current balance for any account can be determined by adding the debit and the credit sides of the T-account and netting the two.

Historically, posting the individual changes shown in each journal entry to the specific T-accounts was a tedious and slow process performed manually. Today, automated systems are designed so that the impact of each entry is simultaneously recorded in the proper T-accounts found in the ledger.

For illustration purposes, the journal entries recorded above have been posted into ledger T-accounts shown in Figure 4.4. Each account includes the previous balance (PB) found in the trial balance shown in Figure 4.3 at the start of the illustrated transactions. The additional debits and credits recorded for each of the fourteen sample transactions include the number of the corresponding journal entry for cross-referencing purposes. The debit and credit sides of each account can be summed and netted at any point to determine the current balance (CB).

FIGURE 4.19 Lawndale Company Ledger

CASH

PB 20,000	
(3) 9,000	(2) 300
(7) 19,000	(5) 700
(8) 5,000	(6) 10,000
(12) 11,000	(9) 2,000
(13) 3,000	(10) 4,000
	(11) 8,000
	(14) 600
67,000	25,600
CB 41,400	

ACCOUNTS RECEIVABLE

PB 9,000	
(4A) 5,000	(8) 5,000
14,000	5,000
CB 9,000	

INVENTORY

PB 8,000	
(1) 2,000	(4B) 2,000
10,000	2,000
CB 8,000	

PREPAID RENT

(10) 4,000	
CB 4,000	

TRUCK

(6) 40,000	
CB 40,000	

LAND

(11) 8,000	(12) 8,000
8,000	8,000
CB 0	

INSURANCE PAYABLE

	PB 700
(5) 700	
700	700
	CB 0

ACCOUNTS PAYABLE

	PB 2,600
(9) 2,000	(1) 2,000
2,000	4,600
	CB 2,600

NOTES PAYABLE

	PB 10,000
	(3) 9,000
	(6) 30,000
	CB 49,000

UNEARNED REVENUE

	(13) 3,000
	CB 3,000

CAPITAL STOCK

	PB 12,000
	(7) 19,000
	CB 31,000

RETAINED EARNINGS

	PB 7,000
	CB 7,000

DIVIDENDS PAID

(14) 600	
CB 600	

SALES OF MERCHANDISE

	PB 22,000
	(4A) 5,000
	CB 27,000

COST OF GOODS SOLD

PB 12,000	
(4B) 2,000	
CB 14,000	

RENT EXPENSE

PB 3,600	
CB 3,600	

SALARY EXPENSE

PB 1,000	
(2) 300	
CB 1,300	

INSURANCE EXPENSE

PB 700	
CB 700	

GAIN ON SALE OF LAND

	(12) 3,000
	CB 3,000

KEY TAKEAWAY

Initial coverage of the recording of basic transactions is concluded here through analysis of the payment of insurance, the contribution of capital, the purchase and sale of land, the receipt of cash prior to work being performed, the payment of dividends to owners, and the like. After the impact of each event is ascertained, debits and credits are used to record these changes. These journal entries are then posted to the appropriate T-accounts used to monitor ever-changing account balances. All the T-accounts are collectively known as a ledger or general ledger. Journal entries document the effect of transactions. T-accounts and the ledger maintain the current balance of every account.

Talking with a Real Investing Pro (Continued)

Following is a continuation of our interview with Kevin G. Burns.

Question: When you were a college student majoring in accounting, you learned all the debit and credit rules as well as about journal entries and the general ledger. In your years as an investment advisor, has this knowledge ever proven to be helpful to you and your career?

Kevin Burns: Although I never planned to be an accountant when I was in college, I found the internal logic of the debit and credit rules quite fascinating. Thinking through transactions and figuring out the proper recording process was a great introduction to business operations. In all honesty, as an investment advisor, I am more interested in asset values and other balance sheet information than the accounting process necessary to gather this information. However, I also happen to own a restaurant and I always find it interesting when I dig through the specific expense accounts looking for ways to be more efficient. For instance, recently when I saw that we had spent a lot of money last year on building maintenance, I could not imagine how that was possible. I dug through the T-account myself and found a recording error that needed to be fixed. My background allowed me to understand the entire process. Frequently, as I study the various debits within our expenses, I am able to spot areas where the restaurant can save money.

Video Clip

Joe talks about the five most important points in Chapter 4.

View the video online at: http://blip.tv/play/sDyBv6xqAA

6. END-OF-CHAPTER EXERCISES

QUESTIONS

1. What is a transaction?
2. Where was the accounting system developed that is still used by businesses today?
3. What is this system called?
4. What are the four steps followed by accounting systems?
5. By what is financial information accumulated?
6. Define T-account.
7. Which accounts are increased with a debit?
8. Which accounts are increased with a credit?
9. What is a journal in the accounting sense?
10. What is a trial balance?
11. Accrual accounting is composed of which two principles? Define each.
12. Define unearned revenue.

TRUE OR FALSE

1. ____ Debits and credits must equal for every transaction.
2. ____ A list of all recorded journal entries is maintained in the ledger.
3. ____ Revenue may not be recorded until cash is collected.
4. ____ A transaction is any event that has a financial impact on a company.
5. ____ An expense account is increased with a credit.
6. ____ Examples of accrued expenses include salary, rent, and interest.
7. ____ Posting refers to process of recording journal entries.
8. ____ A company must recognize an accrued expense as incurred.
9. ____ The matching principle states that expenses should be recognized in the same period as the revenues they help generate.
10. ____ Unearned revenue is a type of revenue account.

MULTIPLE CHOICE

1. Which of the following is ***not*** true about double-entry bookkeeping?
    a. It originated in Italy.
    b. Debits and credits must equal.
    c. It is still used today.
    d. An entry can have no more than one credit and one debit.
2. Which of the following entries could Yeats Company not make when they perform a service for a client?

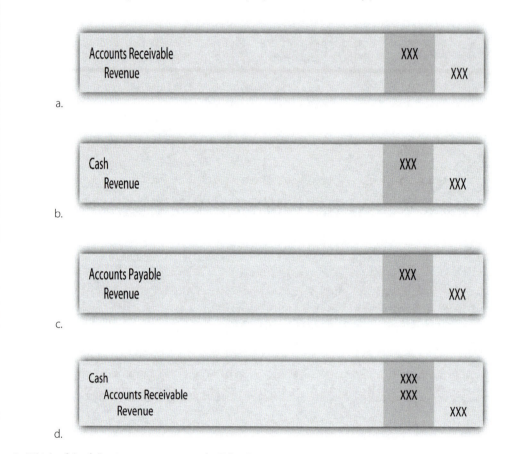

Accounts Receivable	XXX	
Revenue		XXX

a.

Cash	XXX	
Revenue		XXX

b.

Accounts Payable	XXX	
Revenue		XXX

c.

Cash	XXX	
Accounts Receivable	XXX	
Revenue		XXX

d.

3. Which of the following is a transaction for Tyler Corporation?
    a. Tyler pays its employees $400 for work done.
    b. Tyler considers renting office space that will cost $1,500 per month.
    c. Tyler agrees to perform services for a client, which will cost $7,000.
    d. Tyler places an order for supplies that will be delivered in two weeks. The supplies cost $200.
4. Elenor Company sells 400 units of inventory for $40 each. The inventory originally cost Elenor $26 each. What is Elenor's gross profit on this transaction?
    a. $16,000
    b. $10,400
    c. $ 5,600
    d. $ 9,600

5. Which of the following increases with a debit?
    a. Retained earnings
    b. Sales revenue
    c. Inventory
    d. Note payable
6. In January, Rollins Company is paid $500 by a client for work that Rollins will not begin until February. Which of the following is the correct journal entry for Rollins to make when the $500 is received?

Cash	500	
Accounts Receivable		500

a.

Cash	500	
Unearned Revenue		500

b.

Cash	500	
Revenue		500

c.

Accounts Receivable	500	
Revenue		500

d.

PROBLEMS

1. Record the following journal entries for Taylor Company for the month of March:
    a. Borrowed $4,500 from Local Bank and Trust
    b. Investors contributed $10,000 in cash for shares of stock
    c. Bought inventory costing $2,000 on credit
    d. Sold inventory that originally cost $400 for $600 on credit
    e. Purchased a new piece of equipment for $500 cash
    f. Collected $600 in cash from sale of inventory in (d) above
    g. Paid for inventory purchased in (c) above
    h. Paid $1,200 in cash for an insurance policy that covers the next year
    i. Employees earned $3,000 during the month but have not yet been paid
    j. Paid employees $2,900 for wages earned and recorded during February
2. For each of the following transactions, determine if Raymond Corporation has earned revenue during the month of May and, if so, how much it has earned.
    a. Customers paid Raymond $1,500 for work Raymond will perform in June.
    b. Customers purchased $6,000 of inventory for which they have not yet paid.
    c. Raymond performed work for customers and was paid $3,400 in cash.
    d. Customers paid Raymond $2,300 for inventory purchased in April.
3. Record the journal entries for number 2 above.
4. Determine the missing account balance in the following trial balance:

Trial Balance—Ester Company

Ester Company Trial Balance 12/31/20XX

Account Title	Debits	Credits
Cash	$4,600	
Accounts Receivable	11,000	
Inventory	15,090	
Accounts Payable		$3,600
Note Payable		13,000
Capital Stock		5,000
Retained Earnings, 1/1/20XX		2,200
Sales Revenue		19,050
Cost of Goods Sold	?????	
Salary Expense	1,500	

5. State which balance, debit, or credit is normally held by the following accounts:
    a. Cash
    b. Dividends
    c. Notes payable
    d. Unearned revenue
    e. Cost of goods sold
    f. Prepaid rent
    g. Accounts receivable
    h. Capital stock

6. Near the end of her freshman year at college, Heather Miller is faced with the decision of whether to get a summer job, go to summer school, or start a summer dress making business. Heather has had some experience designing and sewing and believes it might be the most lucrative of her summer alternatives. She starts "Sew Cool."

   During June, the first month of business, the following occur:

   a. Heather deposits $1,000 of her own money into Sew Cool's checking account.
   b. Sew Cool purchases equipment for $1,000. The company signs a note payable for this purchase.
   c. Sew Cool purchases $1,000 in sewing supplies and material in cash.
   d. Sew Cool gives Heather's parents a check for $80 for rent and utilities.
   e. Heather sews and sells twenty dresses during the month. Each dress has a price of $60. Cash is received for twelve of the dresses, with customers owing for the remaining eight.
   f. The dresses sold above cost $35 each to make.
   g. Sew Cool purchases advertising for $50 cash.
   h. Sew Cool pays Heather a cash dividend of $10 cash.
   i. Sew Cool's taxes, paid in cash, amount to $87.

      A. Prepare journal entries for the above transactions.
      B. Prepare t-accounts for each account used.
      C. Prepare a trial balance for June.

7. Bowling Corporation had the following transactions occur during February:
    a. Bowling purchased $450,000 in inventory on credit.
    b. Bowling received $13,000 in cash from customers for subscriptions that will not begin until the following month.
    c. Bowling signed a note from Midwest Bank for $67,000.
    d. Bowling sold all the inventory purchased in (a) above for $700,000 on account.
    e. Bowling paid employees $120,000 for services performed during January.
    f. Bowling purchased land for $56,000 in cash.
    g. Bowling received $650,000 in cash from customers paying off January's accounts receivable.
    h. Bowling paid dividends to stockholders in the amount of $4,000.
    i. Bowling owes its employees $123,000 for work performed during February but not yet paid.
    j. Bowling paid $300,000 on its accounts payable.
    k. Bowling paid taxes in cash of $45,000.

    Required:

    A. Prepare journal entries for the above transactions.
    B. Complete the t-accounts below. Numbers already under the accounts represent the prior balance in that account.

Opening T-Account Balances

Account	Debit	Credit
Cash	500,000	
Accounts Receivable	650,000	
Inventory	0	
Land	22,000	
Accounts Payable		100,000
Unearned Revenue		0
Salary Payable		120,000
Note Payable		430,000
Capital Stock		302,000
Retained Earnings		220,000
Sales Revenue		0
Cost of Goods Sold	0	
Salary Expense	0	
Tax Expense	0	
Dividends	0	

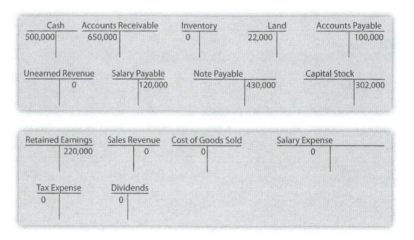

    C. Prepare a trial balance for February.

8. The following events occurred during the month of May for McLain Company.
    a. McLain sells 240 units for $20 each. McLain collects cash for 200 of these units. The units cost McLain $8 each to purchase.
    b. McLain purchases $1,800 worth of inventory on account.
    c. McLain collects $500 in cash on its A/R.
    d. McLain takes out a loan for $400.
    e. McLain pays out $350 cash in dividends.
    f. McLain receives a contribution of $600 from its owners.
    g. McLain purchased a new piece of equipment. The new equipment cost $1,000 and was paid for in cash.
    h. McLain pays $500 of its accounts payable.
    i. McLain incurs $500 in salaries expense, but will not pay workers until next month.
    j. McLain incurs $300 in rent expense and pays it in cash.
    k. McLain prepays $200 in cash for insurance.
    l. Taxes, paid in cash, are $110.

Required:

A. Prepare journal entries for the above transactions.
B. Complete the t-accounts below. Numbers already under the accounts represent the prior balance in that account.

Opening T-Account Balances

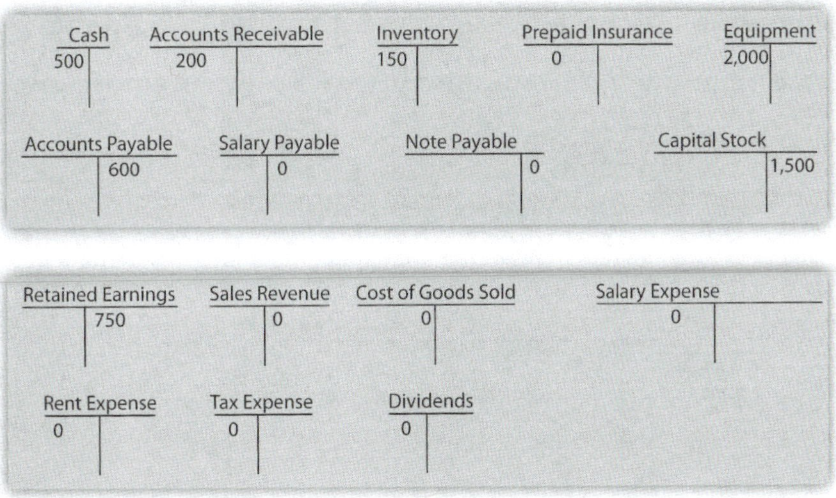

C. Prepare a trial balance for May.

ENDNOTES

1. One method to keep track of these accounts initially is to remember them as the "DEAD" accounts: **d**ebits increase, **e**xpenses and losses, **a**ssets, and **d**ividends paid. Quickly, though, through practice, such mnemonic devices will not be needed.
2. Changes in the balance reported for retained earnings normally do not come as a direct result of a transaction. As discussed previously, this account reflects all the net income earned to date reduced by all dividend payments. Income is made up of revenues, expenses, gains, and losses. Accounting recognition of revenues and gains (which increase with credits) lead to a larger retained earnings balance. Expenses, losses, and dividends paid (which all increase with debits) reduce retained earnings. Consequently, credits cause an increase in retained earnings whereas debits produce a decrease.
3. In larger organizations, similar transactions are often grouped, summed, and recorded together for efficiency. For example, all cash sales at one store might be totaled automatically and recorded at one time at the end of each day. To help focus on the mechanics of the accounting process, the journal entries recorded for the transactions in this textbook will be prepared individually.
4. The parenthetical information is included here only for clarification purposes and does not appear in a true journal entry.

CHAPTER 5

Why Must Financial Information Be Adjusted Prior to the Production of Financial Statements?

Video Clip

Joe introduces Chapter 5 and speaks about the course in general.

View the video online at: http://blip.tv/play/sDyBv68hAA

1. THE NEED FOR ADJUSTING ENTRIES

LEARNING OBJECTIVES

At the end of this section, students should be able to meet the following objectives:

1. **Explain the purpose and necessity of adjusting entries.**
2. **List examples of several typical accounts that require adjusting entries.**
3. **Define an accrued expense.**
4. **Provide examples of adjusting entries for various accrued expenses.**
5. **Describe the reason that accrued expenses often require adjusting entries but not in every situation.**

Question: The first two steps of the accounting process were identified in Chapter 4 as "analyze" and "record." A transaction occurs and the financial effects are ascertained through careful analysis. Once determined, the impact an event has on specific accounts is recorded in the form of a journal entry. Each of the debits and credits is then posted to the corresponding T-account located in the ledger. As needed, current balances can be determined for any or all of these accounts by netting the debits and credits. It is a system as old as the painting of the Mona Lisa.

The third step in this process was listed as "adjust." ***Why do ledger account balances require adjustment?*** *Why are the T-account totals found in Figure 4.3 not simply used by the accountant to produce financial statements for the reporting organization?*

Answer: Financial events take place throughout the year. As indicated, journal entries are recorded with the individual debits and credits then entered into the proper T-accounts. However, not all changes in a company's accounts occur as a result of physical events. Balances frequently increase or decrease simply because of the passage of time. Or, the impact is so gradual that producing individual journal entries is not reasonable. For example, salary is earned by employees every day (actually every minute) but payment is not usually made until the end of the week or month. Other expenses such as utilities, rent, and interest are incurred over time. Supplies such as pens and envelopes are used up on an ongoing basis. Unless an accounting system is programmed to record tiny incremental changes, the financial effects are not captured as they occur.

Following each day of work, few companies take the trouble to record the equivalent amount of salary or other expense and the related liability. When a pad of paper is consumed within an organization, debiting supplies expense for a dollar or two and crediting supplies for the same amount hardly seems worth the effort.

adjusting entries

Changes in account balances recorded prior to making financial statements to update T-accounts because some amounts have increased or decreased gradually over time but not recorded through a normal journal entry.

Prior to producing financial statements, the accountant must search for all such changes that have been omitted. These additional increases or decreases are also recorded in a debit and credit format (often called **adjusting entries** rather than journal entries) with the impact then posted to the appropriate ledger accounts. The process continues until all balances are properly stated. These adjustments are a prerequisite step in the preparation of financial statements. They are physically identical to journal entries recorded for transactions but they occur at a different time and for a different reason.

EXERCISE

Link to multiple-choice question for practice purposes: http://www.quia.com/quiz/2092644.html

Question: Adjusting entries are used to update the ledger for any financial changes that have occurred gradually over time and not recorded through a regular journal entry. ***What kinds of adjustments are normally needed before financial statements are prepared?***

Answer: A variety of adjusting entries will be examined throughout the remainder of this textbook. One of the accountant's primary responsibilities is the careful study of all financial information to ensure that it is all fairly presented before being released. Such investigation can lead to the preparation of numerous adjusting entries. Here, in Chapter 5, only the following four general types of adjustments are introduced. In later chapters, many additional examples will be described and analyzed.

- Accrued expenses (also referred to as accrued liabilities)
- Prepaid expenses
- Accrued revenue
- Unearned revenue (also referred to as deferred revenue)

Usually, at the start of the adjustment process, the accountant prepares an updated trial balance to provide a visual, organized representation of all ledger account balances. This listing aids the accountant in spotting figures that might need adjusting in order to be fairly presented. Therefore, Figure 5.1 takes the ending account balances for the Lawndale Company found in the ledger presented in Figure 4.3 and puts them into the form of a trial balance.

FIGURE 5.1 Updated Trial Balance

Lawndale Company Trial Balance (after recording all new transactions)

Account	Debit Balance	Credit Balance
Cash	$41,400	
Accounts receivable	9,000	
Inventory	8,000	
Prepaid rent	4,000	
Truck	40,000	
Accounts payable		$2,600
Notes payable		49,000
Unearned revenue		3,000
Capital stock		31,000
Retained earnings, beginning of year		7,000
Dividends paid	600	
Sales of merchandise		27,000
Cost of goods sold	14,000	
Rent expense	3,600	
Salary expense	1,300	
Insurance expense	700	
Gain on sale of land		3,000
Totals	$122,600	$122,600

Question: The first adjustment listed is an **accrued expense**. *In Chapter 4, the word "accrue" was defined as "to grow." Thus, an accrued expense is one that increases gradually over time. As indicated previously, some companies program their accounting systems to record such expenses as they are incurred. This accrual process reduces the need for separate adjusting entries. Other companies make few, if any, accruals and update all balances through numerous adjustments. The recording process for such expenses should be designed to meet the informational needs of company officials. Some prefer to have updated balances readily available in the ledger while others are inclined to wait for periodic financial reports to be issued.* ***What are some typical accrued expenses and what is the appropriate adjusting entry if they have not been previously recorded by the accounting system?***

accrued expenses

Expenses (and the related liabilities) that grow gradually over time; impact is recorded prior to preparing financial statements by means of an adjusting entry to update both accounts.

Answer: If a reporting company's accounting system recognizes an expense as it grows, no adjustment is necessary. The balances are recorded properly. They are ready to be included in financial statements. Thus, when statements are prepared, the accountant only needs to search for accrued expenses that have not yet been recognized.

Numerous expenses do get slightly larger each day until paid including salary, rent, insurance, utilities, interest, advertising, income taxes, and the like. For example, on its December 31, 2008, balance sheet, the Hershey Company reported accrued liabilities of approximately $504 million. In the notes to the financial statements, this amount was explained as debts owed on that day for payroll, compensation and benefits, advertising and promotion, and other accrued expenses.

Assume, for illustration purposes, that the accountant reviews the trial balance presented in Figure 5.1 and realizes that utility expenses (such as electricity and water) have not been recorded since the most recent payment. Assume that the Lawndale Company currently owes $900 for those utilities. The following adjustment is needed before financial statements are created. It is an adjusting entry because no physical event took place; this liability simply grew over time and has not yet been paid.

FIGURE 5.2 Adjusting Entry 1: Amount Owed for Utilities

Utilities Expense	900		(increase an asset—debit)
Utilities Payable (or Accrued Liabilities)		900	(increase a liability—credit)

EXERCISE

Link to multiple-choice question for practice purposes: http://www.quia.com/quiz/2092630.html

KEY TAKEAWAY

Adjusting entries are necessary to update all account balances before financial statements can be prepared. These adjustments are not the result of physical events or transactions but are rather caused by the passage of time or small changes in account balances. The accountant examines a current listing of accounts—known as a trial balance—to identify amounts that need to be changed prior to the preparation of financial statements. Although numerous adjustments are studied in this textbook, four general types are especially common: accrued expenses, prepaid expenses, accrued revenues, and unearned revenues. Any expense (such as salary) that grows gradually over time but has not yet been paid is known as an accrued expense. If not automatically recorded by the accounting system, it must be entered into the records by adjustment prior to producing financial statements.

2. PREPARING VARIOUS ADJUSTING ENTRIES

LEARNING OBJECTIVES

At the end of this section, students should be able to meet the following objectives:

1. **Explain the need for an adjusting entry in the reporting of prepaid expenses and be able to prepare that adjustment.**
2. **Explain the need for an adjusting entry in the reporting of accrued revenue and be able to prepare that adjustment.**
3. **Describe the difficulty of determining when the earning process for revenue is substantially complete and discuss possible resolutions.**

prepaid expenses

Assets that are created when an expense is paid in advance; normally recorded as an asset initially and then gradually reassigned to expense over time through adjusting entries.

Question: The second adjustment to be considered here involves the handling of **prepaid expenses**. *In the transactions that were recorded in the previous chapter, Journal Entry 10 reported a $4,000 payment made in advance for four months of rent to use a building. An asset—prepaid rent—was recorded through the normal accounting process. This account is listed on the trial balance in Figure 5.1.* ***Why might a year-end adjusting entry be needed in connection with a prepaid expense?***

Answer: During these four months, the Lawndale Company will use the rented facility to help generate revenue. Over that time, the future economic benefit established by the payment gradually becomes a past benefit. The asset literally changes into an expense day by day. For illustrative purposes, assume that one month has now passed since the original payment. This month of benefit provided by the rent ($1,000 or $4,000/four months) no longer exists; it has been consumed.

As a preliminary step in preparing financial statements, an adjusting entry is needed to reclassify $1,000 from the asset into an expense account. This adjustment leaves $3,000 in the asset (for the remaining three months of rent on the building) while $1,000 is now reported as an expense (for the previous one month of rent).

FIGURE 5.3 Adjusting Entry 2: Previously Rented Facility Is Used

Rent Expense	1,000		(increase an expense—debit)
Prepaid Rent		1,000	(decrease an asset—credit)

The basic purpose of adjusting entries is to take whatever amounts reside in the ledger and align them with the requirements of U.S. generally accepted accounting principles (U.S. GAAP). For this illustration, the original $4,000 payment was classified as a prepaid rent and the adjustment above was created in response to that initial entry.

In recording transactions, some accounting systems mechanically handle events in a different manner than others. Thus, construction of an adjusting entry always depends on the recording that previously took place. To illustrate, assume that when this $4,000 payment was made, the company's computer program had been designed to enter a debit to rent expense rather than to prepaid rent. All money spent for rent was automatically recorded as rent expense. This initial accounting has no impact on the final figures to be reported but does alter the adjustment process.

An adjusting entry still needs to be prepared so that the expense appearing on the income statement is $1,000 (for the past one month) while the asset on the balance sheet is shown as $3,000 (for the next three months). If the entire cost of $4,000 is in rent expense, the following alternative is necessary to arrive at the proper balances. It shifts $3,000 out of the expense and into the asset.

FIGURE 5.4 Adjusting Entry 3: Alternative Based on a Different Initial Recording

Prepaid Rent	3,000		(increase an asset—debit)
Rent Expense		3,000	(decrease an expense—credit)

This entry leaves $1,000 in expense and $3,000 as the asset. Regardless of the account, the accountant first determines the balance that is present in the ledger and then creates the specific adjustment needed to arrive at fairly presented figures.

EXERCISE

Link to multiple-choice question for practice purposes: http://www.quia.com/quiz/2092645.html

Question: Accrued revenue is the third general type of adjustment to be covered here. Based on the title, this revenue is one that grows gradually over time. If not recorded by a company's accounting system, updating is necessary before financial statements are prepared. ***What adjustment is used to recognize accrued revenue that has not previously been recorded?***

Answer: Various types of revenue are earned as time passes rather than through a physical event such as the sale of inventory. To illustrate, assume that a customer comes to the Lawndale Company five days before the end of the year and asks for assistance. The customer must be away for the next thirty days and wants company employees to feed, water, and care for his horses during the period of absence. Everything needed for the job is available at the customer's farm; Lawndale just has to provide the service. The parties agree that the company will receive $100 per day for this work with payment to be made upon the person's return.

No asset changes hands at the start of this task. Thus, the company's accounting system is not likely to make any entry until payment is eventually received. However, assume that after the first five days of work, the company is ready to prepare financial statements and needs to recognize all revenue earned to date. The service to this customer has been carried out for five days at a rate of $100 per day. The company has performed the work to earn $500, an amount that will not be received until latter. This receivable and revenue should be recognized through an adjusting entry so that the reported financial figures are fairly presented. The earning process for the $500 occurred this year and should be recorded in this year.

FIGURE 5.5 Adjusting Entry 4: Revenue Is Earned for Work Done

Accounts Receivable	500		(increase an asset—debit)
Sales of Services		500	(increase a revenue—credit)

No recognition is needed for cost of goods sold. Inventory is not being sold but rather is a service. The $500 receivable will be removed in the subsequent period when the customer eventually pays the company for the services rendered.

Question: As discussed in an earlier chapter, the revenue realization principle (within accrual accounting) provides formal guidance for the timing of revenue reporting. It states in part that the earning process must be substantially complete before revenue can be recognized. That seems reasonable. In the above example, the work has only been performed for five days out of a total of thirty. That is not substantially complete. ***Why is any accrued revenue recognized if the earning process is not substantially complete?***

Answer: This question draws attention to a difficult problem that accountants face frequently in creating a fair portrait of a company. The proper recognition of revenue is one of the most challenging tasks encountered in financial accounting. Here, the simplest way to resolve this issue is to consider the nature of the task to be performed.

Is this job a single task to be carried out by the company over thirty days or is it thirty distinct tasks to be handled once a day over this period of time?

If the work of feeding and caring for the horses is one large task like painting a house, then the earning process is only 5/30 finished at the moment and not substantially complete. No revenue is recognized until the work has been performed for twenty-five more days. The previous adjusting entry is not warranted.

Conversely, if this assignment is thirty separate tasks, then five of them are substantially complete and revenue of $500 is properly recorded by the above entry. Unfortunately, the distinction is not always clear. Because accounting is conservative, revenue should never be recognized unless evidence predominates that the individual tasks are clearly separate events.

EXERCISE

Link to multiple-choice question for practice purposes: http://www.quia.com/quiz/2092646.html

Question: ***In practice, how does an accountant determine whether a specific job is substantially complete?*** *Because of the direct impact on net income, this judgment must be a critical in financial reporting.*

Answer: Accountants spend a lot of time searching for credible evidence as to the true nature of the events they encounter. That can be a challenge. Their goal is to ensure that all information included in financial statements is presented fairly according to U.S. GAAP.

Is a job substantially complete so that revenue can be recognized or not?

That question can often be difficult to answer. Here is one technique that might be applied in analyzing this particular example. Assume that after five days, Lawndale had to quit feeding the customer's horses for some legitimate reason. Should the company be able to demand and collect all $500 for the work done to that point? If so, then those five days are distinct tasks that have been completed. However, if no money would be due based on working just five days, substantial completion has not been achieved by the services performed. Thus, revenue recognition would be inappropriate.

In Adjusting Entry 3, the assumption is made that the daily tasks are separate and that the company could collect for the work accomplished to date. However, this type of judgment can be extremely difficult in the real world. It is often the product of much thought and discussion. The impact on the financial statements can be material, which increases pressure on the accountant.

Students often enter into a financial accounting course believing that little is required other than learning set rules and then following them mechanically. As will be demonstrated many times in this textbook, nothing ever replaces the need for experienced judgment on the part of the accountant.

KEY TAKEAWAY

To align reported balances with the rules of accrual accounting, adjusting entries are created as a step in the preparation of financial statements. Prepaid expenses are normally recorded first as assets and then reclassified to expense as time passes to satisfy the matching principle. The mechanics of this process will vary somewhat based on the initial recording of the payment. Accrued revenues and the corresponding receivables are recognized when the earning process is deemed to be substantially complete. The time at which this benchmark is achieved often depends on whether a single job or a collection of independent tasks is under way. As with so many areas of financial reporting, that decision can rely heavily on professional judgment.

3. PREPARING FINANCIAL STATEMENTS BASED ON ADJUSTED BALANCES

LEARNING OBJECTIVES

At the end of this section, students should be able to meet the following objectives:

1. **Explain the need for an adjusting entry in the reporting of unearned revenue and be able to prepare that adjustment.**
2. **Prepare an income statement, statement of retained earnings, and balance sheet based on the balances in an adjusted trial balance.**
3. **Explain the purpose and construction of closing entries.**

The last adjusting entry to be covered at this time is unearned (or deferred) revenue. Some companies operate in industries where money is received first and then earned gradually over time. Newspaper and magazine businesses, for example, are paid in advance by their subscribers and advertisers. The earning process becomes substantially complete by the subsequent issuance of their products. Thus, the December 28, 2008, balance sheet for the New York Times Company reported a liability titled "unexpired subscriptions" of $81 million. This balance represents payments collected from customers who have not yet received their newspapers.

Question: In Journal Entry 13 in Chapter 4, the Lawndale Company reported receiving $3,000 for services to be rendered at a later date. An unearned revenue account was recorded as a liability for that amount and appears in the trial balance in Figure 5.1. ***When is an adjusting entry needed in connection with the recognition of previously unearned revenue?***

Answer: As indicated, unearned revenue represents a liability recognized when money is received before work is done. After any portion of the required service is carried out so that the earning process is substantially complete, an appropriate amount is reclassified from unearned revenue on the balance sheet to revenue on the income statement. For example, in connection with the $3,000 payment collected by Lawndale, assume that all the work necessary to recognize the first $600 has now been performed. To fairly present this information, an adjusting entry is prepared to reduce the liability and recognize the earned revenue.

FIGURE 5.6 Adjusting Entry 5: Money Previously Received Has Now Been Earned

Unearned Revenue	600		(decrease a liability—debit)
Sales of Services		600	(increase a revenue—credit)

EXERCISE

Link to multiple-choice question for practice purposes: http://www.quia.com/quiz/2092631.html

Question: ***After all adjusting entries have been recorded in the journal and posted to the appropriate T-accounts in the ledger, what happens next in the accounting process?***

Answer: At this point, the accountant believes that all account balances are fairly presented because no material misstatements exist according to U.S. GAAP. As one final check, an adjusted trial balance is produced for a last, careful review. Assuming that no additional concerns are noticed, the accountant prepares an income statement, a statement of retained earnings, and a balance sheet.

The basic financial statements are then completed by the production of a statement of cash flows. In contrast to the previous three, this remaining statement does not report ending ledger account balances but rather discloses the various changes occurring during the period in the composition of the cash account. As indicated in Chapter 3, all cash flows are classified as resulting from operating activities, investing activities, or financing activities.

The reporting process is then completed by the preparation of the explanatory notes that always accompany a set of financial statements.

The final trial balance for the Lawndale Company (including the four adjusting entries produced above) is presented in the appendix to this chapter. After that, each of the individual figures is appropriately placed within the first three financial statements. Revenues and expenses appear in the income statement, assets and liabilities in the balance sheet, and so on. The resulting statements are also exhibited in the appendix for illustrative purposes. No attempt has been made here to record all possible adjusting entries. For example, no income taxes have been recognized and interest expense has not been accrued in connection with notes payable. Depreciation expense of noncurrent assets with finite lives (the truck, in the company's trial balance) will be discussed in detail in a later chapter. However, these illustrations are sufficient to demonstrate the end result of the accounting process as well as the basic structure used for the income statement, statement of retained earnings, and balance sheet.

The statement of cash flows for the Lawndale Company cannot be created based solely on the limited information available in this chapter concerning the cash account. Thus, it has been omitted. Complete coverage of the preparation of a statement of cash flows will be presented in Chapter 17 of this textbook.

Question: Analyze, record, adjust, and report—the four basic steps in the accounting process. ***Is the work year complete for the accountant after financial statements are prepared?***

closing entries

Entries made to reduce all temporary ledger accounts (revenues, expenses, gains, losses, and dividends paid) to zero at the end of an accounting period so that a new measurement for the subsequent period can begin; the net effect of this process is transferred into the retained earnings account to update the beginning balance to the year-end figure.

Answer: One last mechanical process needs to be mentioned. Whether a company is as big as Microsoft or as small as the local convenience store, the final action performed each year by the accountant is the preparation of **closing entries**. Several types of accounts—specifically, revenues, expenses, gains, losses, and dividends paid—reflect the various changes that occur in a company's net assets but just for the current period. In order for the accounting system to start measuring the effects for each new year, all of these specific T-accounts must be returned to a zero balance after the annual financial statements are produced.

- Final credit totals existing in every revenue and gain account are closed out by recording equal and off-setting debits.
- Similarly, ending debit balances for expenses, losses, and dividends paid require a credit entry of the same amount to return each of these T-accounts to a zero balance.

After these "temporary" accounts are closed at year's end, the resulting single figure is the equivalent of the net income reported for the year less dividends paid. This net effect is recorded in the retained earnings T-account. The closing process effectively moves the balance for each revenue, expense, gain, loss, and dividend paid into retained earnings. In the same manner as journal entries and adjusting entries, closing entries are recorded initially in the company's journal and then posted to the ledger. As a result, the beginning retained earnings balance for the year is updated to arrive at the ending total reported on the balance sheet.

Assets, liabilities, capital stock, and retained earnings all start out each year with a balance that is the same as the ending figure reported on the previous balance sheet. Those accounts are not designed to report an impact occurring just during the current year. In contrast, revenues, expenses, gains, losses, and dividends paid all begin the first day of each year with a zero balance—ready to record the events of this new period.

KEY TAKEAWAY

Companies occasionally receive money for services or goods before they are provided. In such cases, an unearned revenue is recorded as a liability to indicate the company's obligation to its customer. Over time, as the earning process becomes substantially complete, the unearned revenue is reclassified as a revenue through adjusting entries. After this adjustment and all others are prepared and recorded, an adjusted trial balance is created and those figures are then used to produce financial statements. Finally, closing entries are prepared for all revenues, expenses, gains, losses, and dividends paid. Through this process, all of these T-accounts are returned to zero balances so that recording for the new year can begin. The various amounts in these temporary accounts are moved to retained earnings. Thus, its beginning balance for the year is increased to equal the ending total reported on the company's balance sheet.

Talking with a Real Investing Pro (Continued)

Following is a continuation of our interview with Kevin G. Burns.

Question: Large companies have millions of transactions to analyze, classify, and record so that they can produce financial statements. That has to be a relatively expensive process that produces no income for the company. From your experience in analyzing companies and their financial statements, do you think companies should spend more money on their accounting systems or would they be wise to spend less and save their resources?

Kevin Burns: Given the situations of the last decade ranging from the accounting scandals of Enron and WorldCom to recent troubles in the major investment banks, the credibility of financial statements and financial officers has eroded significantly. My view is that—particularly today—transparency is absolutely paramount and the more detail the better. Along those lines, I think any amounts spent by corporate officials to increase transparency in their financial reporting, and therefore improve investor confidence, is money well spent.

Video Clip

Joe talks about the five most important points in Chapter 5.

View the video online at: http://blip.tv/play/sDyBv7FAAA

4. CHAPTER APPENDIX

4.1 Final Trial Balance and Financial Statements

FIGURE 5.7 Appendix A

Lawndale Company Final Trial Balance—2009 (including four adjusting entries)

Account	Debit Balance	Credit Balance
Cash	$41,400	
Accounts receivable	9,500	
Inventory	8,000	
Prepaid rent	3,000	
Truck	40,000	
Accounts payable		$2,600
Utilities payable		900
Unearned revenue		2,400
Notes payable		49,000
Capital stock		31,000
Retained earnings, beginning of year		7,000
Dividends paid	600	
Sales of merchandise		27,000
Sales of services		1,100
Cost of goods sold	14,000	
Rent expense	4,600	
Salary expense	1,300	
Utilities expense	900	
Insurance expense	700	
Gain on sale of land		3,000
Totals	$124,000	$124,000

Lawndale Company Income Statement for Year Ended December 31, 2009

Revenues:		
Sales of merchandise	$27,000	
Sales of services	1,100	
Total revenues		$28,100
Expenses:		
Cost of goods sold	14,000	
Rent	4,600	
Salary	1,300	
Utilities	900	
Insurance	700	
Total expenses		(21,500)
Gain on sale of land		3,000
Net income		$9,600

FIGURE 5.8 Appendix B[1]

Lawndale Company Statement of Retained Earnings for Year Ended December 31, 2009		
Retained earnings balance, January 1, 2009		$7,000
Net income reported for 2009	$9,600	
Dividends distributed during 2009	600	
Net income less dividends for 2009		9,000
Retained earnings balance, December 31, 2009		$16,000

Lawndale Company Balance Sheet, December 31, 2009		
Current Assets	Assets	
Cash	$41,400	
Accounts receivable	9,500	
Inventory	8,000	
Prepaid rent	3,000	
Total current assets		$61,900
Noncurrent Assets		
Truck		40,000
Total assets		$101,900

Liabilities and Stockholders' Equity		
	Liabilities	
Current Liabilities		
Accounts payable	$2,600	
Utilities payable	900	
Unearned revenue	2,400	
Total current liabilities		$5,900
Noncurrent Liabilities		
Notes payable		49,000
Total liabilities		$54,900
	Stockholders' Equity	
Capial Stock	$31,000	
Retained Earnings	16,000	
Total stockholders' equity		$47,000
Total liabilities and stockholders' equity		$101,900

5. END-OF-CHAPTER EXERCISES

QUESTIONS

1. What is the purpose of adjusting entries?
2. Name the four general types of adjustments.
3. Give three examples of accrued expenses.
4. Briefly explain why it is difficult for accountants to determine whether or not revenue has been earned if the sales process is not complete.
5. Give an example of business or industry where customers usually pay for the product or service in advance.
6. What type of account is unearned revenue?
7. When should a company reclassify unearned revenue to revenue?
8. Why do companies produce a second trial balance? When is this second trial balance prepared?
9. Why do accountants prepare closing entries?
10. Into which account are revenues and expenses closed?

TRUE OR FALSE

1. ____ Determining when to recognize revenue can be difficult for accountants.
2. ____ Only permanent accounts are closed at the end of the financial statement cycle.
3. ____ Revenue may not be recorded until cash is collected.
4. ____ Some changes to accounts occur because of the passage of time.
5. ____ Accountants do not have to exercise much judgment because there are so many rules to follow.
6. ____ Assets, liabilities and owners' equity accounts will start each financial statement cycle with the same balance they had at the end of the previous cycle.
7. ____ The word "accrue" means "to grow."
8. ____ Companies have some discretion in how and when they record accruals.
9. ____ The purpose of adjusting entries to bring the balance in temporary accounts to zero at the end of the reporting cycle.
10. ____ Only one trial balance is prepared during a financial statement cycle.

MULTIPLE CHOICE

1. Which of the following accounts would be closed at the end of the financial statement cycle?
    a. Accounts receivable
    b. Accounts payable
    c. Cost of goods sold
    d. Unearned revenue
2. Jenkins Company received $600 for a client in May for work Jenkins would perform during May and June. What entry should Jenkins make on May 31 if one-third of the work is complete on that date?

a.

Cash	600	
Unearned Revenue		600

b.

Unearned Revenue	200	
Revenue		200

c.

Cash	600	
Revenue		600

d.

Unearned Revenue	600	
Revenue		600

3. Which of the following accounts would increase retained earnings when closed into it?
    a. Dividends
    b. Sales revenue
    c. Loss of sale of land
    d. Rent expense
4. Which of the following is ***not*** one of the four types of adjustments?
    a. Prepaid revenue
    b. Accrued expenses
    c. Unearned revenue
    d. Prepaid expenses
5. In September 20X3, LaToya Corporation paid for insurance for the next six months in the amount of $42,000. On December 31, LaToya's accountant forgot to make the adjusting entry that was needed. Which of the following is true?
    a. Assets are understated by $42,000.
    b. Net income is understated by $14,000.
    c. Expenses are overstated by $42,000.
    d. Net income is overstated by $28,000.

PROBLEMS

1. Determine if the following adjusting entries are
   - accrued expense (AE)
   - prepaid expense (PE)
   - accrued revenue (AR)
   - unearned revenue (UR)

   a. _____ Atlas Magazine was previously prepaid $400,000 by subscribers and has delivered half of the magazines ordered.

   b. _____ Hornsby Company agreed to provide 1,000 units of its product to Michaels Inc. and has substantially completed the agreement.

   c. _____ Nancy and Sons owes its employees $30,000 for work done over the past two weeks.

   d. _____ Replay Inc. advertised on TV 44 during the month of April, but has not yet made an entry to record the event.

   e. _____ Centurion Company paid Reliable Insurance Company $54,000 for insurance for twelve months, six of which have passed.

   f. _____ Reliable Insurance Company received a payment of $54,000 for insurance for twelve months from Centurion Company and six months have passed.

2. Determine if the following transactions for Marlin Corporation require an adjustment or not. If an adjusting entry is required, give the correct entry.

   a. At the beginning of the month, Marlin agreed to perform services for the next three months for Catsui Corporation for $30,000 per month. Catsui paid Marlin $90,000 in advance. One month has now passed.

   b. Marlin pays its employees every two weeks. At the end of the month, Marlin owes its employees $480,000, but will not pay them until the following week.

   c. Marlin paid $300,000 for rent at the beginning of the month by debiting prepaid rent and crediting cash. The $300,000 covered six months of occupancy, but only one month has passed.

   d. At the beginning of the month, Marlin agreed to perform services for Ryland Company for $16,000 per month for the next six months. Ryland has not yet paid any cash to Marlin and the work is not substantially complete.

3. Keating Inc. rents its headquarters from Starling Enterprises for $10,000 per month. On September 1, 20XX, Keating pays Starling $60,000 for six months worth of rent.

   a. Record the entry that Keating Inc. would make on September 1 when they pay Starling.

   b. Record the entry that Starling Enterprises would make on September 1 when they receive the rent payment from Keating.

   c. Record the adjusting entry that Keating would make on December 31, 20XX, as the company prepares its annual financial statements.

   d. Record the adjusting entry that Starling would make on December 31, 20XX, as the company prepares its annual financial statements.

4. Leon Jackson is ecstatic! First National Bank just approved a loan for Leon to start a Web site design and maintenance business called Webworks. He is now ready to purchase his needed equipment, hire his administrative help, and begin designing sites. During June, his first month of business, the following occur:

   a. Webworks signs a note at the bank and is given $10,000 cash.

   b. Leon deposits $2,000 of his own money into Webworks's checking account.

   c. Webworks purchases a new computer and additional equipment for $3,000.

   d. Webworks purchases supplies worth $200 on account that should last Webworks two months.

   e. Webworks hires Nancy Po to assist with administrative tasks. She will charge $100 per Web site for her assistance.

   f. Webworks begins working on his first two Web sites, one for Juan Sanchez, a friend of his dad's and the other for Pauline Smith, a local businesswoman.

   g. Webworks completes the site for Mr. Sanchez and sends him a bill for $600.

   h. Webworks completes the site for Ms. Smith and sends her a bill for $450.

   i. Webworks collects $600 in cash from Mr. Sanchez.

   j. Webworks pays Nancy $100 for her work on Mr. Sanchez's Web site.

   k. Webworks receives $500 in advance to work on a Web site for a local restaurant. Work on the site will not begin until July.

   l. Webworks pays taxes of $200 in cash.

Required:

A. Prepare journal entries for the above events if needed.
B. Post the journal entries to T-accounts.
C. Prepare an unadjusted trial balance for Webworks for June.
D. Prepare adjusting entries for the following and post them to your T-accounts, adding any additional T-accounts as necessary.

m. Webworks owes Nancy $100 for her work on Ms. Smith's Web site.
n. Leon's parents let him know that Webworks owes $80 toward the electricity bill. Webworks will pay them in July.
o. Webworks only used half of the supplies purchased in (d) above.

A. Prepare an adjusted trial balance for Webworks for June.

5. Jan Haley owns and operates Haley's Dry Cleaners. The following occurred during December:
   a. On December 1, Haley prepaid rent on her store for December and January with $2,000 cash.
   b. On December 1, Haley purchased insurance with cash in the amount of $2,400 that will last six months.
   c. Haley paid $900 of her accounts payable balance.
   d. Haley paid off all of her salaries payable balance.
   e. Haley purchased supplies on account in the amount of $2,400.
   f. Haley paid a salary to her assistant of $1,000 in cash for work done in the first two weeks of December.
   g. Haley dry-cleaned clothes for customers on account in the amount of $8,000.
   h. Haley collected $6,300 of her accounts receivable balance.
   i. Haley paid tax of $750 in cash.

   Required:

   A. Prepare the journal entry for each transaction.
   B. Prepare all necessary T-accounts. Numbers already under the accounts represent the prior balance in that account.

   Opening T-Account Balances

Account	Debit	Credit
Cash	5,000	
Accounts Receivable	6,500	
Prepaid Rent	0	
Prepaid Insurance	0	
Supplies	0	
Accounts Payable		1,200
Salary Payable		1,000
Note Payable		4,000
Capital Stock		3,000
Retained Earnings		2,500
Sales Revenue		0
Supplies Expense	0	
Salary Expense	0	
Rent Expense	0	
Insurance Expense	0	
Tax Expense	0	

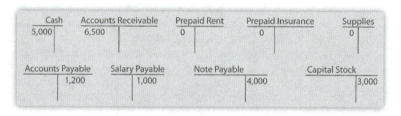

   C. Prepare a trial balance dated 12/31/XX.
   D. Make the following adjusting entries for the month of December and post them to the T-accounts:

   j. Rent expense:
   k. Insurance expense:
   l. Haley owes her assistant $1,000 for work done during the last two weeks of December.
   m. An inventory of supplies shows $400 in supplies remaining on December 31.

   E. Prepare an adjusted trial balance dated 12/31/XX.
   F. Prepare an income statement, statement of retained earnings, and balance sheet for the month ending December 31, 20XX.

6. On January 1, Kevin Reynolds, a student at State U, decides to start a business. Kevin has noticed that various student organizations around campus are having more and more need for mass produced copies of programs on CDs. While a lot of students have a CD drive on their computers that can write to CDs, it is a slow process when a high volume of CDs is needed.

   Kevin believes that with a beginning investment in specialty equipment, he can provide a valuable product to the college community. So on 1/1, Kevin officially begins "Kevin's Kool CD Kopies." Of course, Kevin is very careful to ensure that his customers have full ownership rights to the material on their CDs.

   Part 1:

   The following occur during January.

   1. Kevin deposits $500 of his own money into the company's checking account.
   2. Kevin signs a note payable in the amount of $1,000 from Neighborhood Bank. The note is due in one year.

3. KKCDK (Kevin's Kool CD Kopies) purchases a CD duplicator (a piece of equipment), which can copy seven CDs at one time. The cost is $1,300 and he pays cash.
4. KKCDK purchases 500 blank CDs for $150 on account.
5. KKCDK pays $20 cash for flyers to advertise.
6. KKCDK quickly catches on with the student groups on campus. KKCDK sells 400 CDs to various groups for $0.80 per CD. KKCDK receives cash payment for 300 of the CDs and the student groups owe for the other 100 CDs.
7. KKCDK pays $100 on its accounts payable.
8. KKCDK receives $40 in advance to copy 50 CDs for a student group. He will not begin work on the project until February.
9. KKCDK incurs $40 in tax expense. The taxes will be paid in February.

Required:

A. Prepare journal entries for the above events if needed.
B. Post the journal entries to T-accounts.
C. Prepare an unadjusted trial balance for KKCDK for January.
D. Prepare adjusting entries for the following and post them to your T-accounts.

10. Kevin's roommate, Mark, helps with the CD copying and delivering. KKCDK pays Mark a salary of $50 per month. Mark will get his first check on February 1.
11. KKCDK incurs $10 in interest expense. The interest will be paid with the note.

E. Prepare an adjusted trial balance for KKCDK for January
F. Prepare financial statements for KKCDK for January.

Part II: The following occur in February:

12. Kevin decides to expand outside of the college. On the first day of the month, KKCDK pays $20 in advance for advertising in the local paper. The advertisements will run during February and March.
13. The student groups paid for the 100 CDs not paid for in January.
14. KKCDK paid off its remaining accounts payable, salaries payable, taxes payable and interest payable.
15. KKCDK purchases 450 CDs for $135 on account.
16. KKCDK sells 500 CDs during the month for $0.80 each. KKCDK receives cash for 450 of them and is owed for the other 50.
17. KKCDK completes and delivers the advanced order of 50 CDs described in number 8 above.
18. KKCDK incurs $80 in tax expense. The taxes will be paid in March.

Required:

G. Prepare journal entries for the above events if needed.
H. Post the journal entries to the T-accounts.
I. Prepare an unadjusted trial balance for KKCDK for February.
J. Prepare adjusting entries for the following and post them to your T-accounts.

19. Mark continues to earn his salary of $50 and will be paid on March 1.
20. An adjustment is made for advertising in number 12 above.
21. KKCDK incurs $10 in interest expense. The interest will be paid with the note.

K. Prepare an adjusted trial balance for KKCDK for February.
L. Prepare the financial statements for February.

ENDNOTES

1. In a subsequent chapter, the reporting of noncurrent assets with finite lives will be covered in detail. The cost of such assets is subject to depreciation over their estimated useful lives so that a net book value is reported that falls each period. Therefore, the $40,000 is used here simply to illustrate the placement of the balances.

CHAPTER 6

Why Should Decision Makers Trust Financial Statements?

Video Clip

Joe introduces Chapter 6 and speaks about the course in general.

View the video online at: http://blip.tv/play/sDyBvuBUAA

1. THE NEED FOR THE SECURITIES AND EXCHANGE COMMISSION

LEARNING OBJECTIVES

At the end of this section, students should be able to meet the following objectives:

1. **Understand the reasons that financial statements might not be fairly presented.**
2. **Describe the mission of the Securities and Exchange Commission (SEC).**
3. **Explain the purpose of the EDGAR (Electronic Data Gathering and Retrieval) system.**
4. **Discuss the times when state laws apply to corporate securities rather than the rules and regulations of the SEC.**
5. **Explain the relationship of the SEC and the Financial Accounting Standards Board (FASB).**

Question: The potential importance of financial statements to any person making an analysis of a business or other organization appears rather obvious. The wide range of available information provides a portrait that reflects the company's financial health and potential for future success. However, a degree of skepticism seems only natural when studying such statements because they are prepared by the company's own management.

Decision makers are not naïve. They must harbor some concern about the validity of data that are self-reported. Company officials operate under pressure to present good results consistently, period after period. What prevents less scrupulous members of management from producing fictitious numbers just to appear profitable and financially strong? ***Why should anyone be willing to risk money based on financial statements that the reporting entity itself has created?***

Answer: The possible presence of material misstatements (either accidentally or intentionally) is a fundamental concern that should occur to every individual who studies a set of financial statements. Throughout history, too many instances have arisen where information prepared by a company's management has proven to be fraudulent causing decision makers to lose fortunes. In fact, the colorful term "cooking the books"[1] reflects the very real possibility of that practice. Enron, WorldCom, and Madoff Investment Securities are just recent and wide-ranging examples of such scandals.

The potential for creating misleading financial statements that eventually cause damage to both investors and creditors is not limited to current times and devious individuals. Greed and human weakness have always rendered the likelihood of a perfect reporting environment virtually impossible. In addition, fraud is not the only cause for concern. Often a company's management is simply overly (or occasionally irrationally) optimistic about future possibilities. That is also human nature. Therefore, financial information should never be accepted blindly.

Over the decades, numerous laws have been passed in hopes of creating a system to ensure that distributed financial statements are a fair representation of the underlying organization they profess to report. This is an objective that governments take seriously. Under capitalism, the financial health of the economy depends on the ability of worthy businesses to gain external financing for both operations and expansion. Without trust in the financial reporting process, raising large monetary amounts becomes difficult, if not impossible. As has been seen in recent times, hesitancy on the part of investors and creditors restricts the growth of companies and undermines the strength of the entire economy.

Securities and Exchange Commission (SEC)

Federal government agency holding legal responsibility over the reporting made by companies that issue securities that are publicly traded in the United States; works to ensure that this reporting process works as intended by the government; has opted to leave development of authoritative accounting principles to FASB.

EDGAR (Electronic Data Gathering and Retrieval)

SEC reporting system requiring companies to file their financial statements electronically to allow current and potential investors to obtain this information quickly and easily over the Internet as needed.

In the United States, ultimate responsibility for the availability of complete and reliable information about every organization that issues publicly traded securities[2] lies with the **Securities and Exchange Commission (SEC)**. The SEC is an independent agency within the federal government established by the Securities Exchange Act of 1934. Its mission "is to protect investors, maintain fair, orderly, and efficient markets, and facilitate capital formation."[3]

Virtually all U.S. companies of any significant size—as well as many foreign companies—fall under the jurisdiction of the SEC because their securities are traded publicly within the United States. Financial statements and other formal filings have to be submitted regularly to the SEC by these companies so that they can then be made available to the public through a system known as **EDGAR (Electronic Data Gathering and Retrieval)**.[4] All such statements and other released information must conform to the rules and regulations of the SEC.

Companies that do not issue even a minimum amount of securities to the public normally are required to comply with state laws rather than with the SEC and federal laws. Financial statements for such companies, although not as likely to be public information, are often required by financial institutions and other interested parties. For example, a bank might insist that a local convenience store include financial statements as part of a loan application. The form and distribution of that financial information must conform to state laws (often referred to as "blue sky laws").

Question: Companies such as General Electric or Starbucks that issue securities to the public are required to satisfy all applicable federal laws and regulations. The SEC has authority over the amount and nature of the information that must be provided and the actions that can be taken by both the buyer and the seller of the securities. ***Does the SEC develop the specific accounting principles to be followed in the production of financial statements that are issued by public companies?***

Answer: Legally, the SEC has the ability to establish accounting rules for all companies under its jurisdiction simply by stating that certain information must be presented in a particular manner in the public filings that it requires. However, the SEC has opted to leave the development of authoritative accounting principles to FASB, which is a private (nongovernment) organization.[5] This decision has, at times, been controversial. Some view it as an abdication of an important responsibility by the federal government. The assumption underlying this decision by the SEC is that the members of FASB can be trusted to study each issue meticulously before arriving at a reasoned resolution.

Thus, FASB produces accounting rules to be applied by all for-profit and not-for-profit organizations in the United States. State and local governments follow accounting standards produced by the **Governmental Accounting Standards Board (GASB)**.[6] In July, 2009, *FASB Accounting Standards Codification* was released to serve as the single source of authoritative nongovernmental U.S. generally accepted accounting principles (U.S. GAAP). As a result, all the previous individual rules that had been created over the decades were reclassified into a more logical framework. According to a FASB news release, "The Codification reorganizes the thousands of U.S. GAAP pronouncements into roughly 90 accounting topics and displays all topics using a consistent structure. It also includes relevant Securities and Exchange Commission (SEC) guidance that follows the same topical structure in separate sections in the Codification."[7]

Groups other than FASB also contribute to accounting standards but in a much less significant fashion. The most important of these is the **Emerging Issues Task Force (EITF)**, which was created in 1984 to assist FASB.[8] The EITF examines new problems when they initially arise in hopes of coming to quick agreement as to an appropriate method of reporting based on existing U.S. GAAP. Thus, the EITF is not forming U.S. GAAP as much as helping to apply it to newly created situations. If consensus is achieved (that is, no more than three members object), the conclusions rendered by the EITF are considered to be authoritative until such time—if ever—as FASB provides its own formal guidance. In this way, FASB does not have to issue hasty pronouncements to resolve every unique reporting concern when it first appears.

The SEC itself is not totally absent from the formation of U.S. GAAP. It occasionally issues guidelines to ensure that adequate information is being disclosed to the public through its own rules and interpretive releases. That is especially true in situations where reporting concerns have emerged and adequate official guidance does not exist. The SEC tends to restrict its own power over financial reporting to those areas where U.S. GAAP—for whatever reason—has not yet been well constructed. Assume, for example, that a new type of transaction arises and the EITF is unable to arrive at a consensus resolution. The SEC might specify relevant data to be included in the notes to financial statements or could prohibit certain methods of reporting until FASB had the opportunity to provide a studied ruling.

Governmental Accounting Standards Board (GASB)

Nonprofit organization that holds the authority for establishing accounting standards for state and local government units in the United States

Governmental Accounting Standards Board (GASB)

Nonprofit organization that holds the authority for establishing accounting standards for state and local government units in the United States

Emerging Issues Task Force (EITF)

A group formed to assist FASB by examining new accounting issues as they arise in hopes of arriving at quick agreement as to the appropriate method of reporting based on existing U.S. GAAP.

EXERCISE

Link to multiple-choice question for practice purposes: http://www.quia.com/quiz/2092647.html

KEY TAKEAWAY

The U.S. economy depends on the willingness of investors and creditors to risk their hard-earned financial resources by conveying it to organizations. Financial statements play an important role in providing the information that allows such decisions to be made. However, accounting scandals periodically remind all parties that fraud is possible in the financial reporting process. In the United States, the Securities and Exchange Commission (SEC) is responsible for the fair distribution of information by companies with publicly traded securities. The EDGAR system makes this information readily available. State laws apply to all other organizations. In hopes of creating a well-developed system of considered accounting principles, the SEC has chosen to allow FASB to set U.S. GAAP. The SEC typically only becomes involved with the creation of accounting rules (usually limited to disclosure of information) when current standards are found to be unclear or incomplete.

2. THE ROLE OF THE INDEPENDENT AUDITOR IN FINANCIAL REPORTING

LEARNING OBJECTIVES

At the end of this section, students should be able to meet the following objectives:

1. **Understand the purpose of an independent audit.**
2. **List the two primary components of an independent audit.**
3. **Explain the function of an independent audit firm.**
4. **Describe the steps required to become a Certified Public Accountant (CPA).**
5. **List the various services provided by many public accounting firms.**
6. **Discuss the necessity for the creation of the Public Company Accounting Oversight Board (PCAOB) and describe its function.**

Question: The SEC allows FASB to set U.S. GAAP. ***Does the SEC physically visit each company that issues securities to the public to ensure that periodic financial statements properly follow the rules and guidelines of U.S. GAAP?***

Answer: A detailed examination of the financial statements produced by thousands of publicly traded companies around the world would require a massive work force with an enormous cost. Therefore, this very essential role in the financial reporting process has been left by the SEC to auditing (also known as public accounting) firms that operate both inside and outside of the United States. Before submitting their statements to the SEC and then to the public, reporting companies such as IBM and Wells Fargo must hire one of these independent auditing organizations to

- perform an **audit** (examination) of the financial statements,
- report on whether sufficient supporting evidence was gathered to enable the auditor to provide reasonable assurance that the statements are presented fairly because they contain no material misstatements according to U.S. GAAP.

audit

A examination carried out by an independent auditor of the evidence underlying the balances presented in a set of financial statements followed by the issuance of a public report that provides an opinion as to whether the statements contain material misstatements in accordance with U.S. GAAP; if not, the statements can be viewed as fairly presented, which adds credibility to the information provided.

This written report by the company's independent auditor is then attached to the financial statements for all to see. The report is essential to the integrity of the reporting process. It provides the auditor's expert opinion as to whether decision makers should feel safe in relying on the financial information to make their decisions. The report is a legal requirement for statements provided to the SEC. Even many companies that are not affected by the rules of the SEC have their statements audited by an independent firm to enhance credibility. For example, a convenience store seeking a bank loan could pay for an audit in hopes of increasing the chances that the application will be approved (or because bank officials have required the audit for the bank's own protection).

Not surprisingly, companies that have audits are able to get loans at lower interest rates than comparable organizations that do not have their financial statements subjected to examination.[9] The audit serves to reduce the lender's risk of loss. Thus, a lower interest rate is needed to convince banks and other institutions to provide financial resources.

In the United States, **independent auditing firms** can only be operated by individuals who have been formally recognized by a state government as **Certified Public Accountants (CPAs)**.[10] Such firms range in size from massive (KPMG employs over 135,000 individuals working in 140 countries and generated annual revenues of approximately $22.7 billion for the year ended September 30, 2008[11]) to organizations comprised of just one or two people.

Obviously, for the financial statements of the biggest clients (the ExxonMobils and Wal-Marts of the world), only a public accounting firm of significant size could effectively perform an audit engagement. Consequently, four firms (known collectively as the **Big Four**) are truly huge global organizations:

- Deloitte Touche Tohmatsu
- Ernst & Young
- KPMG
- PricewaterhouseCoopers

However, thousands of smaller independent CPA firms exist providing numerous services such as audit, **tax planning and preparation**, and **advisory work** for a wide range of clients. Ernst & Young indicates on its Web site (http://www.ey.com) that the following services are provided to its clients with each explained in detail: advisory, assurance, tax, transactions, strategic growth markets, and specialty services.

independent auditing firms

Organizations operated by individuals recognized by a state government as Certified Public Accountants (CPAs) to provide independent auditing and other accounting services to the public; also known as CPA firms.

Certified Public Accountants (CPAs)

Individuals who have met state requirements of education, practical experience, and passing the Uniform CPA Examination; the CPA designation is a license that allows a person to provide auditing and other accounting services to the public and serves as a symbol of technical expertise.

Big Four

Term used to encompass the four largest CPA firms operating internationally: Deloitte Touche Tohmatsu, Ernst & Young, KPMG, and PricewaterhouseCoopers; these four firms perform independent audits on most of the world's largest companies.

tax planning and preparation

Professional services performed by many CPA firms including the preparation of tax returns and the creation of tax strategies to help minimize tax payments.

advisory work

Professional services performed by many CPA firms to assist businesses in operating more effectively and efficiently, and therefore, more profitably.

EXERCISE

Link to multiple-choice question for practice purposes: http://www.quia.com/quiz/2092675.html

Question: FASB creates U.S. GAAP, the official standards for the preparation of financial statements. ***What group sets the examination and reporting rules to be followed by independent auditors?*** *Their work is not in accordance with accounting principles. Instead, they are seeking to determine whether U.S. GAAP was applied properly. These auditing firms clearly provide a vital service by adding credibility to reported financial information. How do independent auditors know what actions should be taken in assessing the data reported by a company such as Xerox or Bank of America?*

Answer: When an audit is performed on the financial statements of any organization that issues securities to the U.S. public, the examination and subsequent reporting is regulated by the **Public Company Accounting Oversight Board (PCAOB)**. The PCAOB was brought into existence by the U.S. Congress through the **Sarbanes-Oxley Act of 2002**, a measure passed in response to a number of massive accounting scandals including Enron and WorldCom. Members of Congress apparently felt that the auditing profession had failed to provide adequate protection for the decision makers who were relying on published financial information. Consequently, the federal government became more involved. The PCAOB was established under the oversight and enforcement authority of the SEC. It holds wide-ranging powers that include the creation of official guidelines for the performance of a proper audit. Its mission is stated as follows: "The PCAOB is a private-sector, nonprofit corporation, created by the Sarbanes-Oxley Act of 2002, to oversee the auditors of public companies in order to protect the interests of investors and further the public interest in the preparation of informative, fair, and independent audit reports."[12]

Public Company Accounting Oversight Board (PCAOB)

Private sector, nonprofit corporation brought into existence by the U.S. Congress through the Sarbanes-Oxley Act of 2002 to oversee the auditors of public companies in hopes of protecting investors and furthering the public interest through the preparation of informative, fair, and independent audit reports.

Sarbanes-Oxley Act of 2002

Federal securities law passed by the U.S. Congress in response to the Enron, WorldCom, and other major accounting scandals; it brought about many changes in the audit process and in the relationship between the client and the independent auditor.

If an audit is performed on financial statements that are produced by an organization that does not issue securities to the public, the PCAOB holds no authority. For such smaller engagements, the **Auditing Standards Board (ASB)** officially sets the rules for an appropriate audit. The ASB is a technical committee within the **American Institute of Certified Public Accountants (AICPA)**, a national professional organization of CPAs.

A local convenience store, as mentioned previously, or a medical practice or law firm might choose to have an audit on its financial statements. These audits fall under the guidelines provided by the ASB rather than the PCAOB because the organizations do not issue publicly traded securities. Thus, the rules for performing an audit on a large public company can differ somewhat from those applied to a smaller private one.

Question: If FASB sets U.S. GAAP and the PCAOB (and the ASB) establishes rules for performing an audit, ***what function does the SEC actually serve?***

Auditing Standards Board (ASB)

Technical body within the AICPA that holds the authority and power to set the rules for appropriate audits for organizations that do not issue securities to the public (often referred to as privately held organizations).

American Institute of Certified Public Accountants (AICPA)

A national professional organization of CPAs that sets ethical requirements, conducts research, and helps set a high standard for the profession.

Answer: The goal of the work done by the SEC is summed up in the following statement from its Web site: "The laws and rules that govern the securities industry in the United States derive from a simple and straightforward concept: all investors, whether large institutions or private individuals, should have access to certain basic facts about an investment prior to buying it, and so long as they hold it."[13]

Thus, the SEC strives to make certain that the organizations that fall under its jurisdiction are in total compliance with all laws so that decision makers have ready access to information viewed as relevant. It reviews the required filings submitted by each organization to ensure that the rules and regulations are followed. The SEC also has the power to enforce securities laws and punish companies and individuals who break them. For example, if a company fails to disclose a significant transaction or other event that the SEC believes is necessary, trading of that company's securities can be halted until the matter is resolved. Such regulatory actions can cause a huge financial loss for a business; thus, compliance is viewed as vital.

In addition, if corporate officials provide false or misleading data, fines and jail time are also possible: "L. Dennis Kozlowski, the former CEO of Tyco International, acquired hundreds of companies between 1996 and 2002 and created a conglomerate that made everything from fire suppression systems to health-care products, with worldwide sales of $40 billion. Now, while serving up to 25 years in jail for misleading investors and stealing money from Tyco, he's watching the breakup of all he built."[14]

EXERCISE

Link to multiple-choice question for practice purposes: http://www.quia.com/quiz/2092653.html

KEY TAKEAWAY

Independent auditing firms provide credibility to financial statements by examining the evidence that underlies the information provided and then reporting on those findings. Official oversight of the rules for this process is in the hands of the Public Company Accounting Oversight Board (PCAOB) if the audited company issues securities to the public and the Auditing Standards Board (ASB) if not. The role of the Securities and Exchange Commission (SEC) is to ensure that this reporting process is working as intended by the government. The SEC examines the filings of the various companies and can take disciplinarian action if either the company or its officials fail to act appropriately.

3. PERFORMING AN AUDIT

LEARNING OBJECTIVES

At the end of this section, students should be able to meet the following objectives:

1. **Describe the goal of an auditor in examining an account balance.**
2. **Lists audit tests that might be performed on an account receivable total.**
3. **Understand the reason that an independent auditor only provides reasonable assurance and not absolute assurance.**

Question: A company is preparing a set of financial statements for the most recent year. It has hired an independent firm of CPAs to audit those statements and provide a report that will be attached to them. Perhaps this action is required of the company by the SEC or maybe by a local bank or other lender. ***What work does an independent auditor perform in examining a set of financial statements?*** *The audit firm seeks to provide reasonable assurance to decision makers that these statements are presented fairly and, thus, contain no material misstatements according to U.S. GAAP. How is the auditor able to gain the evidence needed to make that assertion?*

Answer: An independent audit is an elaborate and complicated activity that often requires scores of experienced CPAs many months to complete. A basic understanding of the audit process is best achieved through one or more upper-level college courses as well as years of practical experience. Thus, coverage here must, by necessity, be rather superficial.

The numbers found on a set of financial statements do not appear by magic. For example, if receivables are disclosed on a balance sheet as $12.7 million, a legitimate reason has to exist for reporting that particular figure. In preparing statements, company accountants should document how each balance was derived and why it is considered appropriate according to U.S. GAAP. The statements are the representation of the company; thus, the burden of proof is on that organization and its officials. The independent auditors then examine the available evidence to determine whether reliance on the reported information is advised.

As a simple illustration, assume that a business presents a list of one thousand customers and claims that the total amount due from them is $12.7 million. This figure is reported for "accounts receivable" under the asset section of the company's year-end balance sheet. The independent audit firm seeks to accumulate sufficient, competent evidence to substantiate that this balance is not materially misstated in accordance with U.S. GAAP.

For these receivables, the auditor could carry out several testing procedures to gain the assurance needed. Such techniques might include the following:

- Add the individual account balances to ascertain that the total really is $12.7 million.
- Examine sales documents for a sample of individual customers to determine that the amounts sold are equal to the figures listed within the receivable. For example, if the sales document indicates that Mr. A bought goods at a price of $1,544 is that same dollar amount found in the company's receivable balance?
- Examine cash receipts documents for a sample of customers to ensure that no unrecorded payments were collected prior to the end of the year. If Mr. A paid cash of $1, 544 on December 30, was the corresponding receivable balance reduced by that amount prior to the end of the year?
- Contact a sample of the customers directly to confirm that the balance shown is, indeed, appropriate. "Mr. A: Company records show that you owe $1,544. Is that amount correct?"

Through these and other testing procedures, the auditor hopes to ascertain that $12.7 million is a fairly presented amount for this asset account. All other reported balances are also examined during the independent audit. The quantity and type of audit testing varies considerably based on the nature of the account. Looking at $12.7 million in receivables requires different steps than investigating a building bought for that same amount. Not surprisingly, large balances often require especially extensive testing. In addition, certain accounts (such as cash or inventory) where the risk of misstatement is particularly high draw particular attention from the independent auditors.

If the auditor eventually concludes that sufficient evidence has been obtained to reduce the risk of a material misstatement in the financial statements to an acceptably low level, an audit report can be issued with that opinion. Assuming no problems were encountered, reasonable assurance is provided by the independent auditor to decision makers that the statements are presented fairly and, thus, contain no material misstatements according to U.S. GAAP.

As mentioned, the independent auditor's report is then attached to the financial statements. Upon reading this report, investors and creditors should feel confident relying on the information provided by those statements to make financial decisions about the organization.

EXERCISE

Link to multiple-choice question for practice purposes: http://www.quia.com/quiz/2092676.html

Question: One aspect of the audit process seems particularly puzzling. The independent auditor merely provides reasonable assurance. The risk that a material misstatement is included in the accompanying financial statements is only reduced to a low level and not to zero. Why do decision makers who may be risking significant amounts of money not insist on absolute and complete assurance? Because of the potential for financial loss, decision makers surely must want every possibility of incorrect reporting to be eliminated by the work of the independent auditor. ***Is reasonable assurance that no material misstatements are present truly adequate for decision makers who must rely on a set of financial statements for information?***

Answer: Independent auditors provide reasonable assurance but not absolute assurance that financial statements are presented fairly because they contain no material misstatements according to U.S. GAAP. A number of practical reasons exist as to why the assurance level is limited in this manner.

First, many of the figures found on any set of financial statements are no more than estimations. Auditors do not possess reliable crystal balls that allow them to predict the future. The uncertainty inherent in these estimations immediately eliminates the possibility for absolute assurance. For example, reporting the amount of cash that will be collected from a large group of accounts receivable is simply a carefully considered guess. It is presented according to U.S. GAAP but it is still an estimate.

Second, organizations often take part in so many transactions during a period that uncovering every potential problem or issue is impossible. Usually, in analyzing most account balances, the auditor only has time to test a sample of the entries and adjustments. Without examining every individual event, absolute assurance is not possible. Material misstatements can always be missed if less than 100 percent of the transactions are tested.

Third, an independent auditor visits a company for a few weeks or months each year to carry out testing procedures. Company officials who want to hide financial problems are sometimes successful at concealment. Auditors can never be completely certain that they have not been victimized by an elaborate camouflage scheme perpetrated by management. Thus, they are not comfortable providing absolute assurance.

Fourth, informed decision makers should understand that independent auditors can only provide reasonable assurance. Through appropriate testing procedures, risk of a material misstatement is reduced to an acceptably low level but not eliminated entirely. Investors and creditors need to take that limitation into consideration when assessing the financial health and future well being of an organization presented through a set of financial statements. Although the risk is small, their decisions should factor in the level of uncertainty that is always present.

EXERCISE

Link to multiple-choice question for practice purposes: http://www.quia.com/quiz/2092654.html

KEY TAKEAWAY

Financial statements are the product of company management. An independent auditing firm performs extensive testing of the balances and disclosure reported. Auditors seek to obtain sufficient evidence that the statements are presented fairly because no material misstatements are present according to U.S. GAAP. When the risk of a material misstatement has been reduced to an acceptably low level, reasonable assurance can be provided. Thus, decision makers can feel safe using the information. Absolute assurance is not humanly possible because all statements contain many estimations and the auditors do not have time (or the need) to examine every transaction. Management can, in some cases, also conceal problems from the auditors. Thus, decision makers need to understand that only reasonable assurance of no material misstatements is possible when examining a set of financial statements.

4. THE NEED FOR INTERNAL CONTROL

LEARNING OBJECTIVES

At the end of this section, students should be able to meet the following objectives:

1. **Define internal control.**
2. **Explain a company's need for internal control policies and procedures.**
3. **Describe the effect that a company's internal control has on the work of the independent auditor.**

Question: In the previous discussions, the role of the independent auditor is described as adding credibility to financial statements. The reported figures, though, are still the responsibility of management. ***How do a company and its officials make certain that the information displayed in a set of financial statements is fairly presented?***

Companies like Barnes & Noble and RadioShack participate in millions of transactions in geographically distant store locations as well as internationally through their Web sites. Working with that amount of data, gathered from around the world, can be a daunting technological challenge. Some organizations are able to accumulate massive quantities of information with few—if any—problems; others seem to be overwhelmed by the task. The reliability of the numbers gathered for reporting purposes impacts the amount and type of testing that the independent auditor considers necessary. How do companies make certain that their own information is free of material misstatements?

Answer: The human body is made up of numerous systems that perform specific tasks such as the breathing of air, the circulation of blood, and the digestion of food. Organizations operate in much the same manner. Systems are designed and set in place by management to carry out essential functions such as paying employees, collecting cash from customers, managing inventory levels, and monitoring receivable balances. Within each system, individuals are charged with performing specific tasks, often in a preordained sequence. For example, a cash payment received in the mail from a customer should be handled in a set way every time that it occurs to ensure that it is properly recorded and protected from theft.

To be efficient and effective, these systems must be carefully designed and maintained. They need to keep company assets secure at a minimum cost. In addition, appropriate record keeping is a required aspect of virtually every system. Thus, employees are properly paid when their salary comes due, but also adequate documentation is maintained of the amounts distributed. The entire function is performed according to company guidelines and a record is maintained.

Well-designed systems generate information that poses a reduced threat of material misstatements. However, simply having systems in place—even if they are properly engineered and constructed—is not sufficient to guarantee both the effectiveness of the required actions and the reliability of the collected data. Thus, extra procedures are built into every system by management to help ensure that every operation is performed as intended and the resulting financial data are reliable. All the redundancies added to a system to make certain that it functions properly are known collectively as **internal control**. For example, a rule requiring two designated employees to sign any check for over $5,000 (or some other predetermined amount) is part of a company's internal control. There is no inherent necessity for having a second signature; it is an added safeguard included solely to minimize the chance of theft or error. All actions like this comprise a company's internal control.

internal control

A group of policies and procedures within the accounting and other systems of a company to provide reasonable assurance that they are each operating efficiently and effectively as intended by management.

Internal control policies and procedures can be found throughout the various systems of every company.

- One person counts cash and a second verifies the figure.
- One person requests the purchase of an asset and a second authorizes the request.

Internal control is made up of all the procedures that are performed purely to help make certain that each system operates as intended. Systems cannot be considered well designed without the inclusion of adequate internal control. Management is responsible for the development of effective systems but also for all the internal control rules and requirements to ensure that these systems accomplish their stated objectives.

Question: If a company creates and then maintains good operating systems with appropriate internal control, the financial information that is produced is less likely to contain material misstatements. ***In performing an audit, is the work of the independent CPA affected by the company's internal control?*** *Does the quality of internal control policies and procedures impact the amount and type of audit testing?*

Answer: As a preliminary step in an audit examination, the CPA gains an understanding of the internal control procedures included within each of these systems that relate to reported financial accounts and balances.[15] The auditor then makes an evaluation of the effectiveness of those policies and procedures. In cases where internal control is both well designed and appears to be functioning as intended, a reduction is possible in the amount of audit testing that is needed. The likelihood of a material misstatement is reduced by the company's own internal control.

To illustrate, assume that a company claims to hold accounts receivable totaling $12.7 million. The auditor plans to confirm one hundred of the individual balances directly with the customers to substantiate the separate amounts listed in the accounting records. A letter will be written to each of these individuals asking them whether the specified balance is correct. A stamped return envelope will be included.

Although effective, this confirmation process is slow and expensive. During the year, the reporting company applied several internal control procedures within those systems that maintain the receivables balances. These controls are evaluated by the independent CPA and judged to be excellent. As a result, the auditor might opt to confirm only thirty or forty individual accounts rather than the one hundred that had originally been determined. Because of the quality of internal control in the receivable area, the risk of a material misstatement is already low. Less audit testing is necessary.

Thus, at the beginning of an independent audit, the design of the reporting company's internal control and the effectiveness of its procedures are assessed. Only then does the auditor start to seek sufficient evidence to substantiate that each account balance is presented fairly because no material misstatements are included according to U.S. GAAP.

EXERCISE

Link to multiple-choice question for practice purposes: http://www.quia.com/quiz/2092650.html

KEY TAKEAWAY

All companies operate by means of numerous systems that carry out designated tasks such as the collection of cash and the payment of purchases. These systems need to be well designed and operating as intended to reduce the chance of material misstatements. Additional policies and procedures are included at important junctures in the construction of these systems to ensure that they function appropriately. All such safeguards make up the company's internal control system. The independent auditor evaluates the quality of the internal control found in the various systems. If the risk of material misstatement has been reduced as a result of the internal control in a particular system, less audit testing is required.

5. THE PURPOSE AND CONTENT OF AN INDEPENDENT AUDITOR'S REPORT

LEARNING OBJECTIVES

At the end of this section, students should be able to meet the following objectives:

1. **Describe the purpose of the independent auditor's report.**
2. **Identify the intended beneficiaries of an independent auditor's report.**
3. **Discuss the contents of the introductory, scope, and opinion paragraphs in an independent auditor's report.**
4. **List problems that might impact the contents of an independent auditor's report.**
5. **Indicate the method used by decision makers to determine whether an independent auditor has been unable to issue an unqualified opinion.**

Question: At the conclusion of an audit, a report is issued that will be attached to the financial statements for all to read. Much of this report is boilerplate: The words are virtually identical from one company to the next. ***What information is conveyed by an independent auditor and what should a reader look for when studying an audit report?***

Answer: The **audit report** accompanying the 2007 and 2008 financial statements for the Procter & Gamble Company is found below.

audit report

Formal written opinion issued by an independent auditor to communicate findings at the conclusion of an audit as to whether a specific set of financial statements contain any material misstatements according to U.S. GAAP; if not, the statements are viewed as fairly presented.

To the Board of Directors and Shareholders of the Procter & Gamble Company

We have audited the accompanying Consolidated Balance Sheets of The Procter & Gamble Company and subsidiaries (the "Company") as of June 30, 2008 and 2007, and the related Consolidated Statements of Earnings, Shareholders' Equity, and Cash Flows for each of the three years in the period ended June 30, 2008. These financial statements are the responsibility of the Company's management. Our responsibility is to express an opinion on these financial statements based on our audits.

We conducted our audits in the accordance with the standards of the Public Company Accounting Oversight Board (United States). Those standards require that we plan and perform the audit to obtain reasonable assurance about whether the financial statements are free of material misstatements. An audit includes examining, on a test basis, evidence supporting the amounts and disclosures in the financial statements. An audit also includes assessing the accounting principles used and significant estimates made by management, as well as evaluating the overall financial statement presentation. We believe that our audits provide a reasonable basis for our opinion.

In our opinion, such Consolidated Financial Statements present fairly, in all material respects, the financial position of the Company at June 30, 2008 and 2007, and the results of its operations and cash flows for each of the three years in the period ended June 30, 2008, in conformity with accounting principles generally accepted in the United States of America.

As discussed in Note 1 to the Consolidated Financial Statements, the Company adopted the provisions of FASB Interpretation No. 48, "Accounting for Uncertainty in Income Taxes—an interpretation of FASB Statement No. 109," effective July 1, 2007. Also, as discussed in Note 1 to the Consolidated Financial Statements, the Company adopted the provisions of SFAS No. 158, "Employers' Accounting for Defined Benefit Pension and Other Postretirement Plans, an amendment of FASB Statements No. 87, 88, 106, and 132 (R)," effective June 30, 2007.

We have also audited, in accordance with the standards of the Public Company Accounting Oversight Board (United States), the Company's internal control over financial reporting as of June 30, 2008, based on the criteria established in Internal Control—Integrated Framework issued by the Committee of Sponsoring Organizations of the Treadway Commission and our report dated August 12, 2008 expressed an unqualified opinion on the Company's internal control over financial reporting.

Deloitte & Touche LLP
Cincinnati, Ohio
August 12, 2008

To understand the role of the independent audit within the financial reporting process, a considerable amount of information should be noted in the report found above.

unqualified opinion

An audit opinion informing the reader that attached financial statements are presented fairly, in all material respects, in accordance with U.S. GAAP; thus, the auditor is providing reasonable assurance that the statements contain no material misstatements according to U.S. GAAP and can be relied on by the reader in making financial decisions.

1. The report is addressed to the board of directors (elected by the shareholders) and the shareholders. An audit is not performed for the direct benefit of the reporting company or its management but rather for any person or group studying the financial statements for decision-making purposes. The salutation stresses that those external users (rather than the company itself) are the primary beneficiaries of the work carried out by the independent auditor.

   Interestingly, independent auditors are paid by the reporting company. The concern is raised periodically as to whether an auditor can remain properly independent of the organization that is providing payment for the services rendered. However, audit examinations are quite expensive and no better method of remuneration has yet been devised.
2. To avoid any potential misunderstanding, the first (introductory) paragraph identifies the specific financial statements to which the report relates. In addition, both the responsibility of the management for those financial statements and the responsibility of the independent auditor for providing an opinion on those statements are clearly delineated. The statements are examined by the auditor. The statements are not created by the auditor; that is a job for management.
3. The second (scope) paragraph provides considerable information about the audit work. One key sentence is the second. It explains the purpose of the audit by referring to the standards created by the PCAOB: "Those standards require that we plan and perform the audit to obtain reasonable assurance about whether the financial statements are free of material misstatements." This sentence clearly sets out the purpose of an audit engagement and the level of assurance given by the auditor. No reader should expect absolute assurance.

   The remainder of the second paragraph describes in general terms the steps taken by the auditor:

   - Examine evidence on a test basis to support reported amounts
   - Assess the accounting principles that were applied
   - Assess significant estimations used in creating the statements
   - Evaluate overall presentation
4. The third (opinion) paragraph provides the auditor's opinion of the financial statements. In this illustration, an **unqualified opinion** is being issued meaning that no problems worthy of note were discovered. The auditor provides the reader with reasonable assurance: "In our opinion, such consolidated financial statements present fairly, in all material respects…in conformity with accounting principles generally accepted in the United States of America." Through this sentence, the independent auditor is adding credibility to the financial statements. The auditor believes readers can rely on these statements in making their financial decisions.
5. The fourth (explanatory) paragraph is included whenever the auditor wants to draw the reader's attention to some aspect of the financial statements. The presence of this paragraph does not mean that the information is unreliable, only that the auditor feels some additional explanation is warranted. In this case, the method by which certain accounting events and transactions were handled has been changed because of the creation of new accounting rules (FASB Interpretation No. 48 and FASB SFAS No. 158). Material misstatements are not present; the auditor simply wants to emphasize that changes have taken place because U.S. GAAP has been officially modified.
6. The fifth (control) paragraph provides an additional opinion, this time in connection with the company's internal control. Such an assessment is now required when an audit is performed on a company that is subject to the rules of the PCAOB. Not only is the auditor asserting that the financial statements are presented fairly in conformity with U.S. GAAP (paragraph 3) but also gives an unqualified opinion on the company's internal control over financial reporting. This additional assurance provides the reader with another reason to place reliance on the accompanying financial statements.

Question: The audit report presented here for Procter & Gamble is an unqualified opinion. The independent auditor is providing reasonable assurance to decision makers that the company's financial statements are presented fairly, in all material respects, in conformity with U.S. GAAP. ***What can cause an independent auditor to issue an audit report with less than an unqualified opinion and how is that report physically different?***

Answer: An independent auditor renders an opinion that is not unqualified in two general situations:

- The auditor was not able to obtain sufficient evidence during the audit to justify an unqualified opinion. Perhaps the amount reported for a building or a liability could simply not be substantiated to the auditor's satisfaction. The balance might well be fairly presented according to

U.S. GAAP but evidence was not available to allow the auditor to make that assertion with reasonable assurance.

- The auditor discovers the existence of a material misstatement in the financial statements, a balance or disclosure that does not conform to U.S. GAAP. Because of the potential damage to the credibility of the financial statements, a reporting company will usually make any adjustments necessary to eliminate such misstatements. If not, though, the auditor must clearly warn readers of such problems.

The physical changes made in the report depend on the type of problem that is involved and its magnitude. The key, though, is that a new paragraph is added between the scope and the opinion paragraphs to describe the auditor's concern. Decision makers often scan the audit report solely to see if such a paragraph is contained. If present, a careful reading of its contents (as well as related changes found in the wording of the opinion paragraph) should be made to determine the possible ramifications. Whether evidence was lacking or a material misstatement was uncovered, the auditor is providing a warning for the reader. The presence of an added paragraph—prior to the opinion paragraph—always draws attention.

KEY TAKEAWAY

Upon completion of an audit, the independent auditor's report is attached to the financial statements. It is provided for the benefit of external decision makers. The financial statements are identified and the second (scope) paragraph provides an explanation of the audit process. If no problems are encountered, the report is said to be unqualified and the opinion paragraph provides reasonable assurance to readers that the financial statements are presented fairly because no material misstatements are present according to U.S. GAAP. A qualification arises if the auditor is not able to obtain a satisfactory amount of evidence or if a material misstatement is found. Information about any such problem is then inserted into the audit report between the second (scope) paragraph and the third (opinion) paragraph.

Talking with a Real Investing Pro (Continued)

Following is a continuation of our interview with Kevin G. Burns.

Question: An independent audit is extremely expensive for any reporting company. As an investor, is the benefit gained from seeing the independent auditor's report attached to a set of financial statements actually worth the cost that must be incurred by the company?

Kevin Burns: I think the answer to this question is fairly obvious given the recent scandals, especially in the hedge fund world. An independent audit is absolutely critical for a corporation no matter what the expense. It is an exciting time to be in the accounting profession as investors are demanding additional transparency and independent oversight. Market confidence will be even more critical than usual for any business that wants to obtain money by issuing its equity shares and debt instruments. An internal audit would be perceived as self serving and untrustworthy and perception is 90 percent of reality, especially in today's cynical environment. Given the recent meltdown of financial institutions and stock prices, investors have a right to feel cynical and demand even more assurance before risking their money.

Video Clip

Joe talks about the five most important points in Chapter 6.

View the video online at: http://blip.tv/play/sDyBvupQAA

6. END-OF-CHAPTER EXERCISES

QUESTIONS

1. Why is it important that people and organizations have trust in the financial reporting process?
2. What is the Securities and Exchange Commission?
3. What types of companies fall under the jurisdiction of the SEC?
4. Who has the SEC given responsibility to for setting generally accepted accounting principles (GAAP) in the United States?
5. Who is the Emerging Issues Task Force?
6. Why doesn't the SEC examine all the financial statements submitted to it to ensure their accuracy?
7. For what must public companies hire an auditing firm before they submit their financial statements to the SEC?
8. Why would a nonpublic company have its statements audited?
9. What is a CPA?
10. Which organization sets standards for and regulates firms who audit public companies?
11. Which act established the Public Company Accounting Oversight Board?
12. Which organization sets standards for and regulates firms who do not audit public companies?
13. What type of assurance does an audit provide?
14. Why do audits not provide absolute assurance that financial statements are presented fairly according to GAAP?
15. What are internal controls?
16. How is an auditor's work affected by a company's internal controls?
17. To whom is the audit report addressed?
18. What is an unqualified opinion?
19. Why would an auditor include an explanatory paragraph in an audit report?
20. Why would an auditor not give an unqualified opinion?

TRUE OR FALSE

1. ____ The quality of a company's internal controls has no effect on the work of an auditor.
2. ____ Acquiring the CPA designation requires a candidate to pass an exam, meet education requirements, and meet experience requirements.
3. ____ The SEC is the current accounting standard setting body in the United States.
4. ____ The inclusion of an explanatory paragraph in an audit report is an indication that the financial statements should not be relied on.
5. ____ The PCAOB oversees auditors of public companies.
6. ____ Nonpublic companies have no reason to have an audit of their financial statements performed.
7. ____ Audits are paid for by the creditors and investors of a company.
8. ____ CPAs can work for large, multinational firms, or for small, local firms.
9. ____ Auditors provide reasonable assurance that financial statements are fairly presented in accordance with U.S. GAAP.
10. ____ The Financial Accounting Standards Board is a governmental agency.

MULTIPLE CHOICE

1. Whittington and Company is a CPA firm that audits publicly traded companies. Which of the following is true concerning Whittington and Company?
    a. Whittington and Company are regulated by FASB.
    b. Whittington and Company are hired by the companies they audit.
    c. Whittington and Company should follow the auditing standards set forth by the Auditing Standards Board.
    d. Whittington and Company prepares the financial statements for the companies they audit.
2. Which of the following is ***not*** true about an audit report?
    a. An explanatory paragraph may be included to draw the reader's attention to some aspect of the financial statements.
    b. If a material misstatement exists in the financial statements, the auditor should not issue an unqualified opinion.
    c. The report is addressed to the company's board of directors and shareholders.
    d. If anything other than unqualified opinion is issued, the financial statements must contain a material misstatement.
3. Which of the following is true about the Financial Accounting Standards Board (FASB)?
    a. FASB sets standards that apply to companies throughout the world.
    b. FASB was created by the EITF to handle smaller issues in a timely manner.
    c. FASB produces standards that apply to almost all companies in the United States.
    d. FASB was created by the Securities Exchange Act of 1934.
4. Which pair of organizations are governmental entities?
    a. SEC and PCAOB
    b. SEC and FASB
    c. FASB and EITF
    d. ASB and PCAOB
5. Which of the following is true about the Securities and Exchange Commission (SEC)?
    a. The SEC has the power to set accounting standards in the United States.
    b. The SEC does not have any enforcement powers.
    c. The SEC determines auditing standards for those who audit public companies.
    d. The SEC relies on fees collected from publicly traded companies to operate.

PROBLEM

Match the following organizations to their descriptions.

- ____ FASB
- ____ PCAOB
- ____ SEC
- ____ EITF
- ____ ASB

a. Sets auditing standards for auditors of publicly traded companies
b. Sets U.S. generally accepted accounting principles
c. Helps apply U.S. generally accepted accounting principles to new situations
d. Sets auditing standards for auditors of private companies
e. Created by the Securities Exchange Act of 1934 to protect investors

RESEARCH

1. The chapter mentions the Big Four public accounting firms: Deloitte, Ernst & Young, KPMG, and PricewaterhouseCoopers. We will visit the Web site for one of these—PricewaterhouseCoopers. Go to http://www.pwc.com and answer the following questions:
    a. Name three countries/territories in which PricewaterhouseCoopers (PWC) operates.
    b. Select the United States. Name four services that the firm offers in the United States.
    c. Select the Audit and Assurance function. How does the firm define assurance?

    PricewaterhouseCoopers is currently the auditor of Dell. Go to http://www.dell.com and click on "investor relations" at the bottom of the page. Choose "financials" in the upper left corner. Click on "10-K filings" in the upper right corner. Choose the most recent 10-K. Find the Auditor's Report and read through it.

    d. Is the opinion unqualified?
    e. Are there any explanatory paragraphs?
    f. Is the auditor's opinion on internal control included as part of the audit report?
2. In the United States, audits must be conducted by Certified Public Accountants (CPAs). Each state has different requirements that individuals must meet to become licensed as a CPA. This exercise will give you a chance to discover the rules in your state. Begin by going to the Web site for the National Association of State Boards of Accountancy (NASBA) at http://www.nasba.org.

    Click on the box that says "State Board Listing." A map of the United States will appear. Click on your state. The information for your state board of accountancy will appear in a box. Click on the Web site given. By navigating around the Web site for your state board of accountancy, you should be able to find out what the exam, education, and experience requirements are in your state. Write these down.

ENDNOTES

1. Although often viewed as a relatively recent linguistic creation, variations of the term "cooking the books" had already been in use for over one hundred years when Tobias Smollett included the following phrase in his book *The Adventures of Peregrine Pickle*, first published in 1751: "Some falsified printed accounts, artfully cooked up, on purpose to mislead and deceive." Even over 250 years later, those words aptly describe accounting fraud.
2. For this introductory textbook, a security will include ownership shares of a company as well as debt instruments that can be sold from one party to another. A debt instrument is a promise to pay a stated amount plus a specified rate of interest at a particular point in time.
3. See http://www.sec.gov.
4. Considerable information on accessing the financial data filed with the SEC can be found at http://www.sec.gov/edgar.shtml. Any student considering a career in financial analysis or the like should visit this site to become familiar with its contents, especially the tutorial, so that the EDGAR system can be used to gain information provided by publicly traded companies.
5. As mentioned in Chapter 2, the process of switching authority from U.S. GAAP to International Financial Reporting Standards (IFRS) appears to be at its inception. The SEC has played a major role in this ongoing development and will certainly continue to do so over the next several years.
6. State and local governments follow accounting standards produced by the **Governmental Accounting Standards Board (GASB)**. Information can be found at http://www.gasb.org.
7. News release by FASB, July 1, 2009.
8. In Chapter 2, http://www.fasb.org was mentioned as an excellent source of information about FASB. Another tab available at this site discusses the role of the EITF.
9. David W. Blackwell, Thomas R. Noland, and Drew B. Winters, "The Value of Auditor Assurance: Evidence from Loan Pricing," *Journal of Accounting Research*, Spring 1998, 57–70.
10. The rules for becoming a CPA vary by state but usually include a specific amount and level of education as well as a passing grade on each of the four parts of the uniform CPA Exam. Some states also require a defined length of practical experience such as one or two years. Information about the CPA Exam and state requirements for applying are available at http://www.cpa-exam.org.
11. See http://www.kpmg.com as of July 20, 2009.
12. See http://www.pcaob.com.
13. See http://www.sec.gov.
14. John Kostrzewa, "After the Scandal, a New Tyco," *The Providence Journal*, July 15, 2007, F-1.
15. Some internal controls have nothing to do with a company's financial statement accounts and are not of importance to the work of the independent auditor. For example, a company might establish a review procedure to ensure that only deserving employees receive promotions. This guideline is an important internal control for the operating effectiveness of the company. However, it does not relate to a reported account balance and is not evaluated by the independent auditor.

CHAPTER 7

In a Set of Financial Statements, What Information Is Conveyed about Receivables?

Video Clip

Joe introduces Chapter 7 and speaks about the course in general.

View the video online at: http://blip.tv/play/sDyBvvQiAA

1. ACCOUNTS RECEIVABLE AND NET REALIZABLE VALUE

LEARNING OBJECTIVES

At the end of this section, students should be able to meet the following objectives:

1. **Understand that accounts receivable are reported at net realizable value.**
2. **Know that net realizable value is an estimation of the amount of cash to be collected from a particular asset.**
3. **Appreciate the challenge that uncertainty poses in the reporting of accounts receivable.**
4. **List the factors to be considered by company officials when estimating the net realizable value of accounts receivable.**

Question: The goal of financial accounting is to paint a fairly presented portrait of an organization that enables decision makers to make a reasonable assessment of its financial health and future prospects. This likeness should be communicated based on United States generally accepted accounting principles[1] *(U.S. GAAP) with no material misstatements included. The success of the conveyance is dependent on the ability of an organization's accountants to prepare financial statements that meet this rigorous standard.*

Equally as important, every party analyzing the resulting statements must possess the knowledge necessary to understand the multitude of reported figures and explanations. If appropriate decisions are to result based on this information, both the preparer and the reader need an in-depth knowledge of U.S. GAAP.

For example, the asset section of the balance sheet produced by Dell Inc. as of January 30, 2009, indicates that the company held "accounts receivable, net" amounting to $4.731 billion. What does this figure reflect according to U.S. GAAP? ***What information is communicated to decision makers about a company and its accounts receivable when a single number such as $4.731 billion is reported?***

Answer: One of the most satisfying results of mastering the terminology, rules, and principles of financial accounting is the ability to understand the meaning of amounts and balances disclosed about an organization. In magazines, newspapers, radio, television, and the Internet, such information is presented and analyzed daily. As with any language, failure to comprehend elements of the discussion leaves the listener lost and feeling vulnerable. However, following a reasonable amount of study, the informational content begins to make sense and quickly becomes useful in arriving at logical financial decisions.

accounts receivable

An asset that reports amounts generated by credit sales that are still owed to an organization by its customers.

net realizable value

The amount of cash that is expected to be generated by an asset after costs necessary to obtain the cash are removed; as related to accounts receivable, the amount an organization estimates it will ultimately collect from its customers.

In previous chapters, the term "**accounts receivable**" was introduced to report amounts owed to a company by its customers. Individual balances are generated by sales made on credit. According to U.S. GAAP, the figure that is presented on a balance sheet for accounts receivable is its **net realizable value**—the amount of cash the company estimates will be collected over time from these accounts.

Consequently, officials for Dell Inc. analyzed the company's accounts receivable as of January 30, 2009, and determined that $4.731 billion was the best guess as to the cash that would be collected. The actual total of receivables was higher than that figure but an estimated amount of doubtful accounts had been subtracted in recognition that a portion of these debts could never be collected. For this reason, the asset is identified on the balance sheet as "accounts receivable, net" or, sometimes, "accounts receivable, net of allowance for doubtful accounts" to explain that future losses have already been anticipated and removed.

EXERCISE

Link to multiple-choice question for practice purposes: http://www.quia.com/quiz/2092914.html

Question: As discussed in previous chapters, many of the figures reported in financial accounting cannot be absolutely correct. Although $4.731 billion is the asset balance shown by Dell, the cash eventually collected might be somewhat higher or lower. ***Should the lack of exactness in reporting receivables cause concern for decision makers?***

Answer: No one will ever be able to predict the exact amount of cash to be received from nearly $5 billion in accounts receivable. In fact, Note One to Dell's financial statements specifically states, "The preparation of financial statements in accordance with GAAP requires the use of management's estimates. These estimates are subjective in nature and involve judgments that affect the reported amounts of assets and liabilities, the disclosure of contingent assets and liabilities at fiscal year-end, and the reported amounts of revenues and expenses during the fiscal year. Actual results could differ from those estimates."

Knowledgeable decision makers understand that some degree of uncertainty exists with all such balances. However, a very specific figure does appear on Dell's balance sheet. By including this amount, company officials are asserting that they have obtained sufficient evidence to provide reasonable assurance that the amount collected will not be a materially different figure.[2]

This is the meaning of an accounts receivable balance presented according to U.S. GAAP. Actual receipts are expected to be close enough to $4.731 billion so that an interested party can rely on this number in arriving at considered decisions about the reporting company's financial health and future prospects. Officials believe they have evidence that any eventual difference with the cash collected will be so small that the same decisions would have been made even if the exact outcome had been known at the time of reporting. The difference between reported and actual figures is most likely to be inconsequential. Once again, though, absolute assurance is not given for such reported balances but merely reasonable assurance.

Clearly, the reporting of receivables moves the coverage of financial accounting into more complicated territory. In the transactions and events analyzed previously, uncertainty was rarely mentioned. The financial impact of signing a bank loan or the payment of a salary can be described to the penny except in unusual situations. Here, the normal reporting of accounts receivable introduces the problem of preparing statements where the ultimate outcome is literally unknown. The very nature of such uncertainty forces the accounting process to address such challenges in some logical fashion.

Questions: Inherent uncertainty is associated with the reporting of receivables. No one can know exactly how much cash will be collected. How do company officials obtain sufficient evidence to provide reasonable assurance that the balance is not materially misstated? ***How does any business ever anticipate the amount of cash that will be collected from what can be a massive number of accounts receivable?***

Answer: In accounting, reported balances never represent random guesses. Considerable investigation and analysis goes into arriving at financial statement figures. To determine the net realizable value appropriate for accounts receivable, company officials consider many relevant factors such as the following:

- Historical experience of the company in collecting its receivables
- Efficiency of the company's credit verification policy
- Current economic conditions
- Industry averages and trends
- Current percentage of overdue accounts
- Efficiency of company's collection procedures

Dell Inc. explains this process within the notes to its financial statements by indicating that its estimation "is based on an analysis of historical bad debt experience, current receivables aging, expected future write-offs, as well as an assessment of specific identifiable customer accounts considered at risk or uncollectible."

Additional information disclosed by Dell indicates that the company actually held $4.843 billion in accounts receivable but—at the date of the balance sheet—$112 million of these accounts were anticipated to be uncollectible. Thus, the amount of cash that is estimated to be received is the reported $4.731 billion balance ($4.843 billion total less $112 million expected to be uncollectible). Quite obviously, decision makers studying the company will be interested in comparing this data to the figures disclosed by Dell in previous years as well as the information disseminated by competing organizations such as Hewlett-Packard and Apple. Just determining whether the $112 million in uncollectible accounts is a relatively high or low figure is quite significant in evaluating the efficiency of Dell's current operations.

EXERCISE

Link to multiple-choice question for practice purposes: http://www.quia.com/quiz/2092898.html

KEY TAKEAWAYS

Because of various uncertainties, many of the figures reported in a set of financial statements represent estimations. Accounts receivable is shown at its net realizable value, the amount of cash expected to be collected. Losses from bad accounts are anticipated and removed based on historical trends and other relevant information. Thus, the figure reported in the asset section of the balance sheet is lower than the total amount of receivables held by the company.

2. ACCOUNTING FOR UNCOLLECTIBLE ACCOUNTS

LEARNING OBJECTIVES

At the end of this section, students should be able to meet the following objectives:

1. **Understand the reason for reporting a separate allowance account in connection with accounts receivable.**
2. **Know that bad debt expenses must be anticipated and recorded in the same period as the related sales revenue to conform to the matching principle.**
3. **Prepare the adjusting entry necessary to reduce accounts receivable to net realizable value and recognize the resulting bad debt expense.**

Question: Based on the information provided by Dell Inc., companies seem to maintain two separate ledger accounts in order to report accounts receivables on their balance sheet at net realizable value. One is the sum of all accounts outstanding and the other is an estimation of the amount within that total which will never be collected. Interestingly, the first is a fact and the second is an opinion. The two are then combined to arrive at the net realizable value figure that is shown within the financial statements. ***Is the amount reported for accounts receivable actually the net of the total due from customers less the anticipated amount of doubtful accounts?***

Answer: Yes, companies maintain two separate T-accounts for accounts receivables but that is solely because of the uncertainty involved. If the balance to be collected was known, one account would suffice for reporting purposes. However, that level of certainty is rarely possible.

allowance for doubtful accounts

A contra asset account reflecting the estimated amount of accounts receivable that will eventually fail to be collected and, thus, written off as uncollectible.

- An accounts receivable T-account monitors the total due from all of a company's customers.
- A second account (often called the **allowance for doubtful accounts** or the allowance for uncollectible accounts) reflects the estimated amount that will eventually have to be written off as uncollectible.

Whenever a balance sheet is to be produced, these two accounts are netted to arrive at net realizable value, the figure to be reported for this asset.

contra account

Offset to an account that reduces the total balance to a net amount; in this chapter, the allowance for doubtful accounts always reduces accounts receivable to the amount expected to be collected.

The allowance for doubtful accounts is an example of a "**contra account**," one that always appears with another account but as a direct reduction to lower the reported value. Here, the allowance serves to decrease the receivable balance to its estimated net realizable value. As a contra asset account, debit and credit rules are applied that are the opposite of the normal asset rules. Thus, the allowance increases with a credit (creating a decrease in the net receivable balance) and decreases with a debit. The more accounts receivable a company expects to be bad, the larger the allowance. This increase, in turn, reduces the net realizable value shown on the balance sheet.

By establishing two T-accounts, a company such as Dell can manage a total of $4.843 billion in accounts receivables while setting up a separate allowance balance of $112 million. As a result, the reported figure—as required by U.S. GAAP—is the estimated net realizable value of $4.731 billion.

Question: Accounts receivable and the offsetting allowance for doubtful accounts are netted with the resulting figure reported on the balance sheet.[3] ***How does the existence of doubtful accounts affect the income statement?*** *Sales are made but a portion of the resulting receivables must be reduced because collection is rarely expected to be 100 percent. Does an increase in this allowance create an expense for the reporting company?*

bad debt expense

Estimated expense from making credit sales to customers who will never pay; because of the matching principle, recorded in the same period as the sales revenue.

Answer: Previously, an expense was defined as a measure of the outflow or reduction of net assets caused by the reporting company's attempt to generate revenues. If receivables are recorded that will eventually have to be removed because they cannot be collected, an expense occurs. In financial reporting, terms such as "**bad debt expense**," "doubtful accounts expense," or "the provision for uncollectible accounts" are often encountered.

The inherent uncertainty as to the amount of cash that will actually be received affects the physical recording process. To illustrate, assume that a company makes sales on account to one hundred different customers late in Year One for $1,000 each. The earning process is substantially complete at the time of sale and the amount of cash to be received can be reasonably estimated. According to the revenue realization principle found within accrual accounting, the company should immediately recognize the $100,000 revenue generated by these transactions.[4]

FIGURE 7.1 Journal Entry—Year One—Sales Made on Credit

Accounts Receivable	100,000		(increase an asset—debit)
Sales		100,000	(increase a revenue—credit)

Assume further that the company's past history and other relevant information indicate to officials that approximately 7 percent of all credit sales will prove to be uncollectible. An expense of $7,000 (7 percent of $100,000) is anticipated because only $93,000 in cash is expected from these receivables rather than the full $100,000.

The specific identity and the actual amount of these bad accounts will probably not be known for several months. No physical evidence exists at the time of sale to indicate which will become worthless (buyers rarely make a purchase and then immediately declare bankruptcy or leave town). For convenience, accountants wait until financial statements are to be produced before making their estimation of net realizable value. The necessary reduction is then recorded by means of an adjusting entry.

Question: This company holds $100,000 in accounts receivable but only expects to collect $93,000 based on the available evidence. The $7,000 reduction in the asset is an expense. When should the expense be recognized? These sales were made in Year One but the identity of the specific customers who fail to pay and the exact amounts to be removed will not be determined until Year Two. ***Should bad debt expense be recognized in the same year as the sales by relying on an estimate or delayed until the actual results are eventually finalized?***

Answer: This situation illustrates how accrual accounting plays such a key role within U.S. GAAP. As discussed previously, the timing of expense recognition according to accrual accounting is based on the matching principle. Where possible, expenses are recorded in the same period as the revenues they helped to generate. That guidance is clear. Thus, every company should handle uncollectible accounts in the same manner. The expected expense is the result of making sales to customers who ultimately will never pay. Because the revenue was reported at the time of sale in Year One, the related expense must also be recognized in that year. This handling is appropriate according to accrual accounting even though the $7,000 is only an estimated figure.

Based on U.S. GAAP, when the company produces financial statements at the end of Year One, an adjusting entry is made to (1) reduce the receivables balance to its net realizable value and (2) recognize an expense in the same period as the related revenue.

FIGURE 7.2 Adjusting Entry—End of Year One—Recognition of Bad Debt Expense for the Period

Bad Debt Expense	7,000		(increase an expense—debit)
Allowance for Doubtful Accounts		7,000	(increase a contra asset—credit)

After this entry is made and posted to the ledger, the Year One financial statements contain the following information based on the adjusted T-account balances (assuming for convenience that no other sales were made on credit during the year):

FIGURE 7.3 Year One—Financial Statements

Income Statement (Partial) for Year One	
Revenue	
Sales	$100,000
Operating Expenses	
Bad Debt Expense	7,000
Balance Sheet (Partial) at End of Year One	
Current Assets	
Accounts Receivable	$100,000
Allowance for Doubtful Accounts	7,000
Accounts Receivable, Net	$93,000

From this information, anyone studying these financial statements for Year One should understand that an expense estimated at $7,000 was incurred this year because the company made sales that will never be collected. In addition, year-end accounts receivable total $100,000 but have an anticipated net realizable value of only $93,000. Neither the $7,000 nor the $93,000 figure is expected to be exact but the eventual amounts should not be materially different. This basic portrait provides decision makers with fairly presented information about the accounts receivables held by the reporting company.

EXERCISE

Link to multiple-choice question for practice purposes: http://www.quia.com/quiz/2092899.html

Question: When financial statements are prepared, an expense must be recognized and the receivable balance reduced to net realizable value. However, in the above adjusting entry, why was the accounts receivable account not directly decreased by $7,000 to the anticipated balance of $93,000? This approach is simpler as well as easier to understand. Why was the $7,000 added to an allowance account? ***In reporting receivables, why go to the trouble of setting up a separate allowance?***

Answer: When the company prepares this adjustment at the end of Year One, it does not yet know which accounts will fail to be collected. Officials are only guessing that $7,000 will prove worthless. Plus, on the date of the balance sheet, the company actually does hold $100,000 in accounts receivable. That figure cannot be reduced directly until the specific identity of the accounts to be written off has been determined. Utilizing a separate allowance allows the company to communicate the expected amount of cash while still maintaining a record of all balances in the accounts receivable T-account.

KEY TAKEAWAYS

Sales and the ultimate decision that specific accounts receivable will never be collected can happen months apart. During the interim, bad debts are estimated and recorded on the income statement as an expense and on the balance sheet through an allowance account, a contra asset. In that way, the receivable balance is shown at net realizable value while expenses are recognized in the same period as the sale to correspond with the matching principle. When financial statements are prepared, an estimation of the uncollectible amounts is made and an adjusting entry recorded. Thus, the expense, the allowance account, and the accounts receivable are all presented properly according to U.S. GAAP.

3. THE PROBLEM WITH ESTIMATIONS

LEARNING OBJECTIVES

At the end of this section, students should be able to meet the following objectives:

1. **Record the impact of discovering that a specific receivable is uncollectible.**
2. **Understand the reason that an expense is not recognized when a receivable is deemed to be uncollectible.**
3. **Record the collection of a receivable that has previously been written off as uncollectible.**
4. **Recognize that estimated figures often prove to be erroneous but changes in previous year figures are not made if a reasonable estimate was made.**

Question: The company in this illustration expects to collect an amount from its receivables that will not materially differ from $93,000. The related $7,000 expense is recorded in the same period as the revenue through an adjusting entry. What happens when an actual account is determined to be uncollectible? For example, assume that on March 13, Year Two, a $1,000 balance proves to be worthless. The customer dies, declares bankruptcy, disappears, or just refuses to make payment. This is not a new expense; $7,000 was already anticipated and recognized in Year One. It is merely the first discovery. ***How does the subsequent write-off of a receivable as being uncollectible affect the various T-account balances?***

Answer: When an account proves to be uncollectible, the receivable T-account is decreased. The $1,000 balance is simply removed. It is no longer viewed as an asset because it does not have future economic benefit. Furthermore, the anticipated amount of bad accounts is no longer $7,000. Because this first worthless receivable has been identified and eliminated, only $6,000 remains in the allowance.

The following journal entry is made to write off this account. This entry is repeated whenever a balance is found to be worthless. No additional expense is recognized. The expense was estimated and recorded in the previous period based on applying accrual accounting and the matching principle.

FIGURE 7.4 Journal Entry during Year Two—Write-Off of Specific Account as Uncollectible

Allowance for Doubtful Accounts	1,000		(decrease a contra asset—debit)
Accounts Receivable		1,000	(decrease an asset—credit)

The two basic steps in the recording of doubtful accounts are:

1. The amount of bad accounts is estimated whenever financial statements are to be produced. An adjusting entry then recognizes the expense in the same period as the sales revenue. It also increases the allowance for doubtful accounts (to reduce the reported receivable balance to its anticipated net realizable value).
2. Subsequently, whenever a specific account is deemed to be worthless, the balance is removed from both the accounts receivable and the allowance for doubtful accounts T-accounts. The related expense has been recognized previously and is not affected by the removal of the uncollectible account.

EXERCISE

Link to multiple-choice question for practice purposes: http://www.quia.com/quiz/2092916.html

Question: After an account receivable has been written off as uncollectible, does the company cease in its attempts to collect the amount due from that customer?

Answer: Organizations always make every possible effort to recover any money that they are owed. Writing off an account simply means that the chances of collection are judged to be slim. However, efforts to force payment will continue, often with increasingly aggressive techniques. If money is ever received from a written off account, the company first reinstates the account by reversing the earlier entry. Then, the cash received is recorded in the normal fashion. To illustrate, assume that the above account is eventually collected from this customer.

FIGURE 7.5 Journal Entry—Reinstate Account Previously Thought to Be Worthless

Accounts Receivable	1,000		(increase an asset—debit)
Allowance for Doubtful Accounts		1,000	(increase a contra asset—credit)

FIGURE 7.6 Journal Entry—Collection of Reinstated Account[5]

Cash	1,000		(increase an asset—debit)
Accounts Receivable		1,000	(decrease an asset—credit

Question: In this illustration, at the end of Year One, the company estimated that $7,000 of its accounts receivable will ultimately prove to be uncollectible. However, in Year Two, that figure is likely to be proven wrong. The actual amount might well be $6,000 or $8,000 or many other numbers. When the precise figure is known, does a company return to its Year One financial statements and adjust them to this correct balance? ***Should a company continue reporting an estimated figure once it has been shown to be incorrect?***

Answer: According to U.S. GAAP, if a number is reported based on a reasonable estimation, any subsequent differences with actual amounts are not handled retroactively (by changing the previously released figures). For example, if uncollectible accounts here prove to be $8,000, the company does not adjust the balance reported as the Year One bad debt expense from $7,000 to $8,000. It continues to report $7,000 for that period even though that number is now known to be wrong.[6]

There are several practical reasons for the accountant's unwillingness to adjust previously reported estimations unless they were clearly unreasonable or fraudulent:

1. Most decision makers are well aware that many reported figures only present estimates. Discrepancies are expected and should be taken into consideration when making decisions based on numbers presented in a set of financial statements. In analyzing this company and its financial health, astute investors and creditors anticipate that the total of bad accounts will ultimately turn out to be an amount around $7,000 rather than exactly $7,000.
2. Because an extended period of time often exists between issuing statements and determining actual balances, most parties will have already used the original information to make their decisions. Knowing the exact number now does not allow them to undo those prior actions. There is no discernable benefit from having updated figures as long as the original estimate was reasonable.
3. Financial statements contain numerous estimations and nearly all will prove to be inaccurate to some degree. If exactness were required, correcting each of these previously reported figures would become virtually a never-ending task for a company and its accountants. Scores of updated statements might have to be issued before a "final" set of financial figures became available after several years. For example, the exact life of a building might not be known for fifty years. Decision makers want information that is usable as soon as possible. Speed in reporting is more important than absolute precision.
4. At least theoretically, half of the differences between actual and anticipated results should make the reporting company look better and half make it look worse. If so, the corrections needed to rectify all previous estimation errors will tend to offset and have little overall impact on a company's reported income and financial condition.

Thus, no change is made in financial figures that have already been released whenever a reasonable estimation proves to be wrong. However, differences that arise should be taken into consideration in creating current and subsequent statements. For example, if the Year One bad debts were expected to be 7 percent, but 8 percent actually proved to be uncollectible, the accountant might well choose to use a higher percentage at the end of Year Two to reflect this new knowledge.

Question: To carry this illustration one step further, assume that $400,000 in new credit sales are made during Year Two while cash of $330,000 is collected. Uncollectible receivables totaling $10,000 are written off in that year. ***What balances appear in the various T-accounts at the end of the subsequent year to reflect sales, collections, and the write-offs of receivables?***

Answer: Sales and bad debt expense were reported previously for Year One. However, as income statement accounts, both were closed out so as to begin Year Two with zero balances. They are temporary accounts. In contrast, accounts receivable and the allowance for doubtful accounts appear on the balance sheet and retain their ending figures going into each subsequent period. They are permanent accounts. These two T-accounts will still show $100,000 and $7,000 respectively at the beginning of Year Two.

Assuming that no adjustments have yet been made, these four accounts hold the following balances at the end of Year Two based on appropriate journal entries. Notice that the expense account remains at zero until the end-of-year estimation is made and recorded.

FIGURE 7.7 End of Year Two—Sales, Receivables, and Bad Debt Balances

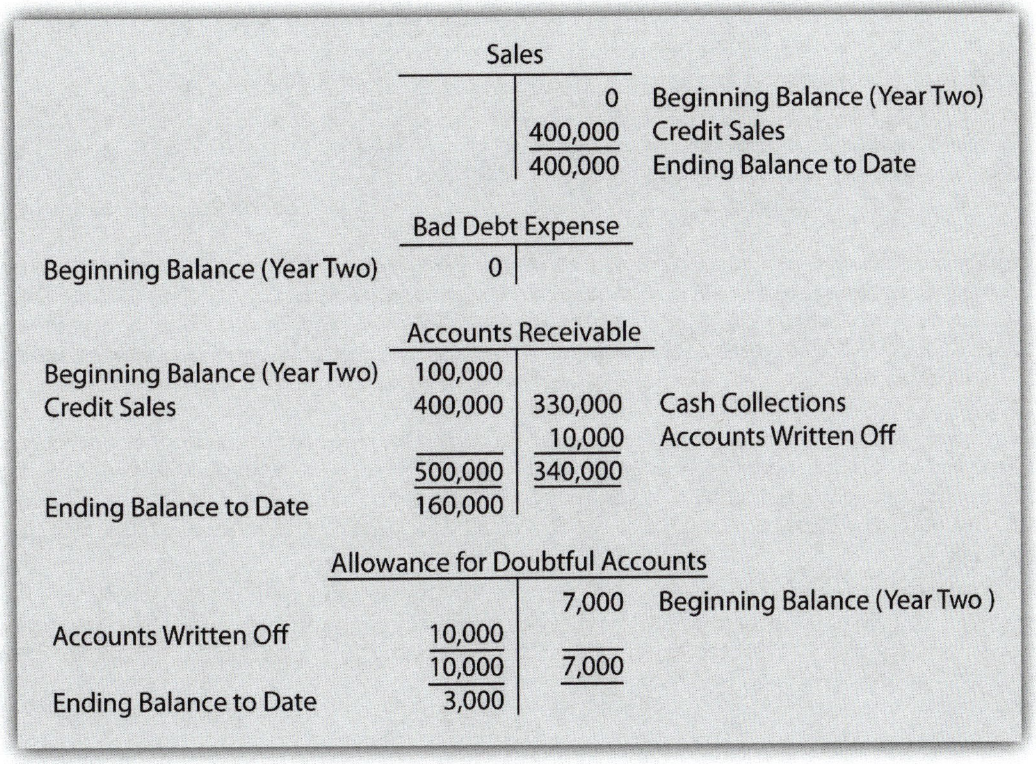

Sales
0 Beginning Balance (Year Two)
400,000 Credit Sales
400,000 Ending Balance to Date
Bad Debt Expense
Beginning Balance (Year Two) 0
Accounts Receivable
Beginning Balance (Year Two) 100,000
Credit Sales 400,000 330,000 Cash Collections
10,000 Accounts Written Off
500,000 340,000
Ending Balance to Date 160,000
Allowance for Doubtful Accounts
7,000 Beginning Balance (Year Two)
Accounts Written Off 10,000
10,000 7,000
Ending Balance to Date 3,000

Question: In the above T-accounts, the balances represent the account totals for Year Two prior to year-end adjusting entries. Why does a debit balance of $3,000 appear in the allowance for doubtful accounts prior to the recording of the necessary adjustment? ***When a debit balance is found in the allowance for doubtful accounts, what does this figure signify?***

Answer: When the Year One financial statements were produced, $7,000 was estimated as the amount of the receivables that would eventually be identified as uncollectible. In Year Two, the actual total written off turned out to be $10,000. The original figure was too low by $3,000. The difference is now reflected by the debit remaining in the allowance account. Until the estimation for the new year is determined and recorded, the balance residing in the allowance account indicates a previous underestimation (an ending debit balance) or overestimation (a credit) of the amount of worthless accounts.[7]

KEY TAKEAWAYS

Bad debt expense is estimated and recorded in the period of sale to correspond with the matching principle. Subsequent write-offs of specific accounts do not affect the expense further. Rather, both the asset and the allowance for doubtful accounts are decreased at that time. If a written off account is subsequently collected, the allowance account is increased to reverse the previous impact. Estimation errors are to be anticipated; perfect predictions are rarely possible. When the amount of uncollectible accounts differs from the original figure recognized, no retroactive adjustment is made if a reasonable estimation was made. Decisions have already been made by investors and creditors based on the original data and cannot be reversed. These readers of the statements should have understood that the information could not possibly reflect exact amounts.

4. ESTIMATING THE AMOUNT OF UNCOLLECTIBLE ACCOUNTS

LEARNING OBJECTIVES

At the end of this section, students should be able to meet the following objectives:

1. **Estimate and record bad debts when the percentage of sales method is applied.**
2. **Estimate and record bad debts when the percentage of receivables method is applied.**
3. **Explain the reason that bad debt expense and the allowance for doubtful accounts will normally report different figures.**
4. **Understand the purpose and maintenance of a subsidiary ledger.**

Question: The final step in reporting receivables at the end of Year Two is the estimation of the bad accounts incurred during this second year and the preparation of the related adjusting entry. According to the ledger balances, sales on credit for the year were $400,000, remaining accounts receivable amount to $160,000, and a $3,000 debit sits in the allowance for doubtful accounts. No entry has yet been made for the Year Two bad debt expense. ***How is the estimation of uncollectible accounts derived each year?***

Answer: Much of financial accounting is quite standardized. However, estimations can be made by any method that is considered logical. After all, it is an estimate. Over the decades, two different approaches have come to predominate when predicting the amount of uncollectible accounts. As long as company officials obtain sufficient evidence to support the reported numbers, either way can be applied.

percentage of sales method

The income statement approach for estimating uncollectible accounts that computes bad debt expense by multiplying credit sales by the percentage that are not expected to be collected.

Percentage of sales method. This alternative computes doubtful accounts expense by anticipating the percentage of sales (or credit sales) that will eventually fail to be collected. The percentage of sales method is sometimes referred to as an income statement approach because the only number being estimated (bad debt expense) appears on the income statement.

Percentage of receivables method. Here, the proper balance for the allowance for doubtful accounts is determined based on the percentage of ending accounts receivable that are presumed to be uncollectible. This method is labeled a balance sheet approach because the one figure being estimated (the allowance for doubtful accounts) is found on the balance sheet. A common variation used by many companies is the "**aging method**," which first categorizes all receivable balances by age and then multiplies each of the individual totals by a different percentage. Normally, a higher rate is used for accounts that are older because they are considered more likely to become uncollectible.

percentage of receivables method

The balance sheet approach for estimating uncollectible accounts that computes the allowance for doubtful accounts by multiplying accounts receivable by the percentage that are not expected to be collected.

aging method

Variation of percentage of receivables method where all receivables are categorized by age; the total of each category is multiplied by an appropriate percentage and then summed to determine the allowance balance.

Question: Assume that this company chooses to use the percentage of sales method. All available evidence is studied by officials who come to believe that 8 percent of credit sales made during Year Two will prove to be worthless. ***In applying the percentage of sales method, what adjusting entry is made at the end of the year so that financial statements can be prepared?***

Answer: According to the general ledger, the company generated $400,000 in credit sales during Year Two. If uncollectible accounts are expected to be 8 percent of that amount, the expense is reported as $32,000 ($400,000 × 8 percent). Bad debt expense (the figure estimated) must be raised from its present zero balance to $32,000.

FIGURE 7.8 Adjusting Entry for Year Two—Bad Accounts Estimated as a Percentage of Sales

Bad Debt Expense	32,000		(increase an expense—debit)
Allowance for Doubtful Accounts		32,000	(increase a contra asset—credit)

This adjustment increases the expense to the appropriate $32,000 figure, the proper percentage of the sales figure. However, the allowance account already held a $3,000 debit balance ($7,000 Year One estimation less $10,000 accounts written off). As can be seen in the T-accounts, the $32,000 recorded expense results in only a $29,000 balance for the allowance for doubtful accounts.

FIGURE 7.9 Resulting T-Accounts, Based on Percentage of Sales Method

Bad Debt Expense

Beginning Balance	0		
Expense Adjustment	32,000		
Ending Balance	32,000		

Allowance for Doubtful Accounts

		7,000	Beginning Balance
Accounts Written Off	10,000	32,000	Expense Adjustment
	10,000	39,000	
		29,000	Ending Balance

After this adjustment, the figures appearing in the financial statements for Year Two are as follows:

FIGURE 7.10 Bad Accounts Estimated Based on 8 Percent of Sales

Income Statement (Partial) for Year Two	
Revenue	
Sales	$400,000
Operating Expenses	
Bad Debt Expense	32,000
Balance Sheet (Partial) at End of Year Two	
Current Assets	
Accounts Receivable	$160,000
Allowance for Doubtful Accounts	29,000
Accounts Receivable, Net	$131,000

EXERCISE

Link to multiple-choice question for practice purposes: http://www.quia.com/quiz/2092879.html

Question: How can bad debt expense be reported as $32,000 while the allowance for doubtful accounts shows a balance of only $29,000? *Should those two numbers not always be identical in every set of financial statements?*

Answer: In this introductory coverage, the difference in these accounts is assumed to be caused solely by the failure of previous estimations to be accurate.[8] Last year, the doubtful accounts expense for this company was reported as $7,000 but accounts with balances totaling $10,000 proved to be uncollectible. Because companies do not go back to the statements of previous years to fix numbers when a reasonable estimate was made, the expense is $3,000 higher in the current period to compensate.

Mechanically, the underestimation still exists in the accounting records in Year Two. It creates the $3,000 debit in the allowance for doubtful accounts before the expense adjustment. Thus, although the current expense is $32,000 (8 percent of sales), the allowance is reported as only $29,000 (the $32,000 expense offset by the $3,000 debit balance remaining from the prior year).

Students are often concerned because these two reported numbers differ. However, both are merely estimates. The actual amount of worthless accounts is likely to be a number somewhat different than either $29,000 or $32,000. Therefore, the disagreement caused by the lingering impact of the $3,000 Year One underestimation should not be an issue as long as company officials believe that neither of the reported balances is materially misstated.

Question: The percentage of receivables method handles this process a bit differently. Assume that the Year Two adjusting entry has not yet been made so that bad debt expense remains at zero and the allowance for doubtful accounts still holds a $3,000 debit balance. However, the company has chosen to use the percentage of receivables method rather than the percentage of sales method. Officials have looked at all available evidence and come to the conclusion that 15 percent of ending accounts receivable ($160,000 × 15 percent or $24,000) is most likely to prove to be uncollectible. ***How does application of the percentage of receivables method affect the recording of doubtful accounts?***

Answer: The percentage of receivables method (or the aging method if that variation is used) views the estimated figure of $24,000 as the proper total for the allowance for doubtful accounts. Thus, the accountant must turn the $3,000 debit balance residing in that contra asset account into the proper $24,000 credit. That change can only be accomplished by recognizing an expense of $27,000. Under the percentage of receivables method, after the adjustment has been recorded, the allowance balance will equal the estimate ($24,000). The expense is the amount needed to arrive at this allowance figure.

FIGURE 7.11 Adjusting Entry for Year Two—Bad Accounts Estimated as a Percentage of Receivables

Bad Debt Expense	27,000		(increase an expense—debit)
Allowance for Doubtful Accounts		27,000	(increase a contra asset—credit)

As shown in the T-accounts below, this entry successfully changes the allowance from a $3,000 debit balance to the desired $24,000 credit. Because bad debt expense had a zero balance prior to this entry, it is now based solely on the $27,000 amount needed to establish the proper allowance.

FIGURE 7.12 Resulting T-Accounts, Based on Percentage of Receivables Method

Allowance for Doubtful Accounts

	Debit	Credit	
		7,000	Beginning Balance
Accounts Written Off	10,000	27,000	Expense Adjustment
	10,000	34,000	
		24,000	Ending Balance

Bad Debt Expense

	Debit	Credit
Beginning Balance	0	
Expense Adjustment	27,000	
Ending Balance	27,000	

After this adjusting entry, the figures appearing in the financial statements for Year Two are as follows:

FIGURE 7.13 Bad Accounts Estimated Based on 15 Percent of Receivables

Income Statement (Partial) for Year Two	
Revenue	
Sales	$400,000
Operating Expenses	
Bad Debt Expense	27,000
Balance Sheet (Partial) at End of Year Two	
Current Assets	
Accounts Receivable	$160,000
Allowance for Doubtful Accounts	24,000
Accounts Receivable, Net	$136,000

Once again, the difference between the expense ($27,000) and the allowance ($24,000) is $3,000 as a result of the estimation being too low in the prior year. The current year expense must be higher.

Either approach can be used as long as adequate support is generated for the numbers reported. They are just two ways to estimate the effect of bad debts. However, financial accounting does stress the importance of consistency to help make the numbers comparable from year to year. Once a method is selected, it normally must continue to be used in all subsequent periods.

Under the percentage of sales method, the expense account is aligned with the volume of sales. In applying the percentage of receivables method, determining the uncollectible portion of ending receivables is the central focus. Regardless of the approach, both bad debt expense and the allowance for doubtful accounts are simply the result of estimating the final outcome of an uncertain event—the collection of accounts receivable.

EXERCISE

Link to multiple-choice question for practice purposes: http://www.quia.com/quiz/2092880.html

Question: A company such as Dell Inc. must have thousands or even hundreds of thousands of separate receivables. The accounts receivable T-account maintains the total dollar amount owed to the company but does not indicate the balance due from each individual customer. ***How does an accounting system monitor all the specific receivable amounts?*** *That has to be essential information for any organization for billing and collection purposes.*

subsidiary ledger

Group of individual accounts whose sum totals (and, therefore, explains) a general ledger account balance.

Answer: As indicated, a general ledger account only reflects the total at the present time. In many cases, as with accounts receivable, the composition of that balance is also important information. For those T-accounts, the accounting system can be expanded to include a **subsidiary ledger** to maintain data about the various individual components making up the account total.

In the previous illustration, the company reports $160,000 as the total of its accounts receivable at the end of Year Two. A separate subsidiary ledger should be in place to monitor the amounts owed by each customer (Mr. A, Ms. B, and so on). The general ledger figure is used whenever financial statements are to be produced. The subsidiary ledger allows the company to access individual account balances so that appropriate action can be taken if specific receivables grow too large or become overdue.

When a subsidiary ledger is maintained, the accounting system can be programmed so that each entry into the designated general ledger T-account requires an immediate parallel increase or decrease to the appropriate individual account. Thus, a $75 sale on credit to Mr. A raises the overall accounts receivable total in the general ledger by that amount while also increasing the balance listed for Mr. A in the subsidiary ledger.

Subsidiary ledgers can be utilized in connection with any general ledger account where the availability of component information is helpful. Other than accounts receivable, they are commonly set up for inventory, equipment, and accounts payable. As might be imagined, big companies maintain subsidiary ledgers for virtually every T-account, whereas small companies are likely to limit use to accounts receivable and—possibly—a few other large balances.

Before computer systems became common, keeping the total of thousands of individual accounts in a subsidiary ledger in agreement with the corresponding general ledger T-account balance was an arduous task. Mechanical errors (mathematical problems as well as debit and credit mistakes) tended to abound. However, current electronic systems are typically designed so that the totals reconcile automatically.

KEY TAKEAWAYS

Each year, an estimation of uncollectible accounts must be made as a preliminary step in the preparation of financial statements. Some companies use the percentage of sales method, which calculates the expense to be recognized, an amount which is then added to the allowance for doubtful accounts. Other companies use the percentage of receivable method (or a variation known as the aging method). It determines the ending balance for the allowance. The reported expense is the amount needed to adjust the allowance to this ending total. Both methods provide no more than an approximation of net realizable value based on the validity of the percentages that are applied.

5. REMEASURING FOREIGN CURRENCY BALANCES

LEARNING OBJECTIVES

At the end of this section, students should be able to meet the following objectives:

1. **Recognize that transactions denominated in a foreign currency are now quite common.**
2. **Understand the necessity of remeasuring foreign currency balances into a company's functional currency prior to the preparation of financial statements.**
3. **Appreciate the problem that fluctuations in exchange rates cause when foreign currency balances are reported in a set of financial statements.**
4. **Know which foreign currency balances are reported using a historical exchange rate and which balances are reported using the exchange rate in effect on the date of the balance sheet.**
5. **Understand that gains and losses are reported on a company's income statement when certain foreign currency balances are remeasured using new currency exchange rates.**

Question: In today's global economy, many U.S. companies make a sizable amount of their sales internationally. The Coca-Cola Company, for example, generated approximately 74 percent of its revenues in 2008 outside of North America. In such cases, U.S. dollars might still be the currency received. However, occasionally and sometimes often, U.S. companies make sales that will be settled in a foreign currency such as the Mexican peso or the Japanese yen. ***What reporting problems are created when a credit sale is denominated in a foreign currency?***

Answer: This situation is a perfect example of why having an authoritative standard for financial accounting, such as U.S. GAAP, is so important for communication purposes. Foreign currency balances are extremely common in today's world. For many companies, sales, purchases, expenses and the like can be denominated in dozens of different currencies. Mechanically, many methods of reporting such figures are available. Without standardization, decision makers would likely be faced with analyzing similar companies possibly reporting foreign balances in a variety of ways. Assessing the comparative financial health and future prospects of organizations using different types of accounting will always pose an extremely difficult challenge.

The basic problem with reporting foreign currency balances is that exchange rates are constantly in flux. The price of one euro in terms of U.S. dollars changes many times each day. If these rates remained constant, a single conversion value could be determined at the time of the initial transaction and then used consistently for reporting purposes. However, exchange rates are rarely fixed; they often change moment by moment. For example, if a sale is made on account with the money to be received in a foreign currency in sixty days, the relative worth of that balance will probably move up and down many times before collection. When such values float, the reporting of foreign currency amounts poses a challenge for financial accounting with no easy resolution.

Question: Exchange rates that vary over time create a reporting problem for companies working in international markets. To illustrate, assume a U.S. company makes a sale of a service to a Mexican company on December 9, Year One, for 100,000 Mexican pesos that will be paid at a later date. The exchange rate when the sale was made is assumed to be 1 peso equal to $0.08. However, by the end of Year One when financial statements are produced, the exchange rate has changed to 1 peso being equal to $0.09. ***What reporting does a U.S. company make of transactions that are denominated in a foreign currency if the exchange rate changes as time passes?***[9]

Answer: At the time of the sale, reporting is easy. The 100,000 pesos has the equivalent value of $8,000 (100,000 pesos × $0.08) so that the following journal entry can be produced. Even though 100,000 pesos will be physically received, $8,000 is reported so that all balances on the seller's financial statements are stated in terms of U.S. dollars.

FIGURE 7.14 Journal Entry—December 9, Year One—Sale of Services Made for 100,000 Pesos

Accounts Receivable	8,000		(increase an asset—debit)
Sale of Services		8,000	(increase a revenue—credit)

By the end of the year, the exchange rate is 1 peso equal to $0.09. The Mexican peso is worth a penny more relative to the U.S. dollar. Thus, 100,000 pesos can now be changed into $9,000 (100,000 × $0.09). When adjusting entries are prepared in connection with the production of financial statements, one or both of the above account balances could remain at $8,000 or be updated to $9,000. The sale took place when the exchange rate was $0.08 but, now, before the money is collected, the peso has risen in value to $0.09. FASB had to set a standard rule as to whether the current rate or the historical rate was appropriate for reporting foreign currency balances.

monetary assets and monetary liabilities

Future sacrifices of economic benefits arising from present obligations, the debts of an organization.

For over twenty-five years, U.S. GAAP has required that **monetary assets and liabilities** denominated in a foreign currency be reported at the current exchange rate as of the balance sheet date. All other balances continue to be shown at the exchange rate in effect on the date of the original transaction. That is the approach that all organizations adhering to U.S. GAAP must follow. Both the individuals who produce financial statements as well as the outside decision makers who use them should understand that this rule is applied.

Monetary assets and liabilities are amounts currently held as cash or that will require a future transfer of a specified amount of cash. In the coverage here, for convenience, such monetary accounts will be limited to cash, receivables, and payables. Because these balances reflect current or future cash amounts, the current exchange rate is always viewed as the most relevant. In this illustration, the actual value of the receivable (a monetary asset) has changed in terms of U.S. dollars. The 100,000 pesos that will be collected now have an equivalent value of $0.09 each rather than $0.08. The reported receivable is updated to $9,000 (100,000 pesos × $0.09).

Cash, receivables, and payables denominated in a foreign currency must be adjusted for reporting purposes whenever exchange rates fluctuate. All other account balances (equipment, sales, rent expense, dividends, and the like) reflect historical events and not future cash flows. Thus, they retain the rate that was appropriate at the time of the original transaction and no further changes are ever needed. The sales figure is not a monetary asset or liability, so the $8,000 balance continues to be reported regardless of the relative value of the peso.

Question: Changes in exchange rates affect the reporting of monetary assets and liabilities. Those amounts are literally worth more or less U.S. dollars as the relative value of the currency fluctuates over time. For the two balances above, the account receivable has to be remeasured on the date of the balance sheet because it is a monetary asset while the sales balance remains $8,000 permanently. How is this change in the receivable accomplished? ***When monetary assets and liabilities denominated in a foreign currency are remeasured for reporting purposes, how is the increase or decrease in value reflected?***

Answer: In this example, the value of the 100,000 peso receivable is raised from $8,000 to $9,000. When the amount reported for monetary assets and liabilities increases or decreases because of changes in currency exchange rates, a gain or loss is recognized on the income statement. Here, the receivable is now reported $1,000 higher. The company's financial condition has improved and a gain is recognized. If the opposite occurs and the reported value of monetary assets declines (or the value of monetary liabilities increases), a loss is recognized. The following adjusting entry is appropriate.

FIGURE 7.15 Adjusting Entry at December 31, Year One—Remeasurement of 100,000 Pesos Receivable

Accounts Receivable	1,000		(increase an asset—debit)
Gain in Value of Foreign Currency Receivable		1,000	(increase a revenue—credit)

On its balance sheet, this company now reports a receivable as of December 31, Year One, of $9,000 while its income statement for that year shows sales revenue of $8,000 as well as the above gain of $1,000. Although the transaction was actually for 100,000 Mexican pesos, the U.S. company records these events in terms of U.S. dollars according to the provisions of U.S. GAAP.

EXERCISE

Link to multiple-choice question for practice purposes: http://www.quia.com/quiz/2092881.html

KEY TAKEAWAYS

Foreign currency balances are common because many companies buy and sell products and services internationally. Although many of these transactions are denominated in foreign currencies, they are reported in U.S. dollars when financial statements are produced for distribution in this country. Because exchange rates often change rapidly, many equivalent values could be used to report these balances. According to U.S. GAAP, monetary assets and liabilities (cash as well as receivables and payables to be settled in cash) are updated for reporting purposes using the exchange rate at the date of the balance sheet. Any change in one of these accounts creates a gain or loss to be recognized on the income statement. All other foreign currency balances (land, buildings, sales, and the like) continue to be shown at the historical exchange rate in effect at the time of the original transaction.

6. A COMPANY'S VITAL SIGNS—ACCOUNTS RECEIVABLE

LEARNING OBJECTIVES

At the end of this section, students should be able to meet the following objectives:

1. **Compute the current ratio, the amount of working capital, and other amounts pertinent to the reporting of accounts receivable.**
2. **Describe the meaning of the current ratio.**
3. **Describe the meaning of the working capital balance.**
4. **Calculate the amount of time that passes before the average accounts receivable is collected and explain the importance of this information.**
5. **List techniques that an organization can implement to speed up the collection of accounts receivable.**

Question: Many individuals analyze financial statements to make logical and appropriate decisions about a company's financial health and well being. This process is somewhat similar to a medical doctor performing a physical examination on a patient. The doctor often begins by checking various vital signs such as heart rate, blood pressure, weight, cholesterol level, and body temperature, looking for any signs of a serious change or problem. For example, if a person's heart rate is higher than expected or if blood pressure has increased significantly since the last visit, the doctor will investigate with special care.

In examining the financial statements of a business or other organization, are there vital signs that should be studied as a routine matter?

Answer: Financial statements are extremely complex and most analysts have certain preferred figures or ratios that they believe to be especially significant when investigating a company. For example, previously, the **current ratio** and the amount of **working capital** were computed based on the amount of current assets (those that will be used or consumed within one year) and current liabilities (those that will be paid within one year):

current ratio

Formula measuring an organization's liquidity (the ability to pay debts as they come due); calculated by dividing current assets by current liabilities.

working capital

Formula measuring an organization's liquidity (the ability to pay debts as they come due); calculated by subtracting current liabilities from current assets.

current ratio = current assets/current liabilities

working capital = current assets – current liabilities.

Both of these figures reflect a company's ability to pay its debts and have enough monetary resources still available to generate profits in the near future. Both investors and creditors frequently calculate, study, and analyze these two amounts. They are vital signs that help to indicate the financial health of a business or other organization.

For example, on December 31, 2008, Avon Products reported a current ratio of 1.22 to 1.00 (current assets of $3.557 billion divided by current liabilities of $2.912 billion) while Caterpillar disclosed working capital of $4.590 billion (current assets of $31.953 billion less current liabilities of $27.363 billion).

Whether these numbers are impressive or worrisome usually depends on a careful comparison with (a) other similar companies and (b) results from prior years.

EXERCISE

Link to multiple-choice question for practice purposes: http://www.quia.com/quiz/2092882.html

Question: Because this chapter deals with accounts receivable, ***what other vital signs might be studied specifically in connection with a company's receivable balance?***

Answer: One indication of a company's financial health is its ability to collect receivables in a timely fashion. Money cannot be put to productive use until it is received. For that reason, companies work to encourage payments being made as quickly as possible. Furthermore, as stated previously, the older a receivable becomes, the more likely it is to prove worthless.

Thus, interested parties (both inside a company as well as external) frequently monitor the time taken to collect receivables. Quick collection is normally viewed as good whereas a slower rate can be a warning sign of possible problems. However, as with most generalizations, exceptions do exist so further investigation is always advised.

The age of a company's receivables is determined by dividing its average sales per day into the receivable balance. Credit sales are used in this computation if known but the total sales figure often has to serve as a substitute because of availability. The sales balance is divided by 365 to derive the amount sold per day. This daily balance is then divided into the reported receivable to arrive at the average number of days that the company waits to collect its accounts. A significant change in the age of receivables will be quickly noted by almost any interested party.

age of receivables = receivables/sales per day

If a company reports sales for the current year of $7,665,000 and currently holds $609,000 in receivables, it requires twenty-nine days on the average to collect a receivable.

sales per day = $7,665,000/365 or $21,000

age of receivables = $609,000/$21,000 or 29 days

As a practical illustration, for the year ended January 30, 2009, Dell Inc. reported net revenue of $61.101 billion. The January 30, 2009, net accounts receivable balance for the company was $4.731 billion, which was down from $5.961 billion as of February 1, 2008. The daily sales figure is calculated as $167.4 million ($61.101 billion/365 days). Thus, the average age of Dell's ending receivable balance at this time was 28.3 days ($4.731 billion/$167.4 million).

receivables turnover

Formula measuring speed of an organization's collections of its accounts receivable; calculated by dividing sales by the average accounts receivable balance for the period.

A similar figure is referred to as the **receivables turnover** and is computed by the following formula:

receivables turnover = sales/average receivables.

For Dell Inc., the average receivable balance for this year was $5.346 billion ([$4.731 billion + $5.961]/2). The receivables turnover can be determined for this company as 11.4 times:

receivables turnover = $61.101 billion/$5.346 billion = 11.4.

The higher the receivable turnover, the faster collections are being received.

EXERCISE

Link to multiple-choice question for practice purposes: http://www.quia.com/quiz/2092900.html

average age of accounts receivable

Formula measuring the average length of time it takes to collect cash from sales; calculated by dividing average accounts receivable for the period by sales per day.

Question: If company officials notice that the **average age of accounts receivable** *is getting older, what type of remedial actions can be taken?* ***How does a company reduce the average number of days that are required to collect receivables so that cash is available more quickly?***

Answer: A number of strategies can be used by astute officials to shorten the time between sales being made and cash collected. Below are a few examples. Unfortunately, all such actions have a cost and can cause a negative impact on the volume of sales or create expenses that might outweigh the benefits of quicker cash inflows. Management should make such decisions with extreme care.

- Require a tighter review of credit worthiness before selling to a customer on credit. If sales on account are only made to individuals and companies with significant financial strength, the quantity of delayed payments should decline.
- Work to make the company's own accounting system more efficient so that bills (sales invoices) are sent to customers in a timely manner. Payments are rarely made—even by the best customers—before initial notification is received. If the billing system is not well designed and effectively operated, that process can be unnecessarily slow.
- Offer a discount if a customer pays quickly. Such reductions reward the customer for fast action.
- Send out second bills more quickly. Customers often need reminding that a debt is due. An invoice marked "late" or "overdue" will often push the recipient into action. A company might send out this notice after thirty days—as an example—rather than wait for forty-five days.
- Instigate a more aggressive collection policy for accounts that are not paid on time. Companies can use numerous strategies to "encourage" payment and begin applying these steps at an earlier point in time.

Most companies monitor the age of receivables very carefully and use some combination of these types of efforts whenever any sign of problem is noted.

KEY TAKEAWAYS

Decision makers analyzing a particular company often look beyond reported balances in search of clues as to its financial strength or weakness. Both the current ratio and the amount of working capital provide an indication of short-term liquidity and profitability. The age of receivables and the receivables turnover are measures of the speed or slowness of cash collections. Any change in the time needed to obtain payments from customers should be carefully considered when studying a company. Management can work to shorten the number of days it takes to receive cash by altering credit, billing, and collection policies or possibly by offering discounts or other incentives for quick payment.

Talking with a Real Investing Pro—Continued

Following is a continuation of our interview with Kevin G. Burns.

Question: Let's say that you are analyzing a particular company and are presently looking at its current assets. When you are studying a company's accounts receivable, what types of information tend to catch your attention?

Kevin Burns: I look at three areas specifically. First, how long does it take for the company to collect its accounts receivable especially compared to previous periods? I don't like to see radical changes in the age of receivables without some logical explanation. Second, how lenient is the company in offering credit? Are they owed money by weak customers or a small concentration of customers? Third, does the company depend on interest income and late charges on their accounts receivable for a significant part of their revenue? Some companies claim to be in business to sell products but they are really finance companies because they make their actual profits from finance charges that are added to the accounts receivable. It is always important to know how a company earns money.

Video Clip

Joe talks about the five most important points in Chapter 7.

View the video online at: http://blip.tv/play/sDyBvvI%2BAA

7. END-OF-CHAPTER EXERCISES

QUESTIONS

1. Define "accounts receivable."
2. How is the "net realizable value" of accounts receivable determined?
3. Name three factors a company might consider when trying to determine the amount of accounts receivable that will be ultimately collected.
4. What does the account "allowance for doubtful accounts" represent?
5. Define contra account.
6. When is bad debt expense recorded?
7. Why do companies set up the allowance for doubtful accounts instead of just decreasing accounts receivable for any expected uncollectible balances?
8. What entry does a company make to write off a specific account that has proven to be uncollectible?
9. Give two reasons why accountants do not restate prior year statements when estimations are not exact.
10. Name the two most popular approaches to estimating uncollectible accounts and briefly explain each.
11. What is the purpose of a company having an accounts receivable subsidiary ledger?
12. Why does reporting balances in foreign currencies create accounting challenges?
13. At what exchange rate are monetary asset and liabilities reported?
14. Define current assets.
15. Define current liabilities.
16. How is the current ratio calculated and what does it indicate about a company's financial health?
17. Why do financial statement users calculate a company's age of receivables?

TRUE OR FALSE

1. _____ Companies use two separate accounts in order to report accounts receivable at its net realizable value.
2. _____ Bad debt expense is reported on the balance sheet as a contra account to accounts receivable.
3. _____ The matching principle says that expenses should be recorded the same period as the revenues they help generate.
4. _____ Once an account has been written off, it can never be reinstated on the books, even if it is later collected.
5. _____ The net accounts receivable number on the balance sheet represents the exact amount the company will collect in cash.
6. _____ All companies perform their estimation of uncollectible accounts in the same manner.
7. _____ Frequently, bad debt expense and the ending balance in the allowance for doubtful accounts will differ.
8. _____ The older a receivable, the less likely it is to be collected.
9. _____ The higher that receivables turnover is, the slower the receivables are being collected.
10. _____ To make statements more accurate, bad debt expense is recorded when a specific account is deemed uncollectible and written off.

MULTIPLE CHOICE

1. Which of the following would ***not*** be used to help a company determine the net realizable value of its accounts receivable?
    a. Industry averages and trends
    b. The company's ability to pay its own debts
    c. Current economic conditions
    d. Efficiency of the company's collection procedures
2. Which principle states that expenses should be recorded in the period in which they help generate revenues?
    a. Matching principle
    b. Going concern principle
    c. Cost/benefit analysis
    d. Measurement principle
3. SunFun Company manufactures lawn furniture that is sold to retailers like big box home improvement stores. During October 20X1, SunFun sold furniture to Home Place on account in the amount of $40,000. At the end of 20X1, the balance was still outstanding. In January 20X2, SunFun decided to write off this particular account as it did not appear the balance would ever be collected. Choose the correct journal entry for this transaction below.

Allowance for Doubtful Accounts	40,000	
Accounts Receivable		40,000

a.

Bad Debt Expense	40,000	
Allowance for Doubtful Accounts		40,000

b.

Bad Debt Expense	40,000	
Accounts Receivable		40,000

c.

Cash	40,000	
Accounts Receivable		40,000

d.

4. Ornate Inc. ended 20X3 with $400 in allowance for bad debts. In 20X4, Ornate wrote off $360 in accounts receivable that appear to be uncollectible. At the end of 20X4, Ornate recorded bad debt expense of $330. What is the balance in the allowance for doubtful accounts at the end of 20X4?
    a. $370
    b. $730
    c. $60
    d. $690

5. Gladson Corporation accrues bad debt expense using the percentage of sales method. At the end of the year, Gladson has $450,000 in accounts receivable and $4,000 in its allowance for doubtful accounts before any entry is made for bad debts. Sales for the year were $1,900,000. The percentage that Gladson has historically used to calculate bad debts is 1 percent of sales. Which of the following is true?
    a. Gladson's bad debt expense for the year is $500.
    b. The percentage of sales method is designed to achieve an accurate balance sheet presentation of the net realizable value of accounts receivable.
    c. Gladson would report an allowance for doubtful accounts of $23,000.
    d. Gladson would need to make an adjustment because the $4,000 remaining balance in the allowance for doubtful accounts indicates they estimated wrong last year.
6. Darlene Corporation has $300,000 in assets, 30 percent of which are current, and $100,000 in liabilities, 40 percent of which are current. Which of the following is true?
    a. Darlene's current ratio is 3 to 1.
    b. Darlene's working capital is $200,000.
    c. Darlene's working capital is $50,000.
    d. The current ratio and working capital are measures of a company's profitability.
7. Fifer Inc. began the year with $450,000 in accounts receivable, ended the year with $590,000 in accounts receivable, and $4,000,000 in sales. Last year Fifer's age of receivables was forty-six days and its receivables turnover was six times. Which of the following is ***not*** true?
    a. Fifer's age of receivables is fifty-four days.
    b. Fifer's receivables turnover is 7.92 times.
    c. Fifer's age of receivables improved this year over last year.
    d. Analysts monitor the time it takes a company to collect its receivables.

PROBLEMS

1. Nuance Company had net credit sales for the year of $500,000. Nuance estimates that 2 percent of its net credit sales will never be collected.
    a. Prepare the entry to record Nuance's bad debt expense for the year.
    b. Nuance had accounts receivable of $100,000 at the end of the year. Show how the net accounts receivable balance would be reported on the balance sheet. Assume that the allowance for doubtful accounts had a beginning balance of zero.
    c. Why is A/R shown at net rather than just showing the full amount?
2. Assume that Nuance in number 1 above used the percentage of receivables method to estimate uncollectible accounts instead of the percentage of sales method. Nuance assumes that 5 percent of accounts receivable will never be collected.
    a. Prepare the entry to record Nuance's bad debt expense for the year.
    b. Show how the net accounts receivable balance would be reported on the balance sheet.
    c. Why are companies allowed to choose between methods of estimating bad debts instead of being required to use one method?
3. Ray's GamePlace sells all the hottest gear and video games. On January 1, 20X7, Ray's had the following account balances:

Accounts Receivable	$27,000
Less Allowance for Doubtful Accounts	(4,000)
Net Accounts Receivable	$23,000

    a. During 20X7, Ray's wrote off $6,000 in uncollectible accounts. Make this journal entry.
    b. One account in the amount of $500 that had been written off in (a) above was collected. Make the journal entries to reinstate the account and show its collection.
    c. During 20X7, Ray's made credit sales of $145,000 and collected $115,000 of accounts receivable. Record these journal entries.
    d. At the end of the year, Ray's determines that approximately 7 percent of its ending accounts receivable balance will not be collected. Ray's uses the percentage of receivables method of calculating bad debts. Make the necessary journal entry.
4. Medwear Corporation is a multinational dealer of uniforms for medical personnel. Medwear is headquartered in a country where dollars are the currency. On March 17, Medwear enters into a transaction to sell uniforms to a hospital in Brussels, Belgium in the amount of 267,000 euros. On this date, the exchange rate was $1.32 for every euro.
    a. Record this transaction for Medwear on March 17 assuming that the uniforms are purchased on account.
    b. On March 31, Medwear prepares financial statements. On this date, the exchange rate is $1.27 per euro. Record the necessary journal entry for Medwear on this date.
5. In Chapter 4, Heather Miller started her own business, Sew Cool. The financial statements for December are shown below.

Sew Cool
Income Statement
As of December 31, 20X8

Revenue	$4,000
Cost of Goods	(2,000)
Gross Profit	2,000
Other Expenses	(1,695)
Earnings before Tax	305
Tax Expense	(107)
Net Income	$198

Sew Cool
Stmt. of Retained Earnings
As of December 31, 20X8

Retained Earnings, December 1, 20X8	$500
Net Income	198
Dividends	(158)
Retained Earnings, December 31, 20X8	$540

Sew Cool
Balance Sheet
December 31, 20X8

Assets		Liabilities	
Current		**Current**	
Cash	$940	Accounts Payable	$900
Accounts Receivable	500	Income Tax Payable	120
Less Allowance for Doubtful Accounts	(20)	Total Current Liabilities	$1,020
Net Accounts Receivable	480		
Inventory	700		
Total Current Assets	$2,120		
Noncurrent		**Noncurrent**	
Equipment	$1,000	Notes Payable	$1,060
		Owners' Equity	
		Capital Stock	$500
		Retained Earnings	540
		Total Owners' Equity	$1,040
Total Assets	$3,120	Total Liabilities & Owners' Equity	$3,120

Based on the financial statements determine the following:

a. Current ratio
b. Working capital
c. Age of receivables
d. Receivables turnover—assume that accounts receivable on 1/1/20X8 were $460.

COMPREHENSIVE PROBLEM

This problem will carry through several chapters, building in difficulty. It allows students to continuously practice skills and knowledge learned in previous chapters.

Recall in Chapter 5 that Leon Jackson started Webworks, a Web site design and maintenance firm. You helped him prepare his adjusted trial balance for June. We are going to continue with this problem, preparing Webworks financial statements for July.

Here are Webworks financial statements as of June 30.

Webworks
Income Statement
As of June 30

Revenue	$1,050
Expenses	(380)
Earning before Tax	670
Tax Expense	(200)
Net Income	$ 470

Webworks
Stmt. of Retained Earnings
As of June 30

Retained Earnings, June 1	$0
Net Income	470
Retained Earnings, June 30	$470

Webworks
Balance Sheet
June 30

Assets		**Liabilities**	
Current		**Current**	
Cash	$9,800	Accounts Payable	$280
Accounts Receivable	450	Salaries Payable	100
Supplies Inventory	100	Unearned Revenue	500
Total Current Assets	$10,350	Total Current Liabilities	$880
Noncurrent		**Noncurrent**	
Equipment	$3,000	Notes Payable	$10,000
		Owners' Equity	
		Capital Stock	$2,000
		Retained Earnings	470
		Total Owners' Equity	$2,470
Total Assets	$13,350	Total Liabilities & Owners' Equity	$13,350

The following events occur during July:

a. Webworks purchases additional equipment for $4,000 cash.

b. Webworks purchases supplies worth $90 on account.

c. Webworks pays off its accounts payable and salaries payable from June.

d. Webworks starts and completes four more sites and bills clients for $1,800.

e. Recall that in June, Webworks received $500 in advance to design a restaurant Web site. Webworks completes this site during July.

f. Webworks collects $1,200 in accounts receivable.

g. Webworks pays Nancy $500 for her work during the first three weeks of July.

h. Webworks receives $200 in advance to work on a Web site for a local dry cleaner and $300 in advance to work on a Web site for a local vet. Work will not begin on the sites until August.

i. Leon's parents have decided to charge rent after seeing how successful his business is and how much space it is taking up in their house. They all agree that rent will be $200 per month. Webworks pays $600 for July, August and September.

j. Webworks pays taxes of $300 in cash.

Required:

A. Prepare journal entries for the above events.

B. Post the journal entries to T-accounts.

C. Prepare an unadjusted trial balance for Webworks for July.

D. Prepare adjusting entries for the following and post them to your T-accounts.

k. Webworks owes Nancy $200 for her work during the last week of July.

l. Leon's parents let him know that Webworks owes $150 toward the electricity bill. Webworks will pay them in August.

m. Webworks determines that it has $50 worth of supplies remaining at the end of July.

n. Prepaid rent should be adjusted for July's portion.

o. In June, Webworks designed a site for Pauline Smith, but has not yet been fully paid. Leon believes the company may not be able to collect all of its accounts receivable. A local CPA helps Leon determine that similar businesses report an allowance for bad debt at an average of 10 percent of their accounts receivable. Webworks will use this method. Make the bad debt accrual for Webworks.

E. Prepare an adjusted trial balance.

F. Prepare financial statements for July.

ENDNOTES

1. As indicated previously, other versions of generally accepted accounting principles do exist. Unless otherwise noted, in this textbook, the presentation of U.S. GAAP is assumed.
2. The independent auditors also analyze the available evidence and must believe that it is sufficient to provide the same reasonable assurance in order to render an unqualified opinion on the financial statements.
3. Some companies include both accounts on the balance sheet to explain the origin of the reported balance. Others show only the single net figure with additional information provided in the notes to the financial statements.
4. Because the focus of the discussion here is on accounts receivable and their collectability, the recognition of cost of goods sold as well as the possible return of any merchandise will be omitted. Those topics are discussed in detail in later chapters.
5. Many companies combine these two entries for convenience. The debit to accounts receivable in the first entry exactly offsets the credit in the second. Thus, the same recording impact is achieved by simply debiting cash and crediting the allowance for doubtful accounts. However, the rationale for that single entry is not always as evident to a beginning student.
6. As will be discussed in subsequent chapters, previously issued financial statements are restated if found to contain material misstatements or in a few other specific circumstances. However, a difference between an actual figure and a reasonable estimation is not handled in this manner. In real life, determining whether a previously reported amount was a reasonable estimation can be the subject of intense debate.
7. The $3,000 debit figure is assumed here for convenience to be solely the result of underestimating uncollectible accounts in Year One. Several other factors may also be present. For example, the balance in the allowance for doubtful accounts will be impacted by credit sales made in the current year that are discovered to be worthless before the end of the period. Such accounts reduce the allowance T-account prior to the recognition of an expense. The residual allowance balance is also affected by the collection of accounts that were written off as worthless in an earlier year. As described earlier, the allowance is actually increased by that event. However, the financial reporting is not altered by the actual cause of the final allowance figure.
8. See immediately preceding endnote for other reasons as to why these balances can differ.
9. As has been stated previously, this is an introductory textbook. Thus, a more in-depth examination of many important topics, such as foreign currency balances, can be found in upper-level accounting texts. The coverage here of foreign currency balances is only designed to introduce students to basic reporting problems and their resolutions.

CHAPTER 8
How Does a Company Gather Information about Its Inventory?

Video Clip

Joe introduces Chapter 8 and speaks about the course in general.

View the video online at: http://blip.tv/play/sDyBvvQhAA

1. DETERMINING AND REPORTING THE COST OF INVENTORY

LEARNING OBJECTIVES

At the end of this section, students should be able to meet the following objectives:

1. **Understand that inventory is recorded initially at its historical cost.**
2. **Provide the guiding rule for identifying expenditures and other costs that must be capitalized in the reporting of inventory.**
3. **Explain the rationale for offering a cash discount for payments made within a specified period of time as well as the accounting for such cost reductions.**

Question: The asset section of the February 28, 2009, balance sheet produced by Best Buy Co. Inc. reports net accounts receivable of $1.868 billion. Based on discussions in the previous chapter, a decision maker should know that this figure reflects net realizable value—the estimation by officials of the amount of cash that will be collected from the receivables owed to the company by its customers. Knowledge of financial accounting rules allows an individual to understand the information being conveyed in a set of financial statements.

As is common, the next account that appears on Best Buy's balance sheet is inventory, all the items held on that date that were acquired for sales purposes—televisions, cameras, computers, and the like. The figure disclosed by the company for this asset is $4.753 billion. Does this balance also indicate net realizable value—the cash expected to be generated from the company's merchandise—or is different information reflected? ***On a balance sheet, what does the amount reported for inventory represent?***

inventory

A current asset bought or manufactured for the purpose of selling in order to generate revenue.

Answer: The challenge of analyzing the various assets reported by an organization would be reduced substantially if every monetary number disclosed the same basic information, such as net realizable value. However, over the decades, virtually every asset has come to have its own individualized method of reporting, one created to address the special peculiarities of that account. Thus, the term "presented fairly" often has a totally different meaning for each asset. Reporting accounts receivables, for example, at net realizable value has no impact on the approach that has come to be accepted for **inventory**.

The reporting of inventory is especially unique because the reported balance is not as standardized as with accounts receivable. For example, under certain circumstances, the balance sheet amount shown for inventory actually can reflect net realizable value. Several other meanings for the reported balance, though, are more likely. The range of accounting alternatives encountered in analyzing this asset emphasizes the importance of reading the notes included with financial statements rather than fixating on a few reported numbers alone. Without careful study of the additional disclosures, a decision maker can simply not know what Best Buy means by the $4.753 billion figure reported for "merchandise inventories." Another company could show the identical number for its inventory and still be reporting considerably different information.

Question: Accounting for inventory seems particularly complicated. A logical approach to the coverage here is needed. In coming to understand the reporting methodology that is utilized with this asset, where should the discussion begin? ***What is the first issue that an accountant faces in establishing an appropriate balance for inventory so that it is reported in conformity with U.S. GAAP?***

Answer: The study of inventory and its financial reporting should begin by defining "cost." In acquiring each item, officials make the decision to allocate a certain amount of scarce resources. What did the company expend to obtain its inventory? That is a reasonable question to address.

To illustrate, assume that a sporting goods company (Rider Inc.) acquires a new bicycle (Model XY-7) to sell. Rider's accounting system should be designed to determine the cost of this piece of inventory, the sacrifice that the company chose to make to obtain the asset. Assume that a price of $250 was charged by the manufacturer (Builder Company) for the bicycle and the purchase was made by Rider on credit. Rider spends another $9 to transport the item from the factory to one of its retail stores and $6 to have the pieces assembled so that the bicycle can be displayed in the salesroom for customers to examine.

In accounting for the acquisition of inventory, cost includes all normal and necessary amounts incurred to get the item into the condition and position to be sold. Hence, by the time this bicycle has reached Rider's retail location and been readied for sale, its cost to the sporting goods company is $265.

FIGURE 8.1 Maintaining a Cost for Inventory Item

Rider, Inc.
Subsidiary Ledger
Bicycle—Model XY-7

Invoice Price—Charged by Manufacturer	$250	
Transportation-in—Delivery to Company's Store	9	
Assembly	6	
Cost of Inventory (Bicycle)	$265	Quantity—1

The charges for delivering this merchandise and assembling the parts were included in the cost of the asset (the traditional term for adding a cost to an asset account, **capitalization**, was introduced previously). Both of these expenditures were properly viewed as normal and necessary to get the bicycle into the condition and position to be resold. Interestingly, any amount later expended to transport the merchandise from the store to a buying customer is recorded as an expense rather than as an asset because that cost is incurred after the sale takes place. At that point, no further future value exists since the merchandise has already been sold.

capitalization

The process of recording as an asset all the normal and necessary costs associated with getting the asset into position and condition to be sold (in the case of inventory) or used to help generate revenue (in the case of noncurrent assets such as land, buildings, and equipment).

Occasionally, costs arise where the "normal and necessary" standard may be difficult to apply. To illustrate, assume that the president of a store that sells antiques buys a 120-year-old table for resell purposes. When the table arrives at the store, another $300 must be spent to fix a scratch cut across its surface. Should this added cost be capitalized (added to the reported balance for inventory) or expensed? The answer to this question is not readily apparent and depends on ascertaining all relevant facts. Here are two possibilities.

Scenario one: The table was acquired by the president with the knowledge that the scratch already existed and needed to be fixed prior to offering the merchandise for sale. In that case, repair is a normal and necessary activity to put the table into condition necessary to be sold. The $300 is capitalized, recorded as an addition to the cost of the inventory.

Scenario two: The table was bought without the scratch but was damaged when first moved into the store through an act of employee carelessness. The table must be repaired but the scratch was neither normal nor necessary. This cost could have been avoided. The $300 is not capitalized but rather reported as a repair expense by the store.

As discussed in an earlier chapter, if the accountant cannot make a reasonable determination as to whether a particular cost qualifies as normal and necessary, the conservatism principle that underlies financial accounting requires the $300 to be reported as an expense. When in doubt, the alternative that makes reported figures look best is avoided so that decision makers are not encouraged to be overly optimistic about the company's financial health and future prospects.

EXERCISE

Link to multiple-choice question for practice purposes: http://www.quia.com/quiz/2092919.html

Question: When inventory is acquired, some sellers are willing to accept a reduced amount to encourage fast payment—an offer that is called a cash discount (or a sales discount or purchases discount depending on whether the seller or the buyer is making the entry). Cash becomes available sooner so that the seller can quickly put it back into circulation to make more profits. In addition, the possibility that a receivable will become uncollectible is reduced if the balance due is not allowed to get too old. Tempting buyers to make quick payments to reduce their cost is viewed as a smart business practice by many sellers.

To illustrate, assume the invoice received by the sporting goods company (Rider) for the above bicycle indicates the proper $250 balance due but also includes the notation: 2/10, n/45. What message is being conveyed by the seller? ***How do cash discounts impact the reporting of inventory?***

Answer: Sellers—such as Builder Company in this example—can offer a wide variety of discount terms to encourage speedy payment. One such as 2/10, n/45 is generally read "two ten, net 45." It informs the buyer that a 2 percent discount can be taken if the invoice is paid by the tenth day. Any net amount that remains unpaid (after merchandise returns or partial cash payments) is due on the forty-fifth day. Rider has the option to pay $245 for the bicycle within ten days of receiving the invoice by taking advantage of the $5 discount ($250 × 0.02). Or, the sporting goods company can wait until the forty-fifth day but then is responsible for the entire $250.

Many companies automatically take advantage of these discounts as a matter of policy because of the high rate of interest earned. If Rider does not submit the money in ten days, it must pay an extra $5 in order to hold onto $245 for an additional thirty-five days. This delay equates to a 2.04 percent interest rate over just that short period of time ($5/$245 = 2.04 percent [rounded]). There are over ten thirty-five-day periods in a year. Paying the extra $5 is the equivalent of an annual interest rate in excess of 21 percent.

365 days per year/35 days holding the money = 10.43 time periods per year

2.04% (for 35 days) × 10.43 time periods equals a 21.28% rate for a year

That substantial rate of interest is avoided by making the early payment, a decision chosen by most companies unless they are experiencing serious cash flow difficulties.

Assuming that Rider avails itself of the discount offer, the capitalized cost of the inventory is reduced to $260.

FIGURE 8.2 Cost of Inventory Reduced by Cash Discount

Rider, Inc.
Subsidiary Ledger
Bicycle—Model XY-7

Invoice Price—Charged by Manufacturer	$250	
Discount Taken—2/10, n/45	(5)	
Transportation-in from Seller to Store	9	
Assembly	6	
Cost of Inventory (Bicycle)	$260	Quantity—1

EXERCISE

Link to multiple-choice question for practice purposes: http://www.quia.com/quiz/2092883.html

KEY TAKEAWAYS

Any discussion of the reporting of inventory begins with the calculation of cost, the amount spent to obtain the merchandise. Cost encompasses all payments that are considered normal and necessary to get the merchandise into the condition and possession to be sold. Any other expenditures are expensed as incurred. Cash discounts are often offered to buyers to encourage quick payment. Taking advantage of such discounts is usually a wise decision because they effectively save interest at a relatively high rate.

2. PERPETUAL AND PERIODIC INVENTORY SYSTEMS

LEARNING OBJECTIVES

At the end of this section, students should be able to meet the following objectives:

1. **Identify the attributes as well as both the advantages and disadvantages of a perpetual inventory system.**
2. **Identify the attributes as well as both the advantages and disadvantages of a periodic inventory system.**
3. **Provide journal entries for a variety of transactions involved in the purchase of inventory using both a perpetual and a periodic inventory system.**

Question: In an earlier chapter, differences between a perpetual inventory system and a periodic inventory system were discussed briefly. A perpetual system—which frequently relies on bar coding and computer scanning—maintains an ongoing record of all items present. ***How is the recording of an inventory purchase carried out in a perpetual system?***

Answer: When a **perpetual inventory system** is in use, all additions and reductions are monitored in the inventory T-account. Thus, theoretically, the balance found in that general ledger account at any point in time will be identical to the merchandise physically on hand. In actual practice, recording mistakes as well as losses such as theft and breakage create some (hopefully small) discrepancies. Consequently, even with a perpetual system, the inventory records must be reconciled occasionally with the items actually present to reestablish accuracy.

perpetual inventory system

Accounting system that maintains an ongoing record of all inventory items; records increases and decreases in inventory accounts as they occur as well as the cost of goods sold to date.

In a perpetual inventory system, the maintenance of a separate subsidiary ledger showing data about the individual items on hand is essential. On February 28, 2009, Best Buy reported inventory totaling $4.753 billion. However, the company also needs specific information as to the quantity, type, and location of all televisions, cameras, computers, and the like that make up this sum. That is the significance of a perpetual system; it provides the ability to keep track of the various types of merchandise. The total cost is available in the inventory T-account but detailed data about the composition (the quantity and frequently the cost) of merchandise physically held is maintained in a subsidiary ledger where an individual file can be available for each item.

Below are the journal entries that Rider Inc. (the sporting goods company) makes for its purchase of a bicycle to sell (Model XY-7) if a perpetual inventory system is utilized. A separate subsidiary ledger file (such as shown previously) is also established to record the quantity and cost of the specific items on hand.

The assumption is made here that the transportation and assembly charges are paid in cash. Furthermore, the actual purchase is initially on credit with payment made during the ten-day discount period. The bicycle is recorded at $250 and then reduced by $5 at the time the discount is taken. This approach is known as the "gross method of reporting discounts." As an alternative, companies can choose to anticipate taking the discount and simply make the initial entry for the $245 expected payment. This option is referred to as the "net method of reporting discounts."

FIGURE 8.3 Rider Inc.—Journal Entries—Perpetual Inventory System[1]

Purchased Bicycle (Model XY-7)—Recorded Using Gross Method

Inventory	250		(increase an asset—debit)
Accounts Payable		250	(increase a liability—credit)

Paid for Bicycle after Taking 2 Percent Discount

Accounts Payable	250		(decrease a liability—debit)
Cash		245	(decrease an asset—credit)
Inventory		5	(decrease an asset—credit)

Payment Made to Transport Bicycle to Retail Store

Inventory	9		(increase an asset—debit)
Cash		9	(decrease an asset—credit)

Payment Made to Assemble Bicycle for Display Purposes

Inventory	6		(increase an asset—debit)
Cash		6	(decrease an asset—credit)

After posting these entries, the inventory T-account in the general ledger reports a net cost of $260 ($250 – $5 + $9 + $6) and the separate subsidiary ledger shown previously indicates that one Model XY-7 bicycle is on hand with a cost of $260.

EXERCISE

Link to multiple-choice question for practice purposes: http://www.quia.com/quiz/2092884.html

Question: In a periodic system, no attempt is made to keep an ongoing record of a company's inventory. Instead, the quantity and cost of merchandise is only determined periodically as a preliminary step in preparing financial statements. ***How is the actual recording of an inventory purchase carried out in a periodic system?***

periodic inventory system

Accounting system that does not maintain an ongoing record of all inventory items; instead, ending inventory is determined by a physical count so that a formula (beginning inventory plus purchases less ending inventory) can be used to determine cost of goods sold.

Answer: If a company uses a **periodic system**, neither the cost nor the quantity of the specific inventory items on hand is monitored. These data are not viewed by company officials as worth the cost and effort required to gather it. However, transactions still take place and a record must be maintained of the costs incurred. This information is eventually used for financial reporting but also—more immediately—for control purposes. Regardless of the recording system, companies want to avoid spending unnecessary amounts on inventory as well as tangential expenditures such as transportation and assembly. If the accounting system indicates that a particular cost is growing too rapidly, alternatives can be investigated before the problem becomes serious. Periodic systems are designed to provide such information through the use of separate general ledger T-accounts for each cost incurred.

Assume that Rider uses a periodic inventory system. Its journal entries for the acquisition of the Model XY-7 bicycle are as follows. No subsidiary ledger is maintained. The overall cost of the inventory item is not readily available and the quantity (except by visual inspection) is unknown. At any point in time, company officials do have access to the amounts spent for each of the individual costs (such as transportation and assembly) for monitoring purposes.

Because these costs result from the acquisition of an asset that eventually becomes an expense when sold, they follow the same debit and credit rules as those accounts.

FIGURE 8.4 Rider Inc.—Journal Entries—Periodic Inventory System

Purchased Bicycle (Model XY-7)—Recorded Using Gross Method			
Purchases of Inventory	250		(increase an asset—debit)
Accounts Payable		250	(increase a liability—credit)
Paid for Bicycle after Taking 2 Percent Discount			
Accounts Payable	250		(decrease a liability—debit)
Cash		245	(decrease an asset—credit)
Purchases Discount		5	(decrease an asset—credit)
Payment Made to Transport Bicycle to Retail Stort			
Transportation-in	9		(increase an asset—debit)
Cash		9	(decrease an asset—credit)
Payment Made to Assemble Bicycle for Display Purposes			
Assembly of Inventory	6		(increase an asset—debit)
Cash		6	(decrease an asset—credit)

Note that the choice between using a perpetual and periodic system impacts the following:

- The information available to company officials on a daily basis

- The journal entries to be made
- The cost necessary to operate the accounting system (the technology required by a perpetual system is more expensive)

Regardless of the system, Rider holds one piece of inventory with a cost of $260. The decision as to whether to utilize a perpetual or periodic system is based on the added cost of the perpetual system and the difference in the information generated for use by company officials. The company's inventory is not physically affected by the method selected.

EXERCISE

Link to multiple-choice question for practice purposes: http://www.quia.com/quiz/2092920.html

EXERCISE

Link to multiple-choice question for practice purposes: http://www.quia.com/quiz/2092921.html

Question: ***Given the availability of sophisticated computers, do any companies still use periodic inventory systems?*** *With bar coding and the advanced state of technology, is periodic inventory simply an antiquated system that is no longer found in actual practice?*

Answer: Obviously, in this computer age, perpetual inventory systems have come to dominate because they provide valuable information to company officials. However, some types of businesses will simply never change from the simplicity of a periodic system.

A beauty salon or barber shop, for example, where services are rendered but a small amount of inventory is kept on hand for occasional sales would certainly not need to absorb the cost of a perpetual system. Visual inspection can alert the employees as to the quantity of inventory on hand.

Restaurants, sandwich shops, ice cream stores, and the like might well choose to use a periodic system because purchasing usually takes place at the establishment where quantities are easy to observe and manage. The information provided by a perpetual system does not necessarily provide additional benefit.

"Dollar stores," which have become particularly prevalent in recent years, sell large quantities of low-priced merchandise. Goods tend to be added to a store's inventory as they become available rather than based on any type of managed inventory strategy. Again, officials must decide whether keeping up with the inventory on hand will impact their decision making. If not, the cost of a perpetual system is unnecessary.

Perhaps, most importantly, some companies often use a hybrid system where the units on hand and sold are monitored with a perpetual system. However, to reduce cost, the dollar amounts are only determined using a periodic system at the end of the year to prepare financial statements. In that way, the company gains valuable information (the number of units on hand) at a reduced amount.

KEY TAKEAWAYS

Perpetual inventory systems are designed to maintain updated figures for inventory as a whole as well as for individual items. Separate subsidiary ledger accounts show the balance for each type of inventory so that company officials can know the size, cost, and composition of the merchandise. A periodic system is cheaper to operate because no attempt is made to monitor inventory balances (in total or individually) until financial statements are to be prepared. A periodic system does allow a company to control costs by keeping track of the individual inventory costs as they are incurred.

3. THE CALCULATION OF COST OF GOODS SOLD

LEARNING OBJECTIVES

At the end of this section, students should be able to meet the following objectives:

1. **Explain the meaning of the FOB point in connection with an inventory purchase and its impact on the recording of the transaction.**
2. **Identify the time at which cost of goods sold is computed in a perpetual inventory system as well as the recording made at the time of sale.**
3. **Identify the time at which cost of goods sold is computed in a periodic inventory system as well as the recording made at the time of sale.**
4. **Provide the computation used in a periodic inventory system to derive cost of goods sold along with the adjusting entry necessary to enter the appropriate balances into the accounting system for each period.**
5. **Understand the necessity of taking a physical inventory count.**

Question: Rider Inc. (the sporting goods company) buys a bicycle for resell purposes and records the transaction using either a perpetual or periodic system. ***When should an inventory purchase be recorded?*** *Assume, for example, that Builder Company (the manufacturer of this bicycle) is located in Wisconsin, whereas the retail store operated by Rider is in Kentucky. Delivery takes several days at a minimum. The precise moment for recording the transaction is probably not critical except near the end of the year when the timing of journal entries can impact the balances to be included on the financial statements.*

To illustrate, assume this bicycle is ordered by Rider Inc. on December 27 of Year One. It is shipped by Builder Company from Wisconsin on December 29 of Year One and arrives at the retail store on January 4 of Year Two. When Rider produces its financial statements for Year One, should the inventory cost and related payable be included even though the bicycle was not physically received until Year Two?

Answer: Documents prepared in connection with shipments made from a seller to a buyer are normally marked with an "FOB" point. FOB stands for "Free On Board" (a traditional maritime term that has gained a wider use over the years) and indicates when legal title to property is transferred. That is the moment that the bicycle is assumed to be conveyed from one party to the other. It signifies the appropriate date for recording.

In this illustration, if Builder Company specifies that the sale of this bicycle is made "**FOB shipping point**" and Rider Inc. agrees to this condition, the transaction occurs on December 29, Year One, when the bicycle leaves the seller. Consequently, both the asset and the liability appear on the December 31, Year One, balance sheet prepared by the buyer while Builder records sale revenue in Year One. However, if the contract states that the transaction is made "**FOB destination**," the seller maintains legal ownership until the bicycle arrives at the store on January 4, Year Two. Neither party records the transaction until that time. Near the end of a reporting period, account balances can clearly be altered by the FOB designation.

FOB shipping point

Terms of sale stipulating that legal title to shipped goods passes to the buyer at the time of shipment so that buyer is responsible for transportation costs and any damages or losses in transit.

FOB destination

Terms of sale stipulating that legal title to shipped goods passes to the buyer when they arrive at the final destination so that the seller is responsible for transportation costs and any damages or losses in transit.

The FOB point is often important for two other reasons.

- The company that holds legal title to merchandise during the trip from seller to buyer normally incurs all transportation costs. If no other arrangements are negotiated, "FOB shipping point" means that Rider Inc. as the buyer pays shipping. "FOB destination" assigns this same cost to Builder, as the seller.
- Any losses or damages that occur in route affect the party holding legal title (again, unless other arrangements are specified in a contract). If shipment from Wisconsin to Kentucky was noted as FOB shipping point and the bicycle breaks as the result of an accident in Illinois, it is the buyer's inventory that was hurt. It is the seller's problem, though, if the shipment is marked as FOB destination. The legal owner bears the cost of damages that occur during the physical conveyance of property.

EXERCISE

Link to multiple-choice question for practice purposes: http://www.quia.com/quiz/2092922.html

Question: When a sale is made so that inventory is surrendered, the seller reports an expense that has previously been identified as "cost of goods sold" or "cost of sales." For example, Best Buy reported "cost of goods sold," for the year ended February 28, 2009, as $34.017 billion. ***When should cost of goods sold be determined?***

To illustrate, assume that Rider Inc. begins the current year holding three Model XY-7 bicycles costing $260 each—$780 in total. During the period, another five units of this same model are acquired, again for $260 apiece or $1,300 in total.[2] *Eventually, a customer buys seven of these bicycles for her family and friends paying cash of $440 each or $3,080 in total. No further sales are made of this model. At the end of the period, a single bicycle remains (3 + 5 – 7). One is still in stock while seven have been sold. What is the proper method of recording the company's cost of goods sold?*

Answer: *Perpetual inventory system.* The acquisition and subsequent sale of inventory when a perpetual system is in use was demonstrated briefly in an earlier chapter. The accounting records maintain current balances so that officials are cognizant of (a) the amount of merchandise being held and (b) the cost of goods sold for the year to date. These figures are readily available in general ledger T-accounts. In addition, separate subsidiary ledger balances are usually established for the individual items in stock, showing the quantity on hand and its cost. When each sale is made, the applicable cost is reclassified from the inventory account on the balance sheet to cost of goods sold on the income statement. Simultaneously, the corresponding balance in the subsidiary ledger is lowered.

In this example, bicycles had been acquired by Rider Inc. and seven of them, costing $260 each (a total of $1,820), are sold to a customer for $440 apiece or $3,080. When a perpetual system is in use, two journal entries are prepared at the time of this transaction: one for the sale and a second to shift the cost of the inventory from asset to expense.

FIGURE 8.5 Journal Entries for Sale of Seven Model XY-7 Bicycles—Perpetual Inventory System

Cash	3,080		(increase an asset—debit)
Sales Revenue—Merchandise		3,080	(increase a revenue—credit)
Cost of Goods Sold	1,820		(increase an expense—debit)
Inventory		1,820	(decrease an asset—credit)

Removing $1,820 leaves an inventory balance of $260 ($780 + $1,300 – $1,820) representing the cost of the one remaining unit. The $1,260 difference between revenue and cost of goods sold for this sale ($3,080 minus $1,820) is the mark-up (also known as "**gross profit**" or "gross margin").

gross profit

Difference between sales and cost of goods sold; also called gross margin or mark-up.

Periodic inventory system. In contrast, a periodic system monitors the various inventory expenditures but makes no attempt to keep up with the merchandise on hand or the cost of goods sold during the year. Although cheap to create and operate, the information available to company officials is extremely limited.

periodic inventory system

Accounting system that does not maintain an ongoing record of all inventory items; instead, ending inventory is determined by a physical count so that a formula (beginning inventory plus purchases less ending inventory) can be used to determine cost of goods sold.

At the time the sale of seven bicycles takes place, the first journal entry shown above is still made to recognize the revenue. However, the second entry is omitted if a periodic system is in use. Cost of goods sold is neither calculated nor recorded when a sale occurs. Thus, the inventory balance remains unadjusted throughout the year. Eventually, whenever financial statements are prepared, the amount to be reported for the asset (inventory) must be determined along with the expense (cost of goods sold) for the entire period.

Because updated totals are not maintained, the only accounts found in the general ledger relating to inventory show balances of $780 (beginning balance) and $1,300 (purchases).

General Ledger Balances—Periodic Inventory System	
Inventory (beginning balance remains unadjusted during the period):	3 units at $260 each or $780
Purchases (total inventory costs incurred during the period; for this example, the balance here includes the invoice price, sales discount, transportation-in, assembly, and the like although they would have been recorded separately):	5 units at $260 each or $1,300

Based on this information, total inventory available for to be sold by Rider Inc. during this period is eight units costing $2,080 ($780 plus $1,300)

physical inventory

A count of the inventory on hand; necessary for reporting purposes when using a periodic system but also required for a perpetual system to ensure the accuracy of the records.

When using a periodic system, cost of goods sold is computed as a prerequisite to preparing financial statements. Inventory on hand is counted (a process known as a "**physical inventory**") and all units that are no longer present are assumed to have been sold. The amount of missing inventory is determined in this process. The figure is then reported as the company's cost of goods sold for the period. Because complete inventory records are not available, any units that are lost, stolen, or broken cannot be separately derived. All merchandise that is no longer on hand is included within cost of goods sold.

In this example, a physical inventory count will be taken by the employees of Rider Inc. on or near the last day of the year so that financial statements can be produced. Because eight bicycles (Model XY-7) were available during the year but seven have now been sold, one unit—costing $260—remains (if no accident or theft has occurred). This amount is the inventory figure that appears in the asset section of the balance sheet.

Cost of goods sold is then computed by the following formula.

FIGURE 8.6 Computation of Cost of Goods Sold in a Periodic System[3]

Beginning Inventory	$780
Purchases for the Period	1,300
Goods Available for Sale	2,080
Ending Inventory (one unit at a cost of $260)	(260)
Cost of Goods Sold	$1,820

In a periodic system, three costs are used to arrive at the amount reported as a company's cost of goods sold. It is important to understand how each of these figures is derived.

- *Beginning inventory* was determined by a physical inventory taken at the end of the previous year. The count was followed by a calculation of the cost of those units still present. This balance was recorded in the inventory account at that time and has remained unchanged until the end of the current year. A periodic system only updates the general ledger when financial statements are prepared.
- The *purchases* figure has been maintained throughout the year in the general ledger to provide a record of the amounts expended for all normal and necessary costs (invoice price, discounts, transportation-in, assembly costs, and the like) needed to get the inventory items into position and condition to be sold.
- *Ending inventory* is found by making a new physical count at the end of the current period. The number of units on hand is determined (one, in this case) and then the cost of those items ($260) is used to arrive at the proper inventory total.

EXERCISE

Link to multiple-choice question for practice purposes: http://www.quia.com/quiz/2092885.html

Question: In a perpetual inventory system, cost of goods sold is determined at the time of each sale. Figures retained in a subsidiary ledger provide the cost of the specific item being surrendered so that an immediate reclassification from asset to expense can be made.

With a periodic system, cost of goods sold is not calculated until financial statements are prepared. The beginning inventory balance (the ending amount from the previous year) is combined with the total acquisition costs incurred this period. Merchandise still on hand is counted and its cost is determined. All missing inventory is assumed to reflect the cost of goods sold. ***When a periodic inventory system is in use, how are both the ending inventory and cost of goods sold for the year physically entered into the accounting records?*** *These figures have not been recorded on an ongoing basis so the general ledger must be updated to agree with the reported balances.*

Answer: In the bicycle example, opening inventory for the period was comprised of three items costing $780. Another five were then bought for $1,300. The total cost of these eight units is $2,080. Because the financial impact of lost or broken units cannot be ascertained in a periodic system, the entire $2,080 is assigned to either ending inventory (one unit at a cost of $260) or cost of goods sold ($780 + $1,300 – $260 or $1,820). There is no other account in which to record inventory costs in a periodic system. The goods are assumed to either be on hand or have been sold.

For a periodic inventory system, a year-end adjusting entry is set up so that these computed amounts are reflected as the final account balances.

FIGURE 8.7 Adjusting Entry—Recording Inventory and Cost of Goods Sold as Determined in Periodic Inventory System[4]

Inventory (ending—one unit at $260)	260		(increase an asset—debit)
Cost of Goods Sold (seven units missing at $260 each)	1,820		(increase an expense—debit)
Purchases of Inventory (four units at $260 each)		1,300	(decrease an asset type account —credit)
Inventory (beginning—three units at $260 each)		780	(decrease an asset—credit)

Note that the reported costs on the financial statements ($260 for ending inventory and $1,820 for cost of goods sold) are identical under both perpetual and periodic systems. However, as will be demonstrated in the next chapter, this agreement does not always exist when inventory items are acquired during the year at differing costs.

KEY TAKEAWAYS

The legal conveyance of inventory from seller to buyer establishes the timing for recording and is based on the FOB point specified. This designation also identifies the party responsible for transportation costs and items damaged while in transit. In contrast, the recording of cost of goods sold depends on the inventory system used. For a perpetual system, the reclassification of an item from inventory to expense occurs at the time of each sale. A periodic system makes no attempt to monitor inventory totals; thus, cost of goods sold is unknown until the preparation of financial statements. The expense is found by adding the beginning inventory to the purchase costs for the period and then subtracting ending inventory. A year-end adjusting entry then updates the various general ledger accounts.

4. REPORTING INVENTORY AT THE LOWER-OF-COST-OR-MARKET

LEARNING OBJECTIVES

At the end of this section, students should be able to meet the following objectives:

1. **Explain the need for reporting inventory at the lower-of-cost-or-market.**
2. **Differentiate between a problem caused by a drop in the purchase value of inventory and one coming from the sales value of the merchandise.**
3. **Understand the difference in applying the lower-of-cost-or-market rule under U.S. GAAP and IFRS.**

Question: In the example of Rider Inc., Model XY-7 bicycles have been bought and sold and one unit remains in stock at the end of the year. The cost of this model has held steady at $260. However, its market value is likely to differ from that figure.

Assume that, because of the sales made during the period, company officials believe that a buyer will eventually be found to pay $440 for this last bicycle. ***Is inventory always reported on a balance sheet at historical cost or is market (or fair) value ever taken into consideration?*** *Should this bicycle be shown as an asset at $260, $440, or some other pertinent figure?*

Answer: Under normal conditions, market value is rarely relevant in the reporting of inventory. For Rider Inc. this bicycle will most likely appear as an asset at its cost of $260 until sold. Value is such a subjective figure that it is usually ignored in reporting inventory. The company has no reliable proof that the bicycle will bring in $440 until a sale actually occurs. The conservative nature of accounting resists the temptation to inflate reported inventory figures based purely on the anticipation of a profitable transaction at some point in the future.

An exception to this rule becomes relevant if the value of inventory falls below cost. Once again, the conservatism inherent in financial accounting is easily seen. If market value remains greater than cost, no change is made in the reported balance until a sale occurs. In contrast, if the value drops so that inventory is worth less than cost, a loss is recognized immediately. Accountants often say that losses are anticipated but gains are not. As a note to the June 24, 2009, financial statements for Winn-Dixie Stores states, "Merchandise inventories are stated at the **lower of cost or market**" (emphasis added). Whenever inventory appears to have lost value for any reason, the accountant compares the cost of the item to its market value and the lower figure then appears on the balance sheet.

Question: ***When applying the lower-of-cost-or-market approach to inventory, how does the owner of the merchandise ascertain market value?***

Answer: The practical problem in applying this rule arises from the difficulty in ascertaining an appropriate market value. There are several plausible ways to view the worth of any asset. For inventory, there is both a "purchase value" (replacement cost—the amount needed to acquire the same item again at the present time) and a "sales value" (net realizable value—the amount of cash expected from an eventual sale). When preparing financial statements, if either of these amounts is impaired, recognition of a loss is likely. Thus, the accountant must watch both values and be alert to any potential problems.

Purchase Value. In some cases, often because of bad timing, a company finds that it has paid an excessive amount for inventory. Usually as the result of an increase in supply or a decrease in demand, replacement cost drops after an item is acquired. To illustrate, assume that Builder Company—the manufacturer of bicycle Model XY-7—has trouble selling the expected quantity of this style to retail stores because the design is not viewed as attractive. Near the end of the year, Builder reduces the wholesale price offered for this model by $50 in hopes of stimulating sales. Rider Inc. bought a number of these bicycles earlier at a total cost of $260 each but now, before the last unit is sold, could obtain an identical product for only $210. The bicycle held in Rider's inventory is literally worth less than what the company paid for it. The purchase value, as demonstrated by replacement cost, has fallen to a figure lower than its historical cost.

lower-of-cost-or-market

Conservative approach to inventory valuation used when merchandise values have decreased; a reduction in the asset is recorded to reflect the decline in value if it falls below cost.

When replacement cost for inventory drops below the amount paid, the lower (more conservative) figure is reported on the balance sheet and the related loss is recognized on the income statement. In applying **lower-of-cost-or-market**, the remaining bicycle is now reported by Rider Inc. at its purchase value. A loss of $50 reflects the reduction in the reported inventory account from $260 to $210.

Sales value. Inventory also has a sales value that can, frequently, be independent of replacement cost. The sales value of an item can fall for any number of reasons. For example, technological innovation will almost automatically reduce the amount that can be charged for earlier models. This phenomenon can be seen whenever a new digital camera or cell phone is introduced to the market. Older items still in stock often must be discounted significantly to attract buyers. Similarly, changes in fashions and fads can hurt the sales value of certain types of inventory. Swim suits usually are offered at reduced prices in August and September as the summer season draws to a close. Damage can also impact an owner's ability to recoup the cost of inventory. Advertised sales tempt buyers to stores by offering scratched and dented products such as microwaves and refrigerators at especially low prices.

For accounting purposes, the sales value of inventory is normally defined as its estimated net realizable value. As discussed in the previous chapter, this figure is the amount of cash expected to be derived from an asset. For inventory, net realizable value is the anticipated sales price less any cost required so that the sale will occur. For example, the net realizable value of an older model digital camera might be the expected amount a customer will pay after money is spent to advertise the product. The net realizable value for a scratched refrigerator is likely to be the anticipated price of the item less the cost of any repairs that must be made prior to the sale.

As with purchase value, if the sales value of an inventory item falls below its historical cost, the lower figure is reported along with a loss to mirror the impact of the asset reduction.

Question: Inventory records are maintained at the historical cost of each item. For reporting purposes, this figure is utilized unless the market value is lower. A reduction in value can result because of a drop in replacement cost (a purchase value) or in net realizable value (a sales value). ***How is the comparison of cost and market value actually made when inventory is reported?***

Assume that Rider Inc. is currently preparing financial statements and holds two bicycles in ending inventory. Model XY-7 cost the company $260 while Model AB-9 cost $380. As mentioned, Model XY-7 now has a replacement cost of only $210. Because of market conditions, the exact sales value is uncertain. The other unit, Model AB-9, has been damaged and can only be sold for $400 after $50 is spent for necessary repairs. What should Rider report for its asset inventory?

Answer: As a preliminary step in preparing financial statements, a comparison of the cost and market value of the inventory is made. For Rider, both reported cost amounts here must be reduced and the inventory account shown as $560.[5] However, the market value used for the first item is its purchase value (replacement cost of $210) whereas the market value for the second is the item's sales value of $350 (net realizable value of $400 minus $50). A problem with either value can lead to the reduction of the reported asset causing the recognition of a loss.

FIGURE 8.8 Recognition of a Loss on Impaired Inventory Value

Model	Cost	Impaired Market Value	Lower of Cost or Market Value
XY-7	$260	$210 (replacement cost)	$210
AB-9	380	350 (net realizable value)	350
Totals	$640		$560

Rider Inc. reports its inventory at the conservative $560 amount on its balance sheet with an $80 loss ($640 – $560) appearing in the income statement for this period.

EXERCISE

Link to multiple-choice question for practice purposes: http://www.quia.com/quiz/2092886.html

Talking with an Independent Auditor about International Financial Reporting Standards

Following is a continuation of our interview with Robert A. Vallejo, partner with the accounting firm PricewaterhouseCoopers.

Question: According to U.S. GAAP, in applying lower-of-cost-or-market to inventory, the determination of market value can be either net realizable value or replacement cost depending on whether a sales value or a purchases value is impaired. This process has been used in the United States for decades. How does International Financial Reporting Standards (IFRS) handle this issue? When a company begins to report its financial statements based on IFRS, how will the comparison of cost to market be made for inventory balances?

Rob Vallejo: International Accounting Standards 2, Inventories (IAS 2) states that inventories should be measured at the lower of cost and net realizable value. Net realizable value is defined as the anticipated sales price of the item (in the ordinary course of business) reduced by the estimated costs to complete the item and any estimated costs needed to make the sale. Replacement cost is not taken into consideration. In practice, because replacement cost is not often an issue for U.S. companies, the methodology commonly used for valuing inventory under U.S. GAAP will continue to be utilized to comply with IFRS. Therefore, I do not expect any significant differences in this area of financial reporting (with the exception of some very industry specific circumstances) when the switch to IFRS is made. However, IFRS does allow reversals of previous write-downs if appropriate.

KEY TAKEAWAYS

Inventory is traditionally reported on a company's balance sheet at its historical cost. However, reductions can be made based on applying the conservative lower-of-cost-or-market approach. In some cases, purchase value is in question if the item's replacement cost has dropped since the date of acquisition. For other inventory items, net realizable value (expected sales price less any costs necessary to sale) may become less than cost because of changes in fads or technology or possibly as a result of damage. Consequently, the reported inventory figure should be reduced if either of these market values is below cost.

5. DETERMINING INVENTORY ON HAND

LEARNING OBJECTIVES

At the end of this section, students should be able to meet the following objectives:

1. **Understand the necessity of taking a physical inventory even in a perpetual inventory system.**
2. **Estimate the amount of inventory on hand using historic gross profit percentages and identify the situations when this computation might be necessary.**

Question: In a periodic inventory system, a physical count is always taken at or very near the end of the fiscal year. This procedure is essential. There is no alternative method for determining the final inventory figure and, hence, the cost of goods sold for the period. ***When a company uses a perpetual system, is a count of the goods on hand still needed since both the current inventory balance and cost of goods sold are maintained and available in the accounting records?***

Answer: A physical inventory is necessary even if a company has invested the effort and cost to install a perpetual system. Goods can be lost, broken, or stolen. Errors can occur in the record keeping. Thus, a count is taken on a regular basis simply to ensure that the subsidiary and general ledger balances are kept in alignment with the actual items held. Unless differences become material, this physical inventory can take place at a convenient time rather than at the end of the year. For example, assume that a company sells snow ski apparel. If a perpetual system is in use, the merchandise could be inspected and counted by employees in May when quantities are low and damaged goods easier to spot.

An adjustment is necessary when the count does not agree with the perpetual inventory balance. To illustrate, assume that company records indicate that sixty-five ski jackets are currently in stock costing $70 apiece. The physical inventory finds that only sixty-three items are actually on hand. The inventory account must be reduced (credited) by $140 to mirror the shortfall (two missing units at $70 each).

The other half of the adjusting entry depends on the perceived cause of the shortage. For example, officials might have reason to believe that errors took place in the accounting process during the period. When merchandise is bought and sold, recording miscues do occur. Possibly two ski jackets were sold on a busy afternoon. The clerk got distracted and the cost of this merchandise was never reclassified to expense. This type of mistake means that the cost of goods sold figure is too low. The balance reported for these two jackets needs to be moved to the expense account to rectify the mistake.

FIGURE 8.9 Adjusting Entry—To Bring Perpetual Inventory Records in Line with Physical Count, a Recording Error Is Assumed

Cost of Goods Sold	140		(increase an expense—debit)
Inventory (to reduce inventory for two jackets costing $70 each)		140	(decrease an asset—credit)

Conversely, if differences between actual and recorded inventory amounts occur because of damage, loss, or theft, the reported balance for cost of goods sold should not bear the cost of these items. They were not sold. Instead, a loss occurred.

If the assumption is made here that the two missing jackets were not sold but have been lost or stolen, the following alternative adjustment is appropriate.

FIGURE 8.10 Adjusting Entry—To Bring Perpetual Inventory Records in Line with Physical Count, Theft or Loss Is Assumed

Loss on Inventory Shortage	140		(increase an expense—debit)
Inventory (to reduce inventory for two jackets costing $70 each)		140	(decrease an asset—credit)

In practice, when an inventory count is made and the results differ from the amount of recorded merchandise, the exact cause is often impossible to identify. Whether a loss is reported or a change is made in reporting cost of goods sold, the impact on net income is the same. The construction of the adjustment is often at the discretion of company officials. Normally, consistent application from year to year is the major objective.

Question: A periodic system is cheap and easy to operate. It does, though, present some practical problems. Assume that a company experiences a fire, flood, or other disaster and is attempting to gather evidence—for insurance or tax purposes—as to the amount of merchandise that was destroyed. How does the company support its claim? Or, assume a company wants to produce interim financial statements for a single month or quarter (rather than a full year) without going to the cost and trouble of taking a complete physical inventory count. ***If the information is needed, how can a reasonable approximation of the inventory on hand be derived when a periodic system is in use?***

Answer: One entire branch of accounting—known as "**forensic accounting**"—specializes in investigations where information is limited or not available (or has even been purposely altered to be misleading). For example, assume that a hurricane floods a retail clothing store in Charleston, South Carolina. Only a portion of the merchandise costing $80,000 is salvaged.[6] In trying to determine the resulting loss, the amount of inventory in the building prior to the storm needs to be calculated. A forensic accountant might be hired, by either the owner of the store or the insurance company involved, to produce a reasonable estimate of the merchandise on hand at the time. Obviously, if the company had used a perpetual rather than a periodic system, the need to hire the services of an accounting expert would be less likely unless fraud was suspected.

forensic accounting

A branch of accounting specializing in investigating and reporting on situations where important information is limited or unavailable.

In some cases, arriving at a probable inventory balance is not extremely complicated even if periodic inventory procedures are utilized. When historical trends can be determined with assurance, a valid estimation of the goods on hand is possible at any point in time without the benefit of perpetual records. For the Charleston store, assume that the general ledger is located after the disaster and the T-account balances provide the following information resulting from the periodic system in use:

FIGURE 8.11 Estimating Inventory—General Ledger Balances

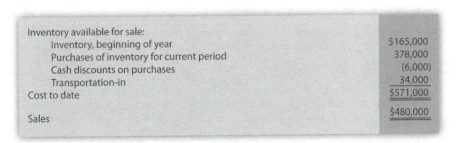

Inventory available for sale:	
Inventory, beginning of year	$165,000
Purchases of inventory for current period	378,000
Cash discounts on purchases	(6,000)
Transportation-in	34,000
Cost to date	$571,000
Sales	$480,000

If no sales had taken place, the inventory on hand would have cost $571,000 as shown by the ledger accounts. Sales did occur prior to the hurricane and a significant amount of merchandise was removed by the customers. However, the $480,000 balance shown in the sales T-account does not reflect the cost of the inventory items that were surrendered. It is a retail amount, the summation of the price charged for all the merchandise sold during the year to date.

To determine the cost of inventory held at the time of the catastrophe, cost of goods sold for the current year has to be approximated and then removed from the $571,000 total. Many companies use a fairly standard mark-up percentage in setting retail prices. By looking at previously reported balances, the accountant is often able to make a reasonable determination of that mark-up. For example, assume that in the preceding year, this company reported sales revenue of $500,000 along with cost of goods sold of $300,000 and, hence, gross profit of $200,000. In this earlier period, cost of goods sold was 60 percent of sales revenue ($300,000/$500,000) while gross profit was 40 percent ($200,000/$500,000).

If available evidence does not indicate any significant changes this year in the method used to set retail prices, the accountant can assume that cost of goods sold during the period prior to the storm was about $288,000 ($480,000 sales revenue × 60 percent). Because the cost of all available inventory was $571,000, approximately $283,000 of those goods were still in stock when the hurricane hit Charleston ($571,000 total cost less $288,000 estimated cost of goods sold). This residual figure can then serve as the basis for the insurance or tax claim. Only goods costing $80,000 were saved. Thus, the estimated loss was $203,000 ($283,000 less $80,000).

The biggest obstacle in this type calculation is the validity of the cost and mark-up percentages. Many companies offer an eclectic variety of products, each with its own specific gross profit. Other companies change their mark-ups frequently based on market conditions. In such cases, determining a reliable percentage can be difficult and the accuracy of the resulting estimation is more questionable.

EXERCISE

Link to multiple-choice question for practice purposes: http://www.quia.com/quiz/2092901.html

KEY TAKEAWAYS

Although perpetual inventory systems are designed to maintain current account balances, a physical count is still required periodically to update the records for errors, theft, and the like. In addition, knowledge of the amount of inventory on hand is sometimes needed in a periodic system even if complete records are not available. If a loss has occurred due to some type of disaster or if interim financial statements are to be prepared, the inventory balance can be estimated. This computation is based on determining the gross profit percentage using historical data. Cost of goods sold for the period is estimated and then removed from the total inventory available for sale.

Talking with a Real Investing Pro—Continued

Following is a continuation of our interview with Kevin G. Burns.

Question: Gross profit is the sales revenue generated by a company less cost of goods sold. In other words, it is the mark-up that a company is able to earn from the sale of its inventory. Goods are bought for a price and then sold at a higher value. In analyzing companies, gross profit is often stated as a percentage. A company's gross profit, for example, might be 37 percent of its sales. When you study a company, how much attention do you pay to changes in gross profit from year to year or differences that exist between one company and another?

Kevin Burns: Actually year to year differences only interest me if there is a significant change. If a company's gross profit margin increases significantly from one year to the next, my radar is activated. I want to know exactly why that happened. Is it temporary or something significant? If gross profit is that volatile, it could also easily go the other direction in the future. I prefer steady as she goes. Predictability and transparency are very important to me. As for gross profit margins between one company and another, the only way that is significant to me is if they are in the same industry and then only if there are big differences. Most companies in mature industries have similar margins and large differences, again, would make me very suspicious.

Video Clip

Joe talks about the five most important points in Chapter 8.

View the video online at: http://blip.tv/play/sDyBvvMSAA

6. END-OF-CHAPTER EXERCISES

QUESTIONS

1. Define "cost" as it relates to determining the value of inventory.
2. What is a cash discount?
3. Explain what the term "3/10 n/30" means.
4. How do cash discounts impact the reported value of inventory?
5. What is a perpetual inventory system?
6. What is a periodic inventory system?
7. Name one advantage of a perpetual inventory system over a periodic inventory system.
8. Name one advantage of a periodic inventory system over a perpetual inventory system.
9. Explain the concept of "free on board."
10. When does ownership transfer if documents specify "FOB shipping point'?
11. When does ownership transfer if documents specify "FOB destination"?
12. What two journal entries are made when inventory is sold under a perpetual system?
13. Give the formula for computing cost of goods sold under a periodic system.
14. Explain the concept of "lower of cost or market."
15. Why would a company that uses a perpetual inventory system still perform a physical inventory count?

TRUE OR FALSE

1. ____ If the market value of a company's inventory increases, the company should record a gain.
2. ____ A company should include costs of transporting an item to its store when determining the cost of the item.
3. ____ A company that uses a perpetual inventory system should still perform a physical inventory count.
4. ____ In a perpetual system, but not a periodic system, cost of goods sold is determined and recorded at the time of sale.
5. ____ If inventory is shipped FOB shipping point, the buyer takes title as soon as the inventory leaves the seller's warehouse.
6. ____ Companies infrequently take advantage of purchase discounts because they amount to so little savings.
7. ____ Periodic inventory systems are, in general, less expensive to operate than perpetual systems.
8. ____ In a periodic system, cost of goods sold is the difference between what a company has available for sale (beginning inventory and purchases) and what they didn't sell (ending inventory).
9. ____ Companies only follow the "lower of cost or market" guideline if they use a periodic inventory system.
10. ____ The "purchases" account is not used in a perpetual inventory system.

MULTIPLE CHOICE

1. On February 13, North Carolina Furniture purchases three sofas from a manufacturer for $300 each. The terms of the sale are 2/10 n/45. North Carolina Furniture pays the invoice on February 21. How much did they pay?
    a. $300
    b. $900
    c. $882
    d. $810
2. Crayson Inc. started the year with $490,000 in beginning inventory. During the year, Crayson purchased an additional $1,060,000 in inventory. At the end of the year, Crayson employees performed a physical count and determined that ending inventory amounted to $450,000. What was Crayson's cost of goods sold for the year?
    a. $1,100,000
    b. $1,020,000
    c. $120,000
    d. $1,060,000
3. Raceway Corporation manufactures miniature cars and racetracks for collectors and enthusiasts. Raceway placed an order for supplies from Delta Inc. on December 1. The sales staff at Delta informed Raceway that the supplies would not be available to ship out until December 22 and Raceway accepted this arrangement. The supplies actually shipped, FOB shipping point, on December 26 and arrived at Raceway's receiving dock on January 2. On which date should Raceway include the supplies in its inventory?
    a. December 1
    b. December 22
    c. December 26
    d. January 2
4. Which of the following concerning the "lower of cost or market" rule is ***not*** true?
    a. If the replacement cost of an inventory item falls below its historical cost, the value of the item should be written down.
    b. If the market value of an item exceeds its historical cost, it should be written up and a gain should be recorded.
    c. It is possible for an item's net realizable value to fall below its historical cost.
    d. Lower of cost or market is an example of the conservatism principle.
5. Romulus Company sells maps. At the end of the year, Romulus's inventory account indicated that it had 2,900 maps of Italy on hand that had originally cost $30 each. An inventory count showed that only 2,875 were actually in ending inventory. What journal entry should Romulus make to if management believes the discrepancy is due to errors in the accounting process?

Cost of Goods Sold	750	
Loss on Inventory Shortage		750

a.

Loss on Inventory Shortage	30	
Inventory		30

b.

c.

Loss on Inventory Shortage	750	
Inventory		750

d.

Cost of Goods Sold	750	
Inventory		750

6. Real South Products has $400,000 worth of inventory on hand on January 1. Between January and March 13, Real South purchased an additional $190,000 in inventory and sales of $530,000 had been made. On March 13, Real South's warehouse flooded and all but $15,000 worth of inventory was ruined. Real South has an average gross profit percentage of 25 percent. What would be the approximate value of the inventory destroyed in the flood?
    a. $240,000
    b. $275,000
    c. $207,500
    d. $177,500

PROBLEMS

1. ConnecTech bought 400 computers in December 20X2 for $300 each. It paid $260 to have them delivered to its store. In January 20X3, ConnecTech sold 220 of the computers for $550 each. ConnecTech uses a perpetual inventory system.
    a. Prepare the journal entry(ies) to record ConnecTech's purchase of the computers.
    b. Determine the balance in ConnecTech's ending inventory on December 31, 20X2.
    c. Prepare the journal entry(ies) to record the sale of the computers.
    d. Determine the balance in ConnecTech's ending inventory on January 31, 20X3.
2. Montez Muffins and More is a bakery located in New York. Montez purchases a great deal of flour in bulk from a wholesaler. The wholesaler offers purchase discounts for fast payment. Montez purchased 600 pounds of flour for $100 on May 1, under terms 2/10 n/30. Determine the amount Montez should pay under the following scenarios:
    a. Montez pays the full balance on May 25.
    b. Montez pays the full balance on May 10.
    c. Montez pays half the balance on May 10 and half on May 25.
3. Racers ATVs sells many makes and models of all terrain vehicles. Racers uses a periodic inventory system. On January 1, Racers had a beginning inventory of AXVs costing $28,600. On January 14, Racers received a shipment of Model AXVs with a purchase price of $14,700 and transportation costs of $400. On May 19, Racers received a second shipment of AXVs with a purchase price of $16,900 and transportation costs of $450. On November 1, Racers received its before Christmas shipment of AXVs with a purchase price of $27,800 and transportation costs of $750.
    a. Make the necessary journal entries for January 14, May 19, and November 1 to show the purchase of the inventory.
    b. Assume that a physical inventory count on December 31 showed an ending inventory of AXVs of $25,800. Determine cost of goods sold for the AXV model for the year.
    c. If sales of AXVs were $96,700, what profit did Racers make on this model?
    d. Racers is considering replacing its periodic inventory system with a perpetual one. Write a memo to Racers management giving the pros and cons of this switch.
4. Magic Carpets Inc. sells a full line of area rugs, from top quality to bargain basement. Economic conditions have hit the textile industry, and Magic Carpets accountant is concerned that its rug inventory may not worth the amount Magic paid for it. Information about three lines of rugs is found below:

	Cost	Replacement Cost	Sales Price	Cost to Sell	Number in Inventory
High Flyers	$230	$240	$350	$40	80
Midflight	150	120	220	25	125
Under the Radar	100	100	110	20	165

    a. Determine market value for each type of rug.
    b. Determine lower of cost or market for each type of rug.
    c. Determine if Magic Carpets has suffered a loss of value on its inventory, and if so, what the amount of loss is.
5. Costello Corporation uses a perpetual inventory system. At the end of the year, the inventory balance reported by its system is $45,270. Costello performs an inventory count and determines that the actual ending inventory is $39,780.
    a. Discuss why a company that uses a perpetual inventory system would perform a physical inventory count.
    b. Why might the ending balance in inventory differ between the perpetual inventory system and physical inventory count?
    c. Assume that Costello determines that the difference is due to a part of its inventory being damaged when a warehouse worker backed into a shelf with his forklift. What journal entry should Costello make?
    d. Assume that Costello believes the difference is due to errors made by its accounting staff. The staff failed to transfer inventory to cost of goods sold when sales were made. Record the journal entry Costello should make in this case.

6. Fabulous Fay's is a boutique clothing store in San Diego. Fay's uses a perpetual inventory system. In March, Fay's purchased a type of swimwear designed to be slimming to the wearer. It purchased twenty suits of varying sizes for $40 each and priced them at $120 each. They sold out almost immediately, so Fay purchased forty more suits in April for $40 each and sold thirty-eight of them for $130 each. Again in July, Fay made one more purchase of twenty suits at $40 each and sold fifteen of them for $130 each. Fay decided not to put the rest of her inventory on sale at the end of the summer, but to hold onto it until cruise season started the following winter. She believed she could sell the rest then without having to mark them down.
    a. Make the journal entries for the purchases Fay made.
    b. Make the journal entries for the sales Fay made.
    c. Determine the balance in ending inventory on December 31.
    d. Fay performed a physical count on December 31 and determined that three of the swimsuits had been severely damaged due to a leaky pipe. Make the journal entry to show the loss of this inventory.
7. Nakatobi Company has a warehouse in Fargo, ND. The company utilizes a periodic inventory system. At the beginning of the year, the warehouse contained $369,000 worth of inventory. During the first quarter, Nakatobi purchased another $218,000 worth of inventory and made sales of $450,000. On April 1, a flood hit Fargo and destroyed half of the inventory housed in the warehouse. Nakatobi needs to estimate the value of the inventory for insurance purposes. The only additional information Nakatobi has is that typically its cost of goods sold is 55 percent of sales.
    a. Determine the value of the inventory on March 31, before the flood hit.
    b. Determine Nakatobi's loss on April 1.

COMPREHENSIVE PROBLEM

This problem will carry through several chapters, building in difficulty. It allows students to continuously practice skills and knowledge learned in previous chapters.

In Chapter 7, you prepared Webworks statements for July. They are included here as a starting point for August.

Here are Webworks financial statements as of July 31.

Webworks
Income Statement
As of July 31

Revenue	$2,300
Expenses	(1,295)
Earning before Tax	1,005
Tax Expense	(300)
Net Income	$705

Webworks
Stmt. Of Retained Earnings
As of July 31

Retained Earnings, July 1	$470
Net Income	705
Retained Earnings, July 31	$1,175

Webworks
Balance Sheet
July 31

Assets		**Liabilities**	
Current		**Current**	
Cash	$5,720	Accounts Payable	$240
Accounts Receivable	1,050	Salaries Payable	200
Less Allowance for Doubtful Accounts	(105)	Unearned Revenue	500
Net Accounts Receivable	945	Total Current Liabilities	$940
Supplies Inventory	50		
Prepaid Rent	400		
Total Current Assets	$7,115		
Noncurrent		**Noncurrent**	
Equipment	$7,000	Notes Payable	$10,000
		Owners' Equity	
		Capital Stock	$2,000
		Retained Earnings	1,175
		Total Owners' Equity	$3,175
Total Assets	$14,115	Total Liabilities & Owners' Equity	$14,115

The following events occur during August:

a. Webworks decides to begin selling a limited selection of inventory items related to its business. During August, Webworks purchases specialty keyboards for $4,900 on account and flash drives for $3,200 on account with the hopes of selling them to its Web site customers or others who might be interested. Due to the limited amount of inventory, Webworks will use a periodic system. Record these purchases.

b. Webworks purchases supplies worth $100 on account.

c. Webworks starts and completes six more sites and bills clients for $2,700.

d. Recall that in July, Webworks received $500 in advance to design two Web sites. Webworks completes these sites during August.

e. Webworks collects $2,400 in accounts receivable.

f. Webworks pays Nancy $600 for her work during the first three weeks of August.

g. In June, Webworks designed a site for Pauline Smith and billed her. Unfortunately, before she could finish paying the bill, Ms. Smith's business folded. It is unlikely Webworks will collect anything. Record the entry to write off the $100 remaining receivable from Ms. Smith.

h. Webworks sells keyboards for $4,500 and flash drives for $3,000 cash.

i. Webworks pays off its salaries payable from July.

j. Webworks pays off $6,000 of its accounts payable.

k. Webworks receives $100 in advance to work on a Web site for a local dentist. Work will not begin on the site until September.

l. Webworks pays Leon salary of $2,000.

m. Webworks pays taxes of $475 in cash.

Required:

A. Prepare journal entries for the above events.

B. Post the journal entries to T-accounts.

C. Prepare an unadjusted trial balance for Webworks for August.

D. Prepare adjusting entries for the following and post them to your T-accounts.

n. Webworks owes Nancy $250 for her work during the last week of August.

o. Leon's parents let him know that Webworks owes $250 toward the electricity bill. Webworks will pay them in September.

p. Webworks determines that it has $60 worth of supplies remaining at the end of August.

q. Prepaid rent should be adjusted for August's portion.

r. Webworks is continuing to accrue bad debts at 10 percent of accounts receivable.

s. Webworks performs a count of ending inventory and determines that $1,900 in keyboards and $1,100 in flash drives remain. Record cost of goods sold.

E. Prepare an adjusted trial balance.

F. Prepare financial statements for August.

ENDNOTES

1. If the net method is applied by Rider Inc. the initial purchase entry is recorded as $245. Later, if the discount is not taken, the additional cost of $5 is recorded as a loss or an expense rather than as a capitalized cost of the inventory because it is not normal and necessary to pay the extra amount.
2. In this illustration, each bicycle in the company's inventory has the same cost: $260. At this introductory stage, utilizing a single cost for all items eliminates a significant theoretical problem concerning the flow of costs, one that will be discussed in detail in the subsequent chapter.
3. The Purchases figure here could have also been shown by displaying the various cost components such as the invoice price, purchases discount, transportation-in, and assembly. That breakdown is important for internal decision making and control but probably of less interest to external parties.
4. As mentioned previously, if separate T-account balances are established for cost components such as transportation-in, assembly costs, and the like, they must be included in this entry rather than just a single Purchases figure.
5. In applying the lower-of-cost-or-market to inventory, the comparison can be made on an item-by-item basis. For example, XY-7 can be valued based on cost and market value and then, separately, a similar determination can be made for AB-9. A company can also group its inventory (all bicycles, for example, might comprise one group that is separate from all motorcycles) and report the lower amount determined for each of these groups. A third possibility is to sum the cost of all inventory and make a single comparison of that figure to the total of all market values. U.S. GAAP does not specify a mechanical approach to use in applying lower of cost or market value.
6. For a full description of forensic accounting, see Frank J. Grippo and J. W. (Ted) Ibex, "Introduction to forensic accounting," *The National Public Accountant*, June 2003.

CHAPTER 9

Why Does a Company Need a Cost Flow Assumption in Reporting Inventory?

Video Clip

Joe introduces Chapter 9 and speaks about the course in general.

View the video online at: http://blip.tv/play/sDyBv7UNAA

1. THE NECESSITY OF ADOPTING A COST FLOW ASSUMPTION

LEARNING OBJECTIVES

At the end of this section, students should be able to meet the following objectives:

1. **Understand the reason that accounting rules are often standardized so that all companies report many events in the same manner.**
2. **Know that the selection of a particular cost flow assumption is necessary when inventory is sold.**
3. **Apply the following cost flow assumptions to determine reported balances for ending inventory and cost of goods sold: specific identification, FIFO, LIFO, and averaging.**

Question: In the coverage of financial accounting to this point, general standardization has been evident. Most transactions are recorded in an identical fashion by all companies. This defined structure helps to ensure understanding. It also enhances the ability of decision makers to compare results from one year to the next or from one company to another. For example, inventory—except in unusual circumstances—is always reported at historical cost unless its value is lower. Experienced decision makers should be well aware of that criterion when they are reviewing the inventory figures reported by a company.

However, an examination of the notes to financial statements for some well-known businesses shows an interesting inconsistency in the reporting of inventory (emphasis added).

Mitsui & Co. (U.S.A.) Inc.—as of March 31, 2009: "Inventories, consisting mainly of commodities and materials for resale, are stated at the lower of cost, principally on the ***specific-identification basis****, or market."*

Johnson & Johnson and Subsidiaries—as of December 28, 2008: "Inventories are stated at the lower of cost or market determined by the ***first-in, first-out method****."*

Safeway Inc. and Subsidiaries—as of December 31, 2008: "Merchandise inventory of $1,740 million at year-end 2008 and $1,866 million at year-end 2007 is valued at the lower of cost on a ***last-in, first-out ('LIFO') basis*** *or market value."*

Bristol-Myers Squibb—as of December 31, 2008: "Inventories are generally stated at ***average cost****, not in excess of market."*

"Specific-identification basis," "first-in, first-out," "last-in, first-out," "average cost" What information do these terms provide? Why are all of these companies using different methods? ***In the financial reporting of inventory, what is the significance of disclosing that a company applies "first-in, first-out," "last-in, first-out," or the like?***

Answer: In the previous chapter, the cost of all inventory items was kept constant over time. Although that helped simplify the initial presentation of relevant accounting issues, such stability is hardly a realistic assumption. For example, the retail price of gasoline has moved up and down like a yo-yo in recent years. The cost of some commodities such as bread and soft drinks has increased gradually for many decades. In other industries, prices actually tend to fall over time. New technology products often start with a high price that drops as the manufacturing process ramps up and becomes more efficient. Several years ago, personal computers cost tens of thousands of dollars and now sell for hundreds.

A key event in accounting for inventory is the transfer of cost from the inventory T-account to cost of goods sold as the result of a sale. The inventory balance is reduced and the related expense is increased. For large organizations, such transactions can take place thousands of times each day. If each item has an identical cost, no problem exists. This standard amount is always reclassified into expense to reflect the sale.

However, if inventory items are acquired at different costs, which cost is moved from asset to expense? At that point, a cost flow assumption must be selected by company officials to guide reporting. That choice can have a significant impact on both the income statement and the balance sheet. It is literally impossible to analyze the reported net income and inventory balance of a company such as ExxonMobil without knowing the cost flow assumption that has been applied.

Question: An example is probably the easiest approach by which to demonstrate cost flow assumptions. Assume a men's retail clothing store holds $120 in cash. On October 26, Year One, one blue dress shirt is bought for $50 in cash for resell purposes. Later, near the end of the year, this style of shirt becomes especially popular. On December 29, Year One, the store's manager buys a second shirt exactly like the first but this time at a cost of $70. Cash on hand has been depleted completely ($120 less $50 and $70) but the company now holds two shirts in its inventory.

Then, on December 31, Year One, a customer buys one of these two shirts by paying cash of $110. Regardless of the cost flow assumption, the company retains one blue dress shirt in inventory at the end of the year and cash of $110. It also reports sales revenue of $110. Those facts are not in doubt.

From an accounting perspective, two questions are left to be resolved (1) what is the cost of goods sold reported for the one shirt that was sold and (2) what is the cost remaining in inventory for the one item still on hand?

In simpler terms, should the $50 or $70 be reclassified to cost of goods sold; should the $50 or $70 remain in ending inventory? For financial accounting, the importance of the answers to those questions cannot be overemphasized. ***What are the various cost flow assumptions and how are they applied to inventory?***

specific identification

Inventory cost flow method in which company physically identifies both its remaining inventory and the inventory that was sold to customers.

Answer: *SPECIFIC IDENTIFICATION.* In a literal sense, **specific identification** is not a cost flow assumption. Companies that use this approach are not making an assumption because they know which item was sold. By some technique, they are able to identify the inventory conveyed to the customer and reclassify its cost to expense.

For some types of inventory, such as automobiles held by a car dealer, specific identification is relatively easy to apply. Each vehicle tends to be somewhat unique and can be tracked through identification numbers. Unfortunately, for many other types of inventory, no practical method exists for determining the physical flow of merchandise.

Thus, if the men's retail store maintains a system where the individual shirts are marked in some way, it will be possible to know whether the $50 shirt or the $70 shirt was actually conveyed to the customer. That cost can be moved from asset to expense.

However, for identical items like shirts, cans of tuna fish, bags of coffee beans, hammers, packs of notebook paper and the like, the idea of maintaining such precise records is ludicrous. What informational benefit could be gained by knowing whether the first blue shirt was sold or the second? In most cases, the cost of creating such a meticulous record-keeping system far outweighs any potential advantages.

FIRST-IN, FIRST-OUT (FIFO). The **FIFO** cost flow assumption is based on the premise that selling the oldest item first is most likely to mirror reality. Stores do not want inventory to grow unnecessarily old and lose freshness. The oldest items are often placed on top in hopes that they will sell first before becoming stale or damaged. Therefore, although the identity of the actual item sold is rarely known, the assumption is made in applying FIFO that the first (or oldest) cost is always moved from inventory to cost of goods sold.

FIFO (first in first out)

Inventory cost flow assumption based on the oldest costs being transferred first from inventory to cost of goods sold so that the most recent costs remain in ending inventory.

Note that it is not the oldest item that is necessarily sold but rather the oldest cost that is reclassified to cost of goods sold. No attempt is made to determine which shirt was purchased by the customer. Here, because the first shirt cost $50, the following entry is made to record the expense and reduce the inventory.

FIGURE 9.1 Journal Entry—Reclassification of the Cost of One Piece of Inventory Using FIFO

Cost of Goods Sold	50	
Inventory		50

For this retail store, the following financial information is reported if FIFO is applied. Two shirts were bought for ($50 and $70) and one shirt was sold for $110.

FIFO	
Cost of Goods Sold (One Unit—the First One)	$50
Gross Profit ($110 less $50)	$60
Ending Inventory (One Unit—the Last One)	$70

In a period of rising prices, the earliest (cheapest) cost moves to cost of goods sold and the latest (more expensive) cost is retained in ending inventory. For this reason, in inflationary times, FIFO is associated with a higher reported net income as well as a higher reported inventory total on the company's balance sheet. Not surprisingly, these characteristics help make it a popular choice.

EXERCISE

Link to multiple-choice question for practice purposes: http://www.quia.com/quiz/2092903.html

Last-in, first-out (LIFO). **LIFO** is the opposite of FIFO: the most recent costs are moved to expense as sales are made.

LIFO (last in first out)

Inventory cost flow assumption based on the most recent costs being transferred first from inventory to cost of goods sold so that the oldest costs remain in ending inventory.

Theoretically, the LIFO assumption is often justified as more in line with the matching principle. Shirt One was bought on October 26 whereas Shirt Two was not acquired until December 29. Revenue was earned on December 31. Proponents of LIFO argue that matching the December 29 cost with the December 31 revenue is more appropriate than using a cost incurred months earlier. According to this reasoning, income is more properly determined with LIFO because a relatively current cost is shown as cost of goods sold rather than a figure that is out-of-date. The difference is especially apparent in periods of high inflation. "By matching current costs against current sales, LIFO produces a truer picture of income; that is, the quality of income produced by the use of LIFO is higher because it more nearly approximates disposable income."[1] Note 1 to the 2008 financial statements for ConocoPhillips reiterates that point: "LIFO is used to better match current inventory costs with current revenues."

The last cost incurred in buying two blue shirts was $70 so that amount is reclassified to expense at the time of the first sale.

FIGURE 9.2 Journal Entry—Reclassification of the Cost of One Piece of Inventory Using LIFO

Cost of Goods Sold	70	
Inventory		70

Although the physical results of these transaction are the same (one unit was sold, one unit was retained, and the company holds $110 in cash), the financial picture painted using the LIFO cost flow assumption is quite different than in the earlier FIFO example.

LIFO	
Cost of Goods Sold (One Unit—the Last One)	$70
Gross Profit ($110 Less $70)	$40
Ending Inventory (One Unit—the First One)	$50

Characteristics commonly associated with LIFO can be seen in this example. When prices rise, LIFO companies report lower net income (the most recent and, thus, the most costly purchases are moved to expense) and a lower inventory account on the balance sheet (because the earlier and cheaper costs remain in the inventory T-account). As will be discussed in a subsequent section, LIFO is popular in the United States because it helps to reduce the amount companies pay in income taxes.

EXERCISE

Link to multiple-choice question for practice purposes: http://www.quia.com/quiz/2092888.html

averaging

Inventory cost flow assumption based on the average cost being transferred from inventory to cost of goods sold so that the same average cost remains in ending inventory.

Averaging. Because the identity of the items conveyed to buyers is unknown, this final cost flow assumption holds that using an average of all costs is the most logical solution. Why choose any individual cost if no evidence exists of its validity? The first item received might have been sold or the last. Selecting either is an arbitrary decision. If items with varying costs are held, using an average provides a very appealing logic. In the shirt example, the two units cost a total of $120 ($50 plus $70) so the average is $60 ($120/2 units).

FIGURE 9.3 Journal Entry—Reclassification of the Cost of One Piece of Inventory Using Averaging

Cost of Goods Sold	60	
Inventory		60

Although no shirt did cost $60, this average serves as the basis for both cost of goods sold as well as the cost of the item still on hand. All costs are included in arriving at each reported figure.

Averaging	
Cost of Goods Sold (One Unit—the Average One)	$60
Gross Profit ($110 less $60)	$50
Ending Inventory (One Unit—the Average One)	$60

Averaging has many supporters. However, it can be a more complicated system to implement especially if costs change frequently. In addition, it does not offer the benefits that make FIFO (higher reported income) and LIFO (lower taxes in the United States) so appealing. Company officials often arrive at such practical decisions based on an evaluation of advantages and disadvantages and not on theoretical merit.

EXERCISE

Link to multiple-choice question for practice purposes: http://www.quia.com/quiz/2092923.html

KEY TAKEAWAYS

U.S. GAAP tends to apply standard reporting rules for many transactions to make financial statements more usable by decision makers. The application of an inventory cost flow assumption is one area where a significant variation is present. A company can choose to use specific identification, first-in, first-out (FIFO), last-in, first-out (LIFO), or averaging. Each of these assumptions determines the cost moved from inventory to cost of goods sold to reflect the sale of merchandise in a different manner. The reported inventory balance as well as the expense on the income statement (and, hence, net income) are dependent on the cost flow assumption that is selected.

2. THE SELECTION OF A COST FLOW ASSUMPTION FOR REPORTING PURPOSES

LEARNING OBJECTIVES

At the end of this section, students should be able to meet the following objectives:

1. **Appreciate that reported inventory and cost of goods sold numbers are not intended to be right or wrong but rather must conform to U.S. GAAP, which includes several different allowable cost flow assumptions.**
2. **Recognize that three cost flow assumptions (FIFO, LIFO, and averaging) are particularly popular in the United States.**
3. **Understand the meaning of the LIFO conformity rule and realize that use of LIFO in the U.S. largely stems from the presence of this tax rule.**
4. **Know that U.S. companies prepare financial statements according to U.S. GAAP and their income tax returns based on the Internal Revenue Code so that significant differences often exist.**

Question: FIFO, LIFO, and averaging can present radically different portraits of identical events. Is the gross profit for this men's clothing store really $60 (FIFO), $40 (LIFO), or $50 (averaging) in connection with the sale of one blue shirt? Analyzing the numbers presented by most companies can be difficult if not impossible without understanding the implications of the assumption applied. ***Which of the cost flow assumptions is viewed as most appropriate in producing fairly presented financial statements?***

Answer: Because specific identification reclassifies the cost of the actual unit that was sold, finding theoretical fault with that approach is difficult. Unfortunately, specific identification is nearly impossible to apply unless easily distinguishable differences exist between similar inventory items. That leaves FIFO, LIFO, and averaging. Arguments over both their merits and problems have raged for decades. Ultimately, the numbers in financial statements must be presented fairly based on the cost flow assumption that is applied.

In Chapter 6, an important distinction was made. The report of the independent auditor never assures decision makers that financial statements are "presented fairly." That is a hopelessly abstract concept like truth and beauty. Instead, the auditor states that the statements are "presented fairly…in conformity with accounting principles generally accepted in the United States of America." That is a substantially more objective standard. Thus, for this men's clothing store, all the following figures are presented fairly but only in conformity with the cost flow assumption used by the reporting company.

FIGURE 9.4 Results of Possible Cost Flows Assumptions Used by Clothing Store

	Gross Profit	Ending Inventory	
Bought Two Units and Sold One	$60	$70	based on application of FIFO
Bought Two Units and Sold One	40	50	based on application of LIFO
Bought Two Units and Sold One	50	60	based on application of averaging

Question: ***Since company officials are allowed to select a cost flow assumption, which of these methods is most typically found in the reporting of companies in the United States?***

Answer: To help interested parties gauge the usage of various accounting principles, a survey is carried out annually of the financial statements of six hundred large companies in this country. The resulting information allows accountants, auditors, and decision makers to weigh the validity of a particular method or presentation. For 2007, that survey found the following frequency of application of cost flow assumptions. Some companies use multiple assumptions: one for a particular part of inventory and a different one for the remainder. Thus, the total here is well above six hundred even though over one hundred of the surveyed companies did not have inventory or mention a cost flow assumption (inventory was probably an immaterial amount). As will be discussed a bit later in this chapter, using multiple assumptions is especially common when a U.S. company has subsidiaries located internationally.

Inventory Cost Flow Assumptions—600 Companies Surveyed[2]	
First-in, First-out (FIFO)	391
Last-in, First-out (LIFO)	213
Averaging	155
Other	24

Interestingly, individual cost flow assumptions tend to be more prevalent in certain industries. In this same survey, 86 percent of the financial statements issued by food and drug stores used LIFO whereas only 10 percent of the companies labeled as "computers, office equipment" had adopted this same approach. That difference could quite possibly be caused by the presence of inflation or deflation. Prices of food and drugs tend to escalate consistently over time while computer prices often fall as technology advances

Question: In periods of inflation, as demonstrated by the previous example, FIFO reports a higher gross profit (and, hence, net income) and a higher inventory balance than does LIFO. Averaging presents figures that normally fall between these two extremes. Such results are widely expected by those readers of financial statements who understand the impact of the various cost flow assumptions.

Any one of these methods is permitted for financial reporting. Why is FIFO not the obvious choice for every organization that anticipates inflation in its inventory costs? Officials must prefer to report figures that make the company look stronger and more profitable. With every rise in prices, FIFO shows a higher income because the earlier (cheaper) costs are transferred to cost of goods sold. Likewise, FIFO reports a higher total inventory on the balance sheet because the later (higher) cost figures are retained in the inventory T-account. The company is no different physically by this decision but FIFO makes it look better. ***Why does any company voluntarily choose LIFO, an approach that reduces reported income and total assets when prices rise?***

LIFO conformity rule

A United States income tax rule that requires LIFO to be used for financial reporting purposes if it is adopted for taxation purposes.

Answer: LIFO might well have faded into oblivion because of its negative impact on key reported figures (during inflationary periods) except for a U.S. income tax requirement known as the **LIFO conformity rule**. Although this tax regulation is not part of U.S. GAAP and looks rather innocuous, it has a huge impact on the way inventory and cost of goods sold are reported to decision makers in this country.

As prices rise, companies prefer to apply LIFO for tax purposes because this assumption reduces reported income and, hence, required cash payments to the government. In the United States, LIFO has come to be universally equated with the saving of tax dollars. When LIFO was first proposed as a tax method in the 1930s, the United States Treasury Department appointed a panel of three experts to consider its validity. The members of this group were split over a final resolution. They eventually agreed to recommend that LIFO be allowed for income tax purposes but only if the company was also willing to use LIFO for financial reporting. At that point, tax rules bled over into U.S. GAAP.

The rationale behind this compromise was that companies were allowed the option but probably would not choose LIFO for their tax returns because of the potential negative effect on figures reported to investors, creditors, and others. During inflationary periods, companies that apply LIFO do not look as financially healthy as those that adopt FIFO. Eventually this recommendation was put into law and the LIFO conformity rule was born. If LIFO is used on a company's income tax return, it must also be applied on the financial statements.

However, as the previous statistics point out, this requirement did not prove to be the deterrent that was anticipated. Actual use of LIFO has become quite popular. For many companies, the savings in income tax dollars more than outweigh the problem of having to report numbers that make the company look a bit weaker. That is a choice that company officials must make.

FIGURE 9.5 Advantages and Disadvantages of FIFO and LIFO

*Assumes a rise in prices over time.

	Advantages*	Disadvantages*
FIFO	Company Looks Financially Stronger	Company Pays More Taxes
LIFO	Company Pays Less Taxes	Company Looks Financially Weaker

EXERCISE

Link to multiple-choice question for practice purposes: http://www.quia.com/quiz/2092924.html

Question: The LIFO conformity rule requires companies that apply LIFO for income tax purposes to also use that same method for their financial reporting to investors, creditors, and other decision makers. ***Is the information submitted to the government for income tax purposes not always the same as that presented to decision makers in a set of financial statements?*** *Reporting different numbers seems unethical.*

Answer: In jokes and in editorials, companies are often derisively accused of "keeping two sets of books." The implication is that one is skewed toward making the company look good (for reporting purposes) whereas the other makes the company look bad (for taxation purposes). However, the existence of separate records is a practical necessity. One set is kept based on applicable tax laws while the other enables the company to prepare its financial statements according to U.S. GAAP. Different rules mean that different numbers result.

In filing income taxes with the United States government, a company must follow the regulations of the Internal Revenue Code.[3] Those laws have several underlying objectives that influence their development.

First, they are designed to raise money for the operation of the federal government. Without adequate funding, the government could not provide hospitals, build roads, maintain a military and the like.

Second, income tax laws enable the government to help regulate the health of the economy. Simply by raising or lowering tax rates, the government can take money out of the economy (and slow public spending) or leave money in the economy (and increase public spending). As an illustration, recently a significant tax break was passed by Congress for first-time home buyers. This move was designed to stimulate the housing market by encouraging additional individuals to consider making a purchase.

Third, income tax laws enable the government to assist certain members of society who are viewed as deserving help. For example, taxpayers who encounter high medical costs or casualty losses are entitled to a tax break. Donations conveyed to an approved charity can also reduce a taxpayer's tax bill. The rules and regulations were designed to provide assistance for specified needs.

In contrast, financial reporting for decision makers must abide by the guidance of U.S. GAAP, which seeks to set rules for the fair presentation of accounting information. That is the reason U.S. GAAP exists. Because the goals are entirely different, there is no particular reason for the resulting financial statements to correspond to the tax figures submitted to the Internal Revenue Service (IRS). Not surprisingly, though, significant overlap is found between tax laws and U.S. GAAP. For example, both normally recognize the cash sale of merchandise as revenue at the time of sale. However, countless differences do exist between the two sets of rules. Depreciation, as just one example, is computed in an entirely different manner for tax purposes than for financial reporting.

Although separately developed, financial statements and income tax returns are tied together at one significant spot: the LIFO conformity rule. If a company chooses to use LIFO for tax purposes, it must do the same for financial reporting. Without that requirement, many companies likely would use FIFO in creating their financial statements and LIFO for their income tax returns. Much of the popularity shown earlier for LIFO is undoubtedly derived from this tax requirement rather than any theoretical merit.

KEY TAKEAWAYS

Information found in financial statements is required to be presented fairly in conformity with U.S. GAAP. Because several inventory cost flow assumptions are allowed, presented numbers can vary significantly from one company to another and still be appropriate. FIFO, LIFO, and averaging are all popular. Understanding and comparing financial statements is quite difficult without knowing the implications of the method selected. LIFO, for example, tends to produce low-income figures in a period of inflation. This assumption probably would not be used extensively except for the LIFO conformity rule that prohibits its use for tax purposes unless also reported on the company's financial statements. Typically, financial reporting and the preparation of income tax returns are unrelated because two sets of rules are used with radically differing objectives. However, the LIFO conformity rule joins these two at this one key spot.

3. PROBLEMS WITH APPLYING LIFO

LEARNING OBJECTIVES

At the end of this section, students should be able to meet the following objectives:

1. **Recognize that theoretical problems with LIFO have led the creators of IFRS rules to prohibit its use.**
2. **Explain that the biggest problem associated with LIFO is an inventory balance that can often show costs from years (or even decades) earlier that are totally irrelevant today.**
3. **Identify the cause of a LIFO liquidation and the reason that it is viewed as a theoretical concern by accountants.**

Question: As a result of the LIFO conformity rule in the tax laws, this cost flow assumption is widely used in the United States. LIFO, though, is not allowed in many other areas of the world. It is not simply unpopular in those locations; its application is strictly forbidden. Thus, international companies are often forced to resort to alternatives in reporting their foreign subsidiaries. For example, a footnote to the 2008 financial statements of American Biltrite Inc. explains that "Inventories are stated at the lower of cost or market. Cost is determined by the last-in, first-out (LIFO) method for most of the Company's domestic inventories. The use of LIFO results in a better matching of costs and revenues. Cost is determined by the first-in, first-out (FIFO) method for the Company's foreign inventories."

Why is LIFO not accepted in most countries outside of the United States?

Answer: Although LIFO can be supported as providing a proper matching of expenses (cost of goods sold) with revenues, a number of serious theoretical problems are created by its application. The most common accusation against LIFO is that it often presents a balance sheet number that is completely out-of-date and useless. When applying this assumption, the latest costs get moved to cost of goods sold so the earlier costs remain in the inventory account—possibly for years and even decades. After some period of time, this asset balance is likely to report a number that has no relevance to today's prices.

For example, in its 2007 financial statements, ExxonMobil reported inventory on its balance sheet at slightly over $11.1 billion based on applying LIFO. In the footnotes to those financial statements, the company disclosed that the current cost to acquire this same inventory was $25.4 billion higher than the number being reported. The asset was shown as $11.1 billion but the price to buy that same inventory was actually $36.5 billion ($11.1 billion plus $25.4). What is the possible informational value of reporting an asset that is being held for sale at an amount more than $25 billion below its current value?[4] That is the essential problem attributed to LIFO.

To illustrate, assume that a gas station has a tank that holds ten thousand gallons of gasoline. On January 1, Year One, the tank is filled at a cost of $1 per gallon. Almost immediately the price of gasoline jumps to $2 per gallon. During the remainder of Year One, the station buys and sells one million gallons of gas. Thus, ten thousand gallons remain in the tank at year's end: ten thousand gallons plus one million gallons bought minus one million gallons sold equals ten thousand gallons. LIFO and FIFO report these results as follows:

LIFO	
Ending Inventory—10,000 gallons at first cost of $1 per gallon	$10,000
Cost of Goods Sold—1,000,000 gallons at last cost of $2 per gallon	2,000,000

FIFO	
Ending Inventory—10,000 gallons at last cost of $2 per gallon	$20,000
Cost of Goods Sold—first 10,000 gallons at $1 per gallon and next 990,000 gallons at $2 per gallon	1,990,000

After just one period, the asset balance shown by LIFO ($1 per gallon) is already beginning to differ from the current cost of $2 per gallon.

If this company continues to buy and sell the same amount annually so that it finishes each year with a full tank of ten thousand gallons (certainly not an unreasonable assumption), LIFO will continue to report this inventory at $1 per gallon for the following decades regardless of current prices. New costs always get transferred to cost of goods sold leaving the first costs ($1 per gallon) in inventory. The tendency to report this asset at a cost expended many years in the past is the single biggest reason that LIFO is viewed as an illegitimate method in many countries. And, that same sentiment would probably exist in the United States except for the LIFO conformity rule.

EXERCISE

Link to multiple-choice question for practice purposes: http://www.quia.com/quiz/2092889.html

Question: LIFO is also criticized because of the possibility of an event known as a **LIFO liquidation**. ***What is a LIFO liquidation and why does it cause a theoretical problem for accountants?***

LIFO liquidation

A decrease in the quantity of inventory on hand when LIFO is applied so that costs incurred in a previous period are mismatched with revenues of the current period; if inflation has occurred, it can cause a significant increase in reported net income.

Answer: As demonstrated above, over time, costs from much earlier years often remain in the inventory T-account when LIFO is applied. A gasoline station that opens in 1972 and ends each year with a full tank of ten thousand gallons of gasoline will report its inventory balance at 1972 costs even in the year 2010 when using LIFO. However, if the quantity of the ending inventory is ever allowed to decrease (accidentally or on purpose), some or all of those 1972 costs move to cost of goods sold. Revenue earned in 2010 is then matched with costs from 1972. That is a LIFO liquidation that can artificially inflate reported earnings if those earlier costs are relatively low.

To illustrate, assume that a station starts 2010 with ten thousand gallons of gasoline. LIFO has been applied over the years so that the inventory is reported at the 1972 cost of $0.42 per gallon. In the current year, gasoline cost $2.55 per gallon to buy and is then sold to the public for $2.70 per gallon creating a normal gross profit of $0.15 per gallon. That is the amount of income that a station is making at this time.

At the beginning of 2010, the station sells its entire stock of ten thousand gallons of gasoline and then ceases to carry this product (perhaps the owners want to focus on groceries or automobile parts). Without any replacement of the inventory, the cost of the gasoline bought in 1972 for $0.42 per gallon is shifted from inventory to cost of goods sold in 2010. Instead of the normal profit margin of $0.15 per gallon or $1,500 for ten thousand gallons, the company reports a gross profit of $2.28 per gallon ($2.70 sales price minus $0.42 cost of goods sold). That amount does not reflect the reality of current market conditions. It allows the company to look overly profitable.

In a LIFO liquidation, costs from an earlier period are matched with revenues of the present year. Revenue is measured in 2010 dollars but cost of goods sold is stated in 1972 prices. Although the reported figures are technically correct, the implication that this station can earn a gross profit of $2.28 per gallon is misleading.

To allow decision makers to properly understand the effect that a LIFO liquidation has on reported net income, disclosure in the company's footnotes is needed whenever costs are mismatched in this manner. According to the footnotes to the 2008 financial statements for Alcoa Inc., "during 2008 and 2007, LIFO inventory quantities were reduced, which resulted in a partial liquidation of the LIFO base.

The impact of this liquidation increased net income by $25 (million) in 2008 and $20 (million) in 2007."

EXERCISE

Link to multiple-choice question for practice purposes: http://www.quia.com/quiz/2092925.html

Talking with an Independent Auditor about International Financial Reporting Standards

Following is a continuation of our interview with Robert A. Vallejo, partner with the accounting firm PricewaterhouseCoopers.

Question: Companies in the United States are allowed to choose FIFO, LIFO, or averaging as an inventory cost flow assumption. Over the years, many U.S. companies have adopted LIFO, in part because of the possibility of reducing income taxes during a period of inflation. However, IFRS rules do not recognize LIFO as appropriate. Why does such strong resistance to LIFO exist outside of the United States? If the United States adopts IFRS will all of these companies that now use LIFO have to switch their accounting systems to FIFO or averaging? How much trouble will that be?

Rob Vallejo: The International Accounting Standards Board revised International Accounting Standard No. 2, Inventories (IAS 2), in 2003. The issue of accounting for inventories using a LIFO costing method was debated and I would encourage anyone seeking additional information to read their basis for conclusion which accompanies IAS 2. The IASB did not believe that the LIFO costing method was a reliable representation of actual inventory flows. In other words, in most industries, older inventory is sold to customers before newer inventory. The standard specifically precludes the use of LIFO, but allows for the use of the FIFO or weighted average costing methods as they view these as better representations of actual inventory flows.

Therefore, when companies have to adopt IFRS, the inventory balances and the related impact on shareholders' equity will be restated as if FIFO or average costing had been used for all periods presented. Most companies keep their books on a FIFO or weighted average cost basis and then apply a LIFO adjustment, so the switch to an alternative method should not be a big issue in a mechanical sense. However, the reason most companies apply the LIFO costing method relates to U.S. tax law. Companies that want to apply LIFO for income tax purposes are required to present their financial information under the LIFO method. The big question still being debated is whether or not U.S. tax law will change to accommodate the move to IFRS. This is very important to U.S. companies, as generally, applying LIFO has had a cumulative impact of deferring the payment of income taxes. If companies must change to FIFO or weighted average costing methods for tax purposes, that could mean substantial cash payments to the IRS. Stay tuned for more debate in this area.

KEY TAKEAWAYS

LIFO is popular in the United States because of the LIFO conformity rule but serious theoretical problems do exist. Because of these concerns, LIFO is prohibited in many places in the world because of the rules established by IFRS. The most recent costs are reclassified to cost of goods sold so earlier costs remain in the inventory account. Consequently, this asset account can continue to show inventory costs from years or even decades earlier—a number that would seem to be of little use to any decision maker. In addition, if these earlier costs are ever transferred to cost of goods sold because of shrinkage in inventory, a LIFO liquidation is said to occur. Revenues are from the current year but cost of goods sold may reflect very old cost numbers. Information about LIFO liquidations appears in the footnotes to the financial statements so readers can weigh the impact.

4. MERGING PERIODIC AND PERPETUAL INVENTORY SYSTEMS WITH A COST FLOW ASSUMPTION

LEARNING OBJECTIVES

At the end of this section, students should be able to meet the following objectives:

1. **Merge a cost flow assumption (FIFO, LIFO, and averaging) with a method of monitoring inventory (periodic or perpetual) to arrive at six different systems for determining reported inventory figures.**
2. **Understand that a cost flow assumption is only applied in computing the cost of ending inventory units in a periodic system but is used for each reclassification from inventory to cost of goods sold in a perpetual system.**
3. **Calculate ending inventory and cost of goods sold under both a periodic and a perpetual FIFO system.**
4. **Recognize that periodic and perpetual FIFO systems will arrive at identical account balances.**

*Question: In the previous chapter, periodic and perpetual inventory systems were introduced. FIFO, LIFO, and averaging have now been presented. How does all of this material come together for reporting purposes? **How does the application of a cost flow assumption impact the operation of a periodic or a perpetual inventory system?***

Answer: Each company that holds inventory must develop a mechanism to both (a) monitor the balances and (b) allow for the creation of financial statements. If a periodic system is used, officials simply wait until financial statements are to be produced before taking a physical count. Then, a formula (beginning inventory plus all purchase costs less ending inventory) is applied to derive cost of goods sold.

In contrast, a perpetual system maintains an ongoing record of the goods that remain on hand and those that have been sold. As noted, both of these systems have advantages and disadvantages.

Companies also select a cost flow assumption to specify the cost that is transferred from inventory to cost of goods sold (and, hence, the cost that remains in the inventory T-account). For a periodic system, the cost flow assumption is only applied when the physical inventory count is taken and the cost of the ending inventory is determined. In a perpetual system, each time a sale is made the cost flow assumption identifies the cost to be reclassified to cost of goods sold. That can occur thousands of times each day.

Therefore, companies normally choose one of six systems to monitor their merchandise balances and determine the cost assignment between ending inventory and cost of goods sold:

- Periodic FIFO
- Perpetual FIFO
- Periodic LIFO
- Perpetual LIFO
- periodic averaging (also called weighted averaging)
- Perpetual averaging (also called moving averaging)

Question: To illustrate, assume that the Mayberry Home Improvement Store starts the new year with four bathtubs (Model WET-5) in its inventory, costing $110 each ($440 in total) when bought on December 9 of the previous period. The following events then take place during the current year.

- *On February 2, three of these bathtubs are sold for $200 each. (revenue $600)*
- *On February 6, three new bathtubs of this model are bought for $120 each. (cost $360)*
- *On June 8, three of these bathtubs are sold for $250 each. (revenue $750)*
- *On June 13, three new bathtubs of this model are bought for $130 each. (cost $390)*
- *On September 9, two of these bathtubs are sold for $300 each. (revenue $600)*
- *On September 22, two new bathtub of this model are bought for $149. (cost $298)*

At the end of the year, on December 31, a physical inventory is taken that finds that four bathtubs, Model WET-5, are in stock (4 – 3 + 3 – 3 + 3 – 2 + 2). None were stolen, lost, or damaged during the period.

How does a periodic FIFO system differ from a perpetual FIFO system in maintaining accounting records and reporting inventory totals?

Answer: Regardless of the inventory system in use, several pieces of information are established in this example. These data are factual, not impacted by accounting.

Data—Purchase and Sale of WET-5 Bathtubs

- Revenue: Eight units were sold for $1,950 ($600 + $750 + $600)
- Beginning Inventory: Four units costing $110 each or $440 in total were on hand
- Purchases: Eight units were bought during the year costing a total of $1,048 ($360 + $390 + $298)
- Ending Inventory: Four units are still held

Periodic FIFO. In a periodic system, the cost of the new purchases is the focus of the record keeping. At the end of the period, the accountant must count and then determine the cost of the items held in ending inventory. When using FIFO, the first costs are transferred to cost of goods sold so the cost of the last four bathtubs remain in the inventory T-account. That is the FIFO assumption. The first costs are now in cost of goods sold while the most recent costs remain in the asset account.

In this illustration, the last four costs (starting at the end of the period and moving forward) are two units at $149 each and two units at $130 each for a total of $558. Only after that cost is assigned to ending inventory can cost of goods sold be calculated.

FIGURE 9.6 Periodic FIFO—Bathtub Model WET-5

Beginning Inventory (carried over from previous year)—4 Units at $110 Each	$440
Purchases—8 Units	1,048
Goods Available for Sale (12 units in total)	$1,488
Ending Inventory (physical count)—2 Units at $149 Each and 2 Units at $130 Each	
Based on Applying FIFO	(558)
Cost of Goods Sold	$930

The last costs for the period remain in ending inventory; the first costs have all been transferred to cost of goods sold. This handling reflects the application of the first-in, first-out cost flow assumption.

Based on the application of FIFO, Mayberry reports gross profit from the sale of bathtubs during this year of $1,020 (revenue of $1,950 minus cost of goods sold of $930).

Perpetual FIFO. Perpetual accounting systems are constructed so that costs can be moved from inventory to cost of goods sold at the time of each new sale. With modern computer processing, that is a relatively simple task. Below is one format that provides the information needed for this home improvement store and its inventory of bathtubs. At points A, B, and C, costs are moved from inventory on hand to cost of goods sold based on FIFO. The cost of the first goods in the "inventory on hand" is reclassified to cost of goods sold at each of those three spots.

FIGURE 9.7 Perpetual FIFO—Bathtub Model WET-5

	Inventory Acquired →	Inventory On Hand →	Cost of Goods Sold
1/1—Beginning Balance		4 Units @ $110	
2/2—3 Units Sold		1 Unit @ 110	(A) 3 Units @ $110 = $330
2/6—3 Units Bought	3 Units @ $120	1 Unit @ 110 3 Units @ 120	
6/8—3 Units Sold		1 Unit @ $120	(B) 1 Unit @ 110 2 Units @ 120 = 350
6/13—3 Units Bought	3 Units @ 130	1 Unit @ 120 3 Units @ 130	
9/9—2 Units Sold		2 Units @ 130	(C) 1 Unit @ 120 1 Unit @ $130 = 250
9/22—2 Units Bought	2 Units @ 149	2 Units @ 130 2 Units @ 149	
Totals		**$260 + $298 = $558**	**$330 + $350 + $250 = $930**

On this perpetual inventory spreadsheet, the final cell in the "inventory on hand" column ($558 or two units @ $130 and two units at $149) provides the cost of the ending inventory. Summation of the "cost of goods sold" column reflects that expense for the period ($930 or $330 + $350 + $250).

One important characteristic of FIFO should be noted here. Under both periodic and perpetual FIFO, ending inventory is $558 and cost of goods sold is $930. The reported numbers are identical. The first cost for the period is always the first cost regardless of when the assignment to expense is made. Thus, the resulting amounts will be the same using either FIFO system. For that reason, many companies that apply FIFO maintain perpetual records to track the units on hand throughout the period but ignore the costs. Then, when financial statements are prepared, they use a periodic computation to determine the cost of ending inventory in order to compute cost of goods sold. That allows the company to monitor its inventory quantities daily without the expense and effort of identifying the cost associated with each new sale.

EXERCISE

Link to multiple-choice question for practice purposes: http://www.quia.com/quiz/2092904.html

KEY TAKEAWAYS

Companies that sell inventory choose a cost flow assumption such as FIFO, LIFO, or averaging. In addition, a method must be applied to monitor inventory balances (either periodic or perpetual). Six combinations of inventory systems can result from these two decisions. With any periodic system, the cost flow assumption is only used to determine the cost of ending inventory so that cost of goods sold can be calculated. For perpetual, the reclassification of costs is performed each time that a sale is made based on the cost flow assumption that was selected. Periodic FIFO and perpetual FIFO systems arrive at the same reported balances because the earliest cost is always the first to be transferred regardless of the method being applied.

5. APPLYING LIFO AND AVERAGING TO DETERMINE REPORTED INVENTORY BALANCES

LEARNING OBJECTIVES

At the end of this section, students should be able to meet the following objectives:

1. **Determine ending inventory and cost of goods sold using a periodic LIFO system.**
2. **Monitor inventory on an ongoing basis through a perpetual LIFO system.**
3. **Understand the reason that periodic LIFO and perpetual LIFO may arrive at different figures.**
4. **Use a weighted average system to report ending inventory and cost of goods sold.**
5. **Calculate inventory balances by applying a moving average inventory system.**

Question: LIFO reverses the FIFO cost flow assumption so that the last costs incurred are the first reclassified to cost of goods sold. ***How is LIFO applied to the inventory of an actual business?*** *If the Mayberry Home Improvement Store adopted LIFO, how would the reported figures have been affected by this decision?*

Answer: *Periodic LIFO.* In a periodic system, only the computation of the ending inventory is altered by the choice of a cost flow assumption.[5] Thus, for this illustration, beginning inventory remains $440 (4 units at $110 each) and the number of units purchased is still eight with a cost of $1,048. The reported figure that changes is the cost of the ending inventory. Four bathtubs remain in stock at the end of the year. According to LIFO, the last costs are transferred to cost of goods sold; only the cost of the first four units remains in ending inventory. That is $110 per unit or $440 in total.

FIGURE 9.8 Periodic LIFO—Bathtub Model WET-5

*If the number of units bought equals the number of units sold—as seen in this example—the quantity of inventory remains unchanged. In a periodic LIFO system, beginning inventory ($440) is then the same as ending inventory ($440) so that cost of goods sold ($1,048) equals the amount spent during the period to purchase inventory ($1,048). Therefore, during the year, company officials can keep track of gross profit by subtracting purchases from revenues.

Beginning Inventory (carried over from previous year)—4 Units at $110 Each	$440
Purchases—8 Units	1,048
Goods Available for Sale (12 units in total)	$1,488
Ending Inventory (physical count)—4 Units at $110 Each Based on Applying LIFO	(440)
Cost of Goods Sold	$1,048*

Mayberry Home Improvement Store reports gross profit using periodic LIFO of $902 (revenue of $1,950 less cost of goods sold of $1,048).

Note here that the anticipated characteristics of LIFO are present. Ending inventory of $440 is lower than that reported by FIFO ($558). Cost of goods sold ($1,048) is higher than under FIFO ($930) so that the reported gross profit (and, hence, net income) is lower by $118 ($1,020 for FIFO versus $902 for LIFO).

EXERCISE

Link to multiple-choice question for practice purposes: http://www.quia.com/quiz/2092905.html

Perpetual LIFO. The mechanical structure for a perpetual LIFO system is the same as that demonstrated for perpetual FIFO except that the most recent costs are moved into cost of goods sold at the time of each sale (points A, B, and C).

FIGURE 9.9 Perpetual LIFO—Bathtub Model WET-5

	Inventory Acquired →	Inventory On Hand →	Cost of Goods Sold
1/1—Beginning Balance		4 Units @ $110	
2/2—3 Units Sold		1 Unit @ 110	(A) 3 Units @ $110 = 330
2/6—3 Units Bought	3 Units @ $120	1 Unit @ 110 3 Units @ 120	
6/8—3 Units Sold		1 Unit @ 110	(B) 3 Units @ 120 = 360
6/13—3 Units Bought	3 Units @ 130	1 Unit @ 110 3 Units @ 130	
9/9—2 Units Sold		1 Unit @ 110 1 Unit @ 130	(C) 2 Units @ 130 = 260
9/22—2 Units Bought	2 Units @ 149	1 Unit @ 110 1 Unit @ 130 2 Units @ 149	
Totals		**$110 + $130 + $298 = $538**	**$330 + $360 + $260 = $950**

Once again, the last cell in the "inventory on hand" column contains the asset figure to be reported on the balance sheet (a total of $538) while the summation of the "cost of goods sold" column provides the amount to be shown on the income statement ($950).

As can be seen here, periodic and perpetual LIFO do not necessarily produce identical numbers.

periodic LIFO: ending inventory $440 and cost of goods sold $1,048

perpetual LIFO: ending inventory $538 and cost of goods sold $950

Periodic and perpetual FIFO always arrive at the same results. In contrast, balances reported by periodic and perpetual LIFO frequently differ. Although the first cost incurred in a period (the cost transferred to expense under FIFO) is the same regardless of the date of sale, this is not true for the last or most recent cost (expensed according to LIFO).

As an illustration, note that two bathtubs were sold on September 9 in this example. Perpetual LIFO immediately determines the cost of this sale and reclassifies the amount. On that date, the cost of the last two units ($130 each) came from the June 13 purchase. That amount is expensed. In contrast, a periodic LIFO system makes that same determination but not until December 31. As viewed from year's end, the last costs were $149 each. Although these items were bought on September 22, which is after the last sale, they are included in the cost of goods sold for a periodic LIFO system.

Two bathtubs were sold on September 9 but the identity of the specific costs to be transferred depends on the date on which the determination is made. A periodic system views the costs from perspective of the end of the year while perpetual does so immediately when a sale is made.

EXERCISE

Link to multiple-choice question for practice purposes: http://www.quia.com/quiz/2092891.html

Question: Not surprisingly, averaging follows a path similar to that of the previous examples. Costs are either moved to cost of goods sold at the end of the year (periodic or weighted average) or at the time of each new sale (perpetual or moving average). The only added variable to this process is the calculation of average cost. ***In the operation of an averaging system, when and how is the average cost of inventory determined?***

Answer: *Periodic (weighted) average.* In the problem being examined here, Mayberry Home Improvement Store eventually held twelve bathtubs. Four of these units were on hand at the start of the year and the other eight were acquired during the period. The beginning inventory cost $440 and the new purchases were bought for a total of $1,048. Thus, these twelve units had a total cost of $1,488 ($440 + $1,048) or $124 per bathtub ($1,488/12 units). When applying a weighted average system, this single average is the basis for both the ending inventory and cost of goods sold to be included in the company's financial statements. No item actually cost $124 but that average is applied to all units.

FIGURE 9.10 Periodic (Weighted) Average—Bathtub Model WET-5

Beginning Inventory (carried over from previous year)—4 Units at $110 Each	$440
Purchases—8 Units	1,048
Goods Available for Sale (12 units in total)	$1,488
Ending Inventory (physical count)—4 Units at $124 Each	
Based on Applying Periodic Averaging	(496)
Cost of Goods Sold (can also be determined	
as 8 units at an average cost of $124 each)	$992

Perpetual (moving) average. In this final approach to maintaining and reporting inventory, each time that a company buys inventory at a new price, the average cost is recalculated. Therefore, a moving average system must be programmed to update the average whenever additional merchandise is acquired.

Below, a new average is computed at points D, E, and F. Each time this figure is found by dividing the number of units on hand after the purchase into the total cost of those items. For example, at point D, the company now has four bathtubs. One cost $110 while the other three were acquired for $120 each or $360 in total. Total cost was $470 ($110 + $360) for these four units for a new average of $117.50 ($470/4 units). That average is then used until the next purchase is made. The applicable average at the time of sale is transferred from inventory to cost of goods sold at points A ($110.00), B ($117.50), and C ($126.88) below.

FIGURE 9.11 Perpetual (Moving) Average—Bathtub Model WET-5

	Inventory Acquired →	Inventory on Hand →	Cost of Goods Sold
1/1—Beginning Balance		4 Units @ $110 = $440	
2/2—3 Units Sold		1 Unit @ 110 = 110	(A) 3 Units @ $110 = $330
2/6—3 Units Bought	3 Units @ $120	1 Unit @ 110 = 110 3 Units @ 120 = 360	
New Average		(D) 4 Units @ 117.50 = 470	
6/8—3 Units Sold		1 Unit @ 117.50	(B) 3 Units @ 117.50 = 352.50
6/13—3 Units Bought	3 Units @ 130	1 Unit @ 117.50 = 117.50 3 Units @ 130 = 390	
New Average		(E) 4 Units @ 126.88 = 507.50	
9/9—2 Units Sold		2 Units @ 126.88 = 253.76	(C) 2 Units @ 126.88 = 253.76
9/22—2 Units Bought	2 Units @ 149	2 Units @ 126.88 = 253.76 2 Units @ 149 = 298	
New Average		(F) 4 Units @ 137.94 = 551.76	
Totals		**$551.76**	**$330 + $352.50 + $253.76 = $936.26**

Summary. The six inventory systems shown here for Mayberry Home Improvement Store provide a number of distinct pictures of ending inventory and cost of goods sold. As stated earlier, these numbers are all fairly presented but only in conformity with the specified principles being applied.

FIGURE 9.12 Six Inventory Systems

	Periodic FIFO	Perpetual FIFO	Periodic LIFO	Perpetual LIFO	Weighted Average	Moving Average
Ending Inventory (4 Units)	$558.00	$558.00	$440.00	$538.00	$496.00	$551.76
Cost of Goods Sold (8 Units)	930.00	930.00	1,048.00	950.00	992.00	936.26
Gross Profit (Sales Revenue of $1,950 Less Cost of Goods Sold)	$1,020.00	$1,020.00	$902.00	$1,000.00	$958.00	$1,013.74

EXERCISE

Link to multiple-choice question for practice purposes: http://www.quia.com/quiz/2092932.html

EXERCISE

Link to multiple-choice question for practice purposes: http://www.quia.com/quiz/2092933.html

KEY TAKEAWAYS

A periodic LIFO inventory system begins by computing the cost of ending inventory at the end of a period and then uses that figure to calculate cost of goods sold. Perpetual LIFO also transfers the most recent cost to cost of goods sold but makes that reclassification at the time of each sale. A weighted average inventory system determines a single average for the entire period and applies that to both ending inventory and the cost of goods sold. A moving average system computes a new average cost whenever merchandise is acquired. That figure is then reclassified to cost of goods sold at the time of each sale until the next purchase is made.

6. ANALYZING REPORTED INVENTORY FIGURES

LEARNING OBJECTIVES

At the end of this section, students should be able to meet the following objectives:

1. **Use information found in footnote disclosure to convert LIFO balance sheet and income statement numbers into their FIFO or current cost equivalents.**
2. **Compute a company's gross profit percentage and explain the relevance of this figure.**
3. **Calculate the average number of days that inventory is held and provide reasons why companies worry if this figure starts moving upward unexpectedly.**
4. **Compute the inventory turnover and explain its meaning.**

Question: The point has been made several times in this chapter that LIFO provides a lower reported net income than does FIFO when prices are rising. In addition, the inventory figure shown on the balance sheet will be below current cost if LIFO is applied during inflation. Comparison between companies that are similar can become difficult, if not impossible, when one uses FIFO and the other LIFO. For example, Rite Aid, the drug store giant, applies LIFO while its rival CVS Caremark applies FIFO to the inventory held in its CVS pharmacies. How can an investor possibly compare the two companies? In that situation, the utility of the financial information seems limited.

How do experienced decision makers manage to compare companies that apply LIFO to others that do not?

Answer: Significant variations in reported balances frequently result from the application of different cost flow assumptions. Because of potential detrimental effects on these figures, companies that use LIFO often provide additional information to help interested parties understand the impact of this choice. For example, a footnote to the 2008 financial statements of Safeway Inc. and Subsidiaries discloses: "merchandise inventory of $1,740 million at year-end 2008 and $1,886 million at year-end 2007 is valued at the lower of cost on a last-in, first-out ('LIFO') basis or market value. Such LIFO inventory had a replacement or current cost of $1,838 million at year-end 2008 and $1,949 million at year-end 2007." Here, the reader is told that this portion of the company's inventory was reported as $1,740 million and $1,886 million although really worth $1,838 million and $1,949 million (the equivalent of using FIFO).

If a decision maker is comparing the 2008 year-end balance sheet of Safeway to another company that did not use LIFO, the inventory balance could be increased from $1,740 million to $1,838 million to show that this asset was worth an additional $98 million ($1,838 million less $1,740 million). Thus, the dampening impact of LIFO on reported assets can be removed easily by the reader. Restatement of financial statements in this manner is a common technique relied on by investment analysts around the world to make available information more usable.

Adjusting Safeway's balance sheet from LIFO to current cost (FIFO) is not difficult because relevant information is available in the footnotes. However, restating the company's income statement to numbers in line with FIFO is a bit more challenging. Safeway reported net income for 2008 of $965.3 million. How would that number have been different with the application of FIFO to all inventory?

As seen in the periodic inventory formula, beginning inventory is added to purchases in determining cost of goods sold while ending inventory is subtracted. With the LIFO figures reported by Safeway, $1,886 million (beginning inventory) was added in arriving at this expense and then $1,740 million (ending inventory) was subtracted. Together, the net effect is an addition of $146 million ($1,886 million less $1,740 million) in computing cost of goods sold for 2008. The expense was $146 million higher than the amount of inventory purchased.

In comparison, if the current cost of the inventory had been used by Safeway, $1,949 million (beginning inventory) would have been added while $1,838 million (ending inventory) subtracted. These two balances produce a net effect on cost of goods sold of adding $111 million.

LIFO: cost of goods sold = purchases + $146 million

FIFO: cost of goods sold = purchases + $111 million

Under LIFO, cost of goods sold is the purchases for the period plus $146 million. Using current cost, cost of goods sold is the purchases plus only $111 million. The purchase figure is the same in both equations. Thus, cost of goods sold will be $35 million higher according to LIFO ($146 million less $111 million) and net income $35 million lower. If FIFO had been used, Safeway's reported income would have been approximately $1 billion instead of $965.3 million. Knowledgeable decision makers can easily make this adjustment for themselves to help in evaluating a company. They can determine the amount of net income to be reported if LIFO had not been selected and can then use that figure for comparison purposes.

In its 2008 financial statements, Sherwin-Williams simplifies this process by disclosing that its reported net income was reduced by $49,184,000 as a result of applying LIFO. Inclusion of this data was explained by clearly stating that "This information is presented to enable the reader to make comparisons with companies using the FIFO method of inventory valuation."

EXERCISE

Link to multiple-choice question for practice purposes: http://www.quia.com/quiz/2092934.html

Question: When analyzing receivables in a previous chapter, the assertion was made that companies have vital signs that can be examined as an indication of financial well-being. These are ratios or other computed amounts considered to be of particular significance. In that earlier coverage, the age of the receivables and the receivable turnover were both calculated and explained. For inventory, do similar vital signs also exist that decision makers should study? ***What vital signs should be determined in connection with inventory when examining the financial health and prospects of a company?***

Answer: No definitive list of ratios and relevant amounts can be identified because different people tend to have their own personal preferences. However, several figures are widely computed and discussed in connection with inventory and cost of goods sold when the financial condition of a company and the likelihood of its prosperity are being evaluated.

Gross profit percentage. The first of these is the **gross profit percentage**, which is found by dividing the **gross profit** for the period by **net sales**.

sales – sales returns and discounts = net sales

net sales – cost of goods sold = gross profit

gross profit/net sales = gross profit percentage

Previously, gross profit has also been referred to as gross margin, markup, or margin of a company. In simplest terms, it is the difference between the amount paid to buy (or manufacture) inventory and the amount received from an eventual sale. Gross profit percentage is often used to compare one company to the next or one time period to the next. If a book store manages to earn a gross profit percentage of 35 percent and another only 25 percent, questions need to be raised about the difference and which percentage is better? One company is making more profit on each sale but, possibly because of higher sales prices, it might be making significantly fewer sales.

For the year ending January 31, 2009, Macy's Inc. reported a gross profit percentage of 39.7 percent but reported net loss for the year of $4.8 billion on sales of nearly $25 billion. At the same time, Wal-Mart earned a gross profit percentage of a mere 23.7 percent but managed to generate net income of over $13 billion on sales of over $401 billion. With these companies, a clear difference in pricing strategy can be seen.

The gross profit percentage is also watched closely from one year to the next. For example, if this figure falls from 37 percent to 34 percent, analysts will be quite interested in the reason. Such changes have a cause and any individual studying the company needs to consider the possibilities.

Are costs rising more quickly than the sales price of the merchandise?
Has a change occurred in the types of inventory being sold?
Was the reduction in the gross profit offset by an increase in sales?

gross profit percentage

Formula measuring profitability calculated by dividing gross profit (sales less cost of goods sold) by sales.

gross profit

Difference between sales and cost of goods sold; also called gross margin or mark-up.

net sales

Sales less sales returns and discounts.

Barnes & Noble Inc. for example, reports that its gross margin was 30.9 percent in 2008 and 30.4 percent in 2007. That is certainly one piece of information to be included in a detailed investigation of this company.

number of days inventory is held

Measures the average number of days that a company takes to sell its inventory items; computed by dividing average inventory for the period by the cost of inventory sold per day.

Number of days inventory is held. A second vital sign is the **number of days inventory is held** on the average. Companies want to turn their merchandise into cash as quickly as possible. Holding inventory can lead to several unfortunate repercussions. The longer it sits in stock the more likely the goods are to get damaged, stolen, or go out of fashion. Such losses can be avoided through quick sales. Furthermore, as long as merchandise is sitting on the shelves, it is not earning any profit for the company. Money is tied up with no return until a sale is made.

Consequently, decision makers (both internal and external to the company) watch this figure closely. A change (especially any lengthening of the time required to sell merchandise) is often a warning of problems.

The number of days inventory is held is found in two steps. First, the company needs to determine the cost of inventory that is sold each day on the average.

cost of goods sold/365 days[6] = cost of inventory sold per day

Then, this daily cost figure is divided into the average amount of inventory held during the period. The average can be based on beginning and ending totals, monthly balances, or other available figures.

average inventory/cost of inventory sold per day = number of days inventory is held

For example, if a company sells inventory costing $40,000 each day and holds an average inventory of $520,000 during the period, the average item takes thirteen days ($520,000/$40,000) to be sold. Again, the significance of that figure depends on the type of inventory, a comparison to similar companies, and the change seen in recent periods of time.

inventory turnover

Ratio used to measure the speed at which a company sells its inventory; computed by dividing cost of goods sold by average inventory for the period.

Inventory turnover. A third vital sign to be presented is the **inventory turnover**, which is simply another way to measure the speed by which a company sells its inventory.

cost of goods sold/average inventory = inventory turnover

The resulting turnover figure indicates the number of times during the period that an amount equal to the average inventory was sold. The larger the turnover number, the faster inventory is selling. For example, Best Buy Co. Inc. recognized cost of goods sold for the year ending February 28, 2009, as $34,017 million. The company also reported beginning inventory for that period of $4,708 million and ending inventory of $4,753 million. Hence, the inventory turnover for this retail electronics giant was 7.23 times during that year.

($4,753 + $4,708)/2 = average inventory of $4,730.5 million

$34,017/$4,703.5 = inventory turnover of 7.23 times

EXERCISE

Link to multiple-choice question for practice purposes: http://www.quia.com/quiz/2092926.html

EXERCISE

Link to multiple-choice question for practice purposes: http://www.quia.com/quiz/2092927.html

KEY TAKEAWAY

Companies that apply LIFO (probably for income tax reasons) often hope decision makers will convert their numbers to FIFO for comparison purposes. Footnote disclosure of FIFO figures can be included to make this conversion possible. In addition, analysts frequently determine several computed amounts and ratios to help illuminate what is happening inside of a company. The gross profit percentage simply determines the average amount of markup on each sale. It demonstrates pricing policies and fluctuations often indicate policy changes or problems in the market. The average number of days in inventory and the inventory turnover both help decision makers know the length of time a company takes to sell its merchandise. Traditionally, a slowing down of sales is bad because inventory is more likely to be damaged, lost, or stolen. Plus, inventory generates no profit for the owner until sold.

Talking with a Real Investing Pro—Continued

Following is a continuation of our interview with Kevin G. Burns.

Question: Companies that sell inventory instead of services must select a cost flow assumption for reporting purposes. What are your thoughts when you are analyzing two similar companies and discover that one has applied FIFO while the other uses LIFO?

Kevin Burns: Truthfully, it is easy to get distracted by issues such as FIFO and LIFO that probably make no difference in the long run. I rarely like to trade stocks quickly. For example, assume a company sells a commodity of some type (jewelry, for example). The commodity fluctuates dramatically in price so when the price is falling you have paid more for the item than the market will now pay you for the finished good. When prices are rising, you reap the benefit by selling at an even greater price than you expected. So if you have two companies dealing with the same issues and one uses LIFO and the other FIFO, the reported results could be dramatically different. However, the underlying facts do not change. Over an extended period of time, the two companies probably end up in the same position regardless of whether they apply LIFO or FIFO. I am much more interested in how they are investing their cash inflows and the quality of the management. On the other hand, a person who trades stocks quickly could well be interested in reported results that might impact stock prices for a short period of time. For example, the trader may well wish to see a company use FIFO as reported profits will be higher for the short term if there is inflation and may believe that he can capitalize on that short-term phenomenon.

Video Clip

Joe talks about the five most important points in Chapter 9.

View the video online at: http://blip.tv/play/sDyBv7xVAA

7. END-OF-CHAPTER EXERCISES

QUESTIONS

1. Why is it unrealistic to assume that inventory costs will remain constant over time?
2. What is a cost flow assumption?
3. Briefly explain the specific identification approach.
4. Briefly explain the first in, first out cost flow assumption.
5. Briefly explain the last in, first out cost flow assumption.
6. Briefly explain the averaging cost flow assumption.
7. Which cost flow assumption will give a higher net income in a period of rising prices?
8. Why don't all companies use specific identification?
9. Which cost flow assumption appears to be used by more companies than any other?
10. What are advantages of using LIFO?
11. Why must a company keep one set of books for financial reporting purposes and another for tax compliance purposes?
12. Why do many countries not permit their companies to use LIFO?
13. Explain LIFO liquidation.
14. How can users compare companies who use different cost flow assumptions?
15. How is gross profit percentage calculated and what does it tell a user about a company?
16. How is number of days in inventory calculated and why would a user want to know this number?
17. What is inventory turnover? What does it tell a user about a company?

TRUE OR FALSE

1. ____ Using the LIFO cost assumption will always result in a lower net income than using the FIFO cost assumption.
2. ____ The United States is the only country that allows LIFO.
3. ____ LIFO tends to provide a better match of costs and expenses than FIFO and averaging.
4. ____ Companies can use LIFO for tax purposes and FIFO for financial reporting.
5. ____ The larger the inventory turnover, the better, in most cases.
6. ____ It is impossible for decision makers to compare a company who uses LIFO with one who uses FIFO.
7. ____ A jewelry store or boat dealership would normally be able to use the specific identification method.
8. ____ The underlying concept of FIFO is that the earliest inventory purchased would be sold first.
9. ____ Gross profit percentage can help users determine how long it takes companies to sell inventory after they purchase it.
10. ____ LIFO liquidation may artificially inflate net income.

MULTIPLE CHOICE

1. Which of the following provides the best matching of revenues and expenses?
   a. Specific Identification
   b. FIFO
   c. LIFO
   d. Averaging
2. Milby Corporation purchased three hats to sell during the year. The first, purchased in February, cost $5. The second, purchased in April, cost $6. The third, purchased in July, cost $8. If Milby sells two hats during the year and uses the FIFO method, what would cost of goods sold be for the year?
   a. $13
   b. $19
   c. $14
   d. $11
3. Which is ***not*** a reason a company would choose to use LIFO for financial reporting?
   a. The company wishes to use LIFO for tax purposes.
   b. The company wants net income to be as high as possible.
   c. The company would like to match the most current costs with revenues.
   d. LIFO best matches the physical flow of its inventory.
4. During the year, Hostel Company had net sales of $4,300,000 and cost of goods sold of $2,800,000. Beginning inventory was $230,000 and ending inventory was $390,000. Which of the following would be Hostel's inventory turnover for the year?
   a. 03 times
   b. 18 times
   c. 84 times
   d. 87 times
5. Traylor Corporation began the year with three items in beginning inventory, each costing $4. During the year Traylor purchased five more items at a cost of $5 each and two more items at a cost of $6.50 each. Traylor sold eight items for $9 each. If Traylor uses LIFO, what would be Traylor's gross profit for the year?
   a. $42
   b. $30
   c. $35
   d. $72

PROBLEMS

1. SuperDuper Company sells top of the line skateboards. SuperDuper is concerned about maintaining high earnings and has chosen to use the periodic FIFO method of inventory costing. At the beginning of the year, SuperDuper had 5,000 skateboards in inventory, each costing $20. In April, SuperDuper purchased 2,000 skateboards at a cost of $22 and in August, purchased 4,000 more at a cost of $23. During the year, SuperDuper sold 9,000 skateboards for $40 each.
    a. Record each purchase SuperDuper made.
    b. Determine SuperDuper's cost of goods sold using FIFO.
2. Assume the same facts as problem 1 above, except that SuperDuper is more concerned with minimizing taxes and uses LIFO. Determine SuperDuper's cost of goods sold using LIFO.
3. Assume the same facts as problem 1 above, except that SuperDuper has decided to use averaging. Determine SuperDuper's cost of goods sold using averaging.
4. Using your answers to problems 1–3, determine the following:
    a. Which of the methods yields the lowest cost of goods sold for SuperDuper?
    b. Which of the methods yields the highest ending inventory for SuperDuper?
5. Ulysses Company uses LIFO costing. It reported beginning inventory of $20,000,000 and ending inventory of $24,500,000. If current costs were used to value inventory, beginning inventory would have been $23,000,000 and ending inventory would have been $26,700,000. Cost of goods sold using LIFO was $34,900,000. Determine what cost of goods sold would be if Ulysses used FIFO.
6. Paula's Parkas sells NorthPlace jackets. At the beginning of the year, Paula's had twenty jackets in stock, each costing $35 and selling for $60. The following table details the purchases and sales made during January:

Date	Number of Items	Cost per Item
January 2	Purchased 12	$36.00
January 8	Purchased 10	36.50
January 10	Sold 15	
January 17	Sold 14	
January 22	Purchased 8	37.00
January 28	Sold 10	

    Assume that Paula's Parkas uses the perpetual FIFO method.
    a. Determine Paula's Parkas cost of goods sold and ending inventory for January.
    b. Determine Parka's gross profit for January.
7. Assume the same facts as in 6 above, but that Paula's Parkas uses the perpetual LIFO method.
    a. Determine Paula's Parkas cost of goods sold and ending inventory for January.
    b. Determine Parka's gross profit for January.
8. Assume the same facts as in 6 above, but that Paula's Parkas uses the moving average method.
    a. Determine Paula's Parkas cost of goods sold and ending inventory for January.
    b. Determine Parka's gross profit for January.
9. The Furn Store sells home furnishings, including bean bag chairs. Furn currently uses the periodic FIFO method of inventory costing, but is considering implementing a perpetual system. It will cost a good deal of money to start and maintain, so Furn would like to see the difference, if any, between the two and is using its bean bag chair inventory to do so. Here is the first quarter information for bean bag chairs:

Date	Number of Items	Cost per Item
Beginning Balance:		
January 1	16	$19
January 17	Purchased 5	20
January 24	Sold 7	
February 10	Purchased 8	21
February 19	Sold 15	
March 1	Purchased 11	22
March 20	Sold 16	

Each bean bag chair sells for $40.

a. Determine Furn's cost of goods sold and ending inventory under periodic FIFO.

b. Determine Furn's cost of goods sold and ending inventory under perpetual FIFO.

10. Rollrbladz Inc. is trying to decide between a periodic or perpetual LIFO system. Management would like to see the effect of each on cost of goods sold and ending inventory for the year. Below is information concerning purchases and sales of its specialty line of rollerblades:

Date	Number of Items	Cost per Item	Sales Price
Beginning Balance:			
January 1	150	$34	
January 22	Purchased 120	35	
February 21	Sold 160		$75
April 8	Purchased 180	36	
June 10	Sold 190		80
August 19	Purchased 110	37	
September 28	Sold 50		82
October 14	Sold 60		82

a. Determine Rollrbladz's cost of goods sold and ending inventory under periodic LIFO.

b. Determine Rollrbladz's cost of goods sold and ending inventory under perpetual LIFO.

11. Highlander Corporation sells swords for decorative purposes. It would like to know the difference in cost of goods sold and ending inventory if it uses the weighted average method or the moving average method. Please find below information to help determine these amounts for the second quarter.

Date	Number of Items	Cost per Item
Beginning Balance:		
April 1	1,700	$70
April 13	Purchased 600	72
May 5	Sold 1,000	
May 25	Purchased 800	73
June 10	Sold 1,500	

Swords retail for $120 each.

a. Determine Highlander's cost of goods sold and ending inventory under weighted average.

b. Determine Highlander's cost of goods sold and ending inventory under moving average.

12. In Chapter 4 and Chapter 7, we met Heather Miller, who started her own business, Sew Cool. The financial statements for December are shown below. To calculate average inventory, assume that inventory on 6/1/20X8, when Sew Cool started business, was zero.

Sew Cool
Income Statement
As of December 31, 20X8

Revenue	$4,000
Cost of Goods	(2,000)
Gross Profit	2,000
Other Expenses	(1,695)
Earning before Tax	305
Tax Expense	(107)
Net Income	$198

Sew Cool
Stmt. of Retained Earnings
As of December 31, 20X8

Retained Earnings, December 1, 20X8	$500
Net Income	198
Dividends	(158)
Retained Earnings, December 31, 20X8	$540

Sew Cool
Balance Sheet
December 31, 20X8

Assets		**Liabilities**	
Current		**Current**	
Cash	$940	Accounts Payable	$900
Accounts Receivable	500	Income Tax Payable	120
Less Allowance for Doubtful Accounts	(20)	Total Current Liabilities	$1,020
Net Accounts Receivable	480		
Inventory	700		
Total Current Assets	$2,120		
Noncurrent		**Noncurrent**	
Equipment	$1,000	Notes Payable	$1,060
		Owners' Equity	
		Capital Stock	$500
		Retained Earnings	540
		Total Owners' Equity	$1,040
Total Assets	$3,120	Total Liabilities & Owners' Equity	$3,120

Based on the financial statements determine the following:

a. Gross profit percentage
b. Number of days inventory is held
c. Inventory turnover

COMPREHENSIVE PROBLEM

This problem will carry through several chapters, building in difficulty. It allows students to continuously practice skills and knowledge learned in previous chapters.

In Chapter 8, you prepared Webworks statements for August. They are included here as a starting point for September.

Here are Webworks financial statements as of August 31.

Webworks
Stmt. of Retained Earnings
As of August 31

Retained Earnings, August 1	$1,175
Net Income	1,615
Retained Earnings, August 31	$2,790

Webworks
Balance Sheet
August 31

Assets		**Liabilities**	
Current		**Current**	
Cash	$6,445	Accounts Payable	$2,690
Accounts Receivable	1,250	Salaries Payable	250
Less Allowance for Doubtful Accounts	(125)	Unearned Revenue	100
Net Accounts Receivable	1,125		
Merchandise Inventory	3,000		
Supplies Inventory	60		
Prepaid Rent	200		
Total Current Assets	$10,830	Total Current Liabilities	$3,040
Noncurrent		**Noncurrent**	
Equipment	$7,000	Notes Payable	$10,000
		Owners' Equity	
		Capital Stock	$2,000
		Retained Earnings	2,790
		Total Owners' Equity	$4,790
Total Assets	$17,830	Total Liabilities & Owners' Equity	$17,830

The following events occur during September:

a. Webworks purchases supplies worth $120 on account.

b. At the beginning of September, Webworks had 19 keyboards costing $100 each and 110 flash drives costing $10 each. Webworks has decided to use periodic FIFO to cost its inventory.

c. On account, Webworks purchases thirty keyboards for $105 each and fifty flash drives for $11 each.

d. Webworks starts and completes five more sites and bills clients for $3,000.

e. Webworks pays Nancy $500 for her work during the first three weeks of September.

f. Webworks sells 40 keyboards for $6,000 and 120 flash drives for $2,400 cash.

g. Webworks collects $2,500 in accounts receivable.

h. Webworks pays off its salaries payable from August.

i. Webworks pays off $5,500 of its accounts payable.

j. Webworks pays off $5,000 of its outstanding note payable.

k. Webworks pays Leon salary of $2,000.

l. Webworks pays taxes of $795 in cash.

Required:

A. Prepare journal entries for the above events.

B. Post the journal entries to T-accounts.

C. Prepare an unadjusted trial balance for Webworks for September.

D. Prepare adjusting entries for the following and post them to your T-accounts.

m. Webworks owes Nancy $300 for her work during the last week of September.

n. Leon's parents let him know that Webworks owes $275 toward the electricity bill. Webworks will pay them in October.

o. Webworks determines that it has $70 worth of supplies remaining at the end of September.

p. Prepaid rent should be adjusted for September's portion.

q. Webworks is continuing to accrue bad debts so that the allowance for doubtful accounts is 10 percent of accounts receivable.

r. Record cost of goods sold.

E. Prepare an adjusted trial balance.

F. Prepare financial statements for September.

ENDNOTES

1. Clayton T. Rumble, "So You Still Have Not Adopted LIFO," *Management Accountant*, October 1983, 50.
2. Yury Iofe, senior editor, and Matthew C. Calderisi, CPA, managing editor, *Accounting Trends & Techniques*, 62nd edition (New York: American Institute of Certified Public Accountants, 2008), 159.
3. Many states also charge a tax on income. These states have their own unique set of laws although they often resemble the tax laws applied by the federal government.
4. As will be seen in the next chapter, similar arguments are made in connection with property and equipment—the reported amount and the value can vary greatly. However, those assets are not normally held for resale purpose so that current worth is of much less interest to decision makers.
5. Because ending inventory for one period becomes the beginning inventory for the next, application of a cost flow assumption does change that figure also. However, the impact is only indirect because the number is simply carried over from the previous period. No current computation of beginning inventory is made based on the cost flow assumption in use.
6. Some analysts prefer to use 360 days to make this computation simpler.

CHAPTER 10

In a Set of Financial Statements, What Information Is Conveyed about Property and Equipment?

Video Clip

Joe introduces Chapter 10 and speaks about the course in general.

View the video online at: http://blip.tv/play/sDyBv71rAA

1. THE REPORTING OF PROPERTY AND EQUIPMENT

LEARNING OBJECTIVES

At the end of this section, students should be able to meet the following objectives:

1. **Recognize that tangible operating assets with lives of over one year (such as property and equipment) are initially reported at historical cost.**
2. **Understand the rationale for assigning the cost of these operating assets to expense over time if the item has a finite life.**
3. **Recognize that these assets are reported on the balance sheet at book value, which is cost less accumulated depreciation.**
4. **Explain the reason for not reporting property and equipment at fair value except in specified circumstances.**

Question: Wal-Mart Stores Inc. owns thousands of huge retail outlets and supercenters located throughout the United States and many foreign countries. These facilities contain a wide variety of machinery, fixtures and the like such as cash registers and shelving. On its January 31, 2009, balance sheet,

Wal-Mart reports "property and equipment, net" of nearly $93 billion, a figure that made up almost 60 percent of the company's total assets. This monetary amount was more than twice as large as any other asset reported by this company. Based on sheer size, the information conveyed about this group of accounts is extremely significant to any decision maker analyzing Wal-Mart or other similar companies. ***In creating financial statements, what is the underlying meaning of the figure reported for property, equipment, and the like?*** *What information is conveyed by the nearly $93 billion balance disclosed by Wal-Mart?*

Answer: According to U.S. GAAP, the starting basis for the monetary figure to be reported by a company for property, equipment, and other tangible operating assets with a life of over one year (as with inventory and several other assets) is historical cost. The amount sacrificed to obtain land, machinery, buildings, furniture, and so forth can be objectively determined based on an arm's length transaction. A willing buyer and a willing seller, both acting in their own self-interests, agreed on this exchange price as being satisfactory.

Thus, the cost incurred to obtain property and equipment provides vital information about management policy and decision making. It also serves as the initial figure appearing on the balance sheet for any item classified in this manner. The buyer has voluntarily chosen to relinquish the specified amount of resources to gain the asset. After the date of acquisition, the reported balance will probably never again reflect fair value.

Subsequently, for any of these operating assets that has a finite life (and most assets other than land do have finite lives), the matching principle necessitates that the historical cost be allocated to expense over the anticipated years of service. This expense is recognized systematically each period as the company utilizes the asset to generate revenue. Expenses are matched with revenues. For example, if equipment is used for ten years, all (or most) of its cost is assigned to expense over that period. This accounting is very similar to the handling of prepaid expenses such as rent as discussed in an earlier chapter. Cost is first recorded as an asset and then moved to expense over time in some logical fashion. At any point, the reported asset is the original cost less the portion of that amount that has been reclassified to expense. That is the most likely meaning of the $93 billion figure reported by Wal-Mart.

Question: The basic accounting for property and equipment certainly resembles that utilized for prepaid expenses such as rent and insurance. ***Do any significant differences exist between the method of reporting prepaid expenses and the handling of operating assets like machinery?***

Answer: One important mechanical distinction does exist when comparing the accounting for prepayments and that used for property and equipment having a finite life. With a prepaid expense (such as rent), the asset is directly reduced over time as the cost is assigned to expense. Prepaid rent balances get smaller each day as the period of usage passes.

In reporting property and equipment, the asset does not physically shrink. As the utility is consumed over time, buildings and equipment do not get smaller; they only get older. To reflect that reality, a separate **accumulated depreciation** account[1] is created to measure the total amount of the asset's cost that has been expensed to date. Through this approach, information about the original cost continues to be available. For example, if equipment is reported as $30,000 and the related accumulated depreciation currently holds a balance of $10,000, the reader knows that the asset originally cost $30,000 but $10,000 of that amount has been moved to expense since the date of acquisition.

For reporting purposes, accumulated depreciation is subtracted from the historical cost of the asset to arrive at the net figure to be shown on the balance sheet. The remaining cost-based amount is often referred to as the net **book value** of the asset. If cost is $30,000 and accumulated depreciation is $10,000, net book value of $20,000 appears in the financial statements. The nearly $93 billion net figure reported by Wal-Mart is the cost of its property and equipment that has not yet been assigned to expense. It is the **historical cost** of those assets (approximately $126 billion) less accumulated depreciation (almost $33 billion—the amount of the cost already recorded as an expense).

Four accounts make up the property and equipment reported by Wal-Mart:

- Land
- Buildings and improvements
- Fixtures and equipment
- Transportation equipment

These are common titles but a variety of other names are also used to report similar asset groups. Examples include property, plant and equipment (abbreviated as PP&E), fixed assets, and plant assets. Regardless of the name that is applied, cost is reported initially and then depreciated unless—like land—the asset has an infinite life.

accumulated depreciation

A contra-asset account created to measure the cost of a depreciable asset (such as buildings and equipment) that has been assigned to expense to date.

book value

Original cost of a depreciable asset such as buildings and equipment less the total amount of accumulated depreciation to date; it is also called net book value or carrying value.

historical cost

All the normal and necessary amounts incurred to get an asset into the position and condition to help generate revenues; it is the starting basis for the balance sheet presentation of assets such as inventory, land, and equipment.

EXERCISE

Link to multiple-choice question for practice purposes: http://www.quia.com/quiz/2092935.html

Question: Wal-Mart reports property and equipment with a book value of $93 billion. However, that figure has virtually nothing to do with the value of these assets. They might actually be worth hundreds of billions. Decision makers analyze financial statements in order to make decisions about an organization at the current moment. Are these decision makers not more interested in the fair value of these assets than in what remains of historical cost? ***Why are property and equipment not reported at fair value?*** *Is fair value not a much more useful piece of information than cost minus accumulated depreciation when assessing the financial health and prospects of a business?*

Answer: The debate among accountants, company officials, investors, creditors, and others over whether various assets should be reported based on historical cost or fair value has raged for decades. There is no easy resolution. Good points can be made on each side of the argument. As financial accounting has evolved, rules for reporting certain assets (such as many types of stock and debt investments where exact market prices can be readily determined) have been changed to abandon historical cost in favor of reflecting fair value. However, no such radical changes in U.S. GAAP have taken place for property and equipment. Reporting has remained relatively unchanged for many decades. Unless the value of one of these assets has been impaired or it is going to be sold in the near future, historical cost remains the basis for balance sheet presentation.

The fair value of property and equipment is a reporting alternative preferred by some decision makers, but only if the amount is objective and reliable. That is where the difficulty begins. Historical cost is both an objective and a reliable measure, determined by a willing buyer and a willing seller. In contrast, any gathering of "experts" could assess the value of a large building or an acre of land at widely differing figures with equal certitude. No definitive value can possibly exist until sold. What is the informational benefit of a number that is so subjective? Additionally, the asset's value might change radically on a daily basis rendering previous assessments useless. For that reason, historical cost, as adjusted for accumulated depreciation, remains the accepted method for reporting property and equipment on an organization's balance sheet.

This use of historical cost is supported by the going concern assumption that has long existed as part of the foundation for financial accounting. In simple terms, a long life is anticipated for virtually all organizations. Officials expect operations to continue for the years required to fulfill the goals that provide the basis for their decisions. They do not plan to sell property and equipment prematurely but rather to utilize these assets for their entire lives. Consequently, financial statements are constructed assuming the organization will function until all of its assets are consumed. Unless impaired or a sale is anticipated in the near future, the fair value of property and equipment is not truly of significance to the operations of a business. It might be interesting information but it is not actually of much importance if no sale is contemplated.

However, the estimated fair value of a company's property and equipment is a factor that does influence the current price of any ownership shares traded actively on a stock exchange. For example, the price of shares of The Coca-Cola Company is certainly impacted by the perceived value of the company's property and equipment. A widely discussed concept known as "**market capitalization**" is one method used to gauge the fair value of a business as a whole. Market capitalization is computed by multiplying the current price of a company's stock times the number of ownership shares that are outstanding. For example, approximately 2.3 billion shares of The Coca-Cola Company were in the hands of investors at December 31, 2008. Because the stock was selling for $45.27 per share on that day, the company's market capitalization was over $104 billion. This figure does not provide a direct valuation for any specific asset but it does give a general idea as to whether fair value approximates book value or is radically different.

market capitalization

Computed by multiplying a company's current stock price times the number of ownership shares outstanding in the hands of the public; it is used to gauge the fair value of a business taken as a whole.

depreciation

A mechanically derived pattern allocating the cost of assets such as buildings and equipment to expense over the expected number of years that they will be used to help generate revenues.

Talking With an Independent Auditor about International Financial Reporting Standards

Following is a continuation of our interview with Robert A. Vallejo, partner with the accounting firm PricewaterhouseCoopers.

Question: In U.S. GAAP, land, buildings, and equipment have traditionally been reported at historical cost less the accumulated **depreciation** recognized to date. Adjustment to fair value is prohibited unless the asset's value has been impaired. Because of the conservative nature of accounting, increases in value are ignored completely until proven through a disposal. Thus, land might be worth $20 million but only shown on the balance sheet as $400,000 if that amount reflects cost. According to IFRS, can increases in the fair value of these assets be reported?

Rob Vallejo: Under IFRS, a company can elect to account for all or specific types of assets using fair value. In that instance, the designated assets are valued each reporting period and written up or down accordingly. Based on my experience working abroad and from speaking with my colleagues in Europe, few companies appear to elect to account for fixed assets using fair value. I am guessing that this decision is because of the administrative challenges of determining fair value and the earnings volatility that would be created by such a policy. Reported net income could bob up and down erratically as fair values fluctuated. Company officials rarely like to see such swings. However, in the right circumstances, using fair value might be a reasonable decision for some companies.

KEY TAKEAWAYS

Land, buildings, and equipment are reported on a company's balance sheet at net book value, which is cost less any of that figure that has been assigned to expense. Over time, the expensed amount is maintained in a contra asset account known as accumulated depreciation. Thus, the asset's cost remains readily apparent as well as the net book value. Land and any other asset that does not have a finite life remain at cost. Unless the value of specific items has been impaired or an asset is to be sold in the near future, fair value is not used for reporting land, buildings, and equipment. It is not viewed as an objective or reliable amount. In addition, because the asset is not expected to be sold, fair value is of limited informational use to decision makers.

2. DETERMINING HISTORICAL COST AND DEPRECIATION EXPENSE

LEARNING OBJECTIVES

At the end of this section, students should be able to meet the following objectives:

1. **Determine the guiding accounting rule that helps ascertain which costs are capitalized in connection with property and equipment and which are expensed.**
2. **List the variables that impact the amount of depreciation to be expensed each period.**
3. **Recognize that the straight-line method predominates in practice but any system that provides a rational approach can be used to create a pattern for depreciation.**

Question: Businesses hold numerous types of assets such as receivables, inventory, cash, investments, and patents. Proper classification is important for the clarity of the reported information. ***What requirements must be met for an asset to be classified as part of a business's property and equipment?***

Answer: To be included within the property and equipment category, an asset must first have tangible physical substance and be expected to be used for longer than a single year. Furthermore, it must serve to generate revenues within the normal operating activities of the business. It cannot be held for immediate resale, like inventory.

A building used as a warehouse and machinery operated in the production of inventory both meet these characteristics. Other examples include computers, furniture, fixtures, and equipment. Conversely, land acquired as a future plant site and a building held for speculative purposes are both classified with investments (or, possibly, "other assets") on the owner's balance sheet rather than as property and equipment. Neither is used at the current time to help generate operating revenues.

Question: The basis for reporting property and equipment is historical cost. What amounts are included in determining the cost of such assets? Assume, for example, that Wal-Mart purchases a parcel of land and then constructs one of its retail stores on the site. Wal-Mart also buys a new cash register to use at this outlet. Initially, such assets are reported at cost. ***For property and equipment, how is historical cost defined?***

Answer: In the previous chapter, the cost of a company's inventory was identified as the sum of all normal and necessary amounts paid to get the merchandise into condition and position to be sold. Property and equipment is not bought for resale so this rule cannot be followed here without some modification. Instead, all expenditures are included within the cost of property and equipment if the amounts are normal and necessary to get the asset into condition and position to assist the company in earning revenues. That is their purpose: to generate profits by helping to create the sale of goods and services.

Land can serve as an example. When purchased, the various normal and necessary expenditures made by the owner to ready the property for its intended use are capitalized to arrive at the cost to be reported. These amounts include payments made to attain ownership as well as any fees required to obtain legal title. If the land is acquired as a building site, money spent for any needed grading and clearing is also included as a cost of the land rather than as a cost of the building or as an expense. These activities readied the land for its ultimate use.

Buildings, machinery, furniture, equipment and the like are all reported in a similar fashion. For example, the cost of constructing a retail store includes money spent for materials and labor as well as charges for permits and the fees charged by architects and engineers. These are normal and necessary to get the structure into condition and position to help generate revenues.

As another example, the cost of a new cash register might well include shipping charges, installation fees, and training sessions to teach employees to use the asset. These costs all meet the criterion for capitalization. They appear to be normal and necessary to permit use of the asset for its intended purpose. Hence, a new cash register bought for $4,100 might actually be reported as an asset by its owner at $5,300 as follows:

FIGURE 10.1 Capitalized Cost of Equipment

Invoice Price—Charged by Seller	$4,100
Shipping Costs from Manufacturer	300
Installation	400
Employee Training Sessions	500
Cost of Cash Register	$5,300

EXERCISE

Link to multiple-choice question for practice purposes: http://www.quia.com/quiz/2092929.html

Question: If a company pays $600,000 on January 1, Year One to rent a building to serve as a store for five years, a prepaid rent account (an asset) is established for that amount. Because the rented facility will be used to generate revenues throughout this period, a portion of the cost is reclassified annually as an expense to comply with the matching principle. At the end of Year One, $120,000 (or one-fifth) of the cost is moved from the asset balance into rent expense by means of an adjusting entry. As a result, the prepaid rent on the balance sheet drops to $480,000, the amount paid for the four remaining years.

If, instead, the company buys a building with an expected five-year life[2] for $600,000, the accounting is quite similar. The initial cost is capitalized to reflect the future economic benefit. Once again, an expense is then recorded at the end of Year One for a portion of this cost to satisfy the matching principle. This expense is referred to as depreciation. Should the Year One depreciation recognized in connection with this acquired building also be $120,000? ***How is the annual amount of depreciation expense determined for reporting purposes?***

Answer: The specific amount of depreciation expense recorded each year for buildings, machinery, furniture, and the like is based on four variables:

1. The historical cost of the asset
2. Its expected useful life
3. Any anticipated residual (or salvage) value
4. An allocation pattern

After total cost is computed, officials estimate the useful life based on company experience with similar assets in the past or other sources of information such as guidelines provided by the manufacturer.[3] In a similar fashion, officials arrive at an expected residual value—an estimate of the likely worth of the asset at the end of its useful life to the company. Because both life expectancy and residual value are no more than guesses, depreciation is simply a mechanically derived pattern that allocates the asset's cost to expense over its expected years of use.

To illustrate, assume a building is purchased by a company on January 1, Year One, for cash of $600,000. Based on experience with similar assets, officials believe that this structure will be worth only $30,000 at the end of an expected five-year life. U.S. GAAP does not require any specific computational method for determining the annual allocation of the asset's cost to expense. Over fifty years ago, the Committee on Accounting Procedure (the authoritative body at the time) issued Accounting Research Bulletin 43 which stated that any method could be used to determine annual depreciation if done in a "systematic and rational manner." This guidance remains in effect today.

straight-line depreciation

Method used to calculate the annual amount of depreciation expense by subtracting any estimated residual value from cost and then dividing this depreciable base by the asset's estimated useful life; a majority of companies in the United States use this method for financial reporting purposes.

Consequently, a vast majority of reporting companies (including Wal-Mart) have chosen to adopt the straight-line method to assign the cost of property and equipment to expense over their useful lives. The estimated residual value is subtracted from cost to arrive at the asset's depreciable base. This figure is then expensed evenly over the expected life. It is systematic and rational: **Straight-line depreciation** allocates an equal expense to each period in which the asset is used to generate revenue.

Straight-line method:

(cost – estimated residual value) = depreciable base

depreciable base/expected useful life = annual depreciation

($600,000 – $30,000) = $570,000/5 years = depreciation expense of $114,000 per year

Question: ***After depreciation has been calculated for the current period, how is this allocation of the asset's cost to expense recorded within the company's accounting system?***

Answer: An adjusting entry is prepared at the end of each period to move the assigned cost from the asset account on the balance sheet to expense on the income statement. To reiterate, the building account is not directly reduced. A separate negative or contra account (accumulated depreciation) is created to reflect the total amount of the cost that has been expensed to date. Thus, the asset's present book value as well as its original historical cost are both still in evidence.

The entries to record the cost of acquiring this building and the annual depreciation expense over the five-year life are as follows. The straight-line method is used here to determine the individual allocations to expense. Now that students should be familiar with using debits and credits for recording, the number in parenthesis is included (where relevant to the discussion) to indicate the total account balance *after* the entry is posted. As indicated in an earlier chapter, revenues, expenses, and dividends are closed out each year. Thus, the depreciation expense reported on each income statement measures only the expense assigned to that period.

FIGURE 10.2 Building Acquisition and Straight-Line Depreciation

1/1/1	Building Cash	$600,000 ($600,000)	 $600,000
12/31/1	Depreciation Expense Accumulated Depreciation —Building	114,000 (114,000)	 114,000 (114,000)
12/31/2	Depreciation Expense Accumulated Depreciation —Building	114,000 (114,000)	 114,000 (228,000)
12/31/3	Depreciation Expense Accumulated Depreciation —Building	114,000 (114,000)	 114,000 (342,000)
12/31/4	Depreciation Expense Accumulated Depreciation —Building	114,000 (114,000)	 114,000 (456,000)
12/31/5	Depreciation Expense Accumulated Depreciation —Building	114,000 (114,000)	 114,000 (570,000)

Because the straight-line method is applied, depreciation expense is a consistent $114,000 each year. As a result, the net book value reported on the balance sheet drops during the asset's useful life from $600,000 to $30,000. At the end of the first year, it is $486,000 ($600,000 cost minus accumulated depreciation $114,000). At the end of the second year, net book value has been reduced to $372,000 ($600,000 cost minus accumulated depreciation of $228,000). This pattern continues over the entire five years.

EXERCISE

Link to multiple-choice question for practice purposes: http://www.quia.com/quiz/2092906.html

KEY TAKEAWAYS

Tangible operating assets with lives of over a year are initially reported at historical cost. All expenditures are capitalized if they are normal and necessary to put the property into the position and condition to assist the company in generating revenue. If the asset has a finite life, this cost is then assigned to expense over the years of expected use in some systematic and rational pattern. Many companies apply the straight-line method, which assigns an equal amount to every full year. In that approach, the expected residual value is subtracted from cost to get the depreciable base that is allocated evenly over the anticipated years of use by the company.

3. RECORDING DEPRECIATION EXPENSE FOR A PARTIAL YEAR

LEARNING OBJECTIVES

At the end of this section, students should be able to meet the following objectives:

1. **Understand the need to record depreciation for the current period prior to the disposal of property or equipment.**
2. **Construct the journal entry to record the disposal of property or equipment and the recognition of a gain or loss.**
3. **Explain the half-year convention and the reason that it is frequently used by companies for reporting purposes.**

Question: Property and equipment are occasionally sold before the end of their estimated lives. A company's operational needs might change or officials could want the benefit of a newer or more efficient model. ***What accounting is necessary in the event that a piece of property or equipment is sold prior to the conclusion of its useful life?*** *In the above example, assume that after the adjusting entry for depreciation is made on December 31, Year Two, the building is sold for $290,000 cash. How is that transaction recorded?*

Answer: Accounting for the disposal of property and equipment is relatively straightforward.

First, to establish account balances that are appropriate at the date of sale, depreciation is recorded for the period of use during the current year. In this way, the expense is matched with any revenues earned in the current period.

Second, the amount received from the sale is recorded while the book value of the asset (both its cost and accumulated depreciation) is removed. If the owner receives less for the asset than this book value, a loss is recognized for the difference, which decreases reported net income. If more is received than book value, the excess is recorded as a gain so that net income increases.

Because the above building is sold for $290,000 on December 31, Year Two, when the book value is $372,000 (cost of $600,000 less accumulated depreciation of $228,000), a loss of $82,000 is reported by the seller ($372,000 book value less $290,000 proceeds). The following entry is recorded after the depreciation adjustment for the period is made.

FIGURE 10.3 Sale of Building at a Loss

12/31/2	Cash	290,000	
	Accumulated Depreciation—Building	228,000	
	Loss on Sale of Building	82,000	
	Building		600,000

Conversely, if this building is sold on that date for $440,000 rather than $290,000, the company receives $68,000 more than book value ($440,000 less $372,000) so that a gain of that amount is recognized.

FIGURE 10.4 Sale of Building at a Gain

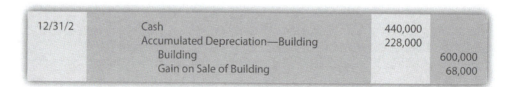

12/31/2	Cash	440,000	
	Accumulated Depreciation—Building	228,000	
	Building		600,000
	Gain on Sale of Building		68,000

Although gains and losses appear on the income statement, they are often shown separately from revenues and expenses. In that way, a decision maker can determine both the income derived from primary operations (revenues less expenses) and the amount that resulted from tangential activities such as the sale of a building or other property (gains less losses).

EXERCISE

Link to multiple-choice question for practice purposes: http://www.quia.com/quiz/2092937.html

Question: In the reporting above, the building was bought on January 1 and sold on December 31 so that depreciation was always determined and recorded for a full year. ***What amount of depreciation is appropriate if property or equipment is held for less than twelve months during a year?*** *Virtually all such assets are bought or sold during the year so that a partial year is appropriate.*

Answer: The recording of depreciation follows the matching principle. If an asset is owned for less than a full year, it does not help generate revenues for all twelve months. The amount of expense should be reduced accordingly. For example, if the above building is purchased on April 1, Year One, depreciation expense of only $85,500 (9/12 of the full-year amount of $114,000) is recognized on December 31, Year One. Similarly, if an asset is sold on a day other than December 31, less than a full year's depreciation is assigned to the year of sale. Once again, revenue is not generated for the entire period; depreciation expense must also be recognized proportionally.

To illustrate, assume the above building was purchased on April 1 of Year One for $600,000 and then sold for $350,000 on September 1 of Year Three. As calculated above, depreciation for Year One is $85,500. Depreciation for the final eight months that it was used in Year Three is $76,000 (8/12 of $114,000). The following journal entries reduce the asset's book value to $324,500 (cost of $600,000 less accumulated depreciation of $275,500). Cash of $350,000 is collected from the sale. Thus, a gain of $25,500 is recognized ($350,000 less $324,500).

FIGURE 10.5 Acquisition, Depreciation, and Sale of Building

4/1/1	Building	$600,000 ($600,000)	
	Cash		$600,000
12/31/1	Depreciation Expense	85,500 ($85,500)	
	Accumulated Depreciation —Building		85,500 (85,500)
12/31/2	Depreciation Expense	114,000 ($114,000)	
	Accumulated Depreciation —Building		114,000 (199,500)
9/1/3	Depreciation Expense	76,000 ($76,000)	
	Accumulated Depreciation —Building		76,000 (275,500)
9/1/3	Cash	350,000	
	Accumulated Depreciation —Building	275,500	
	Building		600,000
	Gain on Sale of Building		25,500

Question: Monitoring the specific days on which depreciable assets are bought and sold seems like a tedious process. ***Do companies use a simpler method for assigning depreciation when a piece of property or equipment is held for less than a full year?***

Answer: Most companies hold many depreciable assets, often thousands. Depreciation is nothing more than a mechanical cost allocation process. It is not an attempt to mirror current value. Consequently, company officials often prefer not to invest the time and effort needed to keep track of the specific number of days or weeks of an asset's use during the years of purchase and sale. As a result, depreciation is often calculated to the nearest month when one of these transactions is made. A full month of expense is recorded if an asset is held for fifteen days or more whereas no depreciation is recognized in a month where usage is less than fifteen days. No genuine informational value comes from monitoring the depreciation of assets down to days, hours, and minutes. An automobile acquired on March 19, for example, is depreciated as if bought on April 1. A computer sold on November 11 is assumed to have been used until October 31.

half-year convention

Method of calculating depreciation for depreciable assets that are held for any period less than a year by automatically taking one-half of year of depreciation; it makes the maintenance of exact records unnecessary.

As another accepted alternative, many companies apply the **half-year convention** (or some variation). When property or equipment is owned for any period less than a full year, a half year of depreciation is automatically assumed. Maintenance of exact records is not necessary. Long-lived assets are typically bought and sold at various times throughout each period so that, on the average, one-half year is a reasonable assumption. As long as such approaches are applied consistently, reported figures are viewed as fairly presented. Property and equipment bought on February 3 or sold on November 27 is depreciated for exactly one-half year in both situations.

EXERCISE

Link to multiple-choice question for practice purposes: http://www.quia.com/quiz/2092938.html

KEY TAKEAWAYS

Depreciation expense is recorded for property and equipment at the end of each fiscal year and also at the time of an asset's disposal. To record a disposal, cost and accumulated depreciation are removed. Any proceeds are recorded and the difference between the amount received and the book value is recognized as a gain (if more than book value is collected) or a loss (if less is collected). Many companies automatically record depreciation for one-half year for any period of less than a full year. The process is much simpler and, as a mechanical allocation process, no need for absolute precision is warranted.

4. ALTERNATIVE DEPRECIATION PATTERNS AND THE RECORDING OF A WASTING ASSET

LEARNING OBJECTIVES

At the end of this section, students should be able to meet the following objectives:

1. **Explain the justification for accelerated methods of depreciation.**
2. **Compute depreciation expense using the double-declining balance method.**
3. **Realize that the overall impact on net income is not affected by a particular cost allocation pattern.**
4. **Describe the units-of-production method including its advantages and disadvantages.**
5. **Compute depletion expense for a wasting asset such as an oil well or a forest of trees.**
6. **Explain the reason that depletion amounts are not directly recorded as an expense.**

Question: Straight-line depreciation certainly qualifies as systematic and rational. The same amount of cost is assigned to expense during each period of use. ***Because no specific method is required by U.S. GAAP, do companies ever use alternative approaches to create other allocation patterns for depreciation?*** *If so, how are these additional methods justified?*

accelerated depreciation

Any method of determining depreciation that assigns larger expenses to the initial years of an asset's service and smaller expenses to the later years; it is justified by the assumption that newer assets generate more revenues than older assets do.

Answer: The most common alternative to the straight-line method is **accelerated depreciation**, which records a larger expense in the initial years of an asset's service. The primary rationale for this pattern is that property and equipment often produce higher revenues earlier in their lives because they are newer. The matching principle would suggest that recognizing more depreciation in these periods is appropriate to better align the expense with the revenues earned.

A second justification for accelerated depreciation is that some types of property and equipment lose value more quickly in their first few years than they do in later years. Automobiles and other vehicles are a typical example of this pattern. Recording a greater expense initially is said to better reflect reality.

Over the decades, a number of equations have been invented to mathematically create an accelerated depreciation pattern, high expense at first with subsequent cost allocations falling throughout the life of the property. The most common is the **double-declining balance method (DDB)**. When using DDB, annual depreciation is determined by multiplying the book value of the asset times two divided by the expected years of life. As book value drops, annual expense drops. This formula has no internal logic except that it creates the desired pattern, an expense that is higher in the first years of operation and less after that. Although residual value is not utilized in this computation, the final amount of depreciation recognized must be manipulated to arrive at this proper ending balance.

double-declining balance method (DDB)

An accelerated method that computes depreciation each year by multiplying the asset's book value (cost less accumulated depreciation) times two divided by the expected useful life.

Depreciation for the building bought above for $600,000 with an expected five-year life and a residual value of $30,000 is calculated as follows if DDB is applied.

(cost – accumulated depreciation) × 2/expected life = depreciation expense for period

Year One:

($600,000 – $0) = $600,000 × 2/5 = $240,000 depreciation expense

Year Two:

($600,000 – $240,000) = $360,000 × 2/5 = $144,000 depreciation expense

Year Three:

($600,000 – $384,000) = $216,000 × 2/5 = $86,400 depreciation expense

Year Four:

($600,000 – $470,400) = $129,600 × 2/5 = $51,840 depreciation expense

Year Five:

($600,000 – $522,240) = $77,760,

so depreciation for Year Five must be set at $47,760 to arrive at the expected residual value of $30,000. This final expense is always the amount needed to arrive at the expected residual value.

Note that the desired expense pattern has resulted. The expense starts at $240,000 and becomes smaller in each subsequent period.

FIGURE 10.6 Building Acquisition and Double-Declining Balance Depreciation

1/1/1	Building	$600,000 ($600,000)	
	Cash		$600,000
12/31/1	Depreciation Expense	240,000 (240,000)	
	Accumulated Depreciation —Building		240,000 (240,000)
12/31/2	Depreciation Expense	144,000 (144,000)	
	Accumulated Depreciation —Building		144,000 (384,000)
12/31/3	Depreciation Expense	86,400 (86,400)	
	Accumulated Depreciation —Building		86,400 (470,400)
12/31/4	Depreciation Expense	51,840 (51,840)	
	Accumulated Depreciation —Building		51,840 (522,240)
12/31/5	Depreciation Expense	47,760 (47,760)	
	Accumulated Depreciation —Building		47,760 (570,000)

When using accelerated depreciation, book value falls quickly at first because of the high initial expense levels. Thus, if the asset is sold early in its life, a reported gain is more likely. For example, in the earlier example where straight-line depreciation was applied, the building was sold after two years for

$290,000 creating an $82,000 loss because the book value was $372,000. The book value was high in comparison to the amount received.

With DDB, if the same building had been sold on December 31, Year Two for $290,000, a $74,000 gain results because book value has dropped all the way to $216,000 ($600,000 cost less $384,000 accumulated depreciation). Accelerated depreciation creates a lower book value, especially in the early years of ownership.

FIGURE 10.7 Building Sold after Two Years

12/31/2	Cash	290,000	
	Accumulated Depreciation—Building	384,000	
	Building		600,000
	Gain on Sale of Building		74,000

Although the annual amounts are quite different, the overall net income is never affected by the allocation pattern in use. In this example, a building was bought for $600,000 and later sold after two years for $290,000. Thus, net income for the entire period of use must be reduced by the $310,000 difference regardless of the approach applied.

FIGURE 10.8 Depreciation Methods—Overall Impact on Net Income

	Straight-Line Method	Double-Declining Balance Method
Year One Depreciation Expense	($114,000)	($240,000)
Year Two Depreciation Expense	(114,000)	(144,000)
Loss on Sale for $290,000	(82,000)	
Gain on Sale for $290,000		+74,000
Overall Impact on Net Income	($310,000)	($310,000)

EXERCISE

Link to multiple-choice question for practice purposes: http://www.quia.com/quiz/2092939.html

Question: The two methods demonstrated here for establishing a depreciation pattern are based on time, five years to be precise. In most cases, though, it is the physical use of the asset rather than the passage of time that is actually relevant to this process. Use is the action that generates revenues. ***How is the depreciation of a long-lived tangible asset determined if usage can be measured?*** *For example, assume that a limousine company buys a new vehicle for $90,000 to serve as an addition to its fleet. Company officials expect this limousine to be driven for three hundred thousand miles and then have no residual value. How is depreciation expense determined each period?*

units-of-production method (UOP)

A method of determining depreciation that is not based on the passage of time but rather on the level of actual usage during the period.

Answer: Depreciation does not have to be based on time; it only has to be computed in a systematic and rational manner. Thus, the **units-of-production method (UOP)** is another alternative that is occasionally encountered. UOP is justified because the periodic expense is matched with the work actually performed. In this illustration, the limousine's depreciation can be computed using the number of miles driven in a year, an easy figure to determine.

($90,000 less $0)/300,000 miles = $0.30 per mile

Depreciation is recorded at a rate of $0.30 per mile. The depreciable cost basis is allocated evenly over the miles that the vehicle is expected to be driven. UOP is a straight-line method but one that is based on usage (miles driven, in this example) rather than years. Because of the direct connection between the expense allocation and the work performed, UOP is a very appealing approach. It truly mirrors the matching principle. Unfortunately, measuring the physical use of most assets is rarely as easy as with a limousine.

For example, if this vehicle is driven 80,000 miles in Year One, 120,000 miles in Year Two, and 100,000 miles in Year Three, depreciation will be $24,000, $36,000, and $30,000 when the $0.30 per mile rate is applied.

FIGURE 10.9 Depreciation—Units-of-Production Method

1/1/1	Vehicle Cash	$90,000 ($90,000)	 $90,000
12/31/1	Depreciation Expense Accumulated Depreciation —Vehicle	24,000 (24,000)	 24,000 (24,000)
12/31/2	Depreciation Expense Accumulated Depreciation —Vehicle	36,000 (36,000)	 36,000 (60,000)
12/31/3	Depreciation Expense Accumulated Depreciation —Vehicle	30,000 (30,000)	 30,000 (90,000)

Estimations rarely prove to be precise reflections of reality. This vehicle will not likely be driven exactly three hundred thousand miles. If used for less and then retired, both the cost and accumulated depreciation are removed. A loss is recorded equal to the remaining book value unless some cash or other asset is received. If driven more than the anticipated number of miles, depreciation stops at three hundred thousand miles. At that point, the cost of the asset will have been depreciated completely.

EXERCISE

Link to multiple-choice question for practice purposes: http://www.quia.com/quiz/2092930.html

Question: The cost of land is not depreciated because it does not have a finite life. However, land is often acquired solely for the natural resources that it might contain such as oil, timber, gold or the like. As the oil is pumped, the timber harvested or the gold extracted, a portion of the value is physically separated from the land. ***How is the reported cost of land affected when its natural resources are removed?***

Answer: Oil, timber, gold and the like are "wasting assets." They are taken from land over time, a process known as **depletion**. Value is literally removed from the asset rather than being consumed through use as with the depreciation of property and equipment. The same mechanical calculation demonstrated above for the units-of-production (UOP) method is applied. The 2008 financial statements for Massey Energy state that "depletion of mining properties owned in fee and leased mineral rights is computed using the units-of-production method over the estimated proven and probable reserve tons."

depletion

A method of allocating the cost of a wasting asset (such as a gold mine or oil well) to expense over the periods during which the value is removed.

Because the value is separated rather than used up, depletion initially leads to the recording of inventory (such as oil or gold, for example). An expense is recognized only at the eventual point of sale.

As with other types of property and equipment, historical cost is the sum of all normal and necessary expenditures to get the wasting asset into condition and position to generate revenues. To illustrate, assume that at the beginning of Year One, land is acquired for $1.6 million cash while another $400,000 is spent to construct a mining operation. Total cost is $2 million. The land is estimated to hold ten thousand tons of ore to be mined and sold. The land will be worth an estimated amount of only $100,000 after all the ore is removed. Depletion is calculated as $190 per ton ([$2,000,000 cost less $100,000 residual value]/10,000 tons). It is a straight-line approach based on units held, an allocation that follows the procedures of the units-of-production method.

Assume that 3,000 tons of ore are extracted in Year One and sold in Year Two for $1 million cash. Another 3,600 tons are removed in the second year for sale at a later time. Depletion is $570,000 in Year One ($190 × 3,000 tons) and $684,000 in Year Two ($190 × 3,600 tons).

FIGURE 10.10 Depletion of Wasting Asset

1/1/1	Land with Mineral Rights	$1,600,000	
	Cash		$1,600,000
1/1/1	Land with Mineral Rights	400,000 (2,000,000)	
	Cash		400,000
12/31/1	Inventory of Ore	570,000	
	Accumulated Depletion		570,000 (570,000)
Year Two	Cash	1,000,000	
	Revenue from Sale of Ore		1,000,000
	Cost of Goods Sold	570,000	
	Inventory of Ore		570,000
12/31/2	Inventory	684,000	
	Accumulated Depletion		684,000 (1,254,000)

For depreciation, expense is recognized immediately as the asset's utility is consumed. With depletion, no expense is recorded until the inventory is eventually sold.

After two years, this land is reported on the company's balance sheet at a net book value of $746,000 based on its historical cost of $2 million. The inventory of ore is reported as an asset at $684,000 until sold.

FIGURE 10.11 Book Value of Land with Mineral Rights

Land with Mineral Rights	$2,000,000
Less: Accumulated Depletion	1,254,000
Net Book Value	$746,000

EXERCISE

Link to multiple-choice question for practice purposes: http://www.quia.com/quiz/2092931.html

KEY TAKEAWAY

Cost allocation patterns for determining depreciation exist beyond just the straight-line method. Accelerated depreciation records more expense in the earlier years of use than in later periods. This pattern is sometimes considered a better matching of expenses with revenues and a closer image of reality. The double-declining balance method is the most common version of accelerated depreciation. Its formula was derived to create the appropriate allocation pattern. The units-of-production method is often used for property and equipment where the quantity of work performed can be easily monitored. This approach is also used in recording the depletion of wasting assets such as oil wells and silver mines.

5. RECORDING ASSET EXCHANGES AND EXPENDITURES THAT AFFECT OLDER ASSETS

LEARNING OBJECTIVES

At the end of this section, students should be able to meet the following objectives:

1. **Record the exchange of one asset for another based on fair value and explain the rationale for this method of recording.**
2. **Determine when the fair value of an asset received is used for recording an exchange rather than the fair value of the property surrendered.**
3. **Compute the allocation of cost between assets when more than one is required in a single transaction.**
4. **Know when expenditures must be capitalized for an asset that has been in use for some time and the impact on future depreciation expense calculations.**

*Question: Some assets are acquired by exchange instead of through purchase (***asset exchange***). For example, the limousine discussed earlier might well be traded away after two years for a newer model. Such transactions are common, especially with vehicles.* ***How is the cost of a new asset determined if obtained through an exchange rather than an acquisition?***

To illustrate, assume that this limousine is traded to an automobile manufacturer for a new model on December 31, Year Two. By that time as shown previously, the net book value had fallen to $30,000 (cost of $90,000 less accumulated depreciation of $60,000). However, because company employees have taken excellent care of the vehicle during those two years, fair value is actually $45,000. As has been discussed, book value rarely equals fair value during the life of property and equipment. Assume that the vehicle being acquired is worth $100,000 so the company also pays $55,000 in cash ($100,000 value received less $45,000 value surrendered) to the manufacturer to complete the trade. How is such an exchange recorded?

asset exchange

A trade of one asset for another in which the book value of the old asset is removed from the records while the new asset is recorded at the fair value surrendered (if known); the difference creates a gain or loss to be reported.

Answer: In virtually all cases, fair value is the accounting basis used to record items received in an exchange. The book value of the old asset is removed from the accounts and the new model is then reported at fair value. Fair value is added; book value is removed. A gain or loss is recognized for the resulting change in the company's reported financial position.

In this example, the company surrenders two assets with a total fair value of $100,000 ($45,000 value for the old limousine plus $55,000 in cash) to obtain the new vehicle. However, the assets given up have a total net book value of only $85,000 ($30,000 and $55,000). A $15,000 gain is recognized on the exchange ($100,000 fair value less $85,000 book value). The gain results because the old limousine had not lost as much value as the depreciation process had expensed. The net book value was reduced to $30,000 but the vehicle was actually worth $45,000.[4]

FIGURE 10.12 Recording Exchange of Assets

Vehicle (New)	100,000	
Accumulated Depreciation	60,000	
Vehicle (Old)		90,000
Cash		55,000
Gain on Exchange of Limousines		15,000

Question: In the previous example, the value of the assets surrendered ($45,000 plus $55,000 or $100,000) equals the value of the new limousine received ($100,000). The trade was exactly even. Because one party has better negotiating skills or a serious need for a quick trade, the two values can differ, at least slightly. For example, the limousine company might give up its old vehicle (worth $45,000) and cash ($55,000) and manage to convince the automobile manufacturer to hand over a new asset worth $110,000. ***If the values are not equal in an exchange, which fair value is used for reporting purposes?*** *Should the new limousine be recorded at the $100,000 value given up or the $110,000 value received?*

Answer: To stay consistent with the historical cost principle, the new asset received in a trade is recorded at the fair value of the item or items surrendered. Giving up the previously owned property is the sacrifice made to obtain the new asset. That is its cost to the new buyer.

Generally, the fair value of the items sacrificed equals the fair value of the items received. Most exchanges involve properties of relatively equal worth; a value of $100,000 is surrendered to acquire a value of $100,000. However, that is not always the case. Thus, if known, the fair value given up always serves as the basis for recording the asset received. Only if the value of the property traded away cannot be readily determined is the new asset recorded at its own fair value.

EXERCISE

Link to multiple-choice question for practice purposes: http://www.quia.com/quiz/2092907.html

Question: At times, two or more assets are acquired for a single price. The most common example is the purchase of a building along with the land on which it is constructed. As has been discussed, the portion of the cost assigned to the building is depreciated over its useful life in some systematic and rational manner. However, land does not have a finite life. Its cost remains an asset so that there is no impact on reported net income over time. ***How does an accountant separate the amount paid for land from the cost assigned to a building when the two are purchased together?***

Assume a business pays $5.0 million for three acres of land along with a five-story building. What part of this cost is attributed to the land and what part to the building? Does management not have a bias to assign more of the $5.0 million to land and less to the building to reduce the future amounts reported as depreciation expense?

basket purchase

The acquisition of more than one asset at a single cost, which is then allocated among those assets based on relative values.

Answer: Companies do occasionally purchase more than one asset at a time. This is sometimes referred to as a **basket purchase**. For example, a manufacturer might buy several machines in a single transaction. The cost assigned to each should be based on their relative values.

For this illustration, assume that the land and building bought for $5.0 have been appraised at $4.5 million and $1.5 million, respectively, for a total of $6.0 million. Perhaps the owner needed cash immediately and was willing to accept a price of only $5.0 million. For the buyer, the land makes up 75 percent of the value received ($4.5 million/$6.0 million) and the building the remaining 25 percent ($1.5 million/$6.0 million). The cost is simply assigned in those same proportions: $3.75 million to the land ($5.0 million × 75 percent) and $1.25 million to the building ($5.0 million × 25 percent).

FIGURE 10.13 Allocation of Cost between Land and Building

Land	3,750,000	
Building	1,250,000	
Cash		5,000,000

In the event that the buyer also has to pay other normal and necessary costs (such as attorney fees, title searches, or the like) for cash of $30,000, the adjusted cost of $5,030,000 must still be allocated based on the relative fair value percentages.

FIGURE 10.14 Total Cost Allocated between Land and Building

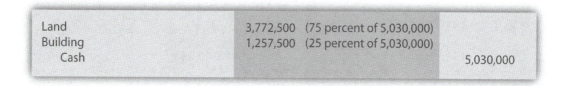

Land	3,772,500 (75 percent of 5,030,000)	
Building	1,257,500 (25 percent of 5,030,000)	
Cash		5,030,000

Occasionally, in a basket purchase, the value can be determined for one of the assets but not for both. As an example, the above land might be worth $4.5 million but no legitimate value is available for the building. Similar structures might not exist in this area for comparison purposes. In such cases, the known value is used with the remainder of the cost assigned to the other property. Assume that the total cost of these properties is $5,030,000. If the land is known to be worth $4.5 million but no reasonable value can be ascribed to the building, the excess $530,000 is arbitrarily allocated to this second asset.

FIGURE 10.15 Allocation Based on Known Value for Land Only

Land	4,500,000	
Building	530,000	
Cash		5,030,000

Does the possibility of bias exist in these allocations? Accounting is managed by human beings and they always face a variety of biases. That potential problem is one of the primary reasons that independent auditors play such an important role in the financial reporting process. These outside experts work to ensure that financial figures are presented fairly and without bias. Obviously, if the buyer assigns more of the cost of a basket purchase to land, future depreciation will be less and reported net income higher. In contrast, if more of the cost is allocated to the building, depreciation expense is higher and taxable income and income tax payments are reduced. That is also a tempting choice.

Thus, the independent auditor must gather evidence to provide reasonable assurance that such allocations are based on reliable appraisal values so that both the land and the building are fairly presented. However, a decision maker is naïve not to realize that potential bias does exist in any reporting process.

Question: Assume that a cost of $1,257,500 is assigned to the building above. Assume further that it has an expected life of twenty years and straight-line depreciation is applied with no residual value. Thus, after eight years, accumulated depreciation is $503,000 ($1,257,500 × 8 years/20 years). At that point, the company spends an additional $150,000 on the building. ***Should an expenditure associated with property and equipment that is already in use be capitalized (added to the asset account) or expensed immediately?***

Answer: The answer to this question depends on the impact that this work has on the building. In many cases, additional money is spent simply to keep the asset operating with no change in expected life or improvement in future productivity. Such costs are recorded as maintenance expense if they were anticipated or repair expense if unexpected. For example, changing the oil in a truck at regular intervals is a maintenance expense whereas fixing a dent from an accident is a repair expense. This distinction has no impact on reported income.

FIGURE 10.16 Recording of Cost to Maintain or Repair Asset

Maintenance (or Repair) Expense	150,000	
Cash		150,000

However, if the $150,000 cost increases the future operating capacity of the asset, the amount should be capitalized. The building might have been made bigger, more efficient, more productive, or less expensive to operate. If the asset has actually been improved by the cost incurred, historical cost is raised.

FIGURE 10.17 Cost Capitalized Because of Increase in Operating Capacity

Building	150,000	
Cash		150,000

Assuming that no change in either the useful life or the residual value occurs as a result of this work, depreciation expense will be $75,375 in each of the subsequent twelve years. The newly increased book value is simply allocated over the useful life that remains.

($1,257,500 +$150,000 – $503,000)/12 remaining years = $75,375

Another possibility does exist. The $150,000 might extend the building's life without creating any other improvement. Because the building will now generate revenue for a longer period of time than previously expected, this cost is capitalized. A clear benefit has been gained from the amount spent. The asset is not physically bigger or improved but its estimated life has been extended. Consequently, the building is not increased directly, but instead, accumulated depreciation is reduced. In effect, this expenditure has recaptured some of the previously expensed utility.

FIGURE 10.18 Cost Capitalized Because Expected Life Is Extended

Accumulated Depreciation	150,000	
Cash		150,000

Assuming the $150,000 payment extends the remaining useful life of the building from twelve years to eighteen with no accompanying change in residual value, depreciation expense will be $50,250 in each of these remaining eighteen years. Once again, the book value has increased but, in this situation, the life of the asset has also been lengthened.

reduced accumulated depreciation: $503,000 – $150,000 = $353,000

adjusted net book value: $1,257,500 – $353,000 = $904,500

annual depreciation: $904,500/18 years = $50,250

EXERCISE

Link to multiple-choice question for practice purposes: http://www.quia.com/quiz/2092959.html

KEY TAKEAWAYS

Assets are occasionally obtained through exchange. Reported cost is established based on the fair value of the property surrendered because that measures the company's sacrifice. The asset received is only recorded at its own fair value if the value of the asset given up cannot be determined. When more than one asset is acquired in a transaction, the cost allocation is based on the relative fair values of the items received. Subsequent costs incurred in connection with property and equipment are capitalized if the asset has been made bigger or better in some way. If the length of the remaining useful life is extended, capitalization is established by reducing accumulated depreciation.

6. REPORTING LAND IMPROVEMENTS AND IMPAIRMENTS IN THE VALUE OF PROPERTY AND EQUIPMENT

LEARNING OBJECTIVES

At the end of this section, students should be able to meet the following objectives:

1. **Recognize the type of assets that are often labeled as land improvements and understand that the distinction between land and land improvements is not always clear.**
2. **Perform the two tests utilized to identify the need to recognize a loss because of impairment in the value of property or equipment.**
3. **Explain the justification for capitalizing interest incurred during the construction of property and equipment.**

Question: Land is not subjected to the recording of depreciation expense because it has an infinite life. Often, though, a parking lot, fence, sidewalk, or the like will be attached to land. They, however, do have finite lives. ***How are attachments to land—such as a sidewalk—reported?*** *Should they be depreciated?*

Answer: Any asset that is attached to land but has a finite life is recorded in a separate account, frequently referred to as **land improvements**, and then depreciated over those estimated number of years. The cost of a parking lot or sidewalk, for example, is capitalized and then written off to expense in the same manner as the accounting for buildings and equipment.

land improvements

Assets attached to land with a finite life such as a parking lot or sidewalk.

In some cases, a distinction between land and improvements is difficult to draw. Accounting rules do not always provide clear guidance for every possible situation. Judgment is occasionally necessary. For example, trees, shrubbery, and sewer systems might be viewed as normal and necessary costs to get land in the condition and position to generate revenues rather than serving as separate assets. Is a sewer system a cost incurred so that land can be utilized or is it truly a distinct asset? U.S. GAAP does not provide absolute rules so such costs may be carried within the land account and not depreciated or reported as land improvements subject to depreciation. Such flexibility in accounting is more prevalent than might be imagined.

Question: Property and equipment is recorded at historical cost, which is subsequently depreciated over its anticipated useful life. At some point, the asset is sold, traded, used up, or disposed of in some other manner. Land is an exception in that it will last forever.

While in use, such assets may lose their value rather rapidly if adverse conditions arise. For example, the economy or the environment might decline and impact the value of such assets. Increases in the fair value of property and equipment are ignored but what about decreases? ***If the value of property and equipment becomes impaired, is any accounting recognition made of that loss prior to disposal?*** *Is historical cost always the basis for reporting regardless of the worth of property and equipment?*

For example, assume that a company constructs a plant for $3 million to manufacture widgets. However, shortly thereafter, the global market for widgets falls precipitously so that the owner has little use for this structure. No one wants to own a manufacturing plant for widgets. Does historical cost continue to be used in accounting for property and equipment even if the value has been damaged significantly?

Answer: Accounting follows the principle of conservatism. Concern always arises when any property or equipment is reported at an amount in excess of fair value. Because temporary swings in value can happen frequently and then rebound, they do not require accounting modification. Historical cost remains the reporting basis. Permanent declines in the worth of an asset, though, need to be noted in some appropriate manner. Consequently, two tests have been created by FASB to determine if the value of property or equipment has been impaired in such a serious fashion that disclosure of the damage is necessary.

recoverability test

A test used to determine whether the value of a long-lived asset has been impaired; if expected future cash flows are less than present book value, a fair value test is performed to determine the amount of impairment.

fair value test

A test to determine the amount, if any, by which the value of a long-lived asset has been impaired; if fair value is less than present book value, the fair value becomes the new basis and an impairment loss is recorded.

If possible impairment of property or equipment is suspected, the owner estimates the total amount of cash that will be generated by the asset during its remaining life. The resulting cash figure is then compared with the asset's current book value to see if it is lower. This **recoverability test** indicates whether a problem exists that is so significant that immediate recognition is warranted.

If expected future cash flows exceed the present book value of property or equipment, no reporting is necessary. The asset can still be used to recover its own book value; no permanent impairment has occurred according to the rules of U.S. GAAP.

Conversely, if an asset cannot even generate sufficient cash to cover its own book value, it has become a detriment to the owner. In that case, the accountant performs a second test (the **fair value test**) to determine the amount of loss to be reported. Book value is compared to present fair value, the amount for which the asset could be sold. For property and equipment, the lower of these two figures is then reported on the balance sheet. Any reduction in the reported asset balance creates a loss to be recognized on the income statement.[5]

The recoverability test. Assume that the $3.0 million building in the above example has been used for a short time so that it now has a net book value of $2.8 million as a result of depreciation. Also assume that because of the change in demand for its product, this building is now expected to generate a net positive cash flow of only $200,000 during each of the next five years or a total of $1.0 million. No amount of cash is expected after that time. This amount is far below the book value of $2.8 million. The company will not be able to recover the asset's book value through these cash flows. As a result, the fair value of the building must be determined to calculate the amount of any loss to be reported.

The fair value test. Assuming that a real estate appraiser believes the building could be sold for only $760,000, fair value is below book value ($2.8 million is obviously greater than $760,000). Therefore, the asset account is reduced to this lower figure creating a reported loss of $2,040,000 ($2.8 million less $760,000).

FIGURE 10.19 Loss on Impaired Value of Building

Loss on Impaired Value of Building	2,240,000	
Building		2,240,000

In its 2007 financial statements, Ford Motor Company describes this process as follows:

> *"We monitor the carrying value of long-lived asset groups held and used for potential impairment when certain triggering events have occurred. These events include current period losses combined with a history of losses or a projection of continuing losses. When a triggering event occurs, a test for recoverability is performed, comparing projected undiscounted future cash flows (utilizing current cash flow information and expected growth rates) to the carrying value of the asset group. If the test for recoverability identifies a possible impairment, the asset group's fair value is measured relying primarily on the discounted cash flow methodology."*

In its 2008 financial statements, Ford provided updated information on the handling of impaired assets from a somewhat different perspective:

> *"Based upon the financial impact of rapidly-changing U.S. market conditions during the second quarter of 2008, we projected a decline in net cash flows for the Ford North America segment. The decline primarily reflected: (1) a more pronounced and accelerated shift in consumer preferences away from full-size trucks and traditional sport utility vehicles ('SUVs') to smaller, more fuel-efficient vehicles as a result of higher fuel prices; (2) lower-than-anticipated U. S. industry demand; and (3) greater-than-anticipated escalation of commodity costs. As a result, in the second quarter of 2008 we tested the long-lived assets of this segment for impairment and recorded in Automotive cost of sales a pre-tax charge of $5.3 billion, representing the amount by which the carrying value of these assets exceeded the estimated fair value."*

Talking with an Independent Auditor about International Financial Reporting Standards

Following is a more of our interview with Robert A. Vallejo, partner with the accounting firm PricewaterhouseCoopers.

Question: The impairment of operational assets is an important reporting issue for many companies because acquired property does not always achieve anticipated levels of profitability. Buildings can be constructed and machinery purchased that simply fail to be as productive as company officials had hoped. According to U.S. GAAP, an asset of this type is viewed as impaired when the total of all future cash flows generated by the asset are expected to be less than its current book value. At that point, the owner cannot even recover the book value of the asset through continued usage. Consequently, the amount reported for the operational asset is reduced to fair value and a loss recognized. Does IFRS handle this type of problem in the same way?

Rob Vallejo: The need to record impairment losses is the same under IFRS but the measurement process is different. The international standards require companies to identify an asset's fair value by calculating the present value of the future cash flows[6] or its net realizable value (anticipated sales price less costs required to sell) if that figure is higher. The asset's value is said to be impaired if this fair value (rather than total cash flows) is below book value. If so, a loss is reported for the reduction from book value to fair value. Also, under IFRS, companies return previously impaired assets to original book value if fair value subsequently increases. In contrast, U.S. GAAP does not allow a write up in value once impairment has been recorded.

EXERCISE

Link to multiple-choice question for practice purposes: http://www.quia.com/quiz/2092960.html

Question: A company is considering buying a building for $1.0 million on January 1, Year One so that a retail store can be opened immediately. The company can borrow the money from a bank that requires payment of $100,000 in interest (an assumed annual rate of 10 percent) at the end of each year starting with Year One. As a second possibility, the company can borrow the same $1.0 million on the first day of the current year and use it to build a similar store to be completed and opened on December 31. Again, $100,000 in interest (10 percent annual rate) must be paid every year, starting at the end of Year One. In each case, the same amount of money is expended to acquire this structure. ***If money is borrowed and a building constructed, is financial reporting the same as if the money had been used to buy property suitable for immediate use?***

Answer: A payment of $1 million is made in both cases for the building. However, the interest is handled differently from an accounting perspective. If a building is purchased, the structure can be used immediately to generate revenue. Payment of the $100,000 interest charge allows the company to open the store and start making sales at the beginning of the year. The matching principle requires this cost to be reported as interest expense for Year One. Expense is matched with the revenue it helps to create.

In contrast, if company officials choose to construct the building, no revenue is generated during all of Year One. Because of the decision to build rather than buy, revenues are postponed. Without any corresponding revenues, expenses are not normally recognized. Choosing to build this structure means that the interest paid during Year One is a normal and necessary cost to get the building ready to use. Thus, the $100,000 interest is **capitalized** rather than expensed. It is reported as part of the building's historical cost to be expensed over the useful life—as depreciation—in the years when revenues are earned.

capitalized interest

Interest cost incurred during the construction of a long-lived asset that is added to historical cost rather than being recorded as interest expense; it is viewed as a normal and necessary expenditure to get the asset into position and condition to generate revenues.

The key distinction is that buying enables the company to generate revenue right away whereas constructing the building means that no revenue will be earned during Year One.

Assume, for example, that this building is expected to generate revenues for twenty years with no expected residual value and that the straight-method is used for depreciation purposes. Notice the difference in many of the reported figures.

Store Bought on January 1, Year One—Revenues Generated Immediately

- Historical cost: $1 million
- Interest expense reported for Year One: $100,000
- Interest expense reported for Year Two: $100,000

- Depreciation expense reported for Year One: $50,000 ($1 million/20 years)
- Depreciation expense reported for Year Two: $50,000
- Net book value at end of Year Two: $900,000 ($1 million less $50,000 and $50,000)

Store Constructed during Year One—No Revenues Generated until Year Two

- Historical cost: $1.1 million (includes Year One interest)[7]
- Interest expense reported for Year One: -0- (no revenues earned)
- Interest expense reported for Year Two: $100,000
- Depreciation expense reported for Year One: Zero (no revenues earned)
- Depreciation expense reported for Year Two: $55,000 ($1.1 million/20 years)
- Net book value at end of Year Two: $1,045,000 ($1.1 million less $55,000)

Question: ***Are there any vital signs in connection with property and equipment that a decision maker might calculate to help in evaluating the financial health of a business?***

fixed asset turnover

Ratio calculated by dividing net sales by the average of the net fixed assets reported for the period; it indicates the efficiency by which these assets have been used to generate sales revenues.

Answer: Ratios and computed amounts are not as common with noncurrent assets as has been seen with current assets. However, the **fixed asset turnover** indicates the efficiency by which a company uses its property and equipment to generate sales revenues. If a company has large amounts reported for various fixed assets but fails to create high revenue balances, the ability of management to make good use of those assets has to be questioned. This figure is calculated by taking net sales for a period and dividing it by the average net book value of the company's property and equipment (fixed assets). For example, a company with $1 million reported for these assets at the beginning of the year but $1.2 million at the end of the year that is able to generate $6.16 million in net sales has a fixed asset turnover of 5.6 times per year. The average of the fixed assets for this period is $1.1 million.

net sales/average net fixed assets

$6,160,000/$1,100,000

5.6 times

KEY TAKEAWAYS

"Land improvements" is an asset category that includes property attached to land (such as a fence or sewer system) that has a finite life and should be depreciated. However, the distinction between land and land improvements can sometimes be difficult to draw.

Over time, property and equipment can lose a significant amount of value for many reasons. If impairment is suspected, a recoverability test is applied to determine whether enough cash will be generated by the asset to cover its current book value. If not, a fair value test is then applied and the asset's book value is reduced to fair value if that number is lower.

During construction of property and equipment, interest is capitalized rather than expensed because revenues are not being generated by the asset. The matching principle requires recognition of this expense be delayed until revenue is earned.

Talking With a Real Investing Pro—Continued

Following is a continuation of our interview with Kevin G. Burns.

Question: On a company's balance sheet, the reporting of land, buildings, and equipment is based on historical cost unless impaired in some manner. Those figures often represent expenditures that were made decades ago. However, fair value is a very subjective and ever changing number in connection with these assets. The debate over the most relevant type of information to provide decision makers is ongoing. Do you think a move should be made to report land, buildings, and equipment at their current fair values?

Kevin Burns: I am a value investor. I look for companies that are worth more than is reflected in the current price of their ownership shares. Therefore, I always like "discovering" little nuggets—like hidden land values—that are still carried at cost after decades of ownership. However in the interest of full disclosure and transparency, I think it would be fairer to the average investor to have some sort of appraisal done to estimate fair market value. This information could be reported or just disclosed. The difficulty is, of course, how often to appraise? I would like to see a revaluation every five years or if a major event occurs that changes the value of the land, building, and equipment by a significant amount.

Video Clip

Joe talks about the five most important points in Chapter 10.

View the video online at: http://blip.tv/play/sDyBv7hpAA

7. END-OF-CHAPTER EXERCISES

QUESTIONS

1. At what value is property, plant, and equipment (PP&E) typically reported on the balance sheet?
2. What is accumulated depreciation?
3. What type of account is accumulated depreciation?
4. Define "book value."
5. Why is property and equipment not reported at its fair value?
6. Why is land not depreciated?
7. Why would land be classified as an investment rather than PP&E?
8. How does a company determine the historical cost of a property and equipment?
9. Define "useful life."
10. Define "residual value."
11. Which method of depreciation allocates an equal amount to each period the asset is used?
12. How does a company determine the gain or loss on the sale of PP&E?
13. What is the half-year convention?
14. What is accelerated depreciation and how is its use justified?
15. How does the units-of-production method differ from straight-line?
16. What is depletion?
17. What is a basket purchase?
18. How are the values attributed to the different assets determined in a basket purchase?
19. When should a subsequent expenditure associated with currently owned property and equipment be capitalized?
20. What are land improvements?
21. How is an impairment loss on PP&E determined?
22. When can a company capitalize interest?

TRUE OR FALSE

1. ____ Almost all property, plant, and equipment (PP&E) is depreciated, which means that its cost is spread over its useful life.
2. ____ PP&E is a long-term asset.
3. ____ If PP&E is found to be permanently impaired, a loss must be recorded.
4. ____ If an expenditure increases the useful life of an asset, it should be capitalized, not expensed.
5. ____ It does not matter how a company divides a basket purchase since all the assets will be depreciated anyway.
6. ____ Companies are allowed to capitalize interest while they are constructing an asset because the asset is not available to generate revenues yet.
7. ____ The only acceptable method of depreciation is straight-line.
8. ____ Accumulated depreciation is a contra-asset account.
9. ____ The purchase price of an asset is capitalized, but costs like transportation and set up of the asset should be expensed as incurred.
10. ____ Both assets used to generate revenue from operations and assets held as investment property are reported as PP&E on the balance sheet.

MULTIPLE CHOICE

1. On January 1, the Rhode Island Redbirds organization purchased new workout equipment for its athletes. The equipment had a cost of $15,600, transportation costs of $450, and set up costs of $290. The Redbirds spent $350 training their trainers and athletes on its proper use. The useful life of the equipment is five years and has no residual value. How much depreciation expense should the Redbirds take in the first year, if straight-line is being used?
   a. $3,120
   b. $3,268
   c. $3,338
   d. $3,210
2. See the information in number 1 above. Assume the Redbirds decide to use the double-declining balance depreciation method instead. What would Year 1 depreciation expense be?
   a. $6,420
   b. $6,676
   c. $6,240
   d. $6,536
3. Kite Corporation wishes to trade equipment it owns for a vehicle owned by the Runner Corporation. Kite's equipment has a book value of $4,000 and a fair value of $4,500. Runner's vehicle has a book value and fair value of $5,100. Kite agrees to pay Runner $600 in cash in addition to giving up the equipment. What would be Kite's gain or loss on this exchange?
   a. $500
   b. $100
   c. $1,100
   d. $600
4. At the beginning of the year, the Kelvin Company owned equipment that appeared on its balance sheet as such:

Equipment	$7,000,000
Accumulated Depreciation	($2,000,000)

   The equipment was purchased two years ago and assigned a useful life of six years and a salvage value of $1,000,000. During the first month of the year, Kelvin made modifications to the equipment that increased its remaining useful life from four years to five years. Its salvage value remained unchanged. The cost of these modifications was $50,000. What would be the balance in the accumulated depreciation account of this equipment on 12/31 of that year?
   a. $2,810,000
   b. $3,000,000
   c. $810,000
   d. $2,000,000
5. On January 3, 20X1, Jewels Inc. purchases a South American mine found to be rich in amethyst for $560,000. Once all the amethyst has been removed, the land is estimated to be worth only $100,000. Experts predict that the mine contains 4,000 pounds of amethyst. Jewels plans on completing the extraction process in four years. No amethyst was extracted during 20X1. What would accumulated depletion be on 12/31/X1?
   a. $115,000
   b. $115
   c. $140
   d. $0
6. Maxwell Corporation wishes to sell a building it has owned for five years. It was purchased for $430,000. Maxwell performed additional modifications to the building, which totaled $45,000. On the proposed date of sale, the accumulated depreciation on the building totaled $75,000. The proposed sales price of the building is $380,000. Maxwell is trying to determine the income statement effect of this transaction. What would be Maxwell's gain or loss on this sale?
   a. $20,000 loss
   b. $25,000 gain
   c. $50,000 loss
   d. $95,000 loss

PROBLEMS

1. Springfield Corporation purchases a new machine on March 3, 20X4 for $35,600 in cash. It pays an additional $3,400 to transport and set up the machine. Springfield's accountant determines that the equipment has no residual value and that the useful life is five years. It is expected to generate 2,400,000 units during its life. Assume Springfield employs the half-year convention.
    a. Record the purchase of the machine.
    b. Assume that Springfield uses the straight-line method of depreciation. Record depreciation expense for the first two years of the machine's life.
    c. Assume that Springfield uses the double-declining balance method of depreciation. Record depreciation expense for the first two years of the machine's life.
    d. Assume that Springfield uses the units-of-production method of depreciation. During Year 1, the machine produces 600,000 units. During Year 2, the machine produces 578,000 units. Record depreciation expense for the first two years of the machine's life.
2. Gameplay Company operates in mall locations and sells videogame equipment and games. The company purchased furniture and fixtures to use in one of its stores for $440,000 in January of 20X5. The furniture and fixtures were being depreciated using the straight-line method over ten years with a residual value of $10,000. In December 20X9, Gameplay decided to close the location and entered into an exchange agreement with Allero Corporation. Allero agreed to give Gameplay vehicles with a fair value of $200,000 and cash of $50,000 in exchange for the furniture and fixtures from this store. The furniture and fixtures have an estimated fair value of $250,000 on the date of exchange.
    a. Make the depreciation entry for the furniture and fixtures that would be necessary in December 20X9, assuming that no entries have been made during the year.
    b. Determine the book value of the furniture and fixtures on the date of exchange.
    c. Record the journal entry Gameplay would make for this exchange.
    d. Where would Gameplay report the gain or loss you determined in part c. above?
3. Fairfield Inc. invested in a plant to manufacture j phones, thinking these would be the next "big thing" and compete with the current maker of the iPhone. Unfortunately, things did not work out so well for the j phone. Complete the following steps to determine if Fairfield will need to record an impairment loss in the current period.
    a. Fairfield purchased the plant on March 1, 20X2, for $46,790,000. Additional costs to get it up and running were $3,780,000. Fairfield assigned a thirty-year useful life and residual value of $4,000,000 and used double-declining balance to depreciate the plant. Record the acquisition of the plant and depreciation for three years, assuming that Fairfield does not use the half-year convention.
    b. On December 31, 20X4, Fairfield's auditors raise concerns that the plant's market value might be below its book value due to the failure of the j phone. They believe this decline is permanent and decide to test for impairment. The accountants and auditors agree that the plant will generate net cash flows of approximately $2,000,000 each year for the next fifteen years. Perform a test of recoverability on the plant.
    c. Assume that you determined that the plant's future cash flows were below its book value. The company must now perform the fair value test. Several appraisers are called in, and the average fair value they give the plant is $15,600,000. Determine if Fairfield must record an impairment loss and, if so, make the journal entry to do so.
4. Janus Corporation was unable to find a store suitable for its business, so it decided to build one. It was able to secure debt financing from the Southeast Bank in the amount of $4,000,000 at an interest rate of 5 percent. During 20X8, Janus spent $2,500,000 on construction, but did not complete the building. Janus continued work on the building into 20X9, eventually completing it on July 1 at a total cost of $3,800,000. Janus does not use the half-year convention.
    a. Determine the amount at which Janus should record the building, including any applicable capitalized interest.
    b. If Janus expects the building to be in use for twenty years with negligible residual value, what would depreciation expense be in 20X9?
5. Markov Corporation owns forests that are harvested and sold to papermaking companies. Markov purchases a new tract of forest on January 1, 20X6, for $360,000. Its experts estimate that 4,000 tons of wood can be harvested from the forest and sold. After that, the land will be worth about $20,000 (of course, Markov could replant trees, changing this value, but for ease of calculations, we'll assume no replanting).
    a. In 20X6, 2,500 tons of wood are harvested and 2,200 are sold for $120 per ton. Make any necessary journal entries.

b. In 20X7, the remaining 1,500 tons are harvested and 1,800 tons are sold for $120 per ton. Make any necessary journal entries.

c. Determine the balance in land account at the end of 20X7. Does this make sense to you? Why?

6. On April 1, 20X1, Chang and Chang Inc. invested in a new machine to manufacture soccer balls. The machine is expected to manufacture 1,400,000 balls over its life of three years and then it will be scrapped. The machine cost $50,000 including normal and necessary costs of setting it up. Chang will use units-of-production to depreciate the machine.

   a. Record depreciation for 20X1 and 20X2 assuming that 450,000 balls were manufactured and sold in 20X1 and 600,000 were manufactured and sold in 20X2.

   b. On January 1, 20X3, Chang decides to get out of the soccer ball business, and sells the machine for $15,000. Record this journal entry.

7. On June 30, Partyplace, a popular spot for receptions and other events, purchased a used limousine and used Hummer from a car dealership as a basket purchase. They received a good deal because they bought the vehicles together, paying only $75,000 for both. The market values were $45,000 for the limo and $40,000 for the Hummer.

   a. Record the purchase of the vehicles.

   b. During the year, Partyplace performed maintenance on the vehicles like oil changes that amounted to $600. Record this.

   c. During the year, Partyplace made some modifications to the limo that should make it more appealing to its customers, thus, in effect, increasing its productivity as it relates to the business. These modifications cost $4,000. Record this.

COMPREHENSIVE PROBLEM

This problem will carry through several chapters, building in difficulty. It allows students to continuously practice skills and knowledge learned in previous chapters.

In Chapter 9, you prepared Webworks statements for September. They are included here as a starting point for October.

Here are Webworks financial statements as of September 30.

Webworks
Income Statement
As of September 30

Revenue	$11,400
Cost of Goods Sold	(5,315)
Gross Profit	6,085
Other Expenses	(3,435)
Earning before Tax	2,650
Tax Expense	(795)
Net Income	$1,855

Webworks
Stmt. of Retained Earnings
As of September 30

Retained Earnings, September 1	$2,790
Net Income	1,855
Retained Earnings, September 30	$4,645

Webworks
Balance Sheet
September 30

Assets		**Liabilities**	
Current		**Current**	
Cash	$3,300	Accounts Payable	$1,285
Accounts Receivable	1,750	Salaries Payable	300
Less Allowance for Doubtful Accounts	(175)	Unearned Revenue	100
Net Accounts Receivable	1,575		
Merchandise Inventory	1,385		
Supplies Inventory	70		
Total Current Assets	$6,330	Total Current Liabilities	$1,685
Noncurrent		**Noncurrent**	
Equipment	$7,000	Notes Payable	$5,000
		Owners' Equity	
		Capital Stock	$2,000
		Retained Earnings	4,645
		Total Owners' Equity	$6,645
Total Assets	$13,330	Total Liabilities & Owners' Equity	$13,330

The following events occur during October:

a. Webworks purchases supplies worth $100 on account.

b. Webworks paid $600 in rent for October, November, and December.

c. At the beginning of October, Webworks had nine keyboards costing $105 each and forty flash drives costing $11 each. Webworks uses periodic FIFO to cost its inventory.

d. On account, Webworks purchases fifty keyboards for $110 each and 100 flash drives for $12 each.

e. Webworks starts and completes seven more sites and bills clients for $3,900.

f. Webworks pays Nancy $700 for her work during the first three weeks of October.

g. Webworks sells 50 keyboards for $7,500 and 110 flash drives for $2,200 cash.

h. The Web site paid for in August and started in September was completed. The client had originally paid $100 in advance.

i. Webworks paid off the remainder of its note payable.

j. Webworks collects $4,000 in accounts receivable.

k. Webworks pays off its salaries payable from October.

l. Webworks pays off $6,000 of its accounts payable.

m. One Web site client is dissatisfied with the work done and refuses to pay his bill. Rather than incur the expense of taking the client to court, Webworks writes off the account in the amount of $200.

n. Webworks pays Leon a salary of $2,000.

o. Webworks purchased office furniture on account for $1,000, including transportation and setup.

p. Webworks pays taxes of $868 in cash.

Required:

A. Prepare journal entries for the above events.

B. Post the journal entries to T-accounts.

C. Prepare an unadjusted trial balance for Webworks for October.

D. Prepare adjusting entries for the following and post them to your T-accounts.

q. Webworks owes Nancy $100 for her work during the last week of October.

r. Leon's parents let him know that Webworks owes $300 toward the electricity bill. Webworks will pay them in November.

s. Webworks determines that it has $50 worth of supplies remaining at the end of October.

t. Prepaid rent should be adjusted for October's portion.

u. Webworks is continuing to accrue bad debts at 10 percent of accounts receivable.

v. A CPA tells Leon that Webworks should be depreciating its equipment and furniture. The CPA recommends that Webworks use the straight-line method with a four-year life for the equipment and a five-year life for the furniture. Normally, when an error is made, such as not depreciating equipment, the company must go back and restate prior financial statements correctly. Since Webworks is only generating these monthly statements for internal information, the CPA recommends that Leon just "catch up" the prior month's depreciation on the equipment this month. So when Webworks records October's equipment depreciation, it will also record the deprecation that should have been taken in July, August and September. The depreciation on the furniture should just be for one month. Round to the nearest whole number.

w. Record cost of goods sold.

E. Prepare an adjusted trial balance.

F. Prepare financial statements for October.

ENDNOTES

1. As discussed in connection with accounts receivable and the allowance for doubtful accounts, an account that appears with another but as a direct reduction is known as a contra account. Accumulated depreciation is a contra account that decreases the reported cost of property and equipment to reflect the portion of that cost that has now be assigned to expense.
2. The estimated lives of property and equipment varies widely. For example, in notes to its financial statements as of January 31, 2009, and for the year then ended, Wal-Mart disclosed that the expected lives of its buildings and improvements ranged from five years to fifty.
3. As mentioned previously, land does not have a finite life and is, therefore, not subjected to the recording of depreciation expense.
4. Accounting rules are created through a slow and meticulous process to avoid unintended consequences. For example, assume that Company A and Company B buy identical antique limousines for $30,000 that then appreciate in value to $100,000 because of their scarcity. Based solely on the accounting rule described in this section, if the two companies exchange these assets, each reports a gain of $70,000 while still retaining possession of an identical vehicle. This reporting is not appropriate because nothing has changed for either party. In reality, no gain occurred since the companies retain the same financial position as before the trade. Thus, in creating its official guidance as described above, FASB held that an exchange must have commercial substance to justify using fair value. In simple terms, the asset acquired has to be different from the asset surrendered as demonstrated by the amount and timing of future cash flows. Without a difference, no rationale exists for making the exchange. If a trade does not have commercial substance, net book value is retained so that no gain is recognized.
5. Mechanically, an impairment loss for property and equipment could be calculated in any one of several ways. FASB established these two tests and required companies to follow them. The Board apparently believed that this information is more understandable to outside decision makers if a single standard process was established. Thus, according to U.S. GAAP, the recoverability test and the fair value test must be used when impairment is suspected. Some might argue that this process is not the best method for determining an impairment loss. Standardization, though, helps to better ensure universal understanding of the figures being reported.
6. As will be demonstrated in Chapter 11, present value is a method used to compute the current worth of a future stream of cash flows by removing the amount of those payments that can be mathematically attributed to interest.
7. As discussed in intermediate accounting textbooks, the full amount of interest is not actually capitalized here because the borrowed money is only tied up in the construction gradually. Until added to the project, any remaining funds can be used to generate revenues. However, for this introductory textbook, focus is on the need to capitalize interest because the decision to build defers the earning of revenue until the project is completed. Complete coverage of the rules to be applied can be obtained in an intermediate accounting textbook.

CHAPTER 11

In a Set of Financial Statements, What Information Is Conveyed about Intangible Assets?

Video Clip

Joe introduces Chapter 11 and speaks about the course in general.

View the video online at: http://blip.tv/play/sDyBv7xZAA

1. IDENTIFYING AND ACCOUNTING FOR INTANGIBLE ASSETS

LEARNING OBJECTIVES

At the end of this section, students should be able to meet the following objectives:

1. **List the characteristics of intangible assets and provide several common examples.**
2. **Understand that intangible assets are becoming more important to businesses and, hence, are gaining increased attention in financial accounting.**
3. **Record the acquisition of an intangible asset.**
4. **Describe the amortization process for intangible assets.**
5. **Explain the accounting used in reporting an intangible asset that has increased in value.**

intangible asset

An asset lacking physical substance that is expected to help generate future revenues for more than one year; common examples are patents, copyrights, and trademarks.

Question: Not so many years ago, most large companies reported significant amounts of property and equipment on their balance sheets but considerably smaller figures for **intangible assets**. *Businesses were often referred to as "bricks and mortar" operations because much of their money was invested in buildings, machinery, and similar long-lived tangible assets.*

Today, the basic nature of many corporate operations has changed dramatically. As of June 30, 2009, Microsoft Corporation reported a total of $14.3 billion for its "goodwill" and "intangible assets, net" versus a mere $7.5 billion in "property and equipment, net of accumulated depreciation." For Yahoo! Inc., the difference is similarly striking. On December 31, 2008, Yahoo! disclosed $3.9 billion of "goodwill" and "intangible assets, net" but only $1.5 billion in "property and equipment, net."

The rise in the value and importance of intangible assets might well be the biggest change experienced in the reporting of businesses over the last ten to twenty years. The sudden growth of Internet and technology companies like Microsoft and Yahoo! has focused attention on the significance of ideas and innovation for achieving profits.

Financial accounting rules evolve as the nature of business moves forward over time. Not surprisingly, much debate has taken place recently concerning the methods by which intangible assets are reported in a set of financial statements. A relatively minor topic in the past has gained a genuine level of importance. Should an idea or an invention be reported in the same manner as a building or a machine? For financial accounting, that is a very important question. As a starting point for this discussion, the basic nature of intangible assets needs to be understood. ***What is an intangible asset and what are some common examples?***

Answer: As the title implies, an intangible asset is one that lacks physical substance. It cannot be touched but is expected to provide future benefits for longer than one year. More specifically, it will assist the reporting company in generating revenues during future periods. Except for a few slight variations, intangible assets are reported in a manner similar to a building or equipment. Historical cost serves as the basis for reporting. If the intangible has a finite life, the depreciation process (although the term "amortization" is normally utilized in connection with intangibles) reclassifies this cost from asset to expense over that estimated period.

In creating the authoritative pronouncement Statement No. 141, *Business Combinations* (issued in 2001 and revised in 2007), FASB attempted to provide structure for the reporting process by placing all intangibles into six major categories:

copyright

An intangible asset that provides the owner with the right to use literary, dramatic, musical, artistic, and certain other intellectual works.

1. Artistic-related (such as **copyrights**)
2. Technology-related (patents)
3. Marketing-related (trademarks)
4. Customer-related (a database of customer information)
5. Contract-related (franchises)
6. Goodwill

Notice that in all cases (except for goodwill, which will be explained later in this chapter), each intangible asset is actually an established right of usage. For example, according to the Web site for the United States Copyright Office, a copyright provides its owner with the right to use "literary, dramatic, musical, artistic, and certain other intellectual works." Similarly, the United States Patent and Trademark Office Web site explains that "a patent for an invention is the grant of a property right to the inventor."

In simple terms, an intangible asset is usually a right that helps the owner to generate revenues.

EXERCISE

Link to multiple-choice question for practice purposes: http://www.quia.com/quiz/2092962.html

Question: Intangible assets are accounted for in a manner that is similar to property and equipment. Assume that an automobile company is creating a television commercial for one of its new products. On January 1, Year One, the company pays $1 million cash to a famous musical group (such as The Rolling Stones) for the right to use a well-known song in this video. The band holds the legal copyright on this piece of music and agrees to share that right with the automobile company so that the song can be played in one or more commercials. ***What accounting is made by a company that acquires an intangible asset such as a copyright?***

Answer: The buyer of an intangible asset prepares a journal entry that is basically identical to the acquisition of inventory, land, or a machine. As with all those other assets, the intangible is recorded initially at historical cost.

FIGURE 11.1 January 1, Year One—Acquisition of Right to Use Copyrighted Song

Copyright	1,000,000	
Cash		1,000,000

Many intangible assets have defined legal lives. For example, copyrights extend for seventy years beyond the creator's life. Acquired intangibles (such as the copyright for this song) often have lives legally limited by the contractual agreement. However, the true useful life of most intangibles is generally only a small number of years. Few intangibles manage to help a company generate revenues for decades. **Amortization** of the cost should extend over the shorter of the asset's useful life or its legal life.

amortization

A mechanically derived pattern allocating an intangible asset's cost to expense over the shorter of the legal life or useful life; it is the equivalent of depreciation but relates to intangible assets.

To illustrate, assume that this piece of music is expected to be included by the automobile company in its commercials for the next four years and then a different advertising campaign will be started. Annual amortization is $250,000 ($1 million cost/4 year life) if the straight-line method is applied (which is normal for intangible assets).

FIGURE 11.2 December 31, Year One—First Year Amortization of Copyright Cost

Amortization Expense	250,000	
Copyright		250,000

At the end of the first year, the copyright appears on the balance sheet of the automobile company as $750,000, the remainder of its historical cost. Note that the credit in this adjusting entry is a direct decrease in the asset account. Although establishing a separate contra account (such as accumulated amortization) is permitted, most companies simply reduce the intangible asset balance because the utility is literally shrinking. Depreciation of a building or equipment does not mean that the asset is getting smaller; a four-story building remains a four-story building throughout its life. Reducing the building account would not reflect reality. In contrast, the above right to use this song did get smaller. The company went from holding a copyright to play this music in its commercials for an expected four years to a copyright that will only be used for three more years.

Question: In the above example, the automobile company acquired the right to use this music for $1 million. That was its historical cost, the figure to be reported for the asset on the company's balance sheet. The number was objectively determined and the accounting straightforward. However, the artist who originally created the music (or his or her company) still holds the original copyright. As indicated by this sale, the rights to this music are extremely valuable. ***How does the creator report an intangible asset such as a copyright?*** *Should the copyright to this piece of music now be reported by the artist (The Rolling Stones) at its proven value of $1 million?*

Answer: Depending on the specific terms of the contract, the creator often continues to possess the copyright and maintains the asset on its own balance sheet. In most cases, the original artist only conveyed permission to the company to use this music for specific purposes or a set time period. However, the copyright does not appear on the creator's books at its $1 million value; rather, it remains at historical cost less any amortization to date. That is the reporting basis for intangible assets according to U.S. GAAP in the same way as for land, buildings, and equipment.

Historical cost for copyrights and other similar intangibles typically includes attorney fees as well as any money spent for legal filings and registration with the appropriate authorities. Subsequently, such intangible assets are sometimes the subject of lawsuits if other parties assert claims to the same ideas and creations. The cost of a successful defense is also capitalized and then amortized over the shorter of the remaining legal life or the estimated useful life.

EXERCISE

Link to multiple-choice question for practice purposes: http://www.quia.com/quiz/2092963.html

Talking With an Independent Auditor about International Financial Reporting Standards

Following is a continuation of our interview with Robert A. Vallejo, partner with the accounting firm PricewaterhouseCoopers.

Question: Under U.S. GAAP, intangible assets with a finite life are reported at historical cost less any accumulated amortization recognized to date. Except in impairment cases, fair value is ignored completely. How are intangible assets reported when IFRS standards are applied?

Robert Vallejo: Unless a company chooses to revalue its intangible assets regularly (an option that is available under IFRS but rarely chosen in practice because it must then be done over time), the accounting under U.S. GAAP and IFRS is basically the same. After initial recognition under IFRS, intangible assets are carried at cost less accumulated amortization (as well as any impairment losses). If an active market is available, fair value of all similar intangible assets can be chosen but, again, that value must then be updated frequently. Per IAS 38, Intangible Assets, the method of amortization that is used should reflect the pattern in which the asset's future economic benefits are expected to be realized by the entity. If that pattern cannot be determined reliably, the straight-line method of amortization must be used.

KEY TAKEAWAY

The reporting of intangible assets has grown in significance in recent years because of the prevalence and success of technology and electronics companies. For the most part, intangible assets provide a company with a right to use an idea, invention, artistic creation, or the like. Copyrights, patents, and trademarks are common examples. They are recorded at historical cost which is then amortized to expense over the shorter of the legal life or the useful life of the intangible. The accounting resembles that of property and equipment so that, for example, increases in value are not reported.

2. THE BALANCE SHEET REPORTING OF INTANGIBLE ASSETS

LEARNING OBJECTIVES

At the end of this section, students should be able to meet the following objectives:

1. **Explain the preferred use of historical cost as the basis for recording property and equipment and intangible assets.**
2. **Realize that the use of historical cost means that a company's intangible assets such as patents and trademarks can be worth much more than is shown on the balance sheet.**
3. **Recognize that large reported intangible asset balances can result from their acquisition either individually or through the purchase of an entire company that holds valuable intangible assets.**
4. **Show the method of recording intangible assets when the owner is acquired by a parent company.**

Question: Much was made in earlier chapters about the importance of painting a portrait that fairly presents the financial health and future prospects of an organization. Many companies develop copyrights and other intangible assets that have incredible value but little or no actual cost. Trademarks provide an excellent example. The golden arches that represent McDonald's must be worth billions but the original design cost was probably not significant and has likely been amortized to zero by now. Could the balance sheet of McDonald's possibly be considered as fairly presented if the value of its primary trademark is omitted?

Many other companies such as Walt Disney, UPS, Google, Apple, Coca-Cola, and Nike rely on trademarks to help create awareness and brand loyalty around the world. ***Are a company's reported assets not understated if the value of a trademark is ignored despite serving as a recognizable symbol to millions of potential customers?*** *With property and equipment, this concern is not as pronounced because those assets tend to have significant costs whether bought or constructed. Internally developed trademarks and other intangibles often have little actual cost despite eventually gaining immense value.*

Answer: Reported figures for intangible assets such as trademarks may indeed be vastly understated on a company's balance sheet when compared to their fair values. Decision makers who rely on financial statements need to understand what they are seeing. U.S. GAAP requires that companies follow the historical cost principle in reporting many assets. A few exceptions do exist and several are examined at various points in this textbook. For example, historical cost may have to be abandoned when applying the lower-of-cost-or-market rule to inventory and also when testing for possible impairment losses of property and equipment. Those particular departures from historical cost were justified because the asset had lost value. Financial accounting tends to follow the principle of conservatism. Reporting an asset at a balance in excess of its historical cost basis is much less common.

In financial accounting, what is the rationale for the prevalence of historical cost, which some might say was an obsession? As discussed in earlier chapters, cost can be reliably and objectively determined. It does not fluctuate from day to day throughout the year. It is based on an agreed-upon exchange price and reflects a resource allocation judgment made by management. Cost is not an estimate so it is less open to manipulation. While fair value may appear to be more relevant, different parties might arrive at significantly different figures. What are the golden arches really worth to McDonald's as a trademark? Is it $100 million or $10 billion? Six appraisals from six experts could suggest six largely different amounts.

Plus, if the asset is not going to be sold, is the fair value of any relevance at the current time?

Cost remains the basis for reporting many assets in financial accounting, though the reporting of fair value has gained considerable momentum. It is not that one way is right and one way is wrong. Instead, decision makers need to understand that historical cost is the generally accepted accounting principle that is currently in use for assets such as intangibles. For reporting purposes, it does have obvious flaws. Unfortunately, any alternative number that can be put forth to replace historical cost also has its own set of problems. At the present time, authoritative accounting literature holds that historical cost is the appropriate basis for reporting intangibles.

Even though fair value accounting seems quite appealing to many decision makers, accountants have proceeded slowly because of potential concerns. For example, the 2001 collapse of Enron Corporation was the most widely discussed accounting scandal to occur in recent decades. Many of Enron's reporting problems began when the company got special permission (because of the unusual nature of its business) to report a number of assets at fair value (a process referred to as "mark to market").[1]

Because fair value was not easy to determine for many of those assets, Enron officials were able to manipulate reported figures to make the company appear especially strong and profitable.[2] Investors then flocked to the company only to lose billions when Enron eventually filed for bankruptcy. A troubling incident of this magnitude makes accountants less eager to embrace the reporting of fair value except in circumstances where very legitimate amounts can be determined. For property and equipment as well as intangible assets, fair value is rarely so objective that the possibility of manipulation can be eliminated.

EXERCISE

Link to multiple-choice question for practice purposes: http://www.quia.com/quiz/2092943.html

goodwill

The price paid by one company to acquire another that is in excess of the fair value of the net identifiable assets and liabilities of the other company; it is often associated with intangibles that cannot be recognized such as employee expertise and customer loyalty, which make the company especially profitable.

Question: Although a historical cost basis is used for intangible assets rather than fair value, Microsoft Corporation still reported $14.3 billion as "goodwill and intangible assets, net" in 2009, while Yahoo! indicated similar balance sheet accounts totaling $3.9 billion. Even the size of these numbers is not particularly unusual for intangible assets in today's economic environment. As of June 30, 2009, for example, the balance sheet for Procter & Gamble listed **goodwill** *of $56.5 billion and trademarks and other intangible assets, net of $32.6 billion.* ***If historical cost is often insignificant, how do companies manage to report such immense amounts of intangible assets?***

Answer: Two possible reasons exist for intangible asset figures to grow to an incredible size on a company's balance sheet. First, instead of being internally developed, assets such as copyrights and patents are often acquired from outside owners. Reported balances then represent the historical costs of these purchases which were likely based on fair value. Large payments may be necessary to acquire such rights if their value has been firmly established.

Second, Microsoft, Yahoo!, and Procter & Gamble could have bought one or more entire companies so that all the assets (including a possible plethora of intangibles) were obtained. In fact, such acquisitions often occur specifically because one company wants to gain valuable intangibles owned by another. In February 2008, Microsoft offered over $44 billion in hopes of purchasing Yahoo! for exactly that reason. Yahoo! certainly did not hold property and equipment worth $44 billion. Microsoft was primarily interested in acquiring a wide variety of intangibles owned by Yahoo! Although this proposed takeover was never completed, the sheer size of the bid demonstrates the staggering value of the intangible assets that today's companies often possess.

If a company buys a single intangible asset directly from its owner, the financial reporting follows the pattern previously described. Whether the asset is a trademark, franchise, copyright, patent, or the like, it is reported at the amount paid with that cost then amortized over the shorter of its useful life or legal life. Intangible assets that do not have finite lives are not amortized and will be discussed later in this chapter.

Reporting the assigned cost of intangible assets acquired when one company (often referred to as "the parent") buys another company ("the subsidiary") is a complex issue discussed in detail in upper-level Advanced Accounting courses. In simple terms, all the subsidiary's assets (inventory, land, buildings, equipment and the like) are valued and recorded at that amount by the parent as the new owner. This process is referred to as the production of consolidated financial statements. Each intangible asset held by the subsidiary that meets certain rules is identified and also consolidated by the parent at its fair value. The assumption is that a portion of the price conveyed to buy the subsidiary is actually being paid to obtain these identified intangible assets. Thus, to the parent company, fair value reflects the cost that was conveyed to gain the intangible asset.

For example, assume Big Company pays $10 million in cash to buy all the stock of Little Company. Among the assets owned by Little are three intangibles (perhaps a copyright, patent, and trademark) that are each worth $1 million. Little also owns land worth $7 million. The previous book value of these assets is not relevant to Big. Following the takeover, Big reports each of the intangibles on its own balance sheet at $1 million. This portion of the acquisition value is assumed to be the historical cost paid by Big to obtain these assets. A company that buys a lot of subsidiaries will often report large intangible asset balances. When Big buys Little Company, it is really gaining control of all of these assets and records the transaction as follows. This entry will lead to the consolidation of the balance sheet figures.

FIGURE 11.3 Big Company Buys Little Company, Which Holds Assets with These Values

Copyright	1,000,000	
Patents	1,000,000	
Trademarks	1,000,000	
Land	7,000,000	
Cash		10,000,000

EXERCISE

Link to multiple-choice question for practice purposes: http://www.quia.com/quiz/2092908.html

KEY TAKEAWAY

Many intangible assets (such as trademarks and copyrights) are reported on the balance sheet of their creator at a value significantly below actual worth. They are shown at cost less any amortization. Development cost is often relatively low in comparison to the worth of the right. However, the reported amount for these assets is not raised to fair value. Such numbers are subjective and open to sudden changes. Furthermore, if the intangible is not held for sale, fair value is of questionable relevance. Companies, though, often pay large amounts to buy intangibles or acquire entire companies that hold numerous intangibles. In accounting for the acquisition of a company, fair value should be assigned to each identifiable subsidiary intangible asset.

3. RECOGNIZING INTANGIBLE ASSETS OWNED BY A SUBSIDIARY

LEARNING OBJECTIVES

At the end of this section, students should be able to meet the following objectives:

1. **Explain that only those subsidiary intangible assets that meet either of two criteria are recognized separately by a parent after an acquisition.**
2. **List the two criteria for subsidiary intangibles to be reported by a parent as assets on its consolidated balance sheet.**
3. **Make the parent's journal entry to record the acquisition of a new subsidiary based on the fair value of its assets and liabilities.**
4. **Compute the amount to be reported as goodwill on a consolidated balance sheet when a parent acquires a new subsidiary.**
5. **Understand that amounts attributed to goodwill are not amortized to expense but rather are checked periodically for loss of value.**

Question: When one company buys another, the subsidiary is often holding rights to numerous intangibles. As mentioned, acquisitions often take place to gain those rights. The parent places those assets that qualify on its own balance sheet at fair value to show that a portion of the amount paid for the subsidiary was the equivalent of an acquisition price for these items. That is a major reason why companies such as Microsoft and Procter & Gamble report billions of dollars in intangible assets. They have probably purchased many of them by acquiring entire companies.

However, according to U.S. GAAP, certain requirements have to be met before such intangibles are recognized as assets on a consolidated balance sheet following a takeover. ***What rules must be satisfied for an acquiring company to record an intangible (previously owned by an acquired company) as an asset?*** *A new subsidiary could very well have hundreds of intangibles: patents, copyrights, databases, smart employees, loyal customers, logos, and the like. When the company is acquired, which of these intangibles are recognized on the consolidated balance sheet produced by the new parent?*

Answer: FASB has stated that a parent company must identify all intangibles held by a subsidiary on the date of acquisition. For consolidation, the fair value of each of these intangibles is recorded by the parent as an asset but only if contractual or other legal rights have been gained or if the intangible can be separated and sold. This guideline serves as a minimum standard for recognition of intangible assets in a corporate takeover:

1. contractual or other legal rights have been gained or
2. the intangible can be separated from the subsidiary and sold.

Patents, copyrights, trademarks, and franchises clearly meet the first of these criteria. Legal rights are held for patents, copyrights, and trademarks while contractual rights provide the right to operate franchises. By acquiring the subsidiary, the parent now owns these same rights and should record them on the consolidated balance sheet at fair value.

Other intangibles that can be separated from the subsidiary and sold should also be consolidated at fair value. For example, an acquired company might have a database containing extensive information about its customers. After purchasing the subsidiary, this information could be separated from that company and sold. Thus, on the date the subsidiary is purchased, the parent should recognize this database as an intangible asset at fair value to reflect the portion of the acquisition price paid to acquire it.

EXERCISE

Link to multiple-choice question for practice purposes: http://www.quia.com/quiz/2092909.html

Question: When one company buys another, payment amounts will likely be negotiated to compensate the seller for intangibles where contractual or legal rights are held or where the asset can be separated and then sold. Thus, parent companies who buy subsidiaries (especially in industries such as technology) will likely recognize significant intangible asset balances on the subsequently consolidated balance sheet.

However, some intangibles have value but fail to meet either of these two criteria. Customer loyalty, for example, is vitally important to the future profitability of a company, but neither contractual nor legal rights are present and loyalty cannot be separated from a company and sold. Hence, customer loyalty is not reported as an intangible asset despite its value. Much the same can be said for brilliant and creative employees. A value exists but neither rule for recognition is met.

The owners of a company that is being acquired will argue for a higher price if attributes such as these are in place because they provide for higher profitability in the future. The amount paid to obtain the subsidiary is impacted although these intangibles do not meet the criteria for separate reporting as assets. How is this additional acquisition cost reported by the parent in producing consolidated financial statements?

Assume Giant Corporation pays $16 million to acquire Tiny Corporation. The subsidiary (Tiny) owns property and equipment worth $4 million. It also holds patents worth $6 million, a database worth $2 million, and copyrights worth $3 million. The total value of those assets is only $15 million. For convenience, assume Tiny has no liabilities. Assume that the parent agrees to pay the extra $1 million because the subsidiary has customer loyalty valued at $600,000 and a talented workforce worth $400,000. How is this additional $1 million reported after the takeover? ***What recording is made when a parent buys a subsidiary and pays an extra amount because intangibles are present that have value but do not meet the criteria for separate reporting?***

Answer: Every subsidiary intangible (such as patents and databases) that meets either of the official criteria is consolidated by the parent at fair value. Any excess price paid over the total fair value of these recorded assets (the extra $1 million in this question) is also reported as an asset. It has a cost and an expected future value. The term that has long been used to report an amount paid to acquire a company that exceeded all the identified and recorded assets is "goodwill." Some amount of goodwill is recognized as a result of most corporate acquisitions. In this example, it specifically reflects the value of the customer loyalty and the quality of the subsidiary's workforce.

If Giant pays $16 million for the stock of Tiny when its reportable assets have a value of only $15 million, the following entry is made by Giant to consolidate the two companies. As shown, the additional $1 million is labeled as goodwill, which will then be included within the intangible assets.

FIGURE 11.4 Giant Company Buys Tiny Company—$1 Million Paid over Fair Value of Assets

Property and Equipment	4,000,000	
Patents	6,000,000	
Database	2,000,000	
Copyrights	3,000,000	
Goodwill	1,000,000	
Cash		16,000,000

Question: In the above illustration, the parent paid this extra $1 million for specified intangibles. However, the customer loyalty and the talented workforce could not be recorded separately as assets because neither met the required criteria. Instead, a goodwill balance was created.

Is the reporting any different if the parent simply paid this amount as a result of serious negotiations? Assume, for example, that Giant agreed to the additional $1 million to obtain Tiny because that company's owners refused to sell for less. Giant believed that the $16 million price was still a good investment even though it required paying $1 million more than the value of the assets (tangible and intangible) that could be identified. ***If an acquiring company pays an additional amount to purchase a subsidiary without a specific rationale, is this cost still recorded as goodwill?***

Answer: The acquisition of one company by another can require months of intense negotiations. One company wants to collect as much as possible; the other wants to pay as little as possible. Compromise is frequently necessary to arrive at a figure that both parties are willing to accept. In most cases, the new parent has to pay more than the sum of the value of all individual assets to entice the owners of the other company to sell.

Sometimes, as in the initial example with the customer loyalty and talented workforce, the reason for the added amount is apparent. More likely, the increased payment is simply necessary in order to make the deal happen. Because the extra amount is sacrificed to gain control of the subsidiary, it is still labeled by the parent as an asset known as goodwill. The rationale does not impact the accounting. Any extra acquisition price settled on to acquire a subsidiary appears in the parent's balance sheet as goodwill and is shown as an intangible asset.

EXERCISE

Link to multiple-choice question for practice purposes: http://www.quia.com/quiz/2092944.html

Question: Buildings, equipment, patents, databases, and the like all have costs that will be assigned to expense over an expected life as they help generate revenues. Goodwill is a different type of asset. It either represents a subsidiary attribute (such as customer loyalty) that is too nebulous to be recognized specifically as an intangible asset or an extra payment made by the parent as a result of the negotiation process. ***What happens to a cost labeled as goodwill after the date a subsidiary is acquired?*** *How does Microsoft or Yahoo! account for their large goodwill balances over time? Is this asset like land that simply continues to be reported at historical cost potentially forever or, possibly, like equipment that is depreciated systematically over some anticipated useful life?*

Answer: Because goodwill is the one asset on a balance sheet that is not tied to an identifiable benefit, no attempt is made to determine an anticipated life. Consequently, unlike most intangibles, the assigned cost is not amortized to expense. A goodwill balance can remain unchanged for decades after a subsidiary is purchased. However, the reported figure is reduced immediately if the value is ever judged to be impaired. Attributes such as customer loyalty or a talented workforce might continue in place for years or disappear in a short period of time. If goodwill is merely a premium paid to acquire a subsidiary, the justification for that excess amount could vanish quickly through poor management decisions or environmental factors. The value of all assets is tentative but probably none is more so than goodwill.

Impairment loss

Reported for long-lived assets when certain rules are met that indicate that fair value has dropped below cost so that the cost cannot be recovered.

Although a cost recorded as goodwill is not amortized over time, its ongoing worth is not assumed. Instead, a test to check for any loss of that value is performed annually. This verification process is more complex than can be covered in an introductory course. The result, though, is important to understand. In the event goodwill has declined in value, an **impairment loss** is recorded to reduce the reported balance. Although not identical, the accounting is similar in some ways to the impairment test for land, buildings, and equipment demonstrated in the previous chapter.

In 2000, Time Warner and America Online (AOL) merged. Because of the perceived benefit of combing these two companies, a huge premium was paid and reported as goodwill on the consolidated balance sheet. Just two years later, it was obvious that the anticipated synergies from this transaction had not developed as expected. In simple terms, too much had been paid by the owners to create the merger. The value of the combined companies had not achieved their overly optimistic projections. Consequently, goodwill was reduced in 2002 by nearly $100 billion with a loss of that amount being reported by the consolidated company. The goodwill account was not amortized to expense but the eventual impairment had to be recognized.

EXERCISE

Link to multiple-choice question for practice purposes: http://www.quia.com/quiz/2092964.html

KEY TAKEAWAY

When a parent acquires another company, all intangibles held by that subsidiary must be identified and consolidated at fair value but only if either of two criteria are met. Recognizing these assets is necessary if legal or contractual rights are held or the intangible can be separated from the company and sold. Other amounts are often included in the acquisition price to compensate for identifiable intangibles (such as customer loyalty) that do not meet either of these criteria. Or, an extra payment is necessary simply to entice the owner to sell. In either situation, this additional amount is reported as goodwill, an intangible asset that then appears on the consolidated balance sheet. Goodwill is not amortized over time but rather is checked periodically for impairment with a loss recognized if the value has declined.

4. ACCOUNTING FOR RESEARCH AND DEVELOPMENT

LEARNING OBJECTIVES

At the end of this section, students should be able to meet the following objectives:

1. **Define the terms "research" and "development."**
2. **Indicate the problem that uncertainty creates in reporting research and development costs.**
3. **Understand the method by which research and development costs are handled in financial accounting as has been established by U.S. GAAP.**
4. **Explain the advantages of handling research and development costs in the required manner.**
5. **Recognize that many companies will report asset balances that are vastly understated as a result of the official handling of research and development costs.**

Question: Many companies create internally developed intangibles such as copyrights and trademarks. As has been mentioned previously, the historical cost for such assets is often relatively small, almost inconsequential. However, monetary amounts spent to arrive at ideas that can be turned into new types of marketable products are often enormous. Such expenditures are essential to the future success of many companies. In 2008 alone, Intel reported spending $5.7 billion on **research** *and* **development** *in hopes of discovering new products to patent and sell. During the same one-year period, Bristol-Myers Squibb incurred costs of $3.6 billion on research and development. Those are clearly not inconsequential amounts. What is meant by the term "research?" What is meant by the term "development?"* ***If a company such as Intel or Bristol-Myers Squibb spends billions on research and development each year, what accounting is appropriate?*** *Should the company recognize an asset or an expense or some combination? The outcome is uncertain, but the money was spent under the assumption that future economic benefits would be derived.*

For example, assume that a technological company or a pharmaceutical company spends $1 million in Year One to do research on Future Product A. The company then spends another $1 million during the period on development costs for Future Product A. At the end of the year, officials believe that a patent is 80 percent likely for Future Product A. If received, sales can be made. During that time, the company also spends another $1 million in research and $1 million in development in connection with Future Product B. However, at year's end, the same officials are less optimistic about these results. They believe that only a 30 percent chance exists that this second product will ever receive a patent so that it can be used to generate revenues. According to U.S. GAAP, what reporting is appropriate for the cost of these two projects?

research

The attempt to find new knowledge with the hope that the results will eventually be useful in creating new products or services or significant improvements in existing products or services; these costs are expensed as incurred according to U.S. GAAP

development

The translation of new knowledge into actual products or services or into significant improvements in existing products or services; these costs are expensed as incurred according to U.S. GAAP.

Answer: Research is an attempt made to find new knowledge with the hope that the results will eventually be useful in creating new products or services or significant improvements in existing products or services. Development is the natural next step. It is the translation of that new knowledge into actual products or services or into significant improvements in existing products or services. In simple terms, research is the search for new ideas; development is the process of turning those ideas into saleable products.

Reporting research and development costs poses incredibly difficult challenges for accountants. As can be seen with Intel and Bristol-Myers Squibb, such costs are often massive because of the importance of new ideas and products to the future of many organizations. Unfortunately, significant uncertainty is inherent in virtually all such projects. The probability of success can be difficult to determine for years and is open to manipulation for most of that time. Often the only piece of information that is known with certainty is the amount that has been spent.

Thus, except for some relatively minor exceptions, all research and development costs are expensed as incurred according to U.S. GAAP.[3] The probability for success is not viewed as relevant to this reporting. Standardization is very apparent. All companies provide the same information in the same manner. The total cost incurred each period for research and development appears on the income statement as an expense regardless of the chance for success.

Consequently, the accounting for Future Product A and Future Product B is identical. Although one is 80 percent likely to be successful while the other is only 30 percent likely, the research and development expenditures for both are expensed as incurred. No asset is reported despite the possibility of future benefits. The rigidity of this rule comes from the inherent uncertainty as to whether revenues will ever be generated and, if so, for how long. Rather than trying to anticipate success, the conservatism found in accounting simply expenses all such costs. The percentages associated with the likelihood of receiving a patent and generating future revenues are ignored.

Two major advantages are provided by this approach. First, the amount spent on research and development each period is easy to determine and then compare with previous years and with other similar companies. Decision makers are quite interested in the amount invested in the search for new ideas and products. Second, the possibility for manipulation is virtually eliminated. No distinction is drawn between a likely success and a probable failure. No reporting advantage is achieved by maneuvering the estimation of a profitable outcome.

EXERCISE

Link to multiple-choice question for practice purposes: http://www.quia.com/quiz/2092945.html

Question: Companies spend billions of dollars on research and development each year in hopes of creating new products that can be sold in the future. This money would never be spent unless officials believed that a reasonable chance existed to recoup such huge investments. However, whether success is 100 percent likely or only 2 percent, no asset are reported on the balance sheet for these costs. ***Because all amounts spent on research and development are expensed automatically, are the assets reported by companies in industries such as technology and pharmaceuticals not omitting many of their most valuable future benefits?*** *If a company spends $5 billion to develop a new drug or electronic device that becomes worth $8 billion, does reporting absolutely no asset make sense?*

Answer: Even a student in an introductory accounting course can quickly recognize the problems created by a rule requiring that all research and development costs be expensed as incurred. Technology, pharmaceutical, and many other companies must exclude items of significant value from their balance sheets by following U.S. GAAP. While this approach is conservative, consistent, and allows for comparability, the rationale is confusing. The balance sheet hardly paints a fair portrait of the underlying organization. Expensing research and development costs also violates the matching principle. These expenditures are made in the hopes of generating future revenues but the expense is recorded immediately.

Capitalizing these costs so that they are reported as assets is logical but measuring the value of future benefits is extremely challenging. Without authoritative guidance, the extreme uncertainty of such projects would leave the accountant in a precarious position. U.S. GAAP "solves" the problem by eliminating the need for any judgment by the accountant. All costs are expensed. No rule could be simpler to apply.

Consequently, any decision maker evaluating a company that invests heavily in research and development needs to recognize that the assets appearing on the balance sheet are incomplete. Such companies spend money to create future benefits that are not being reported. The wisdom of that approach has long been debated but it is the rule under U.S. GAAP. Difficult estimates are not needed and the possibility of manipulation is avoided.

Talking with an Independent Auditor about International Financial Reporting Standards

Following is a continuation of our interview with Robert A. Vallejo, partner with the accounting firm PricewaterhouseCoopers.

Question: Virtually without exception, U.S. GAAP requires that all research and development expenditures must be expensed as incurred. This requirement has existed for over thirty years. Does IFRS handle research and development costs in the same manner?

Robert Vallejo: This is one of the best examples of differences between IFRS and U.S. GAAP. IFRS requires the capitalization of development costs. Guidelines do exist to help determine when a project moves from the research stage into the development stage. However, once the development stage commences, the costs have to be capitalized and amortized over the anticipated useful life. When companies first adopt IFRS, this will be a change that will require some effort, particularly if development costs are significant, and will have a substantial impact on reported net income.

The difference between U.S. GAAP and IFRS is not a question of right or wrong but rather an example of different theories colliding. U.S. GAAP prefers not to address the uncertainty inherent in research and development programs but rather to focus on comparability of amounts spent (between years and between companies). IFRS, on the other hand, views the failure by U.S. GAAP to recognize assets when future benefits are clearly present as a reporting flaw that should not be allowed.

KEY TAKEAWAY

Research and development costs include all amounts spent to create new ideas and then turn them into products that can be sold to generate revenue. Because success is highly uncertain, accounting has long faced the challenge of determining whether such costs should be capitalized or expensed. U.S. GAAP requires that all research and development costs (with a few minor exceptions) be expensed as incurred. This official standard prevents manipulation and allows decision makers to see the amount spent by management for this essential function. However, this method of accounting means that companies (especially in certain industries) often fail to show some of their most valuable assets on their balance sheets.

5. ACQUIRING AN ASSET WITH FUTURE CASH PAYMENTS

LEARNING OBJECTIVES

At the end of this section, students should be able to meet the following objectives:

1. **Realize that if payments for an asset are delayed into the future, part of that cash amount is attributed to the purchase of the asset with the rest deemed to be interest.**
2. **Recognize that a reasonable rate of interest can be stated explicitly and paid when payment for a purchase is delayed so that no present value computation is needed.**
3. **Determine the allocation of cash flows between principal and interest using a present value computation when a reasonable interest rate is not paid.**
4. **Record the acquisition of an intangible asset when a present value computation has been required.**
5. **Define the term "compounding."**
6. **Compute interest to be recognized each period when a transaction was recorded using a present value computation.**
7. **Understand the difference in an annuity due and an ordinary annuity.**

Question: A company buys a patent from an inventor on January 1, Year One, for $1 million to be paid immediately. The accounting is straightforward; the patent is recognized as an intangible asset and reported at the historical cost of $1 million. Accounting rules are clear on the handling of such acquisitions.

Assume, instead, that the company offers to pay this $1 million but not until five years have passed. The seller agrees to that proposal. The purchase is made now but payment is delayed. Is the $1 million still being paid solely for the patent? Does the entire $1 million reflect the historical cost of this intangible? ***What reporting is appropriate if an asset such as a patent, building, or land is bought but payment will not take place for several years?*** *How is historical cost determined?*

Answer: Approximately forty years ago, the authoritative accounting body at the time ruled that when cash is paid for a purchase[4] over an extended period of time in the future, there are always two distinct reasons for the payments.[5]

- The first is obviously the acquisition of the property such as the patent in this example.
- The second is **interest**. Interest is the charge for the use of money over time.

Interest

The charge for using money over time, often associated with long-term loans; even if not specifically mentioned in the debt agreement, U.S. GAAP requires it to be computed and reported based on a reasonable rate.

It was held to be unreasonable to believe that cash payments could be spread over several years without some interest charge being factored into the negotiated amounts. The accounting here is based on that assertion.

In many purchases, interest is explicitly stated. For example, the contract to buy this patent could have required payment of $1 million after five years plus interest at a 7 percent rate to be paid each year. Once again, the accounting is not complicated. The $1 million is the historical cost of the patent while the annual $70,000 payments ($1 million × 7 percent) are recorded each year by the buyer as interest expense. The two amounts are clearly differentiated in the terms of the agreement.

A problem arises if the interest is not explicitly identified in the contract. In the current illustration, the company agrees to make a single $1 million payment in five years with no mention of interest. According to U.S. GAAP, interest is still present because payment has been delayed. Official accounting rules hold that only part of the $1 million is actually paid for the patent with the rest serving as interest. The assertion stands: there is always a charge for using money over time. Payment has been deferred for five years; some part of that payment compensates the seller for having to wait for the money. Even if a rate is not mentioned, the assumption is made that interest for this period of time was taken into consideration when the $1 million figure was set.

present value

The value of future cash flows with all future interest computed at a reasonable rate and then removed; the remainder is literally the present value of those future cash flows.

However, the specific allocation of the $1 million between patent and interest is not readily apparent. To calculate the interest included within the price, an introduction to **present value** computations is necessary.

In simple terms, the present value of future cash flows is the amount left after all future interest is removed (hence the term "present value").

The present value is the cost within the $1 million paid for the patent. The remainder—the interest—will be recognized as expense over the five-year period until payment is made.

To determine the present value of future cash flows, a reasonable interest rate is needed. Then, the amount of interest for these five years can be mathematically calculated. An appropriate interest rate is often viewed as the one the buyer would be charged if this money were borrowed from a local bank.

Assume here that 10 percent is a reasonable annual rate. Present value is then determined which is equal to the payment amount with all interest removed. The formula to determine the present value of $1 at a designated point in the future is $1 divided by $(1 + i)$ raised to the nth power with "n" being the number of periods and "i" the appropriate interest rate. In this case, because payment is due in five years, the present value $1 is $\$1/(1.10)^5$, or 0.62092. This factor can then be multiplied by the actual cash payment to determine its present value.[6]

More simply put, if $1 is paid in five years for an asset and a reasonable rate of interest is 10 percent per year, then the $0.62 (rounded) present value is the portion being paid for the asset with the remaining $0.38 representing interest for those years. The present value computation mathematically determines the interest and then removes it to leave the cost of the asset.

Fortunately, present value tables are available as well as calculators and computer spreadsheets that make this computation relatively easy. On a present value table, the factor is found by looking under the specific interest rate column (10 percent) at the line for the number of applicable time periods (five).

Present value of Single Amount of $1

http://www.principlesofaccounting.com/ART/fv.pv.tables/pvof1.htm

The present value today of paying $1 million in five years assuming a 10 percent annual interest rate is $1 million times 0.62092 or $620,920. This is the amount of the debt at the current moment (known as the principal) before any future interest is accrued over time. Mathematically, the interest for these five years has been computed and removed to arrive at this figure. It is the historical cost of the patent, the present value of the cash flows without any future interest. The remainder of the payment ($379,080) will be reported as interest expense by the buyer over the subsequent five years using a 10 percent annual rate. The total ($620,920 for the patent plus $379,080 interest) equals the $1 million payment.

The journal entries for Year One are as follows. The interest to be recognized for this first year is $62,092 or 10 percent of the principal balance for that year ($620,920).[7]

FIGURE 11.5 Present Value—Acquisition of Patent and Recognition of Year One Interest

1/1/1	Patent	$620,920		($1,000,000 × .620920)
	Note Payable		$620,920	
12/31/1	Interest Expense	62,092		(620,920 × .10)
	Note Payable		62,092	

Notice in the December 31 entry that no interest is actually paid on that date. Payment of this additional charge occurs in five years when the $1 million has to be paid and not just $620,920. Because interest was recognized in Year One but not paid, the amount of the liability (the principal) has grown. Increasing the debt to reflect the accrual of interest is referred to as "compounding." Whenever interest is recognized but not paid, it is compounded which means that it is added to the principal of the liability.

In the second year, interest expense to be recognized is higher because the principal has increased from $620,920 to $683,012 ($620,920 plus $62,092) as a result of compounding the Year One interest. The ongoing compounding raises the principal each year so that the expense also increases.

FIGURE 11.6 Present Value—Recognition and Compounding of Interest[8]

12/31/2	Interest Expense Note Payable	$68,301	 $68,301	(($620,920 + $62,092) × .10)
12/31/3	Interest Expense Note Payable	75,131	 75,131	((683,012 + 68,301) × .10)
12/31/4	Interest Expense Note Payable	82,644	 82,644	((751,313 + 75,131) × .10)
12/31/5	Interest Expense Note Payable	90,912	 90,912	((826,444 + 82,644) × .10)
12/31/5	Note Payable Cash	1,000,000	 1,000,000	

These journal entries show that three goals are achieved by the reporting.

- The patent is recorded at its historical cost of $620,920.
- The liability increases through compounding to $1 million as of its due date.
- Interest expense of $379,080 is recognized over the five-year period ($62,092 + $68,301 + $75,131 + $82,644 + $90,912). Although interest was not mentioned in the contract, U.S. GAAP requires it to be computed and reported over these five years.

EXERCISE

Link to multiple-choice question for practice purposes: http://www.quia.com/quiz/2092946.html

EXERCISE

Link to multiple-choice question for practice purposes: http://www.quia.com/quiz/2092965.html

EXERCISE

Link to multiple-choice question for practice purposes: http://www.quia.com/quiz/2092947.html

EXERCISE

Link to multiple-choice question for practice purposes: http://www.quia.com/quiz/2092966.html

EXERCISE

Link to multiple-choice question for practice purposes: http://www.quia.com/quiz/2092910.html

*Question: Does the application of present value change substantially if cash is paid each year rather than as a lump sum at the end of the term? **What reporting is appropriate if an intangible asset is purchased by making a down payment today followed by a series of payments in the future?***

To illustrate, assume a company acquires a copyright from an artist by paying $10,000 on January 1, Year One, and promising an additional $10,000 at the beginning of each subsequent year with the final payment on January 1, Year Five. The total amount is $50,000. No separate interest is paid. What is the *historical cost to be reported for this intangible asset and what interest should be recorded on the liability over these future years?*

annuity

A series of equal payments made at equal time intervals.

ordinary annuity

Annuity with payments made at the end of each period; it is also called an annuity in arrears.

annuity due

Annuity with payments made at the beginning of each period; it is also called an annuity in advance.

Answer: Although cash is conveyed over an extended period of time in this purchase, a reasonable rate of interest is not being explicitly paid. Thus, once again, a present value computation is necessary to pull out an appropriate amount of interest and leave just the cost of the asset. The present value of the payments (the principal) is the cash paid after all future interest is mathematically removed. That process has not changed. Here, cash is not conveyed as a single amount but rather as an **annuity**—an equal amount paid at equal time intervals. An annuity can be either an **ordinary annuity** with payments made at the end of each period or an **annuity due** with payments starting immediately at the beginning of each period.

The specific series of payments in this question creates an annuity due pattern because the first $10,000 is conveyed when the contract is signed. As before, a mathematical formula can be constructed to determine the applicable present value factor.[9] Tables, a calculator, or a computer spreadsheet can also be used. If a reasonable rate is assumed to be 12 percent per year, the present value of a $1 per year annuity due of five periods with a rate of 12 percent is 4.0374.[10]

Present Value of an Annuity Due of $1 per Period

http://www.principlesofaccounting.com/ART/fv.pv.tables/pvforannuitydue.htm

Assuming a 12 percent annual interest rate, the present value of paying $10,000 annually for five years beginning immediately is $10,000 times 4.03735 or $40,374 (rounded). For annuities, the computation is constructed so that a single payment ($10,000) must be multiplied here rather than the total cash amount ($50,000). Of the total, $40,374 (the present value) is being paid for the copyright with the remaining $9,626 ($50,000 total cash less $40,374) representing the cost of interest over this period. To reiterate, the present value computation removes the interest from the total cash flow so that only the principal (the amount being paid for the asset) remains.

The initial journal entry to record this acquisition is as follows. Because no time has yet passed, interest is omitted.

FIGURE 11.7 Acquisition of Intangible Asset—Present Value of an Annuity Due

1/1/1	Copyright	40,374	
	Cash		10,000
	Note Payable		30,374

At the end of the first year, interest expense on the liability for the period must be recognized along with amortization of the cost of the copyright (assume a life of ten years and no residual value). The interest for the period is the $30,374 principal of the liability times the 12 percent reasonable rate or $3,645 (rounded). Because no interest is explicitly paid in this contract, all the interest is compounded. Amortization of the cost of the asset is $40,374 divided by ten years or $4,037.

FIGURE 11.8 Acquisition of Intangible Asset—Recognition of Interest and Amortization

12/31/1	Interest Expense	3,645	
	Note Payable		3,645
	Amortization Expense	4,037	
	Copyright		4,037

The next scheduled payment is made on January 1, Year Two and reduces the amount of the liability.

FIGURE 11.9 Payment at Start of Year Two

1/1/2	Note Payable	10,000	
	Cash		10,000

At the end of Year Two, both interest on the liability and amortization of the asset's cost must be recognized again to reflect the passage of another period. The amortization figure remains the same (assuming application of the straight-line method) but interest must be recomputed. The principal was $30,374 for the first year but interest of $3,645 was then added to the liability at the end of that period followed by a $10,000 payment.

FIGURE 11.10 Computation of Liability Principal at End of Year Two

Liability Principal—January 1, Year Two ($30,374 plus Year One interest of $3,645)	$34,019
Payment on January 1, Year Two	(10,000)
Liability Principal—December 31, Year Two	$24,019

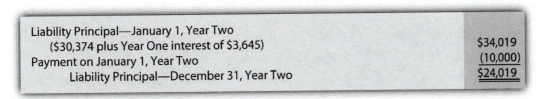

Thus, for the second year, the principal amount of the liability is $24,019 and the interest, at the reasonable rate of 12 percent, is $2,882 (rounded).

FIGURE 11.11 Recognition of Interest and Amortization for Year Two

12/31/2	Interest Expense	2,882	
	Note Payable		2,882
	Amortization Expense	4,037	
	Copyright		4,037

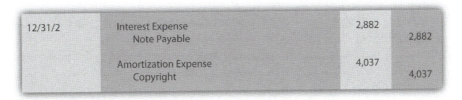

This pattern of entries will continue until the liability has been extinguished and the capitalized cost of the asset amortized completely to expense.

KEY TAKEAWAY

Companies often delay making cash payments for purchases for years. If interest is calculated and paid in the interim, the purchase price and the interest are easy to differentiate. The accounting is straightforward. However, if no interest payments are specified, a present value computation is made to separate the amount paid for the asset from the interest. The resulting amount (the present value) is recognized initially for both the asset and liability. Interest is recognized each period and compounded (added to the principal of the liability) since it is not paid at the time. Cash payments can be a single amount or an annuity (a stream of equal payments made at equal time intervals). An annuity can be an ordinary annuity (payments are made at the end of each period) or an annuity due (payments start immediately and are made at the beginning of each period).

Talking With a Real Investing Pro—Continued

Following is a continuation of our interview with Kevin G. Burns.

Question: Goodwill is one of the most misunderstood balances on any set of financial statements. For example, at the end of 2008, Procter & Gamble reported goodwill of nearly $57 billion. Many serious investors probably are unsure of what to make of that number. How do you factor the reported balance for goodwill into your decision making?

Kevin Burns: I am not a big fan of goodwill. It is way too subjective and frankly I am not sure that it provides credible information. How do you value something from an accounting standpoint that you cannot really measure or touch or feel? You cannot borrow against it. The goodwill balance is irrelevant for the kind of investing I do where I am more interested in asset values and what the real market values are for those assets. My feeling about goodwill is a bit like my feeling for financial footnotes. I prefer companies that can explain how they have value and make money without relying too much on either one.

Video Clip

Joe talks about the five most important points in Chapter 11.

View the video online at: http://blip.tv/play/sDyBv7sKAA

6. END-OF-CHAPTER EXERCISES

QUESTIONS

1. Define "intangible asset."
2. Give three examples of intangible assets.
3. At what value are intangible assets typically reported?
4. How does an intangible asset differ from property and equipment?
5. What is amortization?
6. How does a company typically determine the useful life of an intangible?
7. Under what circumstances could the cost to defend an intangible asset in court be capitalized to the asset account?
8. Why are intangibles, like trademarks, not recorded at their market value, which can greatly exceed historical cost?
9. What are the two reasons intangible assets are reported at more than historical cost plus filing and legal costs?
10. When should a parent (acquiring) company record the intangibles of a subsidiary on its balance sheet?
11. What is "goodwill?"
12. Is goodwill amortized like other intangibles?
13. What should companies do with goodwill each reporting period?
14. Payments made over an extended period of time should be divided into what two items?
15. What is present value?
16. What is an annuity?

TRUE OR FALSE

1. ____ Typically, intangible assets are shown at their fair value.
2. ____ A patent is an example of an intangible asset.
3. ____ Amortization of intangibles is usually done over the asset's legal life.
4. ____ Once a company records goodwill, it will be on the company's books forever because it is not amortized.
5. ____ If an intangible asset is successfully defended from a legal challenge, legal costs may be capitalized to the asset account.
6. ____ When one company acquires another, the acquiring company should continue to report any intangible assets of the purchased company at the same cost used by the purchased company.
7. ____ An intangible asset is a right that helps the owner generate revenues.
8. ____ Research and development costs that help develop successful programs can be capitalized.
9. ____ It is assumed that payments made on a long-term basis include interest.
10. ____ Intangibles purchased from another company are reported at the amount paid for them less any amortization.

MULTIPLE CHOICE

1. Which of the following would not be subject to amortization?
   a. Goodwill
   b. Patent
   c. Copyright
   d. Trademark
2. Mitchell Inc. developed a product, spending $4,900,000 in research to do so. Mitchell applied for and received a patent for the product in January, spending $34,800 in legal and filing fees. The patent is valid for seventeen years. What would be the book value of the patent at the end of Year 1?
   a. $4,644,518
   b. $34,800
   c. $32,753
   d. $4,611,765
3. Kremlin Company pays $2,900,000 for the common stock of Reticular Corporation. Reticular has assets on the balance sheet with a book value of $1,500,000 and a fair value of $2,500,000. What is goodwill in this purchase?
   a. $1,400,000
   b. $1,000,000
   c. $400,000
   d. $0
4. What is the present value of receiving $4,800,000 at the end of 6 years assuming an interest rate of 5 percent?
   a. $3,581,834
   b. $6,432,459
   c. $5,040,000
   d. $4,571,429
5. Which of the following concerning the research and development costs is true?
   a. According to U.S. GAAP, research and development costs must be expensed as incurred.
   b. Current U.S. GAAP reporting for research and development costs violates the matching principle.
   c. International Financial Reporting Standards allow some development costs to be capitalized.
   d. S. GAAP reporting for research and development costs is superior to international reporting.
6. Krypton Corporation offers Earth Company $800,000 for a patent held by Earth Company. The patent is currently on Earth Company's books in the amount of $14,000, the legal costs of registering the patent in the first place. Krypton had appraisers examine the patent before making an offer to purchase it, and the experts determined that it could be worth anywhere from $459,000 to $1,090,000. If the purchase falls through, at what amount should Earth Company now report the patent?
   a. $80,000
   b. $14,000
   c. $459,000
   d. $1,090,000
7. What is the present value of receiving $15,000 per year for the next six years at an interest rate of 7 percent, assuming payments are made at the beginning of the period (annuity due)?
   a. $76,503
   b. $90,000
   c. $59,971
   d. $9,995

PROBLEMS

1. At the beginning of the year, Jaguar Corporation purchased a license from Angel Corporation that gives Jaguar the right to use a process Angel created. The purchase price of the license was $1,500,000, including legal fees. Jaguar will be able to use the process for five years under the license agreement.
    a. Record Jaguar's purchase of the license.
    b. Record amortization of the license at the end of year one.
    c. What is the book value of the license reported on Jaguar's balance sheet at the end of Year One?
2. Yolanda Company created a product for which it was able to obtain a patent. Yolanda sold the patent to Christiana Inc. for $20,780,000 at the beginning of 20X4. Christiana paid an additional $200,000 in legal fees to properly record the patent. At the beginning of 20X4, Christiana determined that the patent had a remaining life of seven years.
    a. Record Christiana's purchase of the patent.
    b. Record amortization of the patent at the end of 20X4 and 20X5.
    c. What is the book value of the patent reported on Christiana's balance sheet at the end of 20X5?
    d. During 20X6, Christiana is sued by Bushnell Corporation, who claims that it has a patent on a product similar to the one held by Christiana and that Bushnell's patent was registered first. After a lengthy court battle, in December of 20X7, Christiana discovers that it has successfully defended its patent. The defense of the patent cost Christiana $1,700,000 in legal fees. Record any necessary journal entries dealing with the court battle.
    e. Christiana reaffirms that the patent has a remaining life of three years on December 31, 20X7. Record amortization expense on this date.
    f. What is the book value of the patent reported on Christiana's balance sheet at the end of 20X7?
3. Star Corporation purchases Trek Inc. for $72,960,000. Star Corporation is gaining the following assets and liabilities:

	Value on Trek's Books	Current Market Value
Inventory	$456,000	$456,000
Land	$1,050,000	$50,000,000
Trademarks	$64,000	$20,004,000
Patent	$15,000	$1,850,000
Accounts Payable	$650,000	$650,000

    Prepare the journal entry for Star to record the purchase of Trek.
4. Assume the same facts as in 3 above, but assume that Star pays $100,000,000 for Trek.
    a. When a purchasing company pays more than the fair market value of the assets of a company being acquired, what is this excess payment called?
    b. Why might Star be willing to pay more than $72,960,000 for Trek?
    c. Record the purchase of Trek by Star given this new purchase amount of $100,000,000.
5. Calculate the present value of each of the following amounts at the given criteria and then answer the questions that follow:

Future Cash Flow	Interest Rate	Number of Periods	Present Value
$400,000	4%	7 years	
$400,000	6%	7 years	
$400,000	4%	12 years	
$400,000	6%	12 years	

    a. Does the present value increase or decrease when the interest rate increases?
    b. Does the present value increase or decrease as the time period increases?
6. On 1/1/X6 Fred Corporation purchases a patent from Barney Company for $10,000,000, payable at the end of three years. The patent itself has an expected life of ten years. No interest rate is stated, but Fred could borrow that amount from a bank at 6 percent interest.
    a. Record the journal entry to record the patent on 1/1/X6.

b. Record the journal entries to record interest expense and amortization expense on 12/31/X6, 12/31/X7, and 12/31/X8.

c. Record the journal entry to show that Fred pays off the note payable on 12/31/X8.

7. Calculate the present value of each of the following amounts at the given criteria. Assume that the payment is made at the beginning of the period (annuity due).

Payment per Period	Interest Rate	Number of Periods	Present Value
$30,000	5%	8 years	
$60,000	4%	7 years	
$25,000	8%	10 years	
$56,000	6%	4 years	

8. Highlight Company purchases the right to use a certain piece of music from the musician. It hopes to make this its "signature song" so it will be a long-term relationship, the contract stating five years. The agreed upon price is $750,000, with no stated interest rate. Highlight could borrow money at 5 percent interest currently. The arrangement states that Highlight will make a down payment on 1/1/X2 of $150,000, and pay $150,000 at the beginning of the following four years, making this an annuity due.

   a. Record the journal entry to record the copyright on 1/1/X2.

   b. Record the journal entries to record interest expense and amortization expense on 12/31/X2, 12/31/X3, 12/31/X4, and 12/31/X5.

   c. Record the journal entries to record the payments on 1/1/X3, 1/1/X4, 1/1/X5, and 1/1/X6.

COMPREHENSIVE PROBLEM

This problem will carry through several chapters, building in difficulty. It allows students to continuously practice skills and knowledge learned in previous chapters.

In Chapter 10, you prepared Webworks statements for October. They are included here as a starting point for November.

Webworks Financial Statements

Webworks
Income Statement
As of October 31

Revenue	$13,700
Cost of Goods Sold	(6,615)
Gross Profit	7,085
Depreciation Expense	(601)
Other Expenses	(3,590)
Earning before Tax	2,894
Tax Expense	(868)
Net Income	$2,026

Webworks
Stmt. of Retained Earnings
As of October 31

Retained Earnings, October 1	$4,645
Net Income	2,026
Retained Earnings, October 31	$6,671

Webworks
Balance Sheet
October 31

Assets		**Liabilities**	
Current		**Current**	
Cash	$1,532	Accounts Payable	$3,385
Accounts Receivable	1,450	Salaries Payable	100
Less Allowance for Doubtful Accounts	(145)		
Net Accounts Receivable	1,305		
Merchandise Inventory	1,470		
Supplies Inventory	50		
Prepaid Rent	400		
Total Current Assets	$4,757	Total Current Liabilities	$3,485
Noncurrent			
Equipment			
Less Accumulated Depreciation	$7,000		
Furniture	(584)		
Less Accumulated	1,000		
Depreciation	(17)		
Total Noncurrent Assets	$7,399		
		Owners' Equity	
		Capital Stock	$2,000
		Retained Earnings	6,671
		Total Owners' Equity	$8,671
Total Assets	$12,156	Total Liabilities & Owners' Equity	$12,156

The following events occur during November:

a. Webworks starts and completes eight more sites and bills clients for $4,600.

b. Webworks purchases supplies worth $80 on account.

c. At the beginning of November, Webworks had nineteen keyboards costing $110 each and forty flash drives costing $12 each. Webworks uses periodic FIFO to cost its inventory.

d. On account, Webworks purchases sixty keyboards for $111 each and ninety flash drives for $13 each.

e. Webworks pays Nancy $800 for her work during the first three weeks of October.

f. Webworks sells 60 keyboards for $9,000 and 120 flash drives for $2,400 cash.

g. A local realtor pays $400 in advance for a Web site. It will not be completed until December.

h. Leon read about a new program that could enhance the Web sites Webworks is developing for clients. He decides to purchase a license to be able to use the program for one year by paying $2,400 cash. This is called a "license agreement" and is an intangible asset.

i. Webworks collects $5,000 in accounts receivable.

j. Webworks pays off its salaries payable from November.

k. Webworks pays off $8,500 of its accounts payable.

l. Webworks pays Leon a salary of $2,000.

m. Webworks wrote off an uncollectible account in the amount of $100.

n. Webworks pays taxes of $1,304 in cash.

Required:

A. Prepare journal entries for the above events.

B. Post the journal entries to T-accounts.

C. Prepare an unadjusted trial balance for Webworks for November.

D. Prepare adjusting entries for the following and post them to your T-accounts.

o. Webworks owes Nancy $150 for her work during the last week of November.

p. Leon's parents let him know that Webworks owes $290 toward the electricity bill. Webworks will pay them in December.

q. Webworks determines that it has $20 worth of supplies remaining at the end of November.

r. Prepaid rent should be adjusted for November's portion.

s. Webworks is continuing to accrue bad debts at 10 percent of accounts receivable.

t. Webworks continues to depreciate its equipment over four years and its furniture over five years, using the straight-line method.

u. The license agreement should be amortized over its one-year life.

v. Record cost of goods sold.

E. Prepare an adjusted trial balance.

F. Prepare financial statements for November.

ENDNOTES

1. Unique accounting rules have long existed in certain industries to address unusual circumstances. College accounting textbooks such as this one tend to focus on general rules rather than delve into the specifics of accounting as it applies to a particular industry.
2. For a complete coverage of the history and ramifications of the Enron scandal, both the movie and the book *The Smartest Guys in the Room* are quite informative and fascinating.
3. FASB, "Accounting for Research and Development Costs," *Statement of Financial Accounting Standards No. 2*, October 1974. Within the new *Accounting Standards Codification*, information on the reporting of research and development can be found at FASB ASC 730-10.
4. Similar rules apply when an asset is sold and the money is to be collected over a period of future years. For convenience, the illustrations in this chapter will focus on cash payments made in an acquisition.
5. The Accounting Principles Board (APB) was the primary group in charge of creating U.S. GAAP from 1962 until 1973 when it was replaced by the Financial Accounting Standards Board (FASB). During those years, the APB produced thirty-one opinions. Its Opinion 21, "Interest of Receivables and Payables" was issued in August 1971 and established the rules described here. Within the new *Accounting Standards Codification*, information on the reporting of interest can be found at FASB ASC 835-30.
6. In an Excel spreadsheet, the present value of $1 at 10 percent for five years can be derived by entering the following into a cell: =PV(.10,5,1,,0).
7. The effective rate method of computing interest is demonstrated here. The principal balance is multiplied by the reasonable interest rate to get the amount of interest to be recorded each period. The effective rate method is the preferred approach according to U.S. GAAP. In Chapter 14, an alternative method known as the straight-line method is also demonstrated. It is also allowed if the differences are not viewed as material.
8. If the computations and entries are all correct, the liability will be $1 million at the end of five years. In the present value computation, the interest was removed at a 10 percent annual rate and then put back in each year through compounding at the same rate. Because some figures are rounded in these computations, the final interest amount may have to be adjusted by a few dollars to arrive at the $1 million total.
9. The mathematical formula to determine the present value of an annuity due of $1 per period is

$$\text{present value of an annuity due} = [(1 - 1/[1 + i]^n)/i] \times (1 + i),$$

where i is the appropriate interest rate and n is the number of payment periods.

The mathematical formula to determine the present value of an ordinary annuity of $1 per period is

$$\text{present value of an ordinary annuity} = (1 - 1/[1 + i]^n)/i,$$

where i is the appropriate interest rate and n is the number of payment periods.

10. On an Excel spreadsheet, the present value of a $1 per year annuity due for five periods at a reasonable rate of 12 percent is computed by typing the following data into a cell: =PV(.12,5,1,,1). If this had been an ordinary annuity because the initial payment was delayed until the end of the first period, present value of that $1 per year ordinary annuity is =PV(.12,5,1,,0).

CHAPTER 12

In a Set of Financial Statements, What Information Is Conveyed about Equity Investments?

Video Clip

Joe introduces Chapter 12 and speaks about the course in general.

View the video online at: http://blip.tv/play/sDyBwKhGAA

1. ACCOUNTING FOR INVESTMENTS IN TRADING SECURITIES

LEARNING OBJECTIVES

At the end of this section, students should be able to meet the following objectives:

1. **Realize that the reporting of investments in the ownership shares of another company depends on the purpose of the acquisition.**
2. **Explain the characteristics of investments that are classified as trading securities.**
3. **Account for changes in the value of investments in trading securities and understand the rationale for this handling.**
4. **Record dividends received from investments classified as trading securities.**
5. **Determine the gain or loss to be recorded on the sale of a trading security.**

Question: Businesses frequently acquire ownership (equity) shares of other companies. At June 30, 2009, Microsoft disclosed that it held investments in the stock of other companies with a value of over $4.4 billion. During 2008, Mars Inc. offered to buy all the ownership shares of Wm. Wrigley Jr. Company for approximately $23 billion. The acquisition of Merrill Lynch by Bank of America made headlines around the *world in the fall of 2008. The purchase of such shares offers many potential benefits.* ***What are the most common reasons for one company to buy the ownership shares of another company?***

Answer: Potentially, many benefits can accrue from obtaining shares of the stock issued by a business. The method of financial reporting applied by the owner depends on the purpose for holding such investments. Thus, the accounting process here is unique. The reporting of most assets does not vary significantly because of the rationale for making the purchase and retaining the property. In contrast, information about the ownership of the stock of another company is presented according to one of several methods based solely on the reason for the investment.

Companies frequently find that they are holding excess cash not needed at the moment for operating purposes. Traditional savings accounts or money market funds offer very low returns for this money. Company officials often seek a greater profit by using surplus cash to buy the ownership shares of other organizations. The hope is that the market price of these shares will appreciate in value and/or dividends will be received before the money is needed for operations. Such investments can be held for a few days (or even hours) or many years. Although earnings can improve through this strategy, the buyer does face additional risk. Share prices do not always go up; they can also decline resulting in losses for the investor.

When equity shares are bought solely as a way to store cash in a possibly lucrative spot, the investor has no interest in influencing or controlling the decisions of the other company. That is not the reason for the purchase; the ownership interest is much too small.

control

Indicates that consolidated financial statements should be reported by bringing together the financial information of two companies; according to U.S. GAAP, it exists when one company owns more than 50 percent of the outstanding common shares of another company.

Investors, though, may also embrace a strategy of acquiring enough shares to gain some degree of influence over the other organization. Often, profitable synergies can be developed by having two companies connected in this way. For example, at the end of 2008, The Coca-Cola Company (CCC) held approximately 35 percent of the outstanding stock of Coca-Cola Enterprises (CCE), its primary bottler and distributor. CCC does not own sufficient shares to **control** the operations of CCE but it certainly can apply significant influence if it so chooses.

Finally, as in the bid by Mars to acquire Wrigley, the investor may seek to obtain a controlling interest in the other company. In many cases, one company even acquires 100 percent ownership of the other. Such acquisitions are actually common as large companies attempt to move into new industries or geographical areas, become bigger players in their current markets, gain access to valuable assets, or simply eliminate competitors. Many smaller companies are started by entrepreneurs with the specific hope that success will eventually attract acquisition interest from a larger organization. Often, a significant profit can be earned by the original owners as a result of the sale of their company.

Question: There are clearly different reasons for buying stock. Assume that Valente Corporation is holding $25,000 in cash that it will not need for several weeks. The money is currently in a money market fund earning only a 1 percent annual rate of return. In hopes of generating a higher profit, the president of Valente has studied the financial statements of Bayless Corporation, a company with capital stock trading on the New York Stock Exchange (NYSE) for $25 per share. On November 30, Year One, the president believes that Bayless stock is primed to have a rather significant jump in market price in the near future. Consequently, Valente uses the $25,000 to acquire one thousand shares of stock in Bayless that will be held for only a few weeks or months. ***How does an owner report an equity investment that is bought with the expectation that the shares will be sold shortly after the purchase is made?***

trading securities

Classification of investments in stocks and bonds when management's intentions are to buy and sell them quickly in the near term; they are reported on the balance sheet at fair value with all changes in value affecting net income.

Answer: If management's intentions are to buy and sell the equity shares of another company in the near term, the purchase is classified on the balance sheet as an investment in **trading securities**. On the acquisition date, the asset is recorded by Valente at historical cost.

FIGURE 12.1 Purchase of Ownership Shares Classified as Trading Securities

Investment in Trading Securities	25,000	
Cash		25,000

As an owner, even for a short period of time, Valente might well receive a cash dividend from Bayless. Many companies distribute dividends to their stockholders periodically as a way of sharing a portion of any income that has been earned.

Assume that Bayless has been profitable and, as a result, a $0.20 per share cash dividend is declared by its board of directors and paid in December. Valente receives $200 of this dividend ($0.20 per share

× one thousand shares) which is reported as revenue on the company's income statement for this period.

FIGURE 12.2 Receipt of Dividend from Investment in Stock

Cash	200	
Dividend Revenue		200

Because of the short-term nature of this investment, Valente might sell these shares prior to the end of the year. The purchase was made anticipating a quick sale. A gain is reported if more than $25,000 is received while a loss results if the shares are sold for less than $25,000. As with dividend revenue, such gains and losses appear on the owner's income statement.

Accounting becomes more complicated if Valente continues to hold this investment at year end. ***Should equity shares held as a trading security be reported in the owner's financial statements at historical cost or current fair value?*** *Which reporting is most helpful to outside decision makers?*

U.S. GAAP requires investments in trading securities to be reported on the balance sheet at fair value. Therefore, if the shares of Bayless are worth $28,000 at December 31, Year One, Valente must adjust the reported value from $25,000 to $28,000 by reporting a gain.

FIGURE 12.3 Shares of Bayless (a Trading Security) Adjusted to Fair Value at End of Year

Investment in Trading Securities	3,000	
Unrealized Gain—Trading Securities		3,000

The gain here is labeled as "**unrealized**" to indicate that the value of the asset has appreciated but no final sale has yet taken place. The gain is not guaranteed; the value might go back down before the shares are sold. However, the unrealized gain is recognized and reported on the owner's Year One income statement.

unrealized gain or loss

A gain or loss created by an increase or decrease in the value of an asset although not yet finalized by a sale.

EXERCISE

Link to multiple-choice question for practice purposes: http://www.quia.com/quiz/2092911.html

Question: The reporting demonstrated above for an investment in a trading security raises a question that has long been debated in financial accounting. Is recognizing a gain (or loss if the value had declined prior to the end of the year) on the owner's income statement appropriate if no actual sale has yet occurred? There is an important related question. In previous chapters, assets such as buildings, copyrights, and inventory were never adjusted to fair value unless an impairment had taken place. ***Why is an investment in a trading security recorded at fair value regardless of whether that value is above or below historical cost?***

Answer: According to U.S. GAAP, changes in the value of trading securities are reported and the resulting gains or losses are shown within current net income for several reasons:

- The Bayless shares sell on a stock exchange and, thus, the reported value of $28,000 can be objectively determined. It is not an estimated amount subject to manipulation as is usually the case with assets such as buildings, copyrights, and inventory.
- The stock can be sold immediately; Valente does not have to find a buyer. The stock exchange provides a workable mechanism to create a sale whenever the owner makes that decision. No question exists that these shares can be liquidating at any time. Once again, the same assertion cannot be made for assets such as buildings, copyrights, and inventory.
- As a trading security, a sale is anticipated in the near term. The owner does not plan to hold the stock for a long period of time. Further changes in value can certainly take place but are less likely

to be severe. The shortness of time prevents many radical fluctuations in value after the balance sheet date.

At year-end, this investment (as a trading security) will be reported on the investor's balance sheet at its fair value of $28,000. On the income statement, both the dividend revenue of $200 and the unrealized gain of $3,000 are shown as increases in net income.

If, instead, the fair value at year-end had been only $21,000, a $4,000 unrealized loss will appear on Valente's income statement to reflect the decline in value ($25,000 historical cost dropping to $21,000 fair value).

EXERCISE

Link to multiple-choice question for practice purposes: http://www.quia.com/quiz/2092969.html

Question: In this ongoing illustration, Valente Corporation had bought one thousand shares of Bayless Corporation which it planned to sell in a relatively short period of time. On the last day of Year One, this trading security was adjusted from the historical cost of $25,000 to the fair value of $28,000. The $3,000 unrealized gain was reported within net income on the Year One income statement.

Assume that these shares are subsequently sold by Valente on February 3, Year Two, for $27,000. ***What reporting is appropriate when an investment in trading securities is sold in a subsequent period?*** *What effect does this final transaction have on reported income?*

Answer: Following the Year One adjustment, this investment is recorded in the general ledger at fair value of $28,000 rather than historical cost. Subsequently, when sold, any difference between the sales price and this carrying amount is recorded as a gain or a loss on the Year Two income statement.

Because the sales price of these shares ($27,000) is less than the reported balance ($28,000), recognition of a $1,000 loss is appropriate. This loss reflects the drop in value that took place during Year Two.

FIGURE 12.4 Sale of Shares of Bayless (a Trading Security) for $27,000 in Year Two

Cash	27,000	
Loss on Sale of Trading Investment	1,000	
Investment in Trading Securities		28,000

This investment was originally bought for $25,000 and eventually sold for $27,000 so an overall gain of $2,000 was earned. For reporting purposes, the income effect is spread between the two years of ownership. A gain of $3,000 was recognized in Year One to reflect the appreciation in value during that period. A loss of $1,000 is reported in Year Two because the stock price fell by $1,000 in that period prior to being sold.

Investments in trading securities are always shown on the owner's balance sheet at fair value. Gains and losses reported in the income statement parallel the movement in value that took place each period.

EXERCISE

Link to multiple-choice question for practice purposes: http://www.quia.com/quiz/2092949.html

KEY TAKEAWAY

Many companies acquire equity shares of other companies. The applicable accounting procedures depend on the purpose for the ownership. If the investment is only to be held for a short period of time, it is labeled a trading security and adjusted to fair value whenever financial statements are to be produced. Any change in value creates a gain or loss that is reported within net income because fair value is objectively determined, the shares can be liquidated easily, and a quick sale is anticipated before a large change in fair value is likely to occur. Dividends received by the owner are recorded as revenue. Whenever trading securities are sold, only the increase or decrease in value during the current year is reported within net income since earlier changes have already been reported in that manner.

2. ACCOUNTING FOR INVESTMENTS IN SECURITIES THAT ARE AVAILABLE FOR SALE

LEARNING OBJECTIVES

At the end of this section, students should be able to meet the following objectives:

1. **Identify the types of investments classified as available-for-sale.**
2. **Record the receipt of dividends from an investment that is viewed as available-for-sale.**
3. **Explain the handling of changes in the fair value of investments in available-for-sale securities.**
4. **Calculate the gain or loss to be reported when available-for-sale securities are eventually sold.**
5. **Understand the need for reporting comprehensive income as well as net income.**
6. **Explain the adjustment of net income utilized to arrive at comprehensive income.**

Question: Not all investments in stock are bought for a quick sale. Assume Valente Corporation buys one thousand shares of Bayless Corporation for $25 in Year One but does not anticipate selling the investment in the near term. Company officials intend to hold these shares for the foreseeable future until the money is clearly needed. Although the stock could be sold at any time, the president of Valente believes this investment might well be retained for years. During Year One, a $200 cash dividend is received from the Bayless shares. At the end of that period, the stock is selling for $28 per share. ***How does the decision to hold equity shares for an extended period of time impact the financial reporting process?***

Answer: Because Valente's intention is to retain these shares for an indefinite period, they will be classified on the company's balance sheet as an investment in **available-for-sale securities** rather than as trading securities. Despite the difference in the plan for these shares, they are—once again—recorded at historical cost when acquired.

available-for-sale securities

Classification of investments in stocks and bonds when management's intentions are to retain them for an indefinite period; they are reported on the balance sheet at fair value although gains and losses are included in stockholders' equity and not within net income.

FIGURE 12.5 Purchase of Ownership Shares Classified as Available-for-Sale Securities

Investment in Available-for-Sale Securities	25,000	
Cash		25,000

The receipt of the dividend is also reported in the same manner as before with the dividend revenue increasing Valente's net income.

FIGURE 12.6 Receipt of Dividend from Investment in Stock

Cash	200	
Dividend Revenue		200

The difference in reporting begins at the end of the year. U.S. GAAP requires available-for-sale investments to be included on the investor's balance sheet at fair value (in the same manner as trading securities). As before, this adjustment to fair value creates an unrealized gain of $3,000. However, reported net income is not affected as it was with the investment in the trading security.

FIGURE 12.7 Shares of Bayless (an Available-for-Sale Security) Adjusted to Fair Value at End of Year

Investment in Available-for-Sale Securities	3,000	
Unrealized Gain on Available-for-Sale Securities		3,000

Question: An immediate question is obvious: If not presented on the income statement, how is the $3,000 unrealized gain in the value of this investment shown by the owner? ***How are changes in the value of available-for-sale securities reported?***

other accumulated comprehensive income

A section of the stockholders' equity of the balance sheet where unrealized gains and losses on available-for-sale securities (as well as a few other specified gains and losses) are shown rather than being included within net income.

Answer: Because no sale is expected in the near term, the fair value of available-for-sale shares will possibly go up and down numerous times before being sold. Hence, the current gain is not viewed as "sure enough." As a result of this uncertainty, a change in the owner's reported net income is not considered appropriate. Instead, any unrealized gain (or loss) in the value of an investment that is classified as available-for-sale is reported within the stockholders' equity section on the balance sheet. The figure is listed either just above or below the retained earnings account. A few other unrealized gains and losses are handled in this manner and are usually combined and reported as "**other accumulated comprehensive income**."

FIGURE 12.8 Stockholders' Equity Including Other Accumulated Comprehensive Income

Contributed Capital (or Capital Stock)	XXX
Retained Earnings	XXX
Other Accumulated Comprehensive Income:	
Unrealized Gain on Available-for-Sale Securities	3,000

- Changes in the value of trading securities create unrealized gains or losses that are reported in the income statement.
- Changes in the value of available-for-sale securities also create unrealized gains and losses but they are shown in stockholders' equity and not net income.

The above procedures were first created in 1993 and have been used since that time. Interestingly, in 2007, FASB passed a rule that allows companies to elect to report available-for-sale investments in the same manner as trading securities. This option must be selected when the investment is purchased. Thus, if that election is made, the $3,000 unrealized gain above is reported on the income statement despite the intention to hold the securities for an indefinite period. This is another example of accounting rules that are not as rigid as sometimes perceived.

EXERCISE

Link to multiple-choice question for practice purposes: http://www.quia.com/quiz/2092972.html

Question: Assume that Valente has chosen not to report the above available-for-sale investment in the same manner as a trading security but rather by means of the traditional approach. Thus, the $3,000 unrealized gain created by the appreciation of value is reported within stockholders' equity at the end of Year One. Subsequently, in Year Two, these shares are sold on the stock exchange for $27,000. What reporting is made at that time? ***How is the eventual sale of investments that are classified as available-for-sale securities reported?***

Answer: When available-for-sale securities are sold, the difference between the original cost ($25,000) and the selling price ($27,000) is reported as a realized gain (or loss) on the income statement. Because no change in net income was reported in the previous year, this entire amount has to be reported at the date of sale. Having put the unrealized gain into stockholders' equity in Year One means that the change in value only touches net income when sold.

However, mechanical complexities now exist. The investment has been adjusted to a $28,000 carrying amount and a $3,000 unrealized gain is still reported within stockholders' equity. As a balance sheet account, this $3,000 figure is not closed out at the end of Year One. When the investment is sold, both the $28,000 asset and the $3,000 unrealized gain must be removed. The net amount mirrors the $25,000 historical cost of these shares. By eliminating the previous gain in this manner, the asset is brought back to the original $25,000. Thus, the appropriate realized gain of $2,000 is recognized: The shares were bought for $25,000 and sold for $27,000.

FIGURE 12.9 Sale of Available-for-Sale Security in Year Two

Cash	27,000	
Unrealized Gain on Available-for-Sale Securities	3,000	
Investment in Available-for-Sale Securities		28,000
Gain on Sale of Available-for-Sale Investment		2,000

EXERCISE

Link to multiple-choice question for practice purposes: http://www.quia.com/quiz/2092950.html

Question: In Year One, Valente's investment in the shares of Bayless Corporation rose in value by $3,000. If those investments are classified as available-for-sale, this unrealized gain does not impact reported net income but, rather, stockholders' equity. This handling is justified because the investor will not necessarily sell these shares in the near future so that numerous subsequent changes in value are likely to take place.

However, net income seems a bit misleading since it does not reflect the increase in the reported worth of this asset. Assume, for example, that Valente reports total net income for Year One of $80,000. That figure includes no part of the $3,000 unrealized gain. ***What reporting is necessary to help investors understand the impact on income of a change in value when investments are labeled as available-for-sale?***

Answer: Indeed, the completeness of reported net income in such situations can be questioned. As noted, changes in the value of available-for-sale securities create unrealized gains or losses that appear in the stockholders' equity section of the balance sheet but not in net income. To help decision makers better evaluate the reporting company, a second income figure is disclosed that does include these gains or losses. The resulting balance is known as **comprehensive income**. It can be shown on the bottom of a company's income statement or in a separate schedule. Here, by adding in the $3,000 change in fair value, Valente's net income figure is adjusted to the more complete total.

comprehensive income

Net income plus any unrealized gains and less any unrealized losses that appear in the stockholders' equity section rather than within net income; it can be shown at the bottom of the income statement or in a separate schedule.

FIGURE 12.10 Net Income Converted to Comprehensive Income

Net Income	$80,000
Unrealized Gain in Available-for-Sale Securities	3,000
Comprehensive Income	$83,000

Decision makers can choose to emphasize one figure (net income) or another (comprehensive income) in their analysis of the reporting company. More appropriately, they can view the two figures as simply different ways to portray the results of the current year and make use of both.

Comprehensive income includes all changes in stockholders' equity other than (a) amounts contributed by stockholders and (b) dividend distributions made to stockholders. Unrealized gains and losses on available-for-sale securities are common but several other unrealized gains and losses are also included in moving from net income to comprehensive income.

For example, for the year ended December 31, 2008, Yahoo! Corporation reported its net income as approximately $424 million. However, the company also disclosed comprehensive income of only $213 million. The $211 million reduction was caused by including gains and losses that resulted from (a) changes in value of available-for-sale securities and (b) translation changes in currency exchange rates reported by subsidiaries operating in foreign countries. According to U.S. GAAP, these gains and losses were not deemed appropriate for inclusion in net income and, instead, were shown in stockholders' equity. However, interested parties can still see their impact on income as reflected in the comprehensive income figure.

EXERCISE

Link to multiple-choice question for practice purposes: http://www.quia.com/quiz/2092951.html

KEY TAKEAWAY

Investments in equity securities are often held by the owner for an indefinite period of time. As such, the asset is classified as available-for-sale and shown at fair value each period. Any changes in the reported amount is not included in net income but is rather listed within other accumulated comprehensive income in the stockholders' equity section of the balance sheet. However, dividends received from the investment are reported as revenue and include in net income. When eventually sold, the difference between original cost and the proceeds received is reported as a gain or loss shown within net income. Because periodic changes in value are not factored into the calculation of net income, they are included in determining comprehensive income. Thus, both net income and comprehensive income are reported to allow decision makers to better understand the impact of these unrealized gains and losses.

3. ACCOUNTING FOR INVESTMENTS BY MEANS OF THE EQUITY METHOD

LEARNING OBJECTIVES

At the end of this section, students should be able to meet the following objectives:

1. **Describe the theoretical criterion for applying the equity method to an investment in stock and explain the alternative standard that is often used.**
2. **Compute the amount of income to be recognized under the equity method and make the journal entry for its recording.**
3. **Understand the handling of dividends that are received when the equity method is applied and make the related journal entry.**
4. **Indicate the impact that a change in fair value has on the reporting of an equity method investment.**
5. **Prepare the journal entry to record the sale of an equity method security.**

Question: Not all investments in corporate stock are made solely for the possibility of gaining dividends and share price appreciation. As mentioned earlier, Coca-Cola Company holds 35 percent ownership of Coca-Cola Enterprises. The relationship between that investor and investee is different. The investor has real power; it can exert some amount of authority over the investee. The Coca-Cola Company owns a large enough stake in CCE so that operating and financing decisions can be influenced. ***When one company holds a sizable portion of another company, is classifying and accounting for the investment as an available-for-sale or trading security a reasonable approach?***

Answer: The answer to this question depends on the size of ownership. As the percentage of shares grows, the investor gradually moves from having little or no authority over the investee to a position where significant influence can be exerted. At that point, the investment no longer qualifies as a trading security or an available-for-sale security. Instead, the shares are reported by means of the **equity method**. The rationale for holding the investment has changed.

equity method

A method of reporting an investment in stock that is applied when the owner has the ability to exert significant influence on the decisions of an investee; it is used to report investments where 20 percent or more and less than or equal to 50 percent of the shares are held, unless evidence exists that significant influence does not exist.

The equity method views the relationship of the two companies in an entirely different fashion. The accounting process applied by the investor must be altered. Consequently, a note to the 2008 financial statements prepared by The Coca-Cola Company states "We use the equity method to account for our investments for which we have the ability to exercise significant influence over operating and financial policies. Consolidated net income includes our Company's proportionate share of the net income or net loss of these companies."

The equity method is applied when the investor has the ability to apply significant influences to the operating and financing decisions of the investee. Unfortunately, the precise point at which one company gains that ability is impossible to ascertain. A bright line distinction simply does not exist. Although certain clues such as membership on the board of directors and the comparative size of other ownership interests can be helpful, the degree of influence is a nebulous criterion. When a question arises as to whether the ability to apply significant influence exists, the percentage of ownership can be used to provide an arbitrary standard.

According to U.S. GAAP, unless signs of significant influence are present, an investor owning less than 20 percent of the outstanding shares of another company reports the investment as either a trading security or available-for-sale security. In contrast, an investor holding 20 percent or more but less than or equal to 50 percent of the shares of another company is assumed to possess the ability to exert significant influence. Unless evidence is present that significant influence does not exist, the equity method is applied by the investor to report all investments in this 20–50 percent range of ownership.

EXERCISE

Link to multiple-choice question for practice purposes: http://www.quia.com/quiz/2092970.html

Question: One company holds shares of another and has the ability to apply significant influence so that the equity method of accounting is appropriate. ***What reporting is made of an investment when the equity method is used?*** *What asset value is reported on the owner's balance sheet and when is income recognized under this approach?*

Answer: When applying the equity method, the investor does not wait until dividends are received to recognize profit from its investment. Because of the close relationship, the investor reports income as it is earned by the investee. If, for example, a company reports net income of $100,000, an investor holding a 40 percent ownership immediately records an increase in its own income of $40,000 ($100,000 × 40 percent). In recording this income, the investor also increases its investment account by $40,000 to reflect the growth in the size of the investee company.

Income is recognized by the investor immediately as it is earned by the investee. Thus, it cannot be reported again when a subsequent dividend is collected. That would double-count the impact. Income must be recognized either when earned by the investee or when later distributed to the investor, but not at both times. The equity method uses the earlier date rather than the latter. Eventual payment of a dividend shrinks the size of the investee company. Thus, the investor decreases the investment account when a dividend is received if the equity method is applied. No additional income is recorded.

Companies are also allowed to report such investments as if they were trading securities. However, few have opted to make this election. If chosen, the investment is reported at fair value despite the degree of ownership with gains and losses in the change of fair value reported in net income.

Question: In applying the equity method, income is recognized by the investor when earned by the investee. Subsequent dividend collections are not reported as revenue by the investor but rather as a reduction in the size of the investment account to avoid including the income twice.

To illustrate, assume that Big Company buys 40 percent of the outstanding stock of Little Company on January 1, Year One, for $900,000. No evidence is present that provides any indication that Big lacks the ability to exert significant influence over the financing and operating decisions of Little. Thus, application of the equity method is appropriate. During Year One, Little reports net income of $200,000 and pays a total cash dividend to its stockholders of $30,000. ***What recording is appropriate for an investor when the equity method is applied to an investment?***

Answer: The purchase of 40 percent of Little Company for cash is merely the exchange of one asset for another. Thus, the investment is recorded initially by Big at its historical cost.

FIGURE 12.11 Acquisition of Shares of Little to Be Reported Using the Equity Method

Investment in Little	900,000	
Cash		900,000

Ownership here is in the 20 to 50 percent range and no evidence is presented to indicate that the ability to apply significant influence is missing. Thus, according to U.S. GAAP, the equity method is applied. Big recognizes its portion of Little's $200,000 net income as soon as it is earned by the investee. As a 40 percent owner, Big accrues income of $80,000. Because earning this income caused Little Company to grow, Big increases its investment account to reflect the change in the size of the investee.

FIGURE 12.12 Income of Investee Recognized by Investor Using the Equity Method

Investment in Little	80,000	
Investment Income—Little		80,000

Big has recognized the income from this investee as it was earned. Consequently, any eventual dividend received from Little is a reduction in the investment in Little account rather than a new revenue. The investee company is smaller as a result of the cash payout. The balance in this investment account rises when the investee reports income but then falls (by $12,000 or 40 percent of the total distribution of $30,000) when that income is later passed through to the stockholders.

FIGURE 12.13 Dividend Received from Investment Accounted for by the Equity Method

Cash	12,000	
Investment in Little		12,000

On Big's income statement for Year One, investment income—Little is shown as $80,000. Because the equity method is applied, the reader knows that this figure is the investor's ownership percentage of the income reported by the investee.

At the end of Year One, the investment in Little account appearing on Big's balance sheet reports $968,000 ($900,000 + 80,000 – 12,000). This total does not reflect fair value as with investments in trading securities and available-for-sale securities. It also does not disclose historical cost. Rather, the $968,000 asset balance is the original cost of the shares plus the investor's share of the investee's subsequent income less any dividends received. Under the equity method, the asset balance is a conglomerate of numbers.

EXERCISE

Link to multiple-choice question for practice purposes: http://www.quia.com/quiz/2092971.html

Question: Assume, at the end of Year One, after the above journal entries have been made, Big sells all of its shares in Little Company for $950,000 in cash. ***When the equity method is applied to an investment, what is the appropriate recording of an eventual sale?***

Answer: An investment reported using the equity method quickly moves away from historical cost as income is earned and dividends received. After just one year, the asset balance reported above by Big has risen from $900,000 to $968,000 (income of $80,000 was added and $12,000 in dividends were subtracted). If these shares are then sold for $950,000, a loss of $18,000 is recognized.

FIGURE 12.14 Sale of Investment Reported Using the Equity Method

Cash	950,000	
Loss on Sale of Equity Method Securities	18,000	
Investment in Little		968,000

If these shares had been sold for more than their $968,000 carrying value, a gain on the sale is recorded.

Summary. All investments in the stock of another company—where ownership is no more than 50 percent—must be accounted for in one of three ways depending on the degree of ownership and the intention of the investor.

FIGURE 12.15 Comparison of Three Methods to Account for Investments

* At the time of acquisition, an investor has the option of accounting for investments that are available for sale or investments where the ability to apply significant influence is present by the same method as that used for trading securities.

	Investment in Trading Securities	Investment in Available for Sale Securities	Investment—Equity Method
Primary Characteristic	Expected to be sold in near term	Will be sold when cash is eventually needed	Investor has ability to apply significant influence (usually shown by 20% to 50% ownership)
Reported Investment Balance	Fair value	Fair value(*)	Cost plus portion of income less portion of dividends(*)
Changes in Fair Value	Included in net income	Included within stockholders' equity and then within comprehensive income	Ignored unless permanent drop in value occurs
Amounts Reported within Investor's Net Income	Dividends received plus change in fair value	Dividends received	Portion of income as earned by Investee
Dividends Received	Included in net income	Included in net income	Reduces investment balance

EXERCISE

Link to multiple-choice question for practice purposes: http://www.quia.com/quiz/2092992.html

EXERCISE

Link to multiple-choice question for practice purposes: http://www.quia.com/quiz/2093013.html

KEY TAKEAWAY

At some point, an owner can gain enough equity shares of another company to have the ability to apply significant influence. Use of the equity method then becomes appropriate. Significant influence is difficult to gauge so ownership of 20–50 percent of the outstanding stock is the normal standard applied in practice. However, if evidence is found indicating that significant influence is either present or does not exist, that takes precedence regardless of the degree of ownership. Under the equity method, income is recognized by the investor as soon as earned by the investee. The investment account also increases as a result of recognizing this income. Conversely, dividends are not reported as income but rather as reductions in the investment balance. Unless a permanent decline occurs, fair value is not taken into consideration in accounting for an equity method investment. When sold, the book value of the asset is removed so that any difference with the amount received can be recognized as a gain or loss.

4. THE REPORTING OF CONSOLIDATED FINANCIAL STATEMENTS

LEARNING OBJECTIVES

At the end of this section, students should be able to meet the following objectives:

1. **List various reasons for one company to seek to gain control over another.**
2. **Recognize that consolidated financial statements must be prepared if one company has control over another which is normally assumed as the ownership of any amount over 50 percent of the company's outstanding stock.**
3. **Explain the reporting of a subsidiary's revenues and expenses when consolidated financial statements are prepared at the date of acquisition.**
4. **Explain the reporting of a subsidiary's assets and liabilities when consolidated financial statements are prepared at the date of acquisition.**
5. **Determine consolidated totals subsequent to the date of acquisition.**
6. **Compute total asset turnover and return on assets (ROA).**

Question: Many companies buy more than 50 percent of the stock of other companies in order to gain control. In a large number of these acquisitions, one company obtains all the outstanding shares of the other so that ownership is complete. If two companies are brought together to form a third, a merger has taken place. If one company simply buys another, the transaction is known as an acquisition. Thomson Financial reported that approximately 35,000 mergers and acquisitions took place around the world during 2006 with a total value of $3.5 trillion. The recent recession has reduced that trend a bit.

Such investments are often made to expand operations into new markets or new industries. Google, for example, acquired YouTube for $1.65 billion to move into the presentation of online videos. As discussed earlier in the coverage of intangible assets, one company might buy another to obtain valuable assets such as patents, real estate, trademarks, technology and the like. Walt Disney's purchase of Pixar and its digital animation expertise appears to fall into this category. Such transactions can also be made to eliminate competition or in hopes of gaining economies of scale. Sprint's $35 billion merger with Nextel was projected to increase profits for the combined companies by lowering operating expenses while also reducing the number of competitors in the wireless communication industry.

To help explain the appropriate method of accounting for such investments, assume that Giant Company acquires 100 percent of Tiny Company. Obviously, control has been obtained. How is the reporting by Giant affected? Because over 50 percent of the stock was purchased, none of the previously described accounting methods are applicable. ***How does a company report the acquisition of another company where control is established?***

Answer: According to U.S. GAAP, control is gained by the acquisition of over 50 percent of the voting stock of a company. The stockholders of Giant now control both Giant and Tiny. As a result, a business combination has been formed from the two previously independent companies. For external reporting purposes, **consolidated financial statements** are required. Giant does not report an investment in Tiny account on its balance sheet as with the other methods described above. Instead, in consolidation, the individual account balances from each organization are put together in a prescribed fashion to represent the single economic entity that has been created. In simple terms, the assets, liabilities, revenues, and expenses of Tiny (the subsidiary) are consolidated with those of Giant (the parent) to reflect the united business.

consolidated financial statements

Statements that are prepared when one company holds control over another company.

Because such acquisitions are common, the financial statements reported by many well-known corporations actually include consolidated financial data from hundreds of different subsidiaries where control has been gained over a number of years. As just one example, Cisco Systems made approximately sixty acquisitions of other companies between 2000 and 2007. Subsequently, the published financial statements for Cisco Systems included the revenues, expenses, assets, and liabilities of each of those subsidiaries.

Consolidation of financial statements is one of the most complex topics in all of financial accounting. However, the basic process is quite straightforward.

Subsidiary revenues and expenses. The revenues and expenses of each subsidiary are included in consolidated figures but only for the period after control is gained. Consequently, if Giant obtains Tiny by buying 100 percent of its stock on April 1, a consolidated income statement for these two companies will contain no revenues and expenses recognized by Tiny prior to that date. Income statement balances accrued under previous owners have no financial impact on the new owner, Giant. Only the revenues and expenses of this subsidiary starting on April 1 are included in the consolidated totals calculated for Giant Company and its consolidated subsidiary.

Subsidiary assets and liabilities. Consolidation of subsidiary assets and liabilities is a more complicated process. On the date of the takeover, a total acquisition price is determined based on the fair value surrendered by the parent in order to gain control. A search is then made to identify all the individual assets and liabilities held by the subsidiary at that time. As discussed in the previous chapter, the parent recognizes all subsidiary assets (1) that provide contractual or legal rights or (2) in which the asset can be separated and then sold. Fair value is established and recorded for each as if the parent were acquiring them individually. A transaction has taken place that brings all of those subsidiary assets and liabilities under the control of the parent company. Consolidation values are reported as if they were bought separately by the parent.

Also, as explained previously, if the acquisition price is more than the total fair value of all these identifiable assets and liabilities, the intangible asset goodwill is reported for the difference. As a going concern, a total value is usually attributed to a company that exceeds the individual values of its assets and liabilities. Having loyal customers and trained employees, for example, helps a company generate more profits than its assets could otherwise earn. When a company is being bought, such anticipated profitability usually leads to an increase in the negotiated price. This excess amount necessitates the recognition of goodwill on the consolidated balance sheet.

EXERCISE

Link to multiple-choice question for practice purposes: http://www.quia.com/quiz/2092973.html

Question: To illustrate the consolidation process, assume that Tiny has earned revenues of $800,000 and incurred expenses of $500,000 during the year to date. In addition, the company reports a single asset, land costing $400,000 but with a $720,000 fair value. The only liability is a $300,000 note payable. Thus, the company's net book value is $100,000 ($400,000 land less $300,000 note payable). Tiny also owns the rights to a well-known trademark that has no book value because it was developed many years ago at little or no cost. However, it is now estimated to be worth $210,000.

The assets and liabilities held by Tiny have a net fair value of $630,000 ($720,000 land plus $210,000 trademark less $300,000 note payable). Because the company has been extremely popular and developed a large customer base, Giant agrees to pay $900,000 to acquire all the outstanding stock. ***If consolidated financial statements are created at the time of a corporate acquisition, what figures are reported by the business combination?***

Answer: In consolidating Giant and its subsidiary Tiny at the date of this acquisition, neither the subsidiary revenues of $800,000 nor its expenses of $500,000 are included. Their financial impact occurred prior to the takeover by Giant; those profits benefitted the previous owners. Therefore, only the revenues and expenses reported by Giant make up consolidated income statement totals determined on the day the parent acquires the subsidiary.

At the same time, consolidated balance sheet totals will not show any "investment in Tiny Company" as in the other methods demonstrated above. Instead, Tiny's land is added to Giant's own totals at its $720,000 fair value. The trademark is consolidated at $210,000 to reflect the amounts paid by Giant to acquire ownership of the subsidiary. The note payable is added to the consolidated figures at $300,000, which was its fair value as well as its book value. Subsidiary assets and liabilities are included in consolidated totals as if purchased by the parent. Mechanically, a $320,000 increase is made to the land account while $210,000 is recorded to recognize the value of the trademark.

The acquisition price of $900,000 paid by Giant exceeds the net value of the subsidiary's identifiable assets and liabilities ($610,000) by $290,000. In consolidation, any excess acquisition payment is assumed to represent goodwill and is reported as an intangible asset.

FIGURE 12.16 Consolidated Totals—Date of Acquisition

Revenues	Parent total only
Expenses	Parent total only
Net Income	Parent total only
Reported Assets and Liabilities	Parent book value plus fair value of subsidiary accounts
Trademark (previously unreported)	Fair value of subsidiary account
Investment in Tiny	Not reported for consolidation—actual assets and liabilities are included instead
Goodwill	Excess payment made to acquire subsidiary
Liabilities	Parent book value plus fair value of subsidiary figures
Stockholders' Equity	Parent total only

EXERCISE

Link to multiple-choice question for practice purposes: http://www.quia.com/quiz/2093014.html

Question: On the date of acquisition, subsidiary revenues and expenses are omitted from consolidation totals but assets and liabilities are included at fair value. Any excess payment made by the parent in purchasing the subsidiary is reported as goodwill. ***In subsequent consolidations, what accounting is made of the subsidiary's revenues, expenses, assets, and liabilities?***

Answer: For subsequent balance sheets created after a business combination is formed, the book value of each of the subsidiary's assets and liabilities is added to the book value of those same accounts within the parent's financial records. However, the initial adjustments made at the date of acquisition to establish fair value must continue to be included because they represent a cost incurred by Giant when the $900,000 payment was made to acquire Tiny Company.

Thus, in future consolidations of these two companies, the $320,000 adjustment recorded to the land account will be present as will the $210,000 portion of the payment assigned to the subsidiary's trademark and the $270,000 goodwill balance. Those costs were not recognized by Tiny but were incurred by Giant at the time of acquisition and must be reflected in the ongoing reporting of those assets.

Recognition of these subsequent adjustments creates one final concern. A trademark has a finite life. Thus, the $210,000 cost paid by the parent and attributed to this asset must be amortized over time. This additional expense is only recognized in the consolidation process since it relates to the purchase of Tiny and not to the operations of either company. Neither land nor goodwill has a finite life so amortization is not appropriate for those purchase price adjustments. As discussed previously, these assets are checked periodically for impairment of value.

Subsequently consolidated income statements report the parent's revenues and expenses plus subsidiary amounts but only those recognized since the acquisition. In addition, the amortization of acquisition cost adjustments, such as for the trademark, will be recognized within the consolidation as an expense.

FIGURE 12.17 Consolidated Totals—Subsequent to Date of Acquisition

Revenues	Parent total plus subsidiary total for the period
Expenses	Parent total plus subsidiary total for the period plus amortization of fair value adjustments (such as for trademark)
Net Income	Consolidated revenues minus consolidated expenses
Reported Assets and Liabilities	Parent book value plus book value of subsidiary accounts plus fair value adjustment less amortization
Trademark (previously unreported)	Fair value adjustment less amortization
Investment in Tiny	Not reported for consolidation—actual assets and liabilities are included instead
Goodwill	Excess payment made to acquire subsidiary remains unchanged unless value is impaired
Stockholders' Equity	Parent total only

EXERCISE

Link to multiple-choice question for practice purposes: http://www.quia.com/quiz/2093016.html

Question: Chapter 12 completes coverage of the assets reported by a company on its balance sheet. In earlier chapters on receivables, inventory, and property and equipment, vital signs were computed and explained as figures and ratios often used in evaluating a company—especially its financial health and future prospects. ***Do any similar vital signs exist for assets as a whole that decision makers typically use as part of an overall evaluation?***

Answer: A company controls a specific amount of assets. Most investors and other decision makers are interested in how effectively management was able to use these resources. Individuals who study companies search for signs that an appropriate level of income was generated from the assets on hand.

total asset turnover

A ratio used to measure the efficient use of assets; it is computed by dividing sales revenue by average total assets for the period.

Total asset turnover. **Total asset turnover** is one such figure. It simply indicates management's efficiency at generating sales. Sales must occur before profits can be earned from normal operations. If assets are not well used to create sales, profits will probably never arise.

total asset turnover = sales revenue/average total assets

For example, here is information reported for 2008 by PepsiCo Inc. and The Coca-Cola Company. Based on this information, the total asset turnover can be computed for each company.

FIGURE 12.18 2008 Comparison of PepsiCo Inc. and The Coca-Cola Company

	PepsiCo	Coca-Cola
Total Assets		
Beginning of Year	$34.6 billion	$43.3 billion
End of Year	36.0 billion	40.5 billion
Average for Year	35.3 billion	41.9 billion
Net Sales Revenue	43.3 billion	31.9 billion
Total Asset Turnover	1.23 times	.76 times

return on assets (ROA)

A ratio used to measure the profitable use of assets, it is computed by dividing net income by average total assets for the period.

Return on assets. Probably one of the most commonly used vital signs employed in studying the financial health of a company is **return on assets**, often known as ROA. It is simply net income divided by average total assets and is viewed by many as an appropriate means of measuring management's efficiency in using company resources.

return on assets (ROA) = net income/average total assets

Some analysts modify the income figure in this computation by removing interest expense to eliminate the impact of different financing strategies.

For 2008, PepsiCo reported net income of $5.1 billion so that its ROA for the year was 14.4 percent ($5.1 net income/$35.3 average total assets). For the same period, The Coca-Cola Company reported net income of $5.8 billion for an ROA of 13.8 percent ($5.8/$41.9).

KEY TAKEAWAY

Companies often attempt to obtain control over other companies for many reasons including gaining access to valuable assets and eliminating competition. According to U.S. GAAP, control is established by acquiring over 50 percent of the ownership shares. At that point, consolidated financial statements must be prepared bringing together the financial accounts from both companies. For the subsidiary, only revenues and expenses since the takeover are included. In consolidating the assets and liabilities of the subsidiary, any difference on the date of acquisition between fair value and book value is computed and assumed to represent an additional cost incurred by the parent. If the asset or liability has a finite life, this amount is then included in all subsequent consolidations after periodic amortization is removed. Goodwill is reported for any unexplained excess payment made in acquiring control over the subsidiary. Many analysts compute total asset turnover and return on assets (ROA) in evaluating the efficiency of management's use of company assets.

Talking With a Real Investing Pro—Continued

Following is a continuation of our interview with Kevin G. Burns.

Question: For the year ended December 31, 2008, Yahoo! Corporation reported its net income as approximately $424 million. The company also disclosed comprehensive income of only $213 million. Does it disturb you that this one company reports two separate income figures and they can be so significantly different? Or, do you find disclosing income in two distinct ways to be helpful when you analyze a company like this?

Kevin Burns: Actually I think the idea of disclosing income in two different ways makes sense. Having said that, if I were a shareholder of Yahoo! I would want to ask, Why these numbers are so far apart? What exactly is included in (or excluded from) each of these income figures? Is the company's core business sound? This question is probably best answered by net income. The reduction in arriving at comprehensive income is likely to have come from losses in the value of available-for-sale investments and from holding foreign currency balances. Is management distracted by trying to manage a large investment portfolio? How much of the difference comes from currency rate changes, and is there a way to hedge this volatility to reduce the impact? If there is a way to hedge the risk, why did company officials not do so?

In sum, the reason I like including both income numbers is that anything that increases disclosure is a positive, especially when investing money. The more transparency the better is my feeling. Then, investors can make up their own minds as to management's competence and the success of the overall business of the company.

Video Clip

Joe talks about the five most important points in Chapter 12.

View the video online at: http://blip.tv/play/sDyBwKhLAA

5. END-OF-CHAPTER EXERCISES

QUESTIONS

1. Give three reasons one company would purchase the stock of another.
2. When is the purchase of stock in one company by another classified as a "trading security?"
3. Where is dividend revenue reported?
4. At what value are trading securities reported on the balance sheet?
5. Why does the accounting for trading securities differ from that of other assets like buildings or inventory?
6. What is an unrealized gain or loss?
7. What is an available-for-sale security?
8. At what value are available-for-sale securities reported on the balance sheet?
9. How does the accounting for unrealized gains and losses on available-for-sale securities differ from trading securities?
10. Define "comprehensive income."
11. Which method of accounting is used when one company owns enough stock in another to exert "significant influence?"
12. When trying to determine if the equity method of accounting should be used, what guidelines are available to help accountants?
13. When and how is income from an equity investment recognized by the owner?
14. How are dividends paid by an investee reported by the owner under the equity method?
15. How much stock must one company own to be considered "in control" of another?
16. Define "consolidation."
17. How is total asset turnover calculated?
18. How is return on assets determined?

TRUE OR FALSE

1. ____ To keep things simpler for financial statement users, all investments are accounted for the same way.
2. ____ If the owner of trading securities is paid a dividend, it should be recorded as revenue and shown on the income statement.
3. ____ If a company owns 35 percent of another, it should use the equity method to account for the investment, regardless of whether or not it has any influence.
4. ____ The higher a company's ROA, the more efficiently the company is using its assets.
5. ____ Gains and losses on available-for-sale securities do not affect net income until the securities are sold.
6. ____ All investments in other companies should be reported at the cost of the investment.
7. ____ When a company owns more than 50 percent of another, the financial statements of the two companies should be consolidated.
8. ____ Equity method investments are reported at their fair value on the balance sheet.
9. ____ Trading securities are defined as those that are held for a short time.
10. ____ Net income and comprehensive income are the same thing.

MULTIPLE CHOICE

1. On March 5, Maxwell Corporation purchased seventy shares of Tyrone Company for $30 per share, planning to hold the investment for a short time. On June 30, Maxwell prepares its quarterly financial statements. On that date, Tyrone is selling for $32 per share. What is the unrealized gain Maxwell will report and where should it be reported?
   a. $140 unrealized gain, owners' equity section of balance sheet
   b. $140 unrealized gain, income statement
   c. $2,240 unrealized gain, income statement
   d. $2,100 unrealized gain, owners' equity section of balance sheet
2. Which of the following is ***not*** a reason investments in trading securities are shown at their fair value on the balance sheet?
   a. Fair values of publicly traded securities are readily available.
   b. Fair value is considered relevant information to financial statement users.
   c. Fair value is an objective amount determined by the market.
   d. Fair value is easier to determine than historical cost.
3. Jackson Corporation purchased 150 shares of Riley Corporation for $46 per share. The investment is available for sale. On 12/31/X5, Riley's stock is selling for $43 per share. Jackson's net income for the year was $235,000. What was Jackson's comprehensive income?
   a. $235,000
   b. $228,100
   c. $234,550
   d. $228,550
4. Anton Company owns 45 percent of Charlotte Corporation and exerts significant influence over it. This investment should be shown as:
   a. An equity method investment
   b. An available-for-sale investment
   c. A consolidation
   d. An investment in trading securities
5. Tried Company began the year with $450,000 in total assets and ended the year with $530,000 in total assets. Sales for the year were $560,000 and net income for the year was $46,000. What was Tried Company's return on assets for the year?
   a. 114%
   b. 4%
   c. 2%
   d. 2%
6. Hydro Company and Aqua Corporation are in the same industry. During 20X9, Hydro had average total assets of $35,000 and sales of $47,800. Aqua had average total assets of $49,000 and sales of $56,900. Which of the following is true?
   a. Aqua Corporation has a total asset turnover of 1.37 times.
   b. Hydro Company is not using is its assets as efficiently as Aqua Corporation.
   c. Aqua Corporation has a higher ROA than Hydro Company.
   d. Hydro Corporation has a total asset turnover of 1.37 times.
7. Lancaster Inc. purchases all the outstanding stock of Lucy Company for $4,500,000. The net assets of Lucy have a fair value of $2,900,000, including a patent with a book value of $4,700 and a fair value of $159,000. At what amount should the patent and any goodwill from this purchase be shown on consolidated financial statements on the date of purchase?
   a. Patent—$4,700, Goodwill—$0
   b. Patent—$159,000, Goodwill—$2,900,000
   c. Patent—$159,000, Goodwill—$1,600,000
   d. Patent—$4,700, Goodwill—$4,500,000
8. On 12/31/X2, Brenda Corporation purchased Kyle Inc. for $3,400,000. Kyle had one asset, a trademark, whose fair value ($45,000) exceeded its book value ($15,000) by $30,000. The trademark has a remaining useful life of five years. Goodwill was also recorded in this purchase in the amount of $146,000. Kyle continued to operate after the purchase, and now on 12/31/X3, Brenda is preparing consolidated

statements for the year. Independent appraisers now believe Kyle's trademark is worth $50,000. Brenda's independent auditors believe that the goodwill has been impaired slightly and is now worth $120,000. At what amounts should the trademark and goodwill be shown on Brenda's consolidated balance sheet on 12/31/X3?

a. Trademark—$36,000, Goodwill—$120,000
b. Trademark—$30,000, Goodwill—$146,000
c. Trademark—$50,000, Goodwill—$120,000
d. Trademark—$50,000, Goodwill—$146,000

PROBLEMS

1. Record the journal entry for each event below:
   a. Investor Corporation purchases 600 shares of stock in Company A for $60 per share on 1/1/X7. This investment is considered a trading security.
   b. On 3/31/X7, Investor prepares quarterly financial statements. At this date, A is selling for $63 per share. Record any unrealized holding gain or loss.
   c. On 4/15/X7, Company A pays a dividend of $2 per share.
   d. On 6/30/X7, Investor prepares quarterly financial statements. At this date, A is selling for $59 per share. Record any unrealized holding gain or loss.
   e. On 8/1/X7, Investor sells all of A for $62 per share.
2. On March 1, Johnson Inc. purchased 500 shares of Thomas Company stock when Thomas' stock was selling for $20 per share. Johnson plans to hold this stock for a short time and hopefully sell it for a gain.

   On December 31, Johnson prepares its financial statements. Thomas' stock is selling for $18 per share.
   a. Determine the unrealized gain or loss Johnson would report on its income statement.
   b. Show how the investment would be reported on Johnson's balance sheet.
3. Record the journal entry for each event below:
   a. Christopher Corporation purchases 1,000 shares of stock in Alpha Company for $30 per share on 7/1/X9. This investment is considered an available-for-sale security.
   b. On 9/30/X9, Christopher prepares quarterly financial statements. At this date, Alpha is selling for $25 per share. Record any unrealized holding gain or loss.
   c. On 12/31/X9, Investor prepares annual financial statements. At this date, Alpha is selling for $28 per share. Record any unrealized holding gain or loss.
   d. On 2/13/X0, Christopher sells 700 shares of Alpha for $31 per share.
   e. On 2/28/X0, Alpha pays a dividend of $0.40 per share.
   f. On 3/31/X0, Christopher prepares quarterly financial statements. At this date, Alpha is selling for $30 per share.
4. On April 16, Yowza Inc. purchased 900 shares of Cool Company stock when Cool's stock was selling for $15 per share. Yowza plans to hold this stock for more than a year.

   On December 31, Yowza prepares its financial statements. Cool's stock is selling for $20 per share.
   a. Determine the unrealized gain or loss Yowza would report in the owners' equity section of the balance sheet.
   b. Show how the investment would be reported on Yowza's balance sheet.
   c. Assume that Yowza's net income for the year was $478,000. What would Yowza's comprehensive income be?
5. Oregon Company, a paper products manufacturer, wishes to enter the Canadian market. The company purchased 30 percent of the outstanding stock of Canadian Paper Inc. on January 1 for $6,000,000. The CEO of Oregon will sit on the board of directors of Canadian, and other evidence of significant influence exists. At the date of purchase, the book value of Canadian's net assets was $20,000,000.
   a. Canadian reported net income of $760,000 for the year. Record the journal entry for Oregon.
   b. Canadian paid a cash dividend of $80,000. Record the journal entry for Oregon.
   c. What amount would Oregon report on its balance sheet as investment in Canadian?
6. On March 1, 20X8, Current Properties paid $1,000,000 for 25 percent of the shares of Sealy Enterprises. Current exerts significant influence over Sealy.
   a. Sealy reported earnings of $400,000 during 20X8. Record this journal entry for Current.
   b. Sealy paid dividends of $50,000 during October 20X8. Record this journal entry for Current.
   c. What amount would Current report on its balance sheet as investment in Sealy?
   d. Sealy reported earnings of $440,000 during 20X9. Record this journal entry for Current.
   e. Sealy paid dividends of $60,000 during October 20X9. Record this journal entry for Current.
   f. On December 30, Current sells its entire investment in Sealy for $1,200,000. Record the journal entry.
7. Teckla Corporation purchases all the outstanding stock of Feather Company on 1/1/X3 for $5,000,000. Teckla's balance sheet on that date ***before the purchase*** looked like this:

Assets and Liabilities of Teckla

Teckla Corporation Balance Sheet January 1, 20X3			
Assets		**Liabilities**	
Cash	$9,400,000	Accounts Payable	$1,950,000
Inventory	700,000	Notes Payable	4,895,000
Land	5,000,000		
		Owners' Equity	
		Capital Stock	$5,000,000
		Retained Earnings	3,255,000
Total Assets	$15,100,000	Total Liabilities & Owners' Equity	$15,100,000

On 1/1/X3, Feather has the following assets and liabilities:

Assets and Liabilities of Feather

	Value on Feather's Books	Current Market Value
Cash	$456,000	$456,000
Inventory	873,000	873,000
Land	50,000	760,000
Patent	5,000	1,000,000
Accounts Payable	500,000	500,000

a. Determine any goodwill that Teckla will show on its consolidated balance sheet.

b. Prepare a consolidated balance sheet for Teckla after it purchases Feather on 1/1/X3.

8. In several past chapters, we have met Heather Miller, who started her own business, Sew Cool. The financial statements for December are shown below. To calculate average total assets, assume that total assets on 6/1/20X8, when Sew Cool started business, were zero.

Sew Cool Financial Statements

Sew Cool
Income Statement
As of December 31, 20X8

Revenue	$4,000
Cost of Goods	(2,000)
Gross Profit	2,000
Other Expenses	(1,695)
Earning before Tax	305
Tax Expense	(107)
Net Income	$198

Sew Cool
Stmt. of Retained Earnings
As of December 31, 20X8

Retained Earnings, December 1, 20X8	$500
Net Income	198
Dividends	(158)
Retained Earnings, December 31, 20X8	$540

Sew Cool
Balance Sheet
December 31, 20X8

Assets		**Liabilities**	
Current		**Current**	
Cash	$940	Accounts Payable	$900
Accounts Receivable	500	Income Tax Payable	120
Less Allowance for Doubtful Accounts	(20)	Total Current Liabilities	$1,020
Net Accounts Receivable	480		
Inventory	700		
Total Current Assets	$2,120		
Noncurrent		**Noncurrent**	
Equipment	$1,000	Notes Payable	$1,060
		Owners' Equity	
		Capital Stock	$500
		Retained Earnings	540
		Total Owners' Equity	$1,040
Total Assets	$3,120	Total Liabilities & Owners' Equity	$3,120

Based on the financial statements determine the following:

a. Total asset turnover

b. Return on assets

COMPREHENSIVE PROBLEM

This problem will carry through several chapters, building in difficulty. It allows students to continuously practice skills and knowledge learned in previous chapters.

In Chapter 11, you prepared Webworks statements for November. They are included here as a starting point for December.

Webworks Financial Statements

Webworks
Income Statement
As of November 30

Revenue	$16,000
Cost of Goods Sold	(8,171)
Gross Profit	7,829
Deprec. and Amort. Expense	(363)
Other Expenses	(3,680)
Earning before Tax	3,786
Tax Expense	(1,135)
Net Income	$2,651

Webworks
Stmt. of Retained Earnings
As of November 30

Retained Earnings, November 1	$6,671
Net Income	2,651
Retained Earnings, November 30	$9,322

Webworks
Balance Sheet
November 30

Assets		**Liabilities**	
Current		**Current**	
Cash	$2,097	Accounts Payable	$2,585
Accounts Receivable	1,750	Salaries Payable	
Less Allowance for Doubtful Accounts	(175)	Unearned Revenue	400
Net Accounts Receivable	1,575		
Merchandise Inventory	1,129		
Supplies Inventory	20		
Prepaid Rent	200		
Total Current Assets	$5,021	Total Current Liabilities	$3,135
Property, Plant, and Equipment			
Equipment	$7,000		
Less Accumulated Depreciation	(730)		
Furniture	1,000		
Less Accumulated Depreciation	(34)		
Total P, P, and E	$7,236		
Other Noncurrent Assets			
Licensing Agreement, Net	$2,200		
		Owners' Equity	
		Capital Stock	$2,000
		Retained Earnings	9,322
		Total Owners' Equity	$11,322
Total Assets	$14,457	Total Liabilities & Owners' Equity	$14,457

The following events occur during December:

a. Webworks starts and completes nine more sites and bills clients for $5,000.

b. Webworks purchases supplies worth $130 on account.

c. At the beginning of December, Webworks had nine keyboards costing $111 each and ten flash drives costing $13 each. Webworks uses periodic FIFO to cost its inventory.

d. On account, Webworks purchases seventy keyboards for $113 each and one hundred flash drives for $15 each.

e. Webworks decides to invest a small amount of its excess cash in the stock market in the hopes of making a quick gain. Webworks purchases sixty shares of stock in XYZ Corporation for $5 per share in cash.

f. Webworks pays Nancy $750 for her work during the first three weeks of December.

g. Webworks sells sixty-five keyboards for $9,750 and ninety flash drives for $1,800 cash.

h. The Web site for the realtor started in November is completed.

i. Webworks collects $4,500 in accounts receivable.

j. Webworks pays off its salaries payable from November.

k. Webworks pays off $10,500 of its accounts payable.

l. XYZ Corporation pays Webworks a dividend of $40.

m. Webworks pays Leon a salary of $2,000.

n. Webworks pays taxes of $1,272 in cash.

Required:

A. Prepare journal entries for the above events.

B. Post the journal entries to T-accounts.

C. Prepare an unadjusted trial balance for Webworks for December.

D. Prepare adjusting entries for the following and post them to your T-accounts.

o. Webworks owes Nancy $200 for her work during the last week of December.

p. Leon's parents let him know that Webworks owes $300 toward the electricity bill. Webworks will pay them in January.

q. Webworks determines that it has $60 worth of supplies remaining at the end of December.

r. Prepaid rent should be adjusted for December's portion.

s. Webworks is continuing to accrue bad debts at 10 percent of accounts receivable.

t. Webworks continues to depreciate its equipment over four years and its furniture over five years, using the straight-line method.

u. The license agreement should continue to be amortized over its one-year life.

v. On December 31, XYZ stock is selling for $6 per share. Record any unrealized gain or loss.

w. Record cost of goods sold.

x. Near the end of December, a new flash drive appears on the market that makes the ones Webworks has been selling virtually obsolete. Leon believes that it might be able to sell the rest of its inventory (twenty flash drives) for $5 each.

E. Prepare an adjusted trial balance.

F. Prepare financial statements for December.

CHAPTER 13

In a Set of Financial Statements, What Information Is Conveyed about Current and Contingent Liabilities?

Video Clip

Joe introduces Chapter 13 and speaks about the course in general.

View the video online at: http://blip.tv/play/sDyBwKhQAA

1. BASIC REPORTING OF LIABILITIES

LEARNING OBJECTIVES

At the end of this section students should be able to meet the following objectives:

1. **Define a liability by listing its essential characteristics.**
2. **Differentiate a current liability from a noncurrent liability.**
3. **Explain the significance that current liabilities have for investors and creditors who are studying the prospects of an organization.**
4. **Compute the current ratio.**
5. **Indicate the appropriate timing for the recognition of a liability.**

liabilities

Future sacrifices of economic benefits arising from present obligations, the debts of an organization.

current liabilities

Debts that will be satisfied within one year from the date of a balance sheet.

Question: The June 30, 2009, consolidated balance sheet for The Procter & Gamble Company and its subsidiaries reports total **liabilities** *of over $71 billion including current liabilities of approximately $31 billion. That seems to be a rather large figure, especially for an organization holding only $3.3 billion in cash and cash equivalents.*

For reporting purposes, the **current liabilities** *were divided into several specific categories:*

- *Accounts payable*
- *Accrued and other liabilities*
- *Debt due within one year*

When creating a balance sheet, what is reported as a liability? Why are some liabilities shown as current whereas others are not? ***How does an accountant draw a distinction between liabilities that are labeled as current and those that are reported as noncurrent (sometimes referred to as long-term liabilities)?***

Answer: A liability is an obligation owed to a party outside of the reporting organization—a debt that can be stated in monetary terms. Liabilities normally require the payment of cash but may at times be settled by the conveyance of other assets or the delivery of services. Some reported liabilities are for definite amounts, although a number are no more than estimations.

noncurrent liabilities

Debts that will not be satisfied within one year from the date of a balance sheet.

The distinction between current and **noncurrent liabilities** is a function of time. A debt that is expected to be satisfied within one year from the date of the balance sheet is classified as a current liability.[1] Amounts owed for rent, insurance, utilities, inventory purchases, and the like usually fall into this category. If payment will not be made until after that one-year interval, the liability is reported as noncurrent. Bonds and notes payable are common examples of noncurrent debts as are liabilities for employee pensions, long-term leases, and deferred income taxes. Current liabilities appear before noncurrent liabilities on a balance sheet.

Question: Below is the liability section of the balance sheet reported by Johnson & Johnson and Subsidiaries as of December 28, 2008. Note that additional information about many of these liabilities is provided in the notes to the company's financial statements.

FIGURE 13.1 Liability Section of Balance Sheet, Johnson & Johnson and Subsidiaries as of December 28, 2008

All numbers in millions.

Current liabilities	
Loans and notes payable (Note 6)	$3,732
Accounts payable	7,503
Accrued liabilities	5,531
Accrued rebates, returns, and promotions	2,237
Accrued salaries, wages, and commissions	1,432
Accrued taxes on income	417
Total current liabilities	20,852
Long-term debt (Note 6)	8,120
Deferred taxes on income (Note 8)	1,432
Employee-related obligations (Notes 5 and 13)	7,791
Other liabilities	4,206
	$42,401

Decision makers who analyze an organization such as Johnson & Johnson usually spend considerable time studying the data available about liabilities, often focusing on current liabilities. ***Why is information describing liabilities, especially the size and composition of current liabilities, considered so important when assessing the financial position and economic health of a business?***

Answer: Liabilities represent claims to assets. Debts must be paid as they come due or the entity risks damaging its future ability to obtain credit or even the possibility of bankruptcy. To stay viable, organizations need to be able to generate sufficient cash on an ongoing basis to meet all obligations. Virtually no other goal can be more important, both to company officials and any external decision makers assessing an entity's financial wellbeing and potential for future success.

In general, the higher a liability total is in comparison to the reported amount of assets, the riskier the financial position. The future is always cloudy for a company when the size of its debts begins to approach the total of its assets. The amount reported as current liabilities is especially significant in this analysis because those debts must be satisfied in the near future. Sufficient cash has to be available quickly, often within weeks or months. Not surprisingly, analysts become concerned when current liabilities grow to be relatively high in comparison with current assets because the organization might not be able to meet those obligations as they come due. In a newspaper account of Advanced Cell Technology, the following warning was issued: "It reported $17 million in current liabilities, but only $1 million in cash and other current assets, an indication it could be forced to file for bankruptcy protection."[2]

As mentioned in an earlier chapter, one tool utilized by decision makers in judging the present level of risk posed by a company's liability requirements is the **current ratio**: current assets divided by current liabilities. This is a simple benchmark that can be computed using available balance sheet information. Although many theories exist as to an appropriate standard, any current ratio below 1.00 to 1.00 signals that the company's current liabilities exceed its current assets.

current ratio

Formula measuring an organization's liquidity (the ability to pay debts as they come due); calculated by dividing current assets by current liabilities.

FIGURE 13.2 Sample of Recent Current Ratios

Exxon-Mobil	1.47 to 1.00 (at 12/31/08)
Oracle	1.81 to 1.00 (at 5/31/08)
Aeropostale	2.25 to 1.00 (at 1/31/09)

EXERCISE

Link to multiple-choice question for practice purposes: http://www.quia.com/quiz/2092994.html

Question: An organization is not inclined to report more liabilities than necessary because of potential damage to the image being portrayed. The inclusion of debts tends to make a company look riskier to creditors and investors. Thus, the danger that officials will report an excessive amount of liabilities seems slight. Balance sheets look better to decision makers if fewer obligations are present to drain off resources. Consequently, where possible, is there not a tendency for officials to limit the debts that are reported? ***At what point does an entity have to recognize a liability?*** *How does U.S. GAAP ensure that all liabilities are appropriately included on a balance sheet?*

Answer: FASB *Statement of Financial Accounting Concepts No. 6* defines many of the elements found in a set of financial statements. According to this guideline, liabilities should be recognized when several specific characteristics all exist:

1. there is a probable future sacrifice
2. of the reporting entity's assets or services
3. arising from a present obligation that is the result of a past transaction or event.

To understand the reporting of liabilities, several aspects of these characteristics are especially important to note. First, the obligation does not have to be absolute before recognition is required. A future sacrifice only has to be "probable." This standard leaves open a degree of uncertainty.

As might be expected, determination as to whether a potential payment is probable can be the point of close scrutiny when independent CPAs audit a set of financial statements. The line between "probable" and "not quite probable" is hardly an easily defined benchmark.

Second, for reporting to be required, a debt must result from a past transaction or event.

- An employee works for a company and is owed a salary. The work is the past event that creates the obligation.
- A vendor delivers merchandise to a business. Acquisition and receipt of these goods is the past event that creates the obligation.

Third, the past transaction or event must create a present obligation. In other words, an actual debt must exist and not just a potential debt. Ordering a piece of equipment is a past event but, in most cases, no immediate obligation is created. In contrast, delivery of this equipment probably does obligate the buyer and, thus, necessitates the reporting of a liability. Often, in deciding whether a liability should be recognized, the key questions for the accountant are (a) what event actually obligates the company and (b) when did that event occur?

Determining the liabilities to be included on a balance sheet often takes considerable thought and analysis. Accountants for the reporting company produce a list of the debts that meet the characteristics listed above. The independent auditor then spends considerable time and energy searching for any other obligations that might have been omitted, either accidentally or on purpose.

KEY TAKEAWAY

Companies are wary of recording liabilities because of the negative impact on reported information. Thus, U.S. GAAP has established rules to help ensure the proper inclusion of liabilities. When specified characteristics are met, a liability is shown. Current liabilities typically are those reported debts that must be satisfied within one year from the balance sheet date. Because a company needs to be able to meet its debts as they come due, analysts pay close attention to this total. The current ratio is also watched closely by many as a sign of financial strength.

2. REPORTING CURRENT LIABILITIES SUCH AS GIFT CARDS

LEARNING OBJECTIVES

At the end of this section students should be able to meet the following objectives:

1. **Define and record accrued liabilities.**
2. **Report the sale and redemption of gift cards.**
3. **Account for gift cards that are not expected to be redeemed.**

Question: Current liabilities often include rent payable, salary payable, insurance payable, and the like. These debts are incurred in connection with day-to-day operations. The amounts are known and payment will be made within a relatively short period of time.

Liabilities that result from physical events such as the purchase of inventory or supplies are often reported as accounts payable. Other current debts (interest payable or rent payable, for example) are sometimes combined under the general title of **accrued liabilities** *because they grow gradually over time rather than through a specific transaction.* ***How does an organization determine the amount of current liabilities to be reported on its balance sheet?***

accrued liabilities

Liabilities that grow gradually because of the passage of time; common examples include salaries and interest.

Answer: As discussed in a previous chapter, the timing for the recognition of a purchase is guided by the FOB point specified by the seller or negotiated by the parties. If marked "FOB shipping point," the liability is reported by the buyer when the goods leave the seller's place of business. "FOB destination" delays recordation until the merchandise is received by the buyer. Unless goods are damaged during transit or a dispute arises over payment for transportation charges, the FOB point is only relevant around the end of a company's fiscal year as the accountant attempts to classify transactions between one period and the next.

Many other liabilities are not created by a specific event but rather grow gradually day by day. Interest and rent are common examples but salaries, insurance, payroll taxes, and utilities also accrue in the same manner. They increase based on the passage of time. Interest on a loan or the amount due to an employee gets larger on a continual basis. For convenience, accounting systems often ignore the growth in these debts until payment is made or financial statements are prepared. Adjusting entries are required at the end of a period to recognize any accrued liabilities that have otherwise been omitted from the general ledger.

To illustrate, assume a large group of employees earns a total of $10,000 per day. They work Monday through Friday with payment made on the final day of each week. If the company's year ends on Wednesday, an adjustment is necessary so that the expense on the income statement and the liability on the balance sheet are both presented fairly for the three days that have passed. The following adjustment is made for $30,000 ($10,000 per day for three days) so that the debt incurred for salaries in the first year is reported properly.

FIGURE 13.3 Year-end Adjusting Entry to Recognize Debt for Three Days' Work

Wages Expense	30,000	
Wages Payable		30,000

As a second example, assume a company borrows $100,000 from a bank at a 6 percent annual interest rate on December 1 with payment to be made in six months. At the end of that year, the company owes interest but only for one month, an amount that is recognized through the following adjusting entry. Accrued interest of $500 ($100,000 principal × 6 percent × 1/12 year) is reported as of December 31.

FIGURE 13.4 Year-end Adjusting Entry to Recognize Interest for One Month

Interest Expense	500	
Interest Payable		500

EXERCISE

Link to multiple-choice question for practice purposes: http://www.quia.com/quiz/2092996.html

gift card liability

An obligation arising when a business accepts cash in exchange for a card that can be redeemed for a specified amount of assets or services.

Question: The February 28, 2009, balance sheet for Best Buy Co. Inc. shows several typical current liability accounts such as accounts payable and accrued liabilities. However, a $479 million figure also appears titled "Unredeemed **Gift Card Liabilities**.*" Over the last decade or so, the importance of gift cards has escalated dramatically for many businesses. By purchasing such cards, customers obtain the right to a specified amount of goods or services. From Starbucks to iTunes, these cards are sold to serve as gifts or merely as a convenient method for handling future payments.* ***How does a company such as Best Buy account for the thousands of gift cards that it sells each year?***

Answer: A liability represents a probable future sacrifice of an asset or service. By selling a gift card, a company has accepted an obligation that will be reported on its balance sheet. Companies such as Best Buy or Barnes & Noble must be willing to hand over inventory items such as cameras or books at the time the gift card is presented. Or, perhaps, some service can be required by the cardholder such as the repair of a computer or a massage. To the seller, a gift card is a liability but one that is not normally settled with cash. Probably the most common type of gift card is a postal stamp. When bought, the stamp provides a person with the right to receive a particular service, the mailing of a letter or package.

To illustrate, assume that a company sells ten thousand gift cards with a redemption value of $50 each. Revenue cannot be recognized when sold because the earning process is not substantially complete. The asset or service has not yet been conveyed to the customer. Rather, a liability (such as "unearned revenue" or "gift card liability") is reported to indicate that the company has an obligation to the holder of the card.

FIGURE 13.5 Sale of Ten Thousand $50 Gift Cards for Cash

Cash	500,000	
Unearned Revenue		500,000

Over time, customers will present their gift cards for selected merchandise. Assume that a person uses the first $50 card to buy goods which had originally cost the company only $32. Upon redemption, the liability is satisfied and the revenue can be recognized. The obligation is met and the earning process has been substantially completed. The second entry below presumes a perpetual inventory system is in use.

FIGURE 13.6 Redemption of Gift Card

Unearned Revenue	50	
Revenue		50
Cost of Goods Sold	32	
Inventory		32

Question: Some gift cards are never redeemed. They might be lost or just forgotten. ***Does the liability for a gift card remain on a company's balance sheet indefinitely if it is unlikely that redemption will ever occur?***

Answer: One reason that gift cards have become so popular with businesses is that some percentage will never be redeemed. They will be misplaced, stolen or the person will move away or die. In such cases, the seller has received money but was never forced to fulfill the obligation. The entire amount of the sale is profit.

A difficult theoretical question arises as to the timing of recognition of the revenue from any such anticipated defaults since the earning process is never substantially completed by redemption. In theory, a company recognizes this revenue when reasonable evidence exists that the card will never be used by the customer. Practically, though, determining this precise point is a matter of speculation.

Companies typically report the revenue from unused gift cards at one of three possible times:

1. When the cards expire if a time limit is imposed.
2. After a specified period of time such as eighteen months or two years.
3. In proportion to the cards that are actually redeemed. For example, assume historically that $8,000 in gift cards are never used by their owners. If 10 percent of the expected gift cards are turned in by customers, the company can also reclassify $800 (10 percent of $8,000) from unearned revenue to revenue to reflect the estimated portion of those cards that will never be presented.

Because of this accounting issue, a note to the financial statements produced by Best Buy explains: "We recognize revenue from gift cards when: (i) the gift card is redeemed by the customer, or (ii) the likelihood of the gift card being redeemed by the customer is remote ("gift card breakage"), and we determine that we do not have a legal obligation to remit the value of unredeemed gift cards to the relevant jurisdictions."

EXERCISE

Link to multiple-choice question for practice purposes: http://www.quia.com/quiz/2092997.html

KEY TAKEAWAY

Accounts payable are created by the purchase of inventory or supplies. Accrued liabilities are those debts that grow gradually over time. All such liabilities must be recorded prior to the preparation of financial statements. In today's retail world, many companies sell gift cards. Because a product or service must be provided to the holder of a gift card, the company has an obligation and a liability is reported. The liability is later reclassified as revenue when the card is redeemed because the earning process is substantially complete. Revenue should also be recorded when it becomes likely that redemption will never occur. This happens when cards are lost, stolen, or the customer has died or left the area. The company must ensure that revenue for such gift cards is not reported until an appropriate point in time.

3. ACCOUNTING FOR CONTINGENCIES

LEARNING OBJECTIVES

At the end of this section students should be able to meet the following objectives:

1. **Define a commitment and explain the method by which it is reported.**
2. **Define a contingency and explain the method by which it is reported.**
3. **Identify the criteria that establish the reporting of a contingent loss.**
4. **Describe the appropriate accounting for those contingent losses that do not qualify for recognition at the present time.**
5. **Explain the handling of a loss that ultimately proves to be different than the originally estimated and recorded balance.**
6. **Provide the proper reporting rules for a contingency.**

Question: The December 31, 2008, balance sheet for E. I. du Pont de Nemours and Company (better known as DuPont) shows total liabilities of approximately $28.7 billion. Immediately following the liability section, a separate category titled "Commitments and Contingent Liabilities" is included but no monetary figure is presented. Note 19 to the financial statements provides further details. In several pages of explanatory material, a number of future matters facing the company are described such as product warranties, environmental actions, litigation, and purchase commitments. ***In financial reporting, what is meant by the terms "commitments" and "contingencies (including loss and gain contingencies)?"***

Answer:

Commitments. Commitments represent unexecuted contracts. For example, assume that a business places an order with a truck company for the purchase of a large truck. The business has made a **commitment** to pay for this new vehicle but only after it has been delivered. Although cash may be needed in the future, no event (delivery of the truck) has yet created a present obligation. There is not yet a liability to report; no journal entry is appropriate.

commitment

An unexecuted contract such as for the future purchase of inventory at a set price; necessitates disclosure of extensive information in the financial statement footnotes although amounts are not reported on the balance sheet or income statement because no transaction has yet occurred.

The information is still of importance to decision makers because future cash payments will be required. However, events have not reached the point where all the characteristics of a liability are present. Thus, extensive information about commitments is included in the notes to financial statements but no amounts are reported on either the income statement or the balance sheet. With a commitment, a step has been taken that will likely lead to a liability.

Contingencies. A **contingency** poses a different reporting quandary. A past event has occurred but the amount of the present obligation (if any) cannot yet be determined. With a contingency, the uncertainty is about the outcome of an action that has already taken place. The accountant is not a fortune teller who can predict the future. For example, assume Wysocki Corporation commits an act that is detrimental to the environment so that the federal government files a lawsuit for damages. The original action against the environment is the past event that creates the contingency. However, both the chance of losing the suit and the possible amount of any penalties might not be known definitively for several years. What, if anything, should be recognized in the interim?

contingency

A potential gain or loss that might arise as a result of a past event; uncertainty exists as to likelihood of the gain or loss occurring and the actual amount, if any, that will result.

Because companies prefer to avoid (or at least minimize) the recognition of losses and liabilities, it is not surprising that structured guidelines are needed for reporting contingencies. Otherwise, few if any contingencies would ever be reported. U.S. GAAP in this area was established in 1975 when FASB issued its Statement Number Five, "Accounting for Contingencies." This pronouncement requires the recognition of a **loss contingency** if

loss contingency

A potential loss resulting from a past event that must be recognized on an entity's financial statements if it is deemed probable and the amount involved can be reasonably estimated.

1. the loss is deemed to be probable and
2. the amount of loss can be reasonably estimated.

When both of these criteria are met, the expected impact of the loss contingency is recorded. To illustrate, assume that the lawsuit above was filed in Year One. Wysocki officials assess the situation. They believe that a loss is probable and that $800,000 is a reasonable estimation of the amount that will eventually have to be paid as a result of the damage done to the environment. Although this amount is only an estimate and the case has not been finalized, this contingency must be recognized.

FIGURE 13.7 Year One—Expected Loss from Lawsuit

Loss from Lawsuit—Estimated	800,000	
Estimated Liability from Lawsuit		800,000

FASB identifies a number of examples of loss contingencies that are evaluated and reported in this same manner including:

- Collectability of receivables
- Obligations related to product warranties and product defects
- Risk of loss or damage of enterprise property by fire, explosion, or other hazards
- Threat of expropriation of assets
- Pending or threatened litigation
- Actual or possible claims and assessments
- Guarantees of indebtedness of others

Question: The likelihood of loss in connection with many contingencies is not always going to be probable or subject to a reasonable estimation. ***What reporting is appropriate for a loss contingency that does not qualify for recording at the present time?***

Answer: If the likelihood of loss is only reasonably possible (rather than probable) or if the amount of a probable loss does not lend itself to a reasonable estimation, only disclosure in the notes to the financial statements is necessary rather than actual recognition. A contingency where the chance of loss is viewed as merely remote can be omitted from the financial statements.

Unfortunately, this official standard provides little specific detail about what constitutes a probable, reasonably possible, or remote loss. "Probable" is described in Statement Number Five as likely to occur and "remote" is a situation where the chance of occurrence is slight. "Reasonably possible" is defined in vague terms as existing when "the chance of the future event or events occurring is more than remote but less than likely" (paragraph 3). The professional judgment of the accountants and auditors is left to determine the exact placement of the likelihood of losses within these categories.

Not surprisingly, many companies contend that future adverse effects from all loss contingencies are only reasonably possible so that no actual amounts are reported. Practical application of official accounting standards is not always theoretically pure, especially when the guidelines are nebulous.

Question: Assume that a company recognizes a contingent loss because it is judged to be probable and subject to a reasonable estimation. Eventually, all estimates are likely to prove wrong, at least in some small amount. ***What happens when a figure is reported in a set of financial statements and the actual total is later found to be different?***

For example, Wysocki Corporation recognized an estimated loss of $800,000 in Year One because of a lawsuit involving environmental damage. Assume the case is eventually settled in Year Two for $900,000. How is the additional loss of $100,000 reported? It relates to an action taken in Year One but the actual amount is not finalized until Year Two. The difference is not apparent until the later period.

Answer: In Year One, because both criteria were met, an $800,000 loss was recognized on the income statement along with a corresponding liability. Notes to the financial statement explain the nature of this lawsuit as well as the range of any reasonably possible losses. Decision makers analyzing the Wysocki Corporation should realize that the amount reported is not a precise measure of the eventual loss. The same is true of all contingencies and other estimations. By the time that the exact amount of loss is determined, investors and creditors have already incorporated the original information into their decisions including the uncertainty of the outcome. Restating the Year One loss to $900,000 does not allow them to undo and change the decisions that were made in the past.

Consequently, no change is made in the $800,000 figure reported for Year One; the additional $100,000 loss is recognized in Year Two. The amount is fixed at the time that a better estimation (or final figure) is available. This same reporting is utilized in correcting any reasonable estimation. Wysocki corrects the balances through the following journal entry that removes the liability and records the remainder of the loss.

FIGURE 13.8 Year Two—Settlement of Lawsuit

Estimated Liability from Lawsuit	800,000	
Additional Loss on Lawsuit	100,000	
Cash		900,000

One important exception to this handling does exist. If the initial estimation was viewed as fraudulent—an attempt to deceive decision makers—the $800,000 figure reported in Year One is physically restated. It simply cannot continue to appear. All the amounts in a set of financial statements have to be presented in good faith. Any reported balance that fails this essential criterion is not allowed to remain. Furthermore, even if there was no overt attempt to deceive, restatement is still required if officials should have known that a reported figure was materially wrong. Such amounts were not reported in good faith; officials have been grossly negligent in reporting the financial information.

From a journal entry perspective, restatement of a previously reported income statement balance is accomplished by adjusting retained earnings. Revenues and expenses (as well as gains, losses, and any dividend paid figures) are closed into retained earnings at the end of each year. That is where the previous year error now resides.

Consequently, upon discovery that the actual loss from this lawsuit is $900,000, that amount is shown by one of the following two approaches:

FIGURE 13.9 Two Ways to Fix an Estimation

Original Estimation Was Reasonable, Made in Good Faith

	Year One Income Statement	Year Two Income Statement
Loss on Lawsuit	$800,000	$100,000

Original Estimation Was Not Made in Good Faith (Restatement Required)

	Year One Income Statement	Year Two Income Statement
Loss on Lawsuit	$900,000	-0-

EXERCISE

Link to multiple-choice question for practice purposes: http://www.quia.com/quiz/2092998.html

gain contingency

A potential gain resulting from a past event that is not recognized in the financial statements until it actually occurs due to the principle of conservatism.

Question: The previous discussion has been about loss contingencies. Companies obviously can also have **gain contingencies**. *In a lawsuit, for example, one party might anticipate winning $800,000 but eventually collect $900,000.* ***Are the rules for reporting gain contingencies the same as those applied to loss contingencies?***

Answer: As a result of the conservatism inherent in financial accounting, the timing used in the recognition of gains does not follow the same rules applied to losses. Losses are anticipated when they become probable; that is a fundamental rule of financial accounting. Recognition of gains is delayed until they actually occur (or, at least until they reach the point of being substantially complete). Disclosure in the notes is still important but the decision as to whether the outcome is probable or reasonably possible is irrelevant in reporting a gain. Gains are not anticipated for reporting purposes.

FIGURE 13.10 Reporting a Gain Contingency

	Year One Income Statement	Year Two Income Statement
Gain on Lawsuit	-0-	$900,000

EXERCISE

Link to multiple-choice question for practice purposes: http://www.quia.com/quiz/2093019.html

Talking with an Independent Auditor about International Financial Reporting Standards

Following is a continuation of our interview with Robert A. Vallejo, partner with the accounting firm PricewaterhouseCoopers.

Question: According to U.S. GAAP, a contingent loss must be recognized when it is probable that it will occur and a reasonable estimation of the amount can be made. That rule has been in place now for over thirty years and is well understood in this country. Are contingent losses handled in the same way by IFRS?

Robert Vallejo: The theory is the same under IFRS but some interesting and subtle differences do exist. If there is a probable future outflow of economic benefits and the company can form a reliable estimate, then that amount must be recognized. However, the term "probable" is defined as "more likely than not" which is much more easily reached than under the requirements of U.S. GAAP. Thus, the reporting of more contingent losses is likely under IFRS than currently under U.S. GAAP.

IAS 37, Provisions, Contingent Liabilities and Contingent Assets, states that the amount recorded should be the best estimate of the expenditure that would be required to settle the present obligation at the balance sheet date. That is the best estimate of the amount that an entity would rationally pay to settle the obligation at the balance sheet date or to transfer it to a third party. Under U.S. GAAP, if there is a range of possible losses but no best estimate exists within that range, the entity records the low end of the range. Under IFRS, the entity records the midpoint of the range. That is a subtle difference in wording, but it is one that could have a significant impact on financial reporting for organizations where expected losses exist within a very wide range.

KEY TAKEAWAY

Entities often make commitments that are future obligations that do not yet qualify as liabilities that must be reported. For accounting purposes, they are only described in the notes to financial statements. Contingencies are potential liabilities that might result because of a past event. The likelihood of loss or the actual amount of the loss is still uncertain. Loss contingencies are recognized when their likelihood is probable and this loss is subject to a reasonable estimation. Reasonably possible losses are only described in the notes and remote contingencies can be omitted entirely from financial statements. Estimations of such losses often prove to be incorrect and normally are simply fixed in the period discovered. However, if fraud, either purposely or through gross negligence, has occurred, amounts reported in prior years are restated. Contingent gains are only reported to decision makers through disclosure within the notes to the financial statements.

4. ACCOUNTING FOR PRODUCT WARRANTIES

LEARNING OBJECTIVES

At the end of this section students should be able to meet the following objectives:

1. **Explain the difference between an embedded and an extended product warranty.**
2. **Account for the liability and expense incurred by a company that provides its customers with an embedded warranty on a purchased product.**
3. **Account for the amount received on the sale of an extended warranty and any subsequent cost incurred as a result of this warranty.**
4. **Compute the average age of accounts payable.**

embedded product warranty

An obligation established by the sale of a product where the seller promises to fix or replace the product if it proves to be defective.

Question: FASB Statement Number 5 includes a **product warranty** *as an example of a contingency. A company sells merchandise such as a car or a microwave and agrees to fix certain problems if they arise within a specified period of time. If the car's transmission breaks, for example, the seller promises to replace it. Making the sale with a warranty attached is the past event that creates this contingency. However, the item acquired by the customer must break before the company has an actual loss. That outcome is uncertain.*

In accounting for contingencies, several estimates are required:

- *The approximate number of claims*
- *The likelihood that claims will result from the warranty*
- *The eventual cost*

As an example, General Electric reported on its December 31, 2008, balance sheet a liability for product warranties totaling over $1.68 billion. That is certainly not a minor obligation. In the notes to the financial statements, the company explains "We provide for estimated product warranty expenses when we sell the related products. Because warranty estimates are forecasts that are based on the best available information—mostly historical claims experience—claims costs may differ from amounts provided." ***How does a company record and report contingencies such as product warranties?***

Answer: In accounting for warranties, cash rebates, the collectability of receivables and other similar contingencies, the likelihood of loss is not an issue. These losses are almost always probable. For the accountant, the challenge is in arriving at a reasonable estimate of that loss. How many microwaves will break and have to be repaired? What percentage of cash rebate coupons will be presented by customers in the allotted time? How often will a transmission need to be replaced?

Many companies utilize such programs on an ongoing basis so that data from previous offers will be available to help determine the amount of the expected loss. However, historical trends cannot be followed blindly. Officials still have to be alert for any changes that could impact previous patterns. For example, in bad economic periods, customers are more likely to take the time to complete the paperwork required to receive a cash rebate. Or, the terms may vary from one warranty program to the next. Even small changes in the wording of an offer can alter the expected number of claims.

To illustrate, assume that a retail store sells ten thousand refrigerators during Year One for $400 cash each. The product is covered by a warranty that extends until the end of Year Three. No claims are made in Year One but similar programs in the past have resulted in repairs being made to 3 percent of the refrigerator at an average cost of $90. Thus, this warranty is expected to cost a total of $27,000 (ten thousand units × 3 percent or three hundred claims × $90 each). Immediate recognition is appropriate because the loss is both probable and subject to reasonable estimation.

Although no repairs are made in Year One, the $27,000 is recognized in that period. All requirements for a liability have been met. In addition, the matching principle states that expenses should be recorded in the same period as the revenues they help to generate. The revenue from the sale of the refrigerators is recognized in Year One so the warranty expense resulting from those revenues is also included at that time.

FIGURE 13.11 Year One—Sale of Ten Thousand Refrigerators for $400 Each

Cash	4,000,000	
Sales of Inventory		4,000,000

FIGURE 13.12 Year One—Recognize Expected Cost of Warranty Claims

Warranty Expense	27,000	
Warranty Payable		27,000

This warranty is in effect until the end of Year Three. Assume in the year following the sale (Year Two) that repairs costing $13,000 are made for these customers at no charge. Refrigerators break and are fixed as promised. The expense has already been recognized in the year of sale so the payments made by the company serve to reduce the recorded liability. They have no additional impact on net income.

FIGURE 13.13 Year Two—Payment for Repairs Covered by Warranty

Warranty Payable	13,000	
Cash		13,000

At the end of Year Two, the warranty payable T-account in the general ledger holds a balance of $14,000 ($27,000 original estimation less $13,000 payout for repairs to date). Because the warranty has not expired, company officials need to evaluate whether this $14,000 liability is still a reasonable estimation of the remaining costs to be incurred. If so, no further adjustment is made.

However, the original $27,000 was an estimate. More information is now available, some of which might suggest that $14,000 is no longer the best number to be utilized for the final period of the warranty. As an illustration, assume that a design flaw has been found in the refrigerators and that $20,000 (rather than $14,000) is now the estimate of the costs to be incurred in the final year of the warranty. The $14,000 is no longer appropriate. The reported figure must be updated to provide a fair presentation of the information that is now available. Estimations should be changed at the point that new data provides a clearer vision of future events.

FIGURE 13.14 December 31, Year Two—Adjust Warranty Liability from $14,000 to Expected $20,000

Warranty Expense	6,000	
Warranty Payable		6,000

In this adjusting entry, the change in the expense is not recorded in the period of the sale. As discussed earlier, no retroactive changes are made in previously reported figures unless fraud occurred or an estimate was held to be so unreasonable that it was not made in good faith.

extended product warranty

An obligation whereby the buyer of a product pays the seller for the equivalent of an insurance policy to protect against breakage or other harm to the product for a specified period of time.

Question: Not all warranties are built into a sales transaction. Many retailers also provide **extended warranties** *but for an additional fee. For example, assume a business sells a high-definition television with an automatic one-year warranty. The buyer receives this warranty as part of the purchase price. The accounting for that first year is the same as just demonstrated; an estimated expense and liability are recognized at the time of sale.*

However, an additional warranty for three more years is also offered at a price of $50. If, on January 1, Year One, a customer chooses to acquire this three-year coverage, what recording is made by the seller? ***Is an extended warranty purchased by a customer reported in the same manner as an automatic warranty embedded within a sales contract?***

Answer: Extended warranties, which are quite popular in some industries, are simply insurance policies. If the customer buys the coverage, the product is insured against breakage or other harm for the specified period of time. In most cases, the company is making the offer in an attempt to earn extra profit. The seller hopes that the amount received for the extended warranty will outweigh the eventual repair costs. Therefore, the accounting differs here from that demonstrated for an embedded warranty that was provided to encourage the sale of the product. Because of the matching principle, the anticipated expense was recognized in the same period as the revenue generated by the sale of the product.

By accepting money for an extended warranty, the seller agrees to provide services in the future. This contract is much like a gift card. The revenue is not earned until the earning process is substantially complete in the future. Thus, the $50 received for the extended warranty is initially recorded as "unearned revenue." This balance is a liability because the company owes a specified service to the customer. As indicated previously, liabilities do not always represent future cash payments.

FIGURE 13.15 January 1, Year One—Sale of Extended Warranty Covering Years 2–4

Cash	50	
Unearned Revenue		50

Note that no expense was estimated and recorded in connection with this warranty. As explained by the matching principle, no expense is recognized until the revenue begins to be reported.

Because of the terms specified, this extended warranty does not become active until January 1, Year Two. The television is then covered for a three-year period. The revenue is recognized, most likely on a straight-line basis, over that time. The $50 will be recognized at the rate of 1/3 per year or $16.66.

FIGURE 13.16 December 31, Year Two (Three and Four)—Recognition of Revenue from Extended Warranty

Unearned Revenue	16.66	
Revenue from Extended Warranty		16.66

In any period in which a repair must be made, the expense is recognized as incurred because revenue from this warranty contract is also being reported. To illustrate, assume that on August 8, Year Two, a slight adjustment must be made to the television at a cost of $9. The product is under warranty so there is no charge to the customer for this service. The expense recognized below is matched with the Year Two revenue recognized above.

FIGURE 13.17 August 8, Year Two—Repair Television under Contract

Warranty Expense	9	
Cash		9

EXERCISE

Link to multiple-choice question for practice purposes: http://www.quia.com/quiz/2092999.html

Question: Previously, the current ratio (current assets divided by current liabilities) and the amount of **working capital** *(current assets minus current liabilities) were discussed. Are there additional vital signs that relate to current liabilities that should be analyzed when looking at an organization?* ***Should decision makers be aware of any specific ratios or amounts in connection with current liabilities that provide especially insightful information about a company's financial health and operations?***

working capital

Formula measuring an organization's liquidity (the ability to pay debts as they come due); calculated by subtracting current liabilities from current assets.

Answer: In studying current liabilities, the number of days a business takes to pay its accounts payable is a figure of interest. If a business begins to struggle, the time of payment tends to lengthen because of the difficulty in generating sufficient cash amounts. Therefore, an unexpected jump in this number is often one of the first signs of financial problems and warrants concern.

To determine the **age of accounts payable** (or the number of days in accounts payable), the amount of inventory purchased during the year is first calculated:

age of accounts payable

A determination of the number of days that a company takes to pay for the inventory that it buys; it is computed by dividing accounts payable by the average inventory purchases per day during the period.

cost of goods sold = beginning inventory + purchases – ending inventory,

Thus,

purchases = cost of goods sold – beginning inventory + ending inventory.

Using this purchases figure, the number of days that a company takes to pay its accounts payable on the average can be found. Either the average accounts payable for the year can be used below or just the ending balance.

purchases/365 = average purchases per day

accounts payable/average purchases per day = average age of accounts payable

As an illustration, the following information comes from the 2008 financial statements for Safeway Inc.

FIGURE 13.18 Information from 2008 Financial Statements for Safeway Inc.

Beginning Inventory	$2.798 billion
Ending Inventory	2.591 billion
Cost of Goods Sold	31.589 billion
Ending Accounts Payable	2.449 billion

The total of inventory purchases by Safeway during 2008 was over $31 billion:

purchases = cost of goods sold – beginning inventory + ending inventory

purchases = $31.589 billion – $2.798 billion + $2.591 billion

purchases = $31.382 billion.

The average purchases amount made each day during 2008 by this company was nearly $86 million:

purchases/365

$31.382/365 = $85.978 million.

The average age of ending accounts payable for Safeway at this time is between twenty-eight and twenty-nine days:

accounts payable/average daily purchases

$2.449 billion/$85.978 million = 28.48 days.

To evaluate that number, a decision maker would need to compare it to previous time periods, the typical payment terms for a business in that industry, and comparable figures from other similar corporations. Interestingly, the same computation for the previous year (2007) showed that Safeway was taking over thirty-four days to pay off its accounts payable during that period.

KEY TAKEAWAY

Many companies incur contingent liabilities as a result of product warranties. If the warranty is given to a customer along with a purchased item, an anticipated expense should be recognized at that time as well as the related liability. If the cost of this type of embedded warranty eventually proves to be incorrect, the correction is made when discovered. Companies also sell extended warranties, primarily as a means of increasing profits. These warranties are recorded initially as liabilities and are reclassified to revenue over the time of the obligation. Subsequent costs are expensed as incurred to align with the matching principle. Expenses are not estimated and recorded in advance. Analysts often determine the average age of accounts payable to determine how quickly liabilities are being paid as an indication of an entity's financial health.

Talking with a Real Investing Pro—Continued

Following is a continuation of our interview with Kevin G. Burns.

Question: Analysts often look closely at current liabilities when evaluating the future prospects of a company. Is there anything in particular that you look for when examining a company and its current liabilities?

Kevin Burns: For almost any company, there are a number of things that I look at in connection with current liabilities. I always have several questions where possible answers can concern me. I am interested in the terms of the current liabilities as well as the age of those liabilities. In other words, is the company current with its payments to vendors? Does the company have a significant amount of current liabilities but only a small amount of current assets? Or, stated more directly, can these liabilities be paid on time? Have current liabilities been growing while business has remained flat or grown much more slowly? Are any of the current liabilities to organizations controlled by corporate insiders? That always makes me suspicious so that, at the very least, I want more information. In sum, I like balance sheets where there are no potential conflicts of interest and the company is a reasonably fast payer of its debts.

Video Clip

Joe talks about the five most important points in Chapter 13.

View the video online at: http://blip.tv/play/sDyBwKhRAA

5. END-OF-CHAPTER EXERCISES

QUESTIONS

1. What is the difference between a current liability and a noncurrent liability?
2. Give an example of a current liability and a noncurrent liability.
3. Why is it important that a company be able to pay its liabilities as they come due?
4. Why are financial statement users particularly concerned about the amount of current liabilities a company has?
5. How is a company's current ratio calculated?
6. What are the three characteristics of liabilities according to FASB?
7. What are "accrued liabilities?"
8. How do companies account for gift cards it has sold?
9. Define "commitments."
10. What two criteria must be met for a company to record a contingency?
11. Give three examples of possible contingencies that a company would report.
12. How would a company report a contingency that is "reasonably possible?"
13. How would a company report a contingency where the chance of loss is "remote?"
14. How are contingent gains reported?
15. How should a company go about estimating liabilities like product warranties?
16. How is the age of accounts payable calculated?

TRUE OR FALSE

1. ____ Contingent gains should only be recorded if they are probable and can be reasonably estimated.
2. ____ A current ratio of less than one means that a company has more current assets than current liabilities.
3. ____ A long-term note payable is an example of a current liability.
4. ____ Restatement of financial statements should occur if a company attempts to mislead investors by understating its liabilities.
5. ____ Embedded and extended warranties should be accounted for in the same way.
6. ____ When estimating its warranty liability, a company should consider things like the state of the economy.
7. ____ Contingent liabilities should be reported on the balance sheet if they are both probable and can be reasonably estimated.
8. ____ Age of accounts payable can help users determine if a company is having trouble paying its bills.
9. ____ Unearned revenue and accounts receivable are examples of current liabilities.
10. ____ Liabilities for gift cards and similar items must be kept on the balance sheet until they are redeemed, regardless of how long that takes.

MULTIPLE CHOICE

1. Which of the following is ***not*** normally a current liability?
    a. Accounts payable
    b. Bonds payable
    c. Interest payable
    d. Income taxes payable
2. Sierra Inc. manufacturers environmentally friendly appliances. It offers a two year warranty standard. In Year 1, Sierra sold 450,000 toasters. Past experience has told Sierra that approximately 4 percent of the toasters require repair at an average cost of $10 each. During Year 1, Sierra actually spends $38,000 and during Year 2, Sierra actually spends $105,000. What is the balance in the warranty liability account at the end of year 2?
    a. $180,000
    b. $143,000
    c. $38,000
    d. $37,000
3. Reporting contingent losses but not contingent gains is an example of which accounting principle?
    a. Matching
    b. Conservatism
    c. Going concern
    d. Cost/benefit
4. Watkins Inc. has the following assets:

Cash	$400
Inventory	$730
Prepaid Rent	$460
Equipment	$4,000

It has the following liabilities

Accounts Payable	$560
Unearned revenue	$200
Long-term Note Payable	$3,500

What is Watkins' current ratio?
    a. 31
    b. 49
    c. 09
    d. 14
5. The following figures appeared on Whazzit's financial statements for the year:

Cost of goods sold	$1,968,000
Beginning inventory	238,000
Ending inventory	249,000
Accounts payable	167,000

What was Whazzit's age of accounts payable?
    a. 1 days
    b. 9 days
    c. 3 days
    d. 8 days

6. Maxout Company sells computers. The computers have an embedded one year warranty, but customers may choose to buy an extended warranty that covers the computer for two years beyond that. The cost of the extended warranty is $200. What journal entry would Maxout make at the end of the second year after the computer is purchased, assuming the customer also purchases the extended warranty?

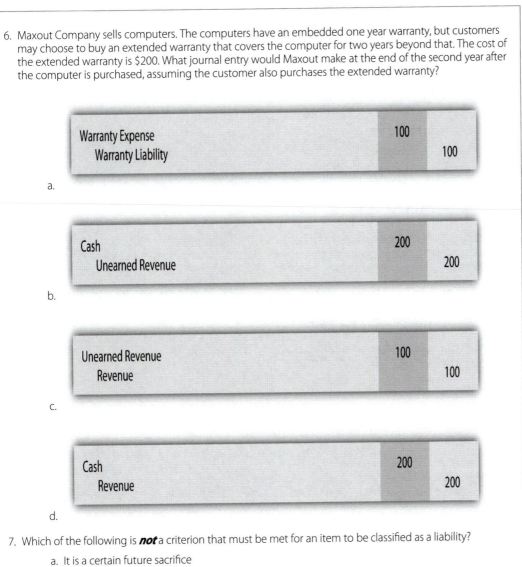

Warranty Expense	100	
Warranty Liability		100

a.

Cash	200	
Unearned Revenue		200

b.

Unearned Revenue	100	
Revenue		100

c.

Cash	200	
Revenue		200

d.

7. Which of the following is ***not*** a criterion that must be met for an item to be classified as a liability?
   a. It is a certain future sacrifice
   b. The sacrifice is from the entity's assets or services
   c. It is a probable future sacrifice
   d. It arises from a present obligation that results from a past transaction

PROBLEMS

1. Knockoff Corporation makes a videogame unit known as the Gii. During the month of June, the following transactions occurred. Record any necessary journal entries for a–e.
   a. Knockoff purchased $300,000 of raw materials inventory on account.
   b. The company incurs salary expense of $45,000, which will not be paid until the beginning of July.
   c. Knockoff owes the IRS and other government entities $120,000 in taxes.
   d. OK Buy places an advance order for Giis and pays Knockoff $23,000. The Giis will be shipped in July.
   e. Knockoff owes a local bank $4,000 in interest.
   f. If Knockoff has $800,000 in current assets, and all current liabilities are given in a–e above, what is Knockoff's current ratio?
   g. Knockoff's main competitor, PlayItAgain, has a current ratio of 2.1. You are trying to decide which company to invest in. Which current ratio do you prefer? Why?
2. OK Buy sells gift cards in various denominations. The company likes to sell these because it receives the cash immediately, but knows that a certain percentage will never be redeemed for merchandise. On December 1, OK Buy had a balance in unearned revenue from sales of gift cards of $728,000.
   a. During December, OK Buy sold an additional $578,000 in gift cards. Prepare this journal entry.
   b. During December, $327,000 worth of gift cards were redeemed to purchase inventory that had originally cost OK Buy $190,000. Prepare these journal entries.
   c. On December 31, OK Buy's accountant determines that 3 percent of the outstanding gift cards will never be redeemed for various reasons. She used past history to help determine this figure. Prepare a journal entry if necessary.
   d. What is the balance in OK Buy's unearned revenue account on December 31 after all of the above transactions have been recorded?
3. Ingalls Company is a fine jeweler located in a mall in a midsize city. During December 20X4, an unfortunate accident happens. Mrs. Rita Yeargin trips over a giant, singing Rudolph set up by the mall management company and went sprawling into Ingalls' store where she cracked her head on a display case. She spent several days in the hospital with a sprained ankle, bruised elbow and a concussion. Prior to the end of the year, Mrs. Yeargin's lawyer files papers to sue both the mall management company and Ingalls for $1,000,000. Ingalls' insurance company tells it that its policy does not cover accidents involving giant, singing Rudolphs. Ingalls's attorney tells it that it is difficult to guess what a jury might do in this case. He estimates that Ingalls will probably be liable for only 20 percent of the $1,000,000 since the Rudolph actually belongs to the mall.
   a. Determine if Ingalls needs to record a journal entry on December 31, 20X4, and if so, record it.
4. Sadler Corporation produces lawnmowers. The lawnmowers come with a three-year warranty. During 20X6, Sadler sold 20,000 lawnmowers that cost $5,800,000 to manufacture for $10,000,000 cash. Sadler's accountant estimates that 10 percent will need to be repaired at some point over the next three years at an average cost of $37 per lawnmower.
   a. Make the journal entry to record the sale of the lawnmowers in 20X6.
   b. Record warranty expense for 20X6.
   c. During 20X7, Sadler spends $24,000 to repair the lawnmowers. Record this.
   d. At the end of 20X7, Sadler's accountant reevaluates the warranty estimates. The accountant believes that the actual warranty liability may be higher than her original estimates. She now believes that an additional $17,000 should be added. Make the necessary journal entry.
   e. During 20X8, Sadler spends $60,000 to repair the lawnmowers. Record this.
5. The Eyes Have It sells custom eyewear with a one-year embedded warranty. Customers may purchase an extended one year warranty beyond that. During 20X7, the company sold 52,000 pairs of eyeglasses for $1,000,000. Customers who purchased 75 percent of those pairs also purchased the one-year extended warranty. This brought in $200,000 cash.
   a. Record the sale of the extended warranties in 20X7.
   b. Assume that during 20X9, the company spent $34,000 to repair glasses under the extended warranty. Record this entry.
   c. Record the entry Eyes will make when the extended warranties expire.
6. In several past chapters, we have met Heather Miller, who started her own business, Sew Cool. The financial statements for December are shown below. To calculate age of accounts payable, assume that beginning inventory on 6/1/20X8, when Sew Cool started business, was zero. *Also, assume that Sew Cool was only in business for 210 days.*

Sew Cool Financial Statements

Sew Cool
Income Statement
As of December 31, 20X8

Revenue	$4,000
Cost of Goods	(2,000)
Gross Profit	2,000
Other Expenses	(1,695)
Earnings before Tax	305
Tax Expense	(107)
Net Income	$198

Sew Cool
Stmt. of Retained Earnings
As of December 31, 20X8

Retained Earnings, December 1, 20X8	$500
Net Income	198
Dividends	(158)
Retained Earnings, December 31, 20X8	$540

Sew Cool
Balance Sheet
December 31, 20X8

Assets		**Liabilities**	
Current		**Current**	
Cash	$940	Accounts Payable	$900
Accounts Receivable	500	Income Tax Payable	120
Less Allowance for Doubtful Accounts	(20)	Total Current Liabilities	$1,020
Net Accounts Receivable	480		
Inventory	700		
Total Current Assets	$2,120		
Noncurrent		**Noncurrent**	
Equipment	$1,000	Notes Payable	$1,060
		Owners' Equity	
		Capital Stock	$500
		Retained Earnings	540
		Total Owners' Equity	$1,040
Total Assets	$3,120	Total Liabilities & Owners' Equity	$3,120

Based on the financial statements determine the following:

a. Current ratio
b. Age of accounts payable

COMPREHENSIVE PROBLEM

This problem will carry through several chapters, building in difficulty. It allows students to continuously practice skills and knowledge learned in previous chapters.

In Chapter 12, you prepared Webworks statements for December. They are included here as a starting point for January.

Webworks Financial Statements

Webworks
Income Statement
As of December 31

Revenue	$16,950
Cost of Goods Sold	(8,657)
Gross Profit	8,293
Deprec. and Amort. Expense	(363)
Other Expenses and Losses	(3,790)
Investment Income	100
Earnings before Tax	4,240
Tax Expense	(1,272)
Net Income	$2,986

Webworks
Stmt. of Retained Earnings
As of December 31

Retained Earnings, December 1	$9,322
Net Income	2,968
Retained Earnings, December 31	$12,290

Webworks
Balance Sheet
December 31

Assets		**Liabilities**	
Current		**Current**	
Cash	$3,215	Accounts Payable	$1,925
Accounts Receivable	2,250	Salaries Payable	200
Less Allowance for Doubtful Accounts	(225)		
Net Accounts Receivable	2,025		
Trading Securities, Net	360		
Merchandise Inventory	1,682		
Supplies Inventory	60		
Total Current Assets	$7,342	Total Current Liabilities	$2,125
Property, Plant, and Equipment			
Equipment	$7,000		
Less Accumulated Depreciation	(876)		
Furniture	1,000		
Less Accumulated Depreciation	(51)		
Total P, P, and E	$7,073		
Other Noncurrent Assets			
Licensing Agreement, Net	$2,200		
		Owners' Equity	
		Capital Stock	$2,000
		Retained Earnings	12,290
		Total Owners' Equity	$14,290
Total Assets	$16,415	Total Liabilities & Owners' Equity	$16,415

The following events occur during January:

a. Webworks starts and completes seven more sites and bills clients for $4,500.

b. Webworks purchases supplies worth $100 on account.

c. At the beginning of January, Webworks had fourteen keyboards costing $113 each and twenty flash drives which had been written down to $5 each in December due to *obsolescence*. Webworks uses periodic FIFO to cost its inventory.

d. On account, Webworks purchases sixty-five keyboards for $117 each and ninety of the new flash drives for $20 each.

e. Webworks pays Nancy $775 for her work during the first three weeks of January.

f. Webworks writes off an account receivable from October in the amount of $150 because collection appears unlikely.

g. Webworks receives $450 in advance to design a Web site for a local salon. Work won't begin on the Web site until February.

h. Webworks sells sixty keyboards for $9,000, all twenty of the old flash drives for $100 and eighty of the new flash drives for $2,400 cash.

i. During January, Webworks receives notice that one of its former clients is not happy with the work performed. When Webworks refuses to refund the client's money, the client decides to sue for what he paid plus damages for his "pain and suffering," which comes to $5,000. An attorney friend of Leon's mom believes that the suit is without merit and that Webworks probably will not have to pay anything.

j. Webworks collects $5,000 in accounts receivable.

k. During January, Webworks sells all of its stock in XYZ Company for $8 per share. Webworks had originally purchased sixty shares for $5 and they were selling for $6 per share on the last balance sheet date.

l. Webworks pays $200 for advertising that will run over the next two months.

m. Webworks pays off its salaries payable from December.

n. Webworks purchased 175 shares of QRS Company for $10 per share. Webworks considers this an available for sale security.

o. Webworks pays off $9,000 of its accounts payable.

p. Webworks pays Leon a salary of $2,000.

q. Webworks prepays $600 for rent for the months of January, February, and March.

r. QRS Company pays Webworks a dividend of $30.

s. Webworks pays taxes of $1,000 in cash.

Required:

A. Prepare journal entries for the above events.

B. Post the journal entries to T-accounts.

C. Prepare an unadjusted trial balance for Webworks for January.

D. Prepare adjusting entries for the following and post them to your T-accounts.

t. Webworks owes Nancy $200 for her work during the last week of January.

u. Leon's parents let him know that Webworks owes $320 toward the electricity bill. Webworks will pay them in February.

v. Webworks determines that it has $40 worth of supplies remaining at the end of January.

w. Prepaid rent should be adjusted for January's portion.

x. Prepaid advertising should be adjusted for January's portion.

y. Webworks is continuing to accrue bad debts at 10 percent of accounts receivable.

z. Webworks continues to depreciate its equipment over four years and its furniture over five years, using the straight-line method.

i. The license agreement should be amortized over its one-year life.

ii. QRS Company is selling for $9 per share on January 31.

iii. Record cost of goods sold.

E. Prepare an adjusted trial balance.

F. Prepare financial statements for January.

ENDNOTES

1. In upper-level accounting courses, the definition of a current liability is refined a bit. It refers to any liability that will require the use of a current asset or the creation of another current liability. However, the one-year standard presented in this textbook is sufficient in a vast majority of cases.
2. Todd Wallack, "Fame-courting biotech running short of cash," *The Boston Globe*, July 17, 2008, A-1.

CHAPTER 14

In a Set of Financial Statements, What Information Is Conveyed about Noncurrent Liabilities Such as Bonds?

Video Clip

Joe introduces Chapter 14 and speaks about the course in general.

View the video online at: http://blip.tv/play/sDyBwKhNAA

1. DEBT FINANCING

LEARNING OBJECTIVES

At the end of this section, students should be able to meet the following objectives:

1. **List and explain the advantages of debt financing.**
2. **List and explain the disadvantages of debt financing.**
3. **Explain and illustrate the use of financial leverage.**
4. **Define notes and bonds as used in debt financing.**

Question: Businesses and other organizations need funds to finance their operations and possible expansions. Such amounts can be quite significant. A portion of this money is normally contributed by investors who choose to become owners through the purchase of shares of capital stock. Cash can also be generated internally by means of profitable operations. If net income exceeds the amount of dividends paid each period, a company has an ongoing source of financing.

However, many companies obtain a large part of the funding needed to support themselves and their growth through borrowing. If those debts will not be paid back within the following year, they are listed on the balance sheet as noncurrent liabilities. Target Corporation, for example, disclosed in its financial statements that it owed $19.9 billion in noncurrent liabilities as of January 31, 2009.

Incurring debts of such large amounts must pose some risks to an organization. Creditors expect to be repaid their entire loan balance plus **interest** *at the specified due date.* ***What problems and potential dangers does an entity face when liabilities—especially those of significant size—are owed?***

interest

The charge for using money over time, often associated with long-term loans; even if not specifically mentioned in the debt agreement, U.S. GAAP requires it to be computed and reported based on a reasonable rate.

Answer: Few things in life are free so the obvious problem with financing through debt is that it has a cost. A bank or other creditor will charge interest for the use of its money. As an example, Target Corporation reported interest expense for the year ending January 31, 2009, of approximately $900 million. The rate of interest will vary based on economic conditions and the financial health of the debtor. As should be expected, strong companies are able to borrow at a lower rate than weaker ones.

In addition, a business must be able to generate enough surplus cash to satisfy its creditors as debts come due. As indicated, Target reports noncurrent liabilities of $19.9 billion. Eventually, company officials have to find sufficient money to satisfy these obligations. Those funds might well be generated by profitable operations or contributed by investors. Or, Target might simply borrow more money to pay off these debts as they mature. This type of rollover financing is common as long as the debtor remains economically strong. Whatever the approach, the company has to manage its financial resources in such a way that all debts can be settled at their maturity date.

The most serious risk associated with debt is the possibility of bankruptcy. As has unfortunately become quite commonplace during the recent economic crisis, organizations that are not able to pay their liabilities as they come due can be forced into legal bankruptcy.[1] The end result of **bankruptcy** is frequently the liquidation of company assets although corporate reorganization and continued existence is also a possibility. The bankruptcy of Circuit City ended with all assets being sold so that the company ceased to exist. Conversely, Delta Air Lines was able to leave bankruptcy in 2007 as a business that had been completely reorganized in hopes of remaining a viable entity.[2]

bankruptcy

A formal court process that often results in the liquidation of a company that cannot pay its liabilities as they come due; in some cases, bankrupt companies are allowed to reorganize their finances and operations so that liquidation is not deemed to be necessary.

Given the cost and risk associated with large amounts of debt, the desire of decision makers to receive adequate and clear financial information is understandable. Few areas of financial accounting have been more discussed over the decades than the reporting of noncurrent liabilities.

Question: Debt is a costly and possibly risky method of financing a company's operations and growth. However, advantages must exist or companies would avoid incurring noncurrent liabilities wherever possible. ***What are the advantages to an organization of using debt to generate funding for operations and other vital activities?***

Answer: One advantage of borrowing money is that interest expense is tax deductible. Therefore, a company will essentially recoup a portion of its interest expense from the government. As mentioned above, Target incurred interest expense of $900 million. This interest reduced the company's taxable income by that amount. If the assumption is made that Target has an effective income tax rate of 35 percent, the income tax total paid to the government is lowered by $315 million (35 percent of $900 million). Target pays interest of $900 million but reduces its income taxes by $315 million so that the net cost of borrowing for the period was $585 million.

Another advantage associated with debt financing is that it can be eliminated. Liabilities are not permanent. If the economic situation changes, a company can rid itself of all debt simply by making payments as balances come due. In contrast, if money is raised by issuing capital stock, the new shareholders can maintain their ownership indefinitely.

However, the biggest advantage commonly linked to debt is the benefit provided by **financial leverage**. This term refers to an organization's ability to increase reported net income by earning more money on borrowed funds than the associated cost of interest. For example, if a company borrows $1 million on a debt that charges interest of 5 percent per year, annual interest is $50,000. If the $1 million can then be used to generate a profit of $80,000, net income has gone up $30,000 ($80,000 – $50,000) using funds provided solely by creditors. The owners did not have to contribute any additional funds to increase profits by $30,000.

financial leverage

A company's ability to earn more on borrowed money than the associated interest cost on those funds; often viewed as a wise business strategy although risks (such as possible bankruptcy) are higher.

Over the decades, many companies have adopted a strategy of being highly leveraged, meaning that most of their funds came from debt financing. If profitable, the owners can make huge profits with little investment of their own. Unfortunately, companies that take this approach have a much greater risk of falling into bankruptcy because of the high volume of debts that have to be serviced.

EXERCISE

Link to multiple-choice question for practice purposes: http://www.quia.com/quiz/2093021.html

Question: Long-term financing typically comes from notes or bonds. ***What are notes and bonds and how do they differ from each other?***

Answer: Both notes and bonds are written contracts (often referred to as indentures) that specify the payment of designated amounts of cash on stated dates. The two terms have become somewhat interchangeable over the years and clear distinctions are not likely to be found in practice. In this textbook, for convenience, the term "note" is used when a contract is negotiated directly between two parties. For example, if officials from Jones Company go to City Street Bank and borrow $1.2 million to construct a new warehouse, the contract between the parties that establishes the specifics of this loan agreement will be referred to as a note.

The term "bond" will describe a contract or group of contracts that is created by a debtor and then sold, often to a number of members of the general public. Jones Company could opt to raise the needed $1.2 million for the new warehouse by printing 1,200 $1,000 bonds that it sells to a wide array of creditors around the world.

Typically, the issuance of debt to multiple parties enables a company to raise extremely large amounts of money. As an example, according to the financial statements published by Marriott International Inc., "$350 million of aggregate principal amount of 6.375 percent Series I Senior Notes due 2017" were issued during 2007. The exact information being conveyed by this disclosure will be described in detail later in this chapter. (This transaction was followed shortly thereafter by the issuance of another $400 million of similar debt for a total of $750 million in debt financing by Marriott within that one year.)

However, if securities are to be issued to the public in this way, the legal rules and regulations of the U.S. Securities and Exchange Commission must be followed, which adds another layer of costs to the raising of funds.

KEY TAKEAWAY

Many companies have a periodic need to raise money for operations and capital improvements. Debt financing is common although it leads to an interest charge and the possibility of bankruptcy. The cost of debt is offset somewhat in that interest expense is tax deductible. Incurring liabilities also allows a company to use financial leverage to boost reported profits if the proceeds can generate more income than the cost of the related interest. Notes and bonds are debt contracts that provide the specific terms that must be followed. In this textbook, notes will indicate that loans have been negotiated between two parties whereas bonds will refer to debt instruments that are sold, often to the public.

2. THE ISSUANCE OF NOTES AND BONDS

LEARNING OBJECTIVES

At the end of this section, students should be able to meet the following objectives:

1. **Identify the various terms that are found in a note or bond contract such as face value, stated cash interest rate, and any types of security or covenants.**
2. **Record notes and bonds issued at face value where periodic interest payments are made on dates other than the year-end.**
3. **Explain the handling of notes and bonds that are sold between interest dates and make the journal entries for both the issuance and the first interest payment.**

Question: Notes and bonds are contracts used in the borrowing of money. They are undoubtedly produced with great care by attorneys knowledgeable in contract law. ***What legal terms are typically included in debt instruments?***

Answer: The specific terms written into a contract or indenture vary depending on what a debtor is willing to promise in order to entice a creditor to turn over needed financial resources. Some of the most common are as follows.

maturity value

Amount of a note or bond to be repaid at the end of the contract; it serves as the basis for computing interest payments and is also known as face value.

note

A written contract to convey money as a loan at a specified interest rate and repayment schedule between two parties.

bond

A written contract created by a debtor that is sold (often to members of the general public) to raise money.

term notes or term bonds

A type of debt instrument where interest is paid at regular time intervals with the entire maturity value due at the end of the contract period.

serial debts

A type of debt instrument where a set amount is paid each period to cover both interest and a portion of the maturity value; home mortgages and automobile loans are common examples.

stated interest rate

Rate established in a debt contract to be paid by the debtor usually at specified time intervals; it is also called cash rate, contract rate or coupon rate.

debenture

A debt contract that does not contain any type of security for the creditor; these contracts are usually offered by debtors that are considered financially strong so that no additional security is required by the creditor to reduce the chance of loss.

Face value or **maturity value**. The **note** or **bond** will specify the amount to be repaid at the end of the contract time. A $1,000 bond, for example, has a face value of $1,000—that amount is to be paid on a designated maturity date. Thus, based on the information presented previously from Marriott's financial statements, that company will eventually be required to pay $350 million to the holders of its Series I notes.

Payment pattern of the face value or maturity value. With some debts, no part of the face value is scheduled for repayment until the conclusion of the contract period. These are often referred to as **term notes or term bonds**. The debtor pays the entire amount (sometimes referred to as a balloon payment) when the contract reaches the end of its term. Based on the information provided, Marriott will be required to pay the $350 million face value of its Series I notes during 2017.

Other debts, **serial debts**, require serial payments where a portion of the face value is paid periodically over time. Home mortgages, for example, are commonly structured as serial notes. Part of each scheduled payment reduces the face value of the obligation so that no large amount remains to be paid on the maturity date.

Notes and bonds can also be set up to allow the debtor to choose to repay part or all of the face value prior to the due date. Such debts are often referred to as "callable." This feature is popular because it permits refinancing if interest rates fall. A new loan is obtained at a cheap interest rate with the money used to pay off old notes or bonds that charge high interest rates. Sometimes a penalty payment is required if a debt is paid prematurely.

Interest rate. Creditors require the promise of interest before they are willing to risk loaning money to a debtor. Therefore, within the debt contract, a stated cash interest rate[3] is normally included. A loan that is identified as having a $100,000 face value with a stated annual interest rate of 5 percent lets both parties know that $5,000 in interest ($100,000 × 5 percent) will be conveyed from debtor to creditor each year.

Therefore, to service the Series I notes issued above, Marriott will be required to make annual interest payments of $22,312,500 ($350 million face value × the **stated interest rate** of 6.375 percent).

Interest payment dates. The stated amount of interest is paid on the dates identified in the contract. Payments can range from monthly to quarterly to semiannually to annually to the final day of the debt term.

Security. Many companies are not able to borrow money (or cannot borrow money without paying a steep rate of interest) unless some additional security is provided for the creditor. Any reduction of risk makes a note or bond instrument more appealing to potential lenders. For example, some loans (often dealing with the purchase of real estate) are mortgage agreements that provide the creditor with an interest in identified property. Although specific rights can vary based on state law and the wording of the contract, this type of security usually allows the creditor to repossess the property or force its liquidation if the debtor fails to make payments in a timely manner. The recent downturn in the housing market has seen many debtor defaults that have led to bank foreclosures on homes across the country.

A **debenture** is a debt contract that does not contain any security. The debtor is viewed as so financially strong that money can be obtained at a reasonable interest rate without having to add extra security agreements to the contract.

Covenants *and other terms.* Notes and bonds can contain an almost infinite list of other agreements. Many of these are promises made by the debtor to help ensure that money will be available to make required payments. For example, the debtor might agree to limit dividend payments until the liability is extinguished, keep its current ratio above a minimum standard, or limit the amount of other debts that it will incur.

covenants

Promises made by the debtor in a debt contract to help ensure that sufficient money will be available to make required payments at the scheduled times.

Debts can also be convertible so that the creditor can swap them for something else of value (often the capital stock of the debtor) if that seems a prudent move. The notes to the financial statements for VeriSign Inc. for December 31, 2008, and the year then ended describe one such noncurrent liability. "The Convertible Debentures are initially convertible, subject to certain conditions, into shares of the Company common stock at a conversion rate of 29.0968 shares of common stock per $1,000 principal amount of Convertible Debentures, representing an initial effective conversion price of approximately $34.37 per share of common stock."

Question: The financial reporting of a debt contract appears to be fairly straightforward. Assume, for example, that Brisbane Company borrows $400,000 in cash from a local bank on May 1, Year One. The face value of this loan is to be repaid in exactly five years. In the interim, interest payments at an annual rate of 6 percent will be made every six months beginning on November 1, Year One. ***What journal entries are appropriate to record a debt issued for a cash amount that is equal to the face value of the contract?***

Answer: Brisbane receives $400,000 in cash but also accepts a noncurrent liability for the same amount.

FIGURE 14.1 May 1, Year One—Cash of $400,000 Borrowed on Long-term Note Payable

Cash	400,000	
Note Payable		400,000

The first semiannual interest payment will be made on November 1, Year One. Because the 6 percent interest rate stated in the contract is for a full year, it must be halved to calculate the payment that covers the six-month intervals. Each of these cash disbursements is for $12,000 which is the $400,000 face value × the 6 percent annual stated interest rate × 1/2 year.

FIGURE 14.2 November 1, Year One—Payment of Interest for Six Months

Interest Expense	12,000	
Cash		12,000

By December 31, Year One, interest for two additional months (November and December) has accrued. This amount ($4,000 or $400,000 × 6 percent × 2/12 year) is recognized so that the financial statements prepared at that time will be presented fairly. No transaction occurs on that date but adjustment is necessary when preparing the Year One statements to report both the expense and the liability for these two months.

FIGURE 14.3 December 31, Year One—Accrual of Interest for Two Months

Interest Expense	4,000	
Interest Payable		4,000

When the next $12,000 interest payment is made by Brisbane on May 1, Year Two, the recorded $4,000 liability is extinguished and interest for four additional months (January through April) is recognized.

The appropriate expense for this period is \$8,000 or \$400,000 × 6 percent × 4/12 year. Mechanically, this payment could be recorded in more than one way but the following journal entry is probably the easiest to follow. Interest expense for the first two months was recorded in Year One with interest for the next four months recorded here in Year Two.

FIGURE 14.4 May 1, Year Two—Payment of Interest for Six Months

Interest Expense	8,000	
Interest Payable	4,000	
Cash		12,000

The interest payments and the recording process will continue in this same way until all five years have passed and the face value is paid.

Except for the initial entry, these events would be recorded in an identical fashion if Brisbane had signed this same note to acquire an asset such as a piece of machinery. No cash is involved in the beginning; the debt is incurred to acquire the property directly. The only reporting difference is that the asset replaces cash in the first journal entry above.

EXERCISE

Link to multiple-choice question for practice purposes: http://www.quia.com/quiz/2092978.html

Question: Bonds can be sold to a group of known investors or to the public in general. Often, companies will print bond indentures but not issue them until the money is needed. Thus, many bonds are sold on a day that falls between two interest dates. Payment must still be made to creditors as specified regardless of the length of time that the debt has been outstanding. If an interest payment is required by the contract, the debtor is legally obligated.

For example, assume that the Brisbane Company plans to issue bonds with a face value of \$400,000 to a consortium of twenty wealthy individuals. As with the previous note arranged with the bank, these bonds pay a 6 percent annual interest rate with payments every May 1 and November 1. However, this sale is not finalized until October 1, Year One. The first six-month interest payment is still required on November 1 as stated in the contract. After just one month, the debtor will be forced to pay interest for six months. That is not fair and Brisbane would be foolish to agree to this arrangement. ***How does a company that issues a bond between interest payment dates ensure that the transaction is fair to both parties?***

Answer: The sale of a bond between interest dates is extremely common. Thus, a standard system of aligning the first interest payment with the time that the debt has been outstanding is necessary. Brisbane will have to pay interest for six months on November 1 even though the cash proceeds from the bond have only been held for one month. At that time, the creditor receives interest for an extra five months.

Consequently, such bonds are normally issued for a stated amount plus accrued interest. The accrued interest is measured from the previous payment date and charged to the buyer. Later, when the first interest payment is made, the net effect reflects just the time that the bond has been outstanding. If issued on October 1, Year One, the creditors should pay for the bonds plus five months of accrued interest. Then, when Brisbane makes the first required interest payment on November 1 for six months, the net effect is interest for one month—the period since the date of issuance (six months minus five months).

Assume that the creditors buy these bonds on October 1, Year One, for face value plus accrued interest. Because five months have passed since the previous interest date (May 1), interest accrued on the bond as of the issuance date is \$400,000 × 6 percent × 5/12 year or \$10,000. The creditors pay \$400,000 for the bond and an additional \$10,000 for the accrued interest to that date. Once again, the actual recording can be made in more than one way but the following seems easiest.

FIGURE 14.5 Issued Bond on October 1 at Face Value plus Accrued Interest Recognized for Five Months

Cash	410,000	
Bonds Payable		400,000
Interest Payable		10,000

After one more month passes, Brisbane makes the first interest payment of $12,000. However, interest expense of only $2,000 is actually recognized in the entry below. That is the appropriate amount of interest for one month ($400,000 × 6 percent × 1/12 year) to reflect the period that the bond has been outstanding. Interest of $10,000 for five months was collected initially; interest of $12,000 was paid for the entire six months; interest expense of $2,000 is the net result for that one month.

FIGURE 14.6 November 1, Year One—Payment of First Interest Payment

Interest Payable	10,000	
Interest Expense	2,000	
Cash		12,000

After this entry, the recording continues on following the same manner as the previous example for the note payable.

EXERCISE

Link to multiple-choice question for practice purposes: http://www.quia.com/quiz/2092979.html

KEY TAKEAWAY

Bond and note contracts include numerous terms to define the specific rights of both debtor and creditor. The face value and the payment patterns should be identified in these indentures as well as cash interest amounts and dates. Security agreements and other covenants are also commonly included. For debts that are issued at face value, interest is recorded as it is paid and also at the end of the year to reflect any accrued amount. Bonds are frequently issued between interest dates so an adjustment in the cash price must be made as well as in the recording of the first interest payment.

3. ACCOUNTING FOR ZERO-COUPON BONDS

LEARNING OBJECTIVES

At the end of this section, students should be able to meet the following objectives:

1. **Identify the characteristics of a zero-coupon bond.**
2. **Explain how interest is earned on a zero-coupon bond.**
3. **Understand the method of arriving at an effective interest rate for a bond.**
4. **Calculate the price of a zero-coupon bond and list the variables that affect this computation.**
5. **Prepare journal entries for a zero-coupon bond using the effective rate method.**
6. **Explain the term "compounding."**
7. **Describe the theoretical problems associated with the straight-line method and identify the situation in which this method can still be applied.**

Question: A wide array of bonds and other types of financial instruments can be purchased from parties seeking money. A zero-coupon bond is one that is popular because of its ease. The face value of a zero-coupon bond is paid to the investor after a specified period of time but no other cash payment is made. There is no stated cash interest. Money is received when the bond is issued and money is paid at the end of the term but no other payments are ever made. ***Why does any investor choose to purchase a zero-coupon bond if no interest is paid?***

Answer: No investor would buy a note or bond that did not pay interest. That makes no economic sense. Because zero-coupon bonds are widely issued, some form of interest must be included. These bonds are sold at a discount below face value with the difference serving as interest. If a bond is issued for $37,000 and the company eventually repays the face value of $40,000, the additional $3,000 is interest on the debt. That is the charge paid for the use of the money that was borrowed. The price reduction below face value can be so significant that zero-coupon bonds are sometimes referred to as deep discount bonds.

To illustrate, assume that on January 1, Year One, a company offers a $20,000 two-year **zero-coupon bond** to the public. A single payment of $20,000 will be made to the bondholder on December 31, Year Two. According to the contract, no other cash is to be paid. An investor who wishes to make a 7 percent annual interest rate can mathematically compute the amount to pay to earn exactly that interest. The debtor must then decide whether to accept this offer.

zero-coupon bond

Bonds that include no interest payments although the entire maturity value is due at the end of a specified time; these debts are issued at a discount so that the difference between the cash paid at the beginning and the cash received on the maturity date represents interest over that time period.

Often, the final exchange price for a bond is the result of a serious negotiation process to determine the interest rate to be earned. As an example, the potential investor might offer an amount that equates to interest at an annual rate of 7 percent. The debtor could then counter by suggesting 5 percent with the two parties finally settling on a price that provides an annual interest rate of 6 percent. In the bond market, interest rates are the subject of intense negotiations. After the **effective rate** (also called the yield or negotiated rate) has been established by the parties, the actual price of the bond is simply a mathematical computation.

effective rate

The interest rate determined by negotiation and market forces that is used to set the price of bonds; it is also called the yield rate or negotiated rate and often varies from the stated interest rate used to establish cash interest payments.

Question: A $20,000 zero-coupon bond is being issued by a company. According to the indenture, it comes due in exactly two years. The parties have negotiated an annual interest rate to be earned of 6 percent. ***How is the price to be paid for a bond determined after an effective rate of interest has been established?***

Answer: Determination of the price of a bond is a present value computation in the same manner as that demonstrated previously in the coverage of intangible assets. Here, a single cash payment of $20,000 is to be made by the debtor to the bondholder in two years. The parties have negotiated an annual 6 percent effective interest rate. Thus, a portion of the future cash ($20,000) serves as interest at an annual rate of 6 percent for this period of time. In a present value computation, total interest at the designated rate is calculated and subtracted to leave the present value amount. That is the price of the bond, often referred to as the principal. Interest is computed at 6 percent for two years and removed. The remainder is the amount paid for the bond.

Present Value of $1

http://www.principlesofaccounting.com/ART/fv.pv.tables/pvof1.htm

The present value of $1 in two years at an annual rate of interest of 6 percent is $0.8900. This can be found by table, by formula, or by use of an Excel spreadsheet.[4] Because the actual payment is $20,000 and not $1, the present value of the cash flows from this bond (its price) can be found as follows:

present value = future cash payment × $0.8900

present value = $20,000 × $0.8900

present value = $17,800

Bond prices are often stated as a percentage of face value. Thus, this bond is sold to the investor at "89" ($17,800/$20,000), which indicates that the price is 89 percent of the face value. The price is the future cash payments with the negotiated rate of interest removed. If the investor pays $17,800 today and the debtor returns $20,000 in two years, the extra $2,200 is the interest. And, mathematically, that extra $2,200 is exactly equal to interest at 6 percent per year.

The issuance is recorded through the following entry.[5]

FIGURE 14.7 January 1, Year One—Zero-Coupon Bond Issued at Effective Annual Rate of 6 Percent

Cash	17,800	
Bond Payable		17,800

EXERCISE

Link to multiple-choice question for practice purposes: http://www.quia.com/quiz/2093023.html

Question: This $20,000 zero-coupon bond is issued for $17,800 so that a 6 percent annual interest rate will be earned. As shown in the above journal entry, the bond is initially recorded at this principal amount. Subsequently, two problems must be addressed by the accountant. First, the company will actually have to pay $20,000. The $17,800 principal balance must be raised to that figure. The liability should be reported as $20,000 at the end of Year Two. Second, the $2,200 difference between the amount received and the eventual repayment ($20,000 less $17,800) has to be recognized as interest for these two years. The additional payment is the cost of the debt, the interest. To arrive at fairly presented figures, these two problems must be resolved. ***How is a zero-coupon bond reported in the period after its issuance?***

Answer: In Chapter 11, the effective rate method of reporting a present value figure over time was demonstrated. It solves both of the accounting problems mentioned here. The debt balance is raised gradually to the face value and interest of 6 percent is reported each year over the entire period.

Interest for Year One should be the $17,800 principal balance multiplied by the effective interest rate of 6 percent to arrive at interest expense for the period of $1,068. However, no payment is made. Thus, this interest is compounded—added to the principal. Interest that is recognized but not paid at that time must be compounded.

FIGURE 14.8 December 31, Year One—Interest on Zero-Coupon Bond at 6 Percent Rate[6]

Interest Expense	1,068	
Bond Payable		1,068

The compounding of this interest raises the principal by $1,068 from $17,800 to $18,868. The balances to be reported in the financial statements at the end of Year One are as follows:

Year One—Interest Expense (Income Statement)	$1,068
December 31, Year One—Bond Payable (Balance Sheet)	$18,868

Interest for Year Two is 6 percent of the new liability balance of $18,868 or $1,132 (rounded). The principal is higher in this second year because of the compounding (addition) of the first year interest. If the principal increases, subsequent interest must also go up.

FIGURE 14.9 December 31, Year Two—Interest on Zero-Coupon Bond at 6 Percent Rate

Interest Expense	1,132	
Bond Payable		1,132

Note that the bond payable balance has now been raised to $20,000 as of the date of payment ($17,800 + $1,068 + $1,132). In addition, interest expense of $2,200 ($1,068 + $1,132) has been recognized over the two years. That was exactly 6 percent of the principal in each of the two years. Total interest reported for this zero-coupon bond is equal to the difference between the amount received by the debtor and the face value repaid. Both of the accounting problems have been resolved through use of the effective rate method.

The $17,800 price of the bond was computed mathematically based on

- the cash payment ($20,000),
- the time periods (two),
- the effective rate of interest (the 6 percent negotiated rate),
- the pattern of cash flows (a single payment in the future).

If interest is then recognized each period based on this same set of variables, the resulting numbers will reconcile. Interest expense for the two years has to be $2,200 and the final liability balance must come back to $20,000.

EXERCISE

Link to multiple-choice question for practice purposes: http://www.quia.com/quiz/2093003.html

EXERCISE

Link to multiple-choice question for practice purposes: http://www.quia.com/quiz/2092980.html

Question: This bond was sold at the present value of its future cash flows based on a rate of interest negotiated by the parties involved. Interest was then recognized periodically by applying the effective rate method. ***Is the effective rate method the only acceptable technique that can be used to compute and report interest when the face value of a debt differs from its issue price?***

Answer: Interest can also be calculated for reporting purposes by a simpler approach known as the straight-line method. Using this technique, an equal amount of the discount is assigned to interest each period over the life of the bond. This zero-coupon bond was sold for $2,200 below face value to provide interest to the buyer. Payment will be made in two years. The straight-line method simply recognizes interest of $1,100 per year ($2,200/2 years).

FIGURE 14.10 December 31, Years One and Two—Interest on Zero-Coupon Bond at 6 Percent Rate—Straight-Line Method

Year 1			
	Interest Expense	1,100	
	Bond Payable		1,100
Year 2			
	Interest Expense	1,100	
	Bond Payable		1,100

Once again, the bond payable balance has been raised to $20,000 at the end of the second year ($17,800 + $1,100 + $1,100) and total interest expense over the life of the bond equals the $2,200 discount ($1,100 + $1,100). However, a question should be raised as to whether the information reported under this method is a fairly presented portrait of the events that took place. Although the bond was sold to earn 6 percent annual interest, this rate is not reported for either period.

Year One: $1,100 interest/$17,800 principal = 6.2 percent

Compounding of the interest raises the principal by $1,100 to $18,900

Year Two: $1,100 interest/$18,900 principal = 5.8 percent

In reality, the parties established an annual rate of 6 percent for the entire two-year period. When applying the straight-line method, this actual rate is not shown for either year. Furthermore, the reported interest rate appears to float (6.2 percent to 5.8 percent) as if a different rate was negotiated for each year. That did not happen; there was a single 6 percent interest rate agreed-upon by the debtor and the creditor.

The straight-line method does not reflect the reality of the transaction. However, it can still be applied according to U.S. GAAP but only if the reported results are not materially different from those derived using the effective rate method.

EXERCISE

Link to multiple-choice question for practice purposes: http://www.quia.com/quiz/2093004.html

KEY TAKEAWAY

Zero-coupon bonds pay no cash interest. They are sold at a discount to provide interest to the buyer. The price of the bond is determined by computing the present value of the required cash flows using the effective interest rate negotiated by the two parties. Present value represents the principal of the debt with all future interest mathematically removed. The bond is recorded at this principal. Interest is subsequently determined each period based on the effective rate. Because no cash interest is paid, the entire amount recognized as interest must be compounded (added) to the principal. The straight-line method can also be used to record interest if the resulting numbers are not materially different from the effective rate method. This alternative assigns an equal amount of the discount to interest each period over the bond's life.

4. PRICING AND REPORTING TERM BONDS

LEARNING OBJECTIVES

At the end of this section, students should be able to meet the following objectives:

1. **Understand the difference between a stated cash interest rate in a debt contract and an effective interest rate negotiated by the debtor and creditor.**
2. **Compute the price of a term bond when the stated cash interest rate is different from the effective interest rate.**
3. **Determine the amount of interest to be compounded each period when the stated cash interest rate is different than effective interest rate.**
4. **Prepare all journal entries for a term bond when the stated cash interest rate is different from the effective interest rate.**

Question: Although zero-coupon bonds are popular, notes and most bonds actually do pay a stated rate of cash interest, one that is specified in the contract. If the buyer and the seller negotiate an effective rate of interest that is the same as this stated rate, an amount equal to face value is paid for the bond. If the stated interest to be paid is 7 percent each year and a negotiated annual rate of 7 percent is accepted by the parties, the bond is issued for face value. No discount or premium results; the debtor and creditor are satisfied with the interest being paid. The effective rate method is not needed because the cash interest and the effective interest are the same—7 percent is paid and recognized as interest.

However, the negotiated rate often differs from the cash rate stated in a bond contract. Market interest rate conditions change quickly. The interest that creditors demand will often shift between the printing of the indenture and the actual issuance day. Or the financial reputation of the company might vary during this time. Information travels so quickly in this technology age that news about companies—both good and bad—spreads rapidly throughout the business community.

To illustrate, assume that Smith Corporation decides to issue $1 million in bonds to the public on January 1, Year One. These bonds come due in four years. In the interim, interest at a stated cash rate of 5 percent will be paid each year starting on December 31, Year One. These are term bonds because interest is conveyed periodically by the debtor but the entire face value is not due until the end of the term.

No investors can be found who want to purchase Smith Corporation bonds with only a 5 percent annual return. Therefore, in setting an issuance price, annual interest of 6 percent is negotiated. Possibly, interest offered by other similar companies is 6 percent so that Smith had to match this rate to entice investors to buy its bonds. Or some event has taken place recently that makes Smith seem slightly more risky causing potential creditors to demand a higher rate of return. A list of market conditions that can impact the price of a bond would be almost unlimited. ***How is the price of a bond calculated when the stated cash rate is different from the effective rate that is negotiated by the two parties involved?***

Answer: The pricing of a bond always begins by identifying the cash flows established by the contract. These amounts are set and not affected by the eventual sales price. The debtor is legally obligated to make these payments regardless of whether the bond is sold for $1 or $10 million.

Here, Smith Corporation must pay $50,000 per year in interest ($1 million × 5 percent) for four years and then the $1 million face value:

Cash Flows in Bond Contract
$50,000 annually for four years
$1,000,000 in four years

After the cash flows are identified, the present value of each is calculated at the negotiated rate. These present values are then summed to get the price to be paid for the bond. The $50,000 interest payments form an annuity since equal amounts are paid at equal time intervals. Because this interest is paid at the end of each period starting on December 31, Year One, these payments constitute an ordinary annuity.[7] As determined by table, formula, or Excel spreadsheet, the present value of an ordinary annuity of $1 at an effective annual interest rate of 6 percent over four years is $3.46511.[8] Thus, the present value of the four interest payments is $50,000 times $3.46511 or $173,256 (rounded). Note that the present value computation requires the multiplication of one annuity payment ($50,000) rather than the total of the interest payments ($200,000).

Present Value of an Ordinary Annuity of $1

http://www.principlesofaccounting.com/ART/fv.pv.tables/pvofordinaryannuity.htm

The second part of the cash flows promised by this bond is a single payment of $1 million in four years. The present value of $1 in four years at a 6 percent annual rate is $0.79209 so the present value of the entire $1 million is $792,090.

Present Value of $1

http://www.principlesofaccounting.com/ART/fv.pv.tables/pvof1.htm

The total present value of the cash flows promised by this bond at an annual 6 percent rate for four years is $173,256 (cash interest) plus $792,090 (face value) or $965,346. Smith will receive this amount on January 1, Year One and pays back $50,000 per year for four years followed by a single payment of $1 million. Mathematically, that is equivalent to earning a 6 percent rate of interest each year for four years.

FIGURE 14.11 January 1, Year One—Term Bonds Issued at an Effective Rate of 6 Percent

Cash	965,346	
Bonds Payable		965,346

EXERCISE

Link to multiple-choice question for practice purposes: http://www.quia.com/quiz/2092981.html

Question: The debtor here has the same accounting problems that were discussed in connection with the previous zero-coupon bonds. First, the recorded principal of this term bond must be raised gradually from $965,346 to the $1 million face value over these four years. Second, the cash interest of 5 percent paid each year has to be adjusted to the annual 6 percent effective rate negotiated by the two parties. ***How does a debtor report a bond payable over its life if the stated interest rate and the effective rate differ?***

Answer: At the end of Year One, Smith Corporation pays $50,000 cash interest to the bondholders ($1 million face value × the 5 percent stated rate) as specified in the contract. However, reported interest on this debt must be recognized at the agreed upon rate of 6 percent that led to the initial principal payment of $965,346. The $34,654 discount below face value ($1 million less $965,346) was accepted by Smith (the debtor) as a means of increasing the actual annual rate of return from 5 percent to 6 percent.

The effective rate is reflected in the financial statements by recognizing interest in Year One of $57,921 (rounded), which is the $965,346 principal times 6 percent. The $7,921 difference between the effective interest expense of $57,921 and the cash interest payment of $50,000 will eventually be paid but not until the end of the four-year term when $1 million rather than $965,346 is conveyed to the bondholders. Therefore, at the end of Year One, this extra $7,921 is compounded. Only the portion of this interest that is not being paid is added to the principal. Earlier, with the zero-coupon bond, the entire amount of interest was compounded because no cash interest payment was made.

FIGURE 14.12 December 31, Year One—Payment of Cash Interest at 5 Percent Rate

Interest Expense	50,000	
Cash		50,000

FIGURE 14.13 Compounding Adjustment to Bring Interest to Effective Annual Rate of 6 Percent[9]

Interest Expense	7,921	
Bond Payable		7,921

Interest expense reported on the income statement for Year One of $57,921 ($50,000 + $7,921) equals the 6 percent effective rate times the principal of the debt for that period. The liability reported for the bond payable at the end of Year One has begun to move closer to the $1 million face value. It is now $973,267 ($965,346 + $7,921) as a result of the compounding.

Reported figures for the remaining three years of this bond contract can be computed to verify that the ending balance does grow to $1 million by the time of payment.

FIGURE 14.14 Reported Bond Figures for the Remaining Three Years until Maturity[10]

	Year Two	Year Three	Year Four
Beginning Bond Principal	$973,267	$981,663	$990,563
Effective Rate	6%	6%	6%
Interest Expense (rounded)	58,396	58,900	59,437
Stated Cash Interest	50,000	50,000	50,000
Interest Compounded (added to principal)	8,396	8,900	9,437
Ending Bond Principal	981,663	990,563	1,000,000

Through the use of the effective rate method, interest expense of 6 percent is recognized each period and the principal balance of the liability gradually grows to equal the face value of the bond.

EXERCISE

Link to multiple-choice question for practice purposes: http://www.quia.com/quiz/2093005.html

KEY TAKEAWAY

In the issuance of a term bond, the stated cash interest rate is often different than the effective interest rate negotiated by the creditor and the debtor. To compute the amount to be exchanged for this bond, the cash flows must be determined based on the specifics of the contract and their present value calculated. The resulting total is the amount paid so that the agreed upon rate of interest is earned over the life of the bond. The bond is initially recorded at present value to reflect its principal at that time. Cash interest payments are recorded thereafter and then adjusted based on the effective interest rate. The interest rate stated in the contract times the face value provides the amount of the cash payments. The principal times the effective rate gives the interest to be recognized for the period. The difference in the effective interest and the cash payment is compounded (added to the principal of the debt).

5. ISSUING AND ACCOUNTING FOR SERIAL BONDS

LEARNING OBJECTIVES

At the end of this section, students should be able to meet the following objectives:

1. **Define a serial bond.**
2. **Identify the steps to calculate the price of a bond and provide the proper accounting.**
3. **Record a serial bond over its life.**
4. **Explain the periodic determination of interest for a serial bond and the amount that must be compounded each period.**

Question: The previous section of this chapter looked at term bonds. Interest was paid each period although payment of the face value did not occur until the end of the four-year term. How does this process differ for a serial bond where both interest and a portion of the face value are paid periodically?

To illustrate, assume that Smith Corporation issues a four-year, $1 million serial bond on January 1, Year One, paying a 5 percent stated interest rate at the end of each year on the unpaid face value for the period. The bond contract specifies that $250,000 of the face value is also to be paid annually at the same time as the interest. Smith and the potential investors negotiate for some time and finally agree on a 6 percent annual effective rate. ***What accounting is appropriate for a serial bond?***

Answer: In reporting a term bond, five steps were taken:

1. The cash flows required by the bond contract are listed.
2. The total present value of these cash flows is computed using the effective rate of interest negotiated by the parties. Present value mathematically removes all future interest at the appropriate rate. Only the principal remains. Thus, this resulting figure is the exact amount to be paid so that the agreed-upon interest rate is earned over the life of the bond.
3. The bond is recorded at the principal (present value) amount paid by the investors.
4. The debtor pays interest periodically on the dates indicated in the contract.
5. The effective rate method is applied. Interest to be reported for each period is determined by multiplying the principal balance of the bond by the effective interest rate. The cash interest figure is adjusted to this calculated amount with the difference compounded (added to the principal).[11]

This same process is applied when a serial bond is issued. The sole difference is that additional payments are made periodically to reduce the face value of the debt.

For the Smith Corporation serial bond described above, the following steps are required.

Identify cash flows specified in the bond contract. As a serial bond, Smith is required to pay $250,000 to reduce the face value each year. In addition, the unpaid face value for Year One is $1 million so the 5 percent stated rate necessitates a $50,000 year-end interest payment. Following the first principal payment, the remaining face value is only $750,000 throughout the second year. Thus, the interest payment at the end of that period falls to $37,500 ($750,000 × 5 percent). Based on the contract, the cash flows required by this bond are as follows.

FIGURE 14.15 Cash Payments Required by Bond Contract

Year	Beginning Face Value	Cash Interest Rate	Cash Interest	Principal Payment	Ending Face Value
One	$1,000,000	5%	$50,000	$250,000	$750,000
Two	750,000	5%	37,500	250,000	500,000
Three	500,000	5%	25,000	250,000	250,000
Four	250,000	5%	12,500	250,000	-0-

Determine present value of the cash flows. These required cash flows can be organized in either of two ways.

1. First, they can be viewed as an ordinary annuity of $250,000 per year for four years plus four separate single amounts of $50,000 (one year), $37,500 (two years), $25,000 (three years) and $12,500 (four years).
2. Second, the payments of the face value and interest can be combined for each year so that there are four separate single amounts of $300,000 (one year), $287,500 (two years), $275,000 (three years), and $262,500 (four years).

The same cash flows are being described so the present value of both patterns will be the same $977,714 whichever approach is followed.

Present Value of an Ordinary Annuity of $1

http://www.principlesofaccounting.com/ART/fv.pv.tables/pvofordinaryannuity.htm

Present Value of $1

http://www.principlesofaccounting.com/ART/fv.pv.tables/pvof1.htm

FIGURE 14.16 Computation of Present Value of Serial Bond—First Pattern of Cash Flows

Computation of Present Value of Serial Bond—First Pattern of Cash Flows

Present value of an ordinary annuity of $250,000 at a 6 percent annual interest rate for four years:

$250,000 (for four years) × 3.46511 = $866,278 (rounded)

Present value of four different single amounts at a 6 percent annual interest rate in each of the next four years:

$50,000 (in one year)	× .94340	=	$47,170
$37,500 (in two years)	× .89000	=	33,375
$25,000 (in three years)	× .83962	=	20,990 (rounded)
$12,500 (in four years)	× .79209	=	9,901 (rounded)
Total present value of single payments			$111,436

Total present value of these cash flows: $866,278 for the ordinary annuity plus $111,436 for the four single payments provides a total present value for all required cash flows of $977,714. If these 5 percent $1 million face value bonds are sold for $977,714 and cash payments are made based on the contract terms, interest at an effective rate of 6 percent is being earned over each of these four years.

FIGURE 14.17 Computation of Present Value of Serial Bond—Second Pattern of Cash Flows

Computation of Present Value of Serial Bond—Second Pattern of Cash Flows

Present value of four different single amounts at a 6 percent annual interest rate in each of the next four years:

$300,000 (in one year)	×	.94340	=	$283,020	
$287,500 (in two years)	×	.89000	=	255,875	
$275,000 (in three years)	×	.83962	=	230,895	(rounded)
$262,500 (in four years)	×	.79209	=	207,924	(rounded)
Total present value of cash flows				$977,714	

Record the principal amount received for the bond. Based on this computation, if $977,714 is paid for this four-year $1 million serial bond with an annual stated rate of 5 percent, the effective rate being earned by these cash flows will be 6 percent per year. Accepting a discount of this amount increases the effective rate of interest from 5 percent to exactly 6 percent. The issuance of the bond is recorded through the following journal entry.

FIGURE 14.18 January 1, Year One—Issuance of $1 Million Serial Bonds Paying 5 Percent Annual Interest with Effective Negotiated Rate of 6 Percent

Cash	977,714	
Bonds Payable		977,714

Payment of stated cash interest at 5 percent annual rate. Because of the terms specified in the contract, interest of $50,000 will be paid at the end of Year One, $37,500 at the end of Year Two, and so on as the face value is also paid. The Year One payment is recorded as follows.

FIGURE 14.19 December 31, Year One—Payment of 5 Percent Interest on Serial Bond

Interest Expense	50,000	
Cash		50,000

This same entry is made each year except that the payments will fall to $37,500, $25,000, and finally $12,500.

Effective rate method is applied to recognize negotiated interest rate. For the first year, the principal balance is the original issuance price of $977,714. The yield rate decided by the two parties was 6 percent so the interest to be recognized is $58,663 (rounded). As shown in the above entry, the cash interest paid is only 5 percent of the face value or $50,000. The extra interest for the period ($8,663) is compounded—added to the principal of the bond payable.

FIGURE 14.20 December 31, Year One—Adjustment of Interest from Cash Rate to Effective Rate

Interest Expense	8,663	
Bonds Payable		8,663

In addition, as a serial bond, the first payment of the face value is made at the end of Year One.

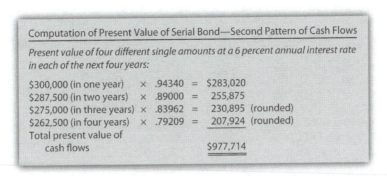

FIGURE 14.21 December 31, Year One—Payment on Face Value of Serial Bond

Bonds Payable	250,000	
Cash		250,000

Whether it is a term bond or a serial bond, the process is the same. All the amounts to be recorded over the four-year life of this bond can be computed to verify that the final payment does remove the debt precisely.

FIGURE 14.22 Balances to be Reported Over the Four-year Life of Serial Bond[12]

	Year One	Year Two	Year Three	Year Four
Beginning Principal Balance	$977,714	$736,377	$493,060	$247,644
Effective Annual Interest Rate	6%	6%	6%	6%
Interest to Be Recognized (principal times effective rate)	58,663	44,183	29,584	14,856
Cash Interest (face value times stated cash rate)	50,000	37,500	25,000	12,500
Compound Interest (difference)	8,663	6,683	4,584	2,356
Face Value Payment	250,000	250,000	250,000	250,000
Ending Principal Balance (beginning balance plus compound interest less face value payment)	736,377	493,060	247,644	-0-

EXERCISE

Link to multiple-choice question for practice purposes: http://www.quia.com/quiz/2093006.html

EXERCISE

Link to multiple-choice question for practice purposes: http://www.quia.com/quiz/2092982.html

KEY TAKEAWAY

The issuance price for bonds can be computed and the subsequent accounting can be outlined in five general steps: determining the cash payments required by the contract, calculating the present value of those cash flows at the negotiated effective rate, recording the bond at this present value amount, recording each periodic cash interest payment, and adjusting the stated cash interest payments to the effective interest rate. A serial bond follows this process although some part of the face value is also paid each period. The principal goes up each period as a result of interest compounding. However, for a serial bond, it also goes down because of the periodic face value payments.

6. BONDS WITH OTHER THAN ANNUAL INTEREST PAYMENTS

LEARNING OBJECTIVES

At the end of this section, students should be able to meet the following objectives:

1. **Realize that interest payments are frequently made more often than annually such as quarterly or semiannually.**
2. **Determine the stated interest rate, the effective interest rate, and the number of time periods to be used in a present value computation when interest payments cover a period of time other than a year.**
3. **Compute the stated cash interest and the effective interest when interest payments are made more frequently than once each year.**
4. **Prepare journal entries for a bond with interest payments made quarterly or semiannually or at some other period shorter than once each year.**

Question: In the previous examples, both the interest rates and payments covered a full year. How is this process affected if interest payments are made at other time intervals such as each quarter or semiannually?

As an illustration, assume that on January 1, Year One, an entity issues bonds with a face value of $500,000 that will come due in six years. Cash interest payments at a 6 percent annual rate are required by the contract but the actual disbursements are made every six months on June 30 and December 31. The debtor and the creditor negotiate an effective interest rate of 8 percent per year. ***How is the price of a bond determined and the debt reported if interest payments occur more often than once each year?***

Answer: None of the five basic steps for issuing and reporting a bond is changed by the frequency of the interest payments. However, both the stated cash rate and the effective rate must be set to agree with the time interval between the payment dates. The number of periods used in the present value computation is also based on the length of this interval.

In this example, interest is paid semiannually so each time period is only six months in length. The stated cash rate to be used for that period is 3 percent or 6/12 of 6 percent. Similarly, the effective interest rate is 4 percent or 6/12 of 8 percent. Both of these interest rates must align with the specific amount of time between payments. Over the six years until maturity, there are twelve of these six-month periods of time.

Thus, the cash flows will be the following:

- *Interest*: $500,000 face value times 3 percent stated rate or $15,000 every six months for twelve periods. Equal payments are made at equal time intervals making this an annuity. Payments are made at the end of each period so it is an ordinary annuity.

Plus

- *Face value*: $500,000 at the end of these same twelve periods. This payment is a single amount.

As indicated, the effective rate to be used in determining the present value of these cash payments is 4 percent per period or 6/12 times 8 percent.

Present Value of $1

http://www.principlesofaccounting.com/ART/fv.pv.tables/pvof1.htm

Present Value of an Ordinary Annuity of $1

http://www.principlesofaccounting.com/ART/fv.pv.tables/pvofordinaryannuity.htm

- The present value of $1 in twelve periods at an effective rate of 4 percent per period is $0.62460.
- The present value of an ordinary annuity of $1 for twelve periods at an effective rate of 4 percent per period is $9.38507.
- The present value of the face value cash payment is $500,000 times $0.62460 or $312,300.

- The present value of the cash interest payments every six months is $15,000 times $9.38507 or $140,776 (rounded).
- Total present value of the cash flows set by this contract is $312,300 plus $140,776 or $453,076. The bond is issued for the present value of $453,076 so that the agreed-upon effective rate of interest (8 percent for a year or 4 percent for each six-month period) is being earned over the entire life of the bond.

FIGURE 14.23 January 1, Year One—Issuance of $500,000 Bond to Yield Effective Rate of 4 Percent Semiannually

Cash	453,076	
Bonds Payable		453,076

On June 30, Year One, the first $15,000 interest payment is made. However, the effective rate of interest for that period is the principal of $453,076 times the six-month negotiated rate of 4 percent or $18,123 (rounded). Therefore, the interest to be compounded for this period is $3,123 ($18,123 interest less $15,000 payment). That is the amount of interest recognized but not paid on this day.

FIGURE 14.24 June 30, Year One—Cash Interest Paid on Bond

Interest Expense	15,000	
Cash		15,000

FIGURE 14.25 June 30, Year One—Interest on Bond Adjusted to Effective Rate

Interest Expense	3,123	
Bonds Payable		3,123

For the second six-months in Year One, the compound interest recorded above raises the bond's principal to $456,199 ($453,076 principal for first six months plus $3,123 in compound interest). Although another $15,000 in cash interest is paid on December 31, Year One, the effective interest for this six-month period is $18,248 (rounded) or $456,199 times 4 percent interest. Compound interest recognized for this second period of time is $3,248 ($18,248 less $15,000).

FIGURE 14.26 December 31, Year One—Cash Interest Paid on Bond

Interest Expense	15,000	
Cash		15,000

FIGURE 14.27 December 31, Year One—Interest on Bond Adjusted to Effective Rate

Interest Expense	3,248	
Bonds Payable		3,248

The Year One income statement will report interest expense of $18,123 for the first six months and $18,248 for the second, giving a total for the year of $36,371.

The December 31, Year One, balance sheet reports the bond payable as a noncurrent liability of $459,447. That is the original principal (present value) of $453,076 plus compound interest of $3,123 (first six months) and $3,248 (second six months).

Once again, interest each period has been adjusted from the cash rate stated in the contract to the effective rate negotiated by the two parties. Here, the annual rates had to be halved because payments were made semiannually. In addition, as a result of the compounding process, the principal balance is moving gradually toward the $500,000 face value that will be paid at the end of the bond term.

EXERCISE

Link to multiple-choice question for practice purposes: http://www.quia.com/quiz/2093024.html

KEY TAKEAWAY

Bonds often pay interest more frequently than once a year. If the stated cash rate and the effective rate differ, present value is still required to arrive at the principal amount to be paid. However, the present value computation must be adjusted to reflect the different pattern of cash flows. The length of time between payments is considered one period. The effective interest rate is then determined for that particular period of time. The number of time periods used in calculating present value is also based on this same definition of a period. The actual accounting and reporting are not affected, merely the method by which the interest rates and the number of periods are calculated.

Talking With a Real Investing Pro—Continued

Following is a continuation of our interview with Kevin G. Burns.

Question: Assume that you are investigating two similar companies because you are thinking about recommending one of them to your clients as an investment possibility. The financial statements look much the same except that one of these companies has an especially low amount of noncurrent liabilities while the other has a noncurrent liability total that seems quite high. Which company are you most likely to recommend?

Kevin Burns: I have done well now for many years by being a conservative investor. My preference is always the company that is debt free or as close to debt free as possible. I do not like leverage, never have. I even paid off my own home mortgage more than ten years ago.

On the other hand, long term liabilities have to be analyzed as they are so very common. Is any of the debt convertible so that it could potentially dilute everyone's ownership in the company? Is the company paying a high stated rate of interest? Why was the debt issued? In other words, how did the company use the money it received? As with virtually every area of a set of financial statements, you have to look behind the numbers to see what is actually happening. If the debt was issued at a low interest rate in order to make a smart acquisition, I am impressed. If the debt has a high interest rate and the money was not well used, that is not attractive to me at all.

Video Clip

Joe talks about the five most important points in Chapter 14.

View the video online at: http://blip.tv/play/sDyBwKhMAA

7. END-OF-CHAPTER EXERCISES

QUESTIONS

1. What are some of the risks for a company of holding debt?
2. What is bankruptcy?
3. Name three advantages of financing with debt.
4. Define "note."
5. Define "bond."
6. How do notes and bonds differ?
7. Define "face value" of a note or bond.
8. What are some of the ways a note or bond repayment can be structured?
9. Define "security."
10. Define "debenture."
11. Why are covenants included in loan agreements?
12. Define "zero coupon" bond.
13. Define "effective interest rate."
14. How do a term bond and a serial bond differ?

TRUE OR FALSE

1. ____ Zero coupon bonds are so named because companies do not record interest expense on them.
2. ____ One advantage of debt financing is that interest is tax deductible.
3. ____ A company's creditors can force it into bankruptcy if it can't pay its debts.
4. ____ Banks typically charge stronger companies higher interest rates than weaker ones because the strong companies can better afford it.
5. ____ Financial leverage refers to a company's ability to pay its debts off early, avoiding interest payments.
6. ____ Debt covenants exist to product the creditor.
7. ____ When a company issues a bond between interest dates, the first interest payment will be lower.
8. ____ Companies must use the effective interest rate method to compute and record interest.
9. ____ A debenture is a debt that is not secured.
10. ____ The maturity value of a bond is amount that the company will need to repay.

MULTIPLE CHOICE

1. Which of the following is ***not*** a type of bond?
   a. Maturity
   b. Zero coupon
   c. Serial
   d. Term
2. Kitten Inc. issued $105,000 in bonds on September 1. The annual interest rate is 6 percent and interest is paid on the bonds every June 30 and December 31. When the bonds are issued on September 1, how much cash will the company collect?
   a. $105,000
   b. $1,050
   c. $106,050
   d. $103,950
3. Which of the following is an agreement which debtors sign as part of getting a loan that serves to protect a creditor?
   a. Security
   b. Term bond
   c. Leverage
   d. Covenant
4. Which of the following is ***not*** a reason companies borrow money?
   a. To raise needed funds
   b. Interest is tax deductible
   c. Creditors have no control over the company
   d. Creditors do not become owners in the company
5. Which of the following refers to an asset a creditor could take from a debtor if the debtor fails to pay back a loan?
   a. Interest
   b. Security
   c. Covenant
   d. Maturity
6. Krystal Corporation issued $100,000 with a 4 percent stated rate of interest on January 1. The effective rate of interest on that date was 6 percent and interest is paid semiannually on June 30 and December 31. The bonds mature ten years from now. What amount would bondholders be willing to pay Krystal on January 1 for the bonds?
   a. $100,000
   b. $85,123
   c. $85,280
   d. $140,000

PROBLEMS

1. Joni Corporation borrows $500,000 from Friendly Bank on February 1, 20X8. The principal will not be repaid until the end of six years, but interest payments are due every February 1 and August 1. The interest rate is 4 percent annually. Record the journal entry necessary for each of the following:
   a. The signing of the loan.
   b. The payment of interest on August 1, 20X8.
   c. The interest accrual on December 31, 20X8.
   d. The payment of interest on February 1, 20X9.
2. Colson Corporation issues bonds to finance an expansion of its hot swimwear line. The $50,000 in bonds is issued on April 1, 20X4 and pay interest in the amount of 5 percent annually. Interest payments are made semiannually, every April 1 and October 1. Record the journal entry necessary for each of the following:
   a. The issuance of the bonds.
   b. The payment of interest on October 1, 20X4.
   c. The interest accrual on December 31, 20X4.
   d. The payment of interest on April 1, 20X4.
3. Assume the same facts as in 2 above, but instead of issuing the bonds on April 1, 20X4, the bonds are issued on July 1, 20X4. Record the journal entry necessary for each of the following.
   a. The issuance of the bonds.
   b. The payment of interest on October 1, 20X4.
   c. The interest accrual on December 31, 20X4.
   d. The payment of interest on April 1, 20X4.
4. Keller Corporation offers a zero-coupon bond of $80,000 on January 1, 20X5. It will come due on December 31, 20X7. Potential bondholders and Keller negotiate an annual interest rate of 7 percent on the bonds.
   a. a.Determine the amount the bondholders would be willing to pay on January 1, 20X5.
   b. Record the issuance of the bonds on January 1, 20X5.
   c. Record the accrual of interest on the bond on December 31, 20X5.
   d. Record the accrual of interest on the bond on December 31, 20X6.
   e. Record the accrual of interest on the bond on December 31, 20X7.
   f. Record the redemption of the bond on December 31, 20X7.
5. Jaguar Corporation issues term bonds with a face value of $300,000 on January 1, 20X1. The bonds have a stated rate of interest of 7 percent and a life of four years. They pay interest annually on December 31. The market value on the date of issuance was 9 percent. Record all necessary journal entries on the following dates.
   a. How much would investors be willing to pay for the bonds on January 1, 20X1?
   b. Determine the amount of each annual cash interest payment.
   c. How much interest expense would Jaguar record for each payment?
6. Collins Company issues term bonds with a face value of $100,000 on May 1, 20X3. The bonds have a stated rate of interest of 4 percent and a life of ten years. They pay interest semiannually on June 30 and December 31. The market value on the date of issuance was 6 percent. Record all necessary journal entries on the following dates:
   a. The issuance of the bonds on May 1, 20X3.
   b. The payment of interest on June 30, 20X3.
   c. The payment of interest on December 31, 20X3.
7. Fitzgerald Corporation issues a $3,000,000 in serial bonds on August 1, 20X2. The terms are as follow:
   - Time to maturity: three years
   - Stated and effective interest rate: 7 percent, paid annually on August 1
   - Principal to be repaid at the end of each year: $1,000,000
   - Determine the journal entries for each of the following dates:

   a. The issuance of the bonds on August 1, 20X2
   b. Accrual of interest expense on December 31, 20X2
   c. Payment of principal and interest on August 1, 20X3
   d. Accrual of interest expense on December 31, 20X3
   e. Payment of principal and interest on August 1, 20X4

f. Accrual of interest expense on December 31, 20X4

g. Payment of principal and interest on August 1, 20X5

8. Chyrsalys Corporation issues $4,000,000 in serial bonds on January 1, 20X5, with a stated interest rate of 3 percent. On this date, investors demand an effective interest rate of 4 percent. The bond terms specify that interest and $2,000,000 in principal will be paid on January 1, 20X6 and 20X7.

    a. What amount would investors be willing to pay for the bonds on January 1, 20X5?

    b. What would interest expense be on December 31, 20X5?

    c. What amount of cash would Chyrsalys pay investors on January 1, 20X6?

    d. What would interest expense be on December 31, 20X6?

    e. What amount of cash would Chyrsalys pay investors on January 1, 20X7?

COMPREHENSIVE PROBLEM

This problem will carry through several chapters, building in difficulty. It allows students to continuously practice skills and knowledge learned in previous chapters.

In Chapter 13, you prepared Webworks statements for January. They are included here as a starting point for February.

Webworks Financial Statements

Webworks
Income Statement
As of January 31

Revenue	$16,000
Cost of Goods Sold	(8,664)
Gross Profit	7,336
Deprec. and Amort. Expense	(363)
Other Expenses and Losses	(3,800)
Investment Income	150
Earning before Tax	3,323
Tax Expense	(1,000)
Net Income	$2,323

Webworks
Stmt. of Retained Earnings
As of January 31

Retained Earnings, January 1	$12,290
Net Income	2,323
Retained Earnings, January 31	$14,613

Webworks
Balance Sheet
January 31

Assets		Liabilities	
Current		**Current**	
Cash	$5,150	Accounts Payable	$2,750
Accounts Receivable	1,600	Salaries Payable	200
Less Allowance for Doubtful Accounts	(160)	Unearned Revenue	450
Net Accounts Receivable	1,440		
Merchandise Inventory	2,423		
Supplies Inventory	40		
Prepaid Rent	400		
Prepaid Advertising	100		
Total Current Assets	$9,553	Total Current Liabilities	$ 3,400
Property, Plant, and Equipment			
Equipment	$7,000		
Less Accumulated Depreciation	(1,022)		
Furniture	1,000		
Less Accumulated Depreciation	(68)		
Total P, P, and E	$6,910		
Other Noncurrent Assets		**Owners' Equity**	
Available for Sale Securities	$1,575	Capital Stock	$2,000
Licensing Agreement, Net	1,800	Retained Earnings	14,613
		Other Accumulated Comprehensive Income:	
		Unrealized Loss on Available for Sale Securities	(175)
		Total Owners' Equity	$16,438
Total Assets	$19,838	Total Liabilities & Owners' Equity	$19,838

The following events occur during February:

a. Webworks starts and completes nine more sites and bills clients for $5,400.

b. Webworks purchases supplies worth $150 on account.

c. At the beginning of February, Webworks had nineteen keyboards costing $117 each and ten flash drives costing $20 each. Webworks uses periodic FIFO to cost its inventory.

d. On account, Webworks purchases seventy keyboards for $118 each and one hundred of the new flash drives for $22 each.

e. On February 1, Webworks borrows $3,000 from Local Area Bank. The loan plus accrued interest will be repaid at the end of two years. The interest rate is 6 percent.

f. Webworks purchases new computer equipment for use in designing Web sites. The equipment costs $5,500 and was paid for in cash.

g. Webworks pays Nancy $800 for her work during the first three weeks of February.

h. Webworks sells seventy-five keyboards for $11,250 and ninety of the new flash drives for $2,700 cash.

i. Webworks collects $5,200 in accounts receivable.

j. Webworks purchases one hundred shares of RST Company for $18 per share in cash. This is considered a trading security.

k. Webworks pays off its salaries payable from January.

l. Webworks is hired to design Web sites for a local photographer and bakery. It is paid $600 in advance.

m. Webworks pays off $11,300 of its accounts payable.

n. Webworks pays Leon a salary of $2,000.

o. Webworks completes the salon Web site and earns the $450 paid in January.

p. RST Company pays Webworks a dividend of $25.

q. Webworks pays taxes of $1,558 in cash.

Required:

A. Prepare journal entries for the above events.

B. Post the journal entries to T-accounts.

C. Prepare an unadjusted trial balance for Webworks for February.

D. Prepare adjusting entries for the following and post them to your T-accounts.

r. Webworks owes Nancy $220 for her work during the last week of February.

s. Leon's parents let him know that Webworks owes $300 toward the electricity bill. Webworks will pay them in March.

t. Webworks determines that it has $70 worth of supplies remaining at the end of January.

u. Prepaid rent should be adjusted for February's portion.

v. Prepaid advertising should be adjusted for February's portion.

w. Webworks is continuing to accrue bad debts at 10 percent of accounts receivable.

x. Webworks continues to depreciate its equipment over four years and its furniture over five years, using the straight-line method. The new equipment will also be depreciated over five years using the straight-line method.

y. The license agreement should be amortized over its one-year life.

z. QRS Company is selling for $12 per share and RST is selling for $16 per share on February 28.

i. Interest should be accrued for February.

ii. Record cost of goods sold.

E. Prepare an adjusted trial balance.

F. Prepare financial statements for February.

ENDNOTES

1. A company can seek protection from its creditors by voluntarily asking the court to allow it to enter bankruptcy. Or, three creditors holding a minimum amount of debt can push a company into bankruptcy, an event known as an involuntary bankruptcy filing.

2. Information on the bankruptcy and subsequent legal reorganization of Delta Air Lines can be found at http://money.cnn.com/2007/04/30/news/companies/delta_bankruptcy/index.htm.

3. The rate for interest on a debt can be identified by any of several terms. Cash rate, stated rate, contract rate, and coupon rate are all examples of the same information: the rate of interest to be paid by the debtor at specified times.

4. As explained in Chapter 11, the present value of $1 can be mathematically determined using the formula $\$1/(1 + i)^n$. Here, i is 0.06 and n is two periods. Present value can also be determined using an Excel spreadsheet. The present value of $1 at 6 percent in two periods is found by typing the following formula into a cell: =PV(.06,2,,1,0).

5. The entry shown here can also be recorded in a slightly different manner. As an alternative, the liability is recorded at its face value of $20,000 with a separate discount of $2,200 also included. The discount serves as a contra account to reduce the net liability balance to its principal amount. Although mechanically different, the liability is still shown as $17,800.

Cash	17,800	
Discount on Bond Payable	2,200	
Bond Payable		20,000

6. If a discount is recorded in the initial entry as is shown in the previous footnote, the credit here is to the Discount account and not directly to the bond payable. The contra account is reduced so the net liability balance increases. Thus, overall reporting of the interest and the liability is not impacted by the method used in recording the issuance of the bond.

7. As mentioned in earlier discussions about intangible assets, an annuity with payments made at the beginning of each period is known as an annuity due. If the interest here had been paid starting on January 1, Year One, the payments would form an annuity due rather than an ordinary annuity. The cash flow pattern for notes and bonds is more likely to be in the form of an ordinary annuity since interest is not typically paid in advance.

8. The mathematical formula to determine the present value of an ordinary annuity of $1 is $(1 - 1/[1 + i]^n)/i$, where i is the appropriate interest rate (6 percent in this illustration) and n is the number of payment periods (four). If using an Excel spreadsheet, the present value of a $1 per period ordinary annuity for four periods at an annual rate of interest of 6 percent can be found by typing the following data into a cell: =PV(.06,4,1,,0).

9. These two entries are often combined. Students should use one entry or two depending on which is easiest to understand.

10. Interest expense for the final year has been increased by $3 so that the final bond payable balance is exactly equal to the $1 million that must be paid. Slight adjustments of this type are common to compensate for numbers having been rounded.

11. The series of steps shown here is also used when a bond is issued at a premium above face value. If the effective rate negotiated by the parties is below the stated cash rate, the amount paid for the bond (the present value) will be above face value rather than below. In effect, the high rate of cash interest makes the bond more valuable. Thereafter, the effective interest recognized each period will be below the cash interest. Adjustment is made to lower the cash interest rate to the effective rate, which also reduces the reported principal balance moving it toward face value. Thus, when the negotiated rate is below the stated cash rate, a premium is created rather than a discount. The subsequent accounting process is not affected except that the increases and decreases are reversed from the examples shown here for a discount.

12. The interest recognized in the final year has been adjusted by $3 to compensate for the rounding of several computations so that the liability balance drops to exactly zero after four years.

CHAPTER 15

In Financial Statements, What Information Is Conveyed about Other Noncurrent Liabilities?

Video Clip

Joe introduces Chapter 15 and speaks about the course in general.

View the video online at: http://blip.tv/play/sDyBwKhKAA

1. ACCOUNTING FOR LEASES

LEARNING OBJECTIVES

At the end of this section, students should be able to meet the following objectives:

1. **Recognize that a lessee can account for a lease as either an operating lease or a capital lease based on the terms of the contract.**
2. **Explain the reason for a lessee to prefer that a lease be reported as an operating lease rather than as a capital lease.**
3. **Understand the concept of off-balance sheet financing especially in connection with the reporting of leases.**
4. **List the four criteria to determine whether a lease contract reflects an operating lease or a capital lease.**
5. **Explain the term "substance over form" and how it applies to the financial reporting of a capital lease.**

Question: Notes and bonds payable serve as the predominant source of reported noncurrent liabilities in the United States. Virtually all companies of any size raise significant sums of money by incurring debts of this type. However, a quick perusal of the financial statements of many well-known companies finds a broad array of other noncurrent liabilities.

- *Sears Holdings Corporation discloses capital lease obligations of approximately $650 million as of January 31, 2009.*
- *Southwest Airlines Co. reports deferred income tax liabilities of over $1.9 billion on December 31, 2008.*
- *The balance sheet for Alcoa Inc. at that same December 31, 2008, date lists a $2.73 billion liability (over 10 percent of the company's total) labeled as "accrued postretirement benefits."*

These other noncurrent liability figures represent large amounts of debts beyond traditional notes and bonds. Some understanding of such balances is necessary in order to comprehend the information being conveyed in a set of financial statements. The reporting of liabilities such as these is explored in great depth in upper-level financial accounting courses. However, a basic level of knowledge is essential for every potential decision maker, not just those few who chose to major in accounting in college.

In this chapter, leases and related liabilities will be explored first. To illustrate, assume that the Abilene Company needs an airplane to use in its daily operations. Rather than buy this asset, an airplane is leased from a business that owns a variety of aircraft. Perhaps Abilene prefers to push the payments off into the future as far as possible. The lease is for seven years at a cost of $100,000 per year. On the day that this lease is signed, should Abilene report a liability and, if so, is the amount the first $100,000 installment, the $700,000 total of all payments, or some other figure? ***How is a liability reported in connection with the lease of an asset?***

lessee

A party that pays cash for the use of an asset in a lease contract.

Answer: For the Abilene Company, the liability balance to be reported here cannot be determined based purely on the information that is provided. When a **lessee** (the party that will make use of the asset) signs an agreement such as this, the lease transaction can be recorded in one of two ways based on the terms of the contract.

- Abilene might be obtaining the use of this airplane through an operating lease, a rental arrangement. If so, the liability to be recognized when the contract is signed is $100,000, only the amount due immediately. Upon payment, reported debt is reduced to zero despite the requirement that six more installments will have to be paid.
- The transaction could also have met the criteria for classification as a capital lease, the equivalent of buying the airplane. In that case, the initial liability recognized by Abilene is the present value of the total $700,000 in cash payments.

EXERCISE

Link to multiple-choice question for practice purposes: http://www.quia.com/quiz/2092984.html

Question: This answer raises a number of immediate questions about lease accounting. Probably the first of these relates to the practical goal of officials who want to produce financial statements that make their company look as healthy and prosperous as possible. A lease agreement might be reported as an **operating lease** *so that only the initial payment is recorded as a liability or as a* **capital lease** *whereby the present value of all payments (a much larger number) is shown as the liability. Officials for the lessee must surely prefer to classify all leases as operating leases if that is possible to reduce the reported debt total.* ***In financial reporting for a lessee, is there not a bias to report operating leases rather than capital leases?*** *This desire has to impact the method by which transactions are constructed.*

operating lease

A rental agreement where the benefits and risks of ownership are not conveyed from the lessor to the lessee.

capital lease

A rental agreement where the benefits and risks of ownership are conveyed from the lessor to the lessee; for accounting purposes, it exists when one of four established criteria are met.

Answer: The answer to this question is obviously "Yes." If a choice exists between reporting a larger liability (capital lease) or a smaller one (operating lease), officials for the lessee are inclined to take whatever measures are necessary to classify each contract as an operating lease. Financial accounting should report events and not influence them. However, at times, authoritative reporting standards impact the method by which events are structured.

Although Abilene Company is bound by the agreement to pay a much larger amount, only the $100,000 balance due at the time the contract is signed is reported as a liability if usage of the airplane is obtained through an operating lease. The term "**off-balance sheet financing**" is commonly used when a company is obligated for an amount of money that is larger than the reported debt. Operating leases are one of the primary examples of "off-balance sheet financing."

off-balance sheet financing

Description used when an entity is obligated for an amount of money that is larger than the amount reported on its balance sheet; for a lessee, an operating lease provides a common example of off-balance sheet financing.

For example, as mentioned at the start of this chapter, Sears Holdings Corporation reports a noncurrent liability of about $650 million in connection with its capital leases. As the notes to those financial statements explain, the company has also signed many other operating leases (for the use of stores, office facilities, warehouses, computers and transportation equipment) that will actually require payment of over $6 billion in the next few years. The debt for that additional $6 billion is "off the balance sheet;" it is not included in the liability section of the company's balance sheet. In accounting for an operating lease, the reported liability balance does not reflect the cash obligation, just the current amount that is due.

EXERCISE

Link to multiple-choice question for practice purposes: http://www.quia.com/quiz/2092985.html

Question: For a lessee, a radical reporting difference exists between operating leases and capital leases. Company officials prefer operating leases so that the amount of reported liabilities is lower. ***What is the distinction between an operating lease and a capital lease?***

Answer: In form, all lease agreements are rental arrangements. One party (the lessor) owns legal title to property while the other (the lessee) rents the use of that property for a specified period of time. However, in substance, a lease agreement may go beyond a pure rental agreement. Financial accounting has long held that a fairly presented portrait of an entity's financial operations and economic health can only be achieved by looking past the form of a transaction in order to report the actual substance of what is taking place. "Substance over form" is a mantra often heard in financial accounting.

Over thirty years ago, FASB issued its *Statement 13*, "Accounting for Leases," to provide authoritative guidance for the financial reporting of leases. In paragraph 60 of that pronouncement, FASB states that "a lease that transfers substantially all of the benefits and risks incident to the ownership of property should be accounted for as the acquisition of an asset and the incurrence of an obligation by the lessee." In substance, the lessee can obtain such a significant stake in leased property that the transaction more resembles a purchase than it does a rental. When the transaction is more like a purchase, it is accounted for as a capital lease. When the transaction is more like a rental, it is accounted for as an operating lease.

- *Capital lease.* Lessee gains substantially all the benefits and risks of ownership. The transaction is reported as a purchase although the legal form is still that of a lease arrangement.
- *Operating lease.* Lessee does not obtain substantially all the benefits and risks of ownership. The transaction is reported as a rental arrangement.

EXERCISE

Link to multiple-choice question for practice purposes: http://www.quia.com/quiz/2093029.html

Question: A capital lease is accounted for as a purchase because it so closely resembles the acquisition of the asset. An operating lease is less like a purchase and more like a rent. The lessee normally prefers to report such transactions as operating leases to reduce the amount of liabilities shown on its balance sheet. ***How does an accountant determine whether a contract qualifies as a capital lease or an operating lease?***

Answer: In establishing reporting guidelines in this area, FASB created four specific criteria to serve as the line of demarcation between the two types of leases. Such rules set a standard that all companies must follow. If any one of these criteria is met, the lease is automatically recorded by the lessee as a capital lease. Both the asset and liability are reported as if an actual purchase took place. Not surprisingly, accountants study these criteria carefully to determine how the rules can be avoided so that each new contract is viewed as an operating lease.

Note in each of these criteria the rationale for classifying the transaction as a capital lease.

lessor

A party that receives cash for granting use of owned property in a lease contract.

1. The lease contract specifies that title to the property will be conveyed to the lessee by the end of the lease term. If legal ownership is to be transferred from **lessor** to lessee, the entire series of payments is simply a method devised to purchase the asset. In substance, the agreement was never intended to be a rental. From the beginning, the property was being acquired.
2. The lease contract allows the lessee to buy the property at a specified time at an amount sufficiently below its expected fair value so that purchase is reasonably assured. The availability of this bargain purchase option indicates, once again, that the true intention of the contract is the conveyance of ownership. The transaction is the equivalent of a purchase if the option price is so low that purchase by the lessee can be anticipated.
3. The lease contract is for a term that is equal to 75 percent or more of the estimated life of the property. This criterion is different from the first two where the transaction was just a disguised purchased. Here, the lessee will never gain ownership. However, the lease is for such an extensive portion of the asset's life that the lessee obtains a vast majority of its utility. Although the 75 percent standard is an arbitrary benchmark, no doubt can exist that the lessee will be the primary beneficiary of the value of the property.
4. The fourth criterion is too complicated to cover in an introductory textbook. The general idea is that the lessee is paying approximately the same amount as would have been charged just to buy the asset. Paying the equivalent of the purchase price (or close to it) indicates that no real difference exists between the nature of the lease transaction and an acquisition.

EXERCISE

Link to multiple-choice question for practice purposes: http://www.quia.com/quiz/2093008.html

KEY TAKEAWAY

A lessee must account for a lease contract as either an operating lease or a capital lease depending on the specific terms of the agreement. Officials working for the lessee are likely to prefer designation as an operating lease because a smaller liability will be reported. Operating leases are common examples of off-balance sheet financing because a significant portion of the contractual payments are not reported as liabilities on the balance sheet. In contrast, for a capital lease, the present value of all future cash flows must be included as a liability. To differentiate operating leases from capital leases, four criteria have been established by FASB. If any one of these criteria is met, the lessee accounts for the transaction as a capital lease. Thus, although a lease in form, the contract is viewed as a purchase in substance and reported in that manner.

2. OPERATING LEASES VERSUS CAPITAL LEASES

LEARNING OBJECTIVES

At the end of this section, students should be able to meet the following objectives:

1. **Account for an operating lease, realizing that the only liability to be reported are amounts that are currently due.**
2. **Understand that the only asset reported in connection with an operating lease is prepaid rent if payments are made in advance.**
3. **Record the initial entry for a capital lease with both the asset and the liability calculated at the present value of the future cash flows.**
4. **Explain the interest rate to be used by the lessee in determining the present value of a capital lease and the amount of interest expense to be recognized each period.**
5. **Determine and recognize the depreciation of a leased asset.**

Question: The Abilene Company has agreed to pay $100,000 per year for seven years to lease an airplane. Assume that legal title will not be exchanged and no purchase option is mentioned in the contract. Further assume that the life of the plane is judged to be ten years and that the amount to be paid does not approximate the fair value of the item. The contract is signed on December 31, Year One, with the first annual payment made immediately. This agreement does not appear to meet any of the four criteria for a capital lease. ***What financial accounting is appropriate for an operating lease?***

Answer: None of the four criteria for a capital lease is being met in this transaction:

1. Legal ownership is not conveyed to the lessee.
2. No bargain purchase option is included in the contract.
3. The life of the lease is less than 75 percent of the life of asset (7 years/10 years or 70 percent).
4. Payments do not approximate the acquisition value of the asset.

Thus, this lease is recorded as an operating lease. The first annual payment was made immediately to cover the subsequent year.

FIGURE 15.1 December 31, Year One—Payment of First Installment of Operating Lease

Prepaid Rent	100,000	
Cash		100,000

Because the first payment has been made, no liability is reported on Abilene's balance sheet although the contract specifies that an additional $600,000 in payments will be required over the subsequent six years. In addition, the airplane itself is not shown as an asset by the lessee because this operating lease is viewed as the equivalent of a rent and not a purchase.

During Year Two, the future value provided by the first prepayment gradually becomes a past value because of the passage of time. The asset balance is reclassified as an expense. At the end of that period, the second payment will also be made.

FIGURE 15.2 December 31, Year Two—Adjustment to Record Rent Expense for Year Two

Rent Expense	100,000	
Prepaid Rent		100,000

FIGURE 15.3 December 31, Year Two—Payment of Second Installment of Operating Lease

Prepaid Rent	100,000	
Cash		100,000

Question: One slight change can move this contract from an operating lease to a capital lease. Assume all the information remains the same in the above example except that the airplane has an expected life of only nine years rather than ten. With that alteration, the life of the lease is 77.8 percent of the life of the asset (seven years out of nine years). That is 75 percent or more of the life of the asset. Because one of the criteria is now met, this contract must be viewed as a capital lease. The change in that one estimation creates a major impact on the reporting process. ***How is a capital lease reported by the lessee?***

Answer: As a capital lease, the transaction is reported in the same manner as a purchase. Abilene has agreed to pay $100,000 per year for seven years but no part of this amount is specifically identified as interest. According to U.S. GAAP, if a reasonable rate of interest is not explicitly paid each period, a present value computation is required to divide the contractual payments between principal (the amount paid for the airplane) and interest (the amount paid to extend payment over this seven-year period). This handling is appropriate for an actual purchase when payments are made over time but also for a capital lease.

Before the lessee starts computing the present value of the future cash flows, one issue must be resolved: the appropriate rate of interest to be applied. In the previous chapter, a negotiated rate was established by the buyer and seller of a bond prior to its issuance. Normally, no such bargained rate exists in connection with a lease. Therefore, the lessee uses its own incremental borrowing rate. That is the interest rate the lessee would be forced to pay if this same amount of money was borrowed from a bank or other lending institution.[1] Assume here that the incremental borrowing rate for Abilene is 10 percent per year. If the company had signed a loan to buy this airplane instead of lease it, the annual interest rate demanded by the lender is assumed to be 10 percent.

Abilene will pay $100,000 annually over these seven years. Because the first payment is made immediately, these payments form an annuity due. As always, the present value calculation computes the interest at the appropriate rate and then removes it to leave the principal: the amount paid for the airplane. Once again, present value can be found by table, by formula, or by Excel spreadsheet.[2]

Present Value of an Annuity Due of $1

http://www.principlesofaccounting.com/ART/fv.pv.tables/pvforannuitydue.htm

Present value of an annuity due of $1 per year for seven years at a 10 percent annual interest rate is $5.35526. The present value of seven payments of $100,000 is $535,526.

$$\text{present value} = \$100{,}000 \times 5.35526$$

$$\text{present value} = \$535{,}526$$

Once present value has been determined, the recording of the capital lease can proceed very much like a purchase made by signing a long-term liability.

FIGURE 15.4 December 31, Year One—Capital Lease Recorded at Present Value

Leased Airplane	535,526	
Lease Liability		535,526

FIGURE 15.5 December 31, Year One—Initial Payment on Capital Lease

Lease Liability	100,000	
Cash		100,000

A comparison at this point between the reporting of an operating lease and a capital lease is striking. The differences are not inconsequential. For the lessee, good reasons exist for seeking an operating lease rather than a capital lease.

FIGURE 15.6 Comparison of Reported Amounts for Operating Lease and for Capital Lease

	Operating Lease	Capital Lease
December 31, Year One		
Asset	Prepaid Rent—$100,000	Leased Airplane—$535,526
Liability (first payment made immediately)	Liability—0	Lease Liability—$435,526

EXERCISE

Link to multiple-choice question for practice purposes: http://www.quia.com/quiz/2092986.html

Question: In a capital lease, the property is not bought but is accounted for as if it had been purchased. Abilene records both the leased airplane and the liability at the present value of the required cash payments. ***What reporting takes place subsequent to the initial recording of a capital lease transaction?***

Answer: As with any purchase of an asset having a finite life where payments extend into the future, the cost of the asset is depreciated and interest is recognized in connection with the liability. This process remains the same whether the asset is bought or obtained by a capital lease.

Depreciation. The airplane will be used by Abilene for the seven-year life of the lease. The recorded cost of the asset is depreciated over this period to match the expense recognition with the revenue that the airplane helps to generate. If the straight-line method is applied, annual depreciation is $76,504 (rounded) or $535,526/7 years.

Interest. The principal of the lease liability during Year Two is $435,526. That is the initial $535,526 present value less the first payment of $100,000. The annual interest rate used in determining the present value was 10 percent so interest expense of $43,553 (rounded) is recognized for this period of time—the principal of $435,526 times this 10 percent annual rate. As in Chapter 14, the effective rate method is applied here. Both the asset and liability are reported as if the asset had been bought for these payments. That is the fundamental idea of a capital lease.

FIGURE 15.7 December 31, Year Two—Depreciation of Airplane Obtained in Capital Lease

Depreciation Expense	76,504	
Accumulated Depreciation		76,504

FIGURE 15.8 December 31, Year Two—Interest on Lease Liability from Capital Lease

Interest Expense	43,553	
Lease Liability		43,553

FIGURE 15.9 December 31, Year Two—Second Payment on Capital Lease

Lease Liability	100,000	
Cash		100,000

EXERCISE

Link to multiple-choice question for practice purposes: http://www.quia.com/quiz/2093031.html

Talking with an Independent Auditor about International Financial Reporting Standards

Following is a continuation of our interview with Robert A. Vallejo, partner with the accounting firm PricewaterhouseCoopers.

Question: In U.S. GAAP, if a lease arrangement meets any one of four criteria, the transaction is reported as a capital lease. Companies often design transactions to either avoid or meet these criteria based on the desired method of accounting. Do IFRS requirements utilize the same set of criteria to determine whether a capital lease or an operating lease has been created?

Rob Vallejo: A lease contact may well be classified differently under IFRS than under U.S. GAAP. This is an example of where U.S. GAAP has rules and IFRS has principles. Under U.S. GAAP, guidance is very specific based on the four rigid criteria established by FASB. However, under IFRS, the guidance focuses on the substance of the transaction and there are no quantitative breakpoints or bright lines to apply. For example, there is no definitive rule such as the "75 percent of the asset's life" criterion found in U.S. GAAP. IFRS simply asks the question: have substantially all the risks and rewards of ownership been transferred? Therefore, this difference could be significant to those organizations that have designed their leases to fit into a certain category under U.S. GAAP. More of these contacts will probably be accounted for as capital leases (which are referred to as finance leases in IFRS). This issue could be resolved in the near term, as FASB and IASB are conducting a joint project to modify their respective standards by 2011.

KEY TAKEAWAY

Operating leases record amounts as they come due and are paid. Therefore, the only reported asset is a prepaid rent and the liability is the current amount due. In contrast, for a capital lease, the present value of the future cash payments is determined using the incremental borrowing rate of the lessee. That amount is recorded as both the leased asset and the lease liability. The asset is then depreciated over the time that the lessee will make use of it while interest expense is recorded (along with periodic payments) in connection with the liability.

3. RECOGNITION OF DEFERRED INCOME TAXES

LEARNING OBJECTIVES

At the end of this section, students should be able to meet the following objectives:

1. **Understand that the recognition of revenues and expenses under U.S. GAAP differs at many critical points from the rules established by the Internal Revenue Code.**
2. **Explain the desire by corporate officials to defer the payment of income taxes.**
3. **Determine the timing for the reporting of a deferred income tax liability and explain the connection to the matching principle.**
4. **Calculate taxable income when the installment sales method is used as well as the related deferred income tax liability.**

Question: At the beginning of this chapter, mention was made that Southwest Airlines reported deferred income taxes at the end of 2008 as a noncurrent liability of $1.9 billion. Such an account balance is not unusual. The Kroger Co. listed a similar $384 million debt on its January 31, 2009, balance sheet. At approximately the same time, Ford Motor Company reported a $614 million **deferred tax liability** *for its automotive business and another $3.28 billion for its financial services division. What is the meaning of these accounts?* ***How is a deferred income tax liability created?***

deferred tax liability

A balance sheet account indicating a smaller current payment of income taxes but with a higher amount due in the future; taxable income will be higher than book income in the future, which necessitates the reporting of the liability.

Answer: The reporting of deferred income tax liabilities is, indeed, quite prevalent. One survey in 2007 found that approximately 70 percent of businesses included a deferred tax balance within their noncurrent liabilities.[3] Decision makers need to have a basic understanding of any account that is so commonly encountered in a set of financial statements.

In the discussion of LIFO presented in Chapter 9, the point was made that financial accounting principles and income tax rules are not identical. In the United States, financial information is presented based on the requirements of U.S. GAAP while income tax figures are determined according to the Internal Revenue Code. At many places, these two sets of guidelines converge. For example, if a grocery store sells a can of tuna fish for $6 in cash, the revenue is $6 on both the reported financial statements and the income tax return. However, at a number of critical junctures, the recognized amounts can be quite different.

Where legal, companies frequently exploit these differences for their own benefit by delaying tax payments. The deferral of income taxes is usually considered a wise business strategy because it allows the company to use its cash for a longer period of time and, hence, generate additional revenues. If an entity makes a 10 percent return on its assets and manages to defer a tax payment of $100 million for one year, the additional profit to be earned is $10 million ($100 million × 10 percent).

Businesses commonly attempt to reduce current taxable income by moving it into the future. In general, this is the likely method used by Southwest, Kroger, and Ford to create their deferred tax liabilities.

- Revenue or a gain might be recognized this year for financial reporting purposes but put off until an upcoming time period for tax purposes. The payment of tax on this income has been pushed to a future year.
- An expense is recognized immediately for tax purposes although it can only be deducted in later years according to financial accounting rules.

In both of these cases, taxable income is reduced in the current period (revenue is moved out or expense is moved in) but increased at a later time (revenue is moved in or expense is moved out). Because a larger tax will have to be paid in the subsequent period, a deferred income tax liability is reported.

Deferred income tax liabilities are easiest to understand conceptually by looking at revenues and gains. Assume that a business reports revenue of $100 on its Year One income statement. Because of certain tax rules and regulations, assume that this amount will not be subject to income taxation until Year Six. The $100 is referred to as a **temporary tax difference**. It is reported for both financial accounting and tax purposes but in two different time periods.

temporary difference

An amount reported as either a revenue or an expense for both financial accounting and income tax purposes but in two different time periods; leads to the recognition of deferred income taxes.

If the effective tax rate is 40 percent, the business records a $40 ($100 × 40 percent) deferred income tax liability on its December 31, Year One, balance sheet. This amount will be paid to the government but not until Year Six when the revenue becomes taxable. The revenue is recognized now according to U.S. GAAP but in a later year for income tax return purposes. Net income is higher in the current year than taxable income, but taxable income will be higher by $100 in the future. Payment of the $40 in income taxes on that $100 difference is delayed until Year Six.

Simply put, a deferred income tax liability[4] is created when an event occurs now that will lead to a higher amount of income tax payment in the future.

EXERCISE

Link to multiple-choice question for practice purposes: http://www.quia.com/quiz/2093032.html

Question: Deferring the payment of an income tax liability does not save a company any money. This process merely delays recognition for tax purposes until a later period. Payment is put off for one or more years. ***If no tax money is saved, why do companies seek to create deferred income tax liabilities?*** *Why not just pay the income tax now and get it over with?*

Answer: As discussed above, delaying the mailing of an income tax check to the government allows a company to make use of its money for a longer period of time. When the cash is paid, it is gone and provides no further benefit to the company. As long as the money is still held, it can be used by management to buy inventory, acquire securities, pay for advertising, invest in research and development activities, and the like. Thus, a common business strategy is to avoid paying taxes for as long as legally possible so that more income can be generated from these funds before they are turned over to the government.

Question: Assume that the Hill Company buys an asset (land, for example) for $150,000. Later, this asset is sold for $250,000 in Year One. The earning process is substantially complete at that point so Hill reports a gain on its Year One income statement of $100,000 ($250,000 less $150,000). Because of the terms of the sales contract, the money will not be collected from the buyer until Year Four (20 percent) and Year Five (80 percent). The buyer is financially strong and expected to pay at the required times. Hill's effective tax rate for this transaction is 30 percent.

Officials for Hill are pleased to recognize the $100,000 gain on this sale in Year One because it makes the company looks better. However, they prefer to wait as long as possible to pay the income tax especially since no cash has yet been collected from the buyer. ***How can the recognition of income be deferred for tax purposes so that a deferred income tax liability is reported?***

Answer: According to U.S. GAAP, this $100,000 gain is recognized in Year One based on accrual accounting. The earning process is substantially complete and the amount to be collected can be reasonably estimated. However, if certain conditions are met, income tax laws permit taxpayers to report such gains using the installment sales method.[5] In simple terms, the installment sales method allows a seller to delay the reporting of a gain until cash is collected. The gain is recognized proportionally based on the amount of cash received. If 20 percent is collected in Year Four, then 20 percent of the gain becomes taxable in that year.

In this illustration, no cash is received in Year One so no taxable income is reported.

FIGURE 15.10 Year One—Comparison of Financial Reporting and Tax Reporting

Year One	Financial Accounting	Income Tax Return
Gain on Sale of Asset	$100,000 (accrual accounting)	0 (installment sales method)

The eventual tax to be paid on the gain will be $30,000 ($100,000 × 30 percent). How is this $30,000 reported in Year One if payment is not required until Years Four and Five?

First, because of the matching principle, an expense of $30,000 is recorded in Year One. As can be seen above, the $100,000 gain is reported on the income statement in that year. Any related expense should be recognized in the same period. That is the basic premise of the matching principle.

Second, the $100,000 gain creates a temporary difference. The amount will become taxable when the cash is collected. At that time, a tax payment of $30,000 is required. Accountants have long debated whether this liability is created when the income is earned or when the payment is to be made. In legal terms, the company does not owe any money to the government until the Year Four and Year Five tax returns are filed. However, U.S. GAAP states that recognition of the gain in Year One creates the need to report the liability. Thus, a deferred income tax liability is also recorded at that time.

Consequently, the following adjusting entry is included at the end of Year One so that both the expense and the liability are properly reported.

FIGURE 15.11 December 31, Year One—Recognition of Deferred Income Tax on Gain

Income Tax Expense—Deferred	30,000	
Deferred Income Tax Liability		30,000

In Year Four, the customer is expected to pay the first 20 percent of the $250,000 sales price ($50,000). If that payment is made at that time, 20 percent of the gain becomes taxable and the related liability comes due. Because $20,000 of the gain (20 percent of the total) is now reported within taxable income, a $6,000 payment ($20,000 gain × 30 percent tax rate) is made to the government, which reduces the deferred income tax liability.

EXERCISE

Link to multiple-choice question for practice purposes: http://www.quia.com/quiz/2092988.html

KEY TAKEAWAY

U.S. GAAP and the Internal Revenue Code are created by separate groups with different goals in mind. Consequently, many differences exist as to amounts and timing of income recognition. Business officials like to use these differences to postpone the payment of income taxes so that the money can remain in use and generate additional profits. Although payment is not made immediately, the matching principle requires the expense to be reported in the same time period as the related revenue. In recognizing this expense, a deferred income tax liability is also created that remains in the financial records until payment is made. One of the most common methods for deferring income tax payments is application of the installment sales method. According to that method, recognition of the profit on a sale is delayed until cash is collected. In the interim, a deferred tax liability is reported to alert decision makers to the eventual payment that will be required.

4. REPORTING POSTRETIREMENT BENEFITS

LEARNING OBJECTIVES

At the end of this section, students should be able to meet the following objectives:

1. **Define the term "postretirement benefits."**
2. **Explain the accounting problems associated with the recognition of accrued postretirement benefits.**
3. **List the steps that are followed to determine a company's reported obligation for postretirement benefits.**
4. **Identify the role of the actuary in accounting for postretirement benefits.**
5. **Calculate the debt-to-equity ratio and explain its meaning.**
6. **Calculate the times interest earned ratio and explain its meaning.**

Question: According to the information at the beginning of this chapter, Alcoa reported a $2.73 billion liability at the end of 2008 for accrued postretirement benefits. ***What constitutes a postretirement benefit?***

Answer: In a note to the Alcoa financial statements, the company explains part of this liability amount as follows:

"Alcoa maintains health care and life insurance benefit plans covering eligible U.S. retired employees and certain retirees from foreign locations. Generally, the medical plans pay a percentage of medical expenses, reduced by deductibles and other coverages. These plans are generally unfunded, except for certain benefits funded through a trust. Life benefits are generally provided by insurance contracts. Alcoa retains the right, subject to existing agreements, to change or eliminate these benefits."

Postretirement benefits cover a broad array of promises that companies make to their employees to boost morale and keep them from seeking other jobs. Alcoa is providing two of the most common: health care insurance and life insurance. Based on stipulations that may be required for eligibility, Alcoa helps employees by paying a portion of their insurance cost even after they have retired. This benefit is apparently earned by working for the company. After a person retires, Alcoa continues to provide these payments as a reward for years of employee service.

Question: Assume that one of the employees for the Michigan Company is currently thirty-four years old and is entitled to retirement benefits starting at the age of sixty-five. Michigan has promised to continue paying health care and life insurance premiums for all retirees as long as they live.[6] *For this employee, no postretirement benefits will be paid for thirty-one years (65 less 34) but then an unknown payment amount will continue for an unknown period of time. In Chapter 2, the challenge presented to accountants as a result of future uncertainty was discussed. Probably no better example can be found than postretirement benefits. For example, if this employee lives to be ninety-four, these insurance payments will continue until sixty years into the future.*

The employee is helping the company generate revenues currently so that, once again, the related expense should be recognized now according to the matching principle. Although this obligation might extend for decades, both the expense and related liability are recorded when the person is actually working for the company and earning these benefits.

How is the amount of this obligation possibly determined? An employee might retire at sixty-five and then die at sixty-six or live to be ninety-nine. Plus, estimating the cost of insurance (especially medical insurance) over several decades into the future seems to be a virtually impossible challenge. The skyrocketing cost of health care is difficult to anticipate months in advance, let alone decades. The dollar amount of the company's obligation for these future costs appears to be a nebulous figure at best. In this textbook, previous liabilities have been contractual or at least subject to a reasonable estimation prior to recognition. ***How is the liability calculated that will be reported by a company for the postretirement benefits promised to its employees?***

Answer: As shown by the Alcoa example, postretirement benefits are estimated and reported according to U.S. GAAP while employees work. Because of the length of time involved and the large number of variables (some of which, such as future health care costs, are quite volatile), a precise determination of this liability is impossible. In fact, it may be the most uncertain number found on any set of financial statements. FASB apparently believes that reporting a dollar amount for postretirement benefits, despite its inexactness, is more helpful than omitting the expense and liability entirely. Decision makers need to understand that these reported balances are no more than approximations.

The actual computation and reporting of postretirement benefits is more complicated than can be covered adequately in an introductory financial accounting textbook. An overview of the basic steps, though, is useful in helping decision makers understand the information that is provided.

actuary

An individual who mathematically computes the likelihood of future events.

To determine the liability to be reported for postretirement benefits that are earned now but only paid after retirement, the Michigan Company takes two primary steps. First, an **actuary** calculates an estimation of the cash amounts that will eventually have to be paid as a result of the terms promised to employees. "An actuary is a business professional who analyzes the financial consequences of risk. Actuaries use mathematics, statistics, and financial theory to study uncertain future events, especially those of concern to insurance and pension programs."[7] In simpler terms, an actuary is an expert who mathematically computes the likelihood of future events.

postretirement benefits

Promises such as pension payments, health care insurance coverage, and life insurance benefits made by employers to eligible employees to be received after they reach a specified retirement age.

For **postretirement benefits**, the actuary has to make a number of estimations such as the average length of the employees' lives and the approximate future costs of health care and life insurance (and any other benefits provided to retirees) based on all available data. For example, an actuary's calculations might indicate that these costs will average $10,000 per year for the twenty years that an employee is expected to live following retirement.

The future payments are estimated by an actuary but they must often be projected decades into the future. Thus, as the second step in this process, the present value of these amounts is calculated to derive the figure to be reported currently on the balance sheet. Once again, as in previous chapters, interest for this period of time is determined mathematically and removed to leave just the principal of the obligation as of the balance sheet date. That is the amount reported within noncurrent liabilities.

Determining Accrued Postretirement Benefits
Step One: Estimate Future Payments
Step Two: Calculate Present Value of Estimated Future Payments

EXERCISE

Link to multiple-choice question for practice purposes: http://www.quia.com/quiz/2093033.html

Question: Alcoa is recognizing an accrued postretirement benefit liability of $2.73 billion. This number is an estimation of the total amount that the company will have to pay starting when each employee retires, a figure that is then subjected to a present value computation. Except for the inherent level of uncertainty, the accounting process seems reasonable. At one time, companies were not required to recognize this obligation. The liability was ignored and costs were simply expensed as paid. Only after advanced computer technology and sophisticated mathematical formulas became available was the reporting of this liability mandated by FASB. ***What is the impact of reporting postretirement benefits if the number is only an approximation?***

Answer: Organizations typically prefer not to report data that appears to weaken the portrait of their economic health and vitality. However, better decisions are made by all parties when more information is readily available. Transparency is a primary goal of financial accounting. Arguments can be made that some part of the problems that automobile and some other businesses currently face are the result of promises that were made over the past few decades where the eventual costs were not properly understood.

As the result of the evolution of U.S. GAAP, decision makers (both inside and outside of the company) can now better see the costs associated with postretirement benefits. Not surprisingly, once disclosed, some companies opted to cut back on the amounts promised to retirees. The note quoted above for Alcoa goes on further to say, "All U.S. salaried and certain hourly employees hired after January 1, 2002, will **not** have postretirement health care benefits. All U.S. salaried and certain hourly employees that retire on or after April 1, 2008, will **not** have postretirement life insurance benefits" (emphasis added).

For the employees directly impacted, these decisions may have been quite alarming. However, by forcing the company to recognize this liability, U.S. GAAP has helped to draw attention to the costs of making such promises.

EXERCISE

Link to multiple-choice question for practice purposes: http://www.quia.com/quiz/2092990.html

Question: In previous chapters, various vital signs have been examined—numbers, ratios, and the like that help decision makers evaluate an entity's financial condition and future prospects. ***In connection with liabilities, do any specific vital signs exist that are frequently relied on to help assess the economic health of a business or other organization?***

Answer: One vital sign that is often studied by decision makers is the **debt-to-equity ratio**. This figure is simply the total liabilities reported by a company divided by total stockholders' equity. The resulting number indicates whether the company gets most of its assets from borrowing and other debt or from its operations and owners. A high debt-to-equity ratio indicates that a company is highly leveraged. As discussed in Chapter 14, that raises the level of risk but also increases the possible profits earned by stockholders. Relying on debt financing makes a company more vulnerable to bankruptcy and other financial problems but also provides owners with the chance for higher financial rewards.

debt-to-equity ratio

A measure of a company's use of debt for financing purposes; it is computed by dividing total liabilities by total stockholders' equity

Recent debt-to-equity ratios shown below for several prominent companies show a wide range of results. No single financing strategy is evident here. The debt-to-equity ratio is not just indicative of a company's selected policy. In some industries, debt levels tend to be higher than in others. Also, individual responses to the recent economic recession might have impacted some companies more than others.

FIGURE 15.12 Recent Debt-to-Equity Ratios for Several Prominent Companies

Company	Debt-to-Equity Ratio
Kellogg Company	6.56 to 1.00 (as of January 3, 2009)
J. C. Penney Company	1.89 to 1.00 (as of January 31, 2009)
Monsanto Company	0.87 to 1.00 (as of August 31, 2008)
The Walt Disney Company	0.93 to 1.00 (as of September 27, 2008)

times interest earned (TIE)

A measure of a company's ability to meet its obligations as they come due; it is computed by taking EBIT (earnings before interest expense and income taxes) and dividing that number by interest expense for the period

Another method to evaluate the potential problem posed by debts is to compute the **times interest earned (TIE)** ratio. Normally, debt only becomes a risk if interest cannot be paid when due. This calculation helps measure how easily a company has been able to meet its interest obligations through current operations.

Times interest earned begins with the company's net income before both interest expense and income taxes are removed (a number commonly referred to as EBIT). Interest expense for the period is then divided into this income figure. For example, if EBIT is $500,000 and interest expense is $100,000, the reporting company earned enough during the year to cover the required interest obligations five times.

FIGURE 15.13 Recent Times Interest Earned for Several Prominent Companies

Company	Times Interest Earned
Kellogg Company	6.3 times (year ended January 3, 2009)
J. C. Penney Company	5.1 times (year ended January 31, 2009)
Monsanto Company	27.6 times (year ended August 31, 2008)
The Walt Disney Company	14.5 times (year ended September 27, 2008)

EXERCISE

Link to multiple-choice question for practice purposes: http://www.quia.com/quiz/2092991.html

KEY TAKEAWAY

Businesses and other organizations often promise benefits (such as medical insurance and life insurance coverage) to eligible employees for the years after they reach retirement age. Determining the related liability poses a significant challenge for accountants because the eventual payment amounts are so uncertain. An actuary uses historical data, computer programs, and statistical models to estimate these amounts. The present value of these projected cash payments is then calculated and recognized as a noncurrent liability. The size of this debt can be quite large but the numbers are no more than approximations. Decision makers often analyze the level of a company's debt by computing the debt-to-equity ratio and the times interest earned ratio. Both of these calculations help decision makers evaluate the risk and possible advantage of the current degree of debt financing.

Talking With a Real Investing Pro—Continued

Following is a continuation of our interview with Kevin G. Burns.

Question: Lease arrangements are quite common in today's business environment. For a capital lease, the present value of the future payments is reported by the lessee as a liability. In contrast, for an operating lease, only the amount currently due is included on the balance sheet as a liability. The reporting of such off-balance sheet financing has been criticized because businesses often go out of their way to create operating leases to minimize the total shown for their debts. However, information about these operating leases must be clearly disclosed in the notes to the financial statements. Are you concerned when you see a company with a lot of off-balance sheet financing? Would you prefer a system where companies had to report more of their debts from leasing arrangements? Do you believe off-balance sheet financing is a problem for the users of financial accounting information?

Kevin Burns: I hate off balance sheet financing. It is trickery in my opinion. As usual, I prefer full or even too much disclosure. A lease is a liability. It should be categorized as such. It is really quite simple—show the liability. Having information in the notes helps but liabilities should be reported on the balance sheet for all to see easily. Anything that reduces transparency is bad for the accounting industry and the people relying on reported financial information.

Video Clip

Joe talks about the five most important points in Chapter 15.

View the video online at: http://blip.tv/play/sDyBwKhHAA

5. END-OF-CHAPTER EXERCISES

QUESTIONS

1. Define "lease."
2. Who are the parties involved in a lease?
3. Name the two types of leases from a lessee's perspective.
4. Define "off-balance sheet financing."
5. Define "capital lease."
6. Define "operating lease."
7. Briefly list the four criteria that require capital lease reporting by a lessee.
8. How many of the four criteria must be met to require capital lease accounting?
9. Define "incremental borrowing rate."
10. Why do deferred tax liabilities exist?
11. Define "deferred tax liability."
12. Define "postretirement benefits."
13. Give two examples of postretirement benefits.
14. How is a company's debt-to-equity ratio calculated?
15. How is a company's times interest earned determined?

TRUE OR FALSE

1. ____ A lessee recording a lease as a capital lease will record depreciation on the leased property.
2. ____ Because taxable income is lower in the current period, a deferral of income recognition is called a deferred tax asset.
3. ____ Postretirement benefits are some of the largest estimates on financial statements.
4. ____ A lease must meet at least two of the criteria set down in Statement of Financial Accounting Standard 13 to be a capital lease.
5. ____ Postretirement benefits are not expensed until they are paid.
6. ____ Lessees usually prefer to record leases as operating leases rather than capital leases.
7. ____ The goals of financial reporting and income tax reporting are not the same.
8. ____ The only postretirement benefit typically paid by companies is pensions.
9. ____ Depreciation and interest are recorded by a lessee under a capital lease, but not an operating lease.
10. ____ Actuaries are business professionals who deal with risk.

MULTIPLE CHOICE

1. Which of the following is ***not*** a criterion that triggers capital lease recording?
   a. Lease covers at least 75 percent of an asset's life.
   b. Lease contains a bargain purchase option.
   c. Payments cover at least 50 percent of the asset's fair value.
   d. Asset transfers to lessee at end of lease.

2. Charlotte Company leases a piece of equipment on February 1. The lease covers two years and the life of the equipment is four years. There is no bargain purchase option, the equipment does not transfer to Charlotte at the end of the lease, and the payments do not approximate the fair value of the equipment. The payments are $4,000 due each February 1, starting with the current one. Charlotte's incremental borrow rate is 5 percent. What journal entry(ies) should Charlotte make on February 1?

Leased Equipment	8,000	
Lease Liability		8,000
Lease Liability	4,000	
Cash		4,000

a.

Prepaid Rent	4,000	
Cash		4,000

b.

Leased Equipment	7,810	
Lease Liability		7,810
Lease Liability	4,000	
Cash		4,000

c.

Rent Expense	4,000	
Cash		4,000

d.

3. Sellers Corporation has assets of $450,000 and liabilities of $200,000. What is Sellers' debt to equity ratio?
   a. 80 to 1.00
   b. 25 to 1.00
   c. 25 to 1.00
   d. 44 to 1.00

4. Which of the following is ***not*** a true statement about postretirement benefits?
   a. A company's liability for postretirement benefits is difficult to estimate.
   b. An expense for an employee's future benefits should be recognized during the period the employee helps generate income (the matching principle).
   c. The liability for postretirement benefits is reported at its present value.
   d. Investors do not pay much attention to the liability for postretirement benefits since it is difficult to estimate.

5. Which of the following concerning deferred tax liabilities are true?
   a. Deferred tax liabilities are created when an event occurs now that leads to lower income tax payments in the future.
   b. Deferred tax liabilities represent money a company will never have to pay in taxes.

c. Deferred tax liabilities arise because of differences in U.S. GAAP and the tax code.
d. Deferred tax liabilities are reported, but deferred tax assets are not reported because of conservatism.

6. Myers Company leases a boat on January 1, 20X9. The lease qualifies as a capital lease. The lease covers four years, with payments of $20,000 annually, beginning on January 1, 20X9. The expected life of the boat is six years. Myers incremental borrowing rate is 4 percent. What amount of depreciation (rounded) should Myers recognize on the boat on December 31, 20X9 if Myers uses the straight-line method?
   a. $18,875
   b. $12,584
   c. $20,000
   d. $13,333
7. Which of the following is true concerning leases?
   a. Lessees would prefer to classify a lease as a capital lease than as an operating lease.
   b. Capital lease liabilities are shown at their present value.
   c. Interest is recorded on both capital and operating leases.
   d. Most capital leases are ordinary annuities.
8. Hyde Corporation has long-term liabilities, such as bonds, notes and leases, for which interest expense must be accrued. During 20X7, Hyde had earnings before interest and taxes of $45,890 and interest expense of $9,920. Which of the following is Hyde's times interest earned?
   a. 28 times
   b. 6 times
   c. 4 times
   d. 63 times
9. Fargo Corporation earns revenue in 20X2 that will be reported on its 20X2 income statement, but will not be reported on its tax return until 20X4. The revenue amounts to $800,000 and Fargo's tax rate is 40 percent. Which of the following is a true statement?
   a. Fargo should report a deferred tax liability of $800,000 in 20X2.
   b. Fargo should not recognize a deferred tax liability until 20X4.
   c. Fargo should report a deferred tax liability of $320,000 in 20X2.
   d. Fargo should never report a deferred tax liability.

PROBLEMS

1. United Company leases an office space in a downtown building. This qualifies as an operating lease. United pays $30,000 in advance for rent every quarter. Record journal entries for United for the following:
    a. United pays $30,000 for the last quarter (three months) of the year on October 1.
    b. Rent expense on October 31.
    c. Rent expense on November 30.
    d. Rent expense on December 31.
2. Ralph Corporation agreed to lease a piece of equipment to Amy Company on January 1, 20X4. The following info relates to the lease:
    - The lease term is five years, at the end of which time the equipment will revert back to Ralph. The life of the equipment is six years.
    - The fair value of the equipment is $500,000.
    - Payments of $115,952 will be due at the beginning of the year, with the first payment due at lease signing.
    - Amy's incremental borrowing rate is 8 percent.

    Prepare the following journal entries for Amy.
    a. Record the capital lease.
    b. Record the first payment on 1/1/X4.
    c. Record depreciation on the equipment on 12/31/X4.
    d. Record interest expense on 12/31/X4.
    e. Record the second payment on 1/1/X5.
3. Landon Corporation has decided to rent crew trucks rather than purchasing them. On April 1, 20X5, Landon enters into an agreement with TuffEnough Trucks to lease three trucks worth $200,000. The lease agreement will span six years and the life of the trucks is estimated to be seven years. Landon's incremental borrowing rate is 6 percent. The payments per year amount to $38,370, payable each April 1, beginning with 20X5.
    a. Record the capital lease.
    b. Record the first payment on 4/1/X5.
    c. Record depreciation on the equipment on 12/31/X5.
    d. Record interest expense on 12/31/X5.
    e. Record the second payment on 4/1/X5.
4. Rollins Company purchased stock in Yuma Corporation for $40,000. Rollins considered this purchase to be a trading security. At the end of the year, Rollin's investment in Yuma yielded an unrealized gain of $8,000. While the $8,000 unrealized gain must be reported on this year's income statement, Rollins will not report the gain on its tax return until the investment in Yuma is sold. If Rollins has a tax rate of 35 percent, prepare the journal entry Rollins should use to record this deferred tax liability.
5. In several past chapters, we have met Heather Miller, who started her own business, Sew Cool. The financial statements for December are shown below.

Sew Cool Financial Statements

Sew Cool
Income Statement
As of December 31, 20X8

Revenue	$4,000
Cost of Goods	(2,000)
Gross Profit	2,000
Other Expenses	(1,665)
Earnings before Interest and Tax	335
Interest Expense	(30)
Earnings before Tax	305
Tax Expense	(107)
Net Income	$198

Sew Cool
Stmt. of Retained Earnings
As of December 31, 20X8

Retained Earnings, December 1, 20X8	$500
Net Income	198
Dividends	(158)
Retained Earnings, December 31, 20X8	$540

Sew Cool
Balance Sheet
December 31, 20X8

Assets		**Liabilities**	
Current		**Current**	
Cash	$940	Accounts Payable	$900
Accounts Receivable	500	Income Tax Payable	120
Less Allowance for Doubtful Accounts	(20)		
Net Accounts Receivable	480		
Inventory	700		
Total Current Assets	$2,120	Total Current Liabilities	$1,020
Noncurrent		**Noncurrent**	
Equipment	$1,000	Notes Payable	$1,060
		Owners' Equity	
		Capital Stock	$500
		Retained Earnings	540
		Total Owners' Equity	$1,040
Total Assets	$3,120	Total Liabilities & Owners' Equity	$3,120

Based on the financial statements determine the following:

a. Debt to equity ratio

b. Times interest earned

6. Lori Company borrowed $10,000 from Secure Bank on January 1, 20X9. The interest rate on the loan is 6 percent annually. Lori also signed a five-year capital lease on January 1, 20X9. The payments are $5,000 each January 1, beginning with the current one. Lori's incremental borrowing rate is 6 percent *and the value of the leased asset is $22,326.*

   a. Determine Lori's 20X9 interest expense.

   b. If Lori's earnings before interest and taxes are $25,710, determine Lori's times interest earned.

7. Myrtle Inc. begins 20X8 with liabilities of $456,000 and owners' equity of $320,000. On the first day of 20X8, the following occur:

   - Myrtle enters into an operating lease where it agrees to pay $50,000 per month for warehouse space.
   - Myrtle borrows $103,000 from Community Bank.
   - Owners' invest an additional $57,000 into the company.

   a. Determine Myrtle's debt-to-equity ratio before the above transactions occur.

   b. Determine Myrtle's debt-to-equity ratio considering the effect of the above transactions.

COMPREHENSIVE PROBLEM

This problem will carry through several chapters, building in difficulty. It allows students to continuously practice skills and knowledge learned in previous chapters.

In Chapter 14, you prepared Webworks statements for February. They are included here as a starting point for March.

Webworks Financial Statements

Webworks
Income Statement
As of February 28

Revenue	$19,800
Cost of Goods Sold	(10,201)
Gross Profit	9,599
Deprec. and Amort. Expense	(455)
Other Expenses and Losses	(3,760)
Investment Income (Loss)	175
Earnings before Interest and Tax	5,209
Interest Expense	(15)
Earnings before Tax	5,194
Tax Expense	(1,558)
Net Income	$3,636

Webworks
Stmt. of Retained Earnings
As of February 28

Retained Earnings, February 1	$14,613
Net Income	3,636
Retained Earnings, February 28	$18,249

Webworks
Balance Sheet
February 28

Assets		**Liabilities**	
Current		**Current**	
Cash	$4,767	Accounts Payable	$2,360
Accounts Receivable	1,800	Salaries Payable	220
Less Allowance for Doubtful Accounts	(180)	Interest Payable	15
		Unearned Revenue	600
Net Accounts Receivable	1,620		
Trading Securities, Net	1,600		
Merchandise Inventory	2,682		
Supplies Inventory	70		
Prepaid Rent	200		
Total Current Assets	$10,939	Total Current Liabilities	$3,195
Property, Plant, and Equipment		**Noncurrent**	
		Note Payable	$3,000
Equipment	$12,500		
Less Accumulated Depreciation	(1,260)		
Furniture	1,000		
Less Accumulated Depreciation	(85)		
Total P, P, and E	$12,155		
Other Noncurrent Assets		**Owners' Equity**	
Available for Sale Securities	$2,100	Capital Stock	$2,000
Licensing Agreement, Net	1,600	Retained Earnings	18,249
		Other Accumulated Comprehensive Income:	
		Unrealized Gain on Available for Sale Securities	(350)
		Total Owners' Equity	$20,599
Total Assets	$26,794	Total Liabilities & Owners' Equity	$26,794

The following events occur during March:

a. Webworks starts and completes seven more sites and bills clients for $5,000.

b. Webworks purchases supplies worth $110 on account.

c. At the beginning of March, Webworks had nineteen keyboards costing $118 each and twenty flash drives costing $22 each. Webworks uses periodic FIFO to cost its inventory.

d. On account, Webworks purchases 80 keyboards for $120 each and 100 flash drives for $23 each.

e. Webworks sells eighty-five keyboards for $12,750 and ninety-two of the flash drives for $2,760 cash.

f. Webworks collects $5,000 in accounts receivable.

g. Webworks pays off $12,000 of its accounts payable.

h. Leon determines that some of his equipment is not being used and sells it. The equipment sold originally cost $2,000 and had accumulated depreciation of $297. Webworks sold the equipment for $1,650 cash.

i. Webworks pays Nancy $750 for her work during the first three weeks of March.

j. Leon and Nancy are having trouble completing all their work now that the business has grown. Leon hires another assistant, Juan. Webworks pays Juan $550 for his help during the first three weeks of March.

k. Webworks writes off an account receivable from December in the amount of $200 because collection appears unlikely.

l. Webworks pays off its salaries payable from March.

m. Webworks pays Leon a salary of $3,500.

n. Webworks completes the design for the bakery, but not the photographer for which it was paid in February. Only $300 of the unearned revenue should be reclassified to revenue.

o. Webworks decides that more space is needed than that which is available in the home of Leon's parents (much to his parents' relief). His parents return the $200 he prepaid for March. Webworks signs a six-month lease in a nearby office building. Webworks will pay $500 at the beginning of each month, starting on March 1. The life of the building is forty years, and no bargain purchase option exists, nor do the payments come close to paying the market value of the space.

p. Webworks pays taxes of $580 in cash.

Required:

A. Prepare journal entries for the above events.

B. Post the journal entries to T-accounts.

C. Prepare an unadjusted trial balance for Webworks for March.

D. Prepare adjusting entries for the following and post them to your T-accounts.

q. Webworks owes Nancy $200 and Juan $150 for their work during the last week of March.

r. Webworks receives an electric bill for $400. Webworks will pay the bill in April.

s. Webworks determines that it has $50 worth of supplies remaining at the end of March.

t. Webworks is continuing to accrue bad debts at 10 percent of accounts receivable.

u. Webworks continues to depreciate its equipment over four years and its furniture over five years, using the straight-line method.

v. The license agreement should be amortized over its one-year life.

w. QRS Company is selling for $13 per share and RST Company is selling for $18 per share on March 31.

x. Interest should be accrued for March.

y. Record cost of goods sold.

E. Prepare an adjusted trial balance.

F. Prepare financial statements for March.

ENDNOTES

1. As explained in upper-level accounting textbooks and courses, under certain circumstances, the lessee might use the implicit interest rate built into the lease contract by the lessor.

2. The mathematical formula to determine the present value of an annuity due of $1 per period is $[(1 - 1/[1 + i]^n)/i] \times (1 + i)$, where i is the appropriate interest rate and n is the number of payment periods. On an Excel spreadsheet, the present value of a $1 per period annuity due for seven periods at an assumed annual interest rate of 10 percent is computed by typing the following data into a cell: =PV(.10,7,1,,1).

3. Yury Iofe, senior editor, and Matthew C. Calderisi, CPA, managing editor, *Accounting Trends & Techniques*, 62nd edition (New York: American Institute of Certified Public Accountants, 2008), 266.

4. Many companies also report deferred income tax assets that arise because of other differences in U.S. GAAP and the Internal Revenue Code. For example, Southwest Airlines included a deferred income tax asset of $365 million on its December 31, 2008, balance sheet. Accounting for such assets is especially complex and will not be covered in this textbook. Some portion of this asset balance, although certainly not all, is likely to be the equivalent of a prepaid income tax where the company was required to make payments by the tax laws in advance of recognition according to U.S. GAAP.

5. The installment sales method can also be used for financial reporting purposes but only under very limited circumstances.

6. Health care and life insurance benefits paid by an employer while an employee is still working do not pose an accounting issue. The amounts are known and can be expensed as incurred. These expenses are matched with the revenues being earned at the current time.

7. http://www.math.purdue.edu/academic/actuary/what.php?p=what.

CHAPTER 16

In a Set of Financial Statements, What Information Is Conveyed about Shareholders' Equity?

Video Clip

Joe introduces Chapter 16 and speaks about the course in general.

View the video online at: http://blip.tv/play/sDyBwKhPAA

1. SELECTING A LEGAL FORM FOR A BUSINESS

LEARNING OBJECTIVES

At the end of this section students should be able to meet the following objectives:

1. **Describe the three primary legal forms available for a business.**
2. **List and discuss the advantages and disadvantages of incorporating a business rather than maintaining a sole proprietorship or partnership.**
3. **Explain the double taxation that is inherent in operating a corporate organization.**
4. **Describe the impact that the possibility of issuing capital stock has on a corporation.**

proprietorship

A business created, owned, and operated by a single individual; business is not legally separated from its owner through incorporation; it is also referred to as a sole proprietorship.

partnership

A business created, owned, and operated by more than one individual; business is not legally separate from its owners through incorporation.

corporation

An organization that has been formally recognized by the state government as a legal entity so that it can sell ownership shares to raise money for capital expenditures and operations; business is legally separated from its owners.

Question: In the United States, businesses and other organizations must operate under one of three legal forms.[1] *A* **proprietorship** *is created by a single owner whereas a* **partnership** *is started and owned by two or more parties. Establishing ownership is often quite informal. In contrast, a* **corporation** *comes into existence by means of a formal request made to the state government. The number of owners is usually not relevant in creating a corporation. Because corporations are the dominant legal form (at least monetarily) in the world, they have been the primary emphasis throughout this text. Numerically, more proprietorships and partnerships do exist but virtually every business of any size operates as a corporation.* ***How is a corporation established, and what characteristics make it attractive?***

Answer: Incorporation of an entity is only required in one state regardless of its size. To start this process, the original owners submit articles of incorporation to that government.[2] Rules, regulations, and requirements vary significantly so that these procedures are more complicated in some states than others. For example, many well-known businesses are incorporated in Delaware because of the ease of the laws in that state.

After all documents have been filed and all other requirements met, the state government issues a corporate charter that recognizes the organization as a legal entity separate from its ownership. This separation of the ownership is what differentiates a corporation from a partnership or proprietorship. Following incorporation in one state, the entity is then allowed to operate in any other state.

As mentioned in a previous chapter, ownership of a corporation is divided into shares of stock that are issued to raise funds. In general, these shares are referred to as capital stock and the owners as shareholders or stockholders. For example, at December 31, 2008, the stockholders of Raytheon Company held approximately 400 million of these shares. Unless restricted contractually, capital stock can be exchanged freely. Once issued by a corporation, shares can be resold dozens or even hundreds of times. Operations are usually unaffected by these ownership changes. Information about the current market price of most stocks as well as a considerable amount of other information can be found at http://www.google.com/finance and http://www.yahoo.com/finance.

Thus, a corporation is able to continue in existence even after owners die or decide to switch to other investments. In partnerships and proprietorships, capital stock does not exist. Consequently, the transfer of an ownership interest is much more complicated. Partnerships and proprietorships often operate only for as long as the original owners are willing and able to continue being actively involved.

As a result of the legal separation of ownership and business, shareholders have no personal liability for the debts of the corporation.[3] An owner of a share of Raytheon is not responsible for any of the liabilities of that company. The maximum loss a shareholder can suffer is the amount contributed to the business (or paid to a previous owner) in acquiring capital stock.

In contrast, the owners of a partnership or proprietorship are personally liable for all business debts. No separation exists between the business and the ownership. A partner or proprietor could invest $1,000 but wind up losing almost any amount if funds are borrowed by the business that cannot be repaid. Such potential losses are especially worrisome in a partnership where each partner serves as an agent for the entire organization. Under the concept of **mutual agency**, any partner can obligate the partnership and, if the debt is not paid when due, the creditor can seek redress from any other partner. The **limited liability** offered by a corporation is one of the primary reasons for its popularity. Investors have a strong preference for being able to quantify the amount of money at risk.

mutual agency

A characteristic of a partnership whereby any partner can obligate other partners to an agreement without their direct consent; does not have a parallel in corporate ownership.

limited liability

A legal characteristic associated with the ownership of a corporation whereby the maximum amount that can be lost is the owner's capital investment; an attribute of the capital stock of a corporation that does not similarly exist with proprietorships or partnerships.

Question: Ownership shares of most corporations can be transferred. Thus, the life of a corporation can extend indefinitely. Caswell-Massey Co., a "purveyor of luxury personal care products," was incorporated in 1752 in Rhode Island and continues to do business today.

Investors are able to move into and out of these investments quickly. In addition, the availability of limited liability restricts potential losses to the amounts invested. These characteristics help explain the immense popularity of the corporate form. However, a significant number of partnerships and proprietorships still come into existence each year. If no problems were possible, incorporation would be the only practical option. ***What disadvantages are associated with corporations?***

Answer: Incorporation is often a time consuming and costly legal process. However, in most states, proprietorships and partnerships can be created informally with little effort. Owners of many small businesses feel that the creation of a corporation is more trouble than it is worth. Furthermore, corporations are often more susceptible to a plethora of government regulations.

The most obvious problem associated with corporations is the **double taxation** of income. As noted, proprietorships and partnerships are not deemed to be entities separate from their owners. Therefore, income is taxed only one time. Owners pay that tax when the income is earned by their business. For a proprietorship, Schedule C is an income statement attached to the owner's individual Form 1040 income tax return to include the business's profit or loss. A partnership does file its own return on Form 1065 but that is merely for information purposes; no income tax is paid. Instead, the various business revenues and expenses are assigned to the partners for inclusion on their individual tax returns. Any eventual conveyance of this income from business to owner does not create a second tax.

double taxation

A negative feature associated with the corporate form of organization; corporate earnings are taxed first when earned and then taxed again when distributed to owners in the form of dividends.

In contrast, corporations are separate legal entities that pay their own taxes by filing Form 1120 to report all taxable income that has been earned.[4] However, when any dividends are eventually distributed from those earnings to the stockholders, this transfer is also viewed as taxable income to the owner. Income is taxed once when earned by the corporation and again when distributed to the owners. Critics have long argued that the collection of the dividend is not a new earning process. To mitigate the impact of this second tax, the United States Congress has established a maximum tax rate of 15 percent on much of the dividend income collected by individuals. This rate is considerably lower than that applied to most other types of income.

To illustrate, assume that income tax rates are 30 percent except for the 15 percent tax on dividends. A proprietorship (or partnership) earns a profit of $100. In this type business, the $100 is only taxable to the owner or owners when earned. Payment of the resulting $30 income tax ($100 × 30 percent) leaves $70. This is the remaining disposal income. Any distribution of this money has no impact on taxes.

If a corporation reports this same amount of income, a tax of $30 is assessed to the business so that only $70 remains. This income can then be conveyed as a dividend. However, another tax must be paid, this time by the stockholder. The second income tax is $10.50 ($70 × 15 percent). The owner is left with only $59.50 ($70.00 less $10.50) in disposal income. The increase in the amount taken by the government ($40.50 versus $30.00 on $100 of taxable income) is significant enough to reduce the inclination of many owners to incorporate their businesses.

EXERCISE

Link to multiple-choice question for practice purposes: http://www.quia.com/quiz/2092983.html

KEY TAKEAWAY

Businesses can exist as corporations, partnerships, or sole proprietorships. A corporation differs from the other two forms because it is an entity legally separate from its ownership. Thus, the liability of owners is limited to the amount of their investments. Corporations are formed according to individual state laws. Shares of the ownership of a corporation (capital stock) are issued to raise money for operations and growth. In many cases, these shares can be readily sold by one owner to the next, often on a stock exchange. The ability to buy and sell capital shares enables a corporation to raise funds and have a continuous life. Disadvantages associated with the corporate form include the cost and difficulty of incorporation and government regulation. The double taxation of corporate income (which is not found with partnerships and sole proprietorships) is often the biggest drawback to incorporation.

2. THE ISSUANCE OF COMMON STOCK

LEARNING OBJECTIVES

At the end of this section students should be able to meet the following objectives:

1. **Identify the rights normally held by the owners of common stock.**
2. **Describe the responsibilities of a corporation's board of directors.**
3. **Define and explain the terms "authorized," "outstanding," "issued," and "par value" in relationship to common stock.**
4. **Record the issuance of common stock for cash.**
5. **Record the issuance of common stock for a service or for an asset other than cash.**

Question: Several accounts frequently appear in the shareholders' equity section of a balance sheet reported by a corporation. Each has its own particular meaning. For example, as of January 3, 2009, Kellogg Company reported the following information (all numbers in millions).

FIGURE 16.1 Shareholders' Equity—Kellogg Company as of January 3, 2009

Common stock, $.25 par value, 1,000,000,000 shares authorized; Issued: 418,842,707 in 2008	$105
Capital in excess of par value	438
Retained earnings	4,836
Treasury stock at cost; 36,981,580 shares in 2008	(1,790)
Accumulated other comprehensive income (loss)	(2,141)
Total shareholders' equity	$1,448

Some of these terms have been examined previously, others have not. For example, retained earnings was described in early chapters as the increase in net assets generated by net income over the life of a company less any amounts distributed as dividends during that same period. In Chapter 12, "accumulated other comprehensive income" was discussed because it was utilized to record changes in the fair value of available-for-sale securities. Gains and losses in the worth of these investments were not included within net income. Rather, they were reported under this heading within stockholders' equity and subsequently used in computing comprehensive income.

Common stock *has also been mentioned in connection with the capital contributed to a company by its owners. However, Kellogg communicates additional information about its common stock such as the number of authorized and issued shares as well as its par value.* ***What is common stock?*** *That seems the logical first step in analyzing the information provided by a company about its capital shares.*

common stock

A type of capital stock that is issued by every corporation; it provides rights to the owner that are specified by the laws of the state in which the organization is incorporated.

Answer: Common stock represents the basic ownership of a corporation. One survey in 2007 found that common stock is the only type of capital stock issued by approximately 90 percent of corporations.[5] Obtaining ownership of a company's common stock provides several distinct rights. However, the specific rights are set by the laws of the state of incorporation and do vary a bit from state to state.[6]

2.1 Typical Corporate Ownership Structure

- Based on state laws and the corporation's own rules, the owners of common stock are allowed to vote on a few specified issues. By far the most prevalent is the election of the board of directors. As mentioned in Chapter 1, these individuals represent the ownership of the corporation in overseeing the management. The **board of directors** meets periodically (annually, quarterly, or as necessary) to review operating results and the future plans created by management. The board provides guidance and changes where necessary. A list of the individuals (often ten to twenty-five) who serve in this capacity is usually included in a corporation's annual report, often just after its financial statements.
- The responsibilities of the board of directors can vary rather significantly from company to company. Some boards do little whereas others are heavily involved in strategy and policy making. For example, a note to the financial statements of Starbucks Corporation explained that the "Company may repurchase shares of its common stock under a program authorized by its Board of Directors." Apparently, approval of that particular program fell within the designated responsibilities of the Starbucks board.
- One of the most important decisions for any board of directors is the declaration of dividends. Management typically cannot pay dividends to shareholders without specific approval by the board. Dividends cause the company (and specifically its cash balances) to get smaller so careful consideration of the impact must be made before declaration is approved. Stockholders like to receive dividends but do not want the company's future to be imperiled as the size shrinks.
- If dividends are paid on common stock, all the owners share proportionally. Although dividends are never guaranteed, the owners must be treated fairly if dividends are distributed. An owner who holds 12 percent of the outstanding common stock is entitled to 12 percent of any dividends paid on common stock. The board of directors cannot reward some of the common shareholders while ignoring others.
- Should the company ever be liquidated, the common stock shareholders are entitled to share proportionally in any assets that remain after all liabilities and other claims are settled. Unfortunately, most liquidations result from a severe financial crisis so that holding any assets at the end of the process is rare.

board of directors

A group that oversees the management of a corporation; the members are voted to this position by stockholders; it hires the management to run the company on a daily basis and then meets periodically to review operating and financing results and also approve policy and strategy.

Question: "Authorized," "issued," and "par value" are terms mentioned by the Kellogg Company in describing its ownership shares. ***What terms are associated with capital stock and what do they mean?***

Answer:

Authorized. In applying to the state government as part of the initial incorporation process, company officials indicate the maximum number of capital shares they want to be able to issue. This approved limit is the authorized total. Corporations often set this figure so high that they never have to worry about reaching it. However, states do allow the authorization to be raised if necessary.

Issued. The number of issued shares is simply the quantity that has been sold or otherwise conveyed to owners. Kellogg reports that one billion shares of common stock were authorized by the state of Delaware but only about 419 million have actually been issued to stockholders as of the balance sheet date. The remaining unissued shares are still available if the company needs to raise money by selling additional capital stock.

authorized shares

The maximum number of shares that a corporation can issue based on the articles of incorporation approved by the state government at the time of incorporation.

issued shares

The number of shares of a corporation that have been sold or conveyed to owners.

outstanding shares

The number of shares of a corporation that are currently in the hands of the public; it is the shares that have been issued since operations first began less any treasury shares repurchased and still held by the corporation.

par value

A number printed on a stock certificate to indicate the minimum amount of money owners must legally leave in the business; generally set at a low amount to avoid legal complications.

Outstanding. The total amount of stock currently in the hands of the public is referred to as the shares "outstanding." Shares are sometimes bought back from stockholders and recorded as treasury stock. Thus, originally issued shares are not always still outstanding. According to the information provided, Kellogg has acquired nearly thirty-seven million treasury shares. Although not mentioned directly, Kellogg now has only 382 million shares of common stock outstanding in the hands of the stockholders (419 million issued less 37 million treasury shares). This number is important because it serves as the basis for dividend payments as well as any votes taken of the stockholders.

Par value. The most mysterious term on a set of financial statements might well be "par value." The requirement for a par value to be set was created decades ago in connection with the issuance of stock. It is printed on the face of a stock certificate and indicates (again depending on state law) the minimum amount of money that owners must legally leave in the business. By requiring a par value to be specified on the stock certificate, state lawmakers hoped to prevent a corporation from borrowing money that was then distributed to a few owners before bankruptcy was declared.

Traditionally, companies have gotten around this limitation by setting the par value at an extremely low number.[7] For example, Kellogg discloses a par value of $0.25 for its common stock, which is actually quite high. Many companies report par values that fall between a penny and a nickel. The balance sheet for Barnes & Noble Inc. shows a par value for its common stock of one-tenth of a penny.

EXERCISE

Link to multiple-choice question for practice purposes: http://www.quia.com/quiz/2093025.html

Question: Over the years, one residual effect from the requirement to include a par value on stock certificates has remained. This figure is still used in reporting the issuance of capital stock. Thus, if Kellogg sells one share for cash of $46.00 (the approximate value on the New York Stock Exchange during the summer of 2009), the common stock account is increased but only by the $0.25 par value. Kellogg receives $46.00 but the par value is only $0.25. How can this journal entry balance? ***How does a company report the issuance of a share of common stock for more than par value?***

Answer: A potential stockholder contributes assets to a company in order to obtain an ownership interest. In accounting, this conveyance is not viewed as an exchange. It is fundamentally different than selling inventory or a piece of land to an outside party. Instead, the contribution of monetary capital is an expansion of both the company and its ownership. As a result, no gain, loss, or other income effect is ever reported by an organization as a result of transactions occurring in its own stock. An investor is merely transferring assets to a corporation to be allowed to join its ownership.

Consequently, a second shareholders' equity balance is created to report the amount received above par value. Kellogg uses the title "capital in excess of par value" but a number of other terms are frequently encountered such as "additional paid-in capital."

Kellogg records the issuance of a share of $0.25 par value common stock for $46 in cash as follows.[8]

FIGURE 16.2 Issuance of a Share of Common Stock for Cash

Cash	46.00	
Common stock (par value)		.25
Capital in excess of par value		45.75

On the balance sheet, within the stockholders' equity section, the amount that owners put into a corporation when they originally bought stock is the summation of the common stock and capital in excess of par value accounts. This total reflects the assets conveyed to the business in exchange for capital stock. For Kellogg, that figure is $543 million, the amount received from its owners since operations first began.

FIGURE 16.3 Kellogg Common Stock and Capital in Excess of Par Value[9]

Common Stock	$105 million
Capital in Excess of Par Value	438 million
Total Contributed Capital	$543 million

EXERCISE

Link to multiple-choice question for practice purposes: http://www.quia.com/quiz/2093026.html

Question: Common stock is sometimes issued in exchange for property or personal services rather than for cash. Such contributions are especially prevalent when a small corporation is first getting started. Potential owners may hold land, buildings, or other assets needed by the business. Or, an accountant, attorney, or the like might be willing to provide expert services and take payment in stock. This arrangement can be especially helpful if the business is attempting to conserve cash. ***What recording is made if capital stock is issued for a service or an asset other than cash?***

Answer: The issuance of stock for an asset or service is not technically a trade[10] but the accounting rules are the same. The asset or the service received by the corporation is recorded at the fair value of the capital stock surrendered. That is the equivalent of historical cost. It is a measure of the sacrifice made by the business to get the asset or service. However, if the fair value of the shares of stock is not available (which is often the case for new and smaller corporations), the fair value of the property or services received becomes the basis for reporting.

To illustrate, assume that a potential investor is willing to convey land with a fair value of $125,000 to the Maine Company in exchange for an ownership interest. During negotiations, officials for Maine offer to issue ten thousand shares of $1 par value common stock for this property. The shares are currently selling on a stock exchange for $12 each. The investor decides to accept this proposal rather than go to the trouble of trying to sell the land.

The "sacrifice" made by the Maine Company to acquire this land is $120,000 ($12 per share × 10,000 shares). Those shares could have been sold on the stock exchange to raise that much money. Instead, Maine issues them directly in exchange for the land and records the transaction as follows.

FIGURE 16.4 Issue Ten Thousand Shares of Common Stock Worth $12 per Share for Land

Land	120,000	
Common Stock ($1 par value × 10,000 shares)		10,000
Capital in Excess of Par Value ($120,000 less $10,000)		110,000

If this stock was not selling on a stock exchange, fair value might not be apparent. In that situation, the Maine Company should recognize the land at its own fair value of $125,000 with an accompanying $5,000 increase in the capital in excess of par value account.

KEY TAKEAWAY

Common stock forms the basic ownership units of most corporations. The rights of the holders of common stock shares are normally set by state law but include voting for a board of directors to oversee current operations and future plans. Financial statements often indicate the number of authorized shares (the maximum allowed), issued shares (the number that have been sold), and outstanding shares (those currently in the hands of owners). Common stock usually has a par value although the meaning of this number has faded in importance over the decades. Upon issuance, common stock is recorded at par value with any amount received above that figure reported in an account such as capital in excess of par value. If issued for an asset or service instead of cash, the recording is based on the fair value of the shares given up. However, if that value is not available, the fair value of the asset or service is used.

3. ISSUING AND ACCOUNTING FOR PREFERRED STOCK AND TREASURY STOCK

LEARNING OBJECTIVES

At the end of this section students should be able to meet the following objectives:

1. **Explain the difference between preferred stock and common stock.**
2. **Discuss the distribution of dividends to preferred stockholders.**
3. **Record the issuance of preferred stock.**
4. **Define treasury stock and provide reasons for a corporation to spend its money to acquire treasury stock.**
5. **Account for the purchase and resale of treasury stock, with both gains and losses occurring.**

Question: Some corporations also issue a second type of capital stock referred to as preferred stock. Probably about 10–15 percent of companies in the United States have preferred stock outstanding but the practice is more prevalent in some industries. ***How is preferred stock different from common stock?***

Answer: Preferred stock is another version of capital stock where the rights of those owners are set by the contractual terms of the stock certificate rather than state law. In effect, common stockholders are voluntarily surrendering one or more of their rights in hopes of enticing additional investors to contribute money to the corporation. For common stockholders, preferred stock is often another possible method of achieving financial leverage in the same manner as using money raised from bonds and notes.

The term "preferred stock" comes from the preference that is conveyed to these owners. They are being allowed to step in front of common stockholders when the specified rights are applied. A wide variety of benefits can be assigned to the holders of preferred shares including additional voting rights, assured representation on the board of directors, and the right to residual assets if the company ever liquidates.

By far the most typical preference is to cash dividends. As mentioned earlier in this chapter, all common stockholders are entitled to share proportionally in any dividend distributions. However, if a corporation issues preferred stock with a stipulated dividend, that amount must be paid before any money is conveyed to the owners of common stock. No dividend is ever guaranteed, not even one on preferred shares. A dividend is only legally required if declared by the board of directors. But, if declared, the preferred stock dividend comes before any common stock dividend.

Common stock is often referred to as a residual ownership because these shareholders are entitled to all that remains after other claims have been settled including those of preferred stock.

The issuance of preferred stock is accounted for in the same way as common stock. Par value, though, often serves as the basis for specified dividend payments. Thus, the par value listed for a preferred share frequently approximates fair value. To illustrate, assume that a corporation issues ten thousand shares of preferred stock. A $100 per share par value is printed on each stock certificate. If the annual dividend is listed as 4 percent, $4 per year ($100 par value × 4 percent) must be paid on preferred stock before any distribution is made on the common stock.

If ten thousand shares of this preferred stock are each issued for $101 in cash ($1,010,000 in total), the company records the following journal entry.

FIGURE 16.5 Issue Ten Thousand Shares of $100 Par Value Preferred Stock for $101 per Share

Cash	1,010,000	
Preferred Stock (Par Value)		1,000,000
Capital in Excess of Par Value		10,000

Companies often establish two separate "capital in excess of par value" accounts—one for common stock and one for preferred stock. They are then frequently combined in reporting the balances within stockholders' equity.

EXERCISE

Link to multiple-choice question for practice purposes: http://www.quia.com/quiz/2093027.html

Question: An account called **treasury stock** *is often found near the bottom of the shareholders' equity section of the balance sheet. Treasury stock represents issued shares of a corporation's own stock that have been reacquired. For example, the December 31, 2008, balance sheet for Viacom Inc. reports a negative balance of nearly $6 billion identified as treasury stock.*

A 2004 story in the Wall Street Journal *indicated that Viacom had been buying and selling its own stock for a number of years: "The $8 billion buyback program would enable the company to repurchase as much as 13 percent of its shares outstanding. The buyback follows a $3 billion stock-purchase program announced in 2002, under which 40.7 million shares were purchased."*[11]

Why does a company voluntarily give billions of dollars back to stockholders in order to repurchase its own stock? That is a huge amount of money leaving the company. Why not invest these funds in inventory, buildings, investments, research and development, and the like? ***Why does a corporation buy back its own shares as treasury stock?***

treasury stock

Issued shares of a corporation's own stock that have been reacquired; balance is shown within stockholders' equity section of the balance sheet as a negative amount unless the shares are retired (removed from existence).

Answer: Numerous possible reasons exist to justify spending money to reacquire an entity's own stock. Several of these strategies are rather complicated and a more appropriate topic for an upper-level finance course. However, an overview of a few of these should be helpful in understanding the rationale for such transactions.

- As a reward for service, businesses often give shares of their stock to key employees or sell them shares at a relatively low price. In some states, using unissued shares for such purposes can be restricted legally. The same rules do not apply to shares that have been reacquired. Thus, a corporation might acquire treasury shares to have available as needed for compensation purposes.
- Acquisition of treasury stock can be used as a tactic to push up the market price of a company's stock in order to please the remaining stockholders. Usually, a large scale repurchase (such as that made by Viacom) indicates that management believes the stock is undervalued at its current market price. Buying treasury stock reduces the supply of shares in the market and, according to economic theory, forces the price to rise. In addition, because of the announcement of the repurchase, outside investors often rush in to buy the stock ahead of the expected price increase. The supply of shares is decreased while demand for shares is increased. Stock price should go up. Not surprisingly, current stockholders often applaud the decision to buy treasury shares as they anticipate a jump in their investment values.
- Corporations can also repurchase shares of stock to reduce the risk of a hostile takeover. If another company threatens to buy enough shares to gain control, the board of directors of the target company must decide if acquisition is in the best interest of the stockholders.[12] If not, the target might attempt to buy up shares of its own treasury stock in hopes of reducing the number of owners in the market who are willing to sell their shares. It is a defensive strategy designed to make the takeover more difficult to accomplish. Plus, as mentioned above, buying back treasury stock should drive the price up, making purchase more costly for the predator.

Question: To illustrate the financial reporting of treasury stock, assume that the Chauncey Company has issued ten million shares of its $1 par value common stock at an average price of $3.50 per share. The company now reacquires three hundred thousand of these shares for $4 each. ***How is the acquisition of treasury stock reported?***

Answer: Under U.S. GAAP, several methods are allowed for reporting the purchase of treasury stock. Most companies appear to use the cost method because of its simplicity. The acquisition of these shares by Chauncey is recorded at the $1.2 million (three hundred thousand shares at $4 each) that was paid.

FIGURE 16.6 Purchase of Three Hundred Thousand Shares of Treasury Stock at a Cost of $4 Each

Treasury Stock	1,200,000	
Cash		1,200,000

Because the cost of treasury stock represents assets that have left the business, this account balance is shown within stockholders' equity as a negative amount, reflecting a decrease in net assets instead of an increase.

Except for possible legal distinctions, treasury stock is the equivalent of unissued stock. It does not receive **dividends** and has no voting privileges.

dividends

Distributions made by a corporation to its shareholders as a reward when income has been earned; shareholders often receive favorable tax treatment when cash dividends are collected.

Question: Treasury shares can be held forever or eventually sold at prices that might vary greatly from original cost. If sold for more, is a gain recognized? If sold for less, is a loss reported? ***What is the impact on a corporation's financial statements if treasury stock is reissued?*** *To illustrate, assume that Chauncey Company subsequently sells one hundred thousand shares of its treasury stock for $5.00 each. That is $1.00 more than these shares cost to reacquire. Is this excess reported as a gain within net income?*

Answer: As discussed previously, transactions in a corporation's own stock are considered expansions and contractions of the ownership and never impact reported net income. The buying and selling of capital stock are viewed as fundamentally different from the buying and selling of assets. Therefore, this reissuance is recorded by Chauncey through the following journal entry.

FIGURE 16.7 Sale of One Hundred Thousand Shares of Treasury Stock Costing $4 Each for $5 per Share

Cash	500,000	
Treasury Stock (Cost)		400,000
Capital in Excess of Cost—Treasury Stock		100,000

The "capital in excess of cost-treasury stock" is the same type of account as the "capital in excess of par value" that was recorded in connection with the issuance of both common and preferred stocks. Within stockholders' equity, these accounts can be grouped or reported separately.

Question: Assume that Chauncey later sells another one hundred thousand of the treasury shares, but this time for only $2.60 each. The proceeds in this transaction are below the acquisition cost of $4 per share. ***What recording is made if treasury stock is sold at the equivalent of a loss?***

Answer: Interestingly, the selling of treasury stock below cost is a transaction not well covered in U.S. GAAP. Authoritative rules fail to provide a definitive rule for reporting this reduction except that stockholders' equity should be decreased with no direct impact recorded in net income.

The most common approach seems to be to first remove any capital in excess of cost recorded by the sale of earlier shares of treasury stock at above cost. If that balance is not large enough to absorb the entire reduction, a decrease is made in retained earnings as shown below. The $100,000 balance in capital in excess of cost-treasury stock was created in the previous journal entry.

FIGURE 16.8 Sale of One Hundred Thousand Shares of Treasury Stock Costing $4 Each for $2.60 per Share

Cash	260,000	
Capital in Excess of Cost—Treasury Stock	100,000	
Retained Earnings	40,000	
Treasury Stock (Cost)		400,000

One outcome of this handling should be noted. In the early chapters of this textbook, retained earnings was defined as all income reported over the life of a business less all dividend distributions to the owners. Apparently, this definition is not absolutely correct in all possible cases. In the above journal entry, retained earnings are also reduced as a result of a stock transaction where a loss occurred that could not otherwise be reported.

EXERCISE

Link to multiple-choice questions for practice purposes: http://www.quia.com/quiz/2093028.html

EXERCISE

Link to multiple-choice questions for practice purposes: http://www.quia.com/quiz/2093007.html

KEY TAKEAWAY

A corporation can issue preferred stock as well as common stock. Preferred shares are given specific rights that come before those of common stockholders. Usually, these rights involve the distribution of dividends. A set payment amount is often required before common stockholders receive any dividend. Subsequently, capital stock shares can be bought back from investors for a number of reasons. If so, they are known as treasury stock. In acquiring these shares, money flows out of the company so the account is reported as a negative balance within stockholders' equity. If resold, the treasury stock account is reduced and capital in excess of cost is recognized if an amount above cost is received. However, if resold at a loss, any previous capital in excess of cost balance is removed followed by a possible reduction in retained earnings.

4. THE ISSUANCE OF CASH AND STOCK DIVIDENDS

LEARNING OBJECTIVES

At the end of this section students should be able to meet the following objectives:

1. **Identify the various dates associated with a dividend distribution.**
2. **Prepare all journal entries to report a cash dividend payment.**
3. **Define the characteristics of a cumulative dividend.**
4. **Explain the rationale for a stock dividend or stock split.**
5. **Record the issuance of a stock dividend**

Question: As stated in Chapter 1, a vast majority of investors purchase capital stock for only two reasons: price appreciation and dividends. Dividends and long-term capital gains (gains on the sale of certain investments that have been held for over a year) are especially appealing to individual investors because they are taxed at a lower rate than most other types of income.

Dividends are usually paid in cash and represent the profits of a business being passed along to the owners. Because the corporation is effectively giving away its assets, dividends require formal approval by the board of directors—known as a dividend declaration. The board considers current cash balances as well as the projected needs of the business before deciding on the amount, if any, of a dividend payment. ***How does a corporation report the declaration and distribution of a cash dividend?***

Answer: Dividends provide a meaningful signal to investors about the financial health of a business. Some corporations even boast about having paid a constant or rising annual dividend for many years. Unfortunately, one result of recent economic times has been that a number of businesses have been forced to reduce or even eliminate dividend distributions. Such decisions typically lead to a drop in the market price of a corporation's stock because of the negative implications.

Other businesses stress rapid growth and rarely, if ever, pay a cash dividend. The board of directors prefers that all profits remain in the business to stimulate future growth. For example, Netflix Inc. reported net income for 2008 of over $83 million but paid no dividend.

Chronologically, accounting for dividends involves several dates with approximately two to five weeks passing between each:

- The **date of declaration**
- The **date of record** (and the related ex-dividend date)
- The **date of payment** (also known as the date of distribution)

date of declaration

Date on which dividend payments are formally declared (approved) by the board of directors; it is the day on which a liability is recorded by the corporation.

date of record

Date on which stock must be held for a shareholder to be entitled to the receipt of a dividend; the date of record is specified by the board of directors when the dividend is declared.

date of payment

Date on which a cash dividend is distributed to those shareholders who held a corporation's stock on the date of record; it is also known as the date of distribution.

To illustrate, assume that the Hurley Corporation has one million shares of authorized common stock. To date, three hundred thousand of these shares have been issued but twenty thousand shares were recently bought back as treasury stock. Thus, 280,000 shares are presently outstanding, in the hands of investors. Hurley earned a reported net income of $780,000 in the current year. After some deliberations, the board of directors has decided to distribute a $1.00 cash dividend on each share of common stock.

The day on which the Hurley board of directors formally decides on the payment of this dividend is known as the date of declaration. Legally, this action creates a liability for the company that must be reported in the financial statements. Only the owners of the 280,000 shares that are outstanding will receive this distribution.

FIGURE 16.9 $1.00 per Share Dividend Declared by Board of Directors

Retained Earnings	280,000	
Dividends Payable		280,000

As discussed previously, dividend distributions reduce the amount reported as retained earnings but have no impact on reported net income.

When the dividend is declared by the board, the date of record is also set. All shareholders who own the stock on that day qualify for receipt of the dividend. The ex-dividend date is the first day on which an investor is not entitled to the dividend. Because receipt of the dividend has been lost, the market price of the stock typically drops by approximately the amount of the dividend on the ex-dividend date although myriad other market factors always influence the movement of stock prices.

No journal entry is recorded by the corporation on either the date of record or the ex-dividend date because they do not relate to any event or transaction. Those dates simply allow Hurley to identify the owners to whom the dividend will be paid.

On the date of payment, the corporation mails checks to the appropriate recipients, an event recorded as follows.

FIGURE 16.10 Payment of $1.00 per Share Cash Dividend

Dividends Payable	280,000	
Cash		280,000

Question: Assume that Wington Company issues a share of $100 par value preferred stock to an investor on January 1, Year One. The preferred stock certificate discloses an annual dividend rate of 8 percent. Thus, dividend payment is $8 each year ($100 × 8 percent). At the end of Year One, Wington faces a cash shortage and is unable to pay this dividend. Have the owners of the preferred shares lost the right to the Year One dividend? ***Must a corporation report a liability if a preferred stock dividend is not paid at the appointed time?***

Answer: Preferred stock dividends are often identified on the stock certificate as "**cumulative**." This term means that the obligation for all unpaid dividends on these shares must be met before dividends can be distributed on common stock. Cumulative dividends are referred to as "in arrears" when past due.

If the dividend on the preferred shares of Wington is cumulative, the $8 is in arrears at the end of Year One. In the future, this (and any other) missed dividend must be paid before any distribution on common stock can be considered. Conversely, if a preferred stock is noncumulative, a missed dividend is simply lost to the owners. It has no impact on the future allocation of dividends between preferred and common shares.

The existence of a cumulative preferred stock dividend in arrears is information that must be disclosed in financial statements. However, the balance is not reported as a liability. Only dividends that have been formally declared by the board of directors are recorded as liabilities. If cumulative, a note to the financial statements should explain Wington's obligation for any preferred stock dividends in arrears.

cumulative

Feature attached to most types of preferred stock so that any dividend payments that are omitted one year must still be paid before the holders of common stock receive any dividends.

EXERCISE

Link to multiple-choice question for practice purposes: http://www.quia.com/quiz/2093030.html

EXERCISE

Link to multiple-choice question for practice purposes: http://www.quia.com/quiz/2092987.html

EXERCISE

Link to multiple-choice question for practice purposes: http://www.quia.com/quiz/2093009.html

Question: A corporate press release issued on May 19, 2009, informed the public that "Green Mountain Coffee Roasters Inc. today announced that its Board of Directors has approved a three-for-two **stock split** *to be effected in the form of a stock dividend. The Company will distribute one additional share of its common stock to all shareholders of record at the close of business on May 29, 2009, for every two shares of common stock held on that date. The shares will be distributed on June 8, 2009."*

Obviously, as shown by this press release, a corporation can issue additional shares of stock to shareholders instead of distributing only cash dividends. These shares can be issued as a **stock dividend** *or in a slightly different manner as a stock split.*[13] *No assets are distributed in either of these scenarios—just more shares of the company's own stock.* ***Are shareholders better off when they receive additional shares in a stock dividend?***

stock split

A division of each share of outstanding stock to increase the number of those shares; it is a method of reducing the market price of the stock; the process is carried out in hopes that a lower price will generate more market activity in the stock and, therefore, a faster rise in price.

Answer: When a stock dividend is issued, the number of shares held by every investor increases but their percentage ownership stays the same. Their ownership interest in the corporation remains proportionally unchanged.

To illustrate, assume that the Red Company reports net assets of $5 million. Janis Samples owns one thousand of the outstanding ten thousand shares of this company's common stock. She holds a 10 percent ownership interest (1,000/10,000) in a business that holds net assets of $5 million.

The board of directors then declares and distributes a 4 percent stock dividend. For each one hundred shares that a stockholder possesses, Red Company issues an additional 4 shares (4 percent of one hundred). Thus, four hundred new shares are conveyed to the ownership as a whole (4 percent of ten thousand) which raises the total number of outstanding shares to 10,400. However, a stock dividend has no actual impact on the corporation. There are simply more shares outstanding. Nothing else has changed.

Janis Samples receives forty of these newly issued shares (4 percent of one thousand) so that her holdings have grown to 1,040 shares. After this stock dividend, she still owns 10 percent (1,040/10,400) of the outstanding stock of Red Company and it still reports net assets of $5 millions. The investor's financial position has not improved; she has gained nothing as a result of this stock dividend.

Not surprisingly, the investor makes no journal entry in accounting for the receipt of a stock dividend. No change has taken place except for the number of shares being held.

stock dividend

A dividend distributed to shareholders by issuing additional shares of stock rather than cash; it increases the number of shares outstanding but each ownership percentage stays the same; as with a stock split, it reduces the price of the stock in hopes of stimulating market interest.

capital in excess of par value

Figure represents amount received by a corporation from the original issuance of capital stock that is in excess of par value; also called additional paid in capital.

However, the corporation does make a journal entry to record the issuance of a stock dividend although it creates no impact on either assets or liabilities. The retained earnings balance is decreased by the fair value of the shares issued while contributed capital (common stock and **capital in excess of par value**) are increased by the same amount.

According to U.S. GAAP, if a stock dividend is especially large (in excess of 20–25 percent of the outstanding shares), the change in retained earnings and contributed capital is recorded at par value rather than fair value.[14]

EXERCISE

Link to multiple-choice question for practice purposes: http://www.quia.com/quiz/2092989.html

EXERCISE

Link to multiple-choice question for practice purposes: http://www.quia.com/quiz/2093010.html

Question: ***If no changes occur in the makeup of a corporation as the result of a stock dividend, why does a board of directors choose to issue one?***

Answer: The primary purpose served by a stock dividend (or a stock split) is a reduction in the market price of the corporation's capital stock. When the price of a share of stock rises to a high level, fewer investors are willing to make purchases. At some point, market interest wanes. The resulting reduction in demand will likely have a negative impact on the stock price. A growing company might find that a previously escalating trend in its market value has hit a plateau when the price of each share rises too high

By issuing a large quantity of new shares (sometimes two to five times as many shares as were outstanding), the price falls, often precipitously. For example, an owner who held one hundred shares at a market price of $120 per share (total value of $12,000) might now have two hundred shares selling at $60 per share or three hundred shares selling at $40 per share (but with the same total market value of $12,000). The stockholder's investment remains unchanged but, hopefully, the stock is now more attractive to investors at the lower price so that the level of active trading increases.

Stock dividends also provide owners with the possibility of other benefits. For example, cash dividend payments usually drop after a stock dividend but not always in proportion to the change in the number of outstanding shares. An owner might hold one hundred shares of common stock in a corporation that has paid $1 per share as an annual cash dividend over the past few years (a total of $100 per year). After a 2-for-1 stock dividend, this person now owns two hundred shares. The board of directors might then choose to reduce the annual cash dividend to only $0.60 per share so that future payments go up to $120 per year (two hundred shares × $0.60 each). Such a benefit, though, is not guaranteed. The investors can merely hope that additional cash dividends will be received.

KEY TAKEAWAY

Many corporations distribute cash dividends after a formal declaration is passed by the board of directors. Journal entries are required on both the date of declaration and the date of payment. The date of record and the ex-dividend date are important in identifying the owners entitled to receive the dividend but no transaction occurs. Hence, no recording is made on those dates. Preferred stock dividends are often cumulative so that any dividends in arrears must be paid before a common stock distribution can be made. Dividends in arrears are not recorded as liabilities until declared. Stock dividends and stock splits are issued to reduce the market price of capital stock and keep potential investors interested in the possibility of acquiring ownership. A stock dividend is recorded as a reduction in retained earnings and an increase in contributed capital. However, stock dividends have no immediate impact on the financial condition of either the company or its stockholders.

5. THE COMPUTATION OF EARNINGS PER SHARE

LEARNING OBJECTIVES

At the end of this section students should be able to meet the following objectives:

1. **Compute and explain return on equity.**
2. **Discuss the reasons that earnings per share (EPS) figures are so closely watched by investors.**
3. **Calculate basic EPS with or without the existence of preferred stock.**
4. **Explain the relevance of the P/E ratio.**
5. **Identify the informational benefit provided by diluted EPS.**

Question: Throughout this textbook, various vital signs have been presented. They include ratios, numbers, percentages, and the like that are commonly studied by investors as an indication of current financial health and future prosperity. One common measure is **return on equity (ROE)**. ***How does an interested party calculate the return on equity reported by a business?***

return on equity (ROE)

Ratio computed to measure the profitable use of a business's resources; it is determined by dividing net income by average shareholders' equity for the period.

Answer: Return on equity reflects the profitability of a company based on the size of the owners' claim to net assets as shown primarily through contributed capital and retained earnings. It is simply the reported net income divided by average shareholders' equity for the period.

return on equity = net income/average shareholders' equity

For example, PPG Industries began 2008 with total shareholders' equity of $4,151 million and ended that year with a balance of $3,333 million. For the year ended December 31, 2008, PPG reported net income of $538 million for a return on equity of 14.4 percent.

average shareholders' equity: ($4,151 million + $3,333 million)/2 = $3,742 million

return on equity: $538 million/$3,742 million = 14.4%

Question: No single "vital sign" that is computed to help investors analyze a business and its financial health is more obsessively watched than earnings per share (EPS). Corporations even call press conferences to announce their latest EPS figures. According to U.S. GAAP, public companies are required to present EPS for each period that net income is reported. As just one example, Pfizer Inc. disclosed EPS of $1.20 on its income statement for the year ended December 31, 2008. ***Why is the EPS reported by a corporation so closely monitored by the investment community?***

Answer: The simple reason for the public fascination with EPS is that this number is generally considered to be linked to the market price of a company's capital stock. Therefore, constant and wide scale speculation takes place about future EPS figures. If analysts merely predict an increase in EPS, that forecast alone can lead to a surge in stock price.

A **price-earnings ratio (P/E ratio)** is even computed to help quantify this relationship. The P/E ratio is the current price of the stock divided by the latest EPS figure. It enables investors to anticipate movements in the price of a stock based on their projections of earnings per share. If a company's P/E ratio is twenty and is expected to remain constant, then an increase in EPS of $1 should lead to a $20 rise in stock price.

price-earnings ratio (P/E ratio)

A ratio computed by dividing current market price of an entity's stock by the latest earnings per share; it is used to help predict future stock prices based on anticipated EPS figures.

FIGURE 16.11 As of July 8, 2009, the P/E ratio for Several Prominent Companies

IBM	11.1
MetLife	8.5
Pfizer	12.5
Target	13.1

The ongoing debate as to whether EPS and the P/E ratio are over emphasized as investing tools is a controversy better left to upper-level finance courses. The fascination is certainly real regardless of whether the perceived benefits are as great as many believe.

Question: ***How is EPS calculated?***

basic earnings per share

A figure that must be reported by corporations that have their stock publicly traded; it is net income less preferred stock dividends divided by the weighted-average number of shares of common stock outstanding during the same period.

preferred stock

A capital stock issued by some companies that has one or more specified preferences over common shareholders, usually in the form of cash dividends.

Answer: EPS is a common stock computation designed to measure operating results after all other claims have been satisfied. In simplest form, EPS (often referred to as **basic EPS**) is the net income for the period divided by the weighted average number of outstanding shares of common stock. The company's income is allocated equally to each of these shares.

To illustrate, assume a business organization reports net income of $700,000. If an average of 200,000 shares of common stock is outstanding for this period of time, EPS is $700,000/200,000 or $3.50 per share. If the market price of this stock is $35, then the P/E ratio is 35/3.50, or ten.

Because EPS only relates to common stock, this computation is altered slightly if **preferred stock** shares are also outstanding. Preferred stock is normally entitled to its dividend before common stock has any claim. Therefore, in determining basic EPS, any preferred stock dividend must be removed to arrive at the portion of income that is attributed to the ownership of common stock.

Basic EPS

(net income – preferred stock dividend)/average number of common shares outstanding

EXERCISE

Link to multiple-choice questions for practice purposes: http://www.quia.com/quiz/2093052.html

EXERCISE

Link to multiple-choice questions for practice purposes: http://www.quia.com/quiz/2093034.html

Question: For the year ended March 31, 2009, the McKesson Corporation reported basic EPS of $2.99 per share. However, the company also reported a second figure, diluted EPS, that was only $2.95 per share. What is the meaning of diluted EPS? ***Why is diluted EPS also reported by some businesses along with basic EPS?***

Answer: All publicly traded companies must disclose basic EPS. Income reported for the period (after removal of any preferred stock dividends) is allocated evenly over the weighted average number of shares of outstanding common stock. Basic EPS is mechanically derived based on historically reported income and share figures.

Many corporations also have other contractual obligations outstanding that could become common stock and, therefore, potentially affect this computation. Stock options, convertible bonds, and convertible preferred stock can each be exchanged in some manner for common stock shares. That decision is usually up to the holder and out of the control of the company. If these conversions were to transpire, the additional shares could cause EPS to drop—possibly by a significant amount. This potential reduction should be considered by investors in making any assessment of EPS.

diluted earnings per share

Hypothetical computation that reduces basic earnings per share to reflect the possible dilution if outstanding convertible items were actually turned into common stock; it includes the potential impact of stock options, convertible bonds and convertible preferred stock to warn decision makers of the consequences if those convertibles are turned into common stock.

Diluted EPS serves as a warning to decision makers of the possible impact that the existence of these convertibles can have on ownership. It is a hypothetical computation that gives weight to the chance that such conversions will take place. The actual mechanical steps in this process are better left to an intermediate accounting course. However, an understanding of the purpose of reporting diluted EPS is worthwhile.

Stock options, convertible bonds, convertible preferred stocks, and the like could become common stock and reduce a company's earnings per share. Thus, U.S. GAAP requires that this possible impact is calculated and shown by the reporting of a lower diluted EPS. For the McKesson Corporation, if all other transactions stayed the same except that its convertible items were exchanged for common stock, basic EPS would drop from $2.99 to $2.95. That is the possible dilution that could be caused by the presence of items convertible into common stock. For an investor or potential investor, that is information of interest. Including this figure alerts them to the possibility of such conversions and helps them quantify the potential impact.

KEY TAKEAWAY

Return on equity (ROE) is one percentage often computed by market analysts to help evaluate the profitability of a business. However, the reporting of earnings per share (EPS) draws a much greater circle of interest. Basic EPS must be reported by every publicly traded company for each year in which net income is reported. Basic EPS is the net income for the period divided by the weighted average number of shares of common stock outstanding. Because EPS is only determined for common stock, any preferred stock dividends must be removed from net income as a preliminary step in carrying out this computation. The resulting figure is viewed as having a major impact on the movement of the company's stock price. The price-earnings (P/E) ratio even quantifies that effect. If a corporation also has items such as stock options or convertible bonds that can be turned into common stock, conversion could potentially have an adverse impact on EPS. Thus, where such contractual obligations are outstanding, diluted EPS must also be reported to help investors understand the possible impact of future conversions.

Talking With a Real Investing Pro—Continued

Following is a continuation of our interview with Kevin G. Burns.

Question: Investors in the United States seem to have an obsession about the reporting of earnings per share. Even slight movements in projected EPS figures can create significant swings in the market price of a company's stock. Do you think there is an overemphasis on EPS in the public's investing decisions? How closely do you pay attention to EPS figures that are reported by the businesses that you are following?

Kevin Burns: This is a very good question. By now students must realize that accounting is really all about estimates. Although investors would like accounting to be objectively exact, reporting such estimates really requires an awful lot of subjectivity. For example, for many years, General Electric would almost always report EPS a penny or two above market expectations. This was quarter after quarter like clockwork. It got to the point where if the company didn't "beat" the estimates on the street by a penny or two, the market was disappointed. It is absurd to believe that this is meaningful. This is especially true when earnings can also be managed simply by delaying or speeding up a major transaction from one time period to another. So, yes, I believe that EPS, although important, is not the ultimate piece of information that some investors seem to think. I am much more concerned about asset values, growth prospects, and what a company does with the cash it is able to generate.

Video Clip

Joe talks about the five most important points in Chapter 16.

View the video online at: http://blip.tv/play/sDyBwKhOAA

6. END-OF-CHAPTER EXERCISES

QUESTIONS

1. What are the three legal forms of business?
2. How does the number of owners differ among the three forms?
3. What is the process for incorporating a business?
4. What liability do stockholders have for a corporation's debts?
5. Explain the "double taxation" concept as it applies to corporations.
6. Define "common stock."
7. List three rights normally held by common stockholders.
8. Define "authorized" number of shares of common stock.
9. Define "issued" number of shares of common stock.
10. Define "outstanding" shares of common stock.
11. Explain the meaning of "par value" of a share of stock.
12. Why is preferred stock called "preferred?"
13. What is treasury stock?
14. Give three reasons a corporation might want to buy back its own stock.
15. What is a dividend?
16. What is a cumulative dividend?
17. What is a stock dividend?
18. What is the difference in accounting between a small stock dividend and a large stock dividend?
19. Why do corporations issue stock dividends?
20. How is return on equity calculated?
21. How is a company's price-earnings ratio calculated?
22. How is basic earnings per share determined?
23. Why would a company be required to report diluted earnings per share?

TRUE OR FALSE

1. ____ Sole proprietorships are easier to form than corporations.
2. ____ Common stockholders are usually permitted to vote for a corporation's board of directors, but preferred stockholders are not.
3. ____ Earnings per share is one of the most watched metrics of a corporation.
4. ____ Preferred dividends must be paid annually.
5. ____ Partnerships and corporations are both subject to double taxation.
6. ____ A corporation with stock options had to report diluted earnings per share.
7. ____ A small stock dividend will typically result in a smaller debit to retained earnings than a large stock dividend.
8. ____ It is not possible for a corporation to have more outstanding shares of stock than authorized shares of stock.
9. ____ Most companies choose a relatively large par value for their stock.
10. ____ Preferred stockholder dividends are paid before common stockholder dividends.
11. ____ One reason a company might repurchase its own stock is to protect against a hostile takeover.
12. ____ Anyone not a stockholder on the date of declaration of a dividend will not be eligible to participate in that dividend.
13. ____ When referring to dividends, the term "in arrears" refers to the fact that the date of declaration and the date of payment are not the same.
14. ____ A company's price-earnings ratio can help predict changes in its stock price based on movement in its EPS.
15. ____ One disadvantage of a sole proprietorship or partnership is the risk of liability by the owner.

MULTIPLE CHOICE

1. Which of the following forms of business is subject to double taxation?
   a. Partnership
   b. Corporation
   c. Sole proprietorship
   d. S corporation

2. Yancey Corporation issues 50,000 shares of common stock for $30 per share. The stock has a par value of $2 per share. By what amount would Yancey credit capital in excess of par?
   a. $1,500,000
   b. $1,400,000
   c. $100,000
   d. $50,000

3. Landon Corporation sold 16,000 shares of $0.50 par value common stock for $17 per share. Which of the following is the journal entry Landon should make?

Cash	272,000	
Common Stock		8,000
Capital in Excess of Par Value		264,000

a.

Cash	272,000	
Common Stock		272,000

b.

Capital in Excess of Par Value	264,000	
Common Stock		264,000

c.

Cash	8,000	
Common Stock		8,000

d.

4. Jackson Company is authorized to issue 20,000 shares of $0.50 par value stock. On February 1, it issues 4,000 shares. On April 20, an additional 6,000 shares are issued. On September 23, Jackson repurchases 2,000 shares. On November 3, it reissues half of the shares it repurchased in September. How many outstanding shares does Jackson have on December 31?
   a. 20,000
   b. 10,000
   c. 9,000
   d. 8,000

5. Paul Mitchell purchased a licensing agreement for $40,000 prior to going to work for Traylor Corporation. Traylor agreed to issue 2,000 shares of common stock to Mitchell in exchange for his licensing agreement, which now has a value of $30,000. At the time of the stock exchange, Traylor's $2 par value stock was selling for $14 per share. For what amount should Traylor debit the licensing agreement?
   a. $40,000

b. $30,000
c. $28,000
d. $4,000

6. Kramer Company is authorized to issue 45,000 shares of its 7 percent, $100 par value preferred stock. On March 15, Kramer issues 5,000 shares for $200 per share. On November 1, Kramer declares the dividend and pays it on December 1. What amount of cash was paid to the preferred shareholders?
   a. $70,000
   b. $315,000
   c. $630,000
   d. $35,000

7. Portor Corporation is authorized to sell 150,000 shares of its $0.25 par value common stock. It currently has 90,000 shares issued and outstanding. Portor would like to declare a stock dividend and is curious about the effect this will have on retained earnings. Portor's stock has a current market value per share of $26. Portor is trying to decide between a 5 percent stock dividend and a 40 percent stock dividend. Which of the following accurately shows the effect of each on retained earnings?

	5% Stock Dividend	40% Stock Dividend
a.	$117,000	$936,000
b.	$117,000	$9,000
c.	$1,125	$9,000
d.	$1,125	$936,000

8. Falls Church Corporation ended the year with revenues of $45,000 and expenses of $33,000. Its stockholders' equity accounts total $490,000. Which of the following is Falls Church's return on equity for the year?
   a. 18%
   b. 73%
   c. 33%
   d. 45%

9. Fleming Corporation began and ended the year with 50,000 outstanding shares of common stock net income for the year totaled $480,000. Preferred dividends amounted to $30,000. Which of the following would be Fleming's basic earnings per share?
   a. $9.60 per share
   b. $16.00 per share
   c. $6.00 per share
   d. $9.00 per share

10. Which of the following would not force a company to compute diluted earnings per share in addition to basic earnings per share?
   a. Convertible preferred stock
   b. Stock warrants
   c. Nonconvertible preferred stock
   d. Stock options

11. Friar Inc. had a net income for 20X5 of $1,870,000. It had 600,000 shares of common stock outstanding on 1/1/X5 and repurchased 150,000 of those shares on 8/31/X5. It has no preferred stock. On 12/31/X5, Friar's stock was selling for $26 per share. Which of the following is Friar's price-earnings ratio on 12/31/X5?
   a. 65
   b. 33
   c. 25
   d. 00

PROBLEMS

1. Cutlass Corporation is authorized to issue 40,000 shares of $1 par value common stock. On March 15, it issues 1,000 shares for $6 per share. Record this transaction for Cutlass.
2. McNair Corporation is authorized to issue 105,000 shares of 5 percent, $200 par value preferred stock. On May 22, McNair issues 32,000 shares for $325 per share. McNair declares the preferred dividend on September 1 and pays it on October 1.
   a. Record the issuance of the preferred stock.
   b. Record the declaration of the dividend on September 1.
   c. Record the payment of the preferred dividend on October 1.
3. Douglas Company's board of directors approves a plan to buy back shares of its common stock. Prepare journal entries for each of the following transactions. Assume that the transactions occur in the order given.
   a. Douglas buys back 2,500 shares of its $1 common stock for $35 per share.
   b. Douglas resells 1,000 shares for $36.
   c. Douglas resells 500 shares for $34.
   d. Douglas resells 600 shares for $33.
   e. Douglas resells the remaining 400 shares for $35.
4. Grayson Corporation is authorized to sell 2,000,000 shares of its $1 par value common stock to the public. Before 20X7, it had issued 60,000 shares with a market value of $12 per share. During 20X7, Grishom issued another 14,000 shares when the market value per share was $24.

   On 1/1/X7, Grishom had retained earnings of $1,950,000. During 20X7, Grishom earned net income of $80,000 and paid dividends to common stockholders of $19,000. Also during 20X7, Grishom repurchased 11,000 shares of its own stock when the market price was $22.
   a. Record the issuance of the common stock during 20X7.
   b. Determine retained earnings on 12/31/X7.
   c. Record the purchase of the treasury stock.
   d. Prepare the stockholders' equity section of the balance sheet on 12/31/X7.
5. In late 20X2, the Pickins Corporation was formed. The articles of incorporation authorize 5,000,000 shares of common stock carrying a $1 par value, and 1,000,000 shares of $5 par value preferred stock. On January 1, 20X3, 2,000,000 shares of common stock are issued for $15 per share. Also on January 1, 500,000 shares of preferred stock are issued at $30 per share.
   a. Prepare journal entries to record these transactions on January 1.

      During March 20X3, the Pickins Corporation repurchased 100,000 common shares for the treasury at a price of $13 per share. During August 20X3, all 100,000 treasury shares are reissued at $16 per share.
   b. Prepare journal entries to record these transactions.

      During November 20X3, Pickins issues a 25 percent stock dividend on all outstanding shares when its stock was selling for $50 per share. On December 1, 20X3, Pickens declares a $0.75 per share cash dividend on common stock and a $2.00 per share cash dividend on preferred stock. Payment is scheduled for December 20, 20X3, to shareholders of record on December 10, 20X3.
   c. Prepare journal entries to record the declaration and payment of these stock and cash dividends.
6. On March 1, St. George Company declares a stock dividend on its $1 par value stock. It had 1,000 shares outstanding and the market value was $13 per share.
   a. What would be the debit to retained earnings for a 10 percent stock dividend?
   b. What would be the debit to retained earnings for a 30 percent stock dividend?
7. Rawlings Company has the following equity accounts at the beginning and end of 20X3:

	1/1/X3	12/31/X3
Preferred Stock, 6%, $100 par value	$2,000,000	$2,000,000
Common Stock, $1 Par Value	$160,000	$200,000
Capital in Excess of Par, Common	$12,000,000	$16,000,000
Retained Earnings	$1,100,000	$1,800,000

   The additional 40,000 shares of common stock were issued on September 1, 20X3. Preferred stock was paid its dividend during year. Net income for the year was $1,200,000.

   Determine Rawlings' basic EPS on December 31, 20X3.

8. Information on Massaff Corporation's stock accounts follows:

	December 31	20X7	20X8
Outstanding shares of:			
	Common stock	300,000	330,000
	Nonconvertible preferred stock	10,000	10,000

The following additional information is available:

- On July 1, 20X8, Massaff sold 30,000 additional shares of common stock.
- Net income for the year ended December 31, 20X8, was $750,000.
- During 20X8 Massaff paid dividends of $3.00 per share on its nonconvertible preferred stock.

Compute Massaff's basic earnings per common share for the year ended December 31, 20X8.

9. In several past chapters, we have met Heather Miller, who started her own business, Sew Cool. The financial statements for December are shown below.

Sew Cool Financial Statements

Sew Cool
Income Statement
As of December 31, 20X8

Revenue	$4,000
Cost of Goods	(2,000)
Gross Profit	2,000
Other Expenses	(1,695)
Earnings before Interest and Tax	335
Interest Expense	(30)
Earnings before Tax	305
Tax Expense	(107)
Net Income	$198

Sew Cool
Stmt. of Retained Earnings
As of December 31, 20X8

Retained Earnings, December 1, 20X8	$500
Net Income	198
Dividends	(158)
Retained Earnings, December 31, 20X8	$540

Sew Cool
Balance Sheet
December 31, 20X8

Assets		**Liabilities**	
Current		**Current**	
Cash	$940	Accounts Payable	$900
Accounts Receivable	500	Income Tax Payable	120
Less Allowance for Doubtful Accounts	(20)		
Net Accounts Receivable	480		
Inventory	700		
Total Current Assets	$2,120	Total Current Liabilities	$1,020
Noncurrent		**Noncurrent**	
Equipment	$1,000	Notes Payable	$1,060
		Owners' Equity	
		Capital Stock	$500
		Retained Earnings	540
		Total Owners' Equity	$1,040
Total Assets	$3,120	Total Liabilities & Owners' Equity	$3,120

Based on the financial statements determine Sew Cool's return on equity.

COMPREHENSIVE PROBLEM

This problem will carry through several chapters, building in difficulty. It allows students to continuously practice skills and knowledge learned in previous chapters.

In Chapter 15, you prepared Webworks statements for March. They are included here as a starting point for April.

Here are Webworks financial statements as of March 31.

Webworks Financial Statements

Webworks
Income Statement
As of March 31

Revenue	$20,810
Cost of Goods Sold	(12,258)
Gross Profit	8,552
Deprec. and Amort. Expense	(392)
Other Expenses and Losses	(6,413)
Investment Income (Loss)	200
Earnings before Interest and Tax	1,947
Interest Expense	(15)
Earnings before Tax	1,932
Tax Expense	(580)
Net Income	$1,352

Webworks
Stmt. of Retained Earnings
As of March 31

Retained Earnings, March 1	$18,249
Net Income	1,352
Retained Earnings, March 31	$19,601

Webworks
Balance Sheet
March 31

Assets		**Liabilities**	
Current		**Current**	
Cash	$9,027	Accounts Payable	$2,770
Accounts Receivable	1,600	Salaries Payable	350
Less Allowance for Doubtful Accounts	(160)	Interest Payable	30
		Unearned Revenue	300
Net Accounts Receivable	1,440		
Trading Securities, Net	1,800		
Merchandise Inventory	2,324		
Supplies Inventory	50		
Total Current Assets	$14,641	Total Current Liabilities	$3,450
Property, Plant, and Equipment		**Noncurrent**	
		Note Payable	$3,000
Equipment	$10,500		
Less Accumulated Depreciation	(1,138)		
Furniture	1,000		
Less Accumulated Depreciation	(102)		
Total P, P, and E	$10,260		
Other Noncurrent Assets		**Owners' Equity**	
		Capital Stock	$2,000
Available-for-Sale Securities	$2,275	Retained Earnings	19,601
Licensing Agreement, Net	1,400	Other Accumulated Comprehensive Income:	
		Unrealized Gain on Available-for-Sale Securities	525
		Total Owners' Equity	$22,126
Total Assets	$28,576	Total Liabilities & Owners' Equity	$28,576

The following events occur during April:

a. Webworks starts and completes ten more sites and bills clients for $7,000.

b. Leon invites Nancy to invest money in the business. She contributes $2,000 and becomes an equal owner with Leon.

c. Webworks purchases supplies worth $125 on account.

d. At the beginning of March, Webworks had fourteen keyboards costing $120 each and twenty-eight flash drives costing $23 each. Webworks uses periodic FIFO to cost its inventory.

e. On account, Webworks purchases ninety-five keyboards for $121 each and ninety flash drives for $25 each.

f. Webworks sells eighty-seven keyboards for $13,050 and ninety-five of the flash drives for $2,850 cash.

g. Webworks collects $6,400 in accounts receivable.

h. Webworks pays its $500 rent.

i. Webworks pays off $14,000 of its accounts payable.

j. Webworks sells all of its shares of RST stock for $20 per share.

k. Webworks pays Juan $700 for his work during the first three weeks of April.

l. Webworks writes off an account receivable from December in the amount of $150 because collection appears unlikely.

m. Webworks pays off its salaries payable from March.

n. Webworks pays Leon and Nancy a salary of $3,500 each.

o. Webworks completes the design for the photographer for which it was paid in February. The $300 of the unearned revenue should be reclassified to revenue.

p. Webworks pays Nancy and Leon a dividend of $250 each.

q. Webworks pays taxes of $372 in cash.

Required:

A. Prepare journal entries for the above events.

B. Post the journal entries to T-accounts.

C. Prepare an unadjusted trial balance for Webworks for April.

D. Prepare adjusting entries for the following and post them to your T-accounts.

r. Webworks owes Juan $100 for his work during the last week of April.

s. Webworks receives an electric bill for $440. Webworks will pay the bill in May.

t. Webworks determines that it has $65 worth of supplies remaining at the end of April.

u. Webworks is continuing to accrue bad debts at 10 percent of accounts receivable.

v. Webworks continues to depreciate its equipment over four years and its furniture over five years, using the straight-line method.

w. The license agreement should be amortized over its one-year life.

x. QRS Company is selling for $14 per share on April 30.

y. Interest should be accrued for April.

z. Record cost of goods sold.

E. Prepare an adjusted trial balance.

F. Prepare financial statements for April.

ENDNOTES

1. In recent decades, a number of variations of these legal forms have been allowed, each with its own particular characteristics. For example, limited liability companies (LLC) and limited liability partnerships (LLP) are hybrids that exhibit characteristics of both partnerships and corporations and are permitted to exist in certain states.
2. A list of the typical contents of the articles of incorporation can be found at "Articles of Incorporation," http://en.wikipedia.org/wiki/Articles_of_Incorporation.
3. When money is loaned to a corporation, especially one that is either new or small, the lender might require the owners to personally guarantee the debt. However, unless such a guarantee is made, the debt is that of the corporation and not the members of the ownership.
4. Tax rules do allow smaller corporations to file their income taxes as S corporations if certain guidelines are met. S corporations follow virtually the same tax rules as partnerships so that income is only taxed one time when initially earned.
5. Yury Iofe, senior editor, and Matthew C. Calderisi, CPA, managing editor, *Accounting Trends & Techniques*, 62nd edition (New York: American Institute of Certified Public Accountants, 2008), 289.
6. Although the Kellogg Company has its headquarters in Battle Creek, Michigan, the company is incorporated in the state of Delaware. Thus, the laws of Delaware set the rights of the common stock shares for this company.
7. Many other laws have been passed over the years that have been much more effective at protecting both creditors and stockholders.
8. A few states allow companies to issue stock without a par value. In that situation, the entire amount received is entered in the common stock account.
9. As mentioned in the previous chapter, the sales of capital stock that occur on the New York Stock Exchange or other stock markets are between investors and have no direct effect on the company. Those transactions simply create a change in ownership.
10. As mentioned earlier, the issuance of capital stock is not viewed as a trade by the corporation because it merely increases the number of capital shares outstanding. It is an expansion of both the company and its ownership. That is different than, for example, giving up an asset such as a truck in exchange for a computer or some other type of property.
11. Joe Flint, "Viacom Plans Stock Buy Back, Swings to Loss on Blockbuster," *The Wall Street Journal*, October 29, 2004, B-2.
12. If the board of directors does agree to the purchase of the corporation by an outside party, the two sides then negotiate a price for the shares as well as any other terms of the acquisition.
13. As can be seen in this press release, the terms "stock dividend" and "stock split" have come to be virtually interchangeable to the public. Both terms were used by Green Mountain. However, minor legal differences do exist that actually impact reporting. Par value is changed to create a stock split but not for a stock dividend. Interestingly, stock splits have no reportable impact on financial statements but stock dividends do. Therefore, only stock dividends will be described in this textbook.
14. A stock dividend of between 20 and 25 percent can be recorded at either fair value or par value.

CHAPTER 17
In a Set of Financial Statements, What Information Is Conveyed by the Statement of Cash Flows?

Video Clip

Joe introduces Chapter 17 and speaks about the course in general.

View the video online at: http://blip.tv/play/sDyBwKhIAA

1. THE STRUCTURE OF A STATEMENT OF CASH FLOWS

LEARNING OBJECTIVES

At the end of this section, students should be able to meet the following objectives:

1. **Describe the purpose of a statement of cash flows.**
2. **Define cash and cash equivalents.**
3. **Identify the three categories of cash flows used for reporting purposes.**
4. **Indicate the type of transactions that are reported as operating activities and provide common examples.**
5. **Indicate the type of transactions that are reported as investing activities and provide common examples.**
6. **Indicate the type of transactions that are reported as financing activities and provide common examples.**

Question: Thus far in this textbook, the balance sheet and the income statement have been studied in comprehensive detail along with the computation of retained earnings. At this point, a student should be able to access a set of financial statements (on the Internet, for example) and understand much of the reported information. Terms such as FIFO, accumulated depreciation, goodwill, capital stock, bad debt expense, and the like that might have sounded like a foreign language at the start of this exploration into financial accounting should now have a genuine meaning.

Examination of one last statement is necessary to complete the financial portrait of a reporting entity: the statement of cash flows. This statement was introduced briefly in Chapter 3. Why is it needed by decision makers? ***What is the rationale for presenting a statement of cash flows?*** *Is it required by U.S. GAAP?*

Answer: Coverage of the statement of cash flows has been delayed because the figures presented do not come directly from ending T-account balances found in a business's general ledger. Instead, the accounts and amounts shown here are derived from the other financial statements. Thus, an understanding of those statements is a helpful prerequisite for the construction of a statement of cash flows.

The delay in examining the statement of cash flows should not be taken as an indication of its lack of significance. In fact, some decision makers view it as the most important of the financial statements. They are able to see how corporate officials managed to get and then make use of the ultimate asset: cash. The acquisition of other assets, the payment of debts, and the distribution of dividends inevitably leads back to a company's ability to generate sufficient amounts of cash. Consequently, presentation of a statement of cash flows is required by US GAAP for every period in which an income statement is reported.

To reiterate the importance of this information, Michael Dell, founder of Dell Inc., states in his book *Direct from Dell: Strategies That Revolutionized an Industry* (written with Catherine Fredman): "We were always focused on our profit and loss statement. But cash flow was not a regularly discussed topic. It was as if we were driving along, watching only the speedometer, when in fact we were running out of gas."[1]

The income statement and the statement of cash flows connect the balance sheets from the beginning of the year to the end. During the course of that time, total reported net assets either increase or decrease as does the entity's cash balance. The individual causes of those changes are explained by means of the income statement and the statement of cash flows.

The purpose of the statement of cash flows is virtually self-evident: it reports the cash receipts (cash inflows) and the cash disbursements (cash outflows) to explain the changes taking place during the year in the cash balance. However, the physical structure of this statement is not self-evident. As illustrated in Chapter 3, all cash flows are classified within three distinct categories. Chapter 17 is designed to demonstrate the logic of this classification system and the method by which the reported numbers are derived.

cash equivalents

Short-term, highly liquid investments with original maturities of ninety days or fewer that are readily converted into known amounts of cash.

Question: Because current assets are listed in order of liquidity, most businesses present "cash and **cash equivalents** *" as the first account on their balance sheets. For example, as of December 31, 2008, Ball Corporation reported cash and cash equivalents totaling $127.4 million. The statement of cash flows uses this same terminology as it explains the drop of $24.2 million in Ball's cash and cash equivalents that took place during 2008.* ***What constitutes cash and what are cash equivalents?***

Answer: Cash consists of coins, currencies, bank deposits (both checking accounts and savings accounts) and some negotiable instruments (money orders, checks, and bank drafts). Cash equivalents are short-term, highly liquid investments that are readily convertible into known amounts of cash. They are so near their maturity date that significant changes in value are unlikely. Only securities with original maturities of ninety days or fewer are eligible to be classified as cash equivalents. Cash equivalents held by most companies usually include Treasury bills[2] , commercial paper[3] , and money market funds.

Going forward, FASB is considering the elimination of the cash equivalents category. Any of these items other than cash will then appear in the financial statements as temporary investments. For simplicity purposes, cash will be used in the examples presented throughout this chapter. However, until the authoritative rules are changed, the accounting for cash equivalents is the same as that for cash.

EXERCISE

Link to multiple-choice question for practice purposes: http://www.quia.com/quiz/2093012.html

Question: For reporting purposes all cash flows are classified within one of three categories: operating activities, investing activities, and financing activities. ***What transactions are specifically identified as operating activities?***

Answer: **Operating activities** generally involve producing and delivering goods and providing services. These events are those that transpire on virtually a daily basis as a result of the organization's primary function. For a business like Borders, operating activities include the buying and selling of books (and other inventory items) as well as the multitude of other tasks required by that company's retail function. In simple terms, operating activities are those that are expected to take place regularly in the normal course of business.

operating activities

A statement of cash flow category used to disclose cash receipts and disbursements arising from the primary activities of the reporting organization.

FIGURE 17.1 Typical Operating Activity Cash Inflows and Outflows

Cash Inflows	Cash Outflows
Receipts from the Sale of Goods or Services	Payments for Inventory Payments to Employees Payments for Taxes Payments for Rents, Insurance, Advertising, and the Like

The net number (the inflows compared to the outflows) is presented as the cash flows generated from operating activities. This figure is viewed as a good measure of a company's ability to prosper. Analysts obviously prefer to see a positive number, one that increases from year to year. Some decision makers believe that this figure is a better reflection of a company's financial health than reported net income because the ultimate goal of a business is to generate cash.

For example, International Paper reported a net loss on its income statement for the year ended December 31, 2008, of $1,282 million (considerably worse than any of the previous five years). However, its statement of cash flows for the same period reported a net cash inflow from operating activities of $2,669 million (considerably better than any of the previous five years). No one could blame a decision maker for being puzzled. Did the company do poorly during 2008 or wonderfully well? That is the problem with relying on only a few of the numbers in a set of financial statements without a closer and more complete inspection. What caused this company to lose over $1.2 billion dollars? How did the company still manage to generate nearly $2.7 billion in cash from its operating activities? In-depth analysis of financial statements is never quick and easy. It requires patience and knowledge and the willingness to dig through all the available information.

Question: On the statement of cash flows for the year ended August 31, 2008, Walgreen Co. reported that a net of over $2.8 billion in cash was spent in connection with a variety of investing activities. This company's management obviously made decisions that required considerable sums of money. Details about those expenditures should be of interest to virtually any party analyzing this company. ***What cash transactions are specifically included in investing activities?***

Answer: **Investing activities** encompass the acquisition and disposition of assets in transactions that are separate from the central activity of the reporting organization. These exchanges do not occur daily.

- For a delicatessen, the purchase of bread or onions is an operating activity but the acquisition of a refrigerator or stove is an investing activity.
- For a pharmacy, the sale of aspirin or penicillin is an operating activity but the disposal of a delivery vehicle or cash register is an investing activity.

All of these cash transactions involve assets but, if classified as an investing activity, they are only tangentially related to the day-to-day operation of the business.

investing activities

A statement of cash flow category used to disclose cash receipts and disbursements arising from an asset transaction other than one relating to the primary activities of the reporting organization.

FIGURE 17.2 Walgreen Statement of Cash Flows Shows Four Investing Activity Cash Flows for the Year Ended August 31, 2008

Additions to Property and Equipment	($2,225) million
Proceeds from Sale of Assets	17 million
Business and Intangible Asset Acquisition Net of Cash Received	(620) million
Net Proceeds from Corporate-Owned Life Insurance Policies	10 million

Healthy, growing companies normally expect cash flows from investing activities to be negative (a net outflow) as money is invested by management especially in new noncurrent assets. As can be seen here, Walgreen's spent over $2.2 billion in cash during this one year to buy property and equipment. The company apparently had sufficient cash available to fund this type of significant expansion.

Question: The third category of cash flows lists the amounts received and disbursed in financing activities. For the year ended June 28, 2008, Sara Lee Corporation reported that cash had been reduced by over $1.8 billion as a result of its financing activities. Again, that is a lot of money leaving the company. ***What cash transactions are specifically identified as financing activities*?**

financing activities

A statement of cash flow category used to disclose cash receipts and disbursements arising from a liability or stockholders' equity transaction other than one relating to the primary activities of the organization.

Answer: **Financing activities** relate primarily to liabilities and shareholders' equity in transactions that are separate from the central, day-to-day activities of the organization. Cash inflows from financing activities usually include issuing capital stock or incurring liabilities such as bonds or notes payable. Outflows are created by the distribution of dividends, the acquisition of treasury stock, the payment of noncurrent liabilities, and the like.

Sara Lee reported five financing activity cash flows for the year ended June 28, 2008. As can be seen in the specific information provided on its statement of cash flows, this company spent nearly $1.5 billion to repay liabilities, another $315 million to repurchase its own stock, and $296 million as dividend payments. Significant information that is readily apparent on this statement.

FIGURE 17.3 Sara Lee Statement of Cash Flows Shows Five Financing Activity Cash Flows for the Year Ended June 28, 2008

Issuances of Common Stock	$5 million
Purchases of Common Stock	(315 million)
Repayments of Long-Term Debt	(1,456 million)
Borrowings (repayments) of Short-Term Debt, Net	251 million
Payment of Dividends	(296 million)

The net result reported for financing activities is frequently positive in some years and negative in others. When a company borrows money or sells capital stock, an overall positive inflow of cash is likely. In years when a large dividend is paid or debt is settled, the net figure for financing activities is more likely to be negative.

EXERCISE

Link to multiple-choice question for practice purposes: http://www.quia.com/quiz/2093015.html

EXERCISE

Link to multiple-choice question for practice purposes: http://www.quia.com/quiz/2093017.html

EXERCISE

Link to multiple-choice question for practice purposes: http://www.quia.com/quiz/2092974.html

Question: Significant investing and financing transactions occasionally occur without a cash component. Land, for example, might be obtained by issuing common stock. Buildings are often bought through the signing of a long-term note payable so that cash payments are deferred into the future. Should that information be omitted from the statement of cash flows? ***If no cash is received or expended, should a transaction be reported on a statement of cash flows?***

Answer: All investing and financing transactions need to be reported in some manner for the benefit of decision makers. They represent choices made by the organization's management. If cash is not involved, such events must still be disclosed in a separate schedule (often just below the statement of cash flows) or explained in the notes to the financial statements. This information is valuable to interested parties who want a complete picture of the decisions made during the reporting period.

For example, in a note to its financial statements for the year ended April 24, 2009, NetApp Inc. disclosed the "acquisition of property and equipment on account" of $13,152,000. Although a noncash transaction, inclusion of the information was still important.

Stock dividends and stock splits, though, are omitted entirely in creating a statement of cash flows. As discussed in the previous chapter, they are viewed as merely techniques to reduce the price of a corporation's stock and are not decisions that impact the allocation of resources.

KEY TAKEAWAY

A statement of cash flows is required by U.S. GAAP whenever an income statement is presented. It explains the changes occurring in cash and cash equivalents during the reporting period. All the various cash inflows and outflows are classified into one of three categories. Operating activities result from the primary or central function of the business. Investing activities are nonoperating and affect an asset (such as the acquisition of a truck or the sale of a patent). Financing activities are nonoperating and involve a liability or a stockholders' equity account (borrowing money on a note, for example, or the acquisition of treasury stock). Investing and financing activities that do not impact cash must still be disclosed.

2. CASH FLOWS FROM OPERATING ACTIVITIES: THE DIRECT METHOD

LEARNING OBJECTIVES

At the end of this section, students should be able to meet the following objectives:

1. **Identify the two methods available for reporting cash flows from operating activities.**
2. **Indicate the method of reporting cash flows from operating activities that is preferred by FASB as well as the one that is most commonly used.**
3. **List the steps to be followed in determining cash flows from operating activities.**
4. **List the income statement accounts that are removed entirely in computing cash flows from operating activities and explain that procedure when the direct method is applied.**
5. **Identify common "connector accounts" that are used to convert accrual accounting figures to the change taking place in the cash balance as a result of these transactions.**
6. **Compute the cash inflows and outflows from common revenues and expenses such as sales, cost of goods sold, rent expense, salary expense, and the like.**

direct method

A mechanical method of reporting the amount of cash flows that a company generates from its operating activities; it is preferred by FASB because the information is easier to understand but it is only rarely encountered in practice.

indirect method

A mechanical method of reporting the amount of cash flows that a company generates from its operating activities; it is allowed by FASB (although the direct method is viewed as superior) but it is used by a vast majority of businesses in the United States.

Question: The net cash inflow or outflow generated by operating activities is especially significant information to any person looking at an organization's financial health and future prospects. According to FASB, that information can be presented within the statement of cash flows by either of two approaches: the **direct method** *or the* **indirect method***. The numerical amount of the change in cash resulting from the company's daily operations is not impacted by this reporting choice. The increase or decrease in cash is a fact that will not vary based on the manner of presentation. Both methods arrive at the same total. The informational value to decision makers, though, is potentially affected by the approach selected.*

FASB has indicated a preference for the direct method. In contrast, reporting companies (by an extremely wide margin) have continued to use the more traditional indirect method. Thus, both will be demonstrated here. The direct method seems a bit easier to explain and will be discussed first. ***How is information presented when the direct method is selected to disclose a company's cash flows from operating activities?***

Answer: The direct method starts with the income statement for the period. Then, each of the separate figures is converted into the amount of cash received or spent in carrying on operating activities. "Sales," for example, is turned into "cash collected from customers." "Salary expense" and "rent expense" are recomputed as "cash paid to employees" and "cash paid to rent facilities."

For illustration purposes, assume that that Liberto Company prepared the following income statement for the year ended December 31, Year One. This statement has been kept rather simple so that the conversion to cash flows from operating activities is not unnecessarily complex. For example, income tax expense has been omitted.

FIGURE 17.4 Liberto Company Income Statement Year Ended December 31, Year One

Revenues:		
Sales to Customers		$480,000
Expenses:		
Cost of Goods Sold	$250,000	
Salary Expense	60,000	
Rent Expense	30,000	
Depreciation Expense	80,000	420,000
Operating Income		60,000
Other Gains and Losses:		
Gain on Sale of Equipment		40,000
Net Income		$100,000

The $100,000 net income figure reported here by Liberto is based on the application of U.S. GAAP. However, the amount of cash generated by the company's operating activities might be considerably more or much less than that income figure. It is a different piece of information.

To transform a company's income statement into its cash flows from operating activities, three distinct steps must be taken. The first step is the complete elimination of any income statement account that does not involve cash. Although such balances are important in arriving at net income, they are not relevant to the cash generated and spent in connection with operations. By far the most obvious example is depreciation. This expense appears on virtually all income statements but has no purpose when cash flows are being determined. It is omitted because depreciation is neither a source nor use of cash. It is an allocation of a historical cost to expense over an asset's useful life. For Liberto, the $80,000 depreciation expense is removed to begin the process of arriving at cash flows from operating activities.

The second step is the removal of any gains and losses that have resulted from investing or financing activities. Although cash was probably involved, this inflow or outflow is reported elsewhere in the statement of cash flows and not within the company's operating activities. For example, Liberto's $40,000 gain on the sale of equipment is germane to the reporting of investing activities, not operating activities. The cash received in this disposal is included on the statement of cash flows but as an investing activity.

Neither noncash items such as depreciation nor nonoperating gains and losses are included when an income statement is converted to the cash flows from operating activities.

Question: After these two balances are deleted, Liberto is left with four income statement accounts:

1. *Sales to customers—$480,000*
2. *Cost of goods sold—$250,000*
3. *Salary expense—$60,000*
4. *Rent expense—$30,000*

These balances all relate to operating activities. However, the numbers reflect the application of U.S. GAAP and accrual accounting rather than the amount of cash exchanged. The cash effects must be determined individually for these accounts. ***How are income statement figures such as sales or rent expense converted into the amount of cash received or expended?***

Answer: For all the remaining income statement accounts, a difference usually exists between the time of recognition as specified by accrual accounting and the exchange of cash. A sale is made on Monday (revenue is recognized) but the money is not collected until Friday. An employee performs work on Monday (expense is recognized) but payment is not made until Friday.

These timing differences occur because accrual accounting is required by U.S. GAAP. Thus, many revenues and expenses are not recorded at the same time as the related cash transactions. In the interim, recognition of an asset or liability balance is necessary. Between the sale on Monday and the collection on Friday, the business reports an account receivable. This asset goes up when the sale is made and down when the cash is collected. Between the employee's work on Monday and the payment on Friday, the business reports a salary payable. This liability goes up when the money is earned and down when the cash payment is made. In this textbook, these interim accounts (such as accounts receivable and salary payable) will be referred to as "connector accounts" because they connect the accrual recording with the cash transaction.

Each income statement account (other than the noncash and nonoperating numbers that have already been eliminated) has at least one asset or liability that is recorded between the time of accounting recognition and the exchange of cash. The changes in these connector accounts are used to convert the individual income statement figures to their cash equivalents. Basically, the increase or decrease is removed to revert the reported number back to the amount of cash involved.

Connector accounts are mostly receivables, payables, and prepaid expenses. For example, see Figure 17.5.

FIGURE 17.5 Common Connector Accounts for Liberto's Four Income Statement Balances[4]

Income Statement Account	Balance Sheet Connector Account
Sales to Customers	Accounts Receivable
Cost of Goods Sold	Inventory and Accounts Payable
Salary Expense	Salary Payable
Rent Expense	Prepaid Rent and Rent Payable

If a connector account is an asset and the balance goes up, the business has less cash (the receivable was not collected, for example). If a connector account is an asset and it goes down, the business has more cash (receivables from previous years were collected in the current period). For a connector account that is an asset, an inverse relationship exists between the change in the balance during the year and the reporting entity's cash balance.

- Increase in connector account that is an asset → Lower cash balance
- Decrease in connector account that is an asset → Higher cash balance

If a connector account is a liability and the balance goes up, the business has saved its cash and holds more (an expense has been incurred but not yet paid, for example). If a connector account is a liability and this balance falls, the business must have used cash to reduce the debt and has less remaining. Consequently, a direct relationship exists between the change in a connector account that is a liability and the cash balance.

- Increase in connector account that is a liability → Higher cash balance
- Decrease in connector account that is a liability → Lower cash balance

Question: Liberto has one revenue and three expenses left on its income statement. To arrive at the net cash flows from operating activities, the cash inflow or outflow relating to each must be determined. Assume that the following changes took place during this year in the related connector accounts:

- *Accounts receivable: up $19,000*
- *Inventory: down $12,000*
- *Prepaid rent: up $4,000*
- *Accounts payable: up $9,000*
- *Salary payable: down $5,000*

In applying the direct method to determine operating activity cash flows, how are the individual figures to be disclosed computed?

Answer:

- Sales to customers were reported on the income statement as $480,000. During that same period, accounts receivable increased by $19,000. Less money was collected than the amount of credit sales. That is what causes a rise in receivables. Consequently, the cash received from customers was only $461,000 ($480,000 less $19,000).
- Salary expense was reported as $60,000. For that time period, salary payable went down by $5,000. More cash must have been paid to cause this drop in the liability. The amount actually paid to employees was $65,000 ($60,000 plus $5,000).

- Rent expense was reported as $30,000. Prepaid rent increased by $4,000 from the first of the year to the end. This connector account is an asset. Because the asset increased, Liberto must have paid an extra amount for rent. Cash paid for rent was $34,000 ($30,000 plus $4,000).
- Cost of goods sold has been left to last because it requires an extra step. The company first determines the quantity of inventory bought this period. Only then can the cash payment made for those acquisitions be determined.
  - Here, cost of goods sold was reported as $250,000. However, the balance held in inventory fell by $12,000. Thus, the company bought $12,000 less inventory than it sold. Fewer purchases cause a drop in inventory. The amount of inventory acquired during the period was only $238,000 ($250,000 less $12,000).
  - Next, the cash paid for those purchases is calculated. As indicated by the information provided, accounts payable went up $9,000. Liabilities increase because less money is paid. Although $238,000 of merchandise was acquired, only $229,000 in cash payments were made ($238,000 less $9,000).

FIGURE 17.6 Liberto Company Statement of Cash Flows for Year One, Operating Activities Reported by Direct Method

Cash Collected from Customers	$461,000
Cash Paid to Acquire Inventory	(229,000)
Cash Paid to Employees	(65,000
Cash Paid for Rent	(34,000)
Cash Generated by Operating Activities	$133,000

Liberto's income statement reported net income of $100,000. However, the cash generated by operating activities during this same period was $133,000. The conversion from accrual accounting to operating cash inflows and outflows required three steps.

1. Noncash revenues and expenses (depreciation, in this example) were removed. These accounts do not represent cash transactions.
2. Nonoperating gains and losses (the gain on sale of equipment, in this example) were removed. These accounts reflect investing and financing activities and the resulting cash flows are reported in those sections rather than within the operating activities.
3. The change in each related connector account during the period is used to adjust the remaining income statement figures to the amount of cash physically exchanged. Accrual accounting figures are converted to cash balances.

EXERCISE

Links to multiple-choice question for practice purposes: http://www.quia.com/quiz/2093018.html

EXERCISE

Links to multiple-choice question for practice purposes: http://www.quia.com/quiz/2092993.html

EXERCISE

Links to multiple-choice question for practice purposes: http://www.quia.com/quiz/2092995.html

EXERCISE

Links to multiple-choice question for practice purposes: http://www.quia.com/quiz/2092975.html

KEY TAKEAWAY

An entity's cash flows from operating activities can be derived and reported by either the direct method or the indirect method. FASB expressed preference for the direct method but the indirect method is used by most businesses in the United States. The process begins with the income for the period (the entire income statement for the direct method but just net income for the indirect method). Noncash items and nonoperating gains and losses are eliminated entirely. In the direct method, the remaining revenue and expense accounts are individually converted into cash figures. For each, the change in one or more related balance sheet connector accounts is taken into consideration. Thus, the reported U.S. GAAP (accrual accounting) figures can be turned into the underlying cash inflows and outflows for reporting purposes.

3. CASH FLOWS FROM OPERATING ACTIVITIES: THE INDIRECT METHOD

LEARNING OBJECTIVES

At the end of this section, students should be able to meet the following objectives:

1. **Explain the difference in the start of the operating activities section of the statement of cash flows when the indirect method is used rather than the direct method.**
2. **Demonstrate the removal of noncash items and nonoperating gains and losses in the application of the indirect method.**
3. **Determine the effect caused by the change in the various connector accounts when the indirect method is used to present cash flows from operating activities.**
4. **Identify the reporting classification for interest revenues, dividend revenues, and interest expense in creating a statement of cash flows and describe the controversy that resulted from this handling.**

Question: As mentioned, most organizations do not choose to present their operating activity cash flows using the direct method despite preference by FASB. Instead, this information is shown within a statement of cash flows by means of the indirect method. ***How does the indirect method of reporting operating activity cash flows differ from the direct method?***

Answer: The indirect method actually follows the same set of procedures as the direct method except that it begins with net income rather than the business's entire income statement. After that, the three steps demonstrated previously are followed although the mechanical process here is different.

1. Noncash items are removed.
2. Nonoperational gains and losses are removed.
3. Adjustments are made, based on the change registered in the various connector accounts, to switch remaining revenues and expenses from accrual accounting to cash accounting.

Question: In the income statement presented above for the Liberto Company, net income was reported as $100,000. That included depreciation expense (a noncash item) of $80,000 and a gain on the sale of equipment (an investing activity rather than an operating activity) of $40,000. ***In applying the indirect method, how are noncash items and nonoperating gains and losses removed from net income?***

Answer: Depreciation is an expense and, hence, a negative component of net income. To eliminate a negative, it is offset by a positive. Adding back depreciation serves to remove its impact from the reporting company's net income.

The gain on sale of equipment also exists within reported income but as a positive figure. It helped to increase profits this period. To eliminate this gain, the $40,000 amount must be subtracted. The cash flows resulting from this transaction came from an investing activity and not an operating activity.

In applying the indirect method, a negative is removed by addition; a positive is removed by subtraction.

FIGURE 17.7 Operating Activity Cash Flows, Indirect Method—Elimination of Noncash and Nonoperating Balances

Net Income	$100,000
Eliminate:	
Depreciation Expense	+80,000
Gain on Sale of Equipment	(40,000)

In the direct method, these two amounts were simply omitted in arriving at the individual cash flows from operating activities. In the indirect method, they are both physically removed from income by reversing their effect. The impact is the same in the indirect method as in the direct method.

Question: After all noncash and nonoperating items are removed from net income, only the changes in the balance sheet connector accounts must be utilized to complete the conversion to cash. For Liberto, those balances were shown previously.

- *Accounts receivable: up $19,000*
- *Inventory: down $12,000*
- *Prepaid rent: up $4,000*
- *Accounts payable: up $9,000*
- *Salary payable: down $5,000*

Each of these increases and decreases was used in the direct method to turn accrual accounting figures into cash balances. That same process is followed in the indirect method. ***How are changes in an entity's connector accounts reflected in the application of the indirect method?***

Answer: Although the procedures appear to be different, the same logic is applied in the indirect method as in the direct method. The change in each of these connector accounts has an impact on the cash amount and it can be logically determined. However, note that the effect is measured on the net income as a whole rather than on individual revenue and expense accounts.

Accounts receivable increased by $19,000. This rise in the receivable balance shows that less money was collected than the sales made during the period. Receivables go up because customers are slow to pay. This change results in a lower cash balance. Thus, the $19,000 should be subtracted in arriving at the cash flow amount generated by operating activities. The cash received was actually less than the figure reported for sales within net income. *Subtract $19,000.*

Inventory decreased by $12,000. A drop in the amount of inventory on hand indicates that less was purchased during the period. Buying less merchandise requires a smaller amount of cash to be paid. That leaves the balance higher. The $12,000 should be added. *Add $12,000.*

Prepaid rent increased by $4,000. An increase in any prepaid expense shows that more of the asset was acquired during the year than was consumed. This additional purchase requires the use of cash; thus, the balance is lowered. The increase in prepaid rent necessitates a $4,000 subtraction in the operating activity cash flow computation. *Subtract $4,000.*

Accounts payable increased by $9,000. Any jump in a liability means that Liberto paid less cash during the period than the debts that were incurred. Postponing liability payments is a common method for saving cash and keeping the reported balance high. The $9,000 should be added. *Add $9,000.*

Salary payable decreased by $5,000. Liability balances fall when additional payments are made. Those cash transactions are reflected in applying the indirect method by a $5,000 subtraction. *Subtract $5,000.*

Therefore, if Liberto Company uses the indirect method to report its cash flows from operating activities, the information will take the following form.

FIGURE 17.8 Liberto Company Statement of Cash Flows for Year One, Operating Activities Reported by Indirect Method

Net Income	$100,000
Eliminate:	
Depreciation Expense	+80,000
Gain on Sale of Equipment	(40,000)
Adjust Revenues and Expenses from Accrual Accounting to Cash:	
Increase in Accounts Receivable	(19,000)
Decrease in Inventory	+12,000
Increase in Prepaid Rent	(4,000)
Increase in Accounts Payable	+9,000
Decrease in Salary Payable	(5,000)
Cash Generated by Operating Activities	$133,000

As with the direct method, the final total is a net cash inflow of $133,000. In both cases, the starting spot was net income (either as a single number or the income statement as a whole). Then, any noncash items were removed as well as nonoperating gains and losses. Finally, the changes in the connector accounts that bridge the time period between U.S. GAAP recognition and the cash exchange are determined and included so that only cash from operating activities remains. The actual cash increase or decrease is not affected by the presentation of this information.

In reporting operating activity cash flows by means of the indirect method, the following pattern exists.

- A change in a connector account that is an asset is reflected on the statement in the opposite fashion. As shown above, increases in both accounts receivable and prepaid rent are subtracted; a decrease in inventory is added.
- A change in a connector account that is a liability is included on the statement as an identical change. An increase in accounts payable is added whereas a decrease in salary payable is subtracted.

A quick visual comparison of the direct method and the indirect method can make the two appear almost completely unrelated. However, when analyzed, the same steps are incorporated in each. They both begin with the income for the period. Noncash items and nonoperating gains and losses are removed. Changes in the connector accounts for the period are factored in so that only the cash from operations remains.

EXERCISE

Link to multiple-choice question for practice purposes: http://www.quia.com/quiz/2092976.html

EXERCISE

Link to multiple-choice question for practice purposes: http://www.quia.com/quiz/2092977.html

Question: When reporting cash flows from operating activities for the year ended December 31, 2008, EMC Corporation listed an inflow of over $240 million labeled as "dividends and interest received" as well as an outflow of nearly $74 million shown as "interest paid."

Unless a company is a bank or financing institution, dividend and interest revenues do not appear to relate to its central operating function. For most businesses, these inflows are fundamentally different than the normal sale of goods and services. Monetary amounts collected as dividends and interest resemble investing activity cash inflows because they are usually generated from noncurrent assets.

Similarly, interest expense is an expenditure normally associated with noncurrent liabilities rather than resulting from daily operations. It could be argued that it is a financing activity cash outflow.

Why is the cash collected as dividends and interest and the cash paid as interest reported within operating activities on a statement of cash flows rather than investing activities and financing activities?

Answer: Authoritative pronouncements that create U.S. GAAP are the subject of years of intense study, discussion, and debate. In this process, controversies often arise. When FASB Statement 95, *Statement of Cash Flows*, was issued in 1987, three of the seven board members voted against its passage. Their opposition, at least in part, came from the handling of interest and dividends. On page ten of that standard, they argue "that interest and dividends received are returns on investments in debt and equity securities that should be classified as cash inflows from investing activities. They believe that interest paid is a cost of obtaining financial resources that should be classified as a cash outflow for financing activities."

The other board members were not convinced. Thus, inclusion of dividends collected, interest collected, and interest paid within an entity's operating activities became a part of U.S. GAAP. Such disagreements arise frequently in the creation of official accounting rules.

The majority of the board apparently felt that—because these transactions occur on a regular ongoing basis—a better portrait of the organization's cash flows is provided by including them within operating activities. At every juncture of financial accounting, multiple possibilities for reporting exist. Rarely is complete consensus ever achieved as to the most appropriate method of presenting financial information.

Talking With an Independent Auditor about International Financial Reporting Standards

Following is the conclusion of our interview with Robert A. Vallejo, partner with the accounting firm PricewaterhouseCoopers.

Question: Any company that follows U.S. GAAP and issues an income statement must also present a statement of cash flows. Cash flows are classified as resulting from operating activities, investing activities, or financing activities. Are IFRS rules the same for the statement of cash flows as those found in U.S. GAAP?

Rob Vallejo: Differences do exist between the two frameworks for the presentation of the statement of cash flows, but they are relatively minor. Probably the most obvious issue involves the reporting of interest and dividends that are received and paid. Under IFRS, interest and dividend collections may be classified as either operating or investing cash flows whereas, in U.S. GAAP, they are both required to be shown within operating activities. A similar difference exists for interest and dividends payments. These cash outflows can be classified as either operating or financing activities according to IFRS. For U.S. GAAP, interest payments are viewed as operating activities whereas dividend payments are considered financing activities. As is common in much of IFRS, more flexibility is available.

KEY TAKEAWAY

Most reporting entities use the indirect method to report cash flows from operating activities. This presentation begins with net income and then eliminates any noncash items (such as depreciation expense) as well as nonoperating gains and losses. Their impact on net income is reversed to create this removal. The changes in balance sheet connector accounts for the year (such as accounts receivables, inventory, accounts payable, and salary payable) must also be taken into consideration in converting from accrual accounting to cash. An analysis is made of the effect on both cash and net income in order to make the proper adjustments. Cash transactions that result from interest revenue, dividend revenue, and interest expense are all left within operating activities because they happen regularly. However, some argue that interest and dividend collections are really derived from investing activities and interest payments relate to financing activities.

4. CASH FLOWS FROM INVESTING AND FINANCING ACTIVITIES

LEARNING OBJECTIVES

At the end of this section, students should be able to meet the following objectives:

1. **Analyze the changes in nonoperational assets to determine cash inflows and outflows from investing activities.**
2. **Analyze the changes in nonoperational liabilities and stockholders' equity accounts to determine cash inflows and outflows from financing activities.**
3. **Recreate journal entries to measure the effect on ledger accounts where several cash transactions have occurred.**

Question: For the year ended September 27, 2008, The Walt Disney Company reported the net outflow of over $2.1 billion in cash as a result of its investing activities during that period (all numbers in millions):

FIGURE 17.9 The Walt Disney Company Investing Activity Cash Flows for Year Ended September 27, 2008

Investments in Parks, Resorts, and Other Property	($1,578)
Sales of Investments	70
Proceeds from Sales of Equity Investments and Businesses	14
Acquisitions	(660)
Proceeds from Sales of Fixed Assets and Other	(8)
Cash Used in Continuing Investing Activities	($2,162)

This portion of Disney's statement of cash flows shows that a number of nonoperating asset transactions created this $2.1 billion reduction in cash. Information about management decisions is readily available. For example, a potential investor can see that officials chose to spend cash of almost $1.6 billion during this year in connection with Disney's parks, resorts and other property. Interestingly, this expenditure level is almost exactly the same as the monetary amount invested in those assets in the previous year. With knowledge of financial accounting, a portrait of a business and its activities begins to become clear.

After the cash amounts are determined, conveyance of this information does not appear particularly complicated. ***How does a company arrive at the investing activity figures that are disclosed within the statement of cash flows?***

Answer: In most cases, an accountant takes the ledger account for each nonoperating asset (land, buildings, equipment, patents, trademarks, and the like) and investigates the individual transactions that took place during the year. The amount of every cash change is identified and reported. A cash sale of land creates an inflow whereas the acquisition of a building probably requires the payment of some cash.

The difficulty in this process can come from having to sort through multiple purchases and sales to compute the exact amount of cash involved in each transaction. At times, determining these cash effects resembles the work required to solve a puzzle with many connecting pieces. Often, the accountant must replicate the journal entries that were made originally. Even then, the cash portion of these transactions may have to be determined by mathematical logic. To illustrate, assume that a company reports the following account balances.

FIGURE 17.10 Account Balances for Illustration Purposes

	January 1, Year One	December 31, Year One
Balance Sheet:		
Equipment	$730,000	$967,000
Accumulated Depreciation	300,000	450,000
Income Statement:		
Depreciation Expense		230,000
Gain on Sale of Equipment		74,000

In looking through business records for Year One, assume that the accountant finds two additional pieces of information about the above accounts:

- Equipment costing $600,000 was sold this year for cash.
- Other equipment was acquired, also for cash.

Sale of equipment. This transaction is analyzed first because the cost of the equipment is already provided. However, the accumulated depreciation relating to the disposed asset is not known. The accountant must study the available data to determine that missing number because that balance is also removed when the asset is sold.

Accumulated depreciation at the start of the year was $300,000 but depreciation expense of $230,000 was then reported as shown above. This expense was recognized through the following year-end adjustment.

FIGURE 17.11 Assumed Adjusting Entry for Depreciation

Depreciation Expense	230,000	
Accumulated Depreciation		230,000

The entry here increases the accumulated depreciation account to $530,000 ($300,000 plus $230,000). However, the end balance is not $530,000 but only $450,000. What caused the $80,000 drop in this contra asset account?

Accumulated depreciation represents the cost of a long-lived asset that has already been expensed. Virtually the only situation in which accumulated depreciation is reduced is the disposal of the related asset. Here, the accountant knows that equipment was sold. Although the amount of accumulated depreciation relating to that asset is unknown, the assumption can be made that it is equal to this reduction of $80,000. No other possible decrease in accumulated depreciation is mentioned.

Thus, the accountant believes equipment costing $600,000 but with accumulated depreciation of $80,000 (and, hence, a net book value of $520,000) was sold for an amount resulting in the $74,000 gain that is shown in the reported figures presented above.

A hypothetical journal entry can be constructed from this information.

FIGURE 17.12 Assumed Journal Entry for Sale of Equipment

Cash	???	
Accumulated Depreciation	80,000	
Equipment		600,000
Gain on Sale of Equipment		74,000

This journal entry only balances if the cash received is $594,000. Equipment with a book value of $520,000 was sold during the year at a reported gain of $74,000. Apparently, $594,000 was received. How does all of this information affect the statement of cash flows?

- A cash inflow of $594,000 is reported within investing activities with a labeling such as cash received from sale of equipment.
- Depreciation of $230,000 is eliminated from net income in computing cash flows from operating activities because this expense had no impact on cash flows.
- The $74,000 gain on sale of equipment is also eliminated from net income but because it does not relate to an operating activity. The $594,000 in cash collected is shown but as an inflow from an investing activity.

Purchase of equipment. According to the information provided, another asset was acquired this year but its cost is unavailable. Once again, the accountant must puzzle out the amount of cash involved in the transaction.

The equipment account began the year with a $730,000 balance. The sale of equipment costing $600,000 was just discussed. This transaction should have dropped the ledger account total to $130,000 ($730,000 less $600,000). However, at the end of the period, the balance reported for this asset is actually $967,000. How does the cost of equipment grow from $130,000 to $967,000? If no other transaction is mentioned, the most reasonable explanation is that equipment was acquired at a cost of $837,000 ($967,000 less $130,000). Unless information is available indicating that part of this purchase was made on credit, the journal entry that was recorded originally must have been as follows.

FIGURE 17.13 Assumed Journal Entry for Purchase of Equipment

Equipment	837,000	
Cash		837,000

At this point, the changes in all related accounts (equipment, accumulated depreciation, depreciation expense, and gain on sale of equipment) have been utilized to determine the two transactions for the period and the cash inflows and outflows. In the statement of cash flows for this company, the investing activities are listed as follows.

FIGURE 17.14 Statement of Cash Flows Investing Activities

Sold Equipment	$594,000
Purchased Equipment	(837,000)
Net Cash Outflow—Investing Activities	($243,000)

EXERCISE

Link to multiple-choice question for practice purposes: http://www.quia.com/quiz/2093020.html

EXERCISE

Link to multiple-choice question for practice purposes: http://www.quia.com/quiz/2093022.html

EXERCISE

Link to multiple-choice question for practice purposes: http://www.quia.com/quiz/2093000.html

Question: For the year ended December 28, 2008, Johnson & Johnson reported a net cash outflow from financing activities of over $7.4 billion. Within its statement of cash flows, that total was broken down into seven specific categories (all numbers in millions).

FIGURE 17.15 Financing Activity Cash Flows Reported by Johnson & Johnson for Year Ended December 28, 2008

Dividends to Shareholders	($5,024)
Repurchase of Common Stock	(6,651)
Proceeds from Short-Term Debt	8,430
Retirement of Short-Term Debt	(7,319)
Proceeds from Long-Term Debt	1,638
Retirement of Long-Term Debt	(24)
Proceeds from the Exercise of Stock Options/Excess Tax Benefits	1,486
Net Cash Used by Financing Activities	($7,464)

In preparing a statement of cash flows, how does a company such as Johnson & Johnson determine the amounts that were paid and received as a result of its various financing activities?

Answer: As has been indicated, financing activities reflect transactions that are not part of a company's central operations and involve either a liability or a stockholders' equity account. Johnson & Johnson paid over $5 billion in cash dividends and nearly $6.7 billion to repurchase common stock (treasury shares). During the same period, approximately $8.4 billion in cash was received from borrowing money on short-term debt and another $1.6 billion from long-term debt. None of these amounts are directly associated with the company's operating activities. However, they do involve liabilities or stockholders' equity and are appropriately reported as financing activities.

The procedures used in determining cash amounts to be reported as financing activities are the same as demonstrated for investing activities. The change in each nonoperating liability and stockholders' equity account is analyzed. The recording of individual transactions can be replicated so that the cash effect is isolated.

To illustrate, various account balances for the Hastings Corporation are presented in the following schedule.

FIGURE 17.16 Account Balances for Illustration Purposes

	January 1, Year One	December 31, Year One
Balance Sheet:		
Note Payable	$680,000	$876,000
Treasury Stock	(400,000)	(300,000)
Capital in Excess of Cost	120,000	160,000
Retained Earnings	454,000	619,000
Income Statement:		
Loss on Early Extinguishment of Debt		25,000
Net Income		200,000

In examining records for the Hastings Corporation for this year, the accountant finds several additional pieces of information:

1. Cash of $400,000 was borrowed by signing a note payable with a local bank.
2. Another note payable was paid off prior to its maturity date because of a drop in interest rates.
3. Treasury stock was sold to the public for cash.
4. A cash dividend was declared and distributed.

Once again, the various changes in each account balance can be analyzed to determine the cash flows, this time to be reported as financing activities.

Borrowing on note payable. Complete information about this transaction is available. Hastings Corporation received $400,000 in cash by signing a note payable with a bank. The journal entry to record the incurrence of this liability is assumed to be as follows.

FIGURE 17.17 Assumed Journal Entry for Signing of Note Payable

Cash	400,000	
Note Payable		400,000

On a statement of cash flows, this transaction is listed within the financing activities as a $400,000 cash inflow.

Paying note payable. Incurring the above $400,000 debt raises the note payable balance from $680,000 to $1,080,000. By the end of the year, this account only shows a total of $876,000. Reported notes payable have decreased in some way by $204,000 ($1,080,000 less $876,000). The information gathered by the accountant indicates that a debt was paid off this year prior to maturity. In addition, the general ledger reports a $25,000 loss on the early extinguishment of a debt. Once again, the journal entry for this transaction can be recreated by logical reasoning.

FIGURE 17.18 Assumed Journal Entry for Extinguishment of Debt

Note Payable	204,000	
Loss on Extinguishment of Debt	25,000	
Cash		???

To balance this entry, cash of $229,000 must have been paid. Spending this amount to settle a $204,000 liability does create the $25,000 reported loss. This cash outflow of $229,000 relates to a liability and is thus listed on the statement of cash flows as a financing activity.

Issuance of treasury stock. This equity balance reflects the cost of repurchased shares. During the year, the total in the T-account fell by $100,000 from $400,000 to $300,000. Apparently, $100,000 was the cost of the shares reissued to the public. At the same time, the capital in excess of cost balance rose from $120,000 to $160,000. That $40,000 increase in contributed capital must have been created by this sale. The shares were sold for more than their purchase price.

FIGURE 17.19 Assumed Journal Entry for Sale of Treasury Stock

Cash	???	
Treasury Stock		100,000
Capital in Excess of Cost		40,000

If the original cost of the treasury stock was $100,000 and an amount $40,000 in excess of cost was recorded, the cash inflow from this transaction was $140,000. Cash received from the issuance of treasury stock is reported as a financing activity of $140,000 because it relates to a stockholders' equity account.

Distribution of dividend. A dividend has been paid but the amount is not shown in the information provided. Net income was reported as $200,000. Those profits always increase retained earnings. As a result, the beginning balance of $454,000 should increase to $654,000. Instead, retained earnings only rose to $619,000 by the end of the year. The unexplained drop of $35,000 ($654,000 less $619,000) must have resulted from the payment of the dividend. No other possible reason is given for this reduction. Hence, a cash dividend distribution of $35,000 is shown within the statement of cash flows as a financing activity.

FIGURE 17.20 Assumed Journal Entry for Payment of Dividend

Retained Earnings (or Dividend Paid)	35,000	
Cash		35,000

In this example, four specific financing activity transactions have been identified as created changes in cash.

FIGURE 17.21 Statement of Cash Flows Financing Activities

Borrowed on Note Payable	$400,000
Extinguishment of Note Payable	(229,000)
Issuance of Treasury Stock	140,000
Distribution of Cash Dividend	(35,000)
Net Cash Inflow—Financing Activities	$276,000

All the sources and uses of this company's cash (as it related to financing activities) are apparent from this schedule. Determining the cash amounts can take some computation but the information is then clear and useful.

EXERCISE

Link to multiple-choice question for practice purposes: http://www.quia.com/quiz/2093001.html

EXERCISE

Link to multiple-choice question for practice purposes: http://www.quia.com/quiz/2093002.html

KEY TAKEAWAY

To determine cash flows from investing activities, the accountant must analyze the changes that have taken place in each nonoperational asset such as buildings and equipment. Journal entries can be recreated to show the amount of any cash inflow or cash outflow. For financing activities, a similar process is applied to each nonoperational liability (notes and bonds payable, for example) and stockholders' equity accounts. Once all changes in these accounts have been determined, the statement of cash flows can be produced.

Talking With a Real Investing Pro—Continued

Following is the conclusion of our interview with Kevin G. Burns.

Question: Many investors watch the movement of a company's reported net income and earnings per share and make investment decisions based on increases or decreases. Other investors argue that the amount of cash flows generated by operating activities is really a more useful figure. When you make investing decisions are you more inclined to look at net income or cash flows generated by operating activities?

Kevin Burns: As I have said previously, net income and earnings per share have a lot of subjectivity to them. Unfortunately, cash flow information can be badly misused also. A lot of investors seem fascinated by EBITDA which is the company's earnings before interest, taxes, depreciation, and amortization. I guess you could say that it is kind of like blending net income and cash flows. But, to me, interest and taxes are real cash expenses so why exclude them? The biggest mistake I ever made as an investor or financial advisor was putting too much credence in EBITDA as a technique for valuing a business. Earnings are earnings and that is important information. A lot of analysts now believe that different cash flow models should be constructed for different industries. If you look around, you can find cable industry cash flow models, theater cash flow models, entertainment industry cash flow models, and the like. I think that is a lot of nonsense. You have to obtain a whole picture to know if an investment is worthwhile. While cash generation is important in creating that picture so are actual earnings and a whole lot of other financial information.

5. APPENDIX

5.1 Comprehensive Illustration—Statement of Cash Flows

Question: The three sections of the statement of cash flows have been presented in this chapter but in separate coverage. Now, through a comprehensive illustration, these categories will be combined into a formal and complete statement.

The following information has been uncovered within the internal records maintained by the Ashe Corporation for the Year 2XX1. The company is a small organization that was incorporated several years ago in the western part of North Carolina.

A few of the significant financial events that occurred during the current year are as follows:

- *Land that had cost Ashe $7,000 several years ago was sold to an outside buyer.*
- *A building was also sold but for $210,000 in cash. This property had an original cost of $230,000. Accumulated depreciation to date on the building was $30,000.*
- *Equipment was purchased for $44,000 in cash to replace other equipment that was sold at the beginning of the year.*
- *An additional $110,000 in cash was borrowed on a note payable.*
- *Common stock was issued to an investor for $5,000.*
- *A cash dividend was declared and paid to the owners near the end of the year.*

Ashe Corporation is now attempting to prepare its first complete set of financial statements as part of an application for a new loan. Company officials have created the following informal balance sheets and income statement.

FIGURE 17.22 Ashe Corporation—2XX1 Beginning and Ending Balance Sheets

	January 1, 2XX1	December 31, 2XX1
Cash	$1,000	$27,000
Accounts Receivable	13,000	28,000
Inventory	17,000	13,000
Land	21,000	14,000
Buildings	390,000	420,000
Less Accumulated Depreciation	(120,000)	(160,000)
Equipment	36,000	50,000
Less Accumulated Depreciation	(17,000)	(20,000)
	$341,000	$372,000
Accounts Payable	18,000	22,000
Wages Payable	1,000	4,000
Interest Payable	2,000	3,000
Taxes Payable	10,000	9,000
Notes Payable	120,000	130,000
Capital Stock	50,000	55,000
Retained Earnings	140,000	149,000
	$341,000	$372,000

FIGURE 17.23 Ashe Corporation—Income Statement for Year Ended December 31, 2XX1

Sales	$274,000
– Loss on Sale of Land	(5,000)
+ Gain on Sale of Building	10,000
– Cost of Goods Sold	(79,000)
– Wages Expense	(40,000)
– Depreciation Expense—Buildings	(70,000)
– Depreciation Expense—Equipment	(30,000)
– Interest Expense	(9,000)
– Income Tax Expense	(11,000)
= Net Income	$40,000

A statement of cash flows now needs to be created for the Ashe Corporation. As shown in the balance sheet, cash increased from $1,000 to $27,000 during the course of this year. That $26,000 change should be explained. ***How does a company construct an entire statement of cash flows?*** *Application of the indirect method for presenting operating activities is so prevalent that company officials have decided to use it.*

5.2 Operating Activities

Answer:

In both the direct and indirect methods, cash flows from operating activities are derived by following several specific steps:

1. Start with net income, either the balance for the period (the indirect method) or the income statement as a whole (the direct method).
2. Remove noncash expenses such as depreciation.

3. Remove nonoperating gains and losses because they relate to either investing activities or financing activities.
4. Convert the remaining revenue and expense balances from accrual accounting to cash accounting by adjusting for the changes occurring during the year in related connector accounts.
    a. Because the indirect method is being used here, the preparation of the operating activities section begins with Ashe Corporation's reported net income of $40,000.
    b. Depreciation is eliminated. This year, the reported amount is $70,000 (buildings) and $30,000 (equipment). As expenses, depreciation is a negative within net income. To remove these two negative amounts, they are added back to the net income figure. Negatives are removed by the inclusion of a positive.
    c. Likewise, both the loss on the sale of land and the gain on sale of a building are removed. Neither relates to an operating activity. The loss is eliminated by an addition to net income while the gain is offset by means of a subtraction.
    d. Only one step remains: adjustment for increases and decreases in the various connector accounts reported by Ashe Corporation in its balance sheet accounts.

FIGURE 17.24 Ashe Corporation—Change in Connector Accounts

Income Statement Account	Connector Account	Change in Connector Account
Sales	Accounts Receivable	Increase of $15,000
Cost of Goods Sold	Inventory	Decrease of $4,000
	Accounts Payable	Increase of $4,000
Wages Expense	Wages Payable	Increase of $3,000
Interest Expense	Interest Payable	Increase of $1,000
Income Tax Expense	Taxes Payable	Decrease of $1,000

The change in each of these six connector accounts—accounts receivable, inventory, accounts payable, wages payable, interest payable, and taxes payable—must be factored into the computation of cash flows from operating activities to arrive at the actual effect on cash for the period.

Accounts receivable—increase of $15,000. The receivables balance rises because more sales are made on credit than cash is collected. The reduction in the cash received causes the receivable to go up. *This decrease in cash collections is reflected by subtracting the $15,000 from net income.*

Inventory—decrease of $4,000. The inventory balance dropped, which indicates that less inventory was bought than was sold this year. Fewer purchases take less money, keeping the cash balance high. *The decrease in inventory and its impact on cash are reported by an addition to net income.*

Accounts payable—increase of $4,000. Liabilities increase because more debt is acquired than the amount of cash paid. Slowness of payment increases accounts payable but also helps keep the company's cash balance high. *This increase in accounts payable must be added to net income to arrive at the cash flows from operating activities.*

Wages payable—increase of $3,000 and interest payable—increase of $1,000. Both of these accrued liabilities went up during this year. Once again, an increase in a liability indicates a reduction in payments. *This saving of cash is shown within the indirect method by adding the increases in wages payable and interest payable to net income.*

Taxes payable—decrease of $1,000. A liability goes down because of cash payments that reduce the obligation. However, they also shrink the amount of cash held. *This effect is mirrored by subtracted the decrease in the liability from net income.*

The steps for determining cash flows generated by operating activities have been completed (using the indirect method) and this part of the statement of cash flows can be prepared.

FIGURE 17.25 Ashe Corporation Cash Flows from Operating Activities for Year Ended December 31, 2XX1—Indirect Method

Net Income	$40,000
Eliminate:	
Depreciation Expense—Buildings	+70,000
Depreciation Expense—Equipment	+30,000
Loss on Sale of Land	+5,000
Gain on Sale of Building	(10,000)
Adjust Revenues and Expenses from Accrual Accounting to Cash:	
Increase in Accounts Receivable	(15,000)
Decrease in Inventory	+4,000
Increase in Accounts Payable	+4,000
Increase in Wages Payable	+3,000
Increase in Interest Payable	+1,000
Decrease in Taxes Payable	(1,000)
Cash Inflow from Operating Activities	$131,000

As can be seen here, cash generated by operating activities ($131,000) is considerably higher than the net income reported for the period ($40,000). That is not uncommon in the world of business especially since depreciation is often a large expense that does not require cash.

Investing Activities

After accounting for operating activities, only three asset accounts remain to be examined (along with their accumulated depreciation balances where appropriate): land, buildings, and equipment. The accountant looks at each individually and attempts to recreate the transactions that brought about the various changes during the year.

Land decreased by $7,000 ($21,000 to $14,000). The information provided states that land costing $7,000 was sold but does not indicate the amount of cash received in the exchange. However, the income statement discloses a $5,000 loss on the sale of land. When land costing $7,000 is sold at a $5,000 loss, only $2,000 in cash is received. The journal entry recorded by Ashe Corporation must have been as follows.

FIGURE 17.26 Assumed Journal Entry for Sale of Land

Cash	2,000	
Loss on Sale of Land	5,000	
Land		7,000

Land is an asset so this inflow of cash will be reported as an investing activity.

Buildings increased by $30,000 ($390,000 to $420,000). According to the introductory information, one building with a cost of $230,000 and a net book value of $200,000 (related accumulated depreciation was identified as $30,000) was sold during this year for $210,000. Those amounts create the $10,000 gain that appears in the company's income statement.

FIGURE 17.27 Assumed Journal Entry for Sale of Building

Cash	210,000	
Accumulated Depreciation	30,000	
Building		230,000
Gain on Sale of Building		10,000

This transaction will be listed as a cash inflow within investing activities. However, the change in the buildings account is not yet fully explained. The above sale drops that account from $390,000 to $160,000 (a $230,000 reduction in cost). The final balance for the year was not $160,000 but rather $420,000, an increase of $260,000. Without mention of additional transactions, the assumption is made that another building was acquired during the period at that price.

FIGURE 17.28 Assumed Journal Entry for Purchase of Building

Buildings	260,000	
Cash		260,000

This second building transaction is also included within the investing activities but as a cash outflow.

Equipment increased by $14,000 ($36,000 to $50,000). The provided information states that one piece of equipment was purchased during the year for $44,000. This transaction identifies another cash outflow to be reported.

FIGURE 17.29 Assumed Journal Entry for Purchase of Equipment

Equipment	44,000	
Cash		44,000

This journal entry does not entirely explain the change that occurred in the equipment account. The beginning balance of $36,000 grew to $80,000 as a result of this purchase. Yet, the ending balance was just $50,000. Another $30,000 reduction ($80,000 less $50,000) took place. Equipment accounts decrease as the result of a sale or some other type of disposal. The $30,000 is the cost of equipment that was sold this period.

In recording the disposal of a long-lived asset, removal of any related accumulated depreciation is also necessary. For the equipment reported by Ashe Corporation, beginning accumulated depreciation was $17,000—a figure that increased by $30,000 due to depreciation for that year (to a balance of $47,000). Ending accumulated depreciation account shows a balance of only $20,000. The apparent reduction of $27,000 ($47,000 less $20,000) must have been the amount relating to the equipment that was sold. That was the accumulated depreciation removed in recording the disposal of this asset.

Because no gain or loss is reported in the income statement on the disposal of equipment, the amount received must have been equal to the $3,000 net book value of the asset ($30,000 less $27,000).

FIGURE 17.30 Assumed Journal Entry for Sale of Equipment

Cash	3,000	
Accumulated Depreciation	27,000	
Equipment		30,000

All the changes in the land, buildings, and equipment accounts have now been examined. Each individual transaction was recreated and the change in cash calculated. The investing activity section of the statement of cash flows is prepared as follows.

FIGURE 17.31 Ashe Corporation Cash Flows from Investing Activities for Year Ended December 31, 2XX1

Sale of Land	$2,000
Sale of Building	210,000
Purchase of Building	(260,000)
Purchase of Equipment	(44,000)
Sale of Equipment	3,000
Cash Outflow from Investing Activities	($89,000)

Financing Activities

Only three accounts remain unexamined: notes payable, capital stock, and retained earnings. They are all either liabilities or stockholders' equity accounts and, thus, lead to financing activities.

Notes payable increased by $10,000 ($120,000 to $130,000). The information gathered from the company disclosed the signing of a note payable for $110,000 in cash. This first transaction is obviously an inflow of that amount of cash.

FIGURE 17.32 Assumed Journal Entry for Signing of Note Payable

Cash	110,000	
Notes Payable		110,000

According to the beginning and ending balance sheets, notes payable did not increase by $110,000 but only by $10,000. Thus, another transaction must have taken place that reduced this liability by $100,000. Notes payable decrease because of cash payments. Because no gain or loss on extinguishment of debt is reported in the income statement, Ashe Corporation must have paid exactly $100,000 to retire that same amount of debt.

FIGURE 17.33 Assumed Journal Entry for Extinguishment of Note Payable

Notes Payable	100,000	
Cash		100,000

The recording of this second transaction leads to the appropriate change in notes payable ($10,000 increase created by a $110,000 liability increase and a $100,000 decrease). It also uncovers another cash flow from financing activities: the $100,000 that was paid on the liability.

Capital stock increased by $5,000 ($50,000 to $55,000). The information states that Ashe Corporation issued stock to an investor for $5,000. That contribution created this account change.

FIGURE 17.34 Assumed Journal Entry for Issuance of Capital Stock

Cash	5,000	
Capital Stock		5,000

The business received this money and must report a financing activity cash inflow of $5,000. No other stock transactions are indicated.

Retained earnings increased by $9,000 ($140,000 to $149,000). This final balance sheet account increased by $40,000 because of the net income earned by Ashe Corporation this year. This amount is closed into retained earnings at the end of the year. The cash flows relating to net income have already been presented above within operating activities.

Retained earnings must have also declined by $31,000 to create the overall change of $9,000. As mentioned previously, other than net income, retained earnings are changed by virtually only one other event: the distribution of dividends. The information mentions that a dividend was paid this year and must have made up this $31,000 difference. Net income of $40,000 and a dividend of $31,000 do arrive at the reported increase in retained earnings of $9,000.

FIGURE 17.35 Assumed Journal Entry for Payment of Cash Dividend

Retained Earnings (or Dividends Paid)	31,000	
Cash		31,000

With this final financing activity, the entire statement of cash flows can be created for the Ashe Corporation. All the transactions that affected cash during the year are included so that investors and other interested parties can gain a picture of the results of operations as well as the investing and financing decisions of management. This picture is an excellent complement to the income statement, statement of retained earnings, and balance sheet.

FIGURE 17.36 Ashe Corporation Statement of Cash Flows Year Ended December 31, 2XX1

Net Income	$40,000
Eliminate:	
Depreciation Expense—Buildings	+70,000
Depreciation Expense—Equipment	+30,000
Loss on Sale of Land	+5,000
Gain on Sale of Building	(10,000)
Adjust Revenues and Expenses from Accrual Accounting to Cash:	
Increase in Accounts Receivable	(15,000)
Decrease in Inventory	+4,000
Increase in Accounts Payable	+4,000
Increase in Wages Payable	+3,000
Increase in Interest Payable	+1,000
Decrease in Taxes Payable	(1,000)
Cash Inflow from Operating Activities	$131,000
Sale of Land	$2,000
Sale of Building	210,000
Purchase of Building	(260,000)
Purchase of Equipment	(44,000)
Sale of Equipment	3,000
Cash Outflow from Investing Activities	($89,000)
Signed Note Payable	$110,000
Paid Note Payable	(100,000)
Issued Common Stock	5,000
Paid Cash Dividend	(31,000)
Cash Outflow from Financing Activities	(16,000)
Increase in Cash during 2XX1	$26,000
Beginning Cash Balance, January 1, 2XX1	1,000
Ending Cash Balance, December 31, 2XX1	$27,000

Video Clip

Joe talks about the five most important points in Chapter 17.

View the video online at: http://blip.tv/play/sDyBwKhJAA

6. END-OF-CHAPTER EXERCISES

QUESTIONS

1. Why are decision makers interested in a company's statement of cash flows?
2. What is the purpose of the statement of cash flows?
3. What is a cash equivalent?
4. What are the three classifications of the statement of cash flows?
5. What is the general definition of operating activities?
6. Give three activities likely to be found in the operating section.
7. What is the general definition of investing activities?
8. Give three activities likely to be found in the investing section.
9. What is the general definition of financing activities?
10. Give three activities likely to be found in the financing section.
11. What are the two methods used to calculate cash flows from operating activities?
12. Name the three steps used to convert a company's income statement to cash flows from operating activities using the direct method.
13. Why are interest and dividend revenue and interest expense included as operating activities?
14. Why can it be difficult to determine cash flows from investing and financing activities?

TRUE OR FALSE

1. ____ Both the indirect and direct methods of calculating cash flows from operations begin with net income.
2. ____ Purchasing treasury stock is an example of a financing activity.
3. ____ Presenting the statement of cash flows is optional according to U.S. GAAP.
4. ____ Some analysts believe the cash flow from operating activities is a better measure of a company than its net income.
5. ____ A loss on the sale of equipment would be shown in the operating section because it is shown on the income statement.
6. ____ Investing and financing activities not involving cash still need to be disclosed.
7. ____ Accrual accounting causes differences to exist between the income statement and operating section of the statement of cash flows.
8. ____ Payment of interest and dividends are both operating activities.
9. ____ Most companies use the direct method of calculating cash flows from operating activities.
10. ____ Depreciation expense is never a cash expense.

MULTIPLE CHOICE

1. Where would cash collected from customers appear on the statement of cash flows?
   a. Operating section
   b. Investing section
   c. Financing section
   d. Supplemental schedule
2. Fritz Corporation began the year with $900,000 in accounts receivable. During the year, revenue totaled $7,000,000. Fritz ended the year with $750,000 in accounts receivable. How much cash did Fritz collect from customers during the year?
   a. $750,000
   b. $7,150,000
   c. $6,850,000
   d. $900,000
3. Where would the redemption of bonds payable appear on the statement of cash flows?
   a. Operating section
   b. Investing section
   c. Financing section
   d. Supplemental schedule
4. During the year, Rafael Corporation paid dividends of $23,000, received cash by signing a note payable of $105,000, purchased a piece of equipment for $29,400 and received dividend income of $12,000. What would be Rafael's cash flow from financing activities for the year?
   a. $64,600
   b. $82,000
   c. $52,600
   d. $94,000
5. Happy Toy Company began 20X9 with $1,000 in inventory and $4,500 in accounts payable. During the year, Happy Toy incurred cost of goods sold of $25,000. Happy Toy ended 20X9 with $2,700 in inventory and $3,800 in accounts payable. How much cash did Happy Toy pay for purchases during 20X9?
   a. $26,000
   b. $22,600
   c. $24,000
   d. $27,400
6. Where would the purchase of available for sale securities appear on the statement of cash flows?
   a. Operating section
   b. Investing section
   c. Financing section
   d. Supplemental schedule
7. Crystal Bell Company generated $48,900 in net income during the year. Included in this number are a deprecation expense of $13,000 and a gain on the sale of equipment of $4,000. In addition, accounts receivable increased by $16,000, inventory decreased by $5,090, accounts payable decreased $4,330 and interest payable increased $1,200. Based on the above information, what would Crystal Bell's cash flow from operations using the indirect method?
   a. $54,120
   b. $71,940
   c. $48,900
   d. $43,860
8. Transportation Inc. incurred rent expense of $98,000 during the year. Prepaid rent increased by $34,000 during the year. How much cash did Transportation pay for rent during the year?
   a. $98,000
   b. $64,000
   c. $132,000
   d. $34,000

PROBLEMS

1. Use the following abbreviations to indicate in which section of the statement of cash flows you would find each item below.

   O = Operating Section
   I = Investing Section
   F = Financing Section

   a. ____ Issuance of bonds payable
   b. ____ Cash paid for interest
   c. ____ Cash collected from customers
   d. ____ Paid dividends
   e. ____ Sold Equipment
   f. ____ Issued preferred stock
   g. ____ Cash paid for inventory purchases
   h. ____ Purchased an equity investment in another company
   i. ____ Cash received from dividend income

2. Roy Company enjoyed sales during 20X1 of $120,000. Roy began the year with $56,000 in accounts receivable and ended the year with $79,000 in accounts receivable. Determine the amount of cash Roy collected from customers during 20X1.
3. Whitmore Corporation had cost of goods sold of $4,793,000 during the year. Whitmore had the following account balances at the beginning and end of the year.

   Change in Inventory and Account Payable Balances

	Beginning of Year	End of Year
Inventory	$893,000	$672,000
Accounts Payable	$569,000	$571,000

   What amount of cash did Whitmore pay for inventory purchases this year?
4. Jamison Company's income statement for 20X6 is below.

   Jamison Company Income Statement as of 12/31/X6

Jamison Company
Income Statement
As of 12/31/X6

Revenue	$76,450
Cost of Goods Sold	(40,740)
Gross Profit	35,710
Depreciation Expense	(8,240)
Other Expenses	(19,000)
Earnings Before Tax	8,740
Tax Expense	(2,076)
Net Income	$6,394

Selected Balance Sheet Accounts from the Beginning and End of 20X6

	1/1/X6	12/31/X6
Accounts Receivable	$32,590	$34,090
Inventory	23,100	35,020
Prepaid Expenses	13,970	11,340
Accounts Payable	39,870	44,960
Salaries Payable	22,030	17,440
Taxes Payable	12,490	11,230

Determine Jamison's cash flow from operations using both the direct and indirect methods.

5. Killian Corporation had several transactions during the year that impacted long term assets and liabilities and owners' equity. Determine if each of the following items would be shown in investing activities, financing activities or neither.

Determination of Cash Flow Balances

	Investing Activity	**Financing Activity**	**Neither**
Sold Common Stock			
Signed a Note Payable for Cash			
Purchased Equipment by Signing a Note Payable			
Sold Land			
Redeemed Bonds Payable			
Declared Dividends to Be Paid Next Year			
Purchased an Investment in Knox Company			

6. Ruthers Corporation began business on January 1, 20X5. The financial statements for Ruthers' first year are given below. Because it is the first year of the company, there are no beginning balances for the balance sheet accounts. This should simplify your preparation of the cash flow statement.

Ruthers Corporation Income Statement as of 12/31/X5

Ruthers Corporation
Income Statement
As of 12/31/X5

Revenue	$14,900
Cost of Goods Sold	(6,780)
Gross Profit	8,120
Other Expenses	(3,910)
Earnings Before Tax	4,210
Tax Expense	(1,263)
Net Income	$2,947

Ruthers Corporation Balance Sheet 12/31/X5

Ruthers Corporation
Balance Sheet
12/31/X5

Assets		**Liabilities**	
Cash	$900	Accounts Payable	$1,830
Accounts Receivable	1,990	Salaries Payable	700
Inventory	2,510	Note Payable	10,000
Prepaid Expenses	577	Total Liabilities	$12,530
Land	14,000		
		Owners' Equity	
		Common Stock	4,500
		Retained Earnings	2,947
		Total Owners' Equity	7,447
Total Assets	$19,977	Total Liabilities & Owners' Equity	$19,977

Additional Information:

a. Ruthers purchased land for $14,000 cash.
b. Common stock was issued for $4,500.
c. A note payable was signed for $10,000 cash.

Prepare Ruthers' statement of cash flows for 20X5 using the indirect method of calculating cash flows from operations.

7. Looney Company is in the process of preparing financial statements for the year ended 12/31/X9. The income statement as of 12/31/X9 and comparative balance sheets are presented below. Note that the Balance Sheet is presented with the most current year first, as is done in practice.

Looney Company Income Statement as of 12/31/X9

Looney Company
Income Statement
As of 12/31/X9

Sales	$6,328
Cost of Goods Sold	(4,740)
Gross Profit	1,588
Selling and Administrative Expenses	(895)
Depreciation Expense	(140)
Earnings Before Interest and Taxes	553
Interest Expense	(100)
Earnings Before Tax	453
Tax Expense	(108)
Net Income	$345

Looney Company Balance Sheet December 31, 20X9 and 20X8

Looney Company
Balance Sheet
December 31, 20X9 and 20X8

	20X9	20X8
Assets		
Cash	$485	$98
Accounts Receivable	960	990
Inventories	1,580	1,802
Property, Plant, and Equipment	1,710	1,620
Less: Accumulated Depreciation	(390)	(250)
Total Assets	$4,345	$4,260
Liabilities and Owners' Equity		
Accounts Payable	$200	$545
Interest Payable	50	80
Income Tax Payable	120	130
Long-Term Debt	1,500	1,430
Total Liabilities	$1,870	$2,185
Capital in Excess of Par	1,164	1,120
Common Stock, $4 Par	291	280
Retained Earnings	1,020	675
Total Owners' Equity	$2,475	$2,075
Total Liabilities and Equity	$4,345	$4,260

The following additional information has been assembled by Looney's accounting department:

a. Equipment was purchased for $90.

b. Long-term debt of $70 was issued for cash.

c. Looney issued eleven shares of common stock for cash during 20X9.

Prepare Looney's statement of cash flows as of 12/31/X9 using the direct method.

8. The following information relates to Henrich's Hat Store Inc. for the year ended December 31, 20X8.

Henrich's Hat Store Inc. Balance Sheet

Henrich's Hat Store, Inc.
Balance Sheet
December 31

	20X8	20X7
Assets		
Current Assets		
Cash	$280,000	$300,000
Accounts Receivable	750,000	690,000
Inventory	660,000	320,000
Total Current Assets	1,690,000	1,310,000
Land	300,000	0
Building and Fixtures	700,000	550,000
Less: Accumulated Depreciation	(100,000)	(80,000)
Total Assets	$2,590,000	$1,780,000
Liabilities		
Current Liabilities		
Accounts Payable	$460,000	$430,000
Taxes Payable	200,000	170,000
Total Current Liabilities	660,000	600,000
Stockholders' Equity		
Common Stock	$200,000	$150,000
Capital in Excess of Par	1,220,000	750,000
Retained Earnings	510,000	280,000
Total Stockholders' Equity	1,930,000	1,180,000
Total Liabilities and Stockholders' Equity	$2,590,000	$1,780,000

Henrich's Hat Store Inc. Income Statement for the Year Ended December 31, 20X8

Henrich's Hat Store, Inc. Income Statement Year Ended December 31, 20X8	
Sales Revenue	$6,000,000
Cost of Goods Sold	(4,600,000)
Gross Profit	1,400,000
Depreciation Expense	(20,000)
Other Expenses	(840,000)
Earnings Before Tax	540,000
Tax Expense	(140,000)
Net Income	$400,000

Other information:

a. The company purchased a building and fixtures with cash during the year, but none were sold.
b. Dividends of $170,000 were declared and paid.
c. Proceeds from the sale of common stock totaled $520,000.
d. Land was purchased for $300,000 cash.

Prepare the statement of cash flows for Henrich's Hat Store Inc. for the year ended December 31, 20X8 using the indirect method of calculating cash flows from operations.

COMPREHENSIVE PROBLEM

This problem has carried through several chapters, building in difficulty. Hopefully, it has allowed students to continuously practice skills and knowledge learned in previous chapters.

In Chapter 16, you prepared Webworks statements for April. They are included here as a starting point for May. This will be your final month of preparing financial statements for Webworks. This month, the statement of cash flows will be added. To simply the problem, fewer transactions than usual are included.

Here are Webworks financial statements as of April 30.

Webworks Financial Statements

Webworks
Income Statement
As of April 30

Revenue	$23,200
Cost of Goods Sold	(12,707)
Gross Profit	10,493
Deprec. and Amort. Expense	(392)
Other Expenses and Losses	(9,045)
Investment Income (Loss)	200
Earnings Before Interest & Tax	1,256
Interest Expense	(15)
Earnings Before Tax	1,241
Tax Expense	(372)
Net Income	$869

Webworks
Stmt. of Retained Earnings
As of April 30

Retained Earnings, April 1	$19,601
Net Income	869
Dividends	(500)
Retained Earnings, April 30	$19,970

Webworks
Balance Sheet
April 30

Assets		**Liabilities**	
Current		**Current**	
Cash	$11,905	Accounts Payable	$3,080
Accounts Receivable	2,050	Salaries Payable	100
Less Allowance for Doubtful Accounts	(205)	Interest Payable	45
Net Accounts Receivable	1,845		
Merchandise Inventory	3,362		
Supplies Inventory	65		
Total Current Assets	$17,177	Total Current Liabilities	$3,225
Property, Plant, and Equipment		**Noncurrent**	
Equipment	$10,500	Note Payable	$3,000
Less Accumulated Depreciation	(1,313)		
Furniture	1,000		
Less Accumulated Depreciation	(119)		
Total P, P, and E	$10,068		
Other Noncurrent Assets		**Owners' Equity**	
Available for Sale Securities	$2,450	Capital Stock	$4,000
Licensing Agreement, Net	1,200	Retained Earnings	19,970
		Other Accumulated Comprehensive Income:	
		Unrealized Gain on Available for Sale Securities	700
		Total Owners' Equity	$24,670
Total Assets	$30,895	Total Liabilities & Owners' Equity	$30,895

The following events occur during May:

a. Webworks starts and completes twelve more sites and bills clients for $9,000.

b. Webworks purchases supplies worth $140 on account.

c. At the beginning of March, Webworks had twenty-two keyboards costing $121 each and twenty-eight flash drives costing $25 each. Webworks uses periodic FIFO to cost its inventory.

d. On account, Webworks purchases eighty-three keyboards for $122 each and ninety flash drives for $26 each.

e. Webworks sells 98 keyboards for $14,700 and 100 of the flash drives for $3,000 cash.

f. Webworks collects $9,000 in accounts receivable.

g. Webworks pays its $500 rent.

h. Webworks pays off $14,000 of its accounts payable.

i. Webworks sells all of its shares of QRS stock for $14 per share.

j. Webworks pays Juan $750 for his work during the first three weeks of May.

k. Webworks pays off its salaries payable from April.

l. Webworks pays Leon and Nancy a salary of $4,000 each.

m. Webworks' note payable permits early payment with no penalty. Leon and Nancy decide to use some of their excess cash and pay off the note and interest payable. The note was paid at the beginning of May, so no interest accrued during May.

n. Webworks pays taxes of $740 in cash.

Required:

A. Prepare journal entries for the above events.

B. Post the journal entries to T-accounts.

C. Prepare an unadjusted trial balance for Webworks for May.

D. Prepare adjusting entries for the following and post them to your T-accounts.

o. Webworks owes Juan $200 for his work during the last week of May.

p. Webworks receives an electric bill for $450. Webworks will pay the bill in June.

q. Webworks determines that it has $70 worth of supplies remaining at the end of May.

r. Webworks is continuing to accrue bad debts at 10 percent of accounts receivable.

s. Webworks continues to depreciate its equipment over four years and its furniture over five years, using the straight-line method.

t. The license agreement should be amortized over its one-year life.

u. Record cost of goods sold.

E. Prepare an adjusted trial balance.

F. Prepare financial statements, including the statement of cash flows, for May. Prepare the operating section using the indirect method.

ENDNOTES

1. Michael Dell with Catherine Fredman, *Direct from Dell: Strategies That Revolutionized an Industry* (New York: HarperBusiness, 1999), 47.
2. A Treasury bill is a popular U.S. government security with a maturity date of one-year or less.
3. The term "commercial paper" refers to securities issued by corporations to solve their short-term cash needs.
4. For convenience, the allowance for doubtful accounts will not be included with accounts receivable. The possibility of bad debts makes the conversion to cash more complicated and is covered in upper-level accounting textbooks.

Index